MARKETING STRATEGY AND MANAGEMENT

Second Edition

Michael J. Baker

MACMILLAN

7|9

First published 1985 by
THE MACMILLAN PRESS LTD
Houndmills, Basingstoke, Hampshire RG21 2XS
and London
Companies and representatives
throughout the world

ISBN 0–333–57643–8 hardcover
ISBN 0–333–57644–6 paperback

A catalogue record for this book is available
from the British Library.

Printed in Hong Kong

Reprinted 1988, 1989, 1990
Second edition 1992
Reprinted 1993

To my family – Sheila, John, Fiona and Anne

Contents

List of Figures   xiv

List of Tables   xvii

Preface to the Second Edition   xix

Acknowledgements   xxii

PART I   MARKETING STRATEGY   1

1   Prologue   3
Introduction   3
The point of departure   3
The strategic perspective in marketing   4
Scope of the book   8

2   Marketing and competition   15
Learning goals   15
Introduction   16
Competition   17
What is marketing?   19
Market structure, conduct and performance   21
Competition and marketing strategy   23
International competition   28
The 'diamond of national advantage'   29
The role of government and chance   33
The development of 'clusters'   34
The creation of competitive advantage   35
Marketing and competitive success   38
Summary   42

3   Marketing and corporate strategy   44
Learning goals   44
Introduction   44
The development of the marketing function   45

Corporate strategy   47
The concept of the firm's business   52
The concept of limited strategic alternatives   57
Corporate strategy or marketing strategy?   60
General management and marketing management   65
Summary   66

4 **Principles of strategic marketing planning**   67
Learning goals   67
Introduction   67
The evolution of management systems   69
Some definitions   73
Formulating objectives   75
A framework for strategic marketing planning   78
Principles of SMP   83
The formulation of corporate strategy   87
Criticisms of and obstacles to strategic planning   89
Summary   96

5 **Analytical frameworks for strategic marketing planning**   98
Learning goals   98
Introduction   99
The product life-cycle   100
Diffusion theory   109
Using the PLC as a planning tool   114
Product portfolio analysis   116
Business portfolio analysis under attack   121
Strategic overviews   125
Gap analysis   130
Scenario planning   132
SWOT   136
Summary   137

6 **The marketing environment**   139
Learning goals   139
Introduction   139
The environment as the ultimate constraint   140
Demographic factors   141
Social and cultural factors   145
Political and governmental factors   146
Economic factors   148
Technological factors   149
Cycles and trends   152

Competition   155
Non-price competition   157
Changing times = changing values   159
What next?   160
Summary   162

✓ 7 **Buyer behaviour   163**
Learning goals   163
Introduction   163
Choice and the social sciences   164
Selective perception   169
Hierarchy of needs   173
Hierarchy of effects   174
Post-purchase dissonance   175
Buy phases   176
Characteristics of goods   177
Buyer behaviour and the decision-maker   178
The Baker composite model   179
Using the model   182
Summary   187

8 **Market segmentation   188**
Learning goals   188
Introduction   188
Product differentiation vs market segmentation   189
Bases for segmentation   191
Procedure and methods   194
Cluster analysis   196
Major segmentation methods   199
Location as a basis for segmentation   200
Demographic segmentation   203
Psychographic and behaviouristic segmentation   203
Usage segmentation   204
Benefit segmentation   207
Segmenting industrial markets   209
When to segment   210
Summary   216

9 **Positioning   218**
Learning goals   218
Introduction   218
Perceptual mapping   219
Positioning in the mind   225

Branding   228
Building a brand reputation   231
Summary   240

10   Situation analysis: the marketing audit   241
Learning goals   241
Introduction   241
Marketing audits   242
Competitor analysis   250
Sales forecasting   253
Summary   259

11   The marketing mix   260
Learning goals   260
Introduction   260
The evolution of the marketing mix concept   261
Identifying the ingredients of the marketing mix   262
Selecting the right mix   266
Managing the mix   271
Summary   275

PART II   MANAGING THE MARKET FUNCTION   277

12   Marketing research   279
Learning goals   279
Introduction   279
The need for marketing research   280
Quantitative or qualitative research?   284
Data collection   287
Secondary sources of data   287
The collection of primary data   289
Probability samples   290
Non-probability samples   292
Field survey methods   292
Market assessment, research checklist   295
Data reduction and analysis   296
Bayesian analysis   299
Developing a decision tree   304
Analysing the decision tree   309
Summary   310

13 Product policy   313
Learning goals   313
Introduction   313
The role of the product in marketing   314
User needs and product characteristics   316
Product classification and marketing strategy   319
Some definitions of the 'product'   321
Product policy   322
Product development   328
The new product development (NPD) cycle   329
Organisation for new product development   333
Managing the product life-cycle   335
Monitoring product performance   344
Summary   347

14 Packaging   348
Learning goals   348
Introduction   348
Definitions   349
Packaging criteria   349
Developing the pack   354
Summary   359

15 Pricing policy and management   360
Learning goals   360
Introduction   360
Theoretical foundations   361
Limitations and contributions of price theory   365
Pricing objectives   367
Profit objectives   369
Sales-oriented objectives   371
Pricing objectives in practice   373
Price determination   374
Cost-plus pricing   375
The contribution approach   376
The role of pricing in the marketing mix   377
Pricing strategies   382
Summary   383

16 Distribution and sales policy   385
Learning goals   385
Introduction   385
Why do channels develop?   387

Functions of a channel   389
Channel composition   391
Factors influencing channel structure   391
Selecting the distribution channel   394
Formulating a distribution policy   399
Vertical marketing systems   401
Personal selling   403
Sales and distribution effort through the product life-cycle   404
Summary   406

17 **Promotion policy and management   408**
Learning goals   408
Introduction   408
The nature of the communication process   410
How does advertising work?   412
Promotion objectives   415
Developing a promotional strategy   421
Setting the advertising budget   423
Measuring advertising effectiveness   430
Summary   433

PART III IMPLEMENTING MARKETING   435

18 **Service   437**
Learning goals   437
Introduction   437
The nature of customer service   438
The scope of customer service   440
The strategic use of customer service   447
Total Quality Management (TQM)   450
Pricing services   452
Measuring service quality   453
Service as a marketing strategy   454
Summary   456

19 **Developing a marketing culture   458**
Learning goals   458
Introduction   458
Organising for marketing   461
Basic business orientations   461
Developing a market-orientated organisation   468
Mission, vision and strategic intent   470

The mission statement   473
Implementing marketing   475
Summary   479

20 The (short-term) marketing plan   480
Learning goals   480
Introduction   480
A framework for marketing planning   481
Essential components of the short-term marketing plan   484
Summary   490

21 Control   491
Learning goals   491
Introduction   491
Profits and performance   492
Cost analysis   494
Other important cost concepts   498
Contribution analysis   500
Cash flow and net present value   505
Management ratios   507
Summary: the importance of control in marketing   513

22 Recapitulation   515
Introduction   515
The 'virtuous circle' of best marketing practice   516
Marketing and competitive success   518
Maxims for marketers   523
A Baker's dozen of key concepts   528

Notes and references   533

Index   553

List of Figures

2.1   The structure–conduct–performance paradigm   22
2.2   Forces governing competition in an industry   25
2.3   Determinants of national competitive advantage   30
2.4   Factors influencing competitive success   41
3.1   Taxonomy of strategic decision-making   53
3.2   Growth vector components   57
3.3   The 'attack' problem   58
3.4   The product life-cycle   61
3.5   Generic strategies   64
4.1   Characteristics of effective strategy statements   81
4.2   The marketing planning process   82
4.3   The cycle of SMP   83
4.4   The strategic condition matrix   86
4.5   A depiction of the strategy centres concept   88
4.6   Phases in the development of strategic planning   91
5.1   Four introductory marketing strategies   102
5.2   Classic fashion good PLC   105
5.3   Innovation of new products postpones the time of total maturity – nylon industry   107
5.4   Distribution of adopters over time   110
5.5   Cumulative adoptions over time   110
5.6   The business portfolio and associated cash flow   120
5.7   Product portfolio sector: strategic guidelines   122
5.8   The stages of planning   124
5.9   The directional policy matrix   125
5.10 3 × 3 chart depicting relative investment opportunity   127
5.11 General Electric's 'stoplight strategy'   130
5.12 The directional policy matrix   131
5.13 Ansoff's gap analysis chart   132
5.14 Gap analysis   133
6.1   UK actual and projected total population, 1945–2010   143
6.2   Significant technological events within a single lifetime   150
6.3   The phases of an economic cycle   153
7.1   Features of a machine tool considered one of the three most important   181
8.1   Alternative perspectives of the total market   190

8.2   Perceptual map   195
8.3   Annual purchase concentration in 18 product categories   206
8.4   Map of the six benefit segments   214
9.1   Hypothetical model of a retail market   223
9.2   Hypothetical model of a retail market, including the position of the 'ideal' store   223
9.3   Hypothetical model of a retail market, including the 'ideal' store and concepts   224
9.4   The relationship between market share and profitability   230
9.5   What is a brand?   232
9.6   Quality and profitability   234
9.7   Timing of market entry and business   235
9.8   The global top 10   236
9.9   The top 10 brands in the UK   237
11.1   Model of the customer market offering dimensions of the marketing mix   263
11.2   Elements of the marketing mix   264
11.3   Typical marketing mix patterns by industry type   269
11.4   The marketing mix and differential advantage: matching customer service wants   275
12.1   Operational research (OR) methods: a taxonomy   281
12.2   Successive focusing   283
12.3   A Bayesian view of the decision process   301
12.4   An exercise in decision-making, showing the possible results of a chance event   305
12.5   The new product development decision   306
12.6   Expected outcomes for NPD   310
12.7   Decision for roll-back   311
13.1   Bar chart showing need elements and need intensity   318
13.2   Ansoff's growth vector matrix   323
13.3   The technology market matrix   327
13.4   New product development costs   332
13.5   Marketing strategy: relationships   337
13.6   A sequential flow diagram for the implementation of the product-elimination decision   342
14.1   Packaging that stands out from the competition: simple designs and vivid colours attract the shopper's attention   358
15.1   Perfect inelasticity   364
15.2   Perfect elasticity   364
15.3   Unit elasticity   364
15.4   Hierarchy of business objectives   368
15.5   Role of pricing in marketing mix – 1980–8   380
16.1   Alternative channels of distribution   392
17.1   Overlap in the field of experience of source and destination   411
17.2   How advertising may work   414

18.1   Composite service organisation for durable goods industries   441
18.2   Composite service organisation for consumer goods industries   442
18.3   Repurchase loyalty to the retailer (new vehicle sales)   445
18.4   The value of customer satisfaction   446
18.5   The relative importance of customer satisfaction factors   447
18.6   A quality-driven planning matrix: strategic response   451
19.1   Financial vs marketing orientations   460
19.2   Organisational sub-systems continuum   466
19.3   Scales of structural characteristics   467
19.4   The Ashridge mission model   471
19.5   Mission statement: Marks & Spencer plc   474
19.6   Mission statement: British Airways plc   475
19.7   Corporate statement: Cable & Wireless   476
20.1   The marketing planning process   482
21.1   Cost curves   495
21.2   Simplified break-even chart   496
21.3   Curvilinear variable cost curve   497
21.4   Break-even   498
21.5   Investment life-cycle of hypothetical new product   500
21.6   Control and operating ratios   508–9
21.7   The business system: an overview   514
22.1   Virtuous circles of marketing practice   516
22.2   Top performer organisation   521
22.3   Top performer marketing activities   521
22.4   Marketing approaches and evolutionary patterns   522

▮ List of Tables

3.1   A comparison of various authors' concepts of strategy and the strategy formulation process in the businesss management field   50–1

4.1   Factors that influence how formal and complex an organisation's planning system should be   69

4.2   Stages of corporate development   70

4.3   Types of strategic planning   72

4.4   Trends in strategic planning   73

4.5   Contrasting strategy requirements   79

4.6   Obstacles to effective strategic planning   92

5.1   Introductory marketing strategies and suitable situations   103

5.2   The classification of adopter categories   114

5.3   How PLC advocates view the implications of the cycle for marketing action   117

5.4   Factors contributing to market attractiveness and business position   126

7.1   Hierarchy-of-effects models   174

7.2   The buy-grid analytic framework for industrial buying situations   176

7.3   Features for effective selling in machine-tool markets   182

7.4   Impact of loss of 0.75% of total market share on various levels of existing market share   185

8.1   Major segmentation variables   200

8.2   ACORN groups in Great Britain   202

8.3   Purchase concentration deciles   205

8.4   Toothpaste market segment description   208

8.5   A summary of product benefits   208

9.1   Critical success factors   221

9.2   Critical success factors: product factors influencing competitiveness   221

9.3   Lindquist's 9 store image attributes   222

10.1   The marketing audit   243–6

10.2   Consumption audit   247

10.3   Weighted services and performance   252

11.1   Wasson's hypotheses about appropriate strategies over the PLC   272–4

12.1   Qualitative vs quantitative research   285

12.2   Methods of data collection   288

13.1   Product characteristics   318

13.2   The market-pull model   326
13.3   Inter-industry variations in dependence on new products   329
14.1   Example of facings analysis: cracker market   357
15.1   A comparison of the Said, Robicheaux, Pass and Udell studies   378
16.1   Intensity of channel coverage   396
16.2   Summary of factors influencing channel length   397–8
17.1   Advertising objectives   419
17.2   Advertising strategy   422
17.3   The most important factors in gaining business in this market   423
17.4   Strengths and weaknesses of major media   425–6
17.5   Methods used to set advertising budgets   428
17.6   Method of setting advertising budget related to company size   428
17.7   Method of setting advertising budget related to product category   429
17.8   Method of setting advertising budget related to profit margin
        achieved   430
17.9   Means of assessment of advertising objectives   432
21.1   Cost distinctions   499
21.2   Break-down by product type   503
21.3   Product characteristics and product benefits segments   504
21.4   Reasons why comparisons of individual annual statements of accounts
        may be of limited value   507
22.1   Company's marketing approach   520
22.2   Company's role for marketing   520

Preface to the Second Edition

Marketing Strategy and Management is one of a trio of books intended to provide a sound foundation for the study of the subject of Marketing. Thus, *Marketing Strategy and Management* builds upon *Marketing: An Introductory Text* (5th edn, 1991) and is complemented by *Research for Marketing* (1991).

The first edition of *Marketing Strategy and Management* was largely written whilst I was the Crowther Foundation Distinguished Visiting Scholar at the Chinese University of Hong Kong in 1983. This break from the routine administrative duties of my appointment at Strathclyde University enabled me to commit to paper the essentials of a course which I have taught for almost twenty years as the capstone to an Honours degree in Marketing. The book thus assumes that the reader has already pursued an introductory course in marketing, such as the Chartered Institute of Marketing's Certificate course or a first year undergraduate programme, and so is familiar with the descriptive aspects of the subject, as well as possessing a reasonable overview of it as a whole. It is quite likely, therefore, that the intended reader of this book will have already read Kotler,[1] Bell,[2] McCarthy and Perrault,[3] Pride and Ferrell,[4] or similar comprehensive text books. Indeed, in the case of the Honours year students at Strathclyde they will probably have read all of these, as well as having studied many sub-areas of marketing, such as advertising, organisational buying behaviour, market research, product development, etc. in some depth. Accordingly, the purpose of this book is to build upon this knowledge by opening in Part I with an analysis of the nature of marketing strategy and strategic marketing planning (SMP), followed by an evaluation of the external forces (i.e. the marketing environment and buyer behaviour) which constrain and proscribe the courses of action available to the organisation. This consideration points to the need for a clear definition of the target market (market segmentation) and the selection of closely defined niches which the organisation can exploit to its advantage (positioning). Part I of the book concludes with a discussion of the situation analysis or marketing audit which captures the threats and opportunities facing the organisation, which are then matched with its strengths in the formulation of a marketing plan.

In order to succeed in an increasingly competitive market-place, the firm must select those opportunities which will enable it to use its *own resources to maximum effect*. Part II of the book looks at the major policy issues which have to be taken into account in designing the most effective marketing mix. Essentially, the purpose here is to remind the reader of the key issues or concepts which have to be considered for each of the mix elements. It is *not* to provide a survey of the latest and most fashionable techniques. Accordingly, while readers will find references to very recent work, they will also find considerable reference to much earlier work on the grounds that many of the key concepts and ideas about marketing were first articulated in the 1950s and 1960s by people like Ted Levitt, Joel Dean and Igor Ansoff (to mention but a few). Thirty or more years later many of these original concepts and ideas are being 'rediscovered', but this hardly seems a sufficient reason for ignoring the original source in favour of the new disciple.

The book concludes in Part III with a section on implementation. During the 1980s a great deal of research was undertaken into the critical success factors which underly competitive success. As one would expect, different studies tend to emphasise particular factors as being especially important. However, virtually all studies are agreed that whilst there is a large number of factors which firms must take into account in devising a successful competitive strategy, in the final analysis it is the *quality of implementation* which tends to distinguish between more and less successful firms. Therefore, in this edition, we give more explicit recognition to the importance of concepts such as vision, corporate mission and corporate culture as the basis for developing an effective organisation. However, implementation depends on more than simple motivation, and Chapter 21 on 'Control' reviews some of the performance indicators which management uses to measure progress. Finally, we conclude with a recapitulation of the more important ideas and issues which have emerged from our review of marketing strategy and management.

Whilst the second edition contains most of the material included in the first, it has been expanded by approximately 20% and extensively restructured. The book now comprises 22 chapters instead of the 16 in the original edition. Two of these – Chapter 2 on Marketing and Competition and Chapter 9 on Positioning – are completely new, whilst the other four are the result of reorganising the first edition material. This restructuring is believed to give a more logical development of the subject and reflects experience with students and managers who have used the book as the basis for formal study of the subject.

The restructuring also reflects some of the changes which occurred in the 1980s after the first edition appeared. Amongst these may be noted the rise of global competition and the growing preoccupation with competitiveness. In turn, this has led to some maturing of views concerning the role of strategic planning and marketing in the organisation. During the 1960s and 1970s there was a tendency to establish separate departments with responsibility for these functions resulting in less involvement on the part of those ultimately responsible for the direction of the firm. The pressures of the recession of the late 1970s and 1980s have made it clear that marketing is the business of all the firm's employees and that strategic planning is too important to be left solely to strategic planners. As a result, there has been a move to dismantle monolithic marketing and planning departments and diffuse the responsibility for these activities more widely through the company. This is not to say that there is not a need for specialist staff advice on these functions but is intended to distinguish between the advisory and executive responsibility for them. Finally, and as noted earlier, familiarity with the latest techniques and procedures is not by itself sufficient to guarantee success. Implementation is the key, and increasing attention is being given to the human factor in management.

As we noted in the first edition's Preface the acid test of this book's utility must be consumer acceptance. Its publishing record and the appearance of this second edition suggest that it has met a need and may be considered successful. That it is so owes a great deal to a number of people, some of whom must be singled out for specific acknowledgement. First, there are my students at Strathclyde – under-graduates, postgraduates and practising managers on short courses – who have provided both the challenge and the feedback that have shaped the book's structure and content. Second, there are my colleagues both at Strathclyde and my many friends in the Marketing Education Group who have helped develop and inform my own understanding of the subject. Third, there are my secretary, June Peffer and research assistant, Jennifer Skene. Between us we have managed to produce two new books and four revised editions of other books in the space of the last eighteen months. Only other secretaries and research assistants can probably appreciate just how much work this has involved. To all of you my special thanks.

University of Strathclyde   M. J. BAKER
October 1991

Acknowledgements

The author and publishers wish to thank the following for permission to reproduce copyright material.

Irwin, for Table 21.1, from J.A. Howard, *Marketing Management* (1957) and Figure 21.7, from E.A. Helfert, *Techniques of Financial Analysis* (1982).

The Journal of Business and Industrial Management, for Figure 15.5, from B.J. Coe, 'Strategy in Retreat : Pricing Drops Out' (1990).

Journal of Marketing Management, for Figure 19.1, from P. Doyle, 'What are the Excellent Companies?' (1992) and Figure 20.1, from J.W. Leppard and M.H.B. McDonald, 'Marketing Planning and Corporate Culture' (1991).

The Journal of Business Strategy, for Figure 5.8, from G. Day, 'Gaining insights through strategy analysis' (1983).

Modern Textiles Magazine, for Figure 5.3, from J.P. Yale 'Innovation of new products postpones the time of total maturity – nylon industry' (1964).

University of Bradford Management Centre, for Figure 5.7, from G.J. Hooley, *MBA Core Course Lecture Notes 1979/80* and Tables 22.1 and 22.2, from J. Lynch, G. Hooley and J. Shepherd, *Effectiveness of British Marketing*.

Shell International Chemical Co., for Figure 5.9, from *The Directional Policy Matrix : a New Aid to Corporate Planning* (1975).

McGraw-Hill, for Figure 5.11, from *Business Week* (28 April 1975) and Figure 13.2, from I. Ansoff, *Corporate Strategy* (1965).

Office of Population Censuses and Surveys, for Figure 6.1.

George Allen & Unwin, for Figure 6.3, from J.J. van Duijn, *The Long Wave in Economic Life* (1983) and Table 17.2, from J. O'Shaughnessy, *Competitive Marketing : a Strategic Approach* (1984).

Goodyear, for Figure 8.1, from B.M. Enis, *Marketing Principles* (1977).

Paul Chapman Publishing, for Figures 9.1 and 9.2, from G. Davies and J. Brooks, *Positioning Strategy in Retailing* (1989).

Collier Macmillan, for Figures 9.4 and 9.6, from R.D. Buzzell and B.T. Gale, *The PIMS Principles Linking Strategy to Performance* (1987), and for Figure 9.5, from T. Levitt, *The Marketing Imagination* (1983).

The Landor ImagePower Survey, for Figures 9.8 and 9.9.

John Wiley, for Figure 11.1, from H.A. Lipson and J.R. Darling, *Introduction to Marketing : an Administrative Approach* (1971).

John Martin Publishing, for Figure 11.2, from *Marketing Planning* (1978).

Hutchinson, for Figure 11.3, from P. Guptara, *The Basic Arts of Marketing* (1990) and Figure 19.4, from A. Campbell, M. Devine and D. Young, *A Sense of Mission* (1990).

Butterworth–Heinemann, for Figure 11.4, from M.J. Baker (ed.), *The Marketing Book* (1991).

MCB Publications, for Figure 12.1, from A. Meidan, *Marketing Application of Operational Research Techniques* (1981).

Intertext, for Figure 12.3, from B.M. Enis and C.L. Broome, *Marketing Decisions: a Bayesian Approach* (1973).

Booz, Allen & Hamilton Inc., for Figure 13.4.

Industrial Marketing Management, for Figure 13.6, from G.J. Avlonitis, 'The Product-Elimination Decision and Strategies' (1983).

AMACOM, for Figure 15.4, from A. Oxenfeldt, *Pricing Strategies* (1975).

The Society of Management Accountants and National Society of Accountants, for Figure 16.1, from D.M. Lambert, *The Distribution Channels Decision* (1978).

University of Illinois Press, for Figure 17.1, from W. Schramm, *The Process and Effects of Mass Communication* (1955).

J. Walter Thompson Co., for Figure 17.2, from T. Joyce, *What Do We Know about How Advertising Works?* (1967).

Administrative Science Quarterly, for Figure 19.3, from P.R. Lawrence and J.W. Lorsch, 'Differentiation and Integration in Complex Organizations' (1967).

Marks & Spencer plc, for Figure 19.5, from *Report and Accounts* (1991).

British Airways plc, for Figure 19.6, from *Report and Accounts* (1991).

Cable & Wireless, for Figure 19.7, from *Report and Accounts* (1991).

Prism, for Figure 18.6, from T.J. Erickson, 'Beyond the Quality Revolution: Linking Quality to Corporate Strategy' (1991).

Institute of Marketing, for Table 17.3, from G.J. Hooley, C.J. West and J.E. Lynch, *Marketing Management Today* (1983).

West Publishing, for Table 3.1 and Figure 4.1, from C.W. Hofer and D.E. Schendel, *Strategy Formulation : Analytical Concepts* (1978).

Intercollegiate Case Clearing House, for Table 4.1, from C.W. Hofer, *Conceptual constructs for formulating corporate and business strategies* (1977).

Harvard Business School, for Table 4.2, from M. Salter, *Course notes, MBA Program* (1969).

University of Strathclyde, for Tables 4.3 and 4.4, and for Table 15.1, from H. Said, 'The Relevance of Price Theory to Pricing Practice : an investigation of pricing policies and practices in UK industry' (1981).

Houghton-Mifflin, for Figure 2.1, from F.M. Scherer and D. Ross, *Industrial Market Structure and Economic Performance* (1990).

Long Range Planning, for Figure 4.6 and Table 4.6, from T.G. Marx, 'Removing the Obstacles to Effective Strategic Planning', (1991) and Figure 5.12, from D.F. Hussey, 'Portfolio Analysis : Practical Experience with the Directional Policy Matrix' (1978).

Heinemann, for Figure 4.2, from M.H.B. McDonald, *Marketing Plans* (1984).

American Management Association, for Table 4.5, from E.S. McKay, *Marketing Mystique* (1972) and Figures 18.1 and 18.2, from T.A. Gannon (ed.), *Product Service Management* (1972).

University of Bradford, for Table 5.1, from C. Firth, 'New Approaches to Strategic Marketing Planning' (1980).

Harvard Business Review, for Table 5.3, from N. Dhalla and S. Yuspeh, 'Forget the Product Life Cycle Concept!' (1976), Table 17.4, from S.R. Fajen, 'More for Your Money from the Media' (1978) and Figures 2.2 from M. Porter, 'How competitive forces shape strategy' (1979), 2.3, from M. Porter, 'The Competitive Advantage of Nations' (1990), 3.2 and 13.2, from I. Ansoff, 'Strategies for Diversification' (1957), 12.4, from J.F. Magee, 'Decision Trees for Decision Making' (1964), and 13.3, from S.C. Johnson and C. Jones, 'How to Organize for New Products' (1957).

Prentice-Hall, for Table 5.4 and Figure 5.10, from D.F. Abell and J.S. Hammond, *Strategic Market Planning* (1979). For Figure 5.1, from P. Kotler, *Marketing Management* (1980) and Figure 6.2, from K. Albrecht, *Stress and the Manager* (1979).

Allyn & Bacon, for Figure 3.1, from R.A. Kerin and R.A. Peterson (eds), *Perspectives on Strategic Marketing Management* (1983), Table 7.2, from P.J. Robinson, C.W. Faris and Y. Wind, *Industrial Buying and Creative Marketing* (1967) and Table 11.1, from R.A. Kerin, *Perspectives on Strategic Marketing Management* (1980).

Market Research Society Newsletter, for Table 7.3, from R. Artingstall, *New Product Development* (1980).

Quarterly Review of Marketing, for Table 8.1, from M. Thomas, 'Market Segmentation' (1980).

A.D. Little Inc., for Figures 4.4 and 4.5.

Marketing, for Table 8.2 and for Table 14.1, from R. Head, 'Shedding Light on Design' (1982).

Chicago Tribune, for Table 8.3.

Journal of Marketing, for Table 8.4, from R.I. Haley, 'Benefit Segmentation' (1968).

Scott, Foresman, for Table 8.5, from L.W. Stern and J.R. Grabner, Jr, *Competition in the Market Place* (1970).

Journal of Retailing, for Table 9.3, from J.D. Lindquist, 'Meaning of Image' (1974).

Sloan Management Review, for Table 10.1, from P. Kotler, W. Gregor and W. Rogers, 'The M.A. comes of age' (1977).

Sociological Review, for Table 12.1, from P. Halfpenny, 'The Analysis of Qualitative Data' (1979).

The Design Council, for Table 13.1 and Figure 13.1, from R. Rothwell, P. Gardiner and K. Schott, *Design and the Economy* (1983).

McKinsey Quarterly, for Table 13.2, from R.C. Bennett and R.G. Cooper, 'The Misuse of Marketing : an American Tragedy' (1982).

Penguin Books, for Table 21.4 and Figures 21.5 and 21.6, from J. Sizer, *An Insight into Management Accounting* (1979) and Table 13.3, from M.J. Baker, *Market Development* (1983).

University of Alabama, for Table 16.2, from D.L. Brady, *An analysis of Factors Affecting the Methods of Exporting Used by Small Manufacturing Firms* (1978).

Cranfield School of Management, for Tables 17.1 and 17.9, from D. Corkindale and S. Kennedy, *The Evaluation of Advertising Objectives* (1974).

Philip Allen, for Table 9.2, from M.J. Baker and S. Hart, *Marketing and Competitive Success* (1989).

Sidgwick and Jackson, for Figure 9.7, from D.K. Clifford and R.E. Cavanagh, *The Winning Performance : How America's high-growth midsize companies succeed* (1985).

Gower, for Tables 10.2 and 10.3, from J. Stapleton, *How to Prepare a Marketing Plan* (1989).

Part I

MARKETING STRATEGY

CHAPTER 1

Prologue

■ Introduction

Prologues, like overtures, are intended to achieve at least three objectives:

1 To establish the point of departure;
2 To indicate the direction in which one is to proceed; and
3 To introduce some of the themes which will be encountered as the plot unfolds.

These, then, are the basic goals of this chapter in which we shall seek to define the general scope of the book, the audience for which it is intended, the information and learning objectives to be pursued and the structure to be followed in attempting to meet these objectives.

■ The Point of Departure

Writing in the Spring 1983 issue of the *Journal of Marketing*[1] two well-known American professors of Marketing, Yoram Wind and Thomas S. Robertson, offered the opinion that marketing has reached a point of discontinuity in its development as a discipline from an emphasis upon marketing management to a broadened perspective concerned with marketing strategy.

The early emphasis upon marketing management and the marketing functions – particularly advertising and selling, distribution, market research and product development – is not surprising. The manipulation of these elements of the marketing 'mix' allows tactical responses to the prevailing conditions in the markets in which one is competing. However, tactical manoeuvres tend to be sufficient to cope only with short-term and localised conditions and circumstances. They are only effective in the long term and on a large scale if they are co-ordinated and integrated within a more broadly based strategic framework. As the markets of the advanced industrialised economies of the Western world gradually moved from an endemic condition of under-supplied markets to one of potential over-supply, it was clear that marketing practices had to change.

Tactical management was not able to cope with the intense competition of the new market conditions; something more was required. It was this recognition which led to what I have chosen to characterise as the 'rediscovery' of the marketing concept.

While most authors and commentators date the statement of the marketing concept to the 1950s and identify its articulation with the General Electric Company, it is obvious that such identification is purely a matter of convenience. Marketing did not just happen in the 1950s – its functions had been in daily use in some shape or form from the beginnings of trade and commerce way back in antiquity. What happened was that the changing balance resulted in the conclusion that supply is the servant of demand. Of course this has always been true, but under conditions of general scarcity demand tends to be basic and obvious. One does not require a sophisticated intelligence and planning system to identify attractive market opportunities. Rather one requires the most cost-effective production and distribution system. This encourages the production and sale of standardised products, which can minimise cost thus satisfying more customers. But the combined effects of technological innovation, increased competition, both national and international, and a slowing of growth in population (to mention but a few long-term trends) have resulted in a much more complex and competitive market-place. In this environment survival, let alone success, calls for a new philosophy of business in which the process of manufacture or supply creation should be seen to start with a clear statement of consumer needs – the marketing concept.

■ The Strategic Perspective in Marketing

The adoption of the marketing concept and a marketing orientation[2] does not create nor bring into existence new business functions but it does call for a change in both focus and emphasis and it is this change of focus and emphasis which has led to the need for marketing orientated *strategy*. In Wind and Robertson's view it is this strategic emphasis or perspective which is missing from the development of both marketing thought and practice. Specifically, they identify seven key limitations within the marketing field which are a direct consequence of the emphasis upon management as opposed to strategy, namely:

- A fixation with the brand as the unit of analysis.
- The interdisciplinary isolation of marketing.
- The failure to examine synergy in the design of the marketing program.
- Marketing's short-run orientation.
- The lack of rigorous competitive analysis.
- The lack of an international orientation.
- The lack of an integrated strategic framework.

It has to be said that there is an element of overstatement in these claims. However, Wind and Robertson do have a point and this book represents an attempt to meet the criticisms they voice by providing both a description and analysis of the nature of marketing strategy. But to write a book on marketing strategy without examining its relationship to marketing management would seem to perpetuate the deficiency of a partial treatment which Wind and Robertson criticised in the first place. Accordingly, this book seeks to show how a strategic approach to marketing can be implemented through management of the marketing function.

However, before describing how this is to be attempted in any detail it will be helpful if we anticipate our own advice and spell out:

1 What is the need to be satisfied?
2 What is the objective to be achieved?
3 What assumptions underlie the approach and method selected?

■ Needs

From the preceding section it should be clear that the basic need to be satisfied is a formal description and analysis of both the strategic and managerial aspects of marketing. However the vital question is, how has this need been identified?; for there can be little doubt that few if any practitioners responsible for marketing strategy and management have expressed a demand for a book on the subject. Indeed many practitioners would readily tell you that marketing is an art or craft which you practise and that it is practice or experience, not theorising or book-learning, which makes you proficient.

I reject this lack of overt demand on at least three counts. First, as will become clear in Chapter 4 when discussing the environment, there has been a radical change in the past decade to the extent that the prevailing and likely future conditions differ radically from those of the 1950s and 1960s when most senior managers were acquiring their experience. While some have been able to adjust to the changed conditions the overall sluggishness of the economy and the number of business failures suggest that the majority have not.

Second, the adoption of a marketing orientation is well advanced and no longer confined to the fast-moving consumer goods companies where it originated. All kinds of manufacturing companies now subscribe to the marketing approach as do service organisations in both the public and private sector whether for profit or not-for-profit. This widespread acceptance has resulted in a massive increase in demand for people to fill marketing appointments and it would seem sensible to try and prepare and train young persons to fill such posts rather than pursue a policy of trial and error learning through experience. Third, the body of knowledge based upon experience has now become so extensive that it makes sense to try and distil and codify it so that it can be communicated formally through books and other media. If experience, synthetic or real, is the key to the identification and solution of problems, who needs a book on the subject? Clearly this is an overstatement, for if everyone subscribed to this view there would be no book, nor a reader for these words. As in most things, the truth probably lies between the two extremes – managerial decision-making cannot be learned from books alone, but it is equally unlikely that it can be learned without them other than possibly by a gifted few with an intuitive flair for it.

A balance of formal learning and practice in application is required. Skills such as driving a car certainly fall into this category – flying aeroplanes even more so, for they involve three dimensions as opposed to two. In fact, flying aeroplanes provides a good analogy with managing an organisation – much of the activity is routine and can be handled satisfactorily in an almost reflex manner, thus leaving the practitioner free to concentrate upon two factors critical to continued success in executing the skill – anticipation and planning – while still maintaining the integrity of the system through a feedback and control system.

Like flying, management has become much more complex in this century. Speed is an obvious example and requires very sophisticated systems to maintain the integrity and safety of the machine. Everything must be done to much finer tolerances and the pilot must depend upon aids to his skill which were unknown and unnecessary in the early days of flying. The substitution of radar for visual observation is but one example of a situation where science and technology are required to give sufficient advance warning of hazards to permit evasive action to be taken. Of course, as many near misses bear witness, in the final analysis it is the pilot's observation and skill which are critical. In the management context, speed is the speed of change and demands elaborate forecasting systems to predict the future conditions likely to be met by the organisation. Similarly, size and complexity have increased markedly and require more extensive and more intricate systems to maintain control.

Without wishing to labour the analogy, the point being made is simply that managerial decision-making is a blend of routine and predictable events with occasional but potentially very hazardous interruptions. Therefore, it makes good sense to define and describe the routine occurrences and to develop standard operating procedures to deal with them. By doing so, it will be possible to delegate responsibility for routine to a lower level of management (or to a mechanical or electronic control system) and leave time free for the anticipating and planning functions. It also makes good sense to accept that if standard operating procedures evolve then they should be formalised and codified into a 'rule book' to which reference can be made as appropriate.

■ **Objectives**

And so to the justification for this book. In the author's opinion managerial decision-making itself is amenable to description, definition and codification. Hence, standard procedures for identifying and solving problems may be created. However, it cannot be over-emphasised that providing a framework for managerial decision-making cannot automatically guarantee correct or 'good' decisions. The selection of data to be used and their interpretation is still in the hands of the decision-maker himself.

The real point is that everyone is fallible. For those who are skilled decision-makers this book will provide an *aide-mémoire* – a cockpit check list. While everyone likes to think that the pilot can get his jumbo jet off the ground without such assistance (and, even more important, back down again), it is comforting to know that use of a check list prevents him omitting a vital step in the procedure.

For those less gifted or less experienced, the purpose of the book is the same – to provide a structured approach to managerial problem-solving – but its contribution is likely to be greater. Indeed I would claim that, as many management problems are of a recurrent type and require the exercise of only a minimal amount of judgement, then following the procedures and methods prescribed in this book will lead to a successful outcome in 95 per cent of the problems one is likely to meet. This is not to decry judgement – far from it – merely to put it into perspective.

In light of the above arguments the objective to be achieved may be stated as:

> To provide a comprehensive and integrated framework for the direction and management of the marketing function.

It must be stressed that it is the *framework* which is claimed to be comprehensive and integrated and, while it is hoped that the overall treatment is integrated also it manifestly cannot be comprehensive.

■ Assumptions

Assumption 1 is that *readers have read a basic textbook on the subject and/or have some business experience*. As the author of a basic textbook I have tried to make this work complementary and avoid duplication as far as possible. Of course there are situations where repetition is essential for clarification and desirable for reinforcement, but, in general, *Marketing* is primarily descriptive while this book is analytic and normative.

Assumption 2 is that there is a 'wheel' of management which revolves through a sequence of conceptualisation, planning, implementation, evaluation and feedback. Assumption 3 is that diagnosis must precede prognosis and Assumption 4 is that while firms may be at any stage of the management wheel it will simplify the analysis if a clean sheet start-up is assumed and so start with conceptualisation and diagnosis before proceeding to planning, prognosis, etc., in an ordered sequence (the organising principle for the book as a whole). Assumptions 5 to 8 are:

5 That the majority of cases are in existing organisations/institutions and that action plans must be based on realistic proposals for the transition from the present to the desired future state.

6   That the broad means of achieving one's objective is a strategic decision and that awareness of broad strategic alternatives must precede the formulation of action plans.
7   That the translation of plans into action is a managerial responsibility and that marketing has a primary role to play.
8   That planning and management are iterative and interactive so that measurement of performance, feedback, control and adjustment are essential elements of the managerial task.

■ Scope of the Book

To provide a perspective to the book as a whole a new Chapter 2 addresses the subject of 'Marketing and Competition'. Beginning with a definition of 'competition', and the role it performs in ensuring that scarce resources are used to maximise satisfaction, we then examine the role which marketing plays in this process. The concept of 'market structure' is then introduced both as a consequence of and an influence upon the conduct and performance of firms in competition with one another. The concept of international competition is then introduced and supported by an extended review of Michael Porter's discussion of the *Competitive Advantage of Nations* (1990). The chapter concludes with a broadly based assessment of the contribution of marketing to competitive success.

Chapter 3, 'Marketing and Corporate Strategy', seeks to establish the point of departure by defining the nature of marketing strategy and comparing it with the broader concept of corporate strategy. The conclusion is that the two are very similar, although marketing strategy may be seen as a subset of corporate strategy responsible mainly for anticipating and planning. The larger concept embraces issues of organisation design and control which go beyond marketing *per se*. Then, it is proposed that there is only a small set of strategic options open to the decision-maker and these are defined as a backcloth for an examination of basic marketing strategies. The chapter concludes with a statement of the functions of marketing management – analysis, planning, implementation and control – which serves as an introduction to the extended treatment of the topics in the remainder of the book.

Chapter 4, 'Principles of Strategic Marketing Planning' (SMP), moves to the heart of the issue by proposing definitions, a framework for SMP and some basic principles to be observed in developing and implementing a strategic marketing plan. It is then argued that the need for SMP is continuous in the sense that every innovation contains within itself the seeds of its own destruction in that it will increase the user's awareness and expectations which will prepare the way for new and improved substitutes. Thus marketers need to formulate strategy in terms of the underlying needs and satisfactions of consumers rather than the specific products or services which serve as the means of delivery of these satisfactions. Equally they must be sensitive to the inevitability of change summarised in the concept of the product life-cycle (PLC), an analysis of which leads to a proposal to use it as a key element in the process of SMP.

Chapter 5, 'Analytical Frameworks for Strategic Marketing Planning', builds upon the foundations introduced in Chapter 4 and suggests techniques and procedures for implementing SMP. To begin with we look at the product life-cycle (PLC) concept and propose that it provides a highly useful framework for organising our thinking about the evolution of products, firms and industries and the appropriate strategies and tactics associated with the phases of birth, growth, maturity and decline. The inevitability of this progression prompts the view that an organisation should seek to develop a *portfolio* of products which are at different stages of the cycle and so ensure the firm's long-term survival. The ideas of the product portfolio and portfolio analysis are extended to examine analytical approaches developed by successful companies such as Shell and GEC and the techniques of Gap, Scenario and SWOT analysis, all of which help the decision-maker structure and implement strategic marketing plans.

Chapter 6, 'The Marketing Environment', is based on the proposition that the external environment constitutes the ultimate constraint upon the firm and dictates the boundary conditions within which it must operate.

Following a review of the major forces which influence and shape the environment – demographic, social, cultural, political, economic and technological factors – attention is focused on the argument that there are discernible cyclical and secular trends in the overall pattern of business activity. An analysis of four basic kinds of economic cycle and broad theories of economic growth lend support for the existence of an underlying process or life-cycle and reinforce the use of the PLC as a basic organising principle. The need to take account of the nature of competition in the market place, discussed in Chapter 2, is reviewed with particular emphasis upon the importance of non-price competition and the implications this has for marketing strategy.

Finally the chapter provides some guidelines for the commissioning and execution of an environmental audit as an essential prerequisite to the formulation of a marketing strategy.

Chapter 7 addresses the nature of 'Buyer Behaviour' and poses the fundamental question 'How do buyers choose?' Following a limited and eclectic review of four different disciplinary explanations of choice behaviour, six concepts are examined because of the light they throw on the basic issue of how individuals and organisations choose between alternatives, namely:

- Selective perception.
- The hierarchy of needs.
- The hierarchy of effects.
- Dissonance.
- 'Buy tasks' and 'Buy phases'.
- The characteristics of goods.

In and of themselves none of the basic models nor the key concepts appears sufficient to reflect the complexity of real-world purchase decisions and a composite model of buyer behaviour is proposed which seeks to incorporate and synthesise both objective and subjective considerations.

The need for a composite model of buyer behaviour rests essentially on the fact that the total demand for a product is the aggregate of the demand of all the individuals who have a need for it backed up by purchasing power. In that each of these individuals will bring to the purchase decision his own values and perceptions we have to allow for these when presenting the 'facts' about our product to them. However, with limited exceptions very few suppliers can afford to tailor their output to the precise needs of the individual customer (even services have to be standardised to some degree) and it follows that to compete successfully one must steer a careful course between complete homogeneity and total heterogeneity. To achieve this compromise marketers have developed an extensive range of techniques for aggregating individual demands or, conversely, disaggregating total demand, into worth-while groupings or segments. This practice of 'Market Segmentation' is the subject of Chapter 8 and a wide range of different approaches is considered in some detail – demographic, locational, psychographic and behaviouristic – as a basis for suggesting how and when segmentation should be used as an appropriate strategic approach.

Chapter 9, 'Positioning', is new to the second edition and has been introduced to recognise the fact that a sustainable competitive advantage depends increasingly upon the seller's ability to develop a *distinctive personality and reputation* in the perception of prospective buyers. Key concepts such as positioning, branding, perceptual mapping, niche marketing and the augmented product are defined and described and the chapter concludes with a discussion of the view that in the 1990s companies will come to be seen as brands.

Chapters 10 and 11 deal with 'Situation Analysis: The Marketing Audit' and 'The Marketing Mix', formerly part of the same chapter. User feedback suggested that they would benefit from separate treatment although both mark the transition from the strategic to the managerial aspects of marketing. Thus in Chapter 10 we focus on the analysis necessary to underpin the formulation of a marketing plan. First we look at the Marketing Audit and the need to document the firm's strengths and weaknesses *vis-à-vis* the opportunities and threats (hence SWOT) presented to it by the external environment in which it has to operate. Of particular importance is the activity of competitors, and this is reviewed briefly as are approaches to sales forecasting on which short-term marketing plans are based.

In Chapter 11, 'The Marketing Mix', we recognise that marketing planners have a number of key factors or variables which they can manipulate in seeking to devise a distinctive and differentiated marketing plan. Several approaches to classifying the mix elements from the basic 4 Ps of Product, Price, Promotion and Place to Borden's extended listing of 12 elements are considered. The chapter concludes with an examination of the management of the marketing mix and acts as an introduction to Part II in which we explore each of the major mix elements in some detail.

Chapter 12, 'Marketing Research', opens with a discussion of the factors which create particular difficulties in seeking to apply formal analytical procedures to marketing decisions, namely:

(a) Many marketing problems are more or less unique.
(b) Buyers can think for themselves.
(c) Most marketing problems are very complex.

To help overcome these difficulties it is argued that the first step must be to establish just what information is available or may be acquired, to assess its worth and then combine it with one's own experience and judgement to reach a decision. A review of sources of secondary and primary data leads naturally into a discussion of data reduction and analysis as a means of imposing structure and meaning on what otherwise might constitute an 'information overload'.

The chapter concludes with a review of decision-making under uncertainty and the ways in which a decision-maker may combine objective 'facts' with his own subjective judgement to reach a decision using a Bayesian approach.

Chapter 13, 'Product Policy', begins with a reminder that most business is transacted by existing organisations with commitments to both products and customers. It follows that a preoccupation with one's product is not a negation of the marketing concept, but an essential precondition of survival. Similarly, it is argued that the emphasis upon user needs and product benefits has distracted attention from the product's physical characteristics and it is contended that a more even balance needs to be struck between the two.

The interaction between product and market is implicit in the four core strategies considered earlier – market penetration, market development, product development and diversification – each of which is reviewed in terms of the most appropriate product policy. To a lesser or greater degree all demand development of the product which leads naturally to a discussion of the role and nature of the new product development process and alternative forms for achieving this.

Depending upon its stage in the life-cycle the product will require differing degrees of emphasis upon the other elements and these are summarised in terms of the four major stages – introduction, growth, maturity and decline. The chapter concludes with a discussion of ways and means of monitoring the product's performance.

'Packaging' (the subject of Chapter 14) does not always receive separate treatment in marketing texts despite the fact that it may provide 'the just discernible difference' on which so many choice decisions hinge. In part this may be because packaging is considered an intrinsic element of the product and treated as such, in part because it is seen as a promotional tool and the subject of passing reference alongside the detailed discussion of advertising.

The chapter opens with some definitions of packaging which underline the different roles it plays in protecting and selling goods and is followed by an extended discussion of the five criteria to be considered in developing a package – appearance, protection, function, cost and disposability. To round off the chapter the issues and steps involved in developing a pack are reviewed.

Chapter 15, 'Pricing Policy and Management', acknowledges that, while firms prefer to compete on dimensions other than price, none the less price is of critical importance in the buying decision and calls for a high level of attention. Accordingly, while marketers might deprecate the economists' overwhelming emphasis upon price as the mechanism for adjusting supply and demand in the market-place they can learn many useful lessons from price theory. A number of key concepts such as elasticity, fixed, variable, marginal and opportunity costs are considered as are some of the major limitations of price theory as an explanation of the real world, e.g. its assumption of profit maximisation, lack of dynamism, neglect of subjective factors, etc. Pricing objectives are examined together with the three broad approaches to price determination – cost plus, flexible mark-up and marginal cost. Finally, the role of pricing in the marketing mix is explored as are the three basic strategies – skimming, penetration and value based.

The comparative neglect of 'Distribution and Sales Policy' provides the introduction to Chapter 16. Given the functions performed by channels of distribution and the important role these play in the creation of time, place and possession utilities such neglect is seen as surprising.

The composition and structure of alternative channels and the factors which influence them are described as are the considerations which condition channel selection decisions. In the latter context much will depend upon whether the producer wishes to pursue an undifferentiated, differentiated or concentrated marketing strategy and intends to push or pull the product through the distribution channel, and all these alternatives receive attention.

The chapter concludes with a brief summary of the personal selling function.

Chapter 17 deals with the final element of the marketing mix – 'Promotion Policy and Management'. Like distribution, promotion and particularly mass-media advertising is often regarded as a cost-creating function which adds little or nothing to the value of a product – a viewpoint which finds little or no support in the evidence presented here.

Starting with the argument that awareness is a necessary prerequisite to purchase, Schramm's model of the communication process is reviewed to clarify the essential point that all information has to be transmitted by a sender to a receiver. While personal communication may be the most direct method it is by no means always the most efficient or cost effective and it is here that the impersonal and indirect methods classified collectively as 'promotion' have an important role to play.

Ever since Lord Leverhulme offered the opinion that half of his advertising expenditure was wasted, marketers have been increasingly concerned with the problem of determining which half. To solve this conundrum one must first have some working hypothesis as to how advertising works and the two major schools of thought – that attitudes cause behaviour and vice versa – are analysed to throw light on the problem.

Once one has formed an opinion as to how advertising works it becomes possible to formulate objectives and state policies for their achievement. In turn this leads to a discussion as to how one should set an advertising appropriation and measure the effectiveness of the expenditures incurred.

The chapter concludes with a look at the problems involved in choosing between the various promotional alternatives in order to develop an optimum promotional mix.

Since the publication of the first edition in 1985 the importance of service has become much more widely recognised, to the point that specialised textbooks are now available concerned solely with this aspect of the marketing mix. Within a general text it is not possible to give the topic extended coverage but a new section on Total Quality Management has been added to Chapter 18, together with a discussion of the measurement of service quality. The chapter concludes with a discussion of how one should offer and price customer services and completes Part II.

Part III, 'Implementing Marketing', is a composite of new material and topics covered in the first edition. It comprises four chapters. Chapter 19, 'Developing a Marketing Culture', opens with a discussion of the relationship between organisational structure and strategy formulation. As recognised elsewhere in the book most strategies are developed by organisations which already exist. Only rarely does management have the opportunity of the clean sheet start-up situation so easily assumed in the textbooks. Accordingly, strategy formulation must take place within the constraints of existing structures and the existing values and attitudes associated with them. While marketers naturally emphasise the importance of a marketing orientation it is quite clear that other functional aspects of business may colour an organisation's overall orientation – R&D, Production, Sales and Finance. The nature of these orientations is examined together with the underlying concepts of organisational climate, corporate personality and culture as the basis for determining what is required to develop a marketing orientated organisation. The chapter includes a short discussion of the notions of corporate vision, mission and strategic intent and concludes with a review of the issues involved in implementing marketing.

Chapter 20 takes a brief look at the nature of the short-term Marketing Plan. The need for formal plans is justified and a normative framework proposed. The conditions necessary for producing market plans are spelled out, as are the key elements in the marketing plan itself.

Within the constraints imposed by the environment the firm will seek to control its own actions in order to achieve its corporate objectives in the most effective and efficient way, and 'Control' is the theme of Chapter 21.

The primary concern of the marketer must be to optimise the marketing mix and to do so he must attempt to quantify and measure the contribution of its different parts. To this end cost-volume-profit relationships are examined, as are the concepts of cash flow and present value. Finally, in order to assess both one's own and one's competitors' performance a brief look is taken at the interpretation of corporate accounts through the use of management ratios.

Chapter 22, 'Recapitulation', is just that. Unlike this introduction, which is designed to give a broad overview of the scope and coverage of the book as a whole, the final chapter is much more eclectic in that it seeks to tease out what I regard as the key lessons to be learned from a reasonably extensive and rigorous review of the field as a whole.

Marketing and Competition

Learning Goals

The issues to be addressed in Chapter 2 include:

1 The concept of 'competition'.
2 The nature and value of CUGs (currently useful generalisations).
3 The nature and scope of marketing.
4 The relationship between market structure, the conduct of suppliers and their performance.
5 How these competitive forces shape and influence marketing strategy.
6 The impact and consequences of international trade on competition.
7 Michael Porter's concept of the 'Diamond of National Advantage'.
8 The role of government and chance in determining competitive outcomes.
9 The development of 'clusters' of competitive industries.
10 The nature and sources of competitive advantage.
11 The contribution of marketing to competitive success.

After reading Chapter 2 you will be able to:

1 Define competition and the role it performs in ensuring that scarce resources are used to maximise satisfaction.
2 Appreciate that good theory usually reflects best practice and why learning through knowledge acquisition is more cost effective than learning by experience.
3 Understand the nature and scope of marketing.
4 Appreciate the ways in which market structure and performance influences and is influenced by the conduct of suppliers and their interaction with users.
5 Perceive how these interactions help determine marketing strategy.
6 Recognise and be able to describe the impact of international trade on competition.
7 Understand and be able to describe Porter's concept of the 'Diamond of National Advantage'.
8 Recognise the influence of government policy on competitive activity.
9 Define the nature of competitive advantage and how this leads to the creation of 'clusters' of successful firms and industries.
10 Appreciate the contribution which marketing makes to the achievement of competitive success.

■ Introduction

In the Prologue (Chapter 1) we drew attention to Wind and Robertson's criticisms of the absence of a strategic emphasis in marketing. Central to these criticisms were the interdisciplinary isolation of marketing, the lack of rigorous competitive analysis and the lack of an international orientation. In this chapter, we seek to address all three of these perceived deficiencies.

To begin with we acknowledge the fact that modern explanations of competitive behaviour in the market place draw on over 200 years' rigorous and detailed analysis by economists. While the extent of this dependency has only recently become recognised generally through the writings of people like Michael Porter,[1] it is clear that marketing is indeed a synthetic discipline in the sense that, like medicine and engineering, it *depends fundamentally upon other disciplines*. Where the new discipline of marketing adds value is in its willingness to cross the (artificial) boundaries which are necessary to define the single discipline and link ideas and concepts from a number of disciplines in order to provide a more comprehensive explanation of the complexity of the real world. First, however, it is important to understand precisely what insights the single discipline can offer, so we open the chapter with arguments in favour of getting back to the basics before attempting a more sophisticated and more complex analysis.

Next we attempt a short answer to the question 'What is marketing?' to provide both content and perspective for the book as a whole. Essentially, we argue that the success of an economy in using and allocating resources may be judged in terms of the satisfaction given by their *consumption*. It follows that it is the consumers' perception of value which is fundamental to the whole concept of economic and business success.

The third section 'Market Structure, Conduct and Performance' offers a conceptual framework from the field of industrial economics which helps explain how performance in the market place is the consequence of the interaction between the basic forces of demand and supply as mediated by the structure and operation of the market.

The following section 'International Competition' recognises that technological change and a revolution in communication has transformed the preoccupation with the operation of national economies to a consideration of their global interdependence.

Finally, we address the issue of central concern to readers of a book of this kind – the contribution of marketing to competitive success. It was Kenneth Boulding who coined the memorable doggerel about 'innovation' 'for which we could easily substitute 'marketing':

> We all know innovation
> Benefits both world and nation.
> The question we must answer later,
> Is, 'will it help the innovator?'

In 'Marketing and Competitive Success', we report the findings of a major survey into this question. The answer, and justification for the book, is that marketing is a *necessary*, albeit not a *sufficient*, condition for competitive success.

■ Competition

In their seminal text *Industrial Market Structure and Economic Performance* Scherer and Ross (1990)[2] open their analysis with the observation that:

> Any economy, whatever its cultural and political traditions may be, must decide what products to supply and how much of each to produce, how scarce resources will be apportioned in producing each, and how the end products will be divided up or distributed among the various members of society. There are three alternative methods to solve this bundle of problems. First, decisions can be made to conform with *tradition*. The economic organisation of manors in Europe during feudal times and the caste system of occupational selection in India are prominent examples. Second, the problem can be solved through *central planning*. Illustrations include output and input planning for most industries in the Soviet Union and the elaborate controls the US Department of Defense imposes over its contractors.
>
> Finally, there is the *market system* approach, under which consumers and producers act in response to price signals generated by the interplay of supply and demand in more or less freely operating markets.

With the growth of democracy throughout the world, the collapse of the Soviet economy in the early 1990s and the abandonment of communism it is clear that the market system approach offers the best solution to the central economic problem of maximising satisfaction through the consumption of scarce resources. The process by which this is achieved is *marketing*.

Clearly, the process and function of marketing has existed since the time when man first discovered that by exchanging surpluses with others he could improve his overall satisfaction – an insight which was to lead to acceptance of task specialisation and exchange as the foundation for increased productivity and higher standards of living. From 1760, and the publication of Adam Smith's *Wealth of Nations*,[3] to 1960, and Ted Levitt's 'Marketing Myopia',[4] the formal study of the nature of competition remained the province of the professional economist. As a consequence, and in common with many other professions, much of the substance of the body of knowledge which distinguished the field of study was poorly communicated to others who might have benefited considerably from the insights it was able to offer to the solution of real world problems. Indeed, few managers appreciate that the essence of Michael Porter's influential writings on competition and competitive advantage[5] are derived directly from the sub-field of economics known as 'industrial organisation' or 'industrial economics'.

The point which we are seeking to make is that there is a tradition of more than 200 years' concentrated analysis on the subject of competition. As such, it would be negligent to ignore the contribution such analysis might make to solving contemporary problems as experienced by the managers of individual and independent firms competing one with another.

There is much truth in the adage that 'There is nothing new under the sun'. Despite this, the thirst for novelty frequently results in the pursuit of fashionable new panaceas to the neglect of explanations, methods and techniques which have withstood the test of time. Our own preference is to depend upon what at my time at the Harvard Business School we called *CUGs* – *currently useful generalisations*. In many cases CUGs will be regarded as axioms or theoretical explanations of activities or behaviour. At Harvard the view was (and probably still is) that the complex, dynamic and interdisciplinary nature of management problems was such that they were not easily amenable to the kind of definitive statement and explanation characteristic of the physical sciences. Accordingly, the appropriate test was 'does this seem to work?' If so, then one has a currently useful generalisation which can be depended upon until it is shown not to work. If and when this occurs it is far easier to jettison a CUG than worry how one is to rewrite the textbook.

Of course many of the CUGs which will be deployed in this chapter and throughout the book are regarded as accepted theoretical explanations by the social scientists and others from whom they have been borrowed. But rather than inquire into the reasons why they have achieved this standing, our focus will be on how the insights and conceptual frameworks offered can help improve managerial analysis and decision-making. In other words, 'how can we use this knowledge to do our job better?'

In this spirit we shall revisit some of the key ideas developed by industrial economists as a basis for determining how they can help us better understand the nature of competition and its implications for the formulation of strategy at the level of the individual firm. A word of caution is appropriate here. Over 30 years' experience as a teacher confirms that the biggest danger faced by decision-makers is a tendency to dismiss facts or evidence on the grounds that 'I know all that' and/or 'That's all very well in theory but in practice . . .'. The point about 'theory' is that it is usually distilled wisdom based upon observation and documentation of real world experience, i.e. it *is* what works in practice. It is a CUG and will remain so until you can convince your peers that it doesn't work and so should be discarded. So, before you dismiss the explanation of social scientists as 'academic' bear in mind that these capture the essence of what seems to work or not work in the field of business management. These are the basic relationships which offer structure and understanding for the solution of particular problems and, therefore, of much greater value than the passing popularity of most of the current management best sellers.

Before reviewing the nature of competition it will be useful first to address the question 'what is marketing?' A little earlier we claimed that marketing is the process through which economies address the central problem of allocating resources in a manner which will maximise the satisfaction of the members of that economy. However, 'marketing' has many other connotations – most often those associated with selling and advertising – so some justification of this claim seems called for.

■ What is Marketing?

Marketing is an enigma. At the same time it is both simple and complex, straightforward and intricate, a philosophy or state of mind and dynamic business function; it is new and it is as old as time itself. Cynically, we might observe that marketing is therefore precisely what you want it to be, and thereby everything or nothing. In attempting to resolve this paradox the views expressed must be those of the author, although they clearly owe much to the influence and thinking of others. Similarly, the reader will have to draw his or her own conclusions concerning the boundaries and parameters of marketing. Fundamentally, however, it is felt to be of little consequence whether the reader thinks or agrees that the concept and processes discussed in this book are the province of marketing or of some other discipline or orientation. What is important is the credibility and conviction which can be attached to them.

While the science of economics is founded essentially upon analysis of the interaction of supply and demand, and the causes and consequences of this interaction – one might say the issues of what will be produced and how – so the art of politics is concerned mainly with who will receive what share of the resultant output. In the eyes of marketers this may be restated somewhat as follows, 'The economic problem is to maximise the satisfaction arising from the consumption of scarce resources. Accordingly, we are concerned with consumer satisfaction, and the best judge of such satisfaction is the individual consumer. This must be so, for satisfaction is a subjective concept that varies between individuals and even within individuals over time. We are concerned, therefore, with consumer sovereignty[6] founded upon the basic proposition that supply must be a function of demand'.

In essence, therefore, the marketing concept is concerned with exchange relationships in which the parties to the exchange are seeking to maximise their personal satisfaction. This proposal is fundamental to the discipline of economics, but goes beyond it in its emphasis upon the subjective rather than the so-called rational or objective measurement of satisfaction. The importance of this distinction is made clear by Lawrence Abbott in his book *Quality and Competition*,[7] in which he asserts that 'what people really desire are not products but satisfying experiences'. He then goes on to say: 'what is considered satisfying is a matter for individual decision: it varies according to one's tastes, standards, beliefs and objectives – and these vary greatly depending on individual personality and cultural environment. Here is a foundation for a theory of choice broad enough to embrace Asiatic as well as Eastern cultures, non-conformists as well as slaves to convention, Epicureans, Stoics, Cynics, roisterers, religious fanatics, dullards and intellectual giants alike.'

To put it another way, we are claiming that marketing is concerned with the *establishment of mutually satisfying exchange relationships in which the judgements as to what is satisfying depend upon the perception of the parties to the exchange.*

But the marketing concept goes beyond recognition of the fact that the parties to an exchange do so out of self-interest, whereby each is seeking to maximise his personal satisfaction. The marketing concept stresses that the desired satisfaction of one party should be the motivating force or catalyst behind an exchange, and this party is the consumer *not* the supplier. In fact, as I have noted elsewhere,[8] we are positing a theory of choice founded on consumer sovereignty.

In our modern sophisticated societies it has become necessary to develop a marketing function to bridge the gap which has developed between the two parties to an exchange – producer and consumer, buyer and seller, or supplier and user – which has grown up as a result of task specialisation, the division of labour and the application of technology to the production function.

In the days of a simple barter economy we may safely assume that the two parties to an exchange at least got what they bargained for. To this extent the exchange must have been mutually satisfying, although one can understand how the different values placed upon different goods might necessitate multiple exchanges in order to convert the homogeneous output of one product or service into a variety of desired outputs and services produced by other suppliers. Clearly the development of a medium of exchange greatly facilitates such transactions and encourages the development of formal places of exchange which become known as 'markets'. Initially the development of markets does not necessarily lead to the separation of producer and consumer but, over time, a new class of intermediary begins to emerge whose function is to bring together the outputs of the producers of a related group of products, concentrate these at a point of sale and enter into transactions for the exchange of title to these goods with prospective consumers. It is not difficult to see how economic growth and development leads to an increasing separation between producer and consumer and the development of more and more sophisticated mechanisms for facilitating exchanges between them.

Clearly this separation is not new, and may be traced back to long before major economic changes such as those precipitated by the industrial revolution. On the other hand, it is only in this century, and many would say in the second half of this century, that the balance between supply and demand has reached a point where producers have once again to take the sort of interest in their relationships with a consumer which is inimical to a barter relationship. Thus, in the modern advanced industrial economy we have arrived at a point where the basic capacity to *produce* exceeds the basic propensity to *consume*. In fact, this situation has existed for many decades, but its impact has been greatly reduced by population growth and increased international trade. However, since the mid-1950s population growth in the advanced economies has tended to slow down while technological innovation has accelerated, so continuing the growth in our capacity to produce.

Given the attitudes to work which prevail in industrial economies, most governments have seen it as desirable to maintain full employment and therefore to encourage increased consumption to absorb the output of this employment. Thus two basic trends may be identified. The first of these is *demand stimulation*, which has led to the rediscovery of the marketing concept and the development of a sophisticated marketing function to facilitate its implementation. The second is the redistribution of the working population into less productive or even *non-productive* (unemployed) activities.

Market Structure, Conduct and Performance

The field of economics concerned with market structure, conduct and performance is generally designated as 'industrial organisation' and, in the opinion of Scherer[9], who is a leading authority on the subject, is concerned with the 'market systems' approach to solving economic problems. According to Scherer, the market system operates through producer and consumer responding to the price signals, which result from the interplay of supply and demand in more or less freely operating markets, in an attempt to 'make the best of the market conditions he or she faces'. As a result of this interaction between supply and demand, a *chain of events* is created in which these forces result in the evolution of a particular market structure, the nature of which has significant effects upon the conduct of suppliers and their consequent performance. The causal relationship between the factors is shown in Figure 2.1. As Scherer and Ross (1990) acknowledge, 'The broad descriptive model of these relationships was conceived by Edward S. Mason of Harvard during the 1930s and elaborated by numerous scholars'. They explain the key elements of the model as follows (pp. 4–5):

> *Performance* in particular industries or markets is said to depend upon the *conduct* of sellers and buyers in such matters as pricing policies and practices, overt and tacit interfirm cooperation, product line and advertising strategies, research and development commitments, investment in production facilities, legal tactics (for example, in enforcing patent rights), and so on. Conduct in turn depends upon the *structure* of the relevant market, characterised by the number, size and distribution of sellers and buyers, the degree of physical or subjective differentiation distinguishing competing sellers' products, the presence or absence of barriers to the entry of new firms, the shapes of cost curves, the degree to which firms are vertically integrated from raw material production to retail distribution, and the extent of the firms' product line diversification (conglomerateness).

Market structure is in turn affected by a variety of *basic* conditions.

These basic conditions are summarised as falling into two categories – *supply* and *demand* – and a number of aspects of each is contained in Figure 2.1.

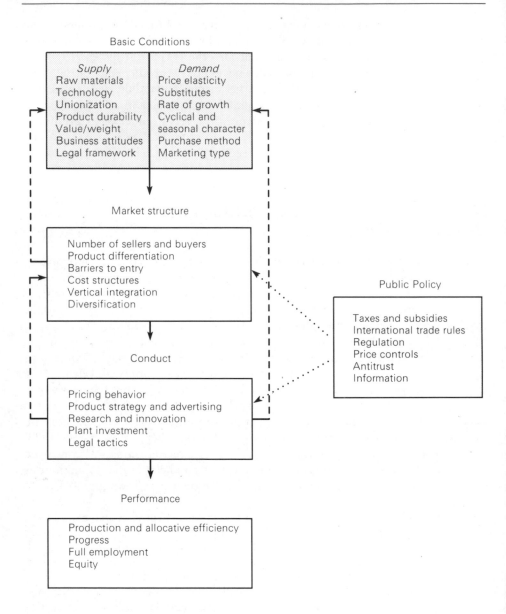

Figure 2.1   The structure–conduct–performance paradigm

Source: F.M. Scherer and D. Ross, *Industrial Market Structure and Economic Performance.*

The study of industrial organisation and the thrust of Scherer and Ross's book is concerned with the causal flows represented by the solid black arrows with the objective of seeking to predict ultimate market performance from the observation of structure, basic conditions, and conduct. However, Figure 2.1 differs in two important respects from that which appeared in the first edition (Figure 4.3, p. 104). First, it contains *feedback loops* (the dotted lines) and, second, it recognises the role and influence of public policy in mediating the 'free operation' of market economies. The feedback loops thus acknowledge that markets are *dynamic systems* and that the forces of supply and demand will be modified by their experience or performance in the market place with satisfactory outcomes leading to reinforcement and repetition, and unsatisfactory outcomes to the selection of alternative courses of action. Similarly, the inclusion of public policy issues recognises that, while in theory 'good economic performance should flow automatically from proper market structure and the conduct to which it gives rise' (Scherer and Ross, 1990), in practice it does not, and government agencies may feel it necessary to intervene to improve performance in accordance with public opinion as to what is the acceptable face of capitalism.

Ultimately it is true that all firms are in competition with one another. But, for practical purposes, most analyses are concerned only with firms which are competing directly with one another in the context of other suppliers producing similar end-use goods or services (an industry) for sale to consumers with closely related needs (the market). It follows that in proceeding from the general to the particular the strategist must move from general considerations of competition and market structure to the specific conditions which characterise the industry or market in which his firm is to operate.

■ Competition and Marketing Strategy

While there is a very extensive economic literature which deals with industrial organisation, comparatively little of this has received any consideration from businessmen. Perhaps this is because businessmen have an intrinsic distrust of economics (often with good cause) but, more likely, it is due to the fact that they have failed to perceive the potential contribution of academic theory to their practical problems. The publication of Michael Porter's book *Competitive Strategy* (1980)[10] did much to redress this deficiency. In this section we will draw heavily upon Porter's exposition (which is strongly recommended as a source book) as it represents a recent and comprehensive review of the applied economist's view of competition. In doing so, however, we would not wish to overlook the existence of a very well-developed and extensive literature dealing with competition that is to be found classified in a library under 'Economics' rather than under 'Business' or 'Management'.

One of the crucial decisions which faces the industry analyst is precisely where to draw the boundaries which define an 'industry'. As we shall see, similar difficulties exist in terms of defining a 'market' and the parameters which one uses will have a major bearing upon the applicability of most, if not all, of the tools and techniques which have been developed to aid management. In particular, therefore, the firm's definition of its industry and its market will be critical to the formulation of its own competitive strategy and the success or otherwise of that strategy. In general, however, and as a prerequisite to such specific definition, it is useful to assume that the industry has been defined so that attention can be concentrated upon the determinants of competition.

Porter uses the economists' concept of substitutability when he offers a working definition of an industry as 'the group of firms producing products that are close substitutes for each other'. In order to define the interaction or state of competition between these firms economists have developed definitions of a continuum of competitive states ranging from zero (monopoly) to absolute ('perfect'). While the theoretical implications of these states are conceptually important (see Chapter 4 on *'Marketing'*[11], and the preceding discussion) it will suffice here if we appreciate that the nature of competition is to ensure that the marginal rate of return on capital will be the same everywhere. Thus the forces of competition work to ensure that capital will flow from less efficient firms in an industry to more efficient firms and from less efficient industries to more efficient industries. The ultimate aim of every strategist should therefore be to have the *most efficient firm* in the *most efficient industry*.

In 'How Competitive Forces Shape Strategy'[12] Michael Porter distinguishes five basic forces which govern competition in an industry – the threat of new entrants, the threat of substitution, the bargaining power of suppliers, the bargaining power of customers and rivalry between current competitors – and depicts their interaction as in Figure 2.2. Porter describes the key features of these five forces along the following lines.

☐ The Threat of New Entrants

Freedom of entry to an industry is widely regarded as a key indicator of an industry's competitiveness such that in the case of a monopoly by definition no other firm can enter while in the case of 'perfect competition' there are no barriers to entry. From the firm's viewpoint the greater the barriers to entry the less the threat from new competitors and the more secure its own position.

Seven major barriers to entry are proposed by Porter:

1. Economies of scale.
2. Product differentiation.
3. Capital requirements.
4. Switching costs.
5. Access to distribution channels.
6. Cost disadvantages independent of scale.
7. Government policy.

A full discussion of these factors is to be found in Porter, and at this juncture we wish only to underline a point to which we will return many times: namely,

25

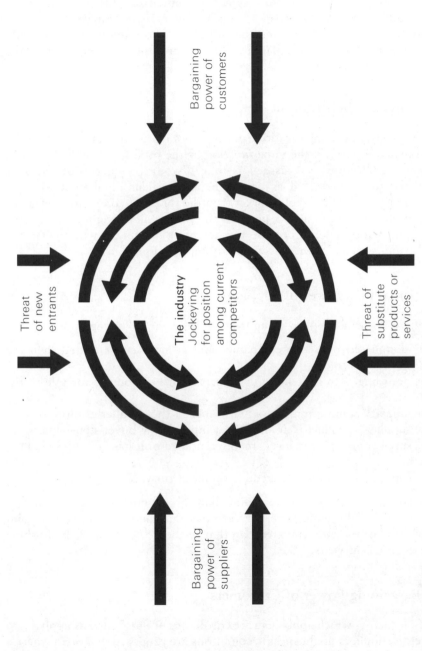

Figure 2.2 Forces governing competition in an industry

Source: M. Porter, 'How competitive forces shape strategy', *Harvard Business Review* (March–April 1979) p. 141.

that product differentiation has become *the* key competitive factor. Simplistically, the reason why this should be so is that if one owns a product which is perceived as differentiated by users then one has a *monopoly* and so is not exposed to competition for as long as one can maintain this position of the perceived difference. As we shall see in Chapter 7 on 'Buyer Behaviour', perception is a subjective state and one which can be influenced significantly by marketing activities, thus explaining the current importance attached to the subject.

☐ The Threat of Substitution

As Porter notes: 'Identifying substitute products is a matter of searching for other products that can perform the same *function* as the product of the industry', a point which underlines our assertion that if your product is sufficiently differentiated to be perceived as unique by a sufficient number of users to comprise an economically viable market then the threat of competition is latent rather than active. Given such a position the danger lies in complacency, for change is inevitable, if only because the act of consumption will *change the consumers* and so make them susceptible to improved products.

☐ The Bargaining Power of Suppliers

According to Porter a supplier group is powerful if the following apply:

(a) It is dominated by a few companies and is more concentrated than the industry it sells to.
(b) It is not obliged to contend with other substitute products for sale to the industry.
(c) The industry is not an important customer of the supplier group.
(d) The supplier's product is an important input to the buyer's business.
(e) The supplier group's products are differentiated or it has built up switching costs.
(f) The supplier group poses a credible threat of forward integration.

   Porter also makes the important point that 'labour must be recognised as a supplier as well, and one that exerts great power in many industries' – a point even more true of the UK economy than that of the USA, albeit of diminishing importance in recent years.

☐ The Bargaining Power of Customers

Many of the factors which apply here are corollaries of those cited as applying to the power of suppliers. Eight specific conditions are proposed by Porter where a buying group will exercise power:

(a) The buyer group is concentrated or purchases large volumes relative to seller sales, e.g. Marks & Spencer *vis-à-vis* its suppliers, or the multiple grocery chains like Tesco or Sainsburys.
(b) The products it purchases from the industry represent a significant fraction of the buyer's costs or purchases.
(c) The products it purchases from the industry are standard or undifferentiated, e.g. basic chemicals, steel, aluminium, etc.
(d) It faces few switching costs.
(e) It earns low profits, i.e. it will be active in seeking cost reductions in bought-in supplies.
(f) Buyers pose a credible threat of backward integration.
(g) The industry's product is unimportant to the quality of the buyers' products or services, e.g. most packaging materials.
(h) The buyer has full information.

☐ Rivalry Between Current Competitors

'Jockeying for position' is the phrase which Porter uses to describe the tactical moves employed by firms to seek an advantage over their competitors. Clearly the greater the degree of skirmishing between the rivals the more active and volatile is the competitive state. The intensity of this rivalry is a function of numerous factors, of which Porter distinguishes eight:

1 Numerous or equally balanced competitors (a basic condition for a state of 'perfect' competition).
2 Slow industry growth, e.g. retail food sales.
3 High fixed or storage costs. On this point Porter makes the important observation that 'The significant characteristic of costs is fixed costs *relative to value added* [emphasis mine], and not fixed costs as a proportion of total costs'.
4 Lack of differentiation or switching costs.
5 Capacity augmented in large increments, e.g. steel, shipbuilding.
6 Diverse competitors – particularly international rivals.
7 High strategic stakes.
8 High exit barriers – e.g. specialised assets with low liquidation values, redundancy costs, social implications, etc.

Porter comments:

> When exit barriers are high, excess capacity does not leave the industry, and companies that lose the competitive battle do not give up. Rather, they grimly hang on and, because of their weakness, have to resort to extreme tactics. The profitability of the entire industry can be persistently low as a result, cf. the world automobile and steel industries.

■ International Competition

Until recently most analyses of competition have focused upon competition *within* a single national economy. Of course the importance of international trade is recognised and prompted Ricardo to articulate his theory of comparative advantage as long ago as 1817. More recently, however, there has developed a recognition that we are now concerned with a global economy and global competition. Developing the ideas introduced in *Competitive Strategy* (1980) and *Competitive Advantage* (1985) Porter extended the scope of his analysis from companies and industries to countries with the publication of his book *The Competitive Advantage of Nations* (1990). Contrary to the views of classical economists who attribute national prosperity to a country's natural endowment of land, labour and capital Porter asserts that prosperity is *created*, not inherited, and depends on its industry's capacity to innovate and upgrade:

> A nation's endowment of factors clearly plays a role in the competitive advantage of a nation's firms, as the rapid growth of manufacturing in low-wage countries such as Hong Kong, Taiwan, and more recently, Thailand attests. But the role of factors is far more complex than is often understood. The factors most important to competitive advantage in most industries, especially the growth in advanced economies, are not inherited but are created within a nation, through processes that differ widely across nations and among industries. Thus, the stock of factors at any particular time is less important than the rate at which they are created, upgraded, and made more specialised to particular industries (p. 74).

> Firms create competitive advantage by perceiving or discovering new and better ways to compete in an industry and bringing them to market, which is ultimately an active innovation. *Innovation* is here defined broadly, to include both improvements in technology and better methods or ways of doing things. It can be manifested in product changes, process changes, new approaches to marketing, new forms of distribution, and new conceptions of scope. Innovators not only respond to possibilities for change, but force it to proceed faster. Much innovation, in practice, is rather mundane and incremental rather than radical. It depends more on accumulation of small insights and advances than on major technological breakthroughs. It often involves ideas that are not 'new' but have never been vigorously diffused. It results from organisational learning as much as from formal R & D. It always involves investment in developing skills and knowledge and usually in physical assets and marketing effort (p. 45).

Frequently, innovation occurs when firms identify a new market opportunity or a segment of a market which has been neglected by those serving the market as they understand it. Thus the Japanese success in world auto markets (both cars and motor cycles) was based upon the production of small, high quality high-performance machines when the prevailing fashion was for large, comparatively low-performance machines. By definition innovation consists of *doing something new* and so must overcome the inertia of the old, established and hitherto successful way of doing things. It is for this reason that innovation is often precipitated by an 'outsider' or a 'newcomer' who is unaware of the thousand and one reasons why the existing way of doing things cannot be changed.

Basically, however, humans possess only a limited range of needs (qv. Maslow's needs hierarchy)[13] so that innovation represents an improved way of serving an existing and known need. It was for this reason that in 'Marketing Myopia' Ted Levitt[14] exhorted suppliers to define markets in terms of the need served such as transportation, entertainment, 'fast food', convenience, etc. rather than in terms of the current products through which these needs were served. Thus the vast majority of innovations are substitute products which offer a more satisfying way of meeting a consumer need. Given that consumers are motivated more by self-interest than by supplier loyalty it is unsurprising that innovations will displace existing products or ideas if they offer enhanced satisfaction.

It follows that a necessary condition for competitive success is that one's own product is at least equivalent to that of one's competitors. Thus the ultimate goal of competition is usually seen as having a 'better' product than one's competitors. Indeed, it is a truism that no company can survive unless a sufficient number of customers hold that view so as to ensure that it can achieve a profitable sales volume. Overall 'better' reflects à combination of both objective and subjective factors as implied by Rogers's (1960)[15] definition of 'relative advantage'. In most cases the objective characteristics of a product are a *sine qua non* of the intending consumers' willingness even to consider it – if you want to buy a washing machine you don't look in a car showroom! However, the value attached to particular objective features of a product will vary significantly according to the intending users' attitudes, knowledge, discretionary purchasing power, etc. In other words, they are *situation specific*. They also *change over time*.

The paradox for both users and suppliers is, therefore, that while they resist change they can improve their (competitive) position only by accepting it. The problem is more acute for suppliers than it is for users and, the more successful a supplier is, the more acute the dilemma – if for no other reason than that they appear to have least to gain and most to lose from changing the status quo. As Porter[16] observes:

> Successful companies tend to develop a bias for predictability and stability; they work on defending what they have. Change is tempered by the fear that there is much to lose. The organisation at all levels filters out information that would suggest new approaches, modifications, or departures from the norm. The internal environment operates like an immune system to isolate or expel 'hostile' individuals who challenge current directions or established thinking.

■ The 'Diamond of National Advantage'

Porter's thesis is that in order to explain how firms may overcome this inertia or complacency one must examine what he terms the 'Diamond of National

Advantage'. As illustrated in Figure 2.3, the 'diamond' is defined by four sets of attributes which Porter describes as follows:

1 *Factor Conditions.* The nation's position in factors of production, such as skilled labour or infrastructure, necessary to compete in a given industry.
2 *Demand Conditions.* The nature of home-market demand for the industry's product or service.
3 *Related and Supporting Industries.* The presence or absence in the nation of supplier industries and other related industries that are internationally competitive.
4 *Firm Strategy, Structure, and Rivalry.* The conditions in the nation governing how companies are created, organised, and managed, as well as the nature of domestic rivalry.

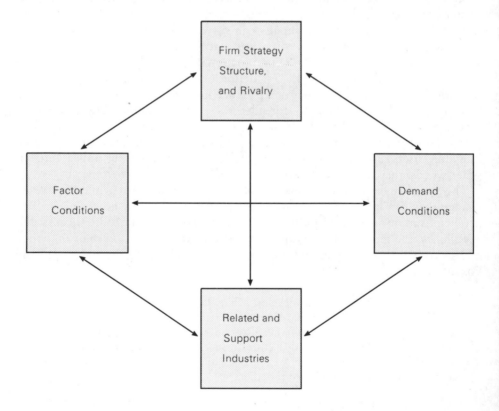

Figure 2.3   Determinants of national competitive advantage

Source: M. Porter, 'The Competitive Advantage of Nations', *Harvard Business Review* (March–April 1990).

According to Porter the classical theory of comparative advantage based upon the concept of factor endowment 'is at best incomplete and at worst incorrect' as an explanation of the competitive advantage of nations. As noted earlier, this is not to say that the factor conditions are unimportant but to emphasise that their contribution depends more upon their utilisation than their mere existence. Indeed, there is much evidence in international competition in the second half of this century to suggest that *factor deficiencies* act as a spur to innovation rather than a deterrent, e.g. Japan's development of just-in-time techniques to economise on expensive space, and the development of steel mini-mills in Northern Italy. Porter also emphasises that the most important factors are those that involve sustained and heavy investment and are specialised, e.g. advanced education and R & D.

The second factor which has a major bearing upon a nation's competitiveness is the *home-market demand*, and *Best of Business*[17] summarises its influence as follows:

> The nature of domestic demand shapes the way companies interpret and respond to customer needs. Nations gain advantage in industry or industry segments where home demand gives local companies a clearer or quicker picture of buyers' needs than foreign rivals can have. Countries also gain advantage when customers push local companies to innovate faster.
>
> Such highly sophisticated and demanding buyers provide a window into the most advanced and stringent customer needs. For example, hot and humid summers make air conditioning highly desirable in Japan. But Japanese homes are small and tightly packed, and a bulky, noisy air conditioner is unacceptable. This, along with the high energy costs, pushed Japanese companies to pioneer energy-saving rotary compressors. A consequence is that Japanese companies have penetrated international markets with their compact, quiet units. Domestic market conditions in Japan have led to an intense effort to innovate by creating products that are *kei-haku-tan-shou*, or 'light, thin, short, small'. The result is a constant stream of compact, portable, multifunctional products that are accepted internationally.

The third point of Porter's diamond is *Related and Supporting Industries*. Few, if any, industries are completely vertically integrated and the strength of any firm in the value chain, which stretches from the extraction of raw materials through to after-sales service, depends significantly on the quality of the firms with which it interacts, particularly on the supply side. Supplier companies which are at the forefront of their own industries act as a catalyst for the transfer of new technology and methods to their customers and, in doing so, enhance and extend both their own and their customers' competitive edge. Examples include the Swiss pharmaceutical industry which grew out of its success in the manufacture of dyestuffs, the Japanese facsimile industry based upon its success with copiers, and Swedish strengths in fabricated steel products like ball bearings and fasteners derived from superior performance in the manufacture of specialty steels.

Finally, *Firm Strategy, Structure and Rivalry* complete the model. Much of the work into international competitiveness in the 1980s came to the conclusion implicit in Porter's model – namely, there is no single source of success. Rather, success depends upon a combination of factors which are appropriate to the needs and context which exist at a point in time: as Shakespeare observed 'There is a tide in the affairs of men, which taken at the flood leads on to fortune' (*Julius Caesar*, Act 4, Sc. 3).

So it is with business. We can define and describe the circumstances which are auspicious but the key issue is whether anyone will recognise and be able to take advantage of an opportunity when it arises. It is for this reason that so much attention has come to be focused on the concepts of organisational climate and culture and the managerial systems and practices through which values and attitudes are translated into competitive behaviour. Given his background as an economist Porter tends to write of management systems rather than cultural differences between nations although these are reflected in his descriptions of the Italians' penchant for strategies which stress focus, customised products, niche marketing, rapid change and breathtaking flexibility while the German system 'works well in technical or engineering-oriented industries – optics, chemicals, complicated machinery – where complex products demand precision manufacturing, a careful development process, after-sales service, and thus a highly disciplined management structure'.

National 'character' also influences attitudes to risk and capital formation, and one of the most trenchant criticisms of UK and US competitive performance over recent decades has been the tendency to go for short-term, more certain and immediate pay-offs rather than adopt a long-term view and 'nurse' emerging technologies and industries through their often difficult formative years. Thus companies and industries which focus on a particular business – 'stick to the knitting' in Peters and Waterman's [18] terms – and confine any diversification to closely related activities are seen as succeeding more than those which pursue unrelated diversification strategies.

Another factor strongly associated with international competitive advantage is the presence of strong domestic competition. In the absence of domestic rivalry and with protected markets the evidence suggests that firms and industries become complacent and flaccid and unable to withstand the rigours of competition from either within or outside their own home market. Given strong competition, firms are forced to innovate and look to the market as the basis for distinguishing specific segments which they can seek to dominate through differentiated products and marketing mixes. Further, the pace of innovation quickens as firms imitate each other's developments and seek to buy in expertise through their hiring policies which enhance labour mobility and the transfer of know-how.

In addition to the four basic determinants of competitive advantage Porter acknowledges the existence of two additional variables which may have an important influence – government and chance.

■ The Role of Government and Chance

As with so many theories developed in the social sciences the academics' attempt to define the boundaries of their subject often leads to greater attention being given to the extreme conditions in their 'purest' form and so being diverted from the intermediate states which are typical of the great majority of cases. Certainly this is so with the concepts of perfect competition and monopoly which rarely, if ever, exist. In the case of government's role in economic affairs and the stimulation of competitiveness (efficiency) the same tendency is apparent in the dichotomy between centrally planned and free market economies. Porter observes:

> Both views are incorrect. Either, followed to its logical conclusion, would lead to the permanent erosion of a country's competitive capabilities. On one hand, advocates of government help for industry frequently propose policies that would actually hurt companies in the long run and only create the demand for more helping. On the other hand, advocates of a diminished government presence ignore the legitimate role that government plays in shaping the context and institutional structure surrounding companies and in creating an environment that stimulates companies to gain competitive advantage.

Porter (and many others) believe that Japan's government has grasped the role governments should play better than any other country. While this is not to say Japan has not made any mistakes it has stimulated the pursuit of both quality and advanced technology which are seen as critical to the forces of the 'diamond'. Thus, while Japanese politicians have not been averse to attempting to manage industry structure, to protect domestic markets and to condone inefficiency to secure political support, they have tempered these typical political responses with a longer view than most other countries. In doing so, they have favoured the policies which Porter argues are vital to nations seeking to gain competitive advantage:

- A focus on specialised factor creation.
- Non-intervention in factor and currency markets.
- The enforcement of strict product, safety and environmental standards.
- The restriction of direct cooperation among industry rivals.
- The promotion of goals that lead to sustained investment.
- The deregulation of competition and the enforcement of strong domestic antitrust policies.
- The rejection of managed trade, i.e. attempts to negotiate levels of trade between markets.

As for 'chance' its effect is important because it creates *discontinuities*. Discontinuities disrupt the established pattern of doing things and create opportunities for innovation – from both established players and newcomers alike.

■ The Development of 'Clusters'

If, then, one regards the 'diamond' as a system, on which chance and government influence impinge, it would appear that competitive industries within a country occur as 'clusters'. Clusters occur as a consequence of both *vertical* relationships with suppliers and customers and also as a result of *horizontal* relationships based upon shared technologies and common customers. Numerous examples demonstrate that clustering is a pervasive phenomenon:

- In Denmark the agricultural dairy-food cluster.
- In the USA leadership in consumer goods contributed to pre-eminence in advertising.
- Japanese strength in consumer electronics skewed strength in semi-conductors towards memory chips and integrated circuits.
- German chemical companies promoted the growth of the pump industry.

Best of Business summarises the impact of clustering as follows:

> Once a cluster has formed, the whole group of industries becomes mutually supporting. Benefits flow forward and backward. Aggressive rivalry in one industry tends to spread to others in the cluster, through the exercise of bargaining power, spin-offs and related diversification by the established companies. Information flows freely, and innovations diffuse through the conduits of suppliers and customers that have contact with multiple competitors.
>
> The presence of a cluster magnifies and accelerates the process of factor creation. Companies from an entire group of interconnected industries *all* invest in specialised but related technologies, information, infrastructure and human resources, and numerous spillovers occur. The scale of the cluster encourages greater investment and specialisation. Government and university attention is heightened, and the pull of size and prestige in attracting talent to the cluster becomes more insistent. The nation's international reputation in the field grows. The cluster of competitive industries thus becomes more than the sum of its parts.

Once again Japan provides a compelling example of the impact of the emergence of clusters on a country's competitive advantage. In Japan *keiretsu* have developed around the major banks and comprise loose groupings of companies with shareholding connections as a result of which cooperation and interaction are encouraged. However, while such collaboration ensures that members of the cluster exchange information and ideas about market needs they are not allowed to dull rivalry or prevent members looking outside the group for more attractive sources of supply or custom. Several other examples of national clusters are given by Porter and it is interesting to note that the 'mechanisms which facilitate interchange within clusters are generally strongest in Japan, Sweden and Italy and weakest in the U.K. and the U.S.' (*Best of Business*).

■ The Creation of Competitive Advantage

Porter's analysis of the factors which give rise to competitive advantage is reflected throughout history in the rise and fall of nation states. Companies and economies appear to grow and prosper by confronting adversity and overcome it through innovation and application. By the same token they decline and decay as a consequence of self satisfaction and complacency which dulls sensitivities and the ability to recognise that change is inevitable as those with a lesser level of advantage seek to improve upon it. The phenomenon is reflected in the North Country saying 'Clogs to clogs in four generations'. The origin of the saying dates from the time of the Industrial Revolution when the lowest paid mill workers wore clogs which, thereby, represented the working class. Members of this class with ambition would seek to improve their lot by sacrificing current consumption to invest in the education of their children who then became white collar workers in the lower paid administrative and professional jobs. In turn they invested in the education of their children who secured top jobs. However, the fourth generation would be brought up in an insulated environment in which everything was provided for them and with no particular pressure to improve themselves. Accordingly, they would squander their inherited wealth leaving their offspring to fend for themselves and initiate another cycle.

Levitt's 'Marketing Myopia' and the rediscovery of marketing emphasise the dangers of complacency, the inevitability of change and the fact that continued success and prosperity depend upon continuous monitoring of one's environment both to anticipate and respond to change. Thus firms and nations lose competitive advantage due to the absence of the reasons which encourage and enhance it. The absence of demanding customers, a deterioration in factor inputs or changes in their relative importance due to technological change, the development of short-termism and a preoccupation with present pleasures to the neglect of long-term investment all initiate the downward spiral from success to failure. Unfortunately, the systemic nature of the 'diamond', which means that improvements in one area can initiate and amplify improvements in the others, works in reverse, too. It is also apparent that homeostasis or equilibrium is very difficult, if not impossible, to achieve.

What is one to do? There is a large measure of truth in the view that people get the politicians and government they deserve – in other words that democratic governments reflect the views and aspirations of the majority. While oppositions may propose and even stimulate change, the gradual convergence of policies in most western democracies suggests that there is more to be gained by swimming with the tide of popular opinion rather than against it. If this is so then change must be initiated by individuals and groups of like minded individuals who organise around them. In terms of economic growth and competitive performance, companies represent the key unit for change. As Porter observes 'Ultimately, only companies themselves can achieve and sustain competitive advantage'. In order to do so there appear to be four basic lessons to be learned.

☐ The First Lesson is that the Fundamental Source of Competitive Advantage is Innovation

Innovation can take many forms from the first radical or 'discontinuous' innovation such as Sony's use of the transistor to build a smaller and lower cost radio. (The transistor was invented at the Bell Laboratories in the USA in 1947. Akio Morita, the president of a small Japanese company, paid $25,000 for a licence to produce it and 2 years later introduced the first portable transistor radio which weighed one-fifth of radios then on the market and cost one-third the price. Morita was the innovator and within 3 years dominated the American market and within 5 years the world market.) Perhaps more important is the capacity for *continuous or incremental innovation* which can be seen in Sony's strategy of portable entertainment systems.

☐ Competitive Advantage Involves the Entire Value System

Stoddard Carpets Limited maintained both volume and profitability in 1989/90 when the UK market crashed as a result of high interest rates. It did so because it combined skills in wool buying with strengths in spinning (which has a major impact upon both design and construction) and weaving, together with excellence in design and marketing, both recognised by national awards. Weakness in any one of these elements would have dulled their competitive edge not only in the carpet market but in all the other consumer durable markets with which it competed for the consumers' discretionary purchasing power.

☐ Competitive Advantage is Sustained Only Through Relentless Improvement

It has been estimated that any innovation is fully diffused and understood within 18 months of its first introduction. Similarly, it is claimed that 10 years after graduation 80% of the knowledge used by a scientist or engineer will have been discovered since he graduated. The message is clear – you cannot afford to stand still but must strive continuously to improve upon the currently successful solution to the markets' needs.

☐ To Sustain an Advantage Requires Continued Investment Over Time

Because objective factors which give rise to competitive advantage can be replicated, imitated or acquired, long-run advantage tends to reside in less tangible subjective factors which together constitute what might be termed 'reputation' and occasionally are reported in a firm's balance sheet as 'goodwill'. In the same context competitive advantage is more often to be found in marketing, distribution and service than in R & D and manufacturing. This is not to say that the latter are less important. On the contrary, investment in them is a necessary condition for success. It is just that, for the reasons given above, they are not *sufficient* to guarantee long-run success.

□ A Global Approach to Strategy is Required

While it is true that successful firms must dominate their domestic market it is also true that it is the challenge of international competition which maintains the competitive edge. Only by continuously testing one's abilities with the most difficult suppliers and demanding customers in the most competitive markets can the firm be sure that it is avoiding complacency and pursuing excellence. In welcoming international competition, however, it is vital to remember that the core strength comes from the domestic market and development of the 'diamond' here must not be neglected.

Finally, however, Porter comes to much the same conclusion as many other analysts of competition in recent decades. As Baker and Hart (1989)[19] put it (in the words of the song) 'it ain't what you do it's the way that you do it'. In other words, there is no royal road to success – one can identify a multiplicity of factors positively associated with success. But while in many instances one can point to the fact that the absence of particular 'critical success factors' (CSFs) will almost certainly lead to failure one cannot guarantee it even if all the CSFs are present. The reason, quite simply, is that competition is a *dynamic state* in which two or more adversaries vie for the patronage of customers. Obviously one will seek to develop objective and measurable advantages over one's rivals but, for the reasons touched on earlier, these tend to be short lived unless continuously improved upon. Thus, from the customer's point of view choice exists when there are two or more equally acceptable alternatives – if there is only one solution then the 'choice' is 'take it or leave it'. The customer's problem is to distinguish between closely similar alternatives and to do so he will draw on previous experience, attitudes (a predisposition to behaviour) and the recommendations of others. It follows that the successful firm or nation is the one which can achieve pre-eminence on performance grounds through innovation and then sustain it.

To sustain competitive advantage demands vision and leadership: vision to be able to perceive the need for continual improvement and change, and leadership to inspire and motivate others to respond to the challenge. 'Leaders believe in change. They possess an insight into how to alter competition, and do not accept constraints in carrying it out. Leaders energise their organisations to meet competitive challenges, to serve demanding needs and, above all, to keep progressing. They find ways to overcome the filters that limit information and prevent innovation' (*Best of Business*).

■ Marketing and Competitive Success

In the preceding section passing reference was made to a study by Baker and Hart published in 1989 as *Marketing and Competitive Success*. Given that our book is concerned primarily with marketing strategy it will be useful here to summarise some of the key findings of this broadly based empirical study into the contribution of marketing to overall competitive success.

In the period following the conclusion of the Second World War there has been a significant acceleration in the scope and intensity of international competition. During the late 1940s and 1950s much economic effort was devoted to making good the losses occasioned by the war so that the emphasis was upon the restoration of national domestic economies. In parallel with the post-war reconstruction taking place in Europe and Japan a number of developing countries sought to improve their economic performance through industrialisation leading to the establishment of a new group of NICs (newly industrialising countries).

Initially much of the increased output of countries like West Germany, Japan, Hong Kong, Singapore, Taiwan, etc. was consumed domestically. But, as growth slowed, these countries began to look to international markets in order to sustain economic growth. Thus, the 1960s and early 1970s witnessed the steady growth of international trade and a marked change in the standing of traditional trading countries such as the USA and the UK. From the mid-1970s onwards the 'threat' of this increasing competition resulted in more and more attention being given to the sources of competitive advantage and the nature of competitive success.

The nature of the threat and the appropriate response are to be found documented in two seminal publications. The first 'Managing our Way to Economic Decline' by Bob Hayes and Bill Abernathy appeared in the July/August 1980 issue of the *Harvard Business Review*. In drawing attention to the USA's decline in competitiveness in international markets and the import penetration of domestic markets, such as automobiles and electronics, which it had 'invented', Hayes and Abernathy pointed out that even the UK had outperformed the USA in terms of economic growth over the past two decades. The diagnosis? – an over-emphasis upon a financial/sales orientation, the key features of which may be summarised as:

- The emphasis tends to be upon short-range profit at the expense of growth and longer-range profit. Budgeting and forecasting frequently pre-empt business planning.
- Efficiency may out-rank effectiveness as a management criterion.
- Pricing, cost, credit, service and other policies may be based on false economy influences and lack of market place realism.
- The business focus is not on the customer and market but on internal considerations and numbers.

The other seminal publication which could be seen as a response to Hayes and Abernathy's concern was the best-selling *In Search of Excellence* by Thomas Peters and Robert Waterman.[20]

The sub-title of Peters and Waterman's book – 'Lessons from America's best run companies' – helps to explain how this book captured the imagination of American managers. This was the real thing, an insight into how eminently successful and widely admired corporations managed their affairs. As Baker and Hart (1989) note, the success of *In Search of Excellence* and other such best sellers is that they themselves conform with a formula for success, namely:

- They assert the superiority of American management and systems.
- They stress entrepreneurial values and the money making ethic which had been so strongly challenged by the consumerist movement in the 1960s and 1970s.
- They are based upon the analysis of the practice and procedure of firms or people who are leaders in their field and manifestly successful.
- They reduce the ingredients of success to simple catechisms or formulae.
- They emphasise that the essential catalyst and hero of the piece is the manager himself.

But the managerial best sellers were not without their critics. Based upon an extensive review of the literature Baker and Hart (Chapter 4) came to a number of conclusions concerning a real understanding of the possible relationship between marketing and competitive performance:

1   While a number of suggestions have been made regarding the *practical* nature of a 'marketing orientation', the majority of writers have been content with a broad and general statement that a marketing orientation enhances success.
2   There is a tendency for many authors to focus solely on the organisational dimensions of marketing: the *trappings* rather than the *substance*.
3   Empirical work has often been concerned with only one or two factors and their effect on corporate success. This means that having carried out a literature review, a broad view is gained of how important the variable under consideration is to the success of the company, but no indication is obtained of the *relative importance* of each variable in the total number of factors. A more comparative investigation of the variables would greatly improve knowledge in the area.
4   Empirical studies, where they have been undertaken, have often been confined to *one industry*, which limits the findings to the industry under investigation.
5   A large number of authors write *normatively*, and this widens the gulf between theory and practice. That theorists and practitioners do not see some managerial issues in the same way is an indication of the work that needs to be done by researchers.

6   The various articles dealing with this subject have been written in different countries at different times and pertain to the economic and social environments which existed *at the time the study was executed*. Such environments, in many cases, are no longer applicable to marketing in the 1980s and 1990s.

7   A number of key empirical studies have identified the characteristics of successful design companies, successful exporting companies, all-round successful companies, etc. without attempting to verify if such characteristics are also present in *less successful* companies. Some progress towards defining what is *exclusive* to successful firms would consolidate findings which would otherwise remain uncontested and unvalidated. It was against this background that Baker and Hart undertook a survey with a rigorous design to try and remedy the weaknesses noted in earlier work.

Readers requiring the full detail of this study must refer to Baker and Hart's original book. However, it will be helpful here to present the multi-factor model which guided both a consideration of other work and the survey of actual practice. In Figure 2.4 it can be seen that five sets of factors – environmental, strategic, marketing, organisational and managerial are generally invoked in seeking to explain business performance. All but managerial factors are the subject of more extended discussion in this book. Based upon extensive qualitative research involving depth interviews with industry leaders, government officials, management writers and other academics, a formal questionnaire was developed for administration to a representative sample of companies with the overall objective of measuring the contribution of marketing factors to competitive success.

In order to avoid the criticisms levelled against earlier studies, it was decided to sample both growth and mature or declining industries (sunrise and sunset). Within these industries respondents were selected who were successful or less successful within the industry by comparison with three performance indicators – sales growth, average profit margin, and average return on capital employed. The details of the final sample composition and the findings of the survey are contained in Baker and Hart's Chapter 6. Based on our analysis the overriding conclusion was that, contrary to the impression gained from many earlier commentators, 'unsuccessful' companies deserve more credit than they are usually given. Given that the data were collected following a major recession in the late 1970s and early 1980s all of the respondents satisfied the minimum criterion of success which was that they had survived. Further, our analysis confirmed that knowledge and use of modern management ideas and techniques were widely diffused and accepted in the 'less successful' companies. Specifically, we found that: 'At the structural level, however, the existence of a particular department's or board titles is as much related to size as to any other factors. In other words, it is fruitless to look at obvious indicators of commitment to marketing. It is therefore necessary to look at more subtle factors, like the extent to which marketing personnel communicate with top level decision-makers, or the extent to which there is a clear and defined *responsibility* for marketing.'

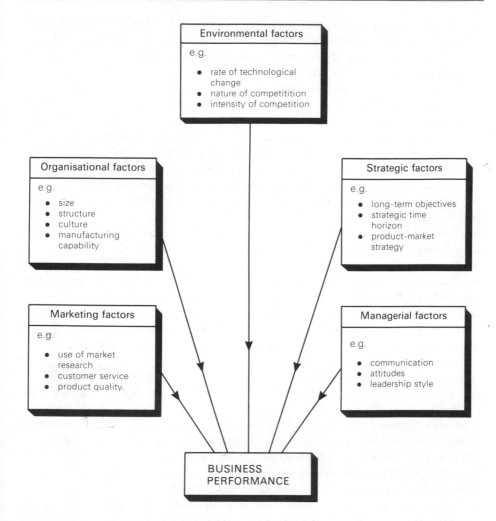

Figure 2.4   Factors influencing competitive success

Source: Michael J. Baker and Susan Hart, *Marketing and Competitive Success* (London: Philip Allan, 1989).

At the *strategic* level, the studies identified a few factors that seem to distinguish between above- and below-average companies: a long-term approach, specific strategic objectives, linking strategic plans closely with changes in markets, and a continuous commitment to new product development are all activities apparent in *more* successful companies rather than *less* successful ones.

At the *tactical* level, market research, market segmentation, and certain promotional techniques are more common in successful companies.

Overall, it is possible to say that relatively few of the factors studied actually accounted for differences in performance. However, the fact that these tightly controlled studies failed to find more factors which distinguish the successful from the less successful is, in itself, very important. Both studies covered a wide range of issues, from the McKinsey 'Southern' Framework[21] and the simultaneous loose–tight structures of Peters and Waterman (1982) to the managerial style reported as being important by Wong, Saunders and Doyle (1992)[22].

Clearly, in order to sustain and improve their competitive edge managers seek information and advice on best practice and seek to incorporate it in their planning and execution. Ultimately, it is clear that it is the quality of implementation that differentiates most between more and less successful competitors. But it is important to emphasise that the quality of implementation will become determinant only provided that the *initial analysis and planning* is of equivalent quality. It is only when one has taken full advantage of the analytical procedures and techniques described in the managerial literature that the quality of implementation will become important. Otherwise, an excellent plan executed by average management will always out-perform a below-average or non-existent plan executed by above-average managers.

Without this belief there would be little if any justification for a book of this kind, the great majority of which is concerned with describing and explaining methods and techniques which are known to improve performance.

■ Summary

The main purpose of Chapter 2 has been to provide a context in which to consider the detailed issues which comprise the substance of the book. As the title indicates, the primary concern has been to describe the nature of competition and the role which marketing has to play in determining the outcome of competition between firms, industries and national economies.

The chapter opened with recognition of the fact that the subject of competition has been central to the formal study of economies for over 200 years. We also observed that, as we move towards the millennium, the market economy has emerged as the principal and preferred mechanism for solving the basic economic problem of maximising satisfaction from the consumption of scarce resources. In parallel with our summary of the key factors which industrial economists have identified as having a major influence on the nature and outcome of competition between firms we warned of the dangers of the implied distinction between theory and practice.

Frequently, theory and practice are presented as if they were polar opposites with little or no relationship to one another. In reality theory (or at least 'normative' theory) should reflect our understanding of real world relationships and so enable us to predict how events will turn out in future given particular and clearly defined sets of circumstances. Knowledge, from which theory is derived, represents distilled experience. While knowledge can never be a complete substitute for experience, its sheer volume predicates that no individual could ever hope to acquire directly the kind of understanding and insight which can be achieved through education as opposed to experiential learning. But rather than digress into a polemic on the importance of theory *per se*, we recommend the pragmatic test adopted by the Harvard Business School in its use of 'Currently Useful Generalisations' (CUGs), namely: 'Does this seem to work?' If it does then the practitioner would be best advised to use the 'theory', 'concept', 'paradigm' or whatever to its best advantage and leave it to the academics to argue over the niceties of the distinctions between the meaning of these terms.

On the assumption that readers of text books are inclined to accept this advice, the remainder of the chapter has reviewed and described some of the more important ideas necessary to an understanding of the nature of competition. First, we explored the view that the interaction between supply and demand (sellers and buyers) resulted in the development of specific markets. The structure of these markets will both influence and be influenced by the actions of suppliers as they compete for the patronage of customers. Their success in this competitive activity will be reflected in their performance and the performance of the industry *vis-à-vis* other industries which are seeking to attract consumers' disposable income.

Within an industry competition is governed by five main forces – the threat of substitutes for the industry's output, the bargaining power of customers and suppliers, the threat of new entrants and the 'jockeying' for position between current competitors. Each of these factors was examined with a view to establishing how they contributed to the creation of competitive advantage. In turn we explored how competitive advantage could be seen to influence and shape marketing strategy.

The analysis of competition was then broadened from the single economy to the case of international trade and exchange. Considerable attention was given to Michael Porter's work, *The Competitive Advantage of Nations*, in which he develops a modern explanation of the theory of comparative advantage as first proposed by Ricardo[23] in the early nineteenth century. This analysis led to an extended statement of the sources of competitive advantage.

Finally, the chapter reviewed the question of the role played by marketing in achieving competitive success. From this review it was apparent that while marketing alone is not a *sufficient* guarantee of success it is certainly an important and, therefore, *necessary* factor contributing to it.

Having established the context within which marketing occurs we proceed in Chapter 3 to define more precisely what marketing is, and its relationship to corporate strategy.

Marketing and Corporate Strategy

Learning Goals

The issues to be addressed in Chapter 3 include:

1 The development of the *marketing function*.
2 The fundamentals of *corporate* vs *marketing strategy* and the context in which they evolve.
3 The identification of *limited strategic alternatives* and *basic strategic options*.

After reading Chapter 3 you will be able to:

1 Describe the *function* of marketing.
2 Recognise the concept of *need satisfaction* in the development of a marketing orientation.
3 Understand the role of *corporate strategy* and be able to describe its *constituent elements*.
4 Distinguish the four factors which create the cycle of business-growth and decay.
5 Identify four alternative strategies of the *growth vector components* and understand the concept of *limited strategic alternatives*.
6 Appreciate the *PLC* as a planning tool and be able to use the concept.
7 Describe three basic marketing strategies – undifferentiated, differentiated and concentrated – and relate these to Porter's generic strategies of cost leadership and differentiation.
8 Describe the four major sub-sets of general management, and show how they differ from marketing management.

■ Introduction

If one is to conduct a reasoned analysis of the nature, scope and role of marketing strategy and management, then it is essential to establish precisely what one means by the terms 'marketing', 'management', and 'strategy'. Even more important, one must also define what one means by marketing management and marketing strategy. This is the essential purpose of Chapter 3, which will be developed as follows.

First we propose to establish why marketing has assumed much greater visibility and importance in the last 30 years or so.

The second task will be to define the terms 'strategy' and 'management' in the business context, and to distinguish between strategy as the formulation of policies to be pursued by the organisation and management as the process by which these policies are translated into action. Philosophically our definition of marketing tends to claim that it is pervasive, and it will be necessary to examine the distinction between corporate strategy and marketing strategy, so as to test its validity.

Given a definition of strategy, it will then be argued that there is only a limited portfolio of basic alternatives open to the decision-maker. It follows that a primary task in devising a strategy is evaluation of these basic alternatives in the light of an organisation's ambitions, objectives and resources, which are the subject of extended treatment in later chapters.

▌The Development of the Marketing Function

With rare and localised exceptions the history of mankind has been one of scarcity. Not until recent times, and even now on only a limited scale, has it been possible to do much more than satisfy the basic physiological needs of people. Thus, the provision and acquisition of food, shelter and clothing has been the major preoccupation of the majority, with only a small and privileged minority able to develop and satisfy demands for higher order needs concerned with leisure, recreation, the arts, etc. In such circumstances the basic choice tends to rest between having and not having, rather than selecting between alternative means of satisfying different needs. In these circumstances the nature of demand tends to be simple and basic and the producer will maximise satisfaction by creating the largest possible output at the lowest possible unit cost.

Such an approach has been characterised as a production orientation and is immortalised in Henry Ford's dictum that 'you can have any colour of car so long as it is black'. In other words, Henry Ford recognised that the basic need which he was satisfying was for a cheap form of personal transportation. Only when this basic demand had been satisfied did consumers become more sophisticated and begin to look for ways of differentiating one motor-car from another, and so express a preference for differentiated motor-cars, including the provision of different colours. Henry Ford has frequently been criticised as an arch example of the old-fashioned production orientation, in which the emphasis was laid upon product standardisation in order to achieve the lowest possible unit cost through pursuit of the economies-of-scale production. Such criticism tends to ignore the fact that when Henry Ford first produced the Model T he was exactly in tune with the needs of his market, and that his failing, if such it was, was in not seeing that the basic demand for cars had become saturated and that the demand needed to be stimulated through the provision of a differentiated product.

From the foregoing comments it is clear that consumer demand must not be regarded as a homogeneous and unchanging entity. In fact, it is just the reverse – it is heterogeneous and dynamic, and it is these factors which decree that one must not only establish the dimensions of consumer needs before setting out to satisfy them, but that one must also anticipate change and adjust one's output to respond to these changes. However, inertia or resistance to change is an endemic human condition. In the short run inertia may appear to work, but in the long run it is inevitably doomed to failure, and retribution is invariably more immediate and final in the case of goods and services (as opposed to ideas, political systems, etc.) for consumers can easily switch or withhold the money votes on which suppliers depend for their existence. Herein, then, lies the essential difference between the marketing orientation with its emphasis upon the future, and the production and/or sales orientations[1] with their emphasis upon the past and present, which result in attempts to mould demand to match the existing and often obsolescent supply.

If one accepts the proposition advanced by Lawrence Abbott which we quoted in Chapter 2, namely that satisfaction is particular to the individual, then it would seem fairly logical that if we wish to maximise consumer satisfaction we must first establish what it is that consumers want. It also seems fairly obvious that perhaps the easiest way to establish what it is that people want is to ask them. Hence, while basic demands may be so obvious as not to require specification, the recognition that all consumers are not alike demands that we try and classify the nature of similarities and differences between individuals in order that we may identify aggregations or segments of sufficient size to warrant the production of a specialised product. Thus it was that in the 1920s and 1930s increasing attention was given to the development of one of the basic elements of the marketing function – marketing research. At the same time producers were also faced with the need to sell what they could make, and this led to a transitional period between the so-called production orientation and the present marketing orientation. In the transitional period the emphasis has to be on sales and promotion, in order to enable the producer to dispose of the products which his existing capital investment is designed to produce. In the short term this is an operational necessity, for unless the investor can capitalise his existing investment he will be unable to generate funds to invest in the new plant and equipment designed to satisfy the new needs of his customers, as identified by and through marketing research.

With increasing affluence the consumer spends less of his disposable income upon basic goods and services for which demand is fairly predictable, and is left with an increasing amount of discretionary purchasing power to spend (or save) in accordance with his or her own personal preferences. In consequence, we can discern two basic tendencies – on the part of producers an increased awareness of the need to establish the precise nature of consumer preference, and on the part of the consumers a desire to satisfy higher order needs. Many of these higher order needs fall into the category of personal services, and so the two trends coalesce with producers seeking to get closer to their consumers in order to establish a closer personal relationship, while consumers seek to extend the satisfaction gained through the consumption of physical goods by increasing their consumption of services, which, by definition, require a high level of personal contact.

In the opinion of marketers, recognition of the need to establish closer contact with the consumer predicates the adoption of a marketing approach, which may be summarised as consisting of the following basic steps:

1   Identification of a need which can be satisfied profitably within the constraints and opportunities represented by the potential supplier's portfolio of resources, and which is consistent with the organisation's declared objectives.
2   Definition of a particular segment or segments of the total demand which offers the best match with the producer's supply capabilities (the target audience).
3   Development of a specific product or service tailored to the particular requirement of the target audience.
4   Preparation of a marketing plan specifying the strategy to be followed in bringing the new offering to the attention of the target audience in a way which will differentiate it from competitive alternatives. (The main elements of such a plan will comprise pricing, promotion, selling and distribution policies.)
5   Execution of the plan.
6   Monitoring of the results and adjustment as necessary to achieve the predetermined objectives.

Collectively these activities constitute the objectives of marketing strategy, and encompass the responsibility of marketing management.

However, as noted earlier, many people would claim that in defining the scope of marketing so broadly we go beyond the province of a function of business and describe business itself. It will help, therefore, if we examine first the nature of corporate strategy as the basis for a comparison with marketing strategy.

■ Corporate Strategy

In recent years the term 'corporate strategy' has been widely adopted by management to describe the activities associated with the statement of an organisation's overall goals or objectives and the means by which they are to be achieved/fulfilled. It is this topic which constitutes the central theme of this section.

However, before embarking upon a discussion of the nature, scope and purpose of corporate strategy, it will be helpful to offer a more precise definition than that given in the preceding paragraph. It will also be helpful to clarify the relationship between business *policy* and *corporate strategy*, for management books and company statements use both terms in many different contexts and with many apparently different connotations.

■ Policy and Strategy

As Ansoff notes when addressing the issue of whether policy and strategy are different names for the same concept,[2] 'the term *policy* has long been a standard part of familiar business vocabulary'. However, he proceeds to distinguish two distinct connotations, only one of which corresponds with his own definition of strategy as '*a rule for making decisions*'. Thus Ansoff argues that a policy is a contingent decision, in that the decision-maker has specified a particular response to a defined set of circumstances whose nature is well understood although their occurrence cannot be specified in advance, as, for example, would be the case in the event of an employee's sickness, or the interruption of work due to a power failure.

Conversely, a strategy is a statement of the action to be adopted under a state of partial *ignorance*, where all the alternatives cannot be recognised and stated in advance of the need for a decision. It follows, therefore, that under this definition the implementation of policy may be delegated, whereas the implementation of strategy cannot, as it depends upon the exercise of judgement by the decision-maker himself, i.e. he cannot pre-define the situation, nor the response, in advance, with sufficient clarity to permit delegation.

Thus, under the Ansoff approach, types of decisions are characterised by reference to the decision-maker's level of ignorance in line with the definitions developed by mathematical decision theorists. Under conditions of *certainty* one *knows* the outcome of the occurrence of a given set of events in advance, and for these circumstances one develops *standard operating procedures*. Under conditions of risk, one knows all the alternatives and the probability of their occurrence in advance, and so may specify the preferred response or *policy*. But, under conditions of *uncertainty*, while one knows the alternatives, one does not know the probability of their occurrence. In the latter situation one may assign a judgemental probability to the likelihood of events and by applying the Bayesian methodology, as developed by Raiffa[3] and Schlaifer,[4] determine which of the possible alternatives is to be preferred in line with one's own judgement and chosen decision criterion. (A decision criterion is the basis selected for choosing between alternatives, e.g. price, profitability, ROI, etc.) Accordingly, under conditions of uncertainty, top management may well be prepared to delegate the authority to make decisions to persons whose judgement they trust, as they can specify:

(a) the alternatives to be evaluated
(b) the decision criterion to be applied.

Under Ansoff's classification such delegation would constitute a policy.

By contrast, with the situations of certainty, risk and uncertainty, described above, a condition of partial ignorance predicates that one is unable to specify all the alternatives open to the decision-maker *in advance*. Clearly, a time must come when a decision has to be made, when one may still be unable to assert categorically that all possible outcomes have been defined. Although Ansoff is not explicit upon the point, one is entitled to infer that unperceived alternatives are ignored or, more likely, subsumed under a generic catch-all such as 'others', and assigned a conditional probability, whereafter one may proceed to make a decision as under conditions of uncertainty.

It is because of this latter possibility that the Ansoff mathematical school of decision theorists' distinctions between strategy and business policy can appear contrived. Certainly there seems to be much to recommend the less precise approach typified by the Harvard Business School Faculty, who have played such an instrumental and major role in developing the field of business policy. In fact, the Faculty at Harvard have included courses in the subject of business policy for over seventy years now, although closer examination reveals that they use the term 'business policy' as synonymous with 'strategy'. This is not to argue that differences between states of knowledge (or ignorance) as characterised by the mathematical theorists, are not important – they are – but to assert that no particularly useful purpose is to be served by attributing precise meanings to the terms 'business policy' and 'strategy' when practitioners appear to find no utility in such a distinction. However, both schools of thought use 'policy' with the connotation 'course of action', and it is this general meaning which is intended hereafter.[5]

■ Defining Corporate Strategy

How then are we to define corporate strategy? Our own preference is for the sense associated with military usage (from which so many apparently new business ideas have been borrowed with little or no acknowledgement), namely, the achievement of a stated purpose through the utilisation of available resources. In a business context we follow the definition proposed by Andrews,[6] namely, 'Corporate strategy is the pattern of major objectives, purposes, or goals, an essential policies and plans for achieving those goals, stated in such a way a define what business the company is in or is to be in, and the kind of compan or is to be.'

However as Table 3.1 clearly indicates there is still a wide diversity of as to the nature of corporate strategy and the reader should consult som sources if he is to appreciate how these different perspectives are jus

TABLE 3.1   A comparison of various authors' concepts of strategy and the

	Chandler	*Andrews*	*Ansoff*	*Cannon*	*Katz*	*Ackoff*
Breadth of strategy definition/concept	Broad	Broad	Narrow	Narrow	Broad	Does not recognise concept
Name for broad concept of strategy	Strategy	Strategy	X	X	Corporate strategy	X
Components of broad concept of strategy	Goals objectives Action Plans Resources allocation	Goals Policies Plans	X	X	Scope Deployments Specifications	X
Name of goals and objectives	Goals and objectives	Goals and objectives	Objectives and constraints	Result strategy	Specifications and strategic criteria	Objectives and goals
Characteristics of objectives	None specified	None specified	Attributes Yardsticks Goals	Attributes Indices Targets and Time Tied to Action Strategies	None specified	None specified
Name of narrow concept strategy	X	X	Strategy	Composite or business strategy	Scope	X
Components of narrow concept strategy	X	X	Product-market scope Growth vector Competitive advantage Synergy	None specified	None specified	X
Names for functional strategies and policies	X	Policies	Policies	Action strategy	Functional policies	Policies
Name for implementation plans	Action plans	Plans	Programs	Commitment strategy	Deployment	Programs, procedures and courses of action
Differentiates between goals and objectives and constraints	No	No	Yes	No	No	Yes
Differentiates between corporate level and business level strategies	No	No	Yes, implicitly	Yes, implicitly	No	No
Differentiates between goal formulation processes and strategy formulation processes	No	No	Yes	No	No	Yes
rentiates en analytical anisational f the	Does not discuss either	Does not discuss organisational aspects	Yes	Yes	Does not discuss organisational aspects	Yes

7. Hofer and D.E. Schendel, *Strategy Formulation: Analytical Concepts* (St Paul,

strategy formulation process in the business management field

McNichols	Newman and Logan	Uyeterhoeven et al.	Paine and Naumes	Glueck	Steiner and Miner	Hofer and Schendel
Narrow	Broad	Both broad and narrow	Narrow	Narrow	Broad	Narrow
X	Master strategy	Strategy	X	X	Master strategy	Grand design
X	Services Technology Synergy Sequencing and timing Targets	Objectives Strategic posture	X	X	Missions Purposes Objectives Policies	Objectives Strategy Policies
Goals and objectives	Targets	Goals and objectives	Objectives	Objectives	Purposes and objectives	Goals and objectives
None specified	None specified	None specified	None specified	Differentiates between official and operative	None specified	Attributes indices targets time
Root strategy	X	Strategic posture	Overall strategy	Strategy	Program strategy	Corporate or business strategy
None specified	Services technology Synergy Sequencing and timing	Scope Competitive posture Self-concept	None specified	None specified	None specified	Domain or scope Resource deployments Competitive advantage Synergy
Operating strategy and policies	Functional policies	Functional strategies and policies	Policies	Functional policies	Functional strategies and policies	Functional strategies and policies
Master plan	Programs and plans	X	Programs and roles	Plans and programs	Programs and plans	Plans for action
No	No	No	Between objectives and constraints	No	No	Yes
No	No	No, but does recognise different organisational levels	No	No	Yes, in places	Yes
No	Yes	No	Not explicitly	Yes	Yes, in places	Yes
Does not discuss organisational aspects	Yes	Does not discuss organisational aspects	No	No	Yes	Yes

Minnesota: West Publishing 1978).

Before leaving the question of how to define strategy, it will be helpful to distinguish between *strategic* and *tactical* decisions.

In their book *Strategic Marketing* Weitz and Wensley[7] cite George Steiner and John Miner's[8] set of 8 dimensions, namely:

1 *Importance*. Strategic decisions are significantly more important than tactical ones.
2 *Level at which conducted*. Strategic decisions are usually made by top management.
3 *Time horizon*. Strategies are long-term; tactics short-term.
4 *Regularity*. The formulation of strategy is continuous and irregular; tactics periodic and fixed time (e.g. annual budget/plan).
5 *Nature of problem*. Strategic problems are usually unstructured and unique and so involve considerable risk and uncertainty. Tactical problems are more structured and repetitive and the risks easier to assess.
6 *Information needed*. Strategies require large amounts of external information much of which relates to the future and is subjective. Tactical decisions depend much more on internally generated accounting or market research information.
7 *Detail*. Strategy broad; tactics narrow and specific.
8 *Ease of evaluation*. Strategic decisions are much more difficult to make.

Weitz and Wensley distinguish between levels of strategic decision-making: 'Strategic decisions at the corporate level are concerned with acquisition, investments, and diversification', i.e. the management of a portfolio of businesses or SBUs. '[A]t the business or SBU level, strategic decisions focus on how to compete in an industry or product-market. Business level strategy deals with achieving and maintaining a competitive advantage. Strategic decisions at the business level are concerned with selecting target market segments and determining the range of products to offer'. It is with this that *Marketing Strategy and Management* is concerned.

Finally, before leaving the issue of definitions, we should note that Donald Melville (1983) provides a useful taxonomy which is reproduced as Figure 3.1.[9] As Melville points out, this is how he intends to use the terms in his work. The reader should be conscious that most authors/planners are not so considerate and be careful to make explicit the meaning they attach to these terms in formal communications originated by them.

■ The Concept of the Firm's Business

Andrews's definition of corporate strategy owes much to a pioneering article by Theodore Levitt on 'Marketing Myopia', which appeared first in the July–August 1960 issue of the *Harvard Business Review* and has been reprinted countless times since. Levitt's thesis is that declining or defunct industries got into such a

Since the words 'strategy', 'objectives', 'goals', 'policy' and 'programs' may have different meanings to individual readers or to various organizational cultures, I have tried to use certain definitions consistently throughout this article. For clarity—not pedantry—these are set forth below:

- A *strategy* is the pattern or plan that integrates an organization's major goals, policies, and action sequences into a cohesive whole. A well-formulated strategy helps marshal and allocate an organization's resources into a unique and viable posture based upon its relative internal competencies and shortcomings, anticipated changes in the environment, and contingent moves by intelligent opponents.
- *Goals (or objectives)* state what is to be achieved and when results are to be accomplished but they do not state how the results are to be achieved. All organizations have multiple goals existing in a complex hierarchy, from 'value objectives', which express the broad value premises toward which the company is to strive, through 'overall organizational objectives', which establish the intended nature of the enterprise and the directions in which it should move, to a series of less permanent goals which define targets for each organizational unit, its subunits, and finally all major program activities within each subunit. Major goals—those which affect the entity's overall direction and viability—are strategic goals.
- *Policies* are rules or guidelines that express the limits within which action should occur. These rules often take the form of contingent decisions for resolving conflicts among specific objectives. For example: 'Don't use nuclear weapons in war unless American cities suffer nuclear attack first' or 'Don't exceed three months' inventory in any item without corporate approval'. Like the objectives they support, policies also exist in a hierarchy throughout the organization. Major policies—those that guide the entity's overall direction and posture or determine its viability—are called strategic policies.
- *Programs* specify the step-by-step sequence of actions necessary to achieve major objectives. They express how objectives will be achieved within the limits set by policy. They insure that resources are committed to achieve goals, and they provide the dynamic track against which progress can be measured. Those major programs that determine the entity's overall thrust and viability are called strategic programs.

Strategic decisions are those that determine the overall direction of an enterprise and its ultimate viability in light of the predictable, the unpredictable, and the unknowable changes that may occur in its most important environments.

Figure 3.1   A taxonomy of strategic decision-making

Source: D.R. Melville, 'Top Management's Role in Strategic Planning', in Roger A. Kerin and Robert A. Peterson (eds), *Perspectives on Strategic Marketing Management* (Boston: Allyn & Bacon, 1983) 2nd edn.

situation due to their being product-orientated rather than customer-orientated. As a result the concept of their business was defined too narrowly. Thus the railroads failed to perceive that they were and are in the transportation business, and so allowed new forms of transportation to woo their customers away from them. Similarly, the film industry suffered severe trauma with the advent of television, in that the new medium was viewed as a direct threat, although not a very serious one, to the traditional movie, as conceived of by the old movie moguls. Levitt contends that the film industry could have avoided all the problems which have beset it in recent years had it defined its business in terms of customer needs and characterised itself as being in the entertainment business.

Levitt goes on to argue that 'the history of every dead and dying "growth" industry shows a self-deceiving cycle of bountiful expansion and undetected decay', and distinguishes four factors which make such a cycle almost inevitable.

1 A belief in growth as a natural consequence of an expanding and increasingly affluent population.
2 A belief that there is no competitive substitute for the industry's major product.
3 A pursuit of the economies of scale through mass production in the belief that lower unit cost will automatically lead to higher consumption and bigger overall profits.
4 Preoccupation with the potential of research and development *per se*, i.e. to the neglect of marketing.

The first of these assumptions is essentially reasonable and will remain valid so long as the population continues to expand and increase in affluence. However, since the 1960s there has developed an increasing awareness that the Earth's resources are finite and that there is a need to conserve and protect these resources, not least through population control.[10] Thus in China, whose population is estimated to reach 1200 million by the year 2000, 50 per cent of whom are under 22 years old, urban families are presently limited to one child and rural families may have a second child only if the first is a girl. While an extreme example, there is ample evidence to suggest that the rate of population growth is diminishing worldwide. On the other hand a direct consequence of this is likely to be an increase in economic welfare so that continued growth in aggregate demand may be anticipated although the composition of this demand is likely to vary considerably.

Similarly, there is substantial evidence to show that, for all but a few products, lower prices will lead to increased consumption always accepting that ultimately there is a finite demand for everything so that consumption is never an automatic consequence of production.

With regard to the fourth proposition, Levitt goes on to argue that even in situations where companies claim to research their market, such research fails in that it only measures preferences between existing alternatives, and so fails to account for switches which may occur in such preferences with the introduction of a new solution to the customer's basic problem or need. In the same vein he argues that much of this type of market research is designed to help companies improve what they are currently doing rather than probe into real needs which may require them to undertake a drastic change of policy.

There can be no doubt that Levitt exaggerates in order to make his point, for firms are certainly not as naive as he tends to infer. Also he falls into the same fault himself, in that his own projections of the changes which are likely to occur have turned out to be little better than those which he criticises. For example, his discussion of the oil companies ignores two fundamental changes which occurred in the 1960s, namely the concern with air pollution and the wish of developing countries to exercise greater control over their own resources.

Further, as Ansoff[11] notes, Levitt's definitions of the firm's business are too broad to be taken literally and lacking in 'what the investment community calls a "common thread" – a relationship between present and future product-markets which would enable outsiders to perceive where the firm is heading and the inside management to give it guidance'.

At the time when he wrote these words Ansoff was prepared to accept that the common thread need not necessarily be strong, for there were a number of eminently successful conglomerate companies operating in the early and middle 1960s. Their fortunes have been more mixed since that time due, in my opinion, to the fact that they were put together by managers particularly skilled in recognising under-utilised assets who acquired them for far less than their true market value. By liquidating assets and ruthlessly disposing of plant and labour surplus to immediate requirements, the conglomerates expanded at an enormous pace.

However, by the mid-1960s cheap acquisitions were less easy to find and the growth of the conglomerates faltered and, in many instances, due to their short-term reorganisation policies, went into reverse. The more astute managements of conglomerates realised that their businesses possessed a common thread, but not in the product-market terms used by Levitt and Ansoff. Their common thread lay in their financial skills. Accordingly, the top managements of the still successful conglomerates have delegated the responsibility for the management of compo-nent parts to managers skilled in the various market interfaces in which they operate and have contented themselves with the allocation of resources between the member companies based upon their perception of their needs and prospects in much the same way as the board of a multi-divisional company operates within an industry. It is our opinion, therefore, that there must be a strong common thread in the product-market sense for the purpose of developing a conventional corporate strategy. A view which is supported by the concept of the Strategic Business Unit (SBU) which is discussed at length in the next chapter.

In the conglomerate form of organisation the board of directors are in a position more akin to the management of an investing institution in that they choose between the apparent merits and demerits of strategies proposed by a number of different companies and so influence the direction of development by either extending or withholding financial resources. In other words, the boards of conglomerate and diversified multi-divisional companies influence the selection of strategy, but are rarely involved in its direct development. On the other hand, one might characterise their activity as grand strategy in that their role and function is to co-ordinate a number of diverse strategies in order to achieve an overall objective. It is our belief, however, that in most instances if one were to try and specify the objectives of grand strategy one would finish up with a generalisation of a very limited practical utility similar to Levitt's 'transportation' or 'entertainment' businesses.

However, we are in agreement with Ansoff when he points out that whereas Levitt's concepts of business may be too broad to be useful, the traditional identification of a firm with a particular industry has become too narrow. Essentially, this is so because many firms have acquired a diverse range of products through policies of vertical and horizontal integration in order to protect their existing markets and also, through new product development, undertaken to exploit technological innovation and to develop new markets with opportunities for growth.

While it is accepted that Western society at large is not as convinced today as it was say a few years ago that the undiluted pursuit of growth is automatically good, none the less it must be recognised that for the vast majority of companies the pursuit of growth is seen as an essential prerequisite of survival. Accordingly, it will be assumed hereafter that growth is a prime objective of most companies. If, therefore, we put together this proposition with that contained in the preceding paragraph, that strategy is evolved in terms of product-market interfaces, then we will find the matrix developed by Ansoff and reproduced as Figure 3.2 of considerable help in identifying basic alternative strategies open to the firm. This matrix first appeared in the September/October 1957 issue of the *Harvard Business Review* in an article entitled 'Strategies for diversification'. In this article Ansoff defined the alternative strategies as follows:

1 Market penetration: the company seeks increased sales for its present products in its present markets through more aggressive promotion and distribution.
2 Market development: the company seeks increased sales by taking its present products into new markets.
3 Product development: the company seeks increased sales by developing improved products for its present markets.
4 Diversification: the company seeks increased sales by developing new products for new markets.

In the original article Ansoff was concerned with what he termed 'intensive growth strategies' and so he did not dwell upon diversification which could hardly be classified as such, although (in *Corporate Strategy*) he does discuss diversification strategies at some length.

At this juncture, however, it would probably be more helpful to consider all the basic alternatives open to a company which I term, perhaps somewhat grandiosely, the concept of limited strategic alternatives.

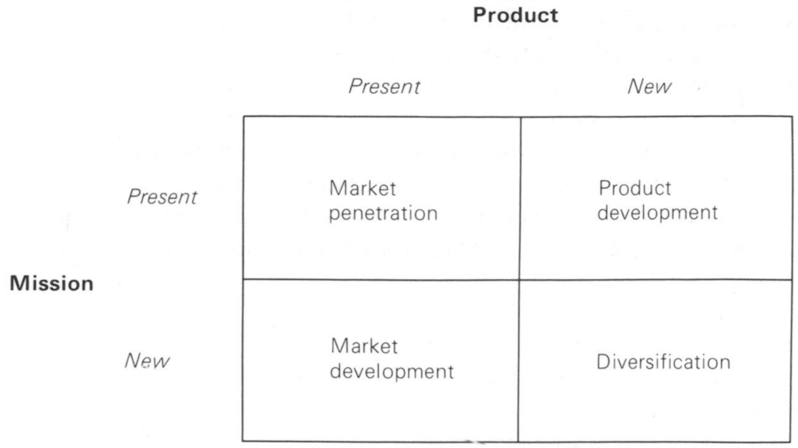

Product

	Present	New
Present	Market penetration	Product development
New	Market development	Diversification

Mission

Figure 3.2   Growth vector components

Source: I. Ansoff, *Corporate Strategy* (New York: McGraw-Hill, 1965); 'Strategies for Diversification', *Harvard Business Review* (September–October 1957).

◼ The Concept of Limited Strategic Alternatives

Many of the basic ideas relating to the formulation of strategy have been developed by the military, accordingly a military analogy should not prove out of place in describing our concept. (After the debacle of Vietnam military analogies found little favour with American managers or academics. Norman Schwarzkopf's success in the Gulf War of 1991 would appear to have radically changed the acceptability of such comparisons!) In war the basic objective is to overcome the enemy's forces and secure control over the territory held by him. Conventionally, therefore, one is faced with a situation in which two armies face each other and each seeks to acquire control over the area occupied by the enemy. However, it is not necessary to consider the complexities faced by the commanders of armies in order to isolate the alternative strategies which are open to them. This may be achieved equally well by considering the alternatives open to a much smaller unit, say an infantry platoon.

Traditionally the problems posed to sub-unit commanders presume a growth strategy in that they emphasise attack and pay much less attention to more negative outcomes such as withdrawal and retreat. Further, as in most purposeful organisations, a strategy of doing nothing is not generally considered as a viable alternative. As a consequence, the usual problem posed is one represented by the simplistic diagram which appears as Figure 3.3 in which our decision-maker is required to advance from *A* to *B* overcoming the resistance offered by the enemy occupying stronghold *S*. Essentially, three alternative solutions are offered to the sub-unit commander faced with this problem:

1   He may continue his advance on a direct line and attack the enemy head on.
2   He may seek to outflank the enemy to either left or right.
3   He may consider that he lacks the resources necessary to achieve his objective and call upon the next sub-unit up in size to assist him.

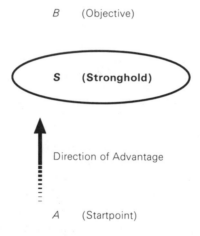

Figure 3.3   The 'attack' problem

In their training most sub-unit commanders are encouraged to believe that the remedy is to be found in alternatives 1 and 2 as otherwise they would not be called upon to exercise their own initiative but would rely upon that of their superior.

It is this necessity to inculcate a positive frame of mind which minimises consideration of the fact that the enemy is rarely a fool and therefore unlikely to have exposed himself to easy defeat by the pursuit of alternatives 1 or 2, i.e. a head-on or flanking attack. Equally, little consideration is given to the possibility of withdrawal or, even worse, retreat. At higher command levels within the military such possibilities are considered and policies and procedures have been developed to cope with them. However, where two opposing forces are equally balanced in terms of resources available to them then it is very likely that a stalemate will develop as was the case during the First World War. Under these circumstances a solution is usually only to be found through what I term the 'bypass strategy'. Fundamentally, the bypass strategy recognises that a stalemate exists due to limitations of current thinking and technology and thus seeks to get round this impasse through technological innovation. In the First World War the invention of the tank constituted such technological innovation although its potential was lost due to premature use. Similarly, much of the swing of fortunes during the Second World War may be attributed to innovations which enabled one adversary to change the rules. Thus, at the present time, neither of the world's basic ideologies appears to possess a sufficient competitive advantage for it to be able to impose its will upon the other by force. Under such circumstances, we may identify a strategy of coexistence.

It is my contention that there is a direct parallel in the world of business in terms of the range of alternative strategies open to a company. Head-on attack may be likened to the economist's concept of price competition between undifferentiated products. Essentially, such a strategy is one of attrition in which the competitor with the greater resources must ultimately win, although only after squandering many of its resources in destroying its competitor. It may also leave them vulnerable to attack by a third party.

The flanking attack may be compared with the strategy of indirect competition wherein the firm seeks to differentiate its output from that of its immediate competitors and pre-empt a segment or segments of the total market. Such differentiation may be objective and accomplished through the firm's product policy, it may be subjective and accomplished through its promotional policy or it may combine elements of both arising from the firm's distribution policy.

Withdrawal and retreat have different connotations. The former suggests one extracts oneself from a situation on one's own terms, whereas the latter suggests that one is compelled to accept another's superiority. Further, withdrawal suggests that the set-back may be only temporary and that one may wish to continue in competition after a period of reorganisation, whereas retreat tends to suggest a cessation of operations. In a business context there are many instances of both strategies. In terms of the Ansoff schemata reproduced as Figure 3.2, a strategy of direct competition may be allied to that of market penetration, while that of indirect competition corresponds closely to product development. Withdrawal suggests primarily market development, although it may also include product development. Cessation of operations is not covered in the matrix, but the diversification alternative bears a close resemblance to our own bypass strategy, in that the company seeks to develop completely new markets through innovation.

Finally, there is a strategy somewhat similar to coexistence, which basically is one of doing nothing. This strategy may prove particularly attractive to a company within an industry which is experiencing considerable competition from a new industry, as has happened, for example, between natural and synthetic fibres, and between glass and metal packaging materials and plastics. In many such situations the majority of companies decide that in order to survive they must diversify into the new industry and acquire the new technology. On the other hand, the 'do nothing' firm adopts a posture that the primary demand for the output of both the old and the new industry is sufficient to ensure a sufficient level of demand to provide an attractive market for it for a long time into the future. Such a firm may also believe that, as many of its competitors leave the old industry to adopt the new technology, so its own competitive standing in the old industry will be improved. Further, in that the 'do nothing' company is not required to make large investments in the new technology, it may well enjoy a period of above average profitability.

If we are correct in our claim that there is a limited set of strategic alternatives open to any company, then it follows that a fundamental activity of the corporate strategist must be an evaluation of these various alternatives in relation to environmental trends and the company's own strengths and weaknesses. In our opinion it is frequently overlooked in management texts dealing with strategy that the role of the decision-maker should be to reduce ignorance to the smallest possible proportions. In turn, this places a premium on the skills of problem definition, data acquisition and analysis, as a means of enabling the decision-maker to choose between the basic alternatives which confront him. We return to these topics in later chapters but at this juncture it will be useful to look at the relationship between corporate strategy and marketing strategy.

■ Corporate Strategy or Marketing Strategy?

We have already noted that a cynic might well regard the posturing of marketing men as a take-over bid for the general management function. Rarely, if ever, do we find the reverse. Thus, while general managers do not claim to be marketing managers and corporate strategists do not claim to be marketing strategists, the marketer would often seem to want to usurp both of these functions. It is my belief that while general managers do not see themselves as marketing managers they *should* be just that, in the sense that they ought to subscribe to the philosophy of business encapsulated in the marketing concept, as we have defined it. Similarly, corporate strategists *must* be marketing strategists, for without a market there is no purpose for the corporation and no role for a corporate strategist, which would not deny any claim that the corporate strategist takes a broader view than the firm's activity in the market place.

However, if we are forced to assess the relative importance of marketing within the corporation as a whole, then we would assert that it is of primary importance – it is a necessary, if not sufficient, condition of survival. As Levitt's analysis in 'Marketing Myopia' makes clear, a firm must adopt a forward orientation and seek to anticipate change so that it can be ready to meet and exploit such change when it occurs. The general manager who loses sight of our simple proposition that supply must be the servant of demand is doomed to join eventually the ranks of the buggy-whip manufacturers, the railroad tycoons and the movie moguls in whatever Valhalla commercial dodos aspire to, for this is the inevitable consequence implicit in the Product Life-Cycle (PLC) concept.

The PLC concept is familiar to students of marketing and draws an analogy between biological life-cycles as experienced by living organisms, and the pattern of sales growth shown by successful products ('successful' is an important but often forgotten qualification, for it is generally accepted that more new products fail than succeed). A typical representation of the PLC is contained in Figure 3.4 and distinguishes four main phases – introduction, growth, maturity and decay. An extensive review[12] of the history of many successful products and ideas confirms that there is a remarkable consistency in the growth pattern they exhibit with regard to the first three phases. However, the comparison between product and biological life-cycles becomes strained in respect of the fourth, decay stage, for, while this is inevitable for living things, many would argue that it can be deferred if not postponed indefinitely for products. In fact, one of the managerial uses for the PLC is as a control device to monitor the onset of maturity, so that action can be taken to avoid decay. Such action may consist of product improvement and/or increased promotional action to extend the mature phase, or a rejuvenation strategy based on either product or market development, which may initiate a new growth phase. While medical science has yet to achieve a comparable level of success, there can be no doubt that it will, and we will have to redraw our life-cycles with much longer mature phases than at present.

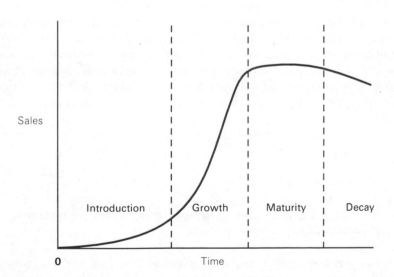

Figure 3.4   The product life-cycle

But none of this denies the fact that decay will set in if action is not taken to prevent it. In a commercial context this means that we must monitor competitive activity, which may suggest new and better ways for consumers to satisfy their basic needs for mobility (cars rather than railways) for entertainment (TV rather than films) for convenience foods (frozen rather than canned or dried) and so on. We must also monitor changes in consumer demand which originate from changes in the structure and composition of the population, from their economic status, and in their taste and preferences due to social change. In other words, we must subscribe to a forward-looking approach, and embrace change if we are to survive – both factors are central to a marketing orientation. Further, while many external factors may impinge on and influence the corporation to change its policies and practices (e.g. health and safety at work, equal opportunities, price controls, etc.), the firm can only conclude an exchange relationship if it has a product or service for which there is a demand, and this alone ensures that the product-market interface is the abiding and continuing focus of the firm's mission. For all these reasons we find it difficult to distinguish between corporate and marketing strategy in a meaningful way. While it is clear that within the overall strategy there will be a need to develop specific policies for each of the main functional areas of the business (R&D, Production, Personnel, Finance and Marketing), all of these will be subordinate to the strategy which specifies how the firm will approach its market.

At a very simple level we can isolate three basic marketing strategies – Undifferentiated, Differentiated and Concentrated.

An undifferentiated strategy exists when the supplier offers the same or undifferentiated product to all persons/organisations believed to have a demand for a product of that type. In light of our earlier comments concerning the individual nature of needs, such an approach might be seen as the antithesis of a marketing orientation, and a classic case of a production orientation. Our own view is that under certain circumstances a production orientation is synonymous with a marketing orientation and reflects a correct appreciation of the priorities – as we observed about Henry Ford – a cheap standard motor-car is preferable to no car at all.

Three sets of circumstances immediately suggest themselves as being suited to an undifferentiated strategy:

1 The introduction of an innovation.
2 The mature/decay stage of the PLC.
3 Commodity marketing where the conditions most closely approximate the economist's model of perfect competition.

When introducing a new product into the market-place – especially a radically different product – several factors may predicate an undifferentiated strategy. For example, it is widely recognised that much of the risk attendant upon a new-product launch is uncertainty as to the scope and nature of demand, which may result in a perceptual mismatch between supplier and potential user. Inertia and commitment to the known and safe product or process, not to mention the capital invested in the current technology, make it very difficult to forecast just what interpretation prospective users will make of the benefits offered by the innovation. Under such circumstances a broad approach may be preferable to an attempt to pre-identify receptive customers – as many of the examples in Corey's[13] book make clear, focusing on the 'obvious' customer often leads to considerable delay in gaining consumer acceptance.[14] While I have argued at length[15] that pre-identification is desirable it may well be more cost effective to pursue an undifferentiated approach when customers will select themselves. (In so far as they will then probably represent a subset or segment of a broader market, it could be argued that this amounts to a 'concentrated' strategy – it is not, for reasons which we discuss below.)

Assuming that a new product is successful and begins to grow rapidly, then an undifferentiated strategy may continue to prove the most suitable, for under these conditions production and distribution problems tend to dominate, with an emphasis upon cashing-in on the rapidly expanding demand. However, as saturation begins to approach so suppliers will seek to differentiate their output from that of their competitors and adopt either a differentiated or concentrated strategy.

A differentiated strategy exists where the supplier seeks to supply a modified version of the basic product to each of the major sub-groups which comprise the basic market. (Methods for segmenting markets are discussed at some length in Chapter 8.) In doing so he will develop a different marketing mix in terms of the product's characteristics, its price, promotion and distribution, although attempts will often be made to standardise on one or more of these factors in the interest of scale economies (usually distribution, e.g. car dealerships, consumer durables, etc.). Such differentiation is only possible for very large firms which can achieve a sufficient volume in each of the segments to remain competitive. For the smaller producer a concentrated strategy may be the only realistic option.

Under this option the producer selects one of the major market segments and concentrates all his efforts upon it. It should be noted that this is different from the user self-selection that we described earlier in connection with an undifferentiated strategy for an innovation. In the latter case the subsets of the market are not clear – the supplier does not possess profiles of different market groupings – and so he cannot devise a targeted or concentrated strategy for matching his output to the needs of one segment. By contrast, in the mature stage of the PLC, the boundaries between different user groups have become apparent and become crystallised as different suppliers seek to pre-empt a segment or segments through consciously devising a differentiated or concentrated marketing strategy.

As demand begins to decline due to competition from new or substitute goods, so the maintenance of a concentrated or differentiated strategy may become uneconomic and suppliers may revert to an undifferentiated strategy. In this situation the dying product is well known and understood by suppliers and users alike, and its marketing will be very similar to that of commodities.

Before leaving the view that there are three basic marketing strategies – undifferentiated, differentiated and concentrated – it will be helpful to relate these to Michael Porter's well known concept of 'generic strategies'. The most recent version of this concept is to be found in *The Competitive Advantage of Nations* (1990)[16] in which he writes:

> In addition to responding to and influencing industry structure, firms must choose a position within the industry. At the heart of positioning is *competitive advantage*. In the long run firms succeed relative to their competitors if they possess sustainable competitive advantage. There are two basic types of competitive advantage: *lower cost* and *differentiation*. Lower cost is the ability of a firm to design, produce, and market a comparable product more efficiently than its competitors. At prices at or near competitors, lower cost translates into superior returns ... Differentiation is the ability to provide unique and superior value to the buyer in terms of product quality, special features, or after-sale service ... Differentiation allows a firm to command a premium price, which leads to superior profitability provided costs are comparable to those of competitors (p. 37).

> The other important variable in positioning is *competitive scope*, or the breadth of the firm's target within its industry. A firm must choose the range of product varieties it will produce, the distribution channels it will employ, the types of buyers it will serve, the geographic areas in which it will sell, and the array of related industries in which it will also compete (p. 38).

Porter proceeds to argue that the type of advantage and scope of advantage may be combined into his notion of generic strategies which offer different approaches to superior performances in an industry. By combining the concepts of competitive advantage and competitive scope Porter offers a simple 2×2 matrix as shown in Figure 3.5.

Competitive advantage

		Lower cost	Differentiation
Competitive scope	Broad target	COST LEADERSHIP	DIFFERENTIATION
	Narrow target	COST FOCUS	FOCUSED DIFFERENTIATION

Figure 3.5   Generic strategies

Source: Michael E. Porter, *The Competitive Advantage of Nations* (London: Macmillan, 1990).

Clearly Porter's reformulation closely resembles that which has been used by marketers for the past 30 years or more. Cost leadership invariably depends upon standardisation and so is equivalent to an undifferentiated marketing strategy. Differentiation is identical in both models. Cost focus and focus differentiation are both variants of a concentrated marketing strategy and involve niche marketing of the kind discussed earlier.

From the foregoing discussion it is clear that the firm's selection of a marketing strategy will influence and affect everything which it does – to this extent then marketing strategy and corporate strategy are inextricably interlinked. However, in the remainder of this book we will focus upon the marketing dimensions of strategy and will largely ignore issues of finance and control, production, research and development, and personnel, except where they impinge directly upon marketing. But before turning to this more detailed analysis it will be useful to complete our review of definitions by considering the role of marketing management within the general management function.

General Management and Marketing Management

In essence, general management is the coordinating and integrative function which both guides and controls the various functional areas of management to ensure that each maximises its contribution to the overall objectives of the firm. To this end the general manager's responsibilities may be subdivided into four major sub-sets:

1 Identifying opportunities.
2 Specifying objectives and the basic policies for their achievement.
3 Delegation of responsibility for performance of tasks necessary to accomplish the firm's mission.
4 Evaluation and control of the tasks so delegated.

The first two areas are concerned with *planning*, and are the primary concern of the strategic function (corporate or 'marketing', according to your preference), while the second two areas are concerned with *execution* of the strategy. Execution is primarily a functional responsibility, and it is a relatively simple matter to distinguish between general management and marketing, or any other functional area of management, by contrast with the difficulty in differentiating between marketing and corporate strategy.

Kotler[17] has defined marketing management as 'the analysis, planning, implementation, and control of programs designed to bring about desired exchanges with target audiences for the purpose of personal or mutual gain. It relies heavily on the adaptation and coordination of product, price, promotion, and place for achieving effective response.' More simply, it is concerned with the management of the marketing mix.

While Kotler makes reference to analysis and planning activities in his definition, this is not to contradict our earlier assertion that these are corporate responsibilities. The distinction rests in the level of the activity. At the general management level we are concerned with setting down the firm's product-market mission, and the broad strategy to be followed in achieving it. At the functional level we are concerned with the detailed analysis and planning within the guidelines or framework laid down in the corporate plan. The activities are tactical rather than strategic.

In other functional areas confusion of the two levels is much less likely to arise than is the case with marketing, for the same reason that, in a marketing orientated company, the focus of both top management and marketing management is the product-market interface. While an interesting subject for debate, extended discussion of points of similarity and difference tends to be rather sterile, and for our purposes it will suffice if the distinction between general and marketing management is that the former embraces all the functional areas while the latter is concerned with only one. Thus while several aspects of marketing, such as identifying and measuring marketing opportunities, will overlap general management activities to a considerable degree, other dimensions of the latter, such as organisational structuring, will receive much less attention in this book.

■ Summary

In Chapter 3 we have attempted to establish the nature and scope of both corporate and marketing strategy in order to highlight the similarities and differences between the two activities. Essentially our position is that in so far as the attainment of corporate objectives is a direct consequence of its success in managing the interface between its output (product or service) and its markets (customers) then corporate strategy is indistinguishable from marketing strategy. That said, it is also clear that the interests and responsibilities of the corporate strategist or general manager extend well beyond the functional interests and responsibilities of the marketing manager. The remaining chapters are concerned largely with clarifying these potentially contradictory propositions, and in Chapter 4 we commence by examining in detail the precise nature of Strategic Marketing Planning.

Principles of Strategic Marketing Planning

Learning Goals

The issues to be addressed in Chapter 4 include:

1 The relevance of *strategic marketing planning* (SMP) to organisations at different stages of their development.
2 The evolution of management and planning *systems*.
3 The formal *definition* of SMP.
4 The nature of *objectives* and their *formulation*.
5 The description of a *framework* for SMP.
6 Identification of some *key principles* of SMP.
7 The formulation of *corporate strategy*.
8 Some *criticisms* of and *obstacles* to SMP.

After reading Chapter 4 you will be able to:

1 Justify the *role* and *importance* of SMP.
2 Trace the development of *alternative approaches* to SMP.
3 *Define* SMP.
4 Define the *nature of objectives* and show how these shape marketing strategies.
5 Describe the *cycle of SMP* and the *stages* involved in it.
6 Illustrate some *key principles* of SMP using a framework developed by Arthur D. Little.
7 Identify and describe the three steps involved in *formulating a corporate strategy.*
8 Spell out some of the *criticisms of* and *obstacles to* the adoption and implementation of SMP.

■ Introduction

In Chapter 3 we attempted to provide some answers to basic questions concerning the nature and scope of marketing and the distinction, if any, between corporate and marketing strategy. Underlying much of the discussion was an implicit recognition of the evolutionary progress of mankind and the inevitability of change in the economic and social environment in which individuals and the organisations to which they belong must live out their lives. While some fatalists might take the view that they can do little if anything to control these environmental forces for change, at the very least management believe that they should seek to anticipate change so that they and their organisation may be best placed to respond to this change when it occurs. However, most managers do not only wish to respond to their environment, they also wish to exercise some control over it through their own actions. It is for this reason that planning plays such an important role in the management task.

In this chapter we shall seek to establish a framework not only for strategic marketing planning (SMP), but also for the book as a whole in the sense that most if not all of the later chapters will seek to expound and clarify specific aspects of marketing planning. However, before looking at SMP as a process it will be helpful if we consider first some of the benefits claimed for formal planning as well as arguments against it. Next we shall establish a framework for SMP and the chapter will conclude with a summary of some of the key principles of SMP and their relationship to the formulation of corporate strategy.

However, before proceeding to a detailed analysis of the nature of SMP, and the different approaches and techniques used in its implementation, it will be helpful to sketch in the stages in the evolution of management systems which have given rise to the current emphasis upon such planning. It is also important to stress that while this textbook is founded on the same basic assumption as most other textbooks – namely, that we are concerned with an established medium- to large-sized company with several products operating in a number of different markets and with a fairly sophisticated management structure – the underlying principles of SMP are just as relevant to the small and newly established firm with a single product and a single market.

The choice of what type of organisational process is used to formulate strategy ranges from the 'back of an envelope' informality of the entrepreneur, to the 'muddling through' or adaptive approach, to the highly formalised systems of planning strategy typically applied by the large multinationals. The stage of development of the organisation is therefore one of the major factors influencing the degree of formality in the process. As Mintzberg notes, different degrees of formality may be found within the same organisation, e.g. the Oil Companies (see Table 4.1).

Clearly the implicit assumption of the large complex organisation is necessary to justify consideration of marketing as a distinct function in its own right, but this does not deny the importance of a marketing orientation and the discipline of formal planning in organisations at an early stage of corporate development. In Table 4.2 we show a concise statement of the stages of corporate development as conceptualised by Malcolm Salter of the Harvard Business School. While the following review will be largely concerned with firms in Stage III and Stage IV, firms in Stages I and II will still benefit considerably from applying the principles discussed here – indeed firms at Stages I and II correspond closely to the 'mini-businesses' or strategic business units which are the basic building blocks of most formal planning systems.

Table 4.1 Factors that influence how formal and complex an organisation's planning system should be

Organisational factors	Informal (simple)	Formal (sophisticated)
Organisational size	small	very large
Organisational complexity	simple	complex
Magnitude of gap between present position and objectives	small	very large
Magnitude of change anticipated in the organisation's strategy	small	very large
Environmental factors		
Rate of change in the organisation's environment	little	rapid change
Degree of competition in the industry	little	rapid change
Length of time for which resources must be committed	short	very long
Process factors		
Need for internal consistency	little	great
Need for comprehensiveness	little	great

Source: C.W. Hofer, *Conceptual constructs for formulating corporate and business strategies* (Boston: Intercollegiate Case Clearing House, #9–378–754,1977) p. 33,

■ The evolution of management systems[1]

In Chapter 3 we traced the development of management through a series of broad orientations from production through sales to marketing and concluded that a marketing orientation is the most satisfactory approach to solving the basic economic problem of maximising satisfaction from the consumption of scarce resources. But while a marketing orientation has dominated practice in the years since the Second World War a closer examination soon reveals a number of distinct phases in the evolution of the management systems used to translate philosophy into action:

1 *The 1950s.* During this decade post-war reconstruction and the reversion to a peace-time economy gave rise to a boom with full employment and significant growth in real incomes. Demand was buoyant and the major emphasis was upon production. However, competition was fierce and efficiency in manufacturing, distribution and sales were all at a premium leading to stress being placed upon professional management, decentralisation and management by objectives. Major car manufacturers (GM and Ford) were at the forefront of thinking and practice during the earlier parts of the decade with companies like General Electric and Pillsbury taking the lead in the later years.

Table 4.2 Stages of corporate development

	Stage I	Stage II	Stage III	Stage IV
Structure of operating units	Single unit managed by a sole proprietor	Single unit managed by a team	Several regional units reporting to a corporate HQ each with structure I or II	Several semi-autonomous units reporting to corporate HQ each with structure I, II or III
Product–market relationships	Small-scale, single line of related products, 1 market, 1 distribution channel	Large-scale, single line of related products, 1 market, 1 distribution channel	Each region produces same product line, single-market, multiple channels	Each unit produces different product line for separate markets, multiple channels
Top management	One-man operation, very little task differentiation	Responsible for single functions, e.g. production, sales, finance	Regional units performing several functions	Product divisions performing all major functions
Quantitative measures of performance	Very few, personalised, not based on formal criteria	Operating budgets for each function	Operating budget, return on sales, ROI	Return on sales, ROI

Source: M. Salter, Course notes MBA program, Harvard Business School (1968).

2   *The 1960s.* Demand and supply were in near equilibrium and producers turned increasingly to marketing as a means of differentiating themselves in the eyes of consumers. Market segmentation and product diversification emerged as key strategies and gave rise to a focus on profit centres and the use of standardised systems of control in order to measure and direct the performance of these distinctive units. A belief developed that the key to continued success was to acquire a portfolio of businesses which complement and reinforce one another – the 'conglomerate', of which ITT and LTV are prime examples. A salient feature of the conglomerate is that top management redeploys capital within the group on the basis of its expectations about future earnings related to the assets employed. With the benefit of hindsight it is now clear that this mechanistic approach gives rise to an emphasis upon the short term and those investments which offer the best opportunity for certain returns – a 'milking' strategy which gives insufficient attention to the inevitable cycle of growth, maturity and decay which characterise the changing fortunes of every industry.

3   *The late 1960s.* Towards the end of the 1960s the underlying dissatisfaction of critics of the materialistic society (Galbraith, Nader, Packard) surfaced as the consumerist movement and forced manufacturers to give even closer attention to products, markets and competition. This concern was sharpened by the intensification of international competition as domestic markets became saturated and firms looked elsewhere for new opportunities for growth.

4   *The 1970s.* The pressure exerted by better informed and more discriminating consumers increases and is given even greater impetus by the oil crisis of 1973. The reverberations of the oil crisis create a climate of turbulence which lends even more force to a competitive, market oriented focus and a change from profit centres to businesses as the key factor in developing strategies for coping with a volatile environment. This trend continues throughout the 1970s.

5   *The 1980s.* Recession is now world wide and the competition is global. Faced with an increasingly complex and often hostile environment firms increase their efforts to develop new products and markets and so exaggerate the intensity of the competitive pressures which they are seeking to escape. The publication of Hayes and Abernathy's pungent criticisms,[2] and Michael Porter's book[3] emphasise the deficiencies of the milking approach favoured by professional managers with a short-term financial orientation. The need to adopt a more flexible and long-term financial orientation which recognises the cyclical nature of competition is acknowledged and puts a premium on strategic analysis and long-range planning.

In parallel with the evolution of management systems there also evolved a series of different approaches to planning. My colleague at Strathclyde University, Professor Lewis Gunn,[4] has produced an excellent summary of the types of strategic planning, which is reproduced as Table 4.3. As well as summarising the main approaches to strategic planning Table 4.3 also reflects the chronology of the development of planning systems from the highly structured top down systems planning of the 1960s and early 1970s to the more marketing-orientated approaches of the late 1970s and early 1980s. In turn, the formalised approaches began to give way to less formalised alternatives – Strategic Issues Planning and Logical Incrementalism – in the mid-to-late 1980s. (Logical incrementalism has always been with us but enjoyed a revival at this time as a reaction against the perceived failures of over-formalised planning approaches.) Now, as we move into the 1990s, the fashion has swung towards the *participative* and *cultural modes* that recognise the need to involve multiple constituencies in the planning process and place particular emphasis upon the underlying value systems which bond people to organisations.

Table 4.3   Types of strategic planning

Systems Planning:	Comprehensive 'Corporate Top Down' 'Paralysis by Analysis'?
SWOT:	Strengths and Weaknesses Opportunities and Threats
Marketing Approaches:	Industry Structure Analysis Competitive Strategy Portfolio Analysis
Strategic Issues Planning:	Selective, Focused Key (make or break) Issues c.f. 'KRA' (Key Results Areas)
Logical Incrementalism:	Muddling Through Opportunism, Side Bets Tentative, Experimental
Political/Participative:	Pluralist, Stakeholder Model Consult, Negotiate, Bargain
Cultural ('Excellence'):	Integrating Corporate 'Culture' 'Framework for Innovation' Avoid 'Paralysis by Analysis'

Source: L. Gunn, University of Strathclyde

Gunn categorises trends in strategic planning (Table 4.4) along three dimensions in terms of their comprehensiveness of approach, degree of participation and emphasis upon the market (as opposed to the organisation itself) and poses the question as to whether all trends are towards the right. At the time of writing, this would certainly seem to be the case.

There is a certain irony in the evolutionary process described above, for it is clear that over the past three decades we have seen a concept of long-range strategic planning turn into an increasingly short-term mechanical and specialised process which has led to its own self-destruction. Such a process is familiar to the student of evolution, for it is clear that while specialisation (i.e. adaptation to the prevailing conditions) may lead to above average short-term rewards, it also puts you at greatest risk if you become so specialised that you cannot accommodate or adapt to a change in the environment. In that 'survival' is generally accepted as the primary object of all organisations it is clear that short-term gain is only to be pursued if it is consistent with the long-term goals of a firm and does not reduce the firm's ability to respond to turbulence in its environment. We are thus faced with the paradox that while 'planning' has fallen into disrepute for leading us into the present impasse it is also seen as offering the greatest potential for escaping from it.

Table 4.4   Trends in strategic planning

Along three dimensions . . .

1. By comprehensiveness of approach:

| VERY BROAD | ———————— | VERY FOCUSED |

| Strategic Planning Systems | SWOT Analysis | Strategic Issues Planning | Logical Incrementalism |

2. By degree of participation:

| TOP-DOWN RATIONALISTIC | ———————— | PARTICIPATIVE POLITICAL |

| Strategic Planning Systems | SWOT | Strategic Issues Planning | Strategic Negotiations | Stakeholder Approach | Incrementalism Partisan Mutual Adjustment |

3. By market-orientation:

| CENTRALISED | ———————— | MARKET-ORIENTATED |

| Strategic Planning Systems | SWOT, etc. | Incrementalism (PMA) | Portfolio Analysis | Competitive Strategy | Framework For Innovation |

ALL TRENDS ARE TO RIGHT?

Source: L. Gunn, University of Strathclyde.

■ Some Definitions

In the preceding paragraph we alluded to the paradox that strategic or long-range planning has been criticised as a major contributor to the mechanistic and inflexible approach to management which underlay many of the economic problems of the late 1970s and 1980s while, at the same time, it is proposed as a palliative if not a cure for these self-same ills. To some degree this misunderstanding would seem to arise from disagreement as to the precise nature of SMP. Accordingly, before conducting our own analysis of this concept and the techniques associated with it, it will be helpful to consider some definitions which indicate what are the salient features of this approach to management.

A review of SMP by Brownlie[5] would seem to support the view that there is no single, universally accepted definition of SMP: he offers us the following seven definitions:

1   The answers to two questions were implicit to Drucker's early conceptualisation of an organisation's strategy: 'What is our business? And what should it be?'
2   Chandler defined strategy as 'the determination of the basic long-term goals and objectives of an enterprise, and the adoption of courses of action and the allocation of resources necessary for carrying out these goals'.
3   Andrews's definition of strategy combines the ideas of Drucker and Chandler: 'strategy is the pattern of objectives, purposes or goals and plans for achieving these goals, stated in such a way as to define what business the company is in or is to be in and the kind of company it is or is to be'.
4   Hofer and Schendel define an organisation's strategy as 'the fundamental pattern of present and planned resource deployments and environmental interactions that indicates how the organisation will achieve its objectives'.
5   According to Abell, strategic planning involves 'the management of any business unit in the dual tasks of anticipating and responding to changes which affect the marketplace for their products'.
6   In 1979, Derek Wynne-Jones, head of the Planning and Strategy division of P.A. Management Consultants, considered that strategic planning 'embraced the overall objective of an organisation in defining its strategy and preparing and subsequently implementing its detailed plans'.
7   Christopher Lorenz, editor of the Management page of the *Financial Times*, considers strategic planning to be 'the process by which top and senior executives decide, direct, delegate and control the generation and allocation of resources within a company'.

But, while these definitions may differ in the particular, there does appear to be a common thread which is that SMP is concerned with establishing the goal or purpose of an organisation and the means chosen for achieving that goal. Perhaps, then, the differences of opinion revolve around how one defines an organisation or 'business'. We have already referred to the stages of corporate development and claimed that SMP is relevant to both complex multinational corporations like IBM as it is to any single-product owner-managed business. That said, we must recognise that differences of size, scale, diversity, complexity, etc., will inevitably result in significant differences between 'firms' and make generalisations about them difficult if not impossible. To overcome or reduce this difficulty most analysts now prefer to define the business in terms of its strategic functions rather than try to define businesses first and then discover that there are major discrepancies in strategic functions between them. As a consequence most discussions of SMP are now focused upon the concept of the strategic business unit (SBU) which has been defined succinctly by Arthur D. Little as:

A Strategic Business Unit – or Strategy Centre – is a business area with an external market place for goods and services, for which management can determine objectives and execute strategies independent of other business areas. It is a business that could probably stand alone if divested. Strategic Business Units are the 'natural' or homogeneous business of a corporation.

Abell and Hammond (1979) also subscribe to the view that SMP should be executed at the level of the 'business unit' which they regard as a 'reasonably autonomous profit centre' normally under the control of its own general manager. More precise definitions than this are seen as impossible due to the diversity encountered in practice but the common features include a wide degree of independence and the existence of the basic functional departments such as R & D, Manufacturing, Sales, etc.

Given this elaboration we can propose a definition of strategic marketing planning as:

> *The establishment of the goal or purpose of a strategic business unit and the means by which this is to be achieved.*

If this definition is acceptable then it would seem that the next logical step would be to look at the manner in which firms formulate objectives and the process by which they seek to achieve them. This we seek to do in the sections which follow.

■ Formulating Objectives

While discussions of planning invariably contain some reference to the need to establish objectives as a prerequisite to formal planning it is rare to find any explicit reference as to just how one should set about formulating these objectives in the first place. As Malcolm McDonald observes:[6]

> The literature on the subject [marketing planning] is, however, not very explicit, which is surprising when it is considered how vital the setting of marketing objectives is.
>
> An objective will ensure that a company knows what its strategies are expected to accomplish and when a particular strategy has accomplished its purpose. In other words, without objectives, strategy decisions and all that follow will take place in a vacuum.

In *Corporate Strategy*[7] Igor Ansoff stresses the importance of objectives as the basis for appraisal, control and coordination and defines an objective as:

> A measure of the efficiency of the resource-conversion process. An objective contains 3 elements: the particular attribute that is chosen as a measure of efficiency, the yardstick, or scale, by which the attribute is measured, and the goal – the particular value on the scale which the firm seeks to attain.

In Chapter 3 we emphasised the critical importance of a clear statement of objectives as the basis for determining where the organisation is headed, the means for reaching that goal, and the basis for determining the progress which has been made. In the particular McKay[8] suggests that it is possible to distinguish two categories of issues to be considered when setting objectives – the general application to all businesses, and the specific which provides for a closer and more detailed examination.

■ General

1   *Business scope*, i.e. What business should we be in?
2   *Business orientation*, i.e. What is the orientation best suited to our business scope and to our continuing purposes of survival, growth and profit?
3   *Business organisation*, i.e. Does our present organisation – in style, structure and staff – fit the orientation chosen?
4   *Public responsibility*, i.e. Are our selections of business opportunities made in light of present and future social and economic needs of the public?
5   *Performance evaluation*, i.e. Does our appraisal system mesh properly with our planning system?

■ Specific

These concern more specific areas for deeper and more precise examination for each SBU, including:

1   *Customer classes*
2   *Competitors*
3   *Markets and distribution*
4   *Technology and products*
5   *Production capability*
6   *Finance*
7   *Environment*

Taken together these issues provide the focus for the marketing audit, which we discuss in detail in Chapter 10, and form the basis for developing the short-term marketing plan based on a manipulation of the elements of the marketing mix.

McDonald cites extensive support for the view that in developing objectives one should move from the general to the particular, from the broad to the narrow and from the long term to the short term. He also stresses the importance of viewing all these objectives as part of a hierarchy which must be internally consistent and mutually reinforcing. It follows then that marketing objectives constitute a sub-set of the overall corporate objective (which will also dictate the objectives for the other major business functions such as R & D and production), and in turn will determine the objectives of other marketing functions such as product development, advertising, selling and distribution.

In discussing marketing objectives Peter Drucker[9] identifies seven which he believes must be given explicit consideration in any company:

1 The desired standing of the existing products in their market in turnover and percentage share measured against direct and indirect competition.
2 The desired standing of existing products in new markets measured as in 1.
3 The existing products which should be phased out and ultimately abandoned, and the future product mix.
4 The new products needed in existing markets, the number, their properties and the share targets.
5 The new markets which new products will help to develop, in size and share.
6 The distribution organisation needed to accomplish the marketing goals and the pricing policy appropriate to them.
7 A service objective, measuring how well the customer should be supplied with what he considers value.

Implicit in this approach is the concept of a portfolio of products which may be at quite different stages in their life-cycle and we shall return to this concept when we examine the analytical framework proposed by the Boston Consulting Group in Chapter 5.

McKay (*Marketing Mystique*) identifies only three basic marketing objectives – to enlarge the market, to increase market share and to improve profitability – but then proceeds to spell out a number of distinct strategies for achieving these objectives:

1 To enlarge the market
(a) By innovation or product development
   1. Through improving existing products or lines to increase use
   2. Through developing new products or lines.
(b) By innovation or market development
   1. Through developing present end-use markets
   2. Through discovering new end-use markets.
2 To increase market share
(a) By emphasising product development and product improvement for competitive advantage
   1. Through product performance
   2. Through product quality
   3. Through product features
(b) By emphasising persuasion effort for competitive advantage
   1. Through sales and distribution
   2. Through advertising and sales promotion
(c) By emphasising customer-service activities for competitive advantage
   1. Through ready availability, order handling and delivery service
   2. Through credit and collection policies

3.   Through after-sale product service
3   To improve profitability
(a)   By emphasising sales volume for profit leverage
1.   Through strengthened sales and distribution effort
2.   Through strengthened advertising and sales promotion effort
3.   Through strengthened advertising effort
(b)   By emphasising elimination of unprofitable activities
1.   Through pruning products and lines
2.   Through pruning sales coverage and distribution
3.   Through pruning customer services
(c)   By emphasising price improvement
1.   Through leadership in initiating needed price increases
2.   Through price improvement gained by differentiating products and services from those of competitors
(d)   By emphasising cost reduction
1.   Through improved effectiveness of marketing tools and methods in product planning, in persuasion activities and in customer service activities.

McKay then proceeds to offer a series of guidelines for formulating objectives and strategies based upon his own extensive review of the literature. The majority of these have already been covered in the preceding discussion, but it is worth stressing the point made by McKay that 'Each strategy carries with it certain essential related commitments, which must be accepted when the strategy is selected.' This assertion is emphasised in Table 4.5, in which push and pull strategies are contrasted in terms of the 'must do', 'might do' and 'don't do' factors.

■ A Framework for Strategic Marketing Planning

In developing a framework for the execution of SMP it will be helpful to conceive of it as a process consisting of a number of discrete steps and governed by a number of specific principles.

The actual number of steps proposed in the SMP process varies according to different authors who have analysed and described the sequential events. However, closer inspection of these alternative models reveals a high degree of consistency between them as will become evident in our review of some of the better-known statements.

The most broadly based models distinguish only three stages or 'cycles' in the process of SMP which may be summarised as:

• Evaluation
• Strategy formulation
• Detailed planning

Table 4.5   Contrasting strategy requirements

Actions	Pull-through strategy	Push-through strategy
Objective	Seek competitive advantage through building brand acceptance and demand direct with customer	Seek competitive advantage by motivating distribution to carry and move your product
Must do	Use communication media to promote desirable image of product or brand, and maintain consistent image Keep improving effectiveness of messages to the customer Price to cover services rendered by distribution plus fair profit	Provide incentives in margins, bonuses and allowances to stimulate volume selling Strive for more and better outlets Maintain standards of distribution service and communications consistent with product and company identity
Might do	Force distribution through customer demand Provide maximum availability so customer stimulation can be promptly satisfied Use direct contacts to assist sales through distributor	Maintain superiority in training and selling assistance provided Encourage distribution commitment to your company and product objectives
Don't do	Continually offer special prices to distributors as incentive to load inventories in distribution channels	Price so distributor has little or no profit Carry on extensive advertising and promotion Assist distributor sales through direct sales effort

Source: E.S. McKay, *The Marketing Mystique* (New York, American Management Association, 1972).

Abell and Hammond (1979) elaborate on this basic framework and state that a strategic market plan may be thought of as involving four sets of related decisions:

1 *Defining the business*, i.e. answering the question 'What business am I in?'. The definition must state:

(a) Product and market *scope*: in particular, which customers are to be served, which customer functions (needs) are to be satisfied and what ways ('technologies') are to be used to satisfy the functions;
(b) Product and market *segmentation*: in particular, whether and how the firm recognises differences among customers in terms of their needs and the ways they are satisfied.

2 *Determining the mission (or role) of the business*, i.e. the set of objectives to be pursued. These should be stated in terms of performance expectations with regard to 'sales growth, market-share, return on investment, net income and

cash' for each distinct product/market and must be based upon a full analysis of the firm's Strengths and Weaknesses, and the Opportunities and Threats which face it (i.e. a SWOT analysis).

3 *Formulating functional strategies*; including marketing, production, etc. Interaction with general management. The results of the strategy formulation process should be completed strategy statements which possess the following characteristics:

(a) They should describe each of the major components of the organisation's strategy, i.e plan scope, distinctive competences, growth vector, competitive advantage, intended synergy.
(b) Should indicate how the strategy will lead to the accomplishment of the organisation's objectives.
(c) The strategy should be described in functional rather than physical forms.
(d) It should be as precise as possible.

Levitt in 'Marketing Myopia'[10] makes the case for functional rather than physical statements of strategy. Drucker[11] points out that Levitt's approach leads to broad impracticable working statements and counsels the use of both specific and precise strategy statements. A good strategy statement would thus appear in cell 3 of Figure 4.1.

4. *Budgeting*, resource allocation decisions, sales forecasts.

Abell and Hammond also distinguished the SMP from a marketing plan (MP) by stressing that the latter is seen as dealing 'primarily with the delineation of target segments and the product, communication, channel and pricing policies for reaching and servicing those segments – the so-called marketing mix', while the former is 'a plan of *all* aspects of an organisation's strategy in the market place'. The essential difference is one of detail. The SMP is more disaggregated than the MP and is concerned with long-term issues. The SMP states clearly who does what, when and with what resources. We return to these distinctions in Chapter 11 ('The Marketing Mix') and Chapter 20 ('The (Short-term) Marketing Plan').

A number of other writers and commentators suggest that SMP, like corporate strategy formulation, should be the result of the answers to a self-examination catechism comprising seven questions. Taylor[12] summarises these as follows:

1 What are the objectives to be achieved and how should we define the scope of our business?
2 What limits are set on these objectives by our personal values and social responsibilities?
3 On which strengths can we build and what are the weaknesses which need to be compensated for?
4 What opportunities are to be taken advantage of and what threats should be avoided?

	Broad	Precise
Functional terms	1 Transportation business	2 Long-distance transportation of low-value, low-density products
Physical terms	3 Railroad business	4 Long-haul, coal-carrying railroad

Figure 4.1   Characteristics of effective strategy statements

Source: C. W. Hofer and D. E. Schendel, *Strategy Formulation: Analytical Concepts* (St Paul, Minnesota: West Publishing, 1978).

5   What are the main decisions to be taken and to what major courses of action must we commit ourselves?
6   What resources will be required and where will these resources come from?
7   What are the risks in this strategy and what contingency plans are required?

M.B. McDonald (*Marketing Plans*) also specifies a seven-step sequence as follows:

1   Defining the business.
2   Situation audit and statement of assumptions.
3   Establishing objectives.
4   Identifying strategic alternatives.
5   Selection of specific courses of action ('strategies').
6   Implementation.
7   Measurement, feedback and control.

From the foregoing summaries it is clear that there is a high degree of consensus on the basic steps in the SMP process and that variations in the number of stages are largely the result of elaboration of that basic framework. Thus McDonald's final model is extended to nine steps as can be seen in Figure 4.2 and could easily be sub-divided still further if it were felt that making a step explicit would improve the clarity of the process and plan.
In Figure 4.2 and much of the preceding discussion we have referred to 'steps' in the marketing planning process. In practice it is more realistic to think of SMP as a *cyclical activity*, as illustrated in Figure 4.3. Such a cycle recognises that the

great majority of companies already exist and so may be at any point on the cycle, whereas flow diagrams imply a once and for all sequence of a new organisation, even when they possess feedback loops as in Figure 4.2.

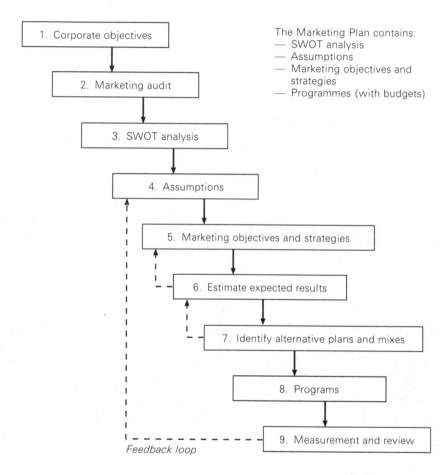

Figure 4.2   The marketing planning process

Source: M. H. B. McDonald, *Marketing Plans* (London: Heinemann, 1984).

So much for the process, what about the principles which are felt to govern it? Again one can find a number of different approaches set out in the literature of SMP, but one of the best developed and comprehensive schemes which has withstood the acid test of implementation is that discussed by Arthur D. Little (ADL). Accordingly, we shall use this as an examplar of a proven approach that works in practice.

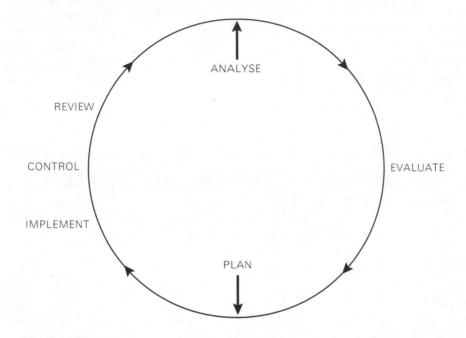

Figure 4.3   The cycle of SMP

■ Principles of SMP

ADL's strategic planning process centres on five principles:

- Strategic Business Units or 'strategy centres'.
- Planning is a data-based activity.
- Business is not random; it is shaped by competitive economics.
- There is a finite set of available strategies for each Business Unit.
- Strategy selection should be condition-driven not ambition-driven.

Much of this book is an elaboration of these points – all of it seeks to conform with them. None the less a summary of the explicit meaning attached to these principles will be a useful prelude to the detailed treatment of later chapters.

We have already adopted ADL's definition of an SBU or strategy centre and noted that all the major writers on the subject now use SBUs as the basic building block for SMP.

The second principle, that 'planning is a data-based activity', also enjoys universal acceptance although, as we shall see in Chapter 12 when dealing with marketing research, most agree that facts can only provide a basis for decision-making. Where facts are not available or uncertainty exists as to their accuracy, reliability or validity then it will be necessary to combine hard data with judgement. (We shall look more closely at this mode of decision-making later.) However, the principle is sound – one should always seek to establish and secure those facts that are available about the environment in general, about the industry in which the firm operates and about the SBU itself and analysis of data should correspond to these three levels. As ADL comment:

- At the market level: an assessment of market size, growth and segmentation in light of macro-forces.
- At the industry level: a strategic segmentation and competitive analysis as a function of industry structure and dynamics.
- At the Business Unit level: an evaluation of operations, performance vs. past strategies, and the determination of key strategic issues.

The third principle that 'Business is not random' predicates that there are discernible patterns to both competition and performance. Much of the discipline of economics is founded on an acceptance of the first proposition and in Chapter 2 we examined the insights which an understanding of market structure, conduct and performance can provide in the formulation and execution of marketing strategy. ADL argue that there are two key factors to examine in determining the strategic condition of a given business – industry maturity and competitive position. Industry maturity is specified in terms of an industry life-cycle as being in an embryonic, growth, mature or ageing state as determined 'by a number of factors including:

- Growth rate/potential.
- Product line breadth/activity.
- Competitor's number/structure.
- Customer loyalty.
- Market-share distribution/stability.
- Ease of entry.
- Technology focus/stability'.

It is claimed that, *inter alia*, industry maturity has implications for the natural strategies available, which lends support to McKay's view that once a basic strategy has been selected or determined there are things you must do, might do, and do not do if you are to maintain consistency. In addition this concept of stages in the life cycle also has significant implications for likely performance and cash generation levels as well as for the most appropriate type of management system. We shall return to these points in Chapter 5 when looking at different approaches to or techniques for strategic planning.

A firm's competitive position is determined by the geographical scope of the industry and the strategic segments (i.e. specific product-market combinations) in which the SBU is competing. Competitive position is more than just market share and is determined by a combination of three factors:

- Market share = the result of past strengths and weaknesses.
- Competitive economics.
- Other factors usually reflecting present strengths and weaknesses, e.g. technology.

The significance of market share as an indicator of a firm's competitive standing tends to increase with industry maturity and we shall return to this proposition when discussing the Boston Consulting Group's product portfolio approach and the Profit Implications of Market Strategy (PIMS) study in Chapter 5.

ADL have developed their own scheme for classifying a firm's competitive position and recognise five categories of positions as follows:

- 'Dominant': Very rare and usually the result of a quasi monopoly or from strongly protected technological leadership, e.g. De Beers in diamonds, Xerox (originally) in photocopying.
- 'Strong': Strong competitors can usually follow strategies of their choice, irrespective of their competitors' moves.
- 'Favourable': When industries are fragmented, with no competitor clearly standing out, the leaders tend to be in a favourable position.
- 'Tenable': Cases where profitability can be sustained through specialisation.
- 'Weak': Either too small to compete effectively or big and inefficient.

By combining maturity and competitive position one obtains a 'strategic condition' matrix, as depicted in Figure 4.4.

Once SBUs have been diagnosed they can be located on the matrix and one can evaluate appropriate strategies for them bearing in mind the fourth principle that 'there is a finite set of available strategies for each Business Unit'. ADL propose six generic strategy groups:

- Market strategies (domestic and international).
- Product strategies.
- Technology strategies.
- Operations strategies.
- Management and systems strategies.
- Retrenchment strategies.

With the exception of the last of these it is clear that ADL are proposing a very different conceptual approach from that underlying the concept of limited

Stages of industry maturity

	Embryonic	Growth	Mature	Aging
Dominant				
Strong				
Favourable				
Tenable				
Weak				

Competitive position

Figure 4.4   The strategic condition matrix

Source: A. D. Little Inc.

strategic alternatives set out in Chapter 3. Clearly the latter are concerned more with the *direction* in which one is seeking to move, while the former are concerned with business functions or the *means* of moving the firm in a chosen direction – an interpretation consistent with ADL's definition of strategies as 'a series of coordinated actions which direct resources'.

In developing strategies the final principle has to be applied, namely, that '*Strategy selection* [should] *be driven by the condition of the business, not the ambition of its Managers*'. As stated, this is clearly a plea for realism in selecting strategies with the inference that one should not overreach oneself. But, towards the end of the chapter when we discuss the advantages and disadvantages of strategic planning it will become evident that the lack of growth in the advanced Western economies in the late 1970s and early 1980s was as much due to a lack of ambition as to an excess of it.

While firms at Stage I and II of corporate development will only have one SBU and so can move to detailed planning and implementation for that SBU, larger and more complex firms at Stages III and IV will have to undertake an additional step which is to ensure that the individual SBU strategies are internally consistent and mutually reinforcing and so conducive to that elusive phenomenon of synergy (the '2 + 2 = 5' concept) in an overall corporate strategy.

■ The Formulation of Corporate Strategy

According to ADL the formulation of a corporate strategy involves three steps:
1 A reconciliation of various internal and external inputs with Business Unit plans and strategy alternatives, to select mutually consistent corporate strategies.
2 Assessment of the implications of the selected strategies in terms of new activities or businesses to be developed and acceptance or modification – we call it revectoring – of specific Business Unit plans, prior to the preparation of a revised corporate plan.
3 Allocation of corporate resources.

In turn, these basic stages call for a formal and detailed assessment of:

- The external environment.
- The internal environment.
- The business portfolio.
- New business opportunities.
- The corporate risk portfolio.
- Corporate human resources and requirements.
- Corporate financial resources and obligations.
- Corporate goals and objectives.

ADL's detailed review of each of these steps reveals a marked overlap with the analytical frameworks developed by other organisations. Thus the review of the internal and external environments comprises the marketing audit and SWOT analysis found in the normative approach to SMP. ADL extend these steps to develop what they term a 'strategic condition matrix', as depicted in Figure 4.4, which proposes four broad alternatives – natural development, selective development, turn around and abandonment – and corresponds closely to Shell's Directional Policy Matrix which we review later (see pp. 125–30).

The third step in ADL's analysis reviews the SBUs in terms of their cash generation/ absorption characteristics using a 'Ronagraph' which bears a striking resemblance to the so-called 'Boston Box' developed by the Boston Consulting Group (see p. 120). Once the potential of the existing businesses has been assessed the analysis is extended to explore possible external opportunities which are then compared with the internal opportunities. This comparison leads naturally to an evaluation of the corporate risk portfolio and eight factors are cited as affecting the risk of each SBU:

1 Industry maturity.
2 Competitive position.
3 Inherent industry risk.
4 Unit objectives.

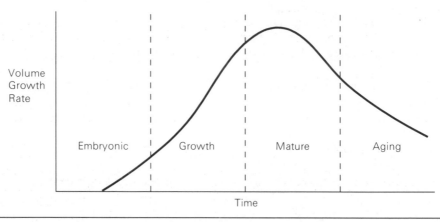

Market	High Growth/Low Share	High Growth/High Share	Low Growth/High Share	Low Growth/Low Share
Financial	Cash hungry Low reported earnings Good P/E High debt level	Self-financing, cash hungry. Good to low reported earnings High P/E. Low–moderate debt level	Cash rich High earnings Fair P/E No debt–High debt capacity	Fair cash flow Low earnings Low P/E Low debt capacity
Managerial	Entrepreneur	Sophisticated manager	Critical administrator	Opportunistic milker
Planning Time Frame	Long enough to draw tentative life cycle (10)	Long-range investment payout (7)	Intermediate (3)	Short range (1)
Structure	Free form or task force	Semi-permanent task force, product or market division	Business Division plus task force for renewal	Pared-down division
Com-pensation	High variable/low fixed, fluctuating with performance	Balanced variable and fixed, individual and group rewards	Low variable–high fixed, group rewards	Fixed only
Com-munication System	Informal/tailor-made	Formal/tailor-made	Formal/uniform	Little or none, command system
Measuring and Reporting	Qualitative marketing, unwritten	Qualitative and quantitative early warning system, all functions	Qualitative, written, production oriented.	Numerical, written, balance sheet oriented

Figure 4.5   A depiction of the strategy centres concept

Source: Arthur D. Little Inc.

5   Unit assumptions.
6   Unit strategies.
7   Past unit performance.
8   Management record.

Once each has been assessed the separate assessments can be combined into an overall corporate risk portfolio.

The same procedure is then repeated in terms of external uncertainties and the likelihood of their affecting each of the SBUs ('exposure'). These are then aggregated into a corporate risk profile which ADL graphed on 8 axes as illustrated in Figure 4.5.

Step 6 is the qualitative and quantitative evaluation of the corporate management resources while step 7 embraces determination of the corporate financial resources and obligations. Finally, these analyses lead to an *explicit* statement of corporate goals and objectives and a timetable for their achievement. Emphasis upon making the process explicit is supported by all the proponents of SMP to ensure that all the key steps have been taken, that the issues considered have been duly recorded so that subsequent reference can be made to them, and to provide an action document for those responsible for implementing the plan. Thus, according to ADL, such a formal plan should cover all the following issues:

1 The key environmental assumptions.
2 The corporate weaknesses requiring attention.
3 The corporate values and objectives.
4 The basic corporate strategic thrusts.
5 Strategic mandates for functional units.
6 Unit strategy revectoring process.
7 New budgeting process.

In running through the process of strategic planning using Arthur D. Little as an examplar frequent reference has been made to 'life-cycles' and in Chapter 5 we will review this concept in some detail as it is fundamental to all major frameworks for strategic marketing planning.

Criticisms of and Obstacles to Strategic Planning

In the aftermath of the recessions precipitated by the energy crises of the 1970s many commentators attributed lacklustre performance (particularly in the USA) to an over-dependence upon formal strategic planning. This issue was the subject of an article in the *Harvard Business Review* by Daniel H. Gray entitled 'Uses and misuses of strategic planning'[13] in which he argued that there was nothing wrong with the concept of strategic planning – it is *faulty preparation and implementation* which causes the problems.

Based upon a year-long research project, Gray concluded that a major problem with strategic planning was (and is) the tendency to regard it as a separate discipline or management function rather than as an instrument to support strategic management: in other words, a tendency for the system to assume a greater importance than its product as an input to the managerial formulation of strategy. With over 500 respondents Gray found a high level of commitment to the concept of formal planning but 87% reported feelings of disappointment and frustration with their systems. 58% of the sample attributed this to difficulties experienced in the implementation of plans while 67% of those from multi-businesses attributed implementation difficulties to faults in the design and management of their system.

More detailed analysis indicated that many of the claimed difficulties in implementation were really due to *pre-implementation factors* which could be summarised as:

1 Poor preparation of line managers.
2 Faulty definition of business units.
3 Vaguely formulated goals.
4 Inadequate information bases for planning.
5 Badly handled reviews of business unit plans
6 Inadequate linkage of strategic planning with other control systems.

Clearly, all these factors are amenable to correction and improvement (Gray provides his own detailed advice as to how to set about this).

In 1987 Michael Porter wrote in *The Economist*[14] that 'Strategic planning was born amid a flurry of optimism and industrial growth in the 1960s and early '70s. It quickly became a fad. Today strategic planning has fallen out of fashion. The criticism is well-deserved. Strategic planning in most companies has not contributed to strategic thinking. The answer is not to abandon planning. The need has never been greater. Instead strategic planning needs to be rethought'.

That said, the sources of resistance to SMP remain much the same as those identified by Malcolm MacDonald[15] namely:

1 The company has made good products without it.
2 Planning is time consuming and prevents people from doing their real job.
3 Plans are constraining, prevent initiative and create inflexibility to rapid change.
4 Plans never come true, and valuable time is wasted writing them.
5 Companies know their business well, there is no point writing down the obvious.
6 No one reads the plan when it is written so it becomes a traditional annual ritual.
7 Some industries are different and do not need plans.
8 Long-range plans are full of meaningless numbers.
9 Plans are based on unrealistic objectives and prepared without hard market information.
10 Departments cannot agree amongst themselves so the plan is never finalised.

In broad terms, the failing enthusiasm for strategic planning may be diagnosed as a problem of *trappings* vs. *substance* following Charles Ames's analysis of a similar disenchantment with the marketing concept in the 1960s.[16] As suggested earlier a contributory factor was that SP had become established as a separate specialist function in its own right and so 'detached' from senior management who were (are) its rightful owners. A further explanation of the 'disarray' in which strategic business planning finds itself is provided by a recent article in *Long Range Planning*.[17]

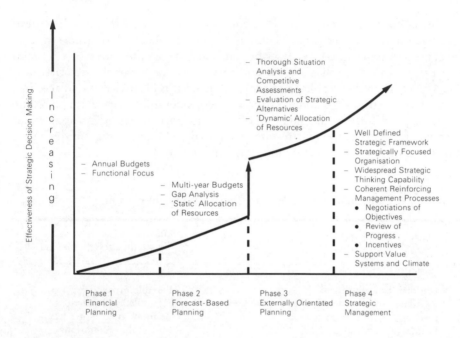

Figure 4.6   Phases in the development of strategic planning

Source: T. G. Marx, 'Removing the Obstacles to Effective Strategic Planning', *Long Range Planning*, 24 (4) (August 1991).

In Dr Marx's view SP has been seen to fail in delivering the promised benefits because of the numerous bureaucratic obstacles put in its path. The obstacles identified occur at each of the four phases of the development of strategic management identified by Gluck *et al.*[18] and illustrated in Figure 4.6. Most companies proceed smoothly through phases 1 and 2 as competitive pressures and investment planning require them to look 3–5 years ahead. But, as Figure 4.6 indicates, there is a step function in both commitment and expenditure to progress from phase 2 to phase 3. Marx comments:

It is in phase 3 of the planning process that the difficult processes really begin. It is here that the company is organised, for planning purposes, into strategic business units (SBU's); extensive training is required; thorough analysis of competitors and the external environment and an inventory of internal strengths and weaknesses are undertaken; and formal business plans are written, reviewed and monitored for the first time. It is also here that the organisational changes are most severe, and that the planning process becomes most vulnerable to its natural enemies – inertia, entrenched interests, and risk aversity.

Unless the firm can overcome these difficulties it is unlikely that it will achieve the transition from externally-orientated planning (phase 3) to true strategic management (phase 4). Marx describes in some detail the kinds of obstacles which can be raised in phase 3 and contrasts these with the characteristics of phase 4 as illustrated in Table 4.6. From Table 4.6 it is clear that if one acquires the trappings of strategic planning (usually at considerable expense) the outcome is virtually antithetical to the intention of the substance of strategic management – dynamic, responsive, flexible, results-orientated and – above all – in the hands of those responsible for direction and implementation.

Table 4.6   Obstacles to effective strategic planning

Phase 3 Obstacles	Phase 4 Characteristics
Planning Processes	
Uniform procedures	Flexible procedures
Regularly scheduled reviews	Scheduled as needed
Strict time limits on reviews	As much time as needed
Formal presentations	Informal presentations
Numerous observers	Decision makers only
Massive paperwork	Ten-page plans
Restricted discussion	Open dialogue
No decisions	Decisions mandatory
Process emphasized	Results emphasized
Content of the Plans	
Data, numbers, facts	Business intelligence
Financial analysis	Strategic analysis
Short-term focus	Long-term focus
Generic strategies	Strategic action plans
Monitoring and Reward Processes	
Random progress reviews	Regular progress reviews
Limited accountability	Strict accountability

Source: T.G. Marx, 'Removing the obstacles to Effective Strategic Planning', *Long Range Planning*, 24(4) (August 1991).

The obstacles encountered in phase 3 are attributed by Marx to one of four basic root causes:

1 Lack of top management commitment.
2 Staff, rather than line management, control of process.
3 Entrenched self-interest.
4 A risk averse corporate culture.

Marx describes and analyses each of these causal factors in some depth and concludes that successful companies which are able to overcome the obstacles progress from the bureaucratic parody of planning of phase 3 to the realities of strategic planning in phase 4. By its nature hands-on strategic planning and management eschews the bureaucracy of its trappings and reduces the practice to its substance. Because of the contrast between trappings and substance some commentators mistakenly believe that phase 4 firms have dropped strategic planning and so may be compared with the Japanese who, the conventional wisdom would have us believe, 'don't plan at all'. Marx observes:

> It is the lack of the most obvious obstacles to effective strategic business planning in the Japanese systems which leads to this misperception. The elimination of formal presentations, large meetings, massive planning books, and regularly scheduled, annual reviews is not the abandonment of planning – it is the liberation of planning!

Support for the above views is reflected in a *Fortune* article entitled 'How to plan for 1995'.[19] According to the author, Ronald Henkoff, the first year of the new decade had confirmed that the turbulence of the 1980s was unlikely to settle down, leading Walker Lewis, head of Strategic Planning Associates in Washington DC to comment 'This may be a time of immense uncertainty, but it is a *certainty* that Western companies are in for ten years of competitive hell'.

Faced with such a prospect, planning for the future assumes even greater importance but it is clear that old methods involving highly formalised procedures are inappropriate to anticipate and capture the surprises and uncertainties in a rapidly changing environment. In Henkoff's view 'At too many companies strategic planning has become overly bureaucratic, absurdly quantitative, and largely irrelevant'. Given the volatility of the market place the strategic planning popularised in the stable 1960s needs to be replaced with a more responsive, hands-on approach in the 1990s – an activity increasingly being referred to as *Strategic Thinking*.

The key characteristics of strategic thinking are seen as *focus* and *flexibility*:

> Focus means figuring out, and building on, what the company does best. It means identifying the evolving needs of your customers, then developing the key skills – often called core competencies – critical to serving them. It means setting a clear, realistic mission and then working tirelessly to make sure everyone – from the chairman to the middle managers to the hourly employee, understands it...

Flexibility means sketching rough scenarios of the future – what General Electric [GE] Chairman Jack Welch calls bands of possibilities – then being ready to pounce on opportunities as they arise (Henkoff, 1990).

As Henkoff observes:

GE was once the corporate citadel of quantitative forecasting. The 350-member planning staff churned out voluminous reports, meticulously detailed and exquisitely packaged. Now GE has but a score of full-time planners. Called business development specialists, they are there only to advise line managers, who have the prime responsibility for formulating strategy.

The heads of GE's 13 businesses each year develop five *one-page* 'charts', memos that alert them to possible opportunities and obstacles in their industries over the next 24 months. When Hungary opened its doors to foreign ownership in state-run companies, GE needed just 60 days to cut a deal for 50% of Tungsram, the country's leading lighting company. Tungsram had been on GE's chart for years.

As noted previously, the challenge of successful strategic thinking/planning is the ability to identify market opportunities and then deploy the organisation's resources to exploit them profitably. It is the ability to think conceptually in terms of the need served and then define this in terms of currently appropriate solutions; to be flexible but control and manage the pace of change so as to optimise present skills and investment while acquiring new skills and releasing capital for new investment. To do this effectively calls for a marketing orientation irrespective of whether one subscribes to the 'technology push' or 'market pull' theory of innovation and change. Market pull lends itself to incremental change, technology push to discontinuities and step changes in the way in which things are done. Market pull works back from existing customers and their consumption behaviour using conventional market research to document possibilities for enhancing current products and services. Technology push arises from insight, intuition and creativity and promises major gains in satisfaction. But, because it is radically different, it engenders resistance which becomes greater the greater the change proposed. Based on over 30 years of experience and research I am convinced that successful innovation – defined as the commercialisation of invention – is highly dependent upon the innovator's ability to identify the *most receptive market segment* – something which depends centrally upon an understanding of markets and customer behaviour. As Henkoff observes 'In a world awash with forecasts, opinions, theories, seminars, consultants, and concepts, many companies have come to the conclusion that the only oracles worth listening to are their customers'.

However, in 'listening to one's customers' it is important to make the distinction implicit in the previous paragraph when discussing the difference between technology push and market pull. Customers are both able and willing to tell suppliers what they like and dislike about current offerings, and it is this feedback which enables the continuous upgrading and improvement of such products where the benefits justify the costs involved. But customers are much less able and willing to speculate about radical change and such theorising and conjecture inevitably falls to the lot of the inventor and entrepreneur. As the record shows the failures of would-be inventors and entrepreneurs greatly exceed the few well documented success stories and it is here that both academic and practitioner have a role to play in seeking to isolate and describe those activities and procedures which appear to enhance the potential for success. Formal strategic planning is an attempt to do just this and the fact that its usefulness has become compromised and open to question should not distract the professional manager from the potential contribution from the activity, *provided* it remains an aid to strategic thinking and not a substitute for it. Because strategic planning practice has degenerated into a form a detailed tactical documentation more akin to the operational budget statement does not mean that the concept of strategic planning is deficient, too. What is needed is a return to the broadly based speculation about alternative futures which was the origin of techniques such as those developed by GE, Shell and the Boston Consulting Group.

In his *Fortune* article Henkoff reports that *scenario planning* has emerged as an approach which combines both focus and flexibility. Describing practice at California Edison, whose painstaking long-range plans had been rendered virtually useless by unanticipated events such as OPEC price-fixing, restrictions on sulphur emissions and accidents at Three Mile Island and Chernobyl, Henkoff comments:

> Looking ahead ten years, the utility came up with 12 possible versions of the future – incorporating an economic boom, a Middle East oil crisis, expanded environment-alism, and other developments. Each scenario carries implications for how much power Edison would need to generate, from 5,000 megawatts more to 5,000 megawatts less than the 15,000 megawatts it was producing in 1987.
>
> To cope with such radical variations in demand, Edison has built flexibility into its system. It can repower or depower oil-and-gas generating plants, buy juice from other utilities and intensify or diminish its campaign to help customers use less electricity. Edison is stepping up conservation in response to new state regulations that reward utilities for encouraging reduced consumption.

Similarly, Royal Dutch/Shell, which has been doing scenario planning for 19 years and is widely regarded as the master of the craft, currently has two 20-year scenarios in place. The first, called "Sustainable World", predicts increased concern about global warming trends and an expanded emphasis on conserva-tion, recycling and emission controls. The second scenario, ominously entitled "Mercantilist World", postulates an increase in protectionism, a slump in world growth, and a de-emphasis on environmentalism.

It is in this spirit of flexibility and broad brush approaches to strategic planning that we have confined the discussion largely to what we have described as CUGs – currently useful generalisations. Such generalisations provide a framework for thinking about and analysis of strategic issues without dulling the mind and spirit with the pseudo-precision of the detailed formal planning systems beloved by the specialist. This is not to suggest that detail has no place in strategic planning but to emphasise that its place is subordinate and supportive – a fact long recognised in successful military organisations where the 'teeth arms' actually do the fighting and the staff and support services attend to the administration, logistics and communications. Accordingly in Chapter 5 we look at some of the techniques and procedures which inform the detailed planning process, but without getting into the detail itself.

■ Summary

In Chapter 4 we have attempted to provide a framework for the remainder of the book by examining some of the principles of strategic marketing planning and, thereby, linking the key areas of marketing, strategy and planning into a single, coherent structure.

To introduce this structure we looked first at the concept of stages of corporate development and concluded that while the degree of detail called for would grow with the increased size and complexity of an organisation, the need for and discipline of strategic planning was appropriate to all forms and size of organisation. This conclusion was reinforced by a brief review of the evolution of management systems and concomitant planning systems which lend considerable support to General Eisehower's often quoted maxim 'The plan is nothing; planning is everything'. In other words, the process is infinitely more important than any specific output from it.

Next we looked at definitions of SMP. As with terms like 'strategy', 'marketing', and 'planning' so it is with their combination into the description of a practice – we can easily agree on the general, it is the particularities which lead to the differences as to precisely what is involved. Accordingly, we proposed that SMP may be defined as:

> *The establishment of the goal or purpose of a strategic business unit and the means by which this is to be achieved.*

If one has a goal or purpose then it is reasonable to expect that one can specify this in the form of a specific objective or objectives. The formulation of objectives was the subject of the next section of the chapter and we drew on the writings of several experts to help spell out the *kinds* of objectives which satisfy our concern for CUGs. In turn, this led us to propose a framework for SMP itself as either a sequence of 'steps' or, more likely, a continuous cycle of activity from analysis to evaluation to planning to implementation to review to analysis and so on. Underlying this cycle we can discern a number of key principles. While acknowledging the universality of these principles we chose to use the framework developed by Arthur D. Little as our exemplar. That said, the frameworks of other leading consultancies such as the Boston Consulting Group or

McKinsey's are just as useful (and very similar!) as a basis for helping decision-makers impose structure on the problems of strategy formulation and planning.

Finally, to conclude the chapter, we considered briefly some of the criticisms of, and obstacles to, the use of strategic marketing planning. In the main the problems associated with SMP reflect the confusion of trappings with substance and the lack of commitment in implementation. These are recurring themes which we address fully in Part III of the book. Meantime we move on to survey some of the techniques and procedures which will help those committed to the principles of SMP to translate it into practice.

Analytical Frameworks for Strategic Marketing Planning

⌐ Learning Goals ⌐

The issues to be address in Chapter 5 include:

1 The concept of the *product life-cycle* (PLC).
2 The *phases* of the PLC – Introduction, Growth, Maturity, Decline – and the basic strategic alternatives associated with them.
3 *Diffusion theory* as confirmation of the existence of the PLC and an input to strategic planning.
4 Using the PLC as a *planning tool*.
5 *Portfolio analysis* as a technique for establishing the firm's current standing and identifying possible future courses of action.
6 *Criticism* of portfolio analysis.
7 *Strategic overviews* and their role in diagnosing current threats and opportunities.
8 *Gap analysis* as a technique for detecting possible mismatches between aspirations and likely outcomes.
9 *Scenario analysis* as a means of coping with increasing environmental uncertainty.
10 *SWOT analysis* as the foundation for formal strategic planning.

After reading Chapter 5 you will be able to:

1 Describe the concept of the product life-cycle and justify its use as a basic *input* to formal planning.
2 Spell out the *strategy alternatives* appropriate to each of the major stages of the PLC – Introduction, Growth, Maturity, Decline.
3 Suggest how *diffusion theory* may be used to aid formal planning.
4 Explain the nature of portfolio analysis and the key *concepts* it embraces – PLC, Market Share, Experience Effects and Scale Effects.
5 Review and critique *criticisms* of portfolio analysis as an approach to SMP.
6 Describe the analytical approaches developed by Shell and GEC as a basis for determining the *strategic threats and opportunities* facing them.
7 Describe and explain the techniques of *gap* and *scenario analysis* and the nature of *SWOT analysis*.

■ Introduction

In Chapter 4 we traced the evolution of management systems during the second half of this century and described how formalised approaches to planning had developed to help professional managers cope better with an increasingly complex and turbulent environment. This review revealed the paradox that much 'planning' appears to have been short-term and responsible for the faltering growth of many western economies – especially those of the UK and USA despite the fact that the normative theory of strategic planning is claimed to offer the best long-term solution to competitive success. However, more recent research in several countries seems to suggest that the problem with strategic planning is similar to that identified by B. Charles Ames regarding the implementation of the marketing concept.

Ames's article 'Trappings versus Substance in Industrial Marketing',[1] was prompted by a growing chorus of complaint from industrial companies that, while marketing might be all very well for fast moving consumer goods firms, it was of little help to them. Ames's analysis and diagnosis was that the reason 'marketing' wasn't working for these industrial companies was because they had mistaken the 'trappings' of the marketing *function* for the 'substance' of the marketing *concept*. Instead of identifying the full implications of becoming market-orientated and customer-driven companies, which usually required a change of both values and corporate culture, management looked for a 'quick fix' by increasing marketing expenditures on advertising and promotion, changing job titles, etc. The consequence, of course, was that little, if anything, happened. Indeed, the increased expenditures often worsened rather than improved corporate fortunes. The need clearly was for a much better understanding of the *philosophy* of marketing, and less emphasis upon its *practice*.

As with marketing, so with strategic planning. Accordingly, the remainder of Chapter 4 was concerned with seeking to establish the objectives, nature and purpose of SMP in order to communicate its substance. In this chapter we turn to issues of implementation and consider a number of analytical frameworks which have proved their worth in converting concept to practice.

Most of the frameworks presented in this chapter satisfy the definition of CUGs (currently useful generalisations) offered in Chapter 2 – they are simple, robust and known to work in practice. Their value lies in their ability to help impose structure on complex problems and reduce them to manageable proportions. Because they are simple, and often reduce problems to only two dimensions, they are frequently criticised or dismissed by theoreticians who can afford the luxury of simulating complex problems without any penalty for failure. Some reference will be made to the more important of these criticisms but, in general, they are rejected on the grounds that experience shows that the methods described in this chapter do help managers solve problems. However, it is important to recognise from the outset that they can offer assistance only in diagnosing, defining and solving problems. As with any other tool or technique, incorrectly selected and applied they will have little or no effect. The skill of the professional manager lies in his or her ability to select the appropriate method from the repertoire available. To do so requires that the manager knows what is in the repertoire.

Accordingly, in this chapter we will look first at the concept of the product life-cycle (PLC) and its close relation to diffusion theory. Next we examine portfolio analysis, as conceived and developed by the Boston Consulting Group, together with some of the criticisms levelled against it. Third, we shall discuss the two dimensional matrices developed by Shell and GEC to provide strategic overviews as a basis for determining the options available in developing a strategy. These considerations are supported by a synopsis of the salient features of scenario and gap analysis. Finally, we consider the role of SWOT analysis. SWOT is an acronym for Strengths, Weaknesses, Opportunities and Threats, and refers to the preliminary analysis which enables the organisation to identify the alternative courses of action available to it. This section will provide a foundation for a series of chapters which explore in greater detail the internal and external factors which must be taken into account in developing a strategic marketing plan.

■ The Product Life-cycle (PLC)

In Chapter 4 we introduced the PLC concept in the context of a discussion of the inevitability of change and of the need for the firm continuously to update its product offering in order to cater for the changing needs of its customers. In this section we shall examine the PLC in greater detail in terms of its value as an input to SMP.

The PLC concept enjoys wide currency in marketing circles and is probably the most widely known yet most misunderstood theoretical construct in marketing. While the supporters of the concept probably outnumber those who denounce it, it is important to make it clear from the start that many highly respected practitioners and academics have rejected the PLC as a useful weapon in the marketer's armoury. Foremost among the critics are Dhalla and Yuspeh whose article[2] found considerable support for their contention that the PLC concept is without empirical support and has led managers to make incorrect decisions particularly concerning products in the mature phase of the cycle.

As a confirmed supporter of the validity of the PLC I reject outright the claim that there is no empirical support for the concept[3] and would argue that the fact that managers have made wrong decisions when seeking to apply the concept is due to their misinterpretation of it rather than an intrinsic deficiency in the concept itself. Such misinterpretation invariably arises from the mistaken belief that the PLC is a precise forecasting tool when in reality it is 'a generalised model of the sale trend for a product class or category over a period of time, and of related changes in competitive behaviour'.[4] As such the PLC may be regarded as an important tool for planning at the strategic level always recognising that it is not of itself deterministic and may be influenced significantly by environmental changes and/or marketing action. In this respect the PLC is remarkably similar to the biological life-cycles on which it is founded, for in favourable conditions species (and products) will proliferate while in adverse circumstances only the strongest and fittest will survive. Similarly, there is no finite length to any stage of the life-cycle and there will be marked differences between different species albeit that some broad parameters may be distinguished for individual members of any given species. It is also important to remember that the PLC is usually presented in a very simplified form comprising only four phases and it would be surprising if such a broad division were able to accommodate detailed variations in action or behaviour. (It is significant that the consumer behaviour life-cycle popularised by Wells *et al.*[5] contains nine phases.) That said, experience shows that dividing a product's life into four distinct phases does enable one to make useful general-isations about the main characteristics of each phase, of the basic strategic alternatives available and of the most appropriate marketing mix for the implementation of each basic strategic option. It will be useful, therefore, to review briefly each of these four phases.

■ Introduction Stage of the Product Life-cycle

While it is obvious, many people overlook the fact that the classic PLC depicts the sales trend for a *successful* new product which survives the pangs of birth and the essentially hostile environment into which it is precipitated. Many new products are stillborn or suffer from basic deformities which severely limit their chances of survival and, while the statistics on new product success and failure are often impressive and contradictory, it is clear that 'infant mortality' is far greater than it should be.

There are numerous reasons why this should be so and many of these are discussed and illustrated in *Market Development*. Fundamentally, these reasons can be classified into half a dozen categories. Thus Buzzell attributes slow initial growth 'to some combination of four possible causes:

1   Delays in expansion of production capacity.
2   Technical problems, i.e. 'working out the bugs'.
3   Delays in making the product available to customers, especially in obtaining adequate distribution through retail outlets.
4   Customer inertia, arising primarily from reluctance to change established behaviour patterns.

Kotler[6] adds two more possible causes 'in the case of expensive new products:

5   Small number of buyers who are attuned to innovation.
6   High cost of the product inhibits purchase.

Put even more simply the success or failure of a new product depends on a number of *technical* factors and the prospective buyer's *behavioural* response to them. In my own research I have usually adopted the simplifying assumption that technical factors such as product characteristics, cost-price, distribution and the like are well known to and under the control or influence of the seller and that, if we are to improve the likelihood of survival then we need to concentrate more attention on the behavioural response of potential users and concentrate our selling efforts on those with the greatest receptivity to innovation. Unfortunately, innovativeness tends to be situation specific and difficult to predict (see the case histories in *Market Development*) which means that it is often simpler to use an undifferentiated strategy emphasising the price and promotion variables as a means to stimulate interest in and early sales of the product. This approach is advocated by Kotler (*Marketing Management*) who proposes four introductory marketing strategies as depicted in Figure 5.1.

		Promotion	
		High	*Low*
Price	*High*	Rapid-skimming strategy	Slow-skimming strategy
	Low	Rapid-penetration strategy	Slow-penetration strategy

Figure 5.1   Four introductory marketing strategies

Source: P. Kotler, *Marketing Management* (Englewood Cliffs, N.J.: Prentice-Hall, 1980) 4th edn.

Kotler then sets out the situations in which each of these strategies may be appropriate, which Firth[7] has tabulated in Table 5.1.

■ Growth

Assuming that a product survives the introductory phase then all the evidence points to a period of rapidly accelerating growth which is exponential in character and may be represented mathematically by some form of logistic curve. In many senses the take-up of a new product may be likened to the spread of an infectious disease in that in the early stages there are large numbers of 'unaffected' consumers so that it is relatively easy to make contact with such a person. However, as progressively more and more persons buy the new thing so

Table 5.1 Introductory marketing strategies and suitable situations

	TYPE OF STRATEGY			
	Rapid skimming	Slow skimming	Rapid penetration	Slow penetration
Suitable situations	1. Large part of the potential market is unaware of the product	1. The market is relatively limited in size	1. The market is large in size	1. The market is large
	2. Those who become aware of the product are eager to have it and are able to pay the asking price	2. Most of the market is aware of the product	2. The market is relatively unaware of the product	2. The market is highly aware of the product
	3. The firm faces potential competition and wants to build up brand preference	3. Those who want the product are prepared to pay a high price	3. Most buyers are price-sensitive	3. The market is price-sensitive
		4. There is little threat of potential competition	4. There is strong potential competition	4. There is some potential competition
			5. The company's unit manufacturing costs fall with the scale of production and accumulated manufacturing experience	

Source: C. Firth, 'New Approaches to Strategic Market Planning', unpublished MBA dissertation, University of Bradford, 1980.

the size of the potential market is reduced and new prospects become increasingly difficult to find until the market is saturated and sales stabilise at the replacement rate.

reason for updating

Critics of the PLC argue that in real life the growth curve seldom assumes the smooth symmetry depicted in the textbooks, nor do its parameters conform to the mathematical formulae that summarise diffusion processes in the physical and natural sciences. Given the number of intervening variables which can interfere with the process it would be very surprising if sales did expand smoothly and the fact that they don't should not be seen as invalidating the broad, underlying trend. Thus supply and/or distribution difficulties, seasonality, competitive reaction, a downturn in the economic climate, etc., could all act to slow down the process, while cheap money, tax changes, new suppliers, etc., could all serve to speed it up. It is also important to take into account the technical complexity of the product, the size and nature of the investment necessary to produce supplies of it and also the existence or not of patent protection. In the case of the latter a firm may well prefer to develop a market more slowly, consolidating its gains as it proceeds and financing further investment from its cash flow. Conversely, where a firm lacks patent protection and/or its product is easily imitated it may well wish to capitalise on its advantage of being first and seek to expand production as quickly as possible. By doing so the firm hopes to capitalise on the economies of both scale and experience and secure cost and marketing advantages which will act as barriers to entry for would-be imitators.

Thus, in assessing the slope of the growth curve it is important always to bear in mind what I have termed a marketing maxim, namely that 'Consumption is a function of availability'. This is not quite the same as Say's Law, which asserts that supply creates demand, but a truism which stresses that the physical availability of an object is the ultimate constraint on its consumption. It follows that if a producer can restrict supply without fear of direct competition he will be able to exercise much greater control over the marketing mix and so earn above average profits. In doing so he will ensure a shallow growth curve quite different from the classic PLC. On the other hand many so-called fad or fashion goods which exhibit almost vertical sales curves do so because there was a sufficient supply to meet all needs almost instantaneously. Indeed for products like hula-hoops, mini or maxi skirts, Rubik cubes, fashion colours, etc., the ease of creating a supply and the absence of barriers to entry will often result in excess supply and large unsold stocks. Further, the very nature of the fashion good dictates that it is unlikely to be repeat-purchased with the result that once the market is saturated sales stop, resulting in the classic fashion good PLC shown in Figure 5.2.

However, the patent protected monopoly and the fashion good (which is usually found in markets approaching conditions of perfect competition) represent boundary states. The great majority of new products are introduced into markets which the economist would define as imperfect in the sense that while competition exists it is restricted to some extent by barriers to entry. In such market conditions (which were analysed in some detail in Chapter 2) we are

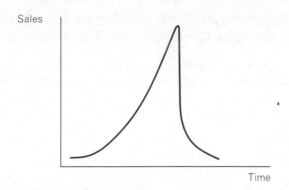

Figure 5.2   The classic fashion good PLC

most likely to find growth characteristics which mirror the traditional PLC as each firm seeks to maximise its share of the expanding market.

Because of the scale and experience effects mentioned earlier profit margins tend to be greatest during the growth phase but actual profits are often small as firms reinvest in new production facilities and in developing new markets through vigorous promotion and distribution policies.

■ Maturity

As the market approaches saturation so the growth rate slows down until eventually it stabilises at a sales level equivalent to the replacement rate together with any natural growth in market size due to demographic changes. Usually this is the longest single phase of the life-cycle and normally will be proportionate to the length of the gestation/introduction phase. That this should be so is logical in that the very forces which accelerate or delay the acceptance of a new product invariably hasten or sustain its decline. For example, consider the forces of resistance to change which slow down the market penetration of many new products. At a conference organised by Sperry Univac in France in 1979 one of the participants argued[8] that 'the future may be further away than people think' and cited the following potential sources of delay:

1   The inherent inertia of human society. [in *Marketing New Industrial Products* we cite 12 reasons why individuals and organisations will resist change in the status quo.] In addition it has to be recognised that the majority of the world's population live in the underdeveloped countries and the potential for radical change in these countries is highly impractical.
2   Resistance to manipulation.
3   The existence of dissident minority. As technology displaces satisfying jobs so the number of dissidents resisting such change will increase. [Not borne out in the UK in the late 1970s and early 1980s, but see 4 below.]

4   The need to keep costs down – if technology destroys jobs wholesale then social security costs may exceed the savings from the new technology, e.g. North Sea oil revenues and the UK in the early 1980s.

5   Communications technology is not really needed, i.e. those who will use services like Ceefax and *Oracle* will be limited to those who used libraries in the past.

Conversely the more closely a new product approximates that for which it is a substitute the more likely its speedy adoption and the more likely that it will in turn be displaced by another incremental innovation.

Although profit margins usually decline through the maturity phase products at this stage of their life-cycle almost invariably comprise the back-bone of an established firm's business and generate most cash for reinvestment in the future. Firth cites seven reasons given by Rogers[9] which account for declining profit margins:

1   Increasing numbers of competitive products leading to over-capacity and intensive competition.

2   Market leaders are under growing pressure from smaller competitors.

3   Strong increase into R & D to find better versions of the product.

4   Cost economies are used up.

5   Decline in product distinctiveness. — *sales forgotten*

6   Dealer apathy and disenchantment with a product with declining sales.

7   Changing market composition where the loyalty of those first to adopt begins to waver.

In turn, and because of this profit erosion, the industry tends to stabilise as a set of well-entrenched competitors all seeking a competitive advantage. This they usually attempt to do by adopting one of four basic strategies which have been characterised as:

1   An offensive or 'take-off' strategy.

2   A defensive strategy.

3   A recycle strategy.

4   A stretching and harvesting strategy.

An offensive strategy has as its objective a major extension of the PLC and will often lead to one or more periods of renewed growth followed by stabilisation at an overall higher level of sales. Perhaps the best-known example of this strategy is that reported by Levitt[10] for nylon in which four quite distinct approaches were used to extend the life-cycle:

1   Promoting more frequent usage among current users.

2   Promoting more varied usage among current users.

3   Attracting new users.

4   Developing new uses for the basic material.

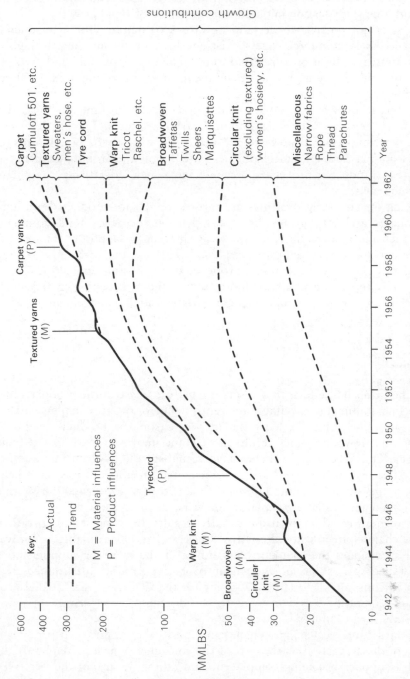

Figure 5.3 Innovation of new products postpones the time of total maturity – nylon industry

Source: Jordan P. Yale, *Modern Textiles Magazine* (February 1964) p. 33.

The collective effect of these strategies is well illustrated in Figure 5.3, from which it can be seen that as usage of nylon for one group of end-products began to level off a new application initiated a fresh period of rapid growth.

Where it is not possible to develop new uses or markets for a product it becomes necessary to protect one's existing share of the market through a defensive strategy. This is often referred to as 'dynamic adaptation' and involves manipulation of the non-product elements of the marketing mix – price, distribution and promotion.

A recycling strategy is most often found in the markets for f.m.c.g., but is also applicable to consumer durables and industrial products. Like a defensive strategy, recycling seeks to preserve a product's market share against erosion through a pre-planned series of relaunches based upon one or more elements of the mix, e.g. product improvements, repackaging, new advertising campaign, different channels, etc.

Stretching or harvesting strategies are most common for products with high market shares and little or no direct competition. Because of its dominant position such a product requires below average marketing support *on a unit basis* and so enjoys above-average profit margins. Products in this category are often described as 'cash cows' – a term first proposed by the Boston Consulting Group (BCG) – and their role is discussed more fully in the next section, which deals with the BCG's product portfolio approach to marketing management.

■ Decline

Despite the firm's best efforts to prolong the mature phase of the product's life-cycle, decline is ultimately inevitable and tends to mirror the growth phase in that it accelerates over time. Perhaps the major reason for product decline is technological innovation which results in new and improved ways of satisfying basic needs. Thus mechanical watches have been displaced by electronic watches and the Swiss watch industry has been decimated, synthetic fibres have been extensively substituted for natural fibres such as cotton and wool and the internal combustion engine has largely replaced the horse as motive power.

While technological innovation usually results in a substitute product, economic change often makes alternative sources of supply available at a lower cost and so changes the competitive standing of the different suppliers to a market. Lower prices for an equivalent or better product are immediately apparent to consumers and largely account for the success of the Japanese car makers in penetrating world markets to the discomfort and demise of many longer-established producers.

Yet a third source of change which can lead to the decline of a product is boredom or dissatisfaction on the part of the consumer, which is frequently the result of a supplier becoming complacent and failing to sustain the perceived value of his offering through aggressive marketing.

Faced with a declining product, management has only three basic options open
to it:

(a) To delete it from the product line (Retreat).
(b) To phase it out over time (Withdrawal).
(c) To attempt to resuscitate it.

Option (c) is rarely a viable one for, if the product is already in decline before
management tries to do anything about it, recovering lost ground is usually a
forlorn hope. It is for this reason that I am such a strong proponent of using the
PLC as a broad framework for strategy formulation and as a basic diagnostic
tool. If the stages of the life-cycle are inevitable and are heralded by changes in the
inflexion of the sales curve then the onset of maturity is the time to consider
rejuvenation strategies when the product is still in good health. Once it has gone
into decline it is much more costly and sometimes impossible to reverse or even
stabilise such a trend.

Of the other two alternatives a phased withdrawal is much to be preferred for,
as we noted in Chapter 3, a withdrawal implies that one retains control over the
process while a retreat means that one is merely reacting to competitive pressures.
One must also consider that in the case of durable products (consumer and
industrial) one has an obligation to provide after sales service, which means that a
retreat could well become a rout or total defeat.

Until recently the elimination/withdrawal decision has received comparatively
little attention, but, due to the pioneering work of Avlonitis, its strategic
importance is now much better appreciated and will be discussed at greater
length in Chapter 13, which is concerned with product policy.

■ Diffusion Theory

My own interest in product life-cycles and their relation to diffusion theory dates
back to the period 1969–71 when I was pursuing research for my doctorate at the
Harvard Business School. A product of this research was published as *Marketing
New Industrial Products*.[11] The purpose of this research was to establish whether
there is an observable pattern for the take-up of new products when introduced
into a market place. Product life-cycle theory clearly suggests that there is, and in
turn this theory may be related directly to a much longer established body of
knowledge associated with the processes of diffusion and other exponential
processes. The following discussion is based on *Marketing New Industrial
Products*.

■ The Diffusion Process

New products are but one manifestation of innovation, just as the manner in
which they penetrate and spread through a market is only one example of the

process we call diffusion. It is now more than three decades since Pemberton[12] identified the tendency for diffusion of an innovation over time to approximate the parameters of the normal distribution such that if one plots the number of adopters of an innovation – assuming that it has fully diffused – against time of adoption since first introduction then the bell-shaped curve in Figure 5.4 results. Alternatively, if one plots the cumulative number of adopters against elapsed time since first introduction then an ogive, or S-shaped curve results similar to that depicted in Figure 5.5. Since Pemberton first focused attention on this relationship many researchers in a diversity of research traditions have observed a similar phenomenon.

Theoretically, once an exponential process has been initiated it will continue to infinity. In reality, however, the process is subject to limiting conditions which invariably result in the existence of an upper boundary, or at least to the presumption that such a boundary exists. A well-documented field is that of

Figure 5.4   Distribution of adopters over time

Source: M. Baker, *Marketing New Industrial Products* (London: Macmillan, 1975).

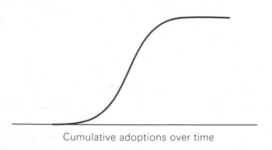

Figure 5.5   Cumulative adoptions over time

Source: M. Baker, *Marketing New Industrial Products* (London: Macmillan, 1975).

biological growth and a simple example drawn from this area will help to clarify these points.

Assume that we possess a simple organism that reproduces itself by cell division then, *ceteris paribus*, we may anticipate that the rate of increase of the population will follow the series 1, 2, 4, 8, 16, 32, 64 . . . Unfortunately for our simple cell it is not immortal, but can only reproduce itself twice before dying so that the population will in fact expand in a series which starts 1, 2, 3, 5, 8, 13, 21 . . . Further, it is also apparent that there must be a finite limit to the resources on which the organism depends for its existence so that growth cannot continue indefinitely. The validity of this contention may easily be demonstrated by placing a simple cell which reproduces itself by division into a restricted environment such as a sealed test-tube. Growth may well continue to the point where the test-tube is visibly filled with cells which are invisible by themselves but, ultimately, the lack of space and necessary nutrients will stabilise growth at some upper limit. In fact, if some factors are in fixed supply then their consumption will eventually lead to the decline and extinction of our population of cells.

However, one must be careful not to assume that decline and extinction will automatically occur for, as Price[13] points out, the existence of a ceiling to exponential growth frequently gives rise to a strong reaction as that ceiling is approached.

Price describes a number of ways in which an exponentially growing phenomenon will seek to avoid a reduction in growth as it nears its ceiling. Two of these – 'escalation' and 'loss of definition' – are viewed as particularly important for they occur more frequently than the 'plain S-shaped ogive' (p. 25).

In the case of escalation, minor modification of the original phenomenon takes place at or near the point of inflection and 'a new logistic curve rises phoenix-like on the ashes of the old'. In a marketing context a close analogy of this is provided by the 'product rejuvenation strategy' whereby further modification of a product is undertaken to revitalise stagnant demand for it.

In many cases, however, it is not possible to raise the ceiling through modification and the phenomenon will fluctuate wildly in an attempt to avoid the inevitable. As a result of these oscillations the phenomenon may become so changed as to be unrecognisable (loss of definition), e.g. the cell described in our earlier example may mutate into a new species of cell suited to the conditions which were limiting the continued growth of the original cell. Alternatively, the phenomenon may accept the inevitable, smoothing out the oscillations and settling in equilibrium at a stable limit, or under different circumstances, slowly decline to nothing.

Recognising that there are several possible forms of S-shaped curve the question arises 'Which variant should be accepted as typical of the diffusion process?'. Dodd[14] has shown that the precise form of the diffusion function may be summarised by a 'brief dimensional formula $[A^m]^{t}$' which he terms the 'power-moments' model. Once one knows how many attributes the innovation possesses, and the means by which these attributes spread among a relevant population, then one can predict whether diffusion will grow in a cumulative normal, exponential or logistic manner.

Addressing this same issue, Zvi Griliches[15] comments that:

> The choice of a particular algebraic form for the trend function is somewhat arbitrary. As the data [diffusion of hybrid seed corn] are markedly S-shaped, several simple S-shaped functions were considered. The cumulative normal and the logistic are used most widely for such purposes. As there is almost no difference between the two over the usual range of data, the logistic was chosen because it is simpler to fit and in our context easier to interpret.

Although this tends to contradict Price's conclusion cited earlier that variants occur more often than the plain S-shaped ogive, there seems to be strong support for Griliches's view that the actual differences between specific functional forms are of minor consequence within the usual range of data. We conclude, therefore, that any of several variants of the S-shaped curve are equally acceptable and that one should use the one which best fits the available data.

The above discussion of the properties of S-shaped curves was prompted by an implied acceptance of Pemberton's observation that such curves are descriptive of the diffusion process. Having described briefly some of the properties of S-shaped curves it will be useful to present some evidence which supports the original inference.

■ The Pervasive Nature of the S-shaped Diffusion Curve

Since Pemberton and Sorokin[16] first focused attention on the fact that innovations tend to diffuse in a consistent manner there has accumulated a growing body of evidence which confirms that if one plots the number of adopters of a given innovation against elapsed time since first introduction then an S-shaped curve will result. However, it must be noted that while Pemberton and Sorokin are generally credited with being the first researchers to *test* for the existence of an S-shaped diffusion curve its existence had long been recognised. Thus Rogers[17] quotes Tarde's[18] observation that an innovation 'shows slow advance in the beginning, followed by rapid and uniformly accelerated progress, followed again by progress that continues to slacken until it finally stops'.

In the rural sociology research tradition the studies of Ryan and Gross,[19] and Griliches on the diffusion of hybrid seed corn convincingly demonstrated an S-shaped cumulative growth curve – a finding which has been confirmed time and time again in parallel studies in the subsequent literature.

Studies of the spread of three new business techniques – Gantt charts, statistical quality control, and critical path techniques – indicate that they diffused in a manner which approximates an S-shaped curve (Wattel[20]).

Mansfield's[21] studies of twelve innovations in four industries led him to conclude that 'the growth in the number of users of an innovation can be approximated by a logistic curve'. More recently, Ray[22] commented, in presenting the preliminary findings of a multinational study of innovation, that, although there were insufficient data to specify the diffusion curves applicable to the innovations studied and so permit unconditional acceptance of Mansfield's logistic curve, none the less the data did suggest 'good cause for using another type of sigmoid or S-shaped curve'.

In the marketing literature, as we have already noted, the widely accepted product life-cycle concept stipulates that over time the sales of a product will exhibit cumulative growth initially, and then stabilise, until either competition results in a decline in sales volume, or further innovation results in renewed growth. In turn, this concept has been successfully applied to help explain some of the variance in the patterns of international investment and trade (see Freeman,[23] Vernon[24] and Well's[25]). A recent OECD publication[26] lends further support to these researchers' findings as analysis of the diffusion of four recent and significant innovations – man-made fibres, plastics, computers and nuclear power – reveal a consistent S-shaped curve in three distinct geographic regions – USA, Europe and Japan.

A similar exponential curve is also reported for numerically-controlled machine tools (*American Machinist's Tenth Inventory*) while Lynn's[27] investigation of the commercial growth of a number of major technological innovations in several diverse fields lends additional substance to the pervasive nature of such diffusion curves.

Taken together, these and many similar findings, predicate that S-shaped diffusion curves are so consistent that one may infer that diffusion is a natural process which obeys immutable laws.

In my view the evidence in support of the existence of a product life-cycle is incontrovertible. However, as we noted earlier, the PLC is 'not of itself deterministic and may be influenced significantly by environmental changes and/or marketing action'. How then can we use the theory to help us plan more effectively?

As we have seen, the most critical phase in a new product's life is its introduction to the market place. While it appears that more professional marketing has reduced the instance of new product failures in recent years, there can be no doubt that this continues to be a major source of significant losses for many companies. The question must be: how do you initiate a life-cycle and how do you sustain the new product in the difficult and dangerous introductory phase? This was the question we addressed directly in *Marketing New Industrial Products* by using the distribution of adopters over time as the basis for seeking to determine whether there were any measurable characteristics which distinguished earlier from later adopters. The concept of adopter categories was first advanced by researchers at Iowa State University[28] who observed that the distribution of adoption over time assumed the characteristics of the normal distribution. Accordingly, they proposed that one could use the parameters of such a distribution (mean and standard deviation) to define different categories of adopter. This they did, as illustrated in Table 5.2. Obviously the question is what, if anything, distinguishes innovators from early adopters and early majority, etc.? Numerous studies have attempted to establish this but, as is often the case, the results are indeterminate.

Table 5.2   The classification of adopter categories

Classification	As % of persons adopting		Cumulative total (%)
Innovators	First	2.5	2.5
Early adopters	Next	13.5	16.0
Early majority	Next	34.0	50.0
Late majority	Next	34.0	84.0
Laggards	Last	16.0	100.0

As a result, many practitioners are tempted to dismiss this as yet another piece of academic theorising of no practical purpose. To do so would be to miss the point that if academic theorists could solve all the real world problems there would be no need for real world managers! The observation that there will always be innovators in any new market is tautologous. The practical pay-off from the theory is that one accepts the existence of such a class of people, recognises that they are likely to differ from product to product, market to market and over time, but then uses one's own knowledge and experience of specific product market interfaces to define the most profitable prospective market segments. It is this issue which we consider in the next section which deals with using the PLC as a planning tool.

■ Using the PLC as a planning tool

In our view the two most important insights offered by the PLC are:

(a) It underlines the inevitability of change.
(b) It makes clear that change is an evolutionary and self-sustaining process with an underlying continuity.

Taken together these factors predicate that ultimately all single product firms are doomed to extinction unless, like the Phoenix, they can rejuvenate themselves. In the case of products based upon a robust core technology this life-span may be considerable, but this does not change the fact that sooner or later it will be displaced by something new. Stone gave way to bronze, bronze gave way to iron, and iron to steel. Steel producers would do well to heed Levitt's warning in 'Marketing Myopia'.[29]

As a generalisation, the more a basic technology is refined and developed, and the closer a product becomes to a consumer convenience good, the shorter its life-cycle. Further, because of competitive pressures such life-cycles are becoming shorter. In the light of this it would seem reasonable to argue that firms should seek to protect their futures by reducing their dependence upon individual products and developing a portfolio of products each of which may be at a different stage in its life-cycle such that products in the growth stage are compensating for those in the decline phase.

In the next section we will look at the product portfolio concept more closely but, before considering the interaction between products at different stages in the life-cycle it will be useful to recognise that each of the main phases calls for a rather different marketing strategy and mix and specify what these are. It will also be helpful to stress that, for multi-product firms with products at different stages of development, it will be necessary to practise what I have termed '3-in-1 marketing'.

3-in-1 marketing recognises that, in its most rudimentary form, SMP is concerned with providing answers to three basic questions:

1   Where are we now?
2   Where do we want to go?
3   How do we get there?

In other words we are concerned with the *present*, the *future* and the intervening or *transitional* period in between, and it would seem self-evident that the successful firm must give consideration to all three if it is to survive, let alone succeed. Thus, while past failings may rightly be attributed to an over-emphasis upon the existing business (the production orientation), there is a very real danger that too much concentration upon the future (the marketing orientation) may result in a dangerous neglect of the existing resource base on which that future must be founded. Similarly, stressing selling (a sales orientation) is an inadequate basis for long-term prosperity, but selling has a vital transitional role to play and deserves greater recognition than it has enjoyed since 'marketing' came on the scene.

Clearly what is required is a careful balance between present capabilities and future aspirations for in a dynamic environment one must possess both a sense of vision (where one wants to go) and a sense of continuity (how one is going to get there). There is no merit in adopting the attitude of the local resident asked for directions by a tourist who responded 'If I was trying to get there I wouldn't start from here', which epitomises so much academic writing – the assumption that we can ignore our pasts, are in possession of infinitely mobile resources and can start every project with a clean sheet of paper.

Essentially then the 3-in-1 approach recognises that the introduction and growth phases of the life-cycle require a future or marketing orientation, maturity a production orientation and decline a sales orientation. This is not to say that the firm requires three different sets of managers, for research[30] by Axel Johne of The City University has provided the important finding that in successful firms the management are able to operate in different modes or roles.

When required to develop plans for the future they adopt organic organisational practices, but the further they proceed towards the actual production and sale of a product the more structured and controlled is their approach so that it corresponds to the so-called mechanistic structure – a process Johne has aptly called 'the mechanistic shift'.

Clearly, a threefold division is a very basic one and is amenable to considerable refinement. As a minimum most writers would argue for a different emphasis as between the introduction and growth phases of the PLC and come up with a summary similar to that proposed by Dhalla and Yuspeh and reproduced as Table 5.3.

Similarly, the emphasis on particular mix elements will vary throughout the growth phase and, as we saw earlier when discussing the mature and decline phases, a number of quite different strategies are available here too. The important point to make is that decision-making is a sequential process and that the main thing is to refine one's focus through a series of choices between limited sets of alternatives. Ideally (as in computer programming) choice should be binary – yes/no, either 'a' or 'b' – but the intrinsic complexity and uncertainty of business decisions usually result in more than two basic options. The greater the number of options the more difficult it becomes to balance the pros and cons of each and the greater the potential for making incorrect decisions. It is for this reason that we advocate simple models and frameworks as the basis for making strategic decisions for, once these have been made correctly, adjustment and refinement may be achieved through the management process.

Finally, we are in sympathy with Firth's conclusion based upon his extensive review of the PLC literature when he states:

> The evidence from this research shows that: (1) Most products do follow a broad life cycle pattern and that competition affects profits as outlined for the various stages. (2) The average length of the PLC is shortening due to rapid economic, technological, social and political changes. (3) There is no common length of time of stages for products. (4) The PLC can be drastically altered by external factors.

■ Product Portfolio Analysis

In the preceding section it was suggested that a major implication of the PLC is that the firm should seek to develop more than one product so that as some mature and decline others are being developed to replace them. Of course, as soon as a company has more than one product it becomes necessary to allocate resources between them and an important tool for achieving this is provided by the Growth-Share Matrix developed by the Boston Consulting Group (BCG).

The Growth-Share Matrix combines elements of the PLC, which plots the growth and decline of sales, with findings concerning the cost and profit implications of varying market shares. With respect to the latter there is a

Table 5.3 How PLC advocates view the implications of the cycle for marketing action

Effects and response	Stages of the PLC			
	Introduction	Growth	Maturity	Decline
Competition	None of importance	Some emulators	Many rivals competing for a small piece of the pie	Few in number with a rapid shakeout of weak members
Overall strategy	Market establishment; persuade early adopters to try the product	Market penetration; persuade mass market to prefer the brand	Defence of brand position; check the inroads of competition	Preparations for removal; milk the brand dry of all possible benefits
Profits	Negligible because of high production and marketing costs	Reach peak levels as a result of high prices and growing demand	Increasing competition cuts into profit margins and ultimately into total profits	Declining volume pushes costs up to levels that eliminate profits entirely
Retail prices	High, to recover some of the excessive costs of launching	High, to take advantage of heavy consumer demand	What the traffic will bear; need to avoid price wars	Low enough to permit quick liquidation of inventory
Distribution	Selective, as distribution is slowly built up	Intensive; employ small trade discounts since dealers are eager to store	Intensive; heavy trade allowances to retain shelf space	Selective; unprofitable outlets slowly phased out
Advertising strategy	Aim at the needs of early adopters	Make the mass market aware of brand benefits	Use advertising as a vehicle for differentiation among otherwise similar brands	Emphasise low price to reduce stock
Advertising emphasis	High, to generate awareness and interest among early adopters and persuade dealers to stock the brand	Moderate, to let sales rise on the sheer momentum of word-of-mouth recommendations	Moderate, since most buyers are aware of brand characteristics	Minimum expenditures required to phase out the product
Consumer sales and promotion expenditures	Heavy, to entice target groups with samples, coupons, and other inducements to try the brand	Moderate, to create brand preference (advertising is better suited to do this job)	Heavy, to encourage brand-switching, hoping to convert some buyers into loyal users	Minimal, to let the brand coast by itself

Source: N.K. Dhalla and S. Yuspeh, 'Forget the Product Life Cycle Concept!', *Harvard Business Review* (January–February 1976) p. 104.

widely held view that as size and market share increase costs will decline and profits will increase. In the early 1970s the Marketing Science Institute (MSI) published the preliminary findings of a study designed, *inter alia*, to explore this relationship, which it designated PIMS – an acronym for Profit Implications of Market Strategy. Early results from a study of 620 firms indicated that market share, investment intensity (ratio of total investment to sales) and product quality are the most important determinants of pre-tax returns on investment (out of 37 contributory factors). As a rough guide a market share of < 40% yields an average pre-tax return on investment (ROI) of 30% which declines to 9.1% with a share of > 10% (i.e. ROI declines at half the pace of market share). The PIMS study now has over 200 companies operating more than 2000 businesses who pool their experience in return for detailed analysis of their own position.

The link between market share and profitability may be explained by a variety of factors of which the most important are economies of scale (scale effects) and what the BCG term 'experience effects'.

• *Scale effects* have long been recognised in manufacturing, where increased size leads to lower unit costs, e.g. Abell cites the rule-of-thumb in process industries in which capital costs increase by the six-tenths power of capacity.[31] Thus a 90-million-ton oil refinery costs $[90/45]^{0.6} = 1.5$ times as much as a 45-million-ton refinery, or put another way, doubling plant size reduces the capital cost per unit of capacity by 25%, reinforced by lower depreciation costs. Similarly, large plants require less labour, proportionately, and can make more effective use of control systems, etc.

Nowadays the greatest economies of scale probably accrue to R & D and marketing, e.g. advertising spend as a barrier to entry. Further in the short run (of which the long run is made up) marketing efficiency/dominance is the best way to ensure full-capacity utilisation and justify the larger initial capital investment.

• *Experience effects*. 'The experience effect, whereby costs fall with cumulative production, is measurable and predictable' (Abell), and applies to all types of products.

Originally the phenomenon was associated only with labour as a component of total cost and resulted in the use of the so-called 'learning-curve' as a planning tool. In the 1960s, however, the BCG demonstrated that the same was true of total value-added costs as well as bought-in supplies and described the relationship between costs and experience in terms of an experience curve. In simple terms experience curves record the decline in costs to be anticipated with cumulative increases in output and are usually reported as a percentage for each doubling in output, e.g. 85% experience curve means that every time output doubles costs decline to 85% of the earlier rate, i.e. a 15% decline for every doubling of output. The main sources of the experience effect are:

1 Labour efficiency
2 Work specialisation and methods improvement
3 New production processes

4   Better performance of equipment (steel mill; oil refineries)
5   Changes in resource mix
6   Product standardisation
7   Product redesign

Abell argues that scale and experience effects exist independently (e.g. Japanese big scale/low experience), but in most cases they occur together and the precise distinction between them is unimportant for purposes of analysis.

If costs do decline with market share then clearly there are significant competitive advantages to be gained by using growth in market share as a basic corporate objective, particularly if such growth is faster than one's immediate competitors.

As noted earlier the Growth-Share Matrix, or Boston Box, developed by the Boston Consulting Group seeks to combine these two sets of relationships into an analytical framework which can provide both broad strategic guidelines as well as detailed monitoring of one's competitive status. In addition, the Growth-Share Matrix is based on four assumptions (Firth, 1982):

1   Margins and cash generated increase with relative market share, due to the experience and scale effects.
2   Sales growth requires cash to finance added capacity and working capital.
3   Increase in market share usually requires cash input to support increased advertising expenditures, lower prices and other share gaining tactics. Alternatively, a decrease in share may make cash available.
4   Growth slows as the product reaches maturity and without losing market position cash generated can be reinvested in other products that are still growing.

Taken together these relationships and assumptions permit the construction of a simple 2 × 2 matrix as shown in Figure 5.6 and the object is to locate each of the firm's products in terms of its market dominance (expressed as the share of market held by the product compared with its largest competitor) and the market growth rate (corrected for inflation). For maximum visual impact the sales of each product should be reflected by the *area* of the circle. (Some practitioners use the diameter of the circle, but this exaggerates the real differences in size.) Relative market share is a more meaningful indicator than actual market share for it captures the competitive position of the firm *vis-à-vis* its largest rival. A ratio of 1 means equality; greater than 1 means you are the market leader; less than 1 a market follower. The division between high and low growth of 10% is purely arbitrary and will vary according to the stage of the product's life-cycle.

Market leadership implies strong cash flows due to the scale and experience effects while followers are more likely to experience weak or even negative cash flows. Similarly, high growth demands heavy investment to sustain it while slow growth makes much smaller demands. Thus products in each of the cells can be distinguished in terms of their cash generation and cash need as follows:

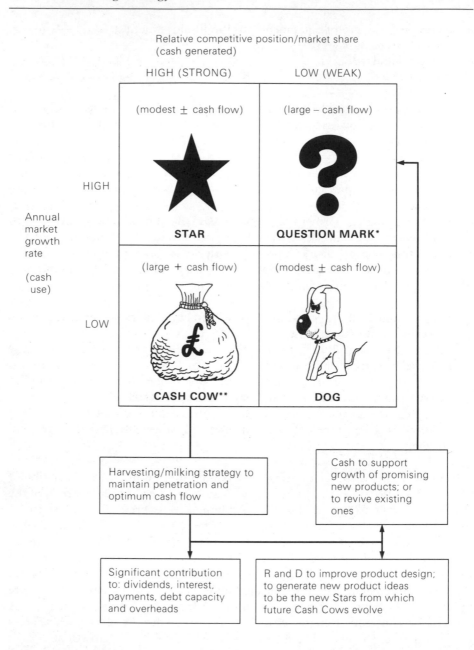

Figure 5.6   The business portfolio and associated cash flow

- Cash cows – generate more cash than they can profitably invest in a slow growth market in which they are already the leader.

- Dogs – low share of slow growth markets equates with low profits barely sufficient to maintain the status quo.
- Problem children – low share of fast-growing markets. A low share means low profits while high growth demands heavy investment. The question is which way will they move?
- Stars – high growth and high share. Cash flow largely used in maintaining market share as market grows.

Once the products are classified one can take decisions regarding product strategy and the composition of the product portfolio. Further, by plotting positions over time using overlays, one can immediately detect important trends in the movement of different firm's market share and competitive standing. (For an extensive analysis of this procedure the reader should refer to Abell and Hammond, 1979.)

Many authors have summarised the strategic and marketing mix implications of the four basic types of product which correspond to the four main phases of the PLC. Two of the best of these summaries are reproduced in Figures 5.7 and 5.6 above. The first of these was prepared by Graham Hooley for his MBA courses at the Bradford Management Centre and the second is taken from Douglas Brownlie's review article (1983).

■ Business portfolio analysis under attack

In recent years Business Portfolio (BP) approaches to SMP have come under considerable criticism.[32] To some extent this criticism has been prompted by the observation that many firms managed to weather the recession of the 1970s and early 1980s not because they had a portfolio of products and a large or dominant market share in certain key markets, but for almost the opposite reason, i.e. they had concentrated their energies upon a single product and have dominated a niche in the market. Similarly, there are many examples of firms in mature industries which continue to operate and survive with products which would clearly be classified as 'dogs' in a BP analysis.

In his overview of 'Analytical frameworks for strategic market planning', Douglas Brownlie[33] summarises these criticisms as follows:

> Additional criticism of the BP approach tends to focus on its over-simplified, and somewhat misleading, representation of possible strategy positions; and its use of the dimensions growth rate and market share, which are themselves considered to be inadequate descriptions of, respectively, industry attractiveness, and competitive position. As Wensley concludes, this approach to strategy development 'encourages the use of general rather than specific criteria as well as implying assumptions about mechanisms of corporate financing and market behaviour which are either unnecessary or false'. Indeed, it has been observed that market leadership does not always offer the benefits of lower costs, more positive cash flow and higher profits.

	Star	Problem children	Cash cow	Dog
Market characteristics	Rapid growth / Market proving itself / Competitors enter / Increasing consumer awareness and trial / Brand preferences start to emerge / Product replacing old products		Growth slows and stops / Market saturation / Concentration – shake out / Awareness at maximum, trials completed / Loyalty established / Beware new products satisfying needs / Growing importance of repeat purchases	
Marketing objectives and strategy	Maintain or improve market share / Market fortification (plug the gaps) / Ensure availability	Improve market share by: (a) all out push (b) segmentation / Abandon if unlikely to achieve growth (harvest & out)	Hold market share / Extend product life (a) Increase frequency of purchases (b) Encourage new product uses (c) Geographic expansion	(a) Harvest (b) Segment and find defensible niche (c) Divest (d) Delete
Product	Improve quality – stay ahead / Product line extension (fill the gaps) / Product differentiation	Improve quality – be better (a) / Look for unfilled gaps (segments) (b) / Buy competitors (a) and (b)	Ensure keeping up with technology but avoid costly revisions of product / Cosmetic revisions	(a) No change (b) Position in selected segments
Price	Will be leader due to experience / Ability to kill competition	Will be follower / May be unable to compete on price (pay more attention to segmentation)	Cut only to kill competition or to protect share / Now is the time to reap rewards	(a) No change or up (b) Depends on segment distinctiveness and price elasticity
Promotion	Heavy brand promotion / Induce awareness and trial / Create brand loyalty	Heavy brand promotion / Direct at new market entrants and specific segments	Lower / Reinforce brand loyalty / Promote new uses 'new', 'improved'	(a) Low. Zero (b) Aim at segment (c) Differentiate
Distribution	Secure channels / Offer better margins through turnover advantage	As not selling so rapidly may need better margins / Look for special innovative outlets	Maintain / Look for new outlets for new uses	(a) Maintain (b) Aim at segment outlets

Figure 5.7 Product portfolio sector: strategic guidelines

Source: G. J. Hooley, MBA Core Course Lecture Notes 1979/80 (Bradford Management Centre).

On the contrary: the number of highly viable companies occupying market 'niches' is legion, and growing by the day. Recent trends that have favoured the development of greater specialisation in some markets include: the growth of private label consumer products; and the emergence of differential preferences in some industrial markets, for example computers, as customers become familiar with products, or develop relevant in-house expertise.

The BP also tends to overlook other important strategic factors which are more a function of the external competitive environment, for example: technological change; barriers to entry; social, legal, political and environmental pressures; union and related human factors; elasticity of demand; and cyclicality of sales. The application of the BP to strategic decision-taking is in the manner of a diagnostic rather than a prescriptive aid in instances where observed cash flow patterns do not conform with those on which the four product-market categories are based. This commonly occurs where changes in product-market strategies have short-term transient effects on cash flow. Further limitations occur in three specific situations:

1   Where barriers to entry are great, so that margins are wide enough in rapid growth to finance further growth and generate cash simultaneously.
2   In a mature market, where price competition reduces margins, so that despite declining financing needs, cash flow deteriorates.
3   If 'experience' or 'scale' effects are small, for example where differences in experience are negated by innovations in production technology which are quickly adopted by competitors; and where capacity utilisation rates differ, or where a competitor has established a low-cost source of raw materials, irrespective of his relative market share.

While these criticisms are well founded and point to the need to exercise caution in applying BP approaches, Brownlie's point that they should be regarded as diagnostic rather than prescriptive cannot be over-emphasised. Our own view, which seems to be shared by the majority of senior managers, is that academics and staff advisers tend to be preoccupied with the detail of techniques and procedures but lack the ability to form a strategic perspective on major issues. Clearly, if one mis-diagnoses a problem then no amount of sophistication applied to the formulation of a solution will be able to remedy this basic deficiency. It is in this respect that portfolio approaches are seen to have their greatest contribution to make for they require the decision-maker to reflect upon the broad dimensions of threats and opportunities to the organisation in terms of its own strengths and weaknesses. It is to these that we turn in Chapter 6, which deals with the marketing environment.

In a review article[34] one of the leading writers on marketing strategy, George Day, has offered a similar view that 'some of the current criticisms [of Business Portfolio analysis methods] are unwarranted, because they reflect a serious misunderstanding of the proper role of these analytical methods'. He goes on to observe: 'what must be realised is that these methods can facilitate the strategic planning process and serve as a rich source of ideas about possible strategic options. But on their own, these methods cannot prescribe the appropriate strategy or predict the consequences of a specific change in strategy.'

Day's review of the various strategy analysis methods is strongly recommended for the perspective it provides upon their contribution to the overall strategic planning process as well as the benefits of using the different methods in combination with one another. As he comments:

> There is a truism in planning circles that the process of strategic planning is more important than the plan. An effective process has broad management participation that encourages a shared understanding of strategic issues and alternatives. The pay-off is in subsequent commitment by these managers to the implementation of strategic decisions. Strategy analysis methods can improve this pay-off by providing a common language and a logical structure that can be used to:
>
> • Isolate areas where critical information is lacking;
> • Communicate judgements and assumptions about strategic issues;
> • Facilitate the generation of alternatives to be given detailed consideration; and
> • Identify trade-offs involved in undertaking various strategic alternatives.
>
> These benefits are primarily realised during the early stages of the planning process within a division or strategic business unit. The strategy analysis methods have virtually no role in later stages of implementation and monitoring (see Figure 5.8).

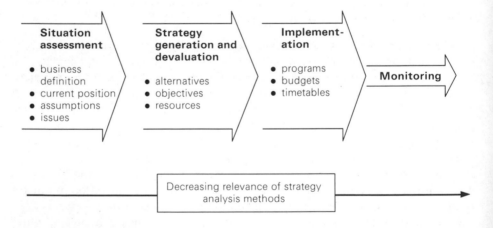

Figure 5.8   The stages of planning

Source: G. Day, 'Gaining insights through strategy analysis', *The Journal of Business Strategy*, 4(1) (Summer 1983).

■ Strategic overviews

As described above, Product Portfolio Analysis constitutes a useful framework for considering the different strategies necessary to sustain a group of products at different stages of their life-cycles and with varying shares of their respective markets. It also possesses the advantage in some people's view that because it depends upon quantitative data for its detailed application it is more objective than the generalised concepts upon which it is based. That said, however, it is clear that:

(a)   On the GIGO (garbage in/garbage out) principle any portfolio analysis will only be as good as the basic data inputs, and many of these are difficult both to define and measure.

(b)   There are many other factors which top management will wish to consider when formulating its basic strategies. While qualitative these factors are usually of much greater significance for longer range planning, e.g. social and political change.

To overcome these potential deficiencies two major companies with a high level of commitment to strategic planning have developed quite similar analytical frameworks: namely, Shell Chemical Company's Directional Policy Matrix and General Electric Company's Strategic Business Planning Grid.

Shell's Directional Policy Matrix (DPM) is based upon two key parameters – the Company's Competitive Capabilities and the Prospects for Sector Profitability – each of which is divided into three categories as shown in Figure 5.9.

Prospects for sector profitability

		Unattractive	*Average*	*Attractive*
	Weak	Disinvest **9**	Phased withdrawal **6** Custodial	Double or quit **3**
Company's competitive capabilities	*Average*	Phased withdrawal **8**	Custodial **5** Growth	Try Harder **2**
	Strong	Cash generation **7**	Growth **4** Leader	Leader **1**

Figure 5.9   The Directional Policy Matrix

Source: *The Directional Policy Matrix: a New Aid to Corporate Planning* (Shell International Chemical Co., 1975).

Table 5.4   Factors contributing to market attractiveness and business position

Attractiveness of your market	*Status/position of your business*
Market factors	
Size (dollars, units or both)	Your share (in equivalent terms)
Size of key segments	Your share of key segments
Growth rate per year:	Your annual growth rate:
Total	Total
Segments	Segments
Diversity of market	Diversity of your participation
Sensitivity to price, service features and external factors	Your influence on the market
Cyclicality	Lags or leads in your sales
Seasonality	
Bargaining power of upstream suppliers	Bargaining power of your suppliers
Bargaining power of downstream suppliers	Bargaining power of your customers
Competition	
Types of competitors	Where you fit, how you compare in terms of
Degree of concentration	products, marketing capability, service,
Changes in type and mix	production strength, financial strength,
	management
Entries and exits	Segments you have entered or left
Changes in share	Your relative share change
Substitution by new technology	Your vulnerability to new technology
Degree and types of integration	Your own level of integration
Financial and economic factors	
Contribution margins	Your margins
Leveraging factors, such as economies of scale and experience	Your scale and experience
Barriers to entry or exit (both financial and non-financial)	Barriers to your entry or exit (both financial and non-financial)
Capacity utilisation	Your capacity utilisation
Technological factors	
Maturity and volatility	Your ability to cope with change
Complexity	Depths of your skills
Differentiation	Types of your technological skills
Patents and copyrights	Your patent protection
Manufacturing process technology required	Your manufacturing technology
Socio-political factors in your environment	
Social attitudes and trends	Your company's responsiveness and flexibility
Laws and government agency regulations	Your company's ability to cope
Influence with pressure groups and government representatives	Your company's aggressiveness
Human factors such as unionisation and community acceptance	Your company's relationships

Source: D. F. Abell and J. S. Hammons, *Strategic Market Planning* (Englewood Cliffs, N.J.: Prentice-Hall, 1979) p. 214.

Abell and Hammond make considerable use of the DPM in their standard work on *Strategic Market Planning*, using slightly different terminology. Thus the Company's Competitive Capabilities are designated 'Business Position', and Prospects for Sector Profitability are termed 'Market Attractiveness', yielding a similar 3 × 3 matrix as shown in Figure 5.10. Abell and Hammond also provide a very useful checklist for assessing Business Position and Market Attractiveness, and this is produced as Table 5.4.

Using these factors, top management can make broad decisions about the location of each of its SBUs on the matrix. Alternatively, by developing a system of weighting and scoring the various factors a more structured evaluation can be made with more precise positioning within the parameters of the matrix. (Abell and Hammond, 1979, describe this technique at p. 219.) Either way the result is to place the SBU in one of three basic areas as shown in Figure 5.10, namely, positions with high, medium or low overall attractiveness. Each of these positions calls for a different marketing strategy.

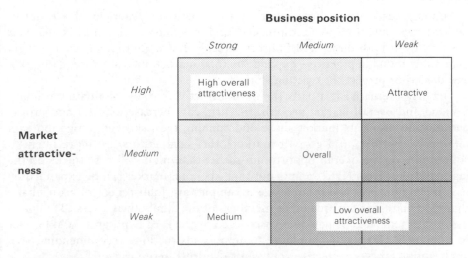

Figure 5.10   3 × 3 chart depicting relative investment opportunity

Source: D.F. Abell and J.S. Hammond, *Strategic Market Planning* (Englewood Cliffs, N.J.: Prentice-Hall, 1979) p. 213.

Further refinement can be achieved by using all nine positions as shown in Figure 5.9. It is immediately obvious that the four corner positions correspond precisely to the equivalent locations in the Boston Box, whereas the remaining five are intermediate between these four basic positions. Strategies appropriate to the various positions may be summarised as:

Market leader (positions 1 and 4). Firms in these positions have the largest share of the market and so enjoy all the advantages outlined in the earlier section on PIMS. Because of its standing the firm with the largest market share is in a strong position to exercise leadership in all aspects of the marketing mix and so dictate the rate and direction of change in the market. The benefits of being 'No 1' are discussed at length by Ries and Trout.[35] They clearly show that attempts by followers to challenge the leader invariably lead to a reinforcement of the leader's position. Thus Pepsi-Cola's 'can you taste the difference?' is countered by Coca-Cola's simple claim 'It's the real thing' and while Avis may try harder, Hertz is still Number 1 in car rentals.

Of course the amount of control a leader firm can exercise will depend very much on the overall structure of the market, which is reflected in the industry concentration ratio (a subject discussed in more detail in Chapter 4) and the firm's size relative to its nearest competitor(s). Leader firms also have to be sensitive to government policies on competition for, in most advanced countries, an organisation with a share of market greater than 25% will be considered a monopoly and so subject to investigation and possible control by the regulatory agencies.

Although leader firms enjoy significant competitive advantages this is not to say that they can afford to be complacent and they must work at protecting their position from both direct and indirect attacks. Three alternative strategies are commonly found in practice – expand the total market, increase share of market and defend or protect the existing share.

The first alternative is usually the most attractive, for, by stimulating primary demand and overall market growth, the firm can increase its sales and profits without increasing its market share and running the risk of investigation as a monopoly. Further, in a growth market other competitors are more likely to concentrate on the overall opportunity rather than mount direct attacks on the market leader. Firth (1962) points out that 'the total market can be expanded by new users, new uses and more usage. Examples are Johnson & Johnson's baby shampoo marketed towards other members of the family (new users), Du Pont's nylon sales extended by new uses discovered by the R & D program and Procter & Gamble's Head and Shoulder shampoo's instructions recommending two applications for more effective control of dandruff (more usage)'.

Increasing one's share of the market requires an aggressive posture towards one's direct competitors and is best pursued when the market is fragmented and one has a relatively low market share and/or when one can demonstrate that the acquisition of a larger share has increased the consumer benefit (a 'defence' against monopoly). Similarly, if one is to protect one's market share it will be necessary to make full use of all the elements of the marketing mix to prevent erosion of one's position through competitive action. In general, firms in this position practise an *undifferentiated* strategy on the precept that what's good for the market is good for them.

Try harder (position 2). While firms in this position are not market leaders they still occupy an attractive position due to the potential of the market. For reasons outlined above it is unlikely that a number 2 or 3 firm in an industry will displace the leader unless the leader becomes complacent and makes mistakes or the follower can achieve a sufficiently significant innovation to by-pass or leapfrog the leader.

In turn 'follower' firms are themselves open to attack and so will usually pursue similar strategies to those of leader firms outlined above. The main difference between leaders and followers normally is that while the former will usually seek to maintain a presence in all the major market segments, followers tend to concentrate their efforts on selected segments which they will seek to dominate – a *differentiated* marketing strategy – and Ries and Trout (1981) provide extensive examples of firms pursuing such focused strategies.

In the case of firms in positions 3, 5 and 7, which are of medium attractiveness, quite different core strategies seem appropriate. Position 3 conforms closely to the 'Question Mark' in the BCG's product portfolio analysis in that it represents a firm with a small share in an attractive market, thus facing it with the problem of whether it can move into a stronger position through further investment and aggressive marketing (usually by a strategy of *concentration*) or whether the odds are too great and it should withdraw and pursue other less competitive opportunities. Position 5 also presents a difficult decision for the strategist, as it represents the average firm in the average market. Through aggressive action it may be able to strengthen its business position, but it is unlikely that it will be able to change the general attractiveness of the market. Conversely if it does nothing its competitive position could weaken and require withdrawal or, if the market declined too, retreat and possible liquidation. On balance a 'custodial' strategy whereby the firm monitors carefully changes in industry and market conditions and is prepared to move quickly in response to perceived threats and opportunities is to be recommended.

As noted earlier position 7 corresponds to the 'cash cow' of the BCG and calls for a milking strategy.

Finally positions 6, 8 and 9 represent situations where the firm would be well advised to consider phased withdrawal and disinvestment. That said, it must be recognised that both positions 6 and 8 may offer opportunities for a more positive approach. For example, a firm in position 8 may well improve its standing in a declining industry if stronger firms decide to withdraw before it. Similarly, if a market begins to grow rapidly firms in position 6 will move to position 3 and will have to decide whether the enhanced opportunity merits investment rather than withdrawal. Position 9 is the BCG's 'dog' and calls for the strategies set out in Figure 5.7.

General Electric's 'Business Screen', is, as already noted, remarkably similar to Shell's DPM as can be seen from Figure 5.11. In this case the two axes are labelled 'Business Strengths' and 'Industry Attractiveness' and each is categorised as high, medium, and low to yield a 3×3 matrix. However, instead of labelling each position, GE uses a simple 'traffic light' coding of red (danger, beware), yellow (proceed with caution), and green (full steam ahead) for the groups with low, medium and high overall attractiveness.

Hussey (1978)[36] summarises the strategic options indicated by the DPM as shown in Figure 5.12.

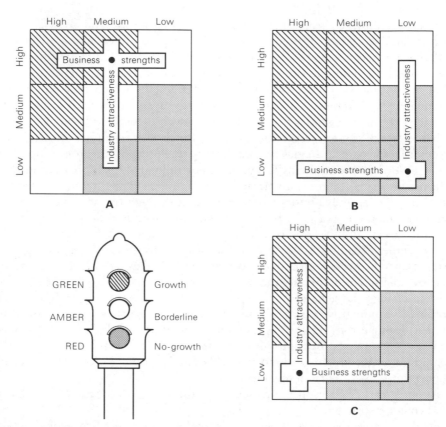

Figure 5.11   General Electric's 'stoplight strategy'

■ Gap Analysis

Gap analysis or 'identification' is a simple and widely used technique to help the firm establish to what extent its current strategies and product-market mix will enable it to achieve its goals. At the corporate level the analysis is best conducted using a single summary statistic (sales, profits, ROI or whatever) and plotting the desired level of performance against the forecasted level of performance. If a gap exits as shown in Figures 5. 13 and 5.14 then clearly there is a need for some remedial action.

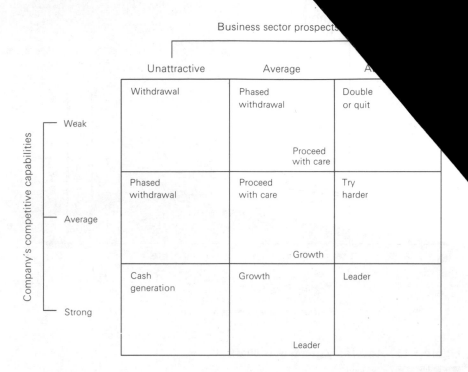

Figure 5.12 The directional policy matrix

Source: Adapted from D. F. Hussey 'Portfolio Analysis: Practical Experience with the Directional Policy Matrix', *Long Range Planning* (August 1978) p. 3.

Where action is needed and what should be done will depend upon a careful analysis of each product in the portfolio using the techniques outlined earlier. The advantage of gap analysis is that it provides a *synoptic overview* of the corporation's overall position. It is, of course, no substitute for the detailed product by product, market by market analysis required when completing a Boston Box or similar portfolio analysis.

As with many concepts in the strategic planning repertoire 'gap analysis' owes much to the original work of Igor Ansoff's *Corporate Strategy*[37] and *Implanting Strategic Management*[38]. Figure 5.13 reproduces Ansoff's Gap Analysis Chart which indicates how it may be used for planning purposes.

Ansoff's chart contains three projection for Sales or ROI (the chosen performance indicator). 1 indicates what will occur if the firm continues with its present strategies and predicts a steady decline. 2 projects the potential opportunity for the firm if it re-deploys its current resources more effectively and 3 represents a possible scenario if the firm can diversify into new areas of activity.

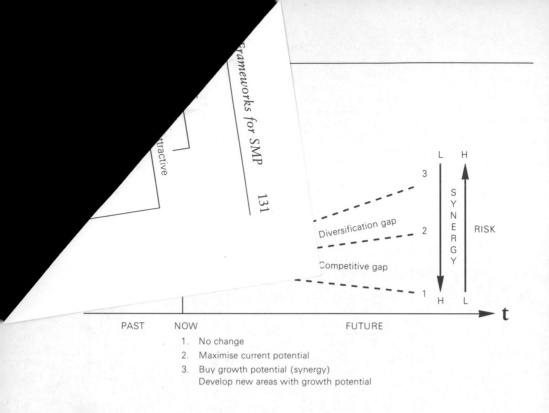

1. No change
2. Maximise current potential
3. Buy growth potential (synergy)
   Develop new areas with growth potential

Figure 5.13   Ansoff's gap analysis chart

Source: H. I. Ansoff, *Corporate Strategy* (New York: McGraw-Hill, 1965).

Thus Ansoff perceives two kinds of gap which he labels 'competitive' and 'diversification' and so provides a link with his growth vector components model introduced in Chapter 3 (see Figure 3.2). Where a competitive gap exists then the three strategies described in Chapter 3 – market penetration, market development and product development – are the ones to consider. But if these are insufficient to close the gap between the firm's objectives and the projected outcomes then it will need to have recourse to the fourth strategic option – *diversification* (see Figure 5.14).

Gap analysis as described here should not be confused with the identification of gaps in the market itself. Such gaps, which represent possible market opportunities, may be identified using the segmentation or positioning techniques described in Chapters 8 and 9 respectively.

■ Scenario Planning

As noted already, recent years have seen a growing disenchantment with formal strategic planning due to the increasing mass of detail associated with it and its inability to respond to the 'surprises' so characteristic of the turbulent 1980s. One

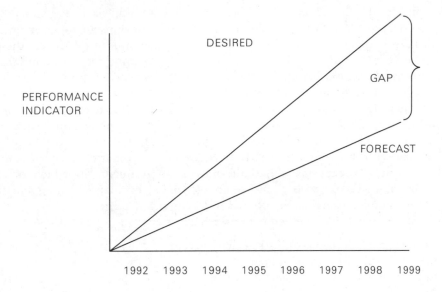

Figure 5.14   Gap analysis

antidote to this dissatisfaction has been the use of scenarios as the basis for analysis and planning.

Scenario analysis is not new and was used successfully by Royal Dutch/Shell to anticipate the oil shortages of 1973–74 and 1979. Indeed in recent years a number of distinctive approaches to scenario planning have been developed and were the subject of a major review article by Huss and Honton in *Long Range Planning* in 1987.[39] The following draws extensively on this source.

Huss and Honton observe that traditional forecasting techniques depend heavily on extrapolation which assumes that tomorrow will be very similar to today. Consequently, such forecasts fail when they are needed most – to help anticipate major change in the business environment. By contrast, scenario analysis encourages planners to think more broadly and creatively about the future and incorporate uncertainty into their projections. Huss and Honton identify three alternative approaches to scenario analysis which they classify as:

1   Intuitive logics as practised by SRI International and Royal Dutch/Shell.
2   Trend-impact analysis as practised by the Futures Group.
3   Cross-impact analysis as practised by the Centre for Futures Research (INTERAX) and Battelle (BASICS).

The main features of these three approaches are discussed below.

■ Intuitive Logics

According to Huss and Honton 'The intuitive logic approach assumes that business decisions are based on a complex set of relationships among economic, political, technological, social, resource and environmental factors. Most of these factors are external to the company but must be understood to provide insights and improve decisions relating to product development, new ventures, capacity expansion, new technologies and business strategies. Some of these variables are precise, quantitative and to some degree, predictable, such as demographics. But many other variables are imprecise, qualitative and less predictable, such as consumer attitudes, politics, financial structure, life style and product demand'.

To cope with this complexity SRI International see scenarios as 'devices for ordering one's perceptions about alternative environments in which one's decisions might be played out' and so enable one to evaluate risks, anticipate key changes and consider trade offs when developing strategy.

The SRI International method comprises eight steps:

1 Analysing the decisions and strategic concerns.
2 Identifying the key decision factors.
3 Identifying the key environmental forces.
4 Analysing the environmental forces.
5 Defining scenario logics.
6 Elaborating the scenarios.
7 Analysing implications for key decision factors.
8 Analysing implications for decision and strategies.

Steps 1–4 are common to most strategic planning methodologies and it is steps 5 and 6 which lie at the heart of and distinguish the SRI International approach. As Huss and Honton explain: scenario logics are organising themes, principles, or assumptions that provide each scenario with a coherent, consistent and plausible logical underpinning. Scenario logics should encompass most of the conditions and uncertainties identified in preceding steps. Scenario logics need not cover every distinct possibility. Trial and error are usually necessary in arriving at useful scenario logics. Workshops are often effective settings for accomplishing this step.

These scenario logics are not simply optimistic/pessimistic or high, medium, low scenarios. Instead they describe alternative futures such as buyer's or seller's markets or a regulated or unregulated market. Each of these scenarios presents opportunities and threats to the user company. Therefore they cannot be considered exclusively optimistic or pessimistic.

In Step 6 the scenarios are combined with the environmental analyses to provide a more focused and detailed picture for comparison with the key decision factors (Step 7). Finally, the full implications of the scenarios are reviewed in the context of a number of specific questions which Huss and Honton list as:

1 Does information about the future validate the original assumptions supporting strategies or proposed decisions?

2   What do the scenarios imply for the design and timing of particular strategies?
3   What threats and opportunities do the scenarios suggest?
4   What critical issues emerge from the scenarios?
5   What special cases deserve to be addressed by specific contingency plans?
6   What kinds of flexibility and resilience do the scenarios suggest are necessary from a company's planning perspective?
7   What factors and forces deserve monitoring in light of information from the scenarios?

The obvious strength of the SRI International method is its 'ability to develop flexible, internally consistent scenarios from an intuitive, logical perspective'. Its obvious weakness is that its subjective nature makes it liable to the dangers of selective perception/distortion and to undue influence by a dominant person or sub-group.

■ Trend-impact Analysis

Trend-impact analysis is a methodology which employs an independent forecast of the key dependent variable which is then modified to reflect the effect of other events impacting upon it. Its advantage is seen in its combination of formal forecasting techniques such as time series analysis and econometrics to establish trends which are then examined in terms of a series of impacting events which may be derived from a Delphi Study, jury of executive opinion or similar well informed but judgemental source. The likelihood or probability of impacting events over time is estimated and used to modify the original independent trend forecast. Finally, narratives are developed for each of the scenarios. Its major disadvantage is that the technique does not explore the effect which the impacting events may have on each other and its focus on a single key decision or forecast variable.

■ Cross-impact Analysis

Cross-impact analysis seeks to overcome the narrow focus of trend-impact analysis and was developed to help interrelate intuitive forecasts of future outcomes derived from methods such as brainstorming, Delphi studies, morphological analysis or even simple opinion surveys. Several companies have developed their own cross-impact methodologies of which two of the better known are INTERAX and BASICS.

INTERAX (Interactive Cross-Impact Simulation) was developed by the Centre for Futures Research in the University of Southern California Graduate School of Business Administration and is 'a forecasting procedure that uses both analytical models and human analysts to develop a better understanding of alternative future environments. It does this by generating scenarios one year at a time so that policy makers can interact with each scenario as it is being generated to experiment with policy options'. The early stages are similar to other methodologies in that one first must define the issue and time period of the analysis. Next one must define the primary variables or key indicators which one is seeking to forecast and these are then projected using independent methods such as time series or econometric analysis. Step 4 seeks to identify impacting events as described for trend-impact analysis but also uses the INTERAX Delphi database derived from an ongoing study of 500 experts on future trends and events. In Steps 5 and 6 the user develops an event probability distribution and then estimates the impact of each event on each indicator variable. In Step 7 the cross-impacts of each event on each indicator variable are analysed and, finally, in Step 8 the computerised model is run until a series of scenarios have been generated.

INTERAX may be run interactively and produces path scenarios which unfold over time. It comes with a comprehensive database which is readily updated and produces 'excellent statistical distributions of outcomes around the average'. However, it has a high start-up cost, is perceived as difficult by many analysts because of its interactive features, and will generate outputs based on the input data irrespective of whether they make sense or not.

BASICS (Battelle Scenario Inputs to Corporate Strategies) was developed in 1977 as a cooperative venture between several laboratories of the Battelle Memorial Institute. 'The BASICS method differs from INTERAX in that it does not use Monte Carlo simulation, and it does not require an independent forecast of the key indicators or variables'. Otherwise BASICS is similar to the methodologies described earlier and the reader should consult Huss and Honton for a detailed description and comparison with these methods.

It was Dwight Eisenhower who observed 'The plan is nothing, planning is everything'. As in so many things the process is more important than a particular outcome at a specific point in time. Experience and personal prejudice predispose the writer to the less sophisticated approaches defined here as intuitive logics. While the power of the computer and formal econometric and statistical analysis may yield many more combinations and permutations than ordinary human analysis they are often as likely to confuse as to inform. Further, the computer or other formal model is rarely able to discriminate between the quality of inputs and so will process them as if all were of equal value. All the models described here have very similar structures – the possible problem is that trend and cross-impact analysis introduce complex analytic methods which may lull the undiscriminating analyst into a false and dangerous sense of security in the quality of the outputs when GIGO – garbage in, garbage out – will always prevail.

■ SWOT

As noted in the Introduction to this chapter, SWOT is an acronym for Strengths, Weaknesses, Opportunities and Threats and defines the desired output from the formal analysis which must precede the selection of strategy and the formulation of plans to implement it.

Successful strategy formulation is essentially a 'marketing' process whereby an organisation seeks to deploy its values and resources in those areas where they will achieve the maximum return. In other words, firms seek to match their strengths with opportunities. In doing so they will be conscious of the need to avoid the threats of external environmental change and competitive activity, and also of the desirability of improving areas of possible weakness. It follows that, to do this effectively, organisations must have a good understanding of all four elements covered by the SWOT analysis – as in most things effective prognosis depends upon accurate diagnosis. This being so each element of the SWOT analysis is given extended treatment.

In Chapter 6, 'The Marketing Environment', it will be argued that to all intents and purposes the external environment or 'market' constitutes the boundary conditions within which firms must compete one with another, to determine who will succeed and who will fail. Thus, while national economies may seek to protect their own firms and industries from external competition (and this tendency is weakening with the growth of global competition) they will seek to encourage it between domestic suppliers to encourage the efficiency which such competition generates. As a very minimum, therefore, one must develop a clear understanding of the threats and opportunities which the current and future environment has to offer.

In addition to understanding the environment sellers also need to understand how users or customers arrive at choice decisions when comparing the competitive offerings available in the market place. This issue is the subject of Chapter 7, 'Buyer Behaviour', which reviews some of the key influences which mediate and shape buying decisions.

Chapter 8 deals with 'Market Segmentation', and addresses this issue from two similar but different perspectives. First, we consider the evaluation of the firm's own strengths and weaknesses through the medium of a marketing audit and, second, we extend the same methodology and techniques to reviewing the strengths and weaknesses of the competition – competitor analysis.

■ Summary

In Chapter 5 we have been concerned with a number of organising frameworks, procedures and techniques designed to assist the planner impose structure upon the complex and multi-dimensional problems he is required to solve. In the course of this review we have sought to emphasise three things:

1   The selection is *eclectic*, not comprehensive. There are many more analytical and problem solving methods described, often at some length, in the literature. Our intention has been to present the better known approaches which appear to satisfy our definition of CUGs. Critics have dismissed some

of these procedures for a variety of reasons and several of the major criticisms of the PLC and portfolio analysis were included to sensitise the reader that they do not enjoy universal support. The acid test, as always, must be 'does it help/work for me?' If it does, use it.

2   *Simplicity* is preferred to complexity.

3   The techniques are an aid to decision-making – *not* a *substitute* for it.

In this spirit we have given considerable attention to the concept of product life-cycles and the theory of diffusion which suggests how the phenomenon may be used in developing marketing strategies. This consideration leads naturally into discussion of portfolio models of the kind first developed by the Boston Consulting Group which use the phases of the PLC as the basis for analysing the performance of products over time. Portfolio analysis is now regarded as old hat by some critics and a summary of some of the major criticisms was reviewed. This review led to much the same conclusion as that made of the PLC itself – the concept provides help in structuring and analysing problems but, in and of itself, it cannot come up with precise solutions to specific problems. This is the responsibility of the decision-maker.

The next section was concerned with another aid to strategic decision-making – the two-dimensional overview of the kind developed by Shell and GEC. These and similar strategic overviews are helpful devices for enabling planners perform a 'first-cut' analysis by classifying products and markets in terms of their intrinsic attractiveness and the firm's capabilities in serving these markets. Such analysis may range from a broad brush judgemental evaluation to one in which hard data on specific performance indicators are provided to give greater precision to the classification of particular products and markets.

The chapter concludes with brief descriptions of three other techniques designed to assist formal strategic planning – gap analysis, scenario analysis and SWOT. Gap analysis is a simple technique for identifying possible discrepancies between an organisation's declared objectives and likely outcomes if current practices are not modified to enable the firm to achieve them. Scenario analysis reflects the difficulty of extrapolating current trends (required by gap analysis) given the rate of change and turbulence in the competitive environment. Scenario analysis thus offers a variety of approaches to help planners capture and model experience and judgement in defining future outcomes.

Finally, SWOT was introduced as an acronym for the process of internal and external analysis through which the firm can establish which opportunities offer it the greatest likelihood of future success so that it can devise strategies and plans to achieve them. It is to these issues which we turn in succeeding chapters.

CHAPTER 6

The Marketing Environment[1]

Learning Goals

The issues to be addressed in Chapter 6 include:

1   The view that the *external environment* is the ultimate constraint upon the courses of action open to a firm.
2   The influence of *demographic factors* on primary demand.
3   The role of other forces – social, cultural, economic, political, technological, etc. – in modifying and shaping *actual demand and consumption patterns*.
4   The pattern of *economic activity* over time and the existence of underlying cycles and trends.
5   The nature of *competition* and the importance of *non-price factors* in developing marketing strategies.
6   The implications of *environmental change* for marketing practice.

On completion of Chapter 6 you will be able to:

1   Define and describe the impact of *environmental forces* on the firm's strategy.
2   Review and describe the main *environmental factors* – demographic, economic, social, technological and political – and their influence upon strategic planning.
3   Distinguish the underlying *cyclical pattern of economic activity* and its implications for strategic planning.
4   Establish the difference between *price* and *non-price competition* and suggest why the latter is central to the development of successful marketing strategies.
5   Appreciate the impact of *environmental change* upon strategic marketing planning.

Introduction

In Chapters 4 and 5 it was argued that significant benefits will accrue to the company which practises Strategic Marketing Planning (SMP). Subsequently a number of broad conceptual frameworks were reviewed and analysed with particular emphasis upon the product life-cycle as a common factor underlying a continuous process of dynamic change to which the firm must respond. We also acknowledged that in order to operationalise the concepts and approaches advocated the firm must be able to define and measure the key factors contained in the various models, particularly market size and share, the state of competition or industry attractiveness, and the stage of the life-cycle in which product or industry is located. It is to these and related issues which we turn in this chapter.

To this end we shall look first at some of the reasons why environmental factors constitute the ultimate constraint upon the firm's strategy. Next we shall review some of the secular trends in the environment with particular reference to the business cycle, the long wave or Kondratieff cycle and some of the factors accounting for the accelerating rate of change especially in the twentieth century. Based upon this analysis we shall argue that the environment establishes the parameters within which firms must operate, but that ultimately their success will depend as much upon their interaction with each other as upon their interpretation of and adaptation to the general environment. Such an argument leads naturally to a consideration of competition as an abstract concept and its application to the real world through industry and market analysis, as discussed in Chapter 2. Finally we conclude the chapter with a synopsis of the main considerations to be taken into account in looking to the future influence of environmental change.

■ The Environment as the Ultimate Constraint

Although the oil crisis of 1974 is now something of a distant memory the reverberations of its impact are still being felt, rather like the after shocks that follow an earthquake. Clearly, conditions are not going to return to the 1960s when most of today's most senior managers gained their first experience of management. Scientific and mechanistic approaches to management have been displaced by a concern for a more subjective and organic conceptualisation of business as a human activity conducted by people on behalf of people. As a consequence the shift in emphasis has moved from the factory to the market place and the managerial orientation from production to marketing. Concomitant with this switch in emphasis has been a growing awareness of the accelerating rate of technological change, of the finite nature of the world's resources and of the present generation's responsibility to husband these carefully for the benefit of future generations.

Taken together, all these trends demand that, if management is fulfilling its primary responsibility to ensure the survival and continued well being of the firm, it must carefully monitor the environment in which it carries out its business. Such monitoring and analysis are essential if the firm is to be able to anticipate change and turn it to its advantage as a marketing opportunity, rather than be surprised by it when it occurs and perceive it as a threat. This ability has certainly characterised the growth and success of firms which have prospered in the turbulent trading conditions of the past twenty years including three major recessions and a major shake-out of marginal performers everywhere. Firms which have succeeded in these difficult times possess many common factors including an adaptive and flexible managerial style, a balanced portfolio of products and a well-developed intelligence and information system designed to monitor and anticipate environmental change.

While most firms have probably always undertaken some form of environmental analysis it is only in the past twenty years or so that attempts have been made to formalise and structure this process. In a 1983 review article[2] John Diffenbach identifies three distinct changes in the evolution of corporate environmental analysis. First, there was an *appreciation* stage stimulated by a number of books and articles, which advocated that one should look beyond short-term market conditions and consider the wider implications of the economic, technological, social and political factors which comprise the general business environment. Acceptance of this proposition leads naturally to the second phase of *analysis* which 'involves finding reliable sources of environmental data, compiling and examining the data to discern trends, developments and key relationships. It also includes monitoring environmental developments and anticipating the future.' In turn this interest led to the publication of numerous books and articles on environmental scanning, scenarios, the Delphi technique, cross-impact and input–output analysis and socio-technological and environmental forecasting. (Diffenbach, 1983 gives references for the more important of these works.)

The third and current phase is that of *application* in which top management seeks to incorporate what are usually staff evaluations into strategies and action plans.

What then are the external environmental factors which the firm must take into account when formulating its strategy? Essentially they may be classified into five major categories:

- Demographic.
- Social and cultural.
- Political.
- Economic.
- Technological.

Although it is immediately obvious that all are interrelated and interdependent, for purposes of analysis it will be useful to consider these separately.

■ Demographic Factors

Ultimately 'markets are people' in the sense that the demand for consumer goods depends directly upon the size of the population. In turn, consumer demand determines the demand for industrial and capital goods – hence 'derived demand'

– as these goods possess value only in so far as they facilitate and satisfy the ultimate consumption needs of individual consumers. It follows that the size and structure of the population is of vital concern to the marketer. Indeed, the rediscovery of marketing was as much due to a slowing down of growth in demand in the advanced economies, in parallel with a slowing down of population growth, as it was due to an increase in supply as a result of technological change. That said, the subject of demographics has received comparatively little attention in the marketing literature until very recently. However, this neglect appears to be coming to an end as business publications such as *Marketing*, *Fortune*, *Business Week*, etc. regularly include demographic projections in their editorial matter. For example, *Marketing* produced a very useful *Guide* on the subject of Demographics prepared by the Henley Centre for Forecasting which has an international reputation for its work in this field. This source provides much of the background for this section.

Derived from the Greek (Demos = the populace, graphein = to write) demography is defined in the *Oxford Dictionary* as the 'study of statistics of births, deaths, disease, etc., as illustrating conditions of life in communities'. Every country in the world compiles such statistics and, while their reliability may vary, these data provide an essential foundation for any forecast about an area or region's potential level of marketing activity.

Of course demographic forecasts rest on assumptions and, like any other forecast, changes in these assumptions can lead to major changes in the actual outcome compared with the forecast. This is clearly illustrated in Figure 6.1 which summarises the UK Government actuaries' projections of the UK population at various dates together with the actual position determined by official censuses. In the case of demographic forecasts the key assumptions relate to births (fertility), mortality and migration, all of which are liable to significant change.

The present century has seen dramatic changes in life expectancy as a consequence of medical developments, public health improvements in water supply, sanitation and housing standards, dietary changes and advances in the preservation and distribution of food, health education, etc. Thus, at the beginning of the century life expectancies in the UK were 48 for males and 52 for females. By the 1980s these had increased to 71 and 77 respectively – an improvement of almost 50%. With declining infant mortality (a major contributory factor to the extension of average life expectancies), and the greater certainty that children would survive to adulthood, so birth rates began to fall resulting in a dramatic slowing down of the overall rate of population growth and the emergence of an aging population.

Given the basic relationship between age – or stage in the family life cycle – and consumption patterns, it is variation in the composition of the population which is of most immediate interest to marketers seeking to project future patterns of demand. Clearly the precise relationship between the numbers in various age groups may alter significantly if there are major changes in birth rates (another baby boom like the 1950s and 1960s), mortality (AIDS or some other unforeseen

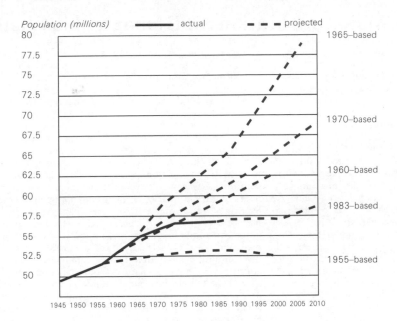

Figure 6.1 UK actual and projected total population, 1945–2010

Source: Office of Population Censuses and Surveys; Government Actuaries' Department.

disease) or migration (less likely given the present distribution of population). It has happened before and can clearly happen again. Nonetheless we possess sufficient information about the numbers in different age groups to essay broadly based scenarios of their implications for business. A good example of such a scenario is provided by the article by Nicola Reeves (see p. 144) which appeared in the Business Section of the *Glasgow Herald* (22 July 1991).

Similar projections to Nicola Reeves's appear regularly in the business pres. But, while the inferences drawn concerning the needs of different age groups are very similar it is important to bear in mind that the position varies markedly from country to country. Europe as a whole has the slowest population growth in the world but countries in the south and east have much higher rates than those in the north. Similarly, while birth rates declined dramatically in the UK in the 1970s they soared in Japan with the result that there will be a major increase in the 20–29 age group in this decade.

While the age of the population is a major determinant of its consumption behaviour this will be mediated by a number of other factors – most importantly, education and income. Recognition of these multiple influences on consumption behaviour has led to the development of a variety of composite measures of which Social Grade, Life Cycle and Geodemographics are among the better

■ Major Implications of Demographic Changes

The huge demographic changes occurring during this decade throughout much of Western Europe, will have major implications for the corporate sector within these countries. At the beginning of this decade, the UK population totalled 57.3 million, with 19% aged under 15 years old. People in the 45–60 age bracket made up 16% of the population, while the old, those over 75, made up only 6.9%.

By the end of the 1990s, this age distribution will have changed markedly with the youngest age group making up 20% of the population, the middle aged 18.5% and the over 75 7.4% of the population.

The pharmaceuticals industry will be a major beneficiary of the aging population. As people grow old, their spending on healthcare rises.

Companies who will benefit from this include Glaxo. Its impressive drugs portfolio includes best-selling Zantac anti-ulcer medicine and research is taking place into cancer and asthma drugs. SmithKline Beecham, which markets a range of antibiotics and the ulcer drug Tagamet alongside a strong line up of over-the-counter medicines, also stands to benefit.

The stores sector is another area which will have to reflect the differing needs of an aging population. Catering to the ever changing fashion trends of the younger age group was the main engine for retail growth in the 1980s which was the heyday for the likes of Next and Burton Group. Although there will be fewer young people, increased home ownership and rising disposable income should ensure steady growth in consumer spending in the future.

Marks and Spencer and the Body Shop are well placed to take advantage of the demographic changes. The demand for personal care and cosmetic products that are environmentally sound should continue to grow at above average rates. Marks and Spencer's traditional customer base is in the 30+ age group. Customer loyalty coupled with quality merchandise should ensure that it continues to have a major slice of the UK clothing market. Other retailers such as Next and Storehouse are busy repositioning their product range.

In the market for food, increased international travel and heightened awareness of healthy lifestyles will raise demand for fruit, organic produce, yogurts, fresh foods and prepared produce. This trend will boost the profit margins of innovative food retailers such as Sainsbury's.

The housing boom of the 1980s was fuelled by the rapid growth in the number of first-time buyers. Although this number will decline in the next decade, the more important factor determining demand for property is housing turnover. As the number of divorces rise, then demand for houses will also increase resulting in greater profits for companies in the construction industry.

Although the building materials and construction sector is bombed out at the moment, longer term the prospects are good. Redland, the construction materials group, is one company which should profit from the demographic changes.

Some of the extra income available, not least from the growing number of people taking early retirement, will be spent on leisure activities. This could lead to the construction of out of town complexes, congregating a range of facilities in one site. Those companies who target the young family market and the over 45 age group will do well.

Given the large amounts of capital investment needed, big companies such as Scottish and Newcastle and Rank Organisation may well grow. Rank is the biggest leisure company in the marketplace with a wide range of activities in the UK and US.

Scottish and Newcastle with its Holiday Club Pontins and Center Parcs, the Dutch operator of all year holiday villages in Europe will find a ready market for its mix of facilities.

Health and fitness-related businesses should also profit from interest by the wealthy middle-aged – the so called 'grey panthers' – as well as business and corporate customers. This is good news for hotel operators such as Trusthouse Forte and Whitbread who have incorporated fitness facilities into their hotels.

The structure and size of the population has a major influence on the economy of a country. In turn, these factors have an enormous role to play in the performance of industry within the country and hence on the values of companies quoted on the equity market. The demographic changes provide sizable long-term opportunities for both companies and investors.

known. These measures are widely used to segment markets and are discussed in more detail in Chapter 8.

In all advanced countries, and many developing ones too, hard data and expert comment of this kind are freely available in official publications and the marketing planner can have no excuse for omitting such vital information from his environmental analysis.

But, while population data and projections may provide an essential starting-point for the assessment of future threats and opportunities in the external environment, it is clear that it is the interpretation of the implications of these data which is vital to SMP. For this interpretation we must look closely at all the other factors.

■ Social and Cultural Factors

One of the recurring themes of this book is the inevitability of change, while a second is that when innovation or change does occur it tends to be an exponential process which accelerates rapidly from slow beginnings.

The cumulative effects of change are vividly described by Karl Albrecht:[3]

> The period from 1900 until the present stands apart from every other period in human history as a time of incredible change. Mankind, at least in the so-called 'developed' countries, has lost its innocence entirely. The great defining character-istics of this period – the first three-quarters of the twentieth century – have been change, impermanence, disruption, newness and obsolescence, and a sense of acceleration in almost every perceptible aspect of American society.
>
> Philosophers, historians, scientists, and economists have given various names to this period. Management consultant Peter F. Drucker (1968)[4] has called it the Age of Discontinuity. Economist John Kenneth Galbraith (1977)[5] has called it the Age of Uncertainty. Media theorist Marshall MacLuhan (1964, 1968)[6] called it the Age of the Global Village. Writer and philosopher Alvin Toffler (1970, 1975)[7] called it the Age of Future Shock. Virtually all thoughtful observers of America, Americans, and American society have remarked with some alarm about the accelerating pace with which our life processes and our surrounds are changing *within the span of a single generation*. And this phenomenon is spreading all over the industrialized world. I call this the Age of Anxiety.

As a result of these changes, Albrecht identifies five significant areas of change in life-style:

1 From rural living to urban living.
2 From stationary to mobile.
3 From self-sufficient to consuming.
4 From isolated to interconnected.
5 From physically active to sedentary.

Albrecht reviews these factors in some detail, mainly to establish his thesis that such change has led to significant physiological and psychological effects and greatly increased the levels of stress among people which, in turn, has become a causal factor in influencing people's life-style.

However, it is also apparent that the writings of authors like Albrecht, Kinsey, Nader, Carson, Packard, Schumacher, Toffler, Meadowes and the Club of Rome, etc., have made us much more aware of ourselves and our environment. Simultaneously, increased affluence in the advanced economies has allowed us to react to this awareness through further social and cultural change which has seen the emergence of consumerism, of concern for equal opportunities, of environmentalism, etc.

At the time of writing the first edition in 1984 few could have anticipated that 'green' issues could have achieved the prominence they enjoy today. With the benefit of hindsight, of course, one can point out that the diffusion of this interest/concern follows the classic pattern of the diffusion/life-cycle curves discussed in Chapter 5. But, as we pointed out when discussing this phenomenon, the difficulty with using the PLC as a predictive device lies in knowing when take-off will occur and what will trigger it. No doubt future historians will be able to chronicle the sequence of events which heightened the awareness in advanced countries of the weakening of the ozone layer, of global warming, of the destruction of non-renewable resources and the threat of unrestricted population growth. The problem is being able to predict when such awareness stopped being the preoccupation of cranks and the creation of 'fad' products, and became of general concern and the rapid introduction of fashionable green products which accelerated the whole process by substituting these for environmentally unfriendly products.

In the final analysis such a matter must be one of judgement and those able to make such judgements will, like Napoleon's 'lucky generals', succeed. One of the justifications for this book, however, is that 'luck' is the product of insight and experience both of which can be increased significantly by knowledge transfer of the kind attempted in text books and formal education. 'Luck', in the context of predicting trends, is a matter of developing a sound understanding of the current position and the events leading up to it, of accepting the inevitability of change and of keeping one's mind open for cues or signals that change is indeed occurring. It follows that the marketer must be sensitive to these changes and the effects they are likely to have on consumption patterns and should make full use of the powerful techniques[8] which have been developed for both monitoring and modelling life-style.

■ Political and Governmental Factors

Once social groups attain a certain size some form of political process becomes necessary to regulate the functioning of the group and the interaction of its members. In most countries, and certainly the great majority with a market economy, the political process leads to the election of a government with a mandate to undertake certain functions on behalf of the society as a whole. These functions are usually very wide-ranging and cover such areas as:

- Security and defence.
- Education.
- Transportation.
- Social security and welfare.
- Health.
- Employment.
- Foreign relations and trade.

Governments develop specific policies for all these areas and support them to varying degrees with investment and expenditure derived from direct and indirect taxation. Accordingly the government will also have an economic policy and this will have a significant influence upon the regulation of competition, upon permissible business practices, upon standards and so on.

It requires little imagination or experience to recognise the extent of political influence upon business activities and it is widely accepted that many of the UK's economic problems may be attributed to the radically different political philosophies of the two major parties which have governed the country in the post-Second World War period. The Conservatives believe basically in a free market economy while the Socialists believe in a state-managed and centrally controlled economy. Given that governments last a maximum of five years before they have to be re-elected it is unsurprising that many businessmen are loath to consider long-term investment when an election may result in a complete U-turn in economic policy.

Writing in 1991, however, it is clear that businessmen in the UK will be less able to plead short-termism as a consequence of political uncertainty than in the past. To a large degree the economic, and so political, fortunes of the UK have become influenced increasingly by membership of the European Community. While it is not felt that 1992 will result in a step-function change, as is frequently implied by references to this particular date, the process of integration into the greatly enlarged European markets has surely and inevitably continued. If anything it can only be accelerated by the union of Germany and the breakdown of the Soviet economy and its recognition of the importance of market forces. Closer to home the Labour party has recognised that, despite growing dissatisfaction with many aspects of Conservative government, the majority of voters are motivated by self-interest rather than ideology and so prefer the more *laissez-faire* market based philosophy. Labour has modified its policies accordingly, to the point that it is becoming increasingly difficult to distinguish them from those of the Conservatives.

In that government policies are invariably made mandatory through legislation no firm can afford to lose touch with political events. However, once the government has published its programme there is a very high probability that it will be enacted and firms may take action accordingly – the real problem lies in the longer term and the possibilities of a change in the government and/or a change in relationships between the country and other countries. For the UK with its dependence on international trade and its involvement in international business such considerations are of vital importance to strategic planning.

■ Economic Factors

Changes in the size and structure of the population and in life-style and consumption patterns together with the prevailing political philosophy all have a significant influence upon economic factors. At their simplest, economies are concerned with the central problem of maximising satisfaction through the utilisation of scarce resources which, in turn, may be classified as land, labour and capital. Land is the source of food and raw materials; labour is necessary to grow the food, extract the raw materials and transform them into consumable products; while capital, particularly in the shape of technology, plant, equipment, transportation, etc., is vital to enhance the efficiency and productivity of this process. To some extent the factors of production may be substituted for one another, but such substitution takes time and can rarely be accomplished in the short to medium term. Thus any major disturbance in the balance between the three factors of production can result in a serious distortion of the economic system. Within a single, self-contained economy such distortion is easier to anticipate and control, but, in the modern world few if any economies are self-contained as the theory of comparative advantage clearly shows that economic welfare will be optimised through international trade. It is because of the development of dependency upon international trade that the Arab increase in oil prices in 1974 had such wide-ranging repercussions upon so many national economies – not necessarily directly, but as a knock-on or domino effect. Thus the immediate effect was felt in the USA and Western Europe where price rises and inflation led to a decline in consumption and a lesser level of demand for imports from Third World countries whose economies declined accordingly.

As noted earlier, given time one can adjust to such a radical distortion and a wide range of responses may be identified. First, most oil-dependent economies instituted energy-saving programmes to extract the maximum benefit and efficiency from the scarce resource. Second, many countries turned to other energy sources such as coal and oil shale which had been uneconomic when oil prices were low. Similarly, the high price of oil prompted the exploitation of many marginal oil-fields and a stepping-up of exploration and development especially of off-shore deposits. Looking even further ahead, research into the potential of renewable sources of energy – wind, wave, solar and nuclear power – was promoted. The net result of these efforts is that in 1982 and 1983 the OPEC producers found it increasingly difficult to sustain a common supply and price policy and had cause to consider the inevitability of product life-cycles and Levitt's observation: 'Every declining industry was once a growth industry.'[9]

In summarising reactions to a swingeing rise in the price of a vital raw material it is apparent that these fell into two major categories – those prompted 'automatically' by market forces and those put into effect by those responsible for overall economic policy and management (governments). The 'automatic' or market response is that which economic theory predicts will occur if one changes the supply of or demand for a product.

The consequence (or cause) of such changes will be a change in the market price and the process which both prompts and reflects this process is competition. Competition was discussed in Chapter 2 and will be returned to later in this chapter while price is the concern of Chapter 15, and we shall discuss these topics more fully there. With regard to governmental response, we have already discussed this briefly and the point is returned to here solely to emphasise the interdependence and interaction between the environmental factors.

■ Technological Factors

As with the other factors, technology and technological change may be both the cause and effect of environmental change. The distinction is a simple one between *technology push*, which is usually associated with a production orientation, and *market pull* which is usually associated with a marketing orientation. As we saw in Chapter 4, firms would be ill-advised to depend solely upon either one or the other of these approaches and should seek a judicious balance between basic research and development in pursuit of radical innovation and applied R&D intended to improve and sustain its current market share.

Earlier in this chapter reference was made to the accelerating rate of technological change and the social and cultural consequences of this. In making this connection Albrecht (*Stress and the Manager*) plots a selection of significant technological innovations on a time continuum from 1900 to 1975. This is reproduced as Figure 6.2 and speaks for itself.

Many of these methods have been proved in practice. In Chapter 5 we discussed the use of scenarios as a means of seeking to capture future uncertainties and in Chapter 12 (Marketing Research) we describe the Bayesian approach for incorporating uncertainty into decisions analysis. At a more prosaic level in Chapter 10 we look at sales forecasting as a basis for developing short- to medium-term extrapolations for use in tactical marketing plans.

More recently (1988) *Fortune* magazine carried an article entitled 'Technology in the year 2000'[10] in which it looked back over the preceding 12 years and offered some predictions of where technology might be by the millennium. In 1976 there were no PCs, no CDs, no VCRs and no genetically engineered vaccines. All were commonplace by 1988. Given the order and magnitude of such changes one might reasonably question the prediction that the next 12 years could bring ten times as much progress.

According to Bylinsky the confidence of the technologists who make such predictions is based upon the fact that 'in contrast with earlier decades of invention, man stands at the dawn of the Age of Insight – a new era of understanding how things work and how to make them work better. In both

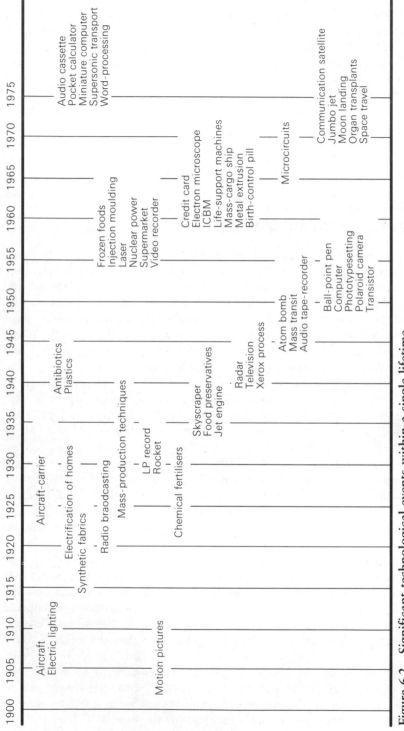

Figure 6.2 Significant technological events within a single lifetime

Source: K. Albrecht, *Stress and the Manager* (Englewood Cliffs, N.J.: Prentice-Hall, 1979).

electronics and biotechnology, the two principle fountainheads of new products, the immediate future holds not just the compilation of more and more data but also some startling new vision'.

Based upon the assessment of some 100 experts in industry, universities, federal agencies and venture capital firms in the USA, Western Europe and Japan *Fortune* set up a number of Probability Panels which came up with a number of specific forecasts including the following:

- In 1970 Intel Corp. pioneered a 1024 bit, or 1-kilobit DRAM (dynamic random access memory) chip which held about 4,000 transistors and related components. In 1988 4-megabit (4 million bit) DRAMs with about 16 million components were in use and by 2000 a 1-billion transistor chip was seen as possible.
- Supercomputers will be able to do 4 trillion complex calculations a second – 1,000 times more than is currently possible, making possible mathematical modelling of enormously complex phenomena.
- 'Visual computing' will enable the output of this mathematical modelling to be presented visually and manipulated in a variety of ways so opening up new areas of scientific inquiry and bring products to market at unheard-of speeds, by allowing the rapid testing of almost infinite product variation.
- Voice recognition and response will be available as will data entry using handwriting and PCs of enormous power the size of paperback books but containing the equivalent memory of 200 volumes.
- In telecommunications voice controlled telephones (78%), colour faxes (77%), combined telephone/computer/TVs (68%) and picture phones (66%) are all seen as highly probable.
- In medicine diagnosis will be possible in minutes rather than days and it should be essentially possible to prevent autoimmune diseases such as rheumatoid arthritis and multiple sclerosis as well as regrow organs in the body rather than replace them with transplants.

Faced with evidence of this kind one is reminded of the question posed previously concerning environmental change as a whole – 'Could we have anticipated it?' to which the answer must be an unequivocal Yes'. The inevitability and accelerating nature of change of this kind is the basic message of the product life-cycle and it is for this reason that we have placed so much emphasis upon the concept. In doing so we have dismissed the criticisms of those who question whether the PLC is a true reflection of reality, but we have been careful not to challenge the complaint that even if PLCs do exist in general they are not very useful as a predictive device in the particular. This criticism is accepted and we must look elsewhere for methods and techniques for predicting particular future events for use in strategic planning, but – and this is the cause of my obsession with the PLC concept – if you don't accept the general implications of the concept first it is unlikely that you would go to the time and trouble of setting-up a formal technological forecasting system.

Because of increased awareness of the need to try and predict the future, considerable effort has been invested into developing techniques for doing this. In the next section we look more closely at some of the secular trends in economic levels of activity which are so heavily influenced by technological factors and of particular importance to long-term strategic planning.

■ Cycles and Trends

With the down-turn in economic activity which accompanied the OPEC price increases of the early 1970s many commentators remarked on the similarity between the period and that of the Great Depression of the 1930s. Such comparisons provoked considerable interest in the assertion as to whether there is an underlying long-term cycle in economic activity with the obvious corollary that, if there is, can such a trend be used for predicting and controlling economies?

Research into long waves or Kondratieff cycles has become a major preoccupation of many economists, particularly in Europe, and there has been a substantial increase in publications dealing with this phenomenon. Much of this research is synthesised in a book by J. J. van Duijn which appeared in 1983 and this section draws heavily on this source.[11]

Cycles vary enormously in general although in the particular all exhibit a basic regularity comprising a number of distinct phases and it is the expectation of changes in direction and the reasons underlying them which are of central interest and concern. In the economic cycle six phases are distinguished (compared with four in the standard PLC) and are shown in Figure 6.3.

While many different types of cycle have been distinguished four enjoy particular support which van Duijn lists as:

(a)   The Kitchin or inventory cycle, with a length of 3–5 years (the 'business cycle').
(b)   The Juglar or investment cycle, with a length of 7–11 years.
(c)   The Kuznets or building cycle, of 15–25 years' duration.
(d)   The long wave or Kondratieff cycle, which is said to be of 45 to 60 years.

The shorter the cycle the more predictable it is, which undoubtedly reinforces the emphasis upon short-term tactical moves to the neglect of long-term strategic planning. Thus it is much easier to adjust inventories to reflect the prevailing supply/demand conditions than to commit oneself to absolute increases or decreases in the level of investment.

As noted, the longer the periodicity of a cycle the more difficult it is to distinguish and define. Accordingly, there is by no means universal agreement upon the existence of long waves in economic activity with life-spans of from 45 to 60 years. However, there is an extensive and growing body of evidence to support the proposition that such long waves do exist and that they may be used to forecast infra-structural change.

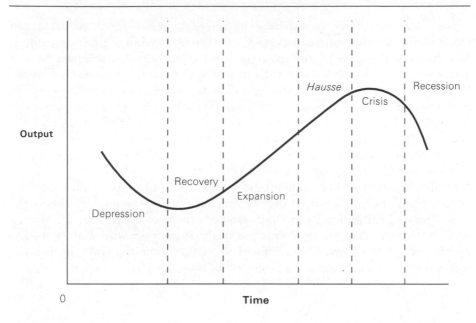

Figure 6.3   The phases of an economic cycle

Source: J. J. van Duijn, *The Long Wave in Economic Life* (London: George Allen & Unwin, 1983).

Views differ as to whether the four cycles are dependent or independent of each other. As van Duijn comments, it is very tempting but also very simplistic to propose that by juggling with the lengths of the various cycles we can come up with an equation which states:

1 Kondratieff = 3 Kuznets = 6 Juglars = 12 Kitchins.

Although it is unlikely that the relationship will ever be so neat, especially now that governments seek to manage their economies, it is equally unlikely that there is no interdependence at all. Certainly, there is a common thread in the normal 'life expectancy' of the four basic types of investment – inventory, plant and equipment, buildings and major infra-structural investments such as railways, motorways, airports, etc. (the Kondratieff cycle). That said, much of the argument in *Marketing New Industrial Products* and *Market Development* is concerned with the contribution of technical innovation to economic growth and change and the role which behavioural factors play in delaying or accelerating such change. It is also apparent that while market pull innovation implies a reaction to express needs technological push frequently ignores such forces and, if sufficiently attractive, may override a natural desire to capitalise fully on investment by depreciating it over its intended life-span, i.e. the original investment criterion may be discarded in the light of new information on comparative cost benefits resulting from innovation.

For those seeking an explanation of the four types of cycle outlined above, van Duijn provides a clear and concise summary (pp. 8–19) and there is a wealth of literature describing the form and parameters of the inventory (business) and investment cycles which is suited to short-to-medium-term economic forecasting. However, for the purposes of strategic planning a longer-term time-horizon is desirable and it is here that van Duijn's analysis of long waves is seen as being of particular value. Fundamental to his analysis (and possibly the reason why it finds favour with this author) is recognition and acceptance of economic growth as an S-shaped phenomenon based on many of the same arguments set out in Chapter 2 of *Marketing New Industrial Products*.

Having established that economic growth in terms of products, industries and even national industrial output over certain time periods, resembles closely the now familiar PLC pattern, van Duijn proceeds to inquire whether an S-shaped curve is also an adequate representation of the secular growth of an economy. Perhaps the best known of theories of secular economic growth is that put forward by Rostow in which he proposes six stages:

1 Traditional society.
2 Preconditions for take-off.
3 Take-off.
4 The drive to technological maturity.
5 The age of high mass consumption.
6 The search for quality.[12]

Evidently there are close parallels between Rostow's stages and the phases of the PLC and van Duijn puts forward considerable evidence to support the existence of the stages and the fact that, like PLCs, growth in *per capita* GNP may be represented by an S-shaped curve. But just as the stylised PLC is unable to provide a complete explanation of the real world so the S-shaped secular growth hypothesis does not provide a complete explanation of the above average growth rates in the period 1948–73. To answer this question van Duijn cites the four explanatory factors proposed by Rostow, namely:

1 The post-war commitment of governments to maintain full employment, backed by a wide range of instruments for affecting the level of effective demand.
2 The backlog of technologies, ready for absorption by Western Europe and Japan; the added impetus of demand for capital goods in countries which had suffered physical war damage.
3 The efforts of the developing regions of Latin America, Africa, the Middle East and Asia to increase investment rates and absorb the backlog of unapplied technologies.
4 An environment of relatively falling energy prices and, from 1951 to 1972, relatively falling or low prices of foodstuffs and raw materials.

Van Duijn poses the question whether these were a one-off occurrence, or are they likely to be repeated. His own opinion inclines to the latter view and provides the justification for suggesting the existence of the long wave acting in conjunction with the secular trend identified by Rostow and others.

The remaining chapters of van Duijn's book are devoted to a review and analysis of a number of different long-wave theories, of the empirical evidence underlying them and of the implications for economic policy particularly during a depression such as that being experienced almost universally during the early 1980s.

Other priorities preclude any further discussion of this important element in the forces which need to be taken into account when making an environmental analysis. However, it is hoped that this cursory commentary will serve to alert the reader to the wealth of insight available from other disciplines to help guide the formulation of basic assumptions which are the essential starting-point for the development of long-term strategic plans. Certainly the environmental forces discussed in the preceding pages provide the framework within which firms must operate. As noted, these conditions are substantially the same for all firms so that to a large degree their success and failure will depend upon their ability to cope with these while interacting with each other in a state of competition. It is to the subject of competition which we now return (Competition was discussed at some length in Chapter 2.).

■ Competition[13]

Although the concept of competition is central to both the study of economics and the practice of business it is seldom that one finds economists attempting to define precisely what they mean by the term. It is equally rare for businessmen to consider the general nature of competition as a basis for making decisions about specific action. A recurring theme of this book is that while the dynamic nature of business means that one is rarely faced twice with exactly the same problem or decision, this is no justification for ignoring the potential contribution from past experience and the statement of theories based upon it. Accordingly, in this section we shall seek to define competition and the different forms it can take, to provide some foundation for the subsequent discussion of the marketing mix and its component elements of product, price, promotion and place.

Lawrence Abbott, a distinguished economist, suggests that *outside* the economic sphere the word 'competition' means a type of activity that involves contestants who are pitted against each other, some common goal sought by them, efforts on the part of each to achieve superiority in attaining the goal, some methods of judging superiority, judges or judging mechanisms to do the judging, the selection of one or perhaps several of the contestants, and rejection of the others. *Within* the field of economics precise definitions of this kind are less easy to come by, and usually finish up not by defining competition *per se*, but the conditions under which it exists, or its consequences. Among the exceptions to this generalisation is J. M. Clark, who sees competition as the 'availability of alternatives', in which availability implies both the existence of alternatives and the ability of participants to choose freely between them.[14]

Proponents of this school of thought approximate much more closely the businessman's view of competition than that of their more traditional professional colleagues, who assume product homogeneity as a basic prerequisite for the study of competition. As we saw in Chapter 2, it was the potential of excess supply for homogeneous products which motivated producers to differentiate their products in an attempt to create and sustain purchase loyalty, and precipitated a switch in orientation from production to selling and marketing. Thus Clark sees competition as a dynamic process, the central element of which is offering the other party a bargain good enough to induce him to deal with you in the face of his free option of dealing with others. Similarly, Abbott sees it as the effort of each producer to get, or to keep, patronage which might go to another. These efforts take the form of striving to make the offer more attractive to the buyers than the offers of competitors. This improved attractiveness of the offer may be a lower price, or it may be improved quality, a more attractive design, a more useful or attractive package, greater convenience of location of the point of sale, the assurance of dependability that comes from a long-established record, improved after sale services, such as repairs or adjustments, and many other features. By contrast, perhaps the ultimate irony is that the economists' so-called 'perfect competition' means the complete absence of all these activities.

According to the classical economist, under conditions of perfect competition the demand curve is horizontal, each supplier has a U-shaped cost curve, and produces a homogeneous product: there is a large number of buyers and sellers, all of whom have perfect knowledge; there is complete freedom of entry and exit from the industry, and the entrepreneurs' sole motivation is profit maximisation. The assumption of perfect knowledge eliminates both the need for, and the economic feasibility of sales promotion, while the assumption of product homogeneity eliminates the possibility of product differentiation, so quantity is the only variable of competitive behaviour, and the unique solution – what price and quantity – is the logical outcome of the assumed impersonal market force. Under these conditions, competition will result in a single price, for no one would buy from a supplier seeking a higher price than other sellers, and no seller would be willing to sell for less.

Such conditions describe a purely competitive market in equilibrium, which is the end result with which price theory is concerned. Before reaching equilibrium, price competition becomes more active when one seller creates a price differential and thus puts his rivals at a disadvantage, which forces them to adjust their own prices to meet competition until equilibrium is reached. At this point no further differential can be advantageous to anyone, and the price adjustment process stops. In other words, price competition does not occur under conditions of equilibrium, but is an institutional device for bringing about price movements towards equilibrium. Without competition a uniform price above equilibrium might persist, buyers would be exploited and resources would not be allocated in the most effective way. Thus, perfect competition represents an ideal situation, and any departure from it is considered to be imperfection in the market, which is undesirable.

The economists' strong emphasis on price relative to the other elements of a company's marketing strategy can be explained according to Philip Kotler by historical, technical and social reasons.[15] The historical reason lies in the environment of the economy at the time when economists such as Adam Smith and Ricardo first began to develop systematic economic theory in conditions dominated by scarcity of resources, low consumer incomes, seller's markets and few economies of large scale. The typical nation's output consisted of raw materials and finished consumer goods, which were highly standardised, and little effort was made to differentiate them through branding, packaging or advertising. The major variable differentiating competitive offerings was price, and the low level of income emphasised the sensitivity of price as a marketing variable.

The technical reason is that price has more tractable properties for purposes of analysis, being quantitative, unambiguous and unidimensional, whereas product quality, product image, customer services, promotion and similar factors are qualitative, ambiguous and multi-dimensional. Similarly for social purposes, the price mechanism provides an efficient and effective method to guide both sellers and buyers in maximising their satisfaction through the use of the scarce resources over which they have control.

Clearly there have been significant changes in the economic environment since Adam Smith's time. As Udell observed in 1972, the present economic environment is characterised by abundant resources, many wealthy consumers, a buyer's market and economies of large scale.[16] As a consequence, competition can no longer be described in terms of a large number of firms offering homogeneous products to buyers with perfect knowledge, nor can a theory of competitive behaviour be restricted to pricing. Instead, today's theory must recognise the role of non-price factors, and it is these which are essentially the domain of marketing, and underlie its recent prominence as a business discipline.

■ Non-price Competition

Udell offers a satisfactory approach to distinguishing between price and non-price competition when he points out that the former implies that the firm accepts its demand curve as given, and manipulates its price to try to attain its objectives, while in non-price competition it seeks to change the location and shape of its demand curve.

The importance of non-price variables in influencing demand was first recognised in the early 1930s, when Joan Robinson[17] and Edwin Chamberlin[18] independently (but almost simultaneously) published their theories of imperfect competition. Chamberlin's theory introduced the notion of product differentiation into the explanation of competitive behaviour when he argued that a general class of product is differentiated if any significant basis exists for distinguishing the goods or services of one seller from those of another. Such a basis may be real or fancied, as long as it is of any importance to buyers and leads to a preference for one variety of product over another. Where such differentiation exists, even though it be slight, buyers will be paired with sellers not by chance, as under competition, but according to their preferences. Chamberlin stated that differentiation may be based upon certain characteristics of the product itself, such as exclusive patented features, trade marks, trade names, peculiarities of the package or container, if any, or singularity in quality, design, colour or style. It may also exist with respect to the condition surrounding its sale, such as the seller's location in retail trade, the general tone of doing business, reputation for fair dealing, and all personal links which attach his customers either to himself or to his establishment.

Chamberlin's theory thus gives explicit recognition to three of marketing's four 'Ps' – product, price and place – and implicitly acknowledges the role of the fourth – promotion – when he refers to branding and personal links between the buyer and seller. These distinctions are also made and further developed in the work of economists such as Knight,[19] Stigler[20] and Machlup,[21] and so provide a sound foundation for the evolution of a theory of competition which is central to the practice of marketing and enshrined in Borden's concept of the marketing mix (see Chapter 7).[22] With four basic sets of variables to manipulate it is clear that the marketer has many more degrees of freedom available to him in developing a unique selling strategy, and one which frees him from the tyranny of having to accept a market price set by impersonal forces outside his own control. As Udell[23] points out, the use of non-price variables is preferable to only manipulating the price to get the customers' patronage for at least four fundamental reasons:

1   The relatively well-to-do customers of today are interested in more than just price. They are interested in product quality, distinctiveness, style, and many other factors which lead to both physical and psychological satisfaction. From product differentiation and sales promotion, the consumer receives a great deal of psychological satisfaction and utility. Consequently, firms try to satisfy consumer desires and increase their sales by product differentiation and sales promotion.

2   The products of moden industry are fairly complex, and buyers often require a substantial amount of information in making purchase decisions. Marketing communications, in addition to being persuasive, are a major source of information about products, prices, and suppliers. Also important is the fact that many marketing communications help to reduce the amount of searching time required of buyers. Therefore, the informative value of sales efforts is important to buyers and sellers alike.

3   In today's competitive economy, supply or production capacity generally exceeds demand and, therefore, nearly all sellers are forced either to be highly competitive or almost collusive in their pricing. Because there may be little or no freedom for a company to deviate from the market price, pricing sometimes is not a meaningful parameter of competitive strategy.

4   It is through successful product differentiation that a manufacturer may obtain
    some pricing freedom. Products known to be identical must be priced identically
    in the market place. However, if a product can be favourably differentiated in
    the eyes of consumers some degree of pricing freedom is usually achieved.

It would seem clear, therefore, that marketing is essentially about non-price
competition, and that this concept is central to its theory and practice. In later
chapters we shall examine the nature of the marketing mix and the development
of specific policies for each of the major factors – product, price, promotion and
place – in some detail and so will not elaborate on them here.

■ Changing Times = Changing Values

From our review it is clear that agreement on broad environmental changes is
widespread. In attempts to manage their economies, governments will continue
to experiment with diametrically opposed policies of regulation and deregulation, and in doing so are unlikely to improve business confidence as to the
continuity of basic policy on competition. We may also look forward to a
continuation of the rapid technological change precipitated by the microelec-
tronics revolution. As a consequence of these three broad trends one can already
detect changes in both values and life-styles.

In essence the change in values and life-styles is away from a Christian ethic of
deferred gratification to a more hedonistic and short-term view of life which
emphasises immediate gratification. The implications of this change were clearly
demonstrated in research undertaken by Leathar into the promotion of non-
smoking by the Scottish Health Education Group.[24] The original campaign,
which was highly thought of by advertising professionals and won several
awards, cited a number of benefits of not smoking and stressed that non-
smokers ran a much lower risk of contracting lung cancer and dying prematurely.
In other words don't smoke, and you may live longer. For the target audience of
teenagers and young adults the promise was both too uncertain (many smokers
don't get lung cancer anyway) and too distant (60 is two lifetimes away when
you're 20). Once this perception was distinguished the theme was changed to one
of more immediate payoffs accenting that non-smokers are nicer to be near and
more socially acceptable. Similarly, advertising on alcohol now underlines
moderation in drinking behaviour rather than total abstinence.

Other examples of society rejecting the traditional values of hard work and
thrift in the anticipation of a better future are legion. When inflation erodes or
wipes out the value of hard-earned savings (the Retail Price Index has increased
fourfold in the past decade) and many in employment are visibly no better off
than the unemployed it is difficult to sustain a belief in the old order. Small
wonder that those made redundant prefer to 'blow' their nest eggs on holidays or
consumer durables which give immediate gratification rather than save-up for the
rainy day which is already here.

Returning to our earlier question as to whether such changes could have been anticipated, we believe that they could, through a combination of strategic planning and focused market research. But, as we suggested, the general climate of opinion rejected the possibility that one economic order was passing and another succeeding it. Given the events of the past few years, most are now persuaded that the future will be different and so are willing to consider a more professional approach to management than they were in the past. So, what should we do next?

■ What Next?

Addressing the question as to the nature of marketing in the 1980s Cox[25] identified four key issues for marketers in the coming decade:

1   How valuable is the strategic planning process for an organisation?
2   What environmental opportunities and threats will influence managers in developing their corporate strategies?
3   How should the functional area of marketing be integrated into the broader organisational concept of strategic planning?
4   What specific marketing strategies will be appropriate?

In light of the prominence accorded to strategic planning in the curricula of business schools, particularly in their executive development programmes, and the extensive coverage given to the subject in management (as opposed to academic) books and journals one might be forgiven if one took a question as to the value of strategic planning as rhetorical. However, one does not have to look far to discover considerable disenchantment with both the concept and practice of strategic planning. In 'Weak Signals from the Unknown' in the October 1984 issue of *International Management* one of the founders of strategic planning, Igor Ansoff, expressed the belief that many firms have lost confidence in or rejected the practice. In Ansoff's view this is largely due to a misunderstanding:

> When an executive says that strategic planning has not worked for him in an era of turbulence, he is stating an obvious truth because it was never designed to do so. You might as well use a lawn mower to drive 200 kilometres.

According to Ansoff, planning has fallen into eras which overlap. The 1950s was the era of long-range planning, which extrapolated the past into the future with confidence the future would unfold as predicted.

The 1960s was the era of strategic planning, which is essentially extrapolation plus some programming, while the 1970s saw the arrival in the more sophisticated companies of strategic issue management, which is primarily concerned with a company's view of the world, its internal organisation and capacity to cope with change. Shell's directional policy matrix (DPM) and G.E's concept of strategic business units (SBUs) being examples of the latter approach.

Looking to the 1980s Ansoff argues that any company which operates in a high-change environment will have to give increased attention to 'weak-signals' and 'surprise' management.

Weak-signals management corresponds closely to Aguilar's concept of scanning the environment in an effort to pick up indications of changes which might affect the organisation.[26] In Ansoff's words – 'the need in the weak signals business is to develop increasing degrees of preparedness in the organisation comparable with the strength of the signals received'.

Clearly the concept is very similar to the military early warning system in which the organisation is brought to higher and higher levels of readiness as signals suggest an increasing probability of a direct threat to the system. Ansoff recognises the contribution of military thinking and practice when he states that surprise management is a 'form of damage control procedure' that recognises that 'no matter how good a radar you have some bombs are going to get through'. In other words surprise management is a contingency plan for how the organisation will respond.

The Argentinian invasion of the Falkland Islands in 1982 provides a dramatic example of the relevance and applicability of such a contingency plan, as well as underlining the fact that existing early-warning systems and intelligence-gathering operations can go sadly wrong – the more so if you ignore weak signals in times of turbulence. A point strongly reinforced by the Gulf War of 1990–1.

Research by Malcolm McDonald at the Cranfield School of Management[27] tends to confirm that formal strategic planning enjoys less popularity than one might expect, as only 10% of his sample of industrial goods manufacturers were found to possess a formal planning system. However, McDonald's research did show that these firms were considerably more successful than those in which there was no formal planning in which he observed 'a commonality of operational problems which centred around declining organisational effectiveness, and confusion over what to do about it'.

Sceptics will no doubt claim that a clear association between the existence of formal strategic planning and business success does not necessarily prove that the former is a causal factor in the existence of the latter – indeed many would argue that it is only successful companies which can afford the trappings of a formal planning system. None the less there is widespread evidence to attest to the value of strategic planning and, like Ansoff, we can only assume that where firms claim to have tried and failed, they have been using an inappropriate set of techniques. It is also possible that they have reposed too much confidence in strategic planning to neglect of the present. If this is the case then it is quite probable that marketing is to blame – or, at least, the commonly held view as to what marketing claims to be.

A third explanation of possible disenchantment with strategic planning also emerged in the course of the interviews with senior industrialists reported in *Marketing and Competitive Success*. In essence many managers who had experienced severe crises during the recession of the late 1970s/early 1980s attributed this not to the failure of strategic planning *per se* but to their own detachment from the process. With the growing expertise and sophisticated techniques which had accompanied the development of formal strategic planning in the 1960s and 1970s top management had delegated more and more responsibility to the professional planners. In consequence they had lost the 'feel' for their markets which had now been reduced to heavily documented formal reports too easily accepted at face value. As we noted earlier, 'luck' is the product of knowledge and experience. Top managers usually receive their appointments because they have these attributes and it is this which enables them to distinguish the relevant and important from the irrelevant and unimportant. Less experienced planners, no matter how good their professional qualifications, are less able to make this distinction so, once again, GIGO prevails. In other words, planning is too important to be left to the planner!

■ Summary

In Chapter 6 we have explored the theme that environmental factors constitute the ultimate constraint upon an organisation's objectives and its ability to achieve them. Commencing with a review of the five basic environmental forces – demographic, social/cultural, political, economic and technological – we looked next at the broad cyclical and secular trends which result from their interaction. It was then argued that while these forces and trends exert a major influence on the firm, its immediate and direct concern is its interaction with other firms producing similar goods for sale into the same end-use market. Accordingly, we looked next at the nature of competition and its effect upon market structure and conduct which prescribes the strategic options available to the firm.

Finally we summarised some of the possible consequences of the environmental changes which we can see all around us at the present time. While it is probably true to say that man has always lived in a state of change all the evidence suggests that the second half of the twentieth century has been more dynamic and turbulent than most with clear effects upon both values and lifestyles.

In order to cope with this turbulence and the uncertainty which it engenders it was proposed that organisations must undertake long-term strategic planning. An essential element of this strategic planning must be a highly developed information-gathering or early-warning system to pick up the first indications of environmental changes which may affect the organisation.

In the next chapter our focus will switch from suppliers, and competition between them, to the forces which determine how consumers discriminate between the competitive alternatives offered to them.

CHAPTER 7

Buyer Behaviour

Learning Goals

The issues to be addressed in Chapter 7 include:

1 A review of alternative explanations of *choice behaviour* to be found in the social sciences – economic, psychological and sociological.
2 The nature of *selective perception* and its influence on choice decisions.
3 The concepts of a *hierarchy of needs* and a *hierarchy of effects*.
4 The role of *post-purchase dissonance*.
5 The sequence of events in a *buying decision* and the effects of novelty/familiarity upon them.
6 The proposition of a composite model of *buyer decision behaviour* and its application in practice.

After reading Chapter 7 you will be able to:

1 Describe and explain the major influences on *choice behaviour*.
2 Define *selective perception* and distinguish its effect on the individual's interpretation of information.
3 Illustrate the concept of a *hierarchy of needs* and its effect on consumer behaviour.
4 Specify the stages through which buyers pass in *making choice decisions*.
5 Propose a *composite model of buyer behaviour* which encompasses and reconciles the foregoing concepts and explains its application in practice.

■ Introduction

The question of how people choose between alternatives is at the very heart of the social sciences and central to the great majority of the managerial disciplines. As a consequence there is a plethora of textbooks which deal with choice behaviour whether on the part of the individual or by the organisation as a subject in its own right. In a book of this sort one can only scratch the surface and at best this chapter can only be an eclectic and perhaps idiosyncratic review of some of the major concepts and phenomena which appear to have a bearing upon this very important question.

Because of my view expressed earlier that it is divisive to make a distinction between consumer and industrial marketing, no distinction will be made between the manner in which individuals make choice decisions as opposed to organisations which comprise collections of individuals. Indeed, on the contrary, a brief discussion of group influence will seem to suggest that group behaviour is patterned on what is acceptable to the individuals comprising that group, so that both individuals and the group will act in a very similar way.

In this chapter we shall first review four different disciplinary explanations of choice behaviour, following a framework proposed by Philip Kotler. Next, we shall examine six key concepts which long experience in management education suggests are most helpful to practising managers to help them understand the multifarious influences which affect choice and at the same time provide them with some useful conceptual frameworks as a basis for organising their own knowledge and experience when taking decisions about buyer behaviour. Finally, I shall propose a very broadly based composite model of buying behaviour which seeks to synthesise the key concepts discussed in this chapter.

■ Choice and the Social Sciences

In his now classic textbook on *Marketing Management*[1] Philip Kotler looks at four major motivation models that have been advanced by different social sciences. These are:

1   The Marshallian model, stressing economic motivations.
2   The Pavlovian model, stressing learning.
3   The Freudian model, stressing psychoanalytic motivations.
4   The Veblenian model, stressing social psychological factors.

As Kotler comments:

> these models represent radically different conceptions of the mainsprings of human and consumer behaviour. Depending upon the product, different variables and behavioural mechanisms may assume particular importance. A psychoanalytic behavioural model might throw much light on the factors operating in cigarette demand, while an economic behavioural model may be useful in explaining the purchase of a home. Sometimes alternative models shed light on different demand aspects of the same product.

As a group economists were the first to construct a specific theory of buyer behaviour, arguing that buying decisions are the result of rational and conscious economic calculations of the satisfaction or utility which will be derived from any given purchase decision. Overall, economic man seeks to maximise his total satisfaction by acquiring a collection of goods and services in which the marginal utility of each is in theory equivalent to the marginal utility of every other item in the collection. This economic view of buyer behaviour is firmly founded in the writings of Adam Smith, who argued that all economic activity is ultimately based upon man's self-interest, and Jeremy Bentham, who refined the idea by arguing that in pursuing his self-interest man carefully calculates the advantages and disadvantages of any given purchase. It is significant that, as Kotler comments: 'Bentham's "felicific calculus" was not applied to consumer behaviour, as opposed to entrepreneurial behaviour, until the late nineteenth century.' It was at the end of the nineteenth century that a number of famous economists developed almost simultaneously the 'marginal utility' theory of value which underlay Adam Smith's explanation but had not been developed by him. Foremost among these economists was Alfred Marshall and it was for this reason that the economists' explanation of buyer behaviour is named after him.

It is an almost universal trait that when offered an explanation of something we almost automatically compare this with our own experience or behaviour to see whether it is consistent. As we shall see later in this chapter, self-reference behaviour may be very misleading indeed. However, this does not prevent us from applying the test and most individuals would probably claim that they wouldn't know a marginal utility if they saw one let alone how to calculate such a statistic. For this reason most marketers would dismiss the concept of *homo economicus* as an inadequate explanation of much buyer behaviour. They would also be able to refer to many analyses of buyer behaviour in which conscious economic calculations have played little part. But, as Kotler points out, there are several ways in which the Marshallian model helps an understanding of buyer behaviour, namely:

1 It is axiomatic that every buyer acts in the light of his own best interest. The question is whether an economist would describe these actions as 'rational' or not.
2 The model is *normative* in the sense that it provides a logical basis for purchase decisions, i.e. how one should decide, rather than being *descriptive*, i.e. how one actually decides.
3 The model suggests a number of useful behavioural hypotheses, e.g. the lower the price, the greater the sales; the lower the price of substitute products, the lower the sales of this product; the lower the price of complementary products, the higher the sales of this product; the higher the real income, the higher the sales of this product, provided that it is not an 'inferior' good; the higher the promotional expenditure, the higher the sales.[2]

However, economics only provides a partial explanation of how buyers choose.

An alternative explanation of choice behaviour is that it is a form of learned behaviour in which one associates a given stimulus with particular outcomes and responds accordingly. This stimulus response theory is based very largely on the pioneering work of Ivan Pavlov, whose experiments with conditioning animals are well known to almost everybody. (One of the best-known of his experiments was to present a dog with two stimuli simultaneously, food and the ringing of a bell, and subsequently remove one of the stimuli (the food) and observe the dog's behaviour. When presented with both stimuli originally the dog's automatic response was to salivate in expectation of food. Subsequently, when the bell was rung by itself the dog had learned that the ringing of the bell was associated with food and began to salivate in expectation of the food which was not present.)

The stimulus response model of behaviour has been developed extensively since Pavlov's original discovery and is based on four central concepts of drive, cue, response and reinforcement. Drives may be physiological or social in origin and constitute an internal stimulus impelling action. By contrast, 'cues are weaker stimuli in the environment and/or in the individual that determine when, where, and how the subject responds.' Thus, cues modify drives into a particular *response*, the nature of which will be influenced substantially by past experience. Depending upon the outcome of the response the individual will learn from this experience which will either reinforce and confirm earlier decisions of the same kind as being satisfactory or, if unsatisfactory, may create uncertainty as to whether to repeat the decision in future or prefer an alternative choice when faced with the same drives and cues.

Clearly there are many applications of stimulus-response theory of relevance to the marketer. For example, much branding and advertising is designed to act as a cue and stimulus to purchase at the point of sale. Thus, in a survey 'How and Why Shoppers Buy' reported in the 28 October 1981 issue of *Marketing* Hugh Davidson reported research which showed that 38% of housewives never made a list before going shopping and a further 36% made only a partial list deciding on the rest of their purchases in the shop. Similarly, research has shown that repeat advertising has an important role to play, both in reminding potential purchasers of past satisfactions received and also in reinforcing the rightness of their decision after the actual purchase event.

The Pavlovian explanation of behaviour is clearly too mechanistic to be an exact replication of the real world. Whereas a great deal of human behaviour may be conditioned and therefore predictable, there are also many situations in which people appear to behave in an unpredictable and idiosyncratic way. One explanation of this unpredictability in human behaviour is provided by Freud's work on motivation. According to Freud a man's psyche or inner spirit is comprised of three parts: the id, the ego and the super-ego. The id is concerned with the strong inherent drives and urges with which he was born, while the ego represents 'his conscious planning centre for finding outlets for his drives', and the super-ego 'channels his instinctive drives into socially approved outlets to avoid the pain of guilt or shame'.

During the 1940s and 1950s the findings of motivational research were used extensively in developing marketing strategy, particularly through the contributions of people such as Ernest Dichter.[3] However, the use of motivational research came under considerable criticism on the grounds that sellers were manipulating buyers and persuading them to act against their own better interests. Much of John Galbraith's criticism of the consumer society is based upon an implicit assumption that buyers can be persuaded to act against their better and, presumably, economic interests.[4] The reaction against motivation research culminated in the publication of Vance Packard's book, *The Hidden Persuaders*,[5] one consequence of which was that this approach to marketing fell out of fashion, although there are now signs of a return of interest in this approach.

The fourth broadly based model of buyer behaviour is that based upon social–psychological interpretations which were first proposed by Thorstein Veblen. Perhaps his best-known work is his *Theory of the Leisure Class*,[6] first published in 1899, in which he argued that many purchases were not motivated by need as much as by concern for one's social standing and prestige. In this sense Veblen may be thought of as the originator of the mythical Joneses with whom the rest of society has to keep up. While Veblen's emphasis upon conspicuous consumption has now been greatly modified by subsequent research and analysis, his contribution in pointing out the importance of social relationships as an influence upon choice cannot be over-stated. A basic concept which has had a pervasive influence on marketing thought is that of social class – a concept which has been widely used as a basis for segmenting markets. Nowadays it is generally recognised that there is considerable mobility between social classes and that in some markets social class may be a very poor predictor of actual attitudes and behaviour. As a consequence newer methods based on life-style using techniques such as psychographics have been found to have much better discriminatory and predictive power. However, even these new techniques recognise the importance of social interaction between individuals and the groups of which they are a part.

In his analysis Kotler includes anthropological concepts of culture and sub-culture within the Veblenian social psychological model. More correctly, the study of culture is the province of the discipline of anthropology and, as one would expect with any complex body of knowledge, is comprised of many different and sometimes conflicting theories and points of view.

In answer to the question 'What is the nature of culture' Bliss[7] observes:

> For some, culture has to do with believing, feeling, and thinking. Are the peoples of a society materialistic or spiritualistic? Do they value tradition rather than innovation? Are they aggressive or passive? What aspirations are they striving towards? The questions imply different values, different cultures.
>
> For others, culture is behaviour – as evidenced in the widespread and persistent pattern of behaviour observable in one country as contrasted with another. In going about their daily activities, people react in a predictable manner, thus making communal life possible. Culture in this sense is behaviour which is taken for granted, which is expected.
>
> For still others, it is the interplay of values and behaviour that defines culture. The tendency to place undue, if not complete, emphasis on behaviour – i.e., the customs and mores of a society – is categorised by Bidney[8] as the positivistic fallacy. On the other hand, to define culture in terms of norms and values and to ignore or minimise actual behaviour, is to commit the normative fallacy.

Thus, as a gross simplification, but none the less a generalisation with which most, if not all, anthropologists would agree, culture is a composite of underlying values and behavioural patterns which, in the words of Bliss, 'give meaning to the lives of its [society's] members and determine the overall climate of activity'.

A concept as powerful as culture must be treated with caution if one is to avoid the dangers of over-generalisation – which leads to stereotyping – or over-specificity which ultimately could lead one to distinguish each individual as a culture in his own right. As with the concept of market segmentation, the practitioner must develop an operationally useful definition which permits an appropriate level of discrimination without falling into the trap of regarding, say, all Americans (or Japanese, or Jews) as being the same or, worse still, completely different from each other. Thus, within any distinct culture one would expect to find a number of sub-cultures each with its own distinctive features and different from other sub-cultures.

Perhaps the most important feature of social science explanations of choice behaviour is that none of them individually provides an adequate explanation of the real world. If we were forced to use one or other of the foregoing explanations then there can be no doubt that in most cases we would be able to classify any given choice decision as being influenced more by one model than another. Thus, if faced with a choice between two objectively similar products, one of which was priced lower than the other, economic man would probably prevail. However, if the two objectively similar products had a similar price then our choice would have to be based on other discriminating factors of a subjective kind. If we had previous experience of one product and knew it to be satisfactory, then the Pavlovian explanation might well apply and we would prefer the known to the unknown product. Alternatively, although both products might be objectively similar, one might appeal more strongly than the other to our subconscious motivations and a Freudian explanation would be appropriate. Finally, if one product were more 'visible' than the others then we might depend upon a Veblenian explanation to account for users preferring it.

In reality what we need is a composite model which incorporates dimensions of each of the separate and independent social science explanations derived from a particular discipline. We shall return to this later in the chapter but at this juncture it will be useful to look at six key concepts which past experience has shown to be very useful in answering the basic question – How do buyers choose? These six key concepts are:

1   Selective perception.
2   The hierarchy of needs.
3   The hierarchy of effects.
4   Post-purchase dissonance.
5   Buy tasks and buy phases.
6   The characteristics of goods.

We shall now consider each of these briefly in turn.

■ Selective Perception

One of the cardinal principles of marketing is that one should always seek to put oneself into the customer's position and analyse the selling proposition from his point of view. The importance of this principle lies in the fact that not only do individuals differ, one from another, they also change themselves over time. Now it is highly probable that there are other people in the world who have opinions and attitudes similar to our own and therefore are likely to behave in a manner similar to ourselves. Indeed, one of the factors which tends to distinguish successful from unsuccessful entrepreneurs is the former's ability to identify a latent need and then satisfy it. However, comparatively few people have this gift, and it is for this reason, if for no other, that so much time and money is now expended on formal management education, and on research to try and predict consumers' behaviour. Without research and information about prospective consumers one is likely to fall into the self-reference trap alluded to earlier and so assume that others will behave in the way in which we ourselves would behave under any given set of circumstances.

The intrinsic danger of making such an assumption can be easily tested by asking a supporter of two opposing teams at football to describe an incident leading to a penalty being imposed upon one side. It was just such a situation which led to the classic example of selective perception which was first reported in a paper by Hastorf and Cantril.[9] Following a particularly acrimonious clash between the college football teams of Dartmouth and Princeton, the two sociologists asked supporters of the team to give their views as to what had led to the incidents involved. While most uninvolved viewers felt that these were the joint responsibility of both teams, supporters of the two sides were almost unanimous in their view that all of the trouble lay in faults of the other team's making. In other words, being a supporter of a team tends to make us extol its virtues and overlook its failings. Accordingly, if one of the players on our team is involved in a clash with a member of the opposing team it is likely that we will interpret this as provocation by the other and justifiable retaliation by our own team member.

In addition to leading us to interpret the world in terms of our expectations of it, the phenomenon of selective perception also plays a very important role in protecting us from information overload. Thus, in the course of a normal day it has been shown that most individuals are exposed to over one thousand different messages concerning products or services which sellers would wish them to buy. Out of this enormous welter of information only six or seven of these messages will catch our conscious attention and lead us to reflect upon whether we wish to pursue our awareness of a new fact any further or just discard it.

One of the most compelling examples of selective perception which I have come across in my own experience relates to some early anti-smoking advertising put out by the Scottish Health Education Unit. The basic principle behind the campaign was straightforward and firmly founded in behavioural research findings. In that young people learn from adults and particularly their parents, it was argued that parents act as exemplars for children. Thus, if adults are seen behaving in a particular way it is likely that children will pattern their own behaviour on this. To this end the SHEU commissioned a series of advertisements in which adults were seen interacting with children in a number of situations. Two particular examples were as follows.

The first advertisement showed a small girl sitting up in bed cuddling a teddy bear, while next to the bed sat a well-dressed woman reading from a storybook. The woman is smoking. At the conclusion of the story the woman emphasises the moral and says, 'you see what I mean, dear?' The woman inhales on her cigarette and the little girl sucks her thumb and says, 'yes, mummy'.

The second domestic scene shows a man and a small boy sitting in what appears to be a kitchen with a bicycle upside down on the table. The man, who has a cigarette in his mouth, is adjusting part of the mechanism of the bike and saying to the boy, 'there, you see how it's done?', to which the boy, sucking on a screwdriver, replies, 'yes, I see'. In order to test the effectiveness of these and other advertisements in the campaign it was decided to do a limited amount of qualitative research, using group depth interviews. Basically the respondents were divided into mixed groups of parents representing the upper and lower socio-economic groupings. When shown the advertisements and asked to comment upon them the results were surprising. In the first place none of the members of the groups picked out the smoking factor at all. When prompted, some respondents thought that the first advertisement in the bedroom was concerned with fire hazards and that the intended message was not to smoke in a bedroom. No associations were perceived in the second advertisement at all. In fact the interpretations placed on the advertisements by the two groups seemed quite bizarre at first, but on reflection could be seen as quite reasonable in terms of the normal frame of reference of the respondents themselves. Thus, in the case of the mother reading a bedtime story, this scene was quite normal in the eyes of the upper social class respondents, who perceived the message as being that it was good for mothers to read to children and that it was part of normal family life. For the respondents from the lower socio-economic groups the scene was quite atypical and led to an interpretation which may be caricatured as follows: 'Her husband is on the nightshift at the factory and she's got a fancy man. That's why she's all dressed up. She's feeling guilty, that's why she's reading a story to the kid because she is going to leave it all alone. You should not leave children alone in a house unattended.' By contrast, in the boy-and-bike advertisement, members of the upper social classes spent most of their time commenting on the unhygienic behaviour of the lower classes who actually took bicycles into their kitchens. Members of the lower socio-economic groupings saw this as a perfectly normal scene from family life and interpreted it as saying that it is important that fathers show sons how to make their bicycles safe so they don't get injured in an accident.

It is instructive that this particular campaign, which was singularly ineffective in communicating any of the objectives of the advertiser to its audience, was highly rated by other advertisers and advertising agents. Only by deliberately setting out to discover how the audience interpreted the advertising did it become clear that a completely different approach was required.

A second case history which exemplifies the importance of understanding how selective perception may result in a very different interpretation of a product from that held by its producer, is provided by the marketing of super plastic aluminium. The full case history of this revolutionary material was reported by myself and Stephen Parkinson in an article entitled 'TI Superform's Academic Launch'.[10] Super plastic aluminium or Supral, as it was called, was the result of considerable research between Tube Investments and the British Aluminium Technological Centre. As a result of this research TI decided to set up a subsidiary (TI Superform) to market the new material. Supral offers significant benefits in the manufacture of complex shapes beyond the capabilities of rubber die pressing, and in quantities below 10 000 off where high tool costs would render multiple pressing or deep drawing of aluminium or steel uneconomic. Further, while Supral is not competitive with plastics on price alone, there are many applications where the high temperature capability of aluminium makes its use preferable. It also seemed possible that with escalating oil prices aluminium could become directly competitive with plastics on price alone which would give it a significant overall advantage.

In light of the basic performance and cost characteristics Superform identified eight basic market sectors as follows:

1   Aerospace.
2   Specialist vehicles.
3   Commercial vehicles.
4   Case shells.
5   Electrical/instrument housings.
6   Gaming/vending machine cases.
7   Architectural panels.
8   Others.

With so many possible end use markets one of the problems which Superform faced was how to focus its selling effort on those with the greatest promise of an early return. This question is one on which I have spent the great majority of my time, both as an industrial salesman and as an academic. While examination of a very large number of distinct cases has enabled me to develop some generalisations[11] perhaps the most important single piece of advice is – put yourself in the shoes of the prospective purchaser and look at your selling proposition from his point of view. Obviously in order to find out what the prospective purchaser's point of view is one has to undertake some research among potential users. To focus our recommendations in the case of Supral, we undertook interviews with those companies which had decided to buy the product as well as those which had declined the offer. In addition to a number of general factors which we shall return to when proposing our own composite model of buying behaviour, there was a significant number of situation specific factors which appeared to have a major influence on the decision whether or not to buy Supral. Among these particular factors were:

1   The potential user's own press-shop/toolroom facilities. Where under-utilised capacity exists manufacturers prefer to use their own facilities rather than buy in, even when buying in offers a piece price saving.
2   The amount of integration in the existing manufacturing process. The greater the integration, the greater the need for material compatibility. In other words, you don't mix steel with aluminium or plastic if you can avoid it.
3   The opportunity to buy in a completed 'bolt on' part will increase interest in cases where substantial hand finishing was necessary before.
4   When the prospective purchaser is developing a new product of his own then the low tooling costs on small runs would appear particularly attractive.
5   Single sourcing – a unique product is seen as much more risky than one available from a number of different competing sources.

Other incentives to early adoption included frequent design changes, the existence of formal value analysis programmes in user companies which substantiated the seller's claim of cost effectiveness (unfortunately these were not very common), and familiarity with similar materials and/or manufacturing technology. Conversely, a number of distinct barriers to adoption were also identified, including:

• Product design/specifications set by a non-UK holding company.
• Use of a performance specification to which all new materials must first conform, e.g. a British Standard (securing a rating often takes a long time for a unique new material).
• Commitment to the known and existing technology.
• The costs of evaluating and testing the new material.
• An existing commitment to suppliers through forward orders and/or investment in capital equipment.
• Ineffective senior management (resistance to change).

While the foregoing factors were specific to a decision as to whether or not to buy Supral, a number of them are felt to have more general application. However, the main point which we are trying to make here is that in any given buying decision it is not the facts themselves which are important but the potential buyer's perception of those facts. Because of selective perception the potential benefits of a new product may look very different to the would-be buyer than from its committed seller's point of view. A simple example of this would be the case where a machine tool manufacturer had introduced Mark II and Mark III versions of a particular tool, each of which offered a 10% increment in capacity over the preceding model. It follows that Mark III offers an increment in capacity of rather better than 20% for owners of the Mark I model, but only 10% for owners of the Mark II model. Thus, the benefits to be gained from purchase of a Mark III model are relative to the capacity and performance of the existing model which one owns and it is this which is most likely to influence the would-be purchaser rather than the absolute capacity rating of the machine.

One concept which is very helpful in assessing the likely saliency of a product to a potential user is to consider where it might be placed in that person's hierarchy of needs.

■ Hierarchy of Needs

Earlier in this chapter when discussing the Pavlovian and Freudian models of buying behaviour, we touched on the nature of drives and motives and their influence upon the individual's choice behaviour. Together, drives and motives are often called 'needs' and there is considerable evidence to support a theory put forward first by Abraham Maslow that needs can be classified into a simple five-step hierarchy as follows:

1 Physiological needs.
2 Safety needs.
3 Love needs.
4 Esteem needs.
5 Self-actualisation needs.

Usually people will seek to satisfy these needs in the order in which they appear in the hierarchy, such that physiological needs will normally take precedence over all others. For example, faced with death from hunger or thirst, the hunter would ignore safety needs and take extreme risks in order to kill an animal. However, once he has first satisfied his thirst and hunger he would then become aware of possible danger from other animals and begin to look for a safe refuge from them. Once the basic physiological and safety needs have been satisfied, the individual seeks to satisfy his need for affection and the feeling of belonging to a group – the so-called love needs. Many consumer products are promoted as having attributes which will enhance one's acceptance with the group, or occasionally are sold on the basis that lack of possession could lead to ostracism or exclusion from the group. Similarly, esteem needs are fertile ground for the marketer as they are concerned with factors such as recognition, status, prestige, etc., most of which can be inferred from an individual's possessions, mode of dress, etc.

The highest level of needs are concerned with self-actualisation or, in the modern idiom, doing one's own thing. People who have achieved this stage are likely to be immune to marketing techniques and have a very clear view of what it is they want and want to do. Indeed, the reason why we qualified the fact that physiological needs override all others is that individuals who are able to self-actualise can override such physiological needs in pursuit of their own higher objectives, e.g. the deaths of the hunger strikers in Northern Ireland.

The value of this basic concept of a hierarchy of needs lies in the fact that it can be used as a first coarse screen for classifying buyer motivations and thus indicate the general kinds of marketing techniques and practices which are likely to be effective. But, to see how to use these we must turn to the third conceptual framework known as the hierarchy of effects.

■ Hierarchy of Effects

The importance of studying buying behaviour is not so much for reasons of maintaining a historical record of what took place, but rather to obtain a better understanding of why such purchase decisions were made. Through such an analysis the marketer hopes that he will be able to determine some pointers which will enable him to predict how prospective buyers will act in future. Based upon past observation, most practitioners subscribe to the view that individuals pass through a number of stages in coming to a decision as to whether or not to buy an object. These stages are succinctly summarised in the salesman's mnemonic AIDA which stands for the four distinct phases of awareness, interest, desire and action. In the jargon of the behavioural sciences AIDA may be classified as a CAC model standing for cognitive, affective and conative or, in more general parlance, knowing, feeling and acting. Such models are also known as hierarchy of effects models in that they propose that a decision to act in a particular way is the consequence of a process which starts with recognition of a stimulus, evaluation of it and then a decision as to how to act upon that information. There is a considerable number of hierarchy of effects models and these are summarised in Table 7.1 reproduced below.

Table 7.1   Hierarchy-of-effects models

	Strong (AIDA)	Lavidge and Steiner	Rogers	Engel, Kollat and Blackwell
Conative (motive)	Action	Purchase Conviction	Adoption Trial	Purchase processes
Affective (emotion)	Desire Interest	Preference Liking	Evaluation Interest	Evaluation and search
Cognitive (thought)	Awareness	Knowledge Awareness	Awareness	Problem recognition
		Unawareness		

Table 7.1 is taken from my basic textbook, *Marketing*, in which the reader will find a much fuller description of the role of hierarchy of effects models. For our present purposes it is sufficient to emphasise that, depending upon one's definition of the various steps in the hierarchy, the model becomes tautological and self-fulfilling. Clearly, one cannot buy a product if one is unaware of its

existence and interest can only follow awareness, while desire can only develop out of interest. That said, hierarchy of effects models have been subjected to much criticism on the grounds that awareness, interest and desire may reflect attitudes towards an object but they do not necessarily imply action or behaviour with regard to those objects. None the less, if we accept the statistic cited earlier that selective perception screens out the vast majority of all marketing stimuli to which the individual is exposed, it would seem reasonable to set marketing objectives in terms of moving people along the hierarchy of effects. Thus, one might set as an objective of an advertising campaign, the achievement of a predetermined level of awareness in the population to whom the advertising message is to be directed. Similarly, once one has achieved a given level of awareness one could set objectives in terms of converting this awareness into interest in the sense that people could recall or play back claims made for the product in its advertising.

■ Post-purchase Dissonance

A fourth general concept of particular value to sellers is that associated with the buyer's feelings after the purchase decision has been made. As we saw earlier when discussing the Pavlovian learning model of consumer behaviour, we identified four concepts of drive, cue, response and reinforcement. In a marketing context purchase is the desired response and the importance of the concept of dissonance is that it describes the purchaser's state of mind after the decision has been taken.

By definition dissonance is the opposite state to consonance by which we understand the individual's effort to organise perceived stimuli into coherent and consistent patterns which are in accord with our knowledge, beliefs and attitudes. It follows that if when considering a particular choice/decision one perceives stimuli which are not consistent with our view of the world, then we are likely to reject that object because it creates dissonance. The need to achieve consonancy between a product and its intended purchaser is so obvious as not to require further discussion here. However, the importance of recent work on dissonance following Leon Festinger's publication of his *Theory of Cognitive Dissonance*[12] has been recognition of the fact that the act of purchase itself may create some uncertainty in the mind of the buyer, who will then seek reassurance that he has made the correct decision. Because of this uncertainty and the need to *reinforce* the buyer in his belief that he has made the correct decision, the importance of the role which after-sales service has to play is emphasised. Thus, research has shown that perception and readership of advertisements relating to products is highest among persons who have just purchased such a product, who would appear to be seeking reinforcement of the correctness of their original decision. Thus, in today's highly competitive markets it is vital that marketers 'follow through' on every purchase and not regard the transaction as finished once the buyer has taken possession of the object.

■ Buy Phases

A fifth concept of considerable practical utility to the marketer is the analytical framework proposed by Robinson, Faris and Wind in their book *Industrial Buying and Creative Marketing*.[13] Although, as the title of the book suggests, this model was developed as a result of research into buying behaviour in industrial companies, it is felt that the framework is of equal value in analysing buying decisions by individuals or small groups.

The analytic framework developed by Robinson, Faris and Wind is based upon two simple classificatory systems – buy phases and buy classes. As can be seen from Table 7.2 there are eight buy phases and three buy classes. The eight buy phases are a slightly extended version of the problem-solving sequence discussed earlier and do not merit any further explanation. Similarly, the buy classes' classification is self-explanatory and reflects the complexity and perceived risk experienced by the prospective buyer when considering a specific purchase. Thus, in the case of a new task, by definition the buyer has not previously evaluated the particular product in question and will have to be moved from a stage of unawareness through to a decision with careful attention to each of the phases, 1 to 6 shown in Table 7.2. In the case of a modified rebuy it is assumed that the

Table 7.2   The buy-grid analytic framework for industrial buying situations

	Buy classes		
Buy phases	New task	Modified rebuy	Straight rebuy
1. Anticipation or recognition of a problem (need) and a general solution			
2. Determination of characteristics and quantity of needed item			
3. Description of characteristics and quantity of needed item			
4. Search for and qualification of potential sources			
5. Acquisition and analysis of proposals			
6. Evaluation of proposals and selection of supplier(s)			
7. Selection of an order routine			
8. Performance feedback and evaluation			

Source: Redrawn from Patrick J. Robinson, Charles W. Faris and Yoram Wind, *Industrial Buying and Creative Marketing* (Boston: Allyn & Bacon, 1967) p. 14.

buyer has previous experience of products of the general category which he is now considering but, whether because of dissatisfaction with a previous purchase, or recognition of improvement in the product since he last purchased it, he wishes to re-evaluate what is available in the market-place. In such a situation the first three buy phases may be skipped over and the process really commence at phase 4. Finally, in the case of a straight rebuy, the purchaser has direct knowledge of the product in question which he has purchased previously from a given source of supply with which he is satisfied. Accordingly, only phases 1 and 7 of the buy phases may be required when placing a reorder for that product.

A major factor influencing the amount of time and effort which will be put into evaluating a potential purchase will depend very much upon the nature of the product itself. Bearing in mind that prospective purchasers will be likely to perceive products differently, i.e. one man's convenience good may be another's shopping or specialty good, it will be helpful to isolate some attributes which will help us to classify how potential purchasers may see a given product.

■ Characteristics of Goods

While many writers have proposed schemata for classifying goods, one of the most well known is that put forward by Leo Aspinwall in 1958,[14] in which he suggested that five product characteristics be used to help decide on the most effective marketing strategy for a product. These are:

1   The replacement rate: the rate at which a good is purchased and consumed by users in order to provide the satisfaction a consumer expects from the product.
2   Gross margin: the difference between the paid in cost and the final realised sales price.
3   Adjustment: the amount of services applied to goods in order to meet the exact needs of the consumer.
4   Time of consumption: the measured time of consumption during which the goods give up the utilities desired.
5   Searching time: the measure of average time and distance from the retail store.

As the last item indicates, Aspinwall was primarily concerned with consumer goods, but it is believed that the general approach is equally relevant to industrial goods.

Aspinwall went on to propose that one could develop a scoring system for each of the five product characteristics and so classify them into broad categories. In his own analysis Aspinwall used three colours to designate three categories of goods, red, orange and yellow, as follows:

Red goods: goods with a high replacement rate and a low gross margin adjustment, time of consumption, and searching time.
Orange goods: goods with a medium score on all five characteristics.
Yellow goods: goods with a low replacement rate and high gross margin,

adjustment, time of consumption, and searching time.

Clearly these three definitions correspond very closely to the distinction between convenience goods, shopping goods and specialty goods in the consumer behaviour literature, and straight rebuy, modified rebuy and new task categories proposed by Robinson *et al*.[15]

■ Buyer Behaviour and the Decision-maker

The foregoing review of four generalised models of buyer behaviour and six key concepts has made it abundantly clear that there is no single simple and easy way in which to predict how potential buyers will act in any given situation. In fact, quite the opposite impression may have been given, namely that buying decisions are complex, dynamic, based upon multiple factors and downright messy to the extent that the theorising of academics merely serves to add to the confusion rather than clarify it. It would be a great pity if this was seen to be the case. As we noted at the beginning of this chapter, its content is eclectic and reflects the idiosyncrasies of the author. Thus, our purpose has not been to present a comprehensive review of buyer behaviour as this goes far beyond the scope of a book of this type. Rather, our objective has been to select a sample of ideas from the literature which seem to provide useful pointers to the ways in which decision-makers can structure their own analysis and thereby arrive at better decisions more often.

Two more things at least need to be stressed. First, the great majority of theoretical work reported here is based on empirical research into the way in which people behave in the real world. If there is bad theory then it is likely that it reflects bad practice, although occasionally it may result from misinterpretation by the researcher. Similarly, if researchers propose what they see as good theory based upon the observed procedures and practices in successful organisations, then failure to conform with such practices and procedures can only be justified after the most thorough of examinations and the identification of unique factors which distinguish the normative recommendation from the reality facing a particular individual or company.

The second important observation to be made upon this chapter is that it is to be hoped that it has indicated to the reader the enormous wealth of ideas and insights which are available to the practitioner to enable him to perform his task better. In exploring this literature one must beware of the trap of only using those ideas which confirm one's own existing prejudices (selective perception is rearing its ugly head again!). Some models and generalisations are much more robust than others and should only be set aside after very careful consideration by the decision-maker. Conversely there are fads and fashions in management thinking as in any other area of activity and equal care must be taken in accepting fashionable new ideas in the absence of strong evidence to support their suitability.

In the final analysis, every decision-maker has to work out that *modus operandi* which is best suited to himself. Experimentation is to be encouraged and practitioners should not leave all the theorising to the academics. Rather, they should seek to develop their own 'currently useful generalisations' as a basis for practice. To this end in the final section of this chapter I present my own so-called model of buyer behaviour. In doing so I am conscious of the fact that some of my fellow academics do not consider this to satisfy the criteria which theorists require of a model. That said, I, and a fairly extensive number of companies – large, medium and small, in growing and declining industries, with high, medium and low technologies – have found this model to be very helpful in organising their thinking about how buyers do choose and how they may develop effective marketing strategies to reflect this behaviour.

■ The Baker Composite Model

■ Notation

The current version of the model may be expressed notationally as follows:

$$P = f[SP(PC, EC, IS, PF, CB, BR)]$$

- P = purchase
- f = a function (unspecified) of
- SP = selective perception
- PC = precipitating circumstances
- EC = enabling conditions
- IS = information search
- PF = performance factors
- CB = cost-benefit
- BR = behavioural response

The first point to be made is that this is a sequential process model very similar to the Buying Decision Process model introduced at p. 176. *PC* is equivalent to problem recognition, *EC* to *interest* (i.e. the problem is accepted as a real one deserving further consideration), *IS*, a new variable corresponds to information search and recognises that if a review of the enabling conditions confirms a continuing interest then one will have to gather additional information on which to make a decision. *PF* and *CB* summarise the objective data concerning performance or 'fitness for purpose' and the economic benefits of acquisition and comprise the 'rational' elements of evaluation. *BR* is a surrogate for the subjective and judgemental factors which will invariably be taken into account when a prospective buyer has more than a Buy–Don't Buy choice, i.e. there are two or more objectively similar products or services which would solve the prospective buyer's consumption problem which initiated the process. Thus *BR* is a composite of one's prior experience and attitudes which may or may not include direct post-purchase experience of the object under consideration.

Second, the precise nature of the function is not specified for the simple reason that it is not known and that it is unlikely, to say the least, that any single functional form could capture the interaction between the other variables in the model.

SP or selective perception is a new variable in the model. In earlier versions the influence of this factor was subsumed within *BR*, which occurs at the end of the process. By placing *SP* at the beginning as a factor mediating the other variables it is possible to communicate that this is a process model and that selective perception will determine whether or not one will even become aware of a purchase opportunity (*EC*) besides conditioning the information selected for evaluation and the interpretation placed upon it.

Finally, the behavioural response may be almost automatic, as, for example, when the preceding evaluation indicates that one option is clearly to be preferred. Alternatively, it may be an extremely difficult and protracted stage when the preceding analysis has failed to suggest one choice before all others – a common occurrence in many markets.

Having described the general model, some elaboration of the variables will indicate what sort of factors one would need to take into account to use it.

In the Pavlovian learning model of buyer behaviour reference is made to the need for some cue or stimulus to activate a drive and initiate action. In our model this factor is termed a 'precipitating circumstance' – what is it that would make a buyer consider a change in the status quo? Clearly, dissatisfaction with existing alternatives constitutes a marketing opportunity, and is one type of precipitating factor. The need to replace or renew a piece of capital equipment or consumer durable is another opportunity, whether the need is caused by breakdown, loss, destruction or a planned replacement policy. Knowing which customers might be in this state would enable the firm to focus its marketing effort to much greater effect, both in terms of the information to be conveyed and the means of conveying it. Similarly, being able to satisfy a known need – we have a faster computer, a more economical car and so forth – is a claim likely to precipitate active consideration of a new purchase.

'Enabling conditions' embraces all those factors which make it possible for a prospective purchaser to benefit from the new product. A television is no use if you have no electricity, nor a gas oven if you have no gas. In the same way, many manufacturers try to avoid mixing materials such as steel, aluminium and plastics, since each requires different skills and techniques in use and increases the investment necessary in both plant and labour. In other words, a new product must be compatible with the user's current status and, in many cases also with their self-image. In the absence of such enabling conditions, interest is likely to be short-lived and unlikely to proceed further to an evaluation.

Technology or performance and the economics or cost-benefit of a purchase are at the very heart of the Marshallian and 'rational' schools of buying behaviour's models – *PF* and *CB* in our model. We have chosen to specify the advantages and disadvantages separately, partly because people do weigh up the pros and cons of courses of action, and partly because, if one is going to use the model, then one should specify as fully as possible what the merits and demerits are, weight these if necessary and only then come up with an overall judgement as to how the new product measures up against the competition.

Some broad guidelines as to the relative importance of different features which go to make up an effective selling proposition in industrial markets generally are shown for machine tools in particular in Table 7.3 and more generally in Figure 7.1. But, while these offer an indication of the relative importance of groups of features, it must always be remembered that the majority of buying decisions turn on highly specific characteristics – another reason why a general model cannot possibly accommodate all conceivable sets of circumstances.

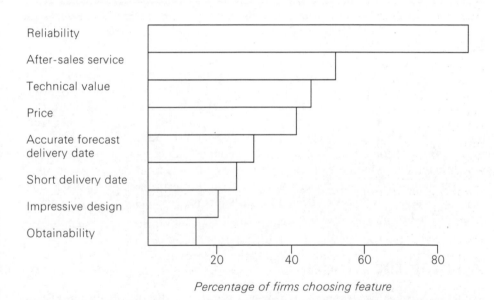

Percentage of firms choosing feature

Figure 7.1 **Features of a machine tool considered one of the three most important**

We have already stipulated that the importance of behavioural response will depend heavily upon the objective evaluation of the available facts (albeit that these are perceived subjectively), and build a better product at an equivalent price or an equivalent product at a lower price' is clearly the best advice to management. But, in most competitive markets, there is often little to choose objectively between alternative offerings, and the buyer will have to make

Table 7.3   Features for effective selling in machine-tool markets

Q. Reviewing the last five years, what factors or reasons appear to discriminate most between success and failure with new products?

	Total *62* *(%)*	*F&D* *34* *(%)*	*Others* *28* *(%)*
Product quality	53	65	39
Uniqueness of product	44	41	47
Level of trade acceptance	39	44	32
Level of advertising investment	36	35	36
Level of distribution achieved	32	35	29
Price	31	38	21
Company commitment	24	24	25
Sales force motivation	23	29	14

Source: R. Artingstall in *New Product Development*, Supplement to *Market Research Society Newsletter*, 168 (March 1980).
Note: The sample comprises '62 major UK manufacturers'.

deliberate recourse to subjective value judgements to assist in distinguishing between the various items available. Because housewives do this daily when preferring Daz to Omo, Sunblest to Mother's Pride and so on and so forth, they are often characterised as choosing irrationally. Nothing could be further from the truth. The important objective decisions about a shopping basket relate to its overall mix and composition *vis-à-vis* the available budget – the choice decision is which detergent, which bread and so on. It would be a fatal mistake to imagine that the industrial buyer doesn't have just the same problems when deciding between Scania, Mercedes or Leyland for his lorries, or Cincinnati or Kearney & Trecker for his machine tools.

■ Using the Model

Much of *Market Development* is taken up with the discussion of actual case histories of the launch and market development of new products and their subsequent success or failure. Where appropriate, the cases are followed by a brief analysis pointing out how the model provides an analytical framework which helps to explain the eventual outcome on the premise that, if this is possible *a posteriori*, then use of the model *a priori* is likely to improve overall success rates in new product development. However, it will be helpful here to provide a broad statement of how to apply the model.

At the outset it must be recognised that in no way does the model contradict the normative approach to market research and market segmentation which is described fully in almost every basic marketing text. Rather it should be seen as reinforcing and amplifying standardised techniques for the identification and measurement of potential demand – indeed, it would not be too extravagant a claim to assert that our analytical framework seeks to emphasise the marketing dimensions of marketing research in that it attempts to address the problem from the perspective of prospective buyers rather than from the standpoint of the seller. That said, it should be clear from our brief statement of the nature of enabling conditions (EC) that this factor seeks to establish a *prima facie* case of primary demand such that EC will describe the maximum potential market for any new product. Thus the existence of EC will define all those individuals or organisations which could conceivably have a use for our new product, more often than not by a process of exclusion rather than of inclusion. Thus, for example, our primary demand specification for baby products would be likely to use the birth rate as a basic parameter in establishing potential market size – being or having a baby constituting a basic qualifying criterion for the existence of EC. (Of course, as we all now know from the example of Johnson & Johnson, to confine the use of baby products to babies actually constrains the potential market since items such as powder and shampoo are widely used by adults. But, if one is launching a new baby product such as nappy liners, it would seem sensible, at least until the product has become established, to regard babies as the primary demand for the product.)

Thus EC is a necessary but not sufficient condition for defining the potential market for a product and constitutes the first crude cut at isolating a group of potential users for a more detailed analysis – for example, the use of two-digit SIC codes. Yet as we have argued earlier, such a basic definition of a target market leaves a great deal to be desired, for it lacks focus and would undoubtedly lead to the dissipation and waste of a great deal of marketing effort. The whole thrust of our approach is to try and identify the most receptive sub-set or segment within the potential market as the target for our initial marketing development work.

To provide a more selective focus, we suggest that one should seek to isolate some cue or stimulus which would have the effect of converting an essentially latent primary demand into an active recognition of the possible means of satisfying a felt need. For firms already operating in a market, for whom a new product frequently represents a product line extension, such identification of a precipitating circumstance (PC) should present much less difficulty than is the case with a firm which has no previous experience of or contact with a potential market. None the less there is considerable evidence to suggest that sellers frequently make inadequate or no use of information available to them through their continuing relationship with present customers, and/or frequently mis-interpret such information as is available to them – the age of the existing stock or holding of a product, for example, which the innovation seeks to replace or substitute for. Perhaps the most obvious yet most frequently committed error, however, is to concentrate early marketing efforts upon the largest potential customers, presumably following the logic that they have most to gain and that by securing orders from them one will stand the best chance of achieving one's initial sales targets. There is considerable evidence, some of it recorded in cases reported in *Market Development*, to suggest that the alternative hypothesis, that small companies are most likely to adopt first, has much to commend it.

In discussing this 'strategy of the indirect approach' in my earlier analysis, I advanced the following arguments in favour of this proposition.

On the assumption that any new product which aspires to success must possess advantages over that which it seeks to replace, then it seems to me that this advantage is potentially of much greater significance to the small rather than the large user. For the large firm, the incentive to increase its share of market is limited. First, there is the possibility that an increase in market share might attract the unwelcome attentions of the Monopolies Commission or its foreign equivalent. Secondly, as any marked increase in market share must be at the expense of major competitors, there is a strong likelihood that any effort to achieve such an increase would result in aggressive retaliation by these competitors, probably to the detriment of all concerned. Thirdly, there may be strong grounds for adopting a 'wait and see' attitude ('anticipatory retardation' in Fellner's terminology), owing to the belief that the present innovation may itself soon be made obsolete by further improvements. Fourthly, there is a marked trend to pursue the 'strategy of the fast second' as described, *inter alia*, by Levitt in his 'Innovative Imitation'. For these reasons alone, many large firms may well adopt a 'don't rock the boat' attitude towards those markets in which they already have a major share, on the grounds that, by disturbing the existing equilibrium, they are much more likely to lose than gain.

For the small firm, with a market share measured as a fraction of 1%, the situation is very different. Assume that such a firm were offered a new raw material with superior properties and a lower or equivalent cost to one of its major inputs. By adopting this new material, the small firm could, in turn, offer end users a superior product at a lower or equivalent price to the inferior substitute which it seeks to replace. Other things being equal, economic rationality predicates that end users will prefer the new product and transfer their demand to its supplier, thereby increasing the latter's market share. If it is assumed that the small firm originally had a 0.25% market share, then it is clear that, even were it to increase this fourfold to 1%, it could only reduce a major supplier's share by 0.75% of the total market. The significance of such a reduction would vary dependent upon the loser's prior market share as indicated in Table 7.4. Of course, the smaller the large firm's present market share, the less likely it becomes that the small firm's gain would be entirely at its expense.

If the foregoing assumptions are correct, then it follows that the small firm has a much greater incentive to adopt than does the large firm. Ignoring for the present the question of variation between small firms in terms of their receptivity to innovation, it has already been established that time to first adoption is a critical determinant of the speed and extent of the overall diffusion process. Once an innovator has secured a successful first adoption, he may use this fact to substantiate his claims as to the value of the innovation in a far more convincing manner than is possible with purely theoretical or 'trial' data. Even though the

Table 7.4   **Impact of loss of 0.75% of total market share on various levels of existing market share.**

Present market share	Reduction in sales volume occasioned by loss of 0.75% of total market
10	−7.50
15	−5.00
20	−3.75
25	−3.00
30	−2.50

small firm's increased share of the market may be insufficient to stimulate the market leaders to adopt the innovation, it may none the less be impressive enough to encourage other small firms to emulate its achievement, giving rise to the so-called 'bandwagon' or 'contagion' effect which underlies exponential growth. Clearly, if this occurs, the cumulative effect of several small firms securing an increased share of market will eventually result in the market leaders suffering a sufficient loss to prompt retaliatory action and so accelerate adoption even further.

Of course, in most markets one is still faced with large numbers of prospective customers, and it is here that the evaluation of the perceived benefits of adoption (technical and economic) will lay considerable weight upon careful and thorough analysis of both the status and needs of likely users. Any standard text on market research will provide a comprehensive review of the techniques available to accomplish this, and only two comments seem appropriate here.

The first is to emphasise yet again that the important, indeed critical thing is to try and look at the 'facts' from the standpoint of the possible buyer; and the second is to underline the value of actually asking the prospective customer for his views. Many sellers appear to be reluctant to attempt a direct approach to customers under the misguided impression that they will not cooperate. My own experience as a salesman, market researcher and consultant is directly contrary to this view since I have always found that buyers are just as anxious to secure information about possible sources of supply as sellers about sources of demand. I have also found that people and companies which have considered purchasing a new product and rejected the idea are very willing to tell you why and are usually much more objective than are actual purchasers seeking to rationalise their behaviour in terms of what they think you want to hear. The message is quite clear: a direct, personal approach to potential customers is likely to pay handsome dividends in defining precisely what they want.

Finally, we return to the influence of behavioural response, which may best be described as conscious selective perception, for whereas selective perception will have conditioned the prospective buyer's view of all the preceding variables, factual or not, its influence will have been largely subconscious, and behavioural response (BR) only assumes any importance when an 'objective' techno-economic analysis still leaves more than one alternative from which to choose. In these circumstances, the would-be buyer recognizes that subjective and qualitative factors have a contribution to make and consciously invokes them. It is for this reason that we argue that marketing has a double role to play, for not only can it influence perception in terms of creating attention, stimulating interest and helping to determine what 'facts' are evaluated, but, in a multiple choice situation, it can prove to be the determinant factor which results in a decision to buy rather than reject or defer purchase.

Ways in which marketing can achieve this discriminating role are manifold and often highly situation-specific, but a few examples will help make the point.

Consider the husband and wife trying to select a consumer durable such as a cooker, fridge or video recorder – the retail outlet has a wide variety on offer and those of comparable size/performance tend to have very similar prices. It is here that personal influence can help to tip the balance, but how many manufacturers offer to help train retail store assistants or otherwise influence them to put their weight behind their particular product? Similarly, how many manufacturers provide an adequate after-sales service to ensure satisfaction and predispose the buyer to repeat purchase when the need comes to replace a durable; or, equally important, try to communicate that, while you shouldn't need service and hope not to collect on your fire or health insurance, if you do it will be forthcoming willingly, speedily and without hassle?

In industrial markets, as we have already suggested, small firms are more often quicker to adopt than large, and because such innovation decisions are proportionately more important to them than is a similar decision in a large firm, where a first purchase may be no more than a trial, they are also more likely to commit themselves fully to making the innovation succeed. But for many small firms cash and technical expertise contribute major barriers to innovation, and it would seem reasonable to propose that sellers should seek to 'normalise' the financial implications by offering a package which makes it possible for the small customer to invest in innovation – after all, if it is going to improve his performance as significantly as you claim, should you not be willing to defer or spread payment until these cash flows are forthcoming? Similarly, technical advice both prior to sale and after installation will enable the seller to ensure that his product is used as intended, will provide information on performance in normal working environments (as opposed to prototypes in laboratories) which may be used for modification and improvement, and give the necessary reassurance to the buyer who might otherwise be put off by the sophistication of the technology. Training operatives also helps to achieve these objectives. In other words, marketing can help to reduce or 'eliminate' key factors in the decision process.

Marketing is essentially a dynamic and creative activity, and it is for these reasons that it is often difficult to prescribe appropriate courses of action. Each situation calls for its own analysis and for an original solution, albeit that the latter may be heavily influenced by either direct or vicarious (reading a book?) experience. It is in this spirit that the model is offered as a framework for structuring one's own analysis and decision making.

■ Summary

Chapter 7 has comprised a very eclectic review of some of the major factors which influence buyer behaviour. The reader should be aware that there are many textbooks which deal with this subject and that most of these make a distinction between *consumer behaviour* (i.e. how individuals make choice decisions) and *organisational buyer behaviour* (OBB). However, based upon a review of the major influences which bear upon choice decisions, we have chosen to propose that all such decisions contain the same elements and follow the same sequence.

Central to our composite model is the view that some cue or stimulus is needed to make a buyer (individual or corporate) aware of a need and so initiate consideration of possible means of satisfying that need. In the process the information considered will be interpreted in the light of the reviewer's own knowledge and experience and the attitudes which have developed out of them. For this reason sellers must seek to establish the precise nature of their intended customers' needs so that they can devise products and/or services which will match these as closely as possible and, also, to enable them to communicate this information effectively to their intended audience.

To achieve this matching process intending sellers need guidance to help them pre-identify those potential buyers who may be prepared to consider their offering. In Chapters 8 and 9 we consider some of the techniques and procedures which have been devised to help disaggregate demand into meaningful market segments and enable the seller to position his product so that it will, at least, attract the intended buyer's attention.

CHAPTER 8
Market Segmentation

Learning Goals

The issues to be addressed in Chapter 8 include:

1 The differences between *product differentiation* and *market segmentation* as alternative competitive strategies.
2 Possible *bases* for *segmenting markets*.
3 *Procedures and methods* for *segmenting markets*.
4 Deciding *when to segment a market*.

After reading Chapter 8 you will be able to:

1 Distinguish between *product differentiation* and *market segmentation* as alternative strategies.
2 Suggest appropriate *ways* for segmenting markets.
3 Define and describe four basic *approaches* – *a priori*, clustering, flexible and componential.
4 Discuss the major *segmentation variables* grouped into four major categories:
   ● Geographic or Location.
   ● Demographic.
   ● Psychographic.
   ● Behaviouristic – Usage.
                  – Benefit.
5 Describe factors to be taken into account when segmenting *industrial markets*.
6 Indicate when it is *appropriate* to segment markets.

Introduction

Chapters 1–7 have been concerned largely with establishing a broadly based strategic overview of marketing and with setting out some of the features which distinguish individual (consumer) and collective (market) behaviour and so provide the framework within which specific marketing decisions must be made. It is timely now to turn from such a comprehensive, and some would argue over-generalised, perspective and begin to narrow the focus on these

188

marketing decisions *per se*. A central and fundamental concept of marketing which provides a bridge between the general and particular, the theoretical and the real world is the notion of *segmentation*.

In Chapter 8 we look, first, at the difference between product differentiation and market segmentation as alternative competitive strategies by which the producer seeks to establish dominance over a subset or subsets of the total market. Next we review a number of different approaches to segmentation each of which would seem to offer particular benefits under given conditions and circumstances.

Such a review leads naturally to consideration of the procedures to be followed in segmenting markets and the various methods available. Here the treatment is concerned with the 'what' and the 'why' rather than 'how' and is intended to provide the decision-maker with an overview of the policy implications of market segmentation rather than a technical description of how to execute a segmentation study which is a subject in its own right.

Product Differentiation vs Market Segmentation

As we have seen, dissatisfaction with the classical economists' explanations of the interaction of supply and demand in the market-place led to the formulation of the theory of imperfect competition in the early 1930s by Joan Robinson and Edwin Chamberlin. It was these theories which were to provide the necessary underpinnings for the statement of the concept of market segmentation by Wendell Smith[1] in 1956 in which he noted that 'diversity or heterogeneity had come to be the rule rather than the exception'. It was recognition of the existence of this heterogeneity in the demand for goods and services which led to the disaggregation of the traditional single demand schedule and acceptance in its place of several separate demand schedules, each of which offers the opportunity to develop products specifically for that sub market or segment. This is not to suggest that suppliers had not previously appreciated thet potential of product differentiation as of course they had. Indeed, the development of imperfect competition is largely attributable to the attempts of the supply side of the market to avoid or minimise the competitive strait-jacket implicit in the production and sale of homogeneous products. The distinction between product differentiation and market segmentation, first made by Smith, is that while the former is supply led (a production orientation) the latter is demand led and so constitutes a marketing orientation, i.e. the product is developed in full recognition and knowledge of the prospective users' needs.

Ultimately each individual consumer might properly be regarded as a distinct market segment in his or her own right, but, with very rare exceptions, such an approach is unrealistic as the costs involved would undoubtedly exceed the potential users' willingness or ability to pay. Thus, market segmentation offers a useful compromise between the extreme approach of both the economist and the behavioural scientist which is readily apparent in Figure 8.1 taken from Enis.[2]

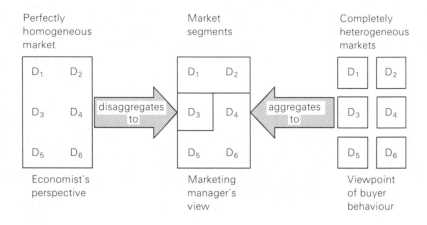

Figure 8.1   Alternative perspectives of the total market

Source: B. M. Enis, *Marketing Principles* (Santa Monica, Calif.: Goodyear, 1977) 3rd edn.

Enis's diagram is particularly useful in clarifying the two 'prototypical research patterns' of real-world segmentation studies distinguished by Wind[3] in a masterly review of the subject, namely:

1   *An* a priori *segmentation design* in which management decides on a basis for segmentation such as product purchase, loyalty, customer type, or other factor. The survey results show the segments' estimated size and their demographic, socioeconomic, psychographic and other relevant character-istics.
2   *A clustering-based segmentation design* in which segments are determined on the basis of a clustering of respondents on a set of 'relevant' variables. Benefit, need, and attitude segmentation are examples of this type of approach. As in *a priori* segmentation studies, the size and other characteristics (demographic, socio-economic, purchase and the like) of the segments are estimated.

Figure 8.1 also makes it clear that the central viewpoint is that of the marketing manager, and it is his responsibility to select the most appropriate basis for defining his target market or markets. Only if this is accomplished effectively will it be possible to design a marketing plan which will maximise the firm's potential. Much of the remainder of this chapter is concerned with examining ways and means of achieving this desired result. However, before looking at some of the bases for segmenting markets and describing some of the available procedures and techniques, it is important to acknowledge that while the majority of marketers are in favour of segmentation there is still a minority who are against it to some extent.

Bliss[4] believes that much dissatisfaction with segmentation as a concept is due to the fact that it is inapplicable in many markets and also because too much emphasis is given to techniques to the neglect of the market itself and the competitive situation within it. Similarly, Resnik, Turney and Mason[5] argue that the soaring costs of products and services, changing values and life-styles call for the opposite approach which they designate 'countersegmentation'. In that Resnik *et al.* appear to have been arguing for larger segments rather than total homogeneity their criticisms may be seen largely as a reaction to the difficult economic climate of the late 1970s and early 1980s with its consequent sharpening of a concern for value for money.

Overall however, segmentation seems to offer more benefits than disadvantages and, in that it can be undertaken to almost any degree of refinement and sophistication, is appropriate to theorist and pragmatist alike.

■ Bases for Segmentation

As Wind[6] notes, the development of a segmentation model requires one to specify a dependent variable which is the basis for segmentation, e.g. usage or time of adoption, and a set of independent variables or 'descriptors' which define the specific segments, e.g. age, occupation, etc. He continues to observe that 'over the years almost all variables have been used as bases for market segmentation' and any superficial review of segmentation studies would readily confirm this to be so. To a large extent the plethora of factors used to define market segments reflects the difficulty of putting the normative theory of marketing segmentation into practice, i.e. the normative theory as proposed by Smith is *proactive* in that one should use knowledge of consumer characteristics to develop a marketing strategy whereas most marketing managers who use segmentation studies do so *reactively* in that they seek to determine the response of different market segments to their marketing strategy. Obviously such information will be used to modify and improve the proposed strategy but a purist would argue that the managerial approach is more closely akin to product differentiation than a normative approach to marketing segmentation.

Perhaps the real difference lies in the time horizon with which the manager is concerned. As we noted earlier (and doubtless will comment on again) a fully fledged theory of marketing needs to recognise the very real constraints which the firm faces in the short term which may be insignificant or unimportant when one takes a long-term view. The difference is perfectly reflected in the cost accountant's distinction between variable and fixed costs and the recognition that in the long term *all* costs are variable, i.e. one can modify one's asset base and change the objectives and direction of the organisation. Thus, in the short term one must sell what one can make and the best way to increase effectiveness and improve performance is to ensure that the product is targeted at those prospective users who can be identified as having a need profile most consistent with the product's performance.

In an ideal world, however, all new product development would stem from a clear identification of a market need. But, as any practising marketing manager would quickly tell you, the major difficulty with following such a counsel of perfection is that few consumers or users are able to specify precisely and in advance just what it is they would like, although they usually have an unerring facility to reject what they don't like once they have seen it. Given such a state of affairs, it may often prove more economical to pursue a trial-and-error approach to new product development, especially where this is of an incremental kind, and let consumers identify themselves though usage rather than expend large amounts on ineffective research. Wind appears to recognise this dilemma when he comments:

> In contrast to the theory of segmentation that implies that there is a *single best* way of segmenting a market, the range and variety of marketing decisions suggest that any attempt to use a single basis for segmentation (such as psychographic, brand preference, or product usage) for *all* marketing decisions may result in incorrect marketing decisions as well as a waste of resources.[7]

So what should the manager do? Wind provides an excellent guide when he tabulates his own preferred bases for segmentation as follows:

For general understanding of a market:
- Benefits sought (in industrial markets, the criterion used is purchase decision).
- Product purchase and usage patterns.
- Needs.
- Brand loyalty and switching pattern.
- A hybrid of the variables above.

For positioning studies.
- Product usage.
- Product preference.
- Benefits sought.
- A hybrid of the variables above.

For new product concepts (and new product introduction).
- Reaction to new concepts (intention to buy, preference over current brand, etc.).
- Benefits sought.

For pricing decisions.
- Price sensitivity.
- Deal proneness.
- Price sensitivity by purchase/usage patterns.

For advertising decisions.
- Benefits sought.
- Media usage.
- Psychographic/life-style.
- A hybrid (of the variables above and/or purchase/usage patterns).

For distribution decisions.
- Store loyalty and patronage.
- Benefits sought in store selection.

The common thread which links all these bases for segmentation is that they focus on the prospective buyer's response to marketing stimuli which is precisely what the manager needs to know when formulating an action plan.

Unfortunately, as hinted earlier, there is no similar consensus about which descriptors will be most useful in helping to define segments in a particular market using one or other of these bases. Wind cites four reasons for this state of affairs which, in my own view, characterise most research in marketing and explain much of the suspicion which exists between academic and practitioner. These four factors are:

1   Lack of a systematic effort (by both academicians and practitioners) to build a *cumulative* body of substantive findings about consumer behaviour.
2   Lack of specific models which link behaviour (and other bases for segmentation) to description variables and thus *predict* which description variables should be used.
3   The non-representative nature of most of the academic studies with respect to sample design (e.g. small, convenient samples), type of respondents (e.g. students) and tasks (e.g. non-marketing-related tasks). Even many of the real-world segmentation studies are based on relatively small and non-representative samples.
4   Lack of comparable conceptual and operational definitions of variables across studies.

Due to these limitations Wind argues that one should regard the literature as a source of hypotheses concerning which variables might be more appropriate in any given situation and provides a useful listing of such hypotheses.

Much of my own research has been concerned with attempting to define innovators for new products on the perhaps simplistic assumption that the diffusion or acceptance of an innovation is functionally related to the speed of the first adoption such that if one can pre-identify early adoptors one will accelerate the acceptance of the new product or process and thereby enhance its prospects of success (or reduce the expense of failure by recognising it sooner!). This research has now covered a period of over twenty years and while I agree with Wind's four factors I am more optimistic than he appears to be in that I think it possible to provide operationally useful models, such as that relating to buyer behaviour in the last chapter, in which certain key variables will have general application although fine tuning the model to a particular product market situation will require the use of situation-specific variables. Further, while I think the literature might provide a useful 'prompt' for the practitioner I consider that the most fruitful source of situation-specific descriptor variables is likely to be the decision-maker's own experience.

■ Procedure and Methods

We have already noted two basic procedures for segmenting markets, namely *a priori* and *clustering*, to which Wind adds two other procedures .which he describes as *flexible* and *componential*. A brief description of these procedures will be given prior to a review of the major segmentation methods which are found in common use.

It would be difficult to improve on Wind's definition of *a priori* segmentation which is a model of clarity and brevity, namely:

> A priori *segmentation models* have had as dependent variable (the basis for segmentation) either product specific variables (e.g. product usage, loyalty) or general customer characteristics (e.g. demographic factors). The typical research design for an *a priori* segmentation model involves seven stages:
>
> 1 Selection of the (*a priori*) basis for segmentation.
> 2 Selection of a set of segment descriptors (including hypotheses on the possible link between these descriptors and the basis for segmentation).
> 3 Sample design – mostly stratified and occasionally a quota sample according to the various classes of the dependent variable.
> 4 Data collection.
> 5 Formation of the segments on a sorting of respondents into categories.
> 6 Establishment of the (conditional) profile of the segments using multiple discriminant analysis, multiple regression analysis, or some other appropriate analytical procedure.
> 7 Translation of the findings about the segments' estimated size and profile into specific marketing strategies, including the selection of target segments and the design or modification of specific marketing strategy.[8]

In practice market segmentation addresses three technical market research problems:

- To construct a spatial representation of consumers' perceptions of products or brands in a category,
- To position consumers' ideal points in the same space and so estimate consumer demand for a product located at any particular point,
- To construct a model which predicts preferences of groups of customers toward new or modified products.

Frequently, it will prove helpful to plot product offerings and/or consumers' perceptions of them on a perceptual map, as shown in Figure 8.2, which illustrates the needs of different end-users[9] for hi-fi equipment in terms of two key dimensions – performance and economy. From such a map it becomes possible to identify the appropriate product configuration and marketing mix for each segment as well as the possible existence of 'gaps' in the market.

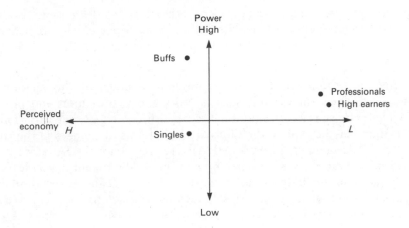

Figure 8.2   Perceptual map

In the case of clustering or *post hoc* segmentation the only significant difference is that the segments are determined after the data have been collected on the basis of perceived groupings or clusters within the data. Frequently such clusters will be determined through the use of factor analysis whereby variables will be grouped on the basis of their correlation with each other (and their lack of correlation with variables included in other factors) and the amount of variance in the dependent variable which they are able to 'explain'.

Flexible segmentation is a dynamic procedure in which conjoint analysis (see below) is combined with a simulation model to allow managers to explore a large number of alternative approaches to segmenting a particular market.

Finally, the componential procedure developed by Green *et al.*[10] is an extension of conjoint analysis and 'shifts the emphasis of the segmentation model from the partitioning of a market to a *prediction* of which person type (described by a particular set of demographic and other psychographic attribute levels) will be most responsive to what type of product feature' (as Wind argues – see above).

Although Wind reports that Green *et al.* have used this technique successfully in a commercial application there is little doubt that many managers regard such procedures with more than a little scepticism. This problem was highlighted in an article by Hooley[11] in which he suggested that three factors encourage practitioners to steer clear of multivariate techniques.

1 Techniques are presented as a panacea for virtually all managerial ills.

2   An over-emphasis upon techniques for their own sake – the 'have technique – will travel' syndrome – in which the merits are highlighted and the limitations glossed over.
3   A general lack of communication between the researcher and the practitioner.

In an attempt to overcome these deficiencies Hooley provides a useful review of multivariate techniques which he dichotomises as being either predictive or descriptive in nature. Among the more common predictive techniques may be numbered:

1   *Multiple regression* which seeks to develop a model of the relationship between a dependent variable such as sales and two or more independent variables such as price, promotional expenditure, etc., so that variations in the former may be explained and predicted in terms of changes in the latter.
2   *Multiple Discriminant Analysis* (MDA). Like regression MDA uses a set of independent variables to predict one or more dependent variables. The technique is particularly useful in marketing as a means of discriminating between market segments in terms of member characteristics.
3   *Conjoint measurement* seeks to identify the relative importance of each product attribute in creating an overall desirability for the product, i.e. you ask respondents to rank order a product in terms of each of the attributes which you consider might be important to potential buyers such as price, ease of use, taste, etc., etc.
4   *Automatic Interaction Detector* (AID) – develops a tree-type diagram in which the factors which help to explain the variance in the dependent variable are successively 'split' into their component parts (independent variables).

Two of the three major descriptive techniques – factor analysis and cluster analysis – have already been mentioned, the third being multidimensional scaling (MDS). MDS is frequently used to develop representations of the relationships between perceived brand images and the individual's product requirements as well as for defining market segments. Hooley notes that MDS possesses the disadvantages that its results are not always clear cut, the segments may be indistinct and may not be applicable to all markets, and that it presents a static rather than a dynamic picture and so requires continuous updating.

Although Hooley designates cluster analysis as a descriptive technique it is, in fact, used for predictive purposes also. Indeed, cluster analysis is often used as a generic term within which are subsumed an enormous variety of specific techniques and a short review of these will be helpful to indicate to the practitioner just what is available.

■ Cluster Analysis[12]

The marketer's interest in segmentation is a particular example of a general problem faced by analysts and decision-makers in virtually all areas of activity, namely: 'Given a sample of N objects or individuals, each of which is measured on each of p variables, devise a classification scheme for grouping the objects into g classes. The number of classes and the characteristics of the classes to be determined.' (Everitt, 1974, p. 1.)

Everitt continues:

> These techniques have been variously referred to as techniques of *cluster analysis, Q-analysis, typology, grouping, clumping, classification, numerical taxonomy* and *unsupervised pattern recognition*. The variety of the nomenclature may be due to the importance of the methods in such diverse fields as psychology, zoology, biology, botany, sociology, artificial intelligence and information retrieval.

In addition to the many fields of study in which different approaches to clustering have been developed, it is also important to recognise that such methods can be used for a number of different purposes. Thus Everitt cites Ball's list of seven possible uses of clustering techniques as follows:

  (i)   Find a true typology.
 (ii)   Model fitting.
(iii)   Prediction based on groups.
 (iv)   Hypothesis testing.
  (v)   Data exploration.
 (vi)   Hypothesis generating.
(vii)   Data reduction.[13]

In market segmentation studies each of these different objectives may be appropriate.

Ideally clusters should be self-evident and capable of identification simply by reviewing a set of data and distinguishing natural groupings within it, e.g. classifying people as male or female. However, for most purposes decision-makers require a much finer discrimination than is possible using the two or three dimensions, which is the maximum which most of us can conceptualise simultaneously. Because of this need for greater sophistication there has been a proliferation of techniques, which Everitt classifies into five types:[14]

- Hierarchical
- Optimisation – partitioning
- Density or mode-seeking
- Clumping
- Others

Hierarchical clustering techniques may be either *agglomerative* or *divisive* in nature. Under the former procedure one would start from the stance of the behavioural scientist in our earlier description of approaches to market segmentation and regard each individual as a potential market in his or her own right. In most cases such an assumption would be unrealistic in economic terms so one would begin to combine individuals into groups. Conversely, the economists' undifferentiated demand schedule would be the logical starting-point for a divisive approach to segmentation. Everitt observes: 'Both types of hierarchical technique may be viewed as attempts to find the most efficient step in some defined sense, at each stage in the progressive subdivision or synthesis of the population.'[15]

Partitioning techniques differ from hierarchical techniques in that they allow for adjustment of the original clusters, created on the basis of a predetermined criterion, through a process of reallocation. Thus, if one's *a priori* expectations as to the optimum way to segment a market lead to groupings which look less than ideal or do not perform as expected one can relocate individuals until an optimum segmentation is achieved.

Density search techniques are, as the name suggests, methods which seek to emulate the human observer's ability to distinguish clusters of higher density surrounded by spaces with a lower density.

The fourth main type of technique, *clumping*, is seen as necessary where overlapping clusters are desirable. The case cited by Everitt is language where, because words tend to have several meanings, they may belong in several places. Finally, there is a number of other techniques such as 'Q' factor analysis, latent structure analysis, etc., which do not conform to any of the previous categories. These techniques, and many more from the other categories, are described at some length in Chapter 2 of Everitt's book.

The existence of so many different clustering techniques is itself evidence of the fact that there is no clear 'best' method and that one can anticipate arguments for and against any given approach. Everitt provides a useful summary of problems associated with cluster analysis, *per se*, and then in the context of the five-fold analysis discussed above. General problems include those of the precise definition of a cluster, the choice of variables, the measurement of similarity and distance and deciding the number of clusters present. These are technical matters beyond the scope of a book of this kind, but Everitt points out that there are various intuitively reasonable ways for validating clusters, namely:

> Firstly, several clustering techniques, based on different assumptions, could be used on the same set of data, and only clusters produced by all or by the majority of methods accepted. Secondly, the data could be randomly divided into two and each half clustered independently. Membership assignment in the partitioned samples should be similar to that of the entire sample, if the clusters are stable. A third method of establishing the underlying stability of groups produced by a clustering program is to make predictions about the effect which the omission of some of the variables would have on the group structure and then to check that the predictions are verified.[16]

The final word should also be given to Everitt, who reinforces the adage that any interpretation of data is only as good as the person making it when he comments that:

> Cluster-analysis is potentially a very useful technique, but it requires care in its application, because of the many associated problems. In many of the applications of the methods that have been reported in the literature the authors have either ignored

or been unaware of these problems, and consequently few results of lasting value can be pointed to. Hopefully future users of these techniques will adopt a more cautious approach, and in addition remember that, along with most other statistical techniques, classification procedures are essentially descriptive techniques for multivariate data, and *solutions given should lead to a proper re-examination of the data matrix rather than a mere acceptance of the clusters produced* (emphasis mine).[17]

Having looked at the variety of clustering methods available to analysts who wish to classify members of a population, we turn now to some of the methods in common usage by marketers.

■ Major Segmentation Methods

There is widespread agreement in the marketing literature that for a segment to merit specific marketing attention it must satisfy at least four conditions. It must be:

1 *Measurable*.
2 *Accessible*.
3 *Substantial*.
4 *Unique* in its response.

To these four conditions which are specified by Frank, Massy and Wind,[18] and endorsed by Louden and Bitta,[19] Kotler[20] and Thomas,[21] Thomas would add a fifth condition:

5 Stability, i.e. can its behaviour be predicted in the future?

In addition to applying to the segment as a whole it is clear that these conditions must also apply to the variables used in defining the segment itself. There are numerous lists of such variables and that shown in Table 8.1 is taken from Thomas.

In this listing Thomas follows Kotler and others in grouping the variables into four major categories:

● Geographic.
● Demographic.
● Psychographic.
● Behaviouristic.

Geographic factors are fairly self-evident and inclined to be taken for granted. But, while they have received comparatively little attention in the USA they have been the focus of considerable interest in the UK as is evident in the development of ACORN and CLS.

Table 8.1   Major segmentation variables

Geographic
Region
County size
City (or SmSA size)
Density – Urban, suburban, rural
Climate
Demographic
Age
Sex
Family size
Family life-cycle
Income
Occupation
Education
Religion
Race
Nationality
Social class

Psychographic	– Producing psychological profiles or types
Life-style	Straights, swingers, long-hairs
Personality	Compulsive, gregarious, ambitious, introverted, passive, authoritarian
Behaviouristic	– Effective marketing must address the needs normal consumers attempt to gratify
Purchase occasion	Should we segment people *or* their consumption occasions?
Benefits sought	Economy, convenience, prestige.
User status	Non-user, Ex-user, Potential user, First-time user, Regular user.
Usage rate	light, medium, heavy users
Loyalty status	none, medium, strong, absolute
Readiness stage	unaware, aware, informed, interested, desirous, intending to buy
Marketing factor	sensitivity Quality, price, service, advertising, sales promotion.

Source: Thomas, M. 'Market Segmentation', *Quarterly Review of Marketing*, 6(1) (Autumn 1980) p. 28.

■ Location as a Basis for Segmentation

The observation that 'birds of a feather flock together' owes much to the fact that people with similar social, economic and life-style characteristics have a tendency to congregate and settle close to one another in particular neighbourhoods. In that this behaviour has been apparent for thousands of years it is surprising that it was not until 1973 that any serious attempt was made to devise a formal methodology for utilising this knowledge as a basis for market segmentation. It was in this year that Richard Webber found that the application of cluster-analysis techniques to official statistics for Liverpool enabled him to define a number of distinctive neighbourhood types. Subsequently, and with the help of the Census Office, Webber found that the same approach on a national scale led to the isolation of thirty-six separate neighbourhood types, 'each of them different in terms of their population, housing and socio-economic character-istics'.[22]

Clark continues:

> The next step came as a result of a seminar at the Centre for Environmental Studies, when one statistician, Ken Baker, associate director of the British Market Research Bureau, promptly saw the system's value as a tool for controlling the fieldwork of the Bureau's Target Group Index. Baker decided to categorise all the 24 000 respondents in the TGI consumer survey geographically according to Webber's neighbourhood groups. The result seemed to show without doubt that respondents in different neighbourhood groups displayed significantly different propensities to buy specific products and services.

Having established the potential for his technique, now designated ACORN (*A Classification of Residential Neighbourhoods*) Webber joined Consolidated Analysis Centers Inc. (CACI) in 1979 and set about improving the method to enable a finer discrimination to be achieved. Accordingly it was decided to adopt the census enumeration districts of which there are 125 000 with an average of 150 households each in place of the 18 000 wards (with populations of up to 10 000 households) which had been used hitherto. However, this resulted in more detail than necessary and CACI and BMRB agreed on a division into eleven groups as summarised in Table 8.2 below. CACI provide a description of each of these groups. For example, for Group A 'the typical household in this type of area is a young family with young or school-age children, living in a modern, medium-sized house. This will have been built by the local authority or as part of a large down-market, private estate. This type of area is most common on the outskirts of the larger urban areas, to which companies and their skilled work-forces have moved from congested inner areas during the past 30 years'.

Each of the smaller groupings comprises 2 or more of the basic 36 types and a finer subdivision can be achieved within groups by reference to the criteria used for these. All told, ACORN uses 40 variables – 15 social and economic, 12 related to age and household composition and 13 concerned with housing type – and so provides much better discriminatory power than more traditional unidimensional measures. A further advantage of ACORN is that not only does it identify particular market segments it also tells you precisely where they are located and so permits better decisions on, for example:

- where to locate new retail outlets;
- which products and services to promote at particular branches;
- how to select sales territories;
- which local media to use;
- where to distribute leaflets.

Table 8.2   ACORN groups in Great Britain

Group	Description	Number of households in 1978*	%
A	Modern family housing for manual workers	1 857 098	9.6
B	Modern family housing, higher incomes	1 436 181	7.4
C	Older housing of intermediate status	2 014 941	10.4
D	Very poor-quality older terraced housing	1 779 150	9.2
E	Rural areas	1 130 237	5.8
F	Urban local authority housing	4 012 342	20.6
G	Housing with most overcrowding	570 965	2.9
H	Low-income areas with immigrants	816 499	4.2
I	Student and high-status non-family areas	835 986	4.3
J	Traditional high-status suburbia	3 714 195	19.1
K	Areas of elderly people (often resorts)	1 245 210	6.4
	Unclassified	31 179	0.2
	TOTAL	19 444 000	100

Source: E. Clark, *Marketing* (16 December 1982).

*1978 population estimates are based on CACI systems for updating local populations using OPCS mid-year estimates apportioned within new local authorities on the basis of changes in the electoral roll at ward/parish level.

Clark provides numerous examples of how a wide spectrum of organisations have used ACORN in selecting and using localised media and also for direct marketing operations including brewers (product mix), building societies (store location), publishers (to build up circulation) and direct mail houses such as Great Universal Stores, American Express and the AA.

CLS stands for *Consumer Location System* (launched early in 1983) and comprises a composite of the Target Group Index (TGI) and ACORN, with the aim of achieving a significant increase in the use of direct mail to reach highly specific target markets. In the words of Michael Rines,[23] 'The new system specifies mass consumer markets in much tighter terms than is possible with any other medium; establishes a rational basis for intermedia cost comparisons; and makes available accurate lists of names and addresses of potential purchasers within specified target markets.'

The system itself is based upon a reduction of the 563 product categories covered by TGI into 135 for which direct mail appears to offer a particularly strong advantage over alternative media. These product categories are then correlated with the ACORN classification to permit precise identification of which out of more than 18 million households are potential customers for the particular product or service in question for each of which CCN Systems can provide address labels, fully personalised letters or a magnetic tape.

■ Demographic Segmentation

The next group of variables which is widely used in marketing studies is that concerned with *demographics*. Demographics and particularly measures of socio-economic status or 'social class' have long enjoyed considerable support as a basis for market segmentation. Some doubt has been cast upon the validity and effectiveness of this approach and led to the establishment of a working party of the Market Research Society in 1979 to investigate their usefulness. The major concern is that traditional social class groupings are overly dependent upon occupation as the key criterion and that this is far less satisfactory as an indicator of economic standing, of cultural tastes, life-styles, purchase behaviour and so on. Francis Quinlan[24] addressed this issue in an article published in 1981 in which he wrote:

'It is suggested that social grading of almost any kind is becoming of only marginal practical interest to most marketers.'

For example, much consumer expenditure relates to *family* purchasing rather than individual purchasing, and there is evidence that the income and expenditure of the household or family unit can be a more reliable indicator of the family's market potential than information about the individual head of the household or the housewife would suggest. It is these same reasons which motivated the claim in the previous chapter that consumer and industrial buyer behaviour possess much in common. Thus, Quinlan concludes that 'teachers and text books of marketing should not continue to refer to social grading for segmentation purposes as if it were as easy as ABC' and advocates the use of the more sophisticated approaches such as ACORN.

■ Psychographic and Behaviouristic Segmentation

Dissatisfaction with demographic criteria alone undoubtedly explains the development of *psychographic* and *behaviouristic* approaches. Segmentation by 'social character' or psychographics owes much to the pioneering work of Riesman *et al.*[25] and their three segment divisions of social character, viz.:

1 Tradition-directed behaviour – things are done 'as in the past' – i.e. behaviour is easy to predict and use for segmentation purposes.
2 Other-directedness – the individual seeks to conform with the current way of doing things as exhibited in the behaviour of his contemporaries or peer group, i.e. success means blending in with the environment.
3 Inner-directedness – one is indifferent to the behaviour of one's peers and contemporaries – the marketer's bête-noire!

While this fairly basic approach to classification has been subject to considerable criticism it possesses the considerable benefit for the practitioner that it is simple, it is robust and best of all, it actually works. Thus a study by McCrohan[26] on automobile purchase showed that other-directed segments bought more prestigious cars to 'fit in' with society while those not concerned to 'fit in' purchased less prestigious cars. While the results are unsurprising in themselves and are intuitively appealing they are *contra* to normal industry practice where *size* of car is the basic segmentation criterion not prestige. Now one may argue that size is a surrogate for prestige, but in a climate where 'small is beautiful', the outstanding performance of the MG Metro suggests this 'ain't necessarily so' and points up one of the basic rules of marketing which is that the act of consumption changes the consumer and one must continuously monitor and react to these changes if one is to remain successful.

The measurement of life-style (another name for psychographics) has progressed a long way since Riesman *et al.*'s major contribution and was the subject of a major review article by William D. Wells.[27] In this article Wells proposes an operational definition of psychographic research as 'Qualitative research intended to place consumers on psychological – as distinguished from demographic – dimensions', a definition which emphasises the distinctive features of the area – it has a quantitative rather than a qualitative orientation and goes beyond demographics. (An extensive review of the method is to be found at pp. 175–9 of my basic textbook *Marketing*, 5th edn).

The final category we distinguished earlier is *behaviouristic* under which Kotler lists such variables as purchase occasion, benefits sought, user status, usage rate, loyalty status, readiness stage and marketing factor sensitivity. Most of these variables are self-evident and in any case are described more than adequately by Kotler. However, two – usage and benefit – deserve some explanation here.

■ Usage Segmentation

The application of Pareto's Law that a small proportion of all the observations related to a phenomenon contain the majority of the information about it – the so-called 80–20 principle – has wide application in marketing. Nowhere is this more so than in the case of usage patterns for products and services where it is commonly referred to as the theory of the 'heavy half'.

The relevance of this theory to the practice of market segmentation was encapsulated in an article by Dik Warren Twedt,[28] first published in 1964, which has become a marketing classic in its own right. Given this status it seems more appropriate to reproduce the opening paragraphs rather than summarise them:

> It's certainly no news that some people buy more gasoline, drink more bourbon, use more paper napkins, eat more candy, chew more gum and even use their credit cards more than other people. But what was news to us, when we began comparing purchase concentration for many different categories of products and services, was the extreme skewness, and the marked similarity of slope, of all these curves [see

Figure 8.3]. Incidentally, the following discussion is limited to relatively mature product categories – it seems unlikely that the same rules would hold for new products.

One first step in the analysis was to eliminate the non-purchasers. Arraying the purchasers by amount consumed, and cumulating the percentage of total volume accounted for by purchasing deciles, it became apparent that for a very wide range of products 'the heavy half' of purchasers – those above the median of usage – account for 80 per cent to 90 per cent of total volume [see Table 8.3]. This relationship appears so consistently that it may be more appropriate to think of it as a marketing law rather than a theory to be proved.

Table 8.3   Purchase concentration deciles

	%/Buying	10	20	30	40	50	60	70	80	90	100
Concentrated fruit juice	72	39	58	72	82	89	94	97	99	99	100
Beer (Dec)	33	42	62	74	82	88	92	95	97	99	100
Margarine	89	31	50	64	75	83	90	94	97	99	100
Dog food	31	34	55	69	80	88	93	97	99	99	100
Cake mixes	75	32	52	67	77	85	90	94	97	99	100
Hair tonics	48	42	60	72	81	87	91	95	98	99	100
RTE cereals	96	36	57	70	80	87	92	96	98	99	100
Soaps and detergents	98	28	46	61	72	81	88	93	97	99	100
Toilet tissue	98	24	40	53	64	74	82	89	94	98	100
Canned hash	32	40	58	70	79	86	90	94	96	98	100
Cola bev'gs (May–Aug)	78	44	65	77	84	90	93	96	98	99	100
Lemon-lime	58	56	72	81	86	91	94	96	98	99	100
Hair fixatives	46	52	68	76	83	88	92	95	98	99	100
Shampoo	82	32	50	63	73	81	87	92	96	98	100
Bourbon whisky	41	48	66	76	84	89	91	92	95	98	100

Source: *Chicago Tribune* Consumer Panel, special analyses of 1962 data.

The evidence for the next five propositions is not quite so well established as the heavy-half relationship, simply because the detailed analyses have not yet been made on all the product categories studied. They are, however, sufficiently well-founded so that I urge each of you to apply the theory to those product categories in which you are most interested. The five propositions are these:

1 In general, demographic characteristics (age, education, income, race, etc.) are such poor predictors of heavy usage that it is usually much more efficient to measure consumption directly, and then cross-tabulate by measures of consumer preference or by advertising vehicle exposure.

2 Heavy usage of different product categories is relatively independent – the fact that a household uses a lot of aluminium foil tells us nothing about how much canned dog food the family will buy. In a study completed last month,

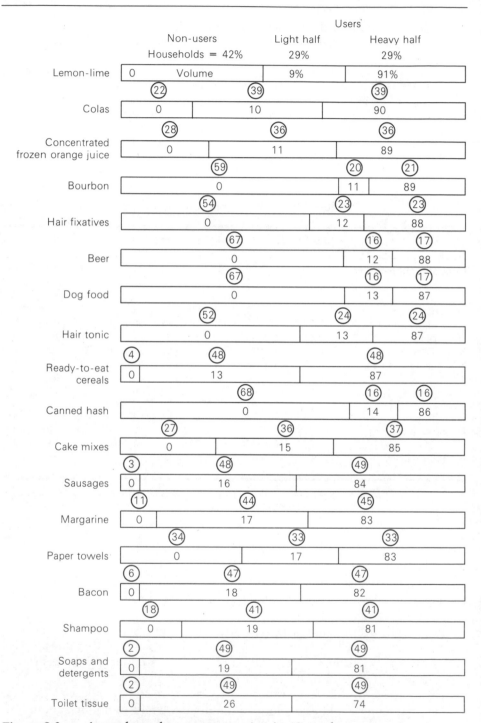

Figure 8.3   Annual purchase concentration in 18 product categories

Source: Twedt, 'How Important to Marketing Strategy is the "Heavy User"', *Journal of Marketing*, January 1964.

intercorrelations of 26 product categories by heavy-half usage were all quite low. The highest relationship was found between bacon and wieners, but even here the phi coefficient was only .37. These low relationships are not surprising when we remember that the more we spend for one product category, the less we have to spend for others.

3   Among the heavy users, there seems to be less, rather than more, brand loyalty. Not only do they buy more – they buy more often, and they buy more different brands.

4   The heavy users are not price buyers. They pay as much, or even a bit more, for a unit of purchase, than do the light users.

5   Although there are changes in consumption patterns as the family's position in the life cycle advances, these changes are usually not so abrupt or so pronounced as to impair the utility of direct consumption measures.[28]

In the period since this article was published there has emerged considerable evidence to support Twedt's five propositions and little to refute them, and usage segmentation must be regarded as a robust method, particularly in mature and established markets.

■ Benefit Segmentation

Much the same status as attaches to Twedt's work is also accorded to the seminal contribution of Russell I. Haley 'Benefit Segmentation: a decision-oriented research tool'.[29] Writing in 1968 Haley identified three segmentation approaches which enjoyed widespread support – geographic, demographic and volume or heavy half – but went on to propose that in and of themselves none of these was sufficiently selective. Specifically, Haley pointed out that while heavy consumers are the most valuable segment they are not 'usually available to the same brand – because they are not all seeking the same kind of benefits from a product'.

In addition, Haley pointed out that all three extant approaches to segmentation were handicapped because 'All are based on an ex-post facto analysis of the kinds of people who make up various segments of a market. They rely on *descriptive* factors rather than *causal* factors. For this reason they are not efficient predictors of future buying behaviour, and it is future buying behaviour that is of central interest to marketers.'

To overcome this deficiency Haley argued that one should seek to establish the benefits which consumers are looking for in a product as these determine their behaviour much more accurately than do demographics or volume of consumption. In his words, 'The benefit segmentation approach is based upon being able to measure consumer value systems in detail, together with what the consumer thinks about various brands in the product category of interest. While this concept seems simple enough, operationally it is very complex. There is no simple straightforward way of handling the volumes of data that have to be generated.

Computers and sophisticated multivariate attitude measurement techniques are a necessity.'

Several such techniques have been described in the preceding pages, but it will be helpful to reproduce Haley's segmentation of the toothpaste market to exemplify the potential output from a study following this approach.

Table 8.4   Toothpaste market segment description

Segment name:	The sensory segment	The sociables	The worriers	The independent segment
Principal benefit sought	Flavor, product appearance	Brightness of teeth	Decay prevention	Price
Demographic strengths:	Children	Teens, young people	Large families	Men
Special behavioral characteristics:	Users of spearmint flavored tooth-paste	Smokers	Heavy users	Heavy users
Brands dispropor-tionately favored:	Colgate, Stripe	Macleans, Plus White, Ultra Brite	Crest	Brands on sale
Personality characteristics:	High self-involvement	High sociability	High hypochon-driasis	High autonomy
Life-style characteristics:	Hedonistic	Active	Conservative	Value-oriented

Source: R. I. Haley, 'Benefit Segmentation: a decision-oriented research tool', *Journal of Marketing*, vol. 32 (July 1968).

Table 8.5   A summary of product benefits

1. Perceived objective performance rendered by the physical aspects of the product.
2. Perceived social benefits represented by the consumption, use, or mere possession of the product.
3. Psychological benefits derived from an association of the product with otherwise irrelevant attributes (e.g. virility, maturity).
4. Objective benefits confirmed by the location, manner, and timing of purchase availability.
5. Subjective satisfactions derived from the purchase location and manner of sale.
6. Instructional, informational, and technical services furnished by the seller in promoting the product.
7. The assurance of dependability and quality imparted by brand or source.
8. An assortment benefit, in the sense of variety of merchandise available or preferred.

Source: C. R. Wasson, F. D. Sturdivant and D. H. McConaughy, *Competition and Human Behaviour* (New York: Appleton-Century-Crofis, 1968) pp. 12–13, cited in Louis W. Sterm, and John R. Grabner, Jr, *Competition in the Market Place* (Glenview, Ill.: Scott, Foresman, 1970).

Given such an analysis the marketer is in a much better position to develop the most effective mix in terms of pricing, product development, packaging, distribution, copy platform, media selection and so on. Indeed, such studies frequently identify gaps or niches in the market-place and allow the producer to develop both a new product and a new strategy.

A useful summary of product benefits for which a consumer might pay is reproduced as Table 8.5.

■ Segmenting Industrial Markets

Although it is a recurring theme of this book that strategically marketing is marketing and the distinction of variants (consumer, industrial, service, not for profit, social, etc.) is counter-productive, it is also acknowledged that in the particular and at the *tactical* level one must be sensitive to situation-specific factors which underlie the wish to regard bank marketing as different from consumer goods marketing and so on. Clearly the selection of a segmentation method is an area where tactical considerations are paramount and it might be helpful to indicate some of the factors which need to be taken into account when segmenting industrial markets to point up the similarities and differences with consumer markets.

While Choffray and Lilien[30] claim that 'most segmentation analysis has been aimed mainly at consumer markets', there is ample evidence that industrial marketers have long used a variety of techniques to help them subdivide markets into meaningful segments. Thus the Standard Industrial Classification (SIC) in the USA provides a closely defined methodology for specifying an organisation's type of activity in broad terms (2-digit code, e.g. 23 = apparel) in precise terms (3-digit code, e.g. 232 = men's, youths' and boys' furnishings, etc.) and pinpoint terms (4-digit codes, e.g. 2322 = underwear). Although 4-digit codes are not available for every industry in every geographical location SIC codes provide an excellent first cut at dividing up a market into meaningful subgroups.

Current thinking on industrial market segmentation is summarised well in an article by Cardozo[31] in which he identifies four dimensions which may be used separately or in combination to classify organisational buying situations:

1 *Familiarity with the buying task*: This dimension is based upon the work of Robinson and Faris[32] in which they identify 3 different types of buying task – *new task, modified rebuy* and *straight rebuy*. Clearly each of these situations will call for a different approach to segmentation.
2 *Product type*: in this case one could segment on the basis of product use in terms of components, material and equipment required which, in turn, may be related to the 'degree of standardisation':

   - *Custom* – a unique design for a particular customer
   - *Modular* – a unique combination of standard components or materials
   - *Standard* – a combination of ingredients that has been offered previously

3 *Importance of the purchase to the buying organisation*
4 *Type of uncertainty in the purchase situation*

The latter two factors are of special interest because they reflect the fact that buyers too try and segment the set of potential suppliers by developing criteria on which to assess them and setting up formal vendor rating schemes. Johnson and Flodhammer[33] support the view that understanding the buyers' needs is as important in industrial as consumer markets when they assert 'Unless there is knowledge of the industrial users' needs the manufactured product usually has the lowest common denominator – price. Quality and service are unknown quantities.'

■ When to Segment

In the preceding pages we have considered several important aspects of market segmentation without addressing directly the key question of under what circumstances a segment will merit the development of a differentiated marketing strategy and mix. Frank, Massy and Wind[34] propose eight criteria for determining whether there is a prima facie case for segmentation, namely:

1 *Size* – is the segment, actual or potential, of sufficient size to justify the development of a differentiated marketing strategy?
2 *Incremental cost* – what additional costs will be incurred in seeking to satisfy a particular segment and will these be recovered with additional profit over that which could be anticipated if the market were not segmented in the first place?
3 *Size of intersegment differences* – the greater these are the more the justification for segmentation and for treating the segments as separate markets.
4 *Durability of differences* – the longer lasting the differences between segments the greater the justification for distinguishing them. A particular case which runs counter to this point is that of new products where one may invest considerable effort to identify innovators and seek to reach them with a distinctive strategy in the knowledge that if the product is successful the segment will, by definition, be eliminated.
5 *Cyclical volatility* – the more stable a segment the better.
6 *Compatibility with other segments* – should seek to define segments which are mutually reinforcing rather than in opposition to one another, i.e. one must be careful not to 'cannibalise' one's own markets.
7 *Degree of 'fit'* – the company should seek to build upon its strengths.
8 *Degree of competition* – the best segments are those in which there is an absence of direct competition, i.e. one should seek to serve a gap in the market rather than select segments in which there are several existing contenders.

Assessment of these criteria comprise the first step in the four-stage procedure recommended by Worcester and Downham[35] which may be summarised as:

- *First stage: background clarification*
- *Second stage: qualitative exploration.* 'Having identified the main behavioural patterns in the market, it is then important to explore the various factors determining or influencing these patterns.'
- *Third stage: developing measuring instruments.* Segments are defined according to a base or basis, and further description of target segments is included in terms of other variables or descriptors.
- *Fourth stage: developing effective marketing programmes*

It is worth noting that many critics of segmentation who claim that it is all very well in theory but not very effective in practice, fall into the trap of paying insufficient attention to the first two stages. As Young *et al.*[36] comment:

> Unfortunately the results of these [segmentation] studies often have been disappointing because the segments derived from the study have not been actionable from a marketing standpoint. A common reason for this lack of applicability is preoccupation with the techniques and method of segmentation such as whether to use generic benefits, problems, lifestyles, psychographics, or preferences and the type of factor or cluster analysis to be performed. In too many instances, marketing researchers have failed to analyse the marketing environment and competitive structure before applying their favorite methodological approach. [cf. Hooley!]

According to Young *et al.* there are many situations where a segmented approach is not even useful and the market should be analysed in its entirety. Specific examples are:

1 The market is so small that marketing to a portion of it is not profitable.
2 Heavy users make up such a large proportion of the sales volume that they are the only relevant target.
3 The brand's the dominant brand in the market.

The authors then provide three case histories to show how a successful segmentation study should be executed and the first of these is reproduced below both as an example of how to conduct and use a segmentation analysis and also of the technical jargon which is so off-putting for most managers.

■ Segmentation on Generic Benefits

The Canadian Government Office of Tourism decided to conduct a marketing segmentation study of the US travel market to obtain a comprehensive picture of Americans who are potential vacation travelers to Canada. Because Canada is a large, diverse country with many different aspects, it truly can be many things to many people. Therefore, a segmentation approach was deemed desirable to ascertain the different groups of potential vacation travelers to Canada and which aspects of Canadian vacations could address their needs and desires. Once the segments had been identified and described, they could be evaluated in terms of the Canadian vacation business potential they offered, and those segments deemed attractive enough to cultivate then could be addressed through advertising and promotion campaigns portraying the advantages for a Canadian vacation of the specific type desired by the target Segment(s).

However, because of the complexity of the travel and vacation business, certain conceptual problems and issues had to be resolved in planning and executing the study.

Though most segmentation studies will not be as complicated as this one, it demonstrates the process the researcher must follow to resolve three critical issues before designing the questionnaire and fielding the study: (1) who should be interviewed, (2) the frame of reference for questioning, and (3) alternative methods of segmentation

Who should be interviewed. This critical consideration must be addressed in all studies. Because the purpose of the travel study was to expand the number of Canadian vacations taken by U.S. travelers, it was insufficient to include only those persons who had been to Canada because they accounted for only 5% of the U.S. population. Instead, it was necessary to define relevant prospect groups to obtain new visitors to Canada.

Consideration of the profitability of various types of tourists to Canada dictated a decision to interview only those who had taken a vacation of at least a week's duration in the past, and the vacation decision maker was the specific person to be questioned. Furthermore, the key analytical decision was dictated by the knowledge that the distance people have traveled on past vacations is a strong indicator of how far they would be willing to travel on future vacations. Therefore, the sample was designed to cover only those persons who had traveled the requisite distance for a Canadian vacation – defined in the study as three quarters of the distance to Canada.

Frame of reference for questioning. This factor was a particularly difficult problem for this study because most individuals were potential prospects for more than one type of vacation. To question about vacations in general was not relevant as needs and desires would vary by type of vacation. Also, asking about the ideal vacation would likely yield fantasized wishes that would have no relationship to the type of vacation a person would or could take. This problem was overcome by asking the respondent to anchor all responses in terms of the last vacation taken. In this way, responses were based on the reality of a specific vacation experience for which behavioural and attitudinal information were obtained.

Alternative methods of market segmentation. As in most segmentation studies, this was the most critical issue. Because the best way to segment or group U.S. travelers for developing marketing programs was far from obvious, the following alternative methods were investigated.

1   By segmenting consumers on *favorability toward Canada* as a vacation area, U.S. travelers could be grouped on the basis of their attitudes toward Canada. This approach could be most appropriate if Canada were a single entity and if attitudes toward vacationing in Canada were polarized. However, these possibilities did not appear to represent reality.

2   By segmenting on *geographic area*, or proximity to selected areas of Canada, respondents would be assigned by their U.S. locality. This approach would be reasonable as an independent segmentation alternative if travelers' vacation behavior and desires varied dramatically by region in the U.S., but they do not.

3   By segmenting consumers on *desires sought* in their last vacation, respondents could be segmented on what they were seeking in a vacation of the last type taken.

A pilot study consisting of 200 interviews was developed to test the meaningfulness of each approach. The last approach (desires sought in the last vacation) was found to be most meaningful in terms of marketing and was the approach used in the major study.

Results

The major study consisted of 1,750 interviews with eligible respondents, i.e., those responsible for making a decision about an extended vacation of at least three-fourths the distance to Canada during the last three years. A national probability sample was used with one callback on the household and one on the eligible respondent.

A benefit segmentation was obtained for those desires sought in planning the most recent vacation meeting the eligibility criteria. The technique of segmentation was a Q-factor analysis. This approach consists of normalizing the profile of the respondents across all benefits to obtain groups of homogeneous respondents through principal components extraction of eigenvalues and their associated eigenvectors, which subsequently are rotated by the varimax procedure [2–4, 8, 9, 12]. To facilitate the analysis and description of the marketing segments, a perceptual map derived by the multiple discriminant analysis technique is shown in Figure 8.4 [4, 10, 11].* The locations of the six segments are shown in circles; the benefit items shown as vectors indicate those desires sought by each group.

---

*   The discriminant analysis was performed by a stepwise computer program to select those benefit items that can best predict group membership [5]. After the items had been selected, their relationship to the Q groups was shown in a two-dimensional space. The procedure was [10, 11]: (1) the eigenvalues and their associated canonical coefficients were computed through the principal components method for those variables that were selected as the best discriminators, (2) each individual then was scored on his first two canonical dimensions and the group means were computed, (3) the canonical scores were correlated with the original items which were plotted as vectors in two-dimensional space to show the relationship of the benefit items to each group.

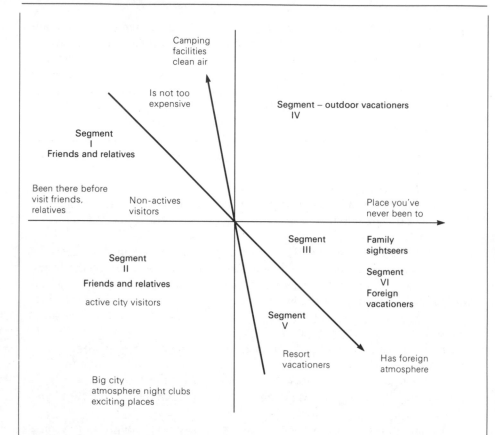

Figure 8.4   Map of the six benefit segments

Segment I. Friends and relatives – nonactive visitor (29%). These vacationers seek familiar surroundings where they can visit friends and relatives. They are not very inclined to participate in any activity.

Segment II. Friends and relatives – active city visitor (12%). These vacationers also seek familiar surroundings where they can visit friends and relatives, but they are more inclined to participate in activities – especially sightseeing, shopping, and cultural and other entertainment.

Segment III. Family sightseers (6%). These vacationers are looking for a new vacation place which would be a treat for the children and an enriching experience.

Segment IV. Outdoor vacationer (19%). These vacationers seek clean air, rest and quiet, and beautiful scenery. Many are campers and availability of recreation facilities is important. Children are also an important factor.

Segment V. Resort vacationer (19%). These vacationers are most interested in water – sports (e.g. swimming) and good weather. They prefer a popular place with a big-city atmosphere.

Segment VI. Foreign vacationer (26%). These vacationers look for vacations in a place they have never been before with a foreign atmosphere and beautiful scenery. Money is not of major concern but good accommodation and service are. They want an exciting, enriching experience.

Because of their relatively low vacation expenditures, segments I and II offered less attractive business potential than was offered by the other segments. Moreover, Canadian vacations could not provide an opportunity to visit with friends and relatives.

The other segments had vacation needs and desires that could be delivered by various areas of Canada through different types of vacations. For each of these segments, data from the questionnaire were used to determine a profile in terms of behavior, psychographics, travel incentives, and image of a Canadian vacation.

Implementation
Unlike a commercial firm, the Canadian Office of Tourism had special problems in implementing the results of the study. It had to rely on an extensive program to inform the many elements of the travel industry of the study findings through meetings, seminars, and publications. As a result of these efforts, improvements were made in the following areas.

1 *Advertising execution.* The tonality or style of the advertising was made more compatible with the personality traits and lifestyles of the target groups. Creatively, the advertising message stressed the specific benefits sought by each segment, reinforced the positive images of Canada that each group already had, and corrected any undesirable impressions they may have held.
2 *Media considerations.* The study facilitated the selection of vehicles compatible with the life style, demographic features, and personality of target groups. The study was not designed to measure individual media habits, but the results allowed a closer look at the media available and comparison of editorial environment of U.S. consumer magazines with the unique audience profiles and desires for each segment. Television commercials were changed in mood, tempo, and emphasis to attract travelers in the most promising segment.
3. *Merchandising and promotional efforts.* Promotional brochures and specific types of vacation 'tours' or packages were developed along the lines suggested by the findings.
4. *Provincial tourist offices.* The results were passed on to the provinces so they could adopt a segmented promotional effort, and to those areas that could deliver the benefits sought by one or more of the target groups.

In addition to providing marketing guidance, the study findings were useful in the planning of new hotels, accommodations, and tourist facilities by the Canadian government and private groups.

Finally, in his review Wind (1978)[37] addresses the issues of translating segmentation findings into strategy and a quotation from this will provide a useful bridge between the broadly based issues which have been the subject of this and previous chapters and Chapter 9 in which we turn to look at the specific case of positioning. Wind observes:

> The most difficult aspect of any segmentation project is the translation of the study results into marketing strategy. No rules can be offered to assure a successful translation and, in fact, little is known (in the published literature) on how this translation occurs.[38]

Informal discussions with and observation of 'successful' and 'unsuccessful' translations suggest a few generalisable conclusions aside from the obvious ones such as:

1   Involving all the relevant users (e.g. product managers, new product developers, advertising personnel, etc.) in the problem definition, research design, and data interpretation stages.
2   Viewing segmentation data as one input to a total marketing information system and combining them with sales and other relevant data.
3   Using the Segmentation data on a continuous basis. The reported study results should be viewed only as the *beginning* of a utilisation program.

Finally, and as a postscript to a chapter which has largely advocated the merits of differentiated or concentrated marketing strategies through the use of segmentation techniques, we should not lose sight of the fact that many firms still prefer to pursue an *undifferentiated* approach. A classic example of this is provided by the world-famous Finnish textile firm Marimekko® whose marketing policy is expressed as follows:

> We make things for ourselves and sell them to people who think like us.
>   This is only slightly exaggerated. People are behind every stage in production at Marimekko and the users are also people.
>   The Marimekko story would indeed have been short had there not been sufficient customers thinking like us. Thank goodness there were and in such abundance that Marimekko can build its future around a steady growth.
>   Marimekko is no colossus able to penetrate the consciousness of people around the world through a massive advertising campaign. It has been compelled to build its marketing around its products and place its faith in them.

■ Summary

In Chapter 8 we started by considering the basic differences between product differentiation and market segmentation as competitive strategies. Essentially the difference resides in the fact that product differentiation originates with the producer while market segmentation has its origins in the market-place. Product differentiation thus reflects the producer's perception of variations in the product which will appeal to different sub-groups of consumers. By contrast, market segmentation starts from the observation that different subgroups or segments of a market exhibit different consumption preferences and then seeks to develop products or services which will match the needs of these segments.

In order to segment markets (the demand for specific products) one needs an appropriate indicator(s). Accordingly, we reviewed a number of different bases for segmentation and the contexts in which each would be appropriate. Four basic procedures – *a priori, clustering, flexible* and *componential* – were discussed and some of the available techniques outlined with a particular emphasis upon *cluster analysis*.

The characteristics of a viable segment were defined – it must be *measurable, accessible, substantial, unique* and *stable* in its response – as were the major segmentation methods. Each of the latter – *geographic, demographic, psychographic* and *behaviouristic* – was then reviewed in some detail to demonstrate its application in practice.

Of course, it is not always appropriate to segment a market and Chapter 8 concluded with a discussion of the circumstances under which a segment will merit the development of a differentiated marketing strategy. A case history conducted by the Canadian Government Office of Tourism of the US travel market exemplifies and reinforces the points made.

In Chapter 9, *Positioning*, we take a closer look at how firms seek to compete with one another *within* market segments.

CHAPTER 9
Positioning

Learning Goals

The issues to be addressed in Chapter 9 include:

1 The nature of *positioning* and its relationship to market segmentation.
2 The role of *perception* in choice decisions and its measurement through *perceptual mapping*.
3 The concepts of *positioning* and '*ladders in the mind*'.
4 The idea of '*niche marketing*'.
5 The nature of *branding* and its use in marketing.
6 The concept of the *augmented product* and its role in developing competitive advantage.
7 The view that increasingly companies will be regarded as *brands*, and marketed as such.

After reading Chapter 9 you will be able to:

1 Define and describe key *concepts* such as:

- Positioning.
- Branding.
- Perceptual mapping.
- Niche marketing.
- Augmented product.

2 Explain the importance of these factors in developing a *sustainable competitive advantage*.
3 Spell out what is involved in *developing successful brands*.
4 Understand why the rapid erosion of objective advantages has led to increased emphasis upon *less tangible and subjective benefits*.
5 Discuss the trend towards marketing companies as *brands* and the factors likely to reinforce this development.

■ Introduction

In Chapter 8 we explored the concept of market segmentation as a bridge between broad generalisations about competition and buyer behaviour and the identification of specific markets. In Chapter 9 we take this process further by considering how firms compete with each other *within* market segments – a procedure which in recent years has come to be known as 'positioning'.

As the *Macmillan Dictionary of Marketing and Advertising* explains, the 'term [positioning] has a simple meaning and a more complicated one. As typically used, it defines what is accurately called product positioning – that is, defining the location of a product (or service) relative to others in the same marketplace and then promoting it in such a way as to reinforce or change its "position". This is easier said than done, however. The process of defining a 'position' requires dimensions along which the competing products can be compared, and the resulting definition must be comparative if it is to be any use as the basis of positioning strategy'. The establishment and measuring of criteria which permit one to distinguish between similar products competing in the same market segment is the province of *perceptual mapping*, and this will be described in some detail below.

So much for the simple definition. What about the complex one? According to Al Ries and Jack Trout[1] 'Positioning starts with a product. A piece of merchandise, a service, a company, an institution, or even a person. Perhaps yourself. But positioning is not what you do to a product. Positioning is what you do in the mind of the prospect. That is, you position the product in the mind of the prospect'.

As the *Dictionary of Marketing and Advertising* points out, the 'collective mind is likely, inconveniently, to be already made up on the subject of products that already exist'. How then does one change peoples' minds? According to Ries and Trout by using simple rather than complex and sophisticated messages – a proposition we look at in greater detail later in this chapter.

In order to position products, services and even companies it is essential to invest them with a distinctive 'personality' or 'brand'. The final part of the chapter examines the nature of branding and demonstrates how, increasingly, it is often the only real basis for differentiating between competitors.

■ Perceptual Mapping

In the composite model of buyer behaviour (p. 179) it was suggested that consumers make choice decisions primarily on the basis of performance factors (i.e. how well does the product meet the precise needs of the intending consumer) related to the cost of acquiring a given supply. However, it was also recognised that these objective characteristics would be 'interpreted' by the prospective purchaser in terms of his or her precise needs, the context in which the decision was being made and prior knowledge and experience, through the process of selective perception. Finally, it was noted that in many competitive markets consumers are faced with a wide choice of offerings which are near-perfect substitutes for each other in terms of performance and cost-benefit factors and so have to resort to other factors to enable them to choose between them. We termed this 'Behavioural response' and so endorsed the view that perception influences decision-making at both the subconscious and the conscious level. At the subconscious level selective perception determines what information we will admit to our conscious mind while at the conscious level it determines how we interpret and use that information. This being the case it is clearly very important that we be able to capture and measure consumer perceptions of competing products. As Urban and Star (1991)[2] observe:

> If we are to make good positioning decisions, we need to know : (1) What dimensions do consumers use to evaluate competitive marketing programs – how many are there, and what should they be named? (2) How important is each of these dimensions in the decision process? (3) How do we and the competition compare on these dimensions? (4) How do consumers make choices on the basis of this information?

In Chapter 8 on 'Market Segmentation' we cited a number of benefits which consumers typically look for when evaluating a product and also showed how these factors could be combined into two primary dimensions to yield a 'perceptual map' (Figure 8.2). First, however, one must identify just what the relevant factors are which prospective users will take into account when evaluating a product. Table 9.1 provides a list of 16 attributes or 'critical success factors' culled from an extensive review of the literature as part of the survey undertaken by Susan Hart and myself into the sources of competitive success.[3] In our survey, we collected data from six different industries and used this to construct a rank ordering of the importance of these factors as shown in Table 9.2. Readers should not be surprised to learn that while it is quite simple to aggregate data in this way it can also be very misleading as there are significant differences between industries. For example, for the six industries we surveyed Design was ranked as the least important of the 16 factors – in a subsequent review of the market for household textiles it was ranked most important! That said, the 16 factors cover most of the attributes considered important in industrial or business markets and so provide a good basis for beginning to construct a perceptual map.

One of the best documented examples of the use of perceptual mapping is to be found in Gary Davies and Janice Brooks's book *Positioning Strategy in Retailing*.[4] In Chapter 6, the authors explain how to use multi-dimensional scaling (MDS) to produce maps for different kinds of retail markets and the following draws heavily on this source.

As noted above, the first problem in measuring the perception or 'image' of a store is to develop a list of criteria which are relevant and unambiguous. Based upon an extensive review of the literature, J.D. Lindquist[5] developed a list of nine major attributes from 32 different elements, as shown in Table 9.3.

Davies and Brooks (1989) suggest that researchers should collect data on as many of these key attributes as possible, but counsel that in doing so one must allow for differences in perception between different groups of the population and also concentrate on specific factors that can be converted into *strategic action*.

Table 9.1   Critical Success Factors

* ★ Sale price
* ★ Style Fashion (Design)
* ★ Durability
* ★ Flexibility and adaptability in use
* ★ Parts availability
* ★ Attractive appearance/shape
* ★ Technical sophistication
* ★ Performance in operation
* ★ Easy to use
* ★ Safe to use
* ★ Reliability
* ★ Easy to maintain
* ★ Quality of after-sales service
* ★ Efficient delivery
* ★ Advertising and promotion
* ★ Operator comfort

Table 9.2   Critical Success Factors : Product Factors Influencing Competitiveness (in rank order)

1. Performance in operation
2. Reliability
3. Sale price
4. Efficient delivery
5. Technical sophistication
6. Quality of after-sales service
7. Durability
8. Ease of use
9. Safety in use
10. Ease of maintenance
11. Parts availability and cost
12. Attractive appearance/shape
13. Flexibility and adaptability in use
14. Advertising and promotion
15. Operator comfort
16. Design

Source: M. J. Baker and S. Hart *Marketing and Competitive Success* (London: Philip Allen, 1989).

Table 9.3   **Lindquist's 9 store image attributes**

Attribute	Contributing factors/components
Mechandise	Quality; selection/assortment; styling/fashion; guarantees; pricing
Service	Service general; sales clerk service; self service; ease of merchandise return; delivery service; credit policies
Clientele	Social class appeal; self-image congruency; store personnel
Physical facilities	Physical facilities, e.g. air-conditioning, washroom; store layout; shopping ease, e.g. width of aisles; architecture
Convenience	Convenience general; locational convenience; parking
Promotion	Sales promotions; advertising; displays; trading stamps; symbols and colour
Store atmosphere	Atmosphere congeniality, i.e. feelings of warmth and acceptance
Institutional factors	Conservative vs modern projection of store; reputation and reliability
Post-transaction satisfaction	Merchandise in use; returns; adjustments

The usual sources of information for identifying appropriate criteria are group discussions, word association tests and analysis of the retailer's own advertising. Such research is likely to generate many more criteria than MDS can cope with (most perceptual maps have only two dimensions) and some means must be found of reducing these to manageable proportions - usually through the use of factor or cluster analysis as described in Chapter 8. Having decided on the attributes to be used Davies and Brooks compare all the chosen retailers and all the chosen concepts in a market research survey structured to represent the known characteristics of the marketplace. Typically, respondents to the survey are asked to compare two retailers, two concepts or a concept and a retailer, and to rate their similarity. The gradings given are averaged for all respondents to produce a semi-matrix . . . which is the final market research data. The MDS analysis that follows is designed only to represent those data in such a way that the hidden structure in the data, the market structure, can be seen more easily. The map or model produced is not a theoretical model . . . but a representation of data in a form that can be used to describe and predict consumer behaviour.

The output of an MDS program (of which there are several variants) is a two-dimensional map in which the distance between two points reflects the similarity

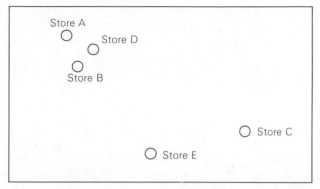

Figure 9.1   Hypothetical model of a retail market

Source: G. Davies and J. Brooks, *Positioning Strategy in Retailing* (London: Paul Chapman Publishing, 1989).

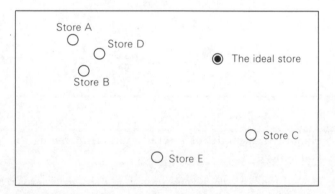

Figure 9.2   Hypothetical model of a retail market, including the position of the 'ideal' store

Source: G. Davies and J. Brooks, *Positioning Strategy in Retailing* (London: Paul Chapman Publishing, 1989).

between them – the smaller the distance the more similar they are and vice versa. Thus the output from an MDS analysis of the survey data might yield a map like that in Figure 9.1, which enables one to make statements that stores A, B & D are quite similar and C & E quite distinctive. However, in order to interpret the map and use it for decision-making purposes a reference point is needed, and in Figure 9.2 this is provided by plotting the 'Ideal Store' based upon the opinion of the shoppers surveyed. Davies and Brooks interpret the map as follows :

> Store C now seems the only really well-placed store in that it is not only differentiated but, because it is placed close if not closest to the ideal, it has the widest appeal. Store

C has adopted the best possible positioning strategy. Store D is also fairly well-placed; being close to the ideal store it has broad appeal. However, stores A & B compete with store D for the particular shopping experience associated by the shopper with all three stores. Stores A & B are worse off in that they appear to be second choices to store D. All things being equal, the shopper will visit store D first and will be better disposed to buying similar merchandise there rather than at store A or B. Store E is clearly out on a limb.

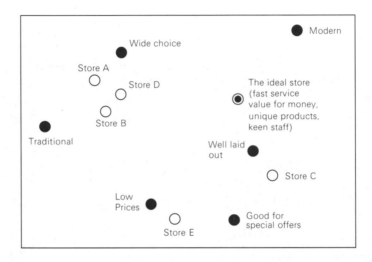

Figure 9.3   Hypothetical model of a retail market, including the 'ideal' store and concepts

Source: G. Davies and J. Brooks, *Positioning Strategy in Retailing* (London: Paul Chapman Publishing, 1989).

In Figure 9.3 the authors include the concepts generated and screened in the market research, which enables one to interpret the positions much more effectively and decide whether and how to reposition oneself. From Figure 9.3 it is apparent that store E is a price leader and, being out on its own, is of greatest appeal to price conscious shoppers.

Davies and Brooks concede that it is not possible to assess the statistical validity of the market maps produced by this technique. That said, their research shows the method is both robust and stable over time and so of considerable benefit to decision-makers. Certainly the technique, and the book describing its use, merit careful study by all those responsible for formulating retail strategies. Similarly, Chapter 8 'Product Positioning' in Urban and Star (1991) will be of value to those seeking a broadly based description of the use of multi-variate techniques to help determine how products are perceived in the marketplace.

■ Positioning in the Mind

Mapping methods of the kind described in the previous section help establish how different competitors are seen in the market, both in relation to each other and to the ideal product. But, as noted in the introduction to this chapter, while this information is valuable the key issue is how to defend or improve/change one's position in the market. To achieve this, one must either reinforce or modify people's perceptions and it is this second aspect of 'positioning' which was addressed in Ries and Trout's book.[6]

According to Ries and Trout 'positioning got started in 1972 when we wrote a series of articles entitled "The Positioning Era" for the trade paper *Advertising Age*'. Ries and Trout are primarily concerned with the impact of advertising in what they describe as 'an overcommunicated society'. They make their point vividly by explaining that (in 1987) the *per capita* consumption of advertising in America was $376.62 per year so that if you have an advertising budget of $1 million per year this is equivalent to less than half a cent spread over 365 days for the average consumer. More important the other advertisers are spending $376.615 to divert his attention from you – odds of over 75,000:1 ! Ries and Trout comment :

> In the communication jungle out there, the only hope to score big is to be selective, to concentrate on narrow targets, to practice segmentation. In a word, 'positioning'.
>
> The mind, as a defence against the volume of today's communications, screens and rejects much of the information offered it. In general, the mind accepts only that which matches prior knowledge or experience. Millions of dollars have been wasted trying to change minds with advertising. Once a mind is made up, it's almost impossible to change it. Certainly, not with a weak force like advertising.

So what is one to do? According to Ries and Trout 'the best approach in our overcommunicated society is the over-simplified message'. But even an over-simplified message will be effective only if communicated at the right time. Hence, 'Positioning is an organised system for finding a window in the mind. It is based on the concept that communication can only take place at the right time and under the right circumstances'.

Ries and Trout cite Harvard psychologist George Miller in support of the view that the human mind has a very limited ready-use capacity – usually, only seven bits or units of information. Hence the popularity of seven-unit lists which have to be remembered – seven-digit phone numbers, seven wonders of the world, Snow White and the seven dwarfs, seven deadly sins, etc. With very important, high involvement topics one may increase the number of units – the Ten Commandments – but with low interest/low involvement topics like product or supplier identities the number may fall to as low as two or three. Further, in the case of product identities, users tend to rank order these in a 'ladder' (hence, ladders in the mind) with the preferred or most important on the top rung. 'A competitor that wants to increase its share of the business must either dislodge the brand above (a task that is usually impossible) or somehow relate its brand to the other company's position' (Ries and Trout, p. 32).

Similarly, with a new kind of product one must build a new ladder and will be most likely to succeed if one can relate it to an existing ladder. This may often be done most effectively by defining what it is *not*, rather than what is, e.g. a horseless carriage, lead-free petrol, sugar-free diet foods, etc.

Ries and Trout provide numerous examples to support their advice for successful positioning. To become a leader one should 'be firstest with the mostest', on the principle that while people can usually recall who was number 1 to achieve something they usually have difficulty in recalling number 2. On the other hand, if you can't be first then relating yourself to Number 1 helps link your name with theirs as an alternative choice – remember 'Avis is No. 2 – and we try harder'.

However, the real benefit of positioning lies in identifying the gap or hole in the marketplace, and then filling it. Of course, to do this one must establish the relevant criteria and then plot the existing alternatives in the same way as the store positioning maps illustrated in Figure 9.3. In some cases the axes of a perceptual map such as that in Figure 9.2 may appear to be opposed to one another (i.e. performance and price). But, as the Japanese have shown in market after market, they are adept at providing high performance at a comparatively low price and so give the greatest value for money – a much more meaningful concept to the consumer than either price or performance on their own. In other cases, however, price may be used to convey images of quality and value, particularly when consumers have difficulty in evaluating more objective performance criteria.

All of these tactics may be summarised within the concept of 'niche marketing'. As noted in Chapter 3 niche strategies tend to be adopted by 'follower' firms with a limited product portfolio who lack the resources to attack on more than one front at the same time. To pursue such a strategy successfully one must identify niches which are :

1   Of sufficient size and purchasing power to be profitable.
2   Growing or having the potential to do so.
3   Neglected by major companies.
4   Ones in which the firm has superior competencies looked for by the customers.
5   Capable of being defended through the establishment of a customer franchise.

Kotler[7] asserts that specialisation is the key to successful niche strategies and suggests 10 specialist roles open to the market nicher, namely:

1   *End-use specialist.* This firm decides to specialise in serving one type of end-use customer. For example, a law firm can decide to specialise in the criminal, civil, or business law markets.

2 *Vertical-level specialist.* This firm specialises at some vertical level of the production–distribution cycle. For example, a copper firm may concentrate on the production of raw copper, copper components, or finished copper products.

3 *Customer-size specialist.* This firm concentrates on selling to either small, medium, or large-size customers. Many nichers specialise in serving small customers because they are neglected by the majors.

4 *Specific-customers specialist.* This firm limits its selling to one (or a few) major customers. Many firms sell their entire output to a single company such as Sears or General Motors.

5 *Geographic specialist.* This firm focuses on the needs of a certain locality, region, or area of the world.

6 *Product or product-line specialist.* This firm produces only one product line or product. Within the laboratory equipment industry are firms that produce only microscopes, or even more narrowly, only lenses for microscopes.

7 *Product-feature specialist.* This firm specialises in producing a certain type of product or product-feature. Rent-a-Junk, for example, is a California car rental agency that rents only 'beat-up' cars.

8 *Job-shop specialist.* This firm stands ready to make customised products as ordered by the customer.

9 *Quality/price specialist.* This firm chooses to operate at the low or high end of the market. For example, Hewlett-Packard specialises in the high-quality, high-price end of the hand-calculator market.

10 *Service specialist.* This firm offers or excels in one or more services not readily available from other firms. An example would be a bank that takes loan requests over the phone or dispatches an officer to deliver the money at the client's home or office.

But what happens if one cannot identify a niche? Ries and Trout counsel that in such circumstances 'The basic underlying marketing strategy has got to be 'reposition the competition'. To do this one must change the perception of consumers of the status quo – a straightforward recommendation which is notoriously difficult to implement. Copernicus showed that the earth revolved round the sun, Columbus proved the earth is not flat and the Wright Brothers that we could fly. How does one provide such proof? Usually by supplying evidence which people can easily verify for themselves or, alternatively, reducing the credibility/acceptance of the received wisdom so that people will look for something else to replace it. Ries and Trout explain how Tylenol 'burst the aspirin bubble' by promoting the negative side effects of aspirin and then claiming that Tylenol avoided all of these. Similarly, Stolichnaya vodka produced and bottled in Russia successfully broke into the US market against established brands like Samovar, Smirnoff, Popov, etc. by simply saying 'Most American vodkas seem Russian' then listing where they were made, followed by the statement 'Stolichnaya is different. It is Russian'. Ries and Trout offer numerous other examples to support their argument, and point out that since the mid-1970s comparative advertising in which one comments adversely on competing brands has been legal in the US and UK and so a perfectly acceptable form of competition (always provided the statements are true!).

Ries and Trout continue 'In the positioning era, the single most important marketing decision you can make is what to name the product'. In recent years the subject of 'branding' has become one of the most widely discussed in the marketing domain. Its importance deserves separate treatment.

■ Branding

One of the most successful and succinct discussions of the nature and role of branding is to be found in Chapter 18 of *The Marketing Book*[8]. Entitled 'Branding' this chapter by Professor Peter Doyle first appeared in the Summer 1989 issue of the *Journal of Marketing Management* and was prompted by a major debate as to whether brands should be valued and included in the balance sheet. At the time a major takeover was being mounted against Rank Hovis McDougall (RHM). In fighting off the bid RHM management successfully persuaded their shareholders that the bid grossly undervalued the real worth of the company if one took into account the value of the international brands such as Cerebos, Hovis, Rank, etc. in its product portfolio. The point was well made as Nestlé's subsequent acquisition of Rowntree Mackintosh took full account of world class brands like Smarties, KitKat and Yorkie.

According to Doyle, a positive or successful brand can be defined as follows:

> *A successful brand is a name, symbol, design, or some combination which identifies the 'product' of a particular organisation as having a sustainable differential advantage* (emphasis in original).

Several points are important about this definition. First, successful brands are positive. In 1990 British Telecom spent over £70 million in redesigning and repositioning its corporate identity or 'brand' in order to try and overcome the negative association of its reputation for poor service. (This sum covered the total costs of changing the company's visual identity and was not, of course, solely for design and promotion.) Second, brands can take many forms – not just names. Third, the 'product' can just as easily be a service, an organisation or even an aspiration. Brands are owned by organisations/people and they confer a sustainable differential/competitive advantage. Doyle defines 'differential advantage' as meaning that customers have a reason for preferring that brand to competitor's brands, while 'sustainable' means an advantage that is not easily copied by competitors and so represents a barrier to entry in the market segment in which the brand competes. Only if a brand has a *sustainable differential advantage* (SDA) should it appear on the balance sheet. Thus neutral or negative brands earn profits through property or distribution efforts (however much is spent on promotion) and so, like short-lived fashion brands, should not be considered as assets in the same way as brands with SDA. Like other assets, brands require continued investment if they are to maintain their value. In the short term it may be possible to increase profits by cutting back on brand investment (i.e. by 'milking' the brand). If this is done, then competition will gradually erode the brand's standing and lead to its depreciation.

The importance of brands for consumers is that they help simplify decision-making. The brand is a form of mental shorthand that neatly summarises the output of the complex process described in our model of choice behaviour in Chapter 7. When introduced to a new product or service we have to execute an evaluation in which we relate performance characteristics to our felt needs and determine whether consumption of the new offering will increase our overall satisfaction compared with our current pattern of behaviour. We have also seen that with low involvement goods the easiest way to resolve this problem is through trial or experience rather than the kind of extended and complex evaluation which will precede even trial of a high involvement (high perceived risk) object. Once we have learned a pattern of behaviour then we will tend to repeat that behaviour in future until some event suggests that by breaking this habit we may increase our satisfaction in some way. Thus, as Ries and Trout point out, we form 'short-lists' of known solutions to possible consumption problems and find it convenient to rank order these in terms of expected outcomes. Brands enable us to identify acceptable solutions without having to remember to recall all the factors which led to our original choice.

But, as Doyle points out, successful brands with SDA do not depend solely on actual experience in use for their reputations. Indeed a great deal of a brand's reputation may be based upon perceptions that have built up over time. In his words 'Such preferences or brand images are based upon cultural, social and personality factors, as well as commercial stimuli like advertising, public relations and prominence of distribution'. As such we can form favourable or unfavourable attitudes towards brands even if we have no actual experience of them. One can like the Marlboro ads and not smoke and think well of Pedigree Chum and not own a dog. Undoubtedly, the 'owners' of such brands value this support from non-users not just because if they become users they will have an immediate preference for the brand, but because this favourable opinion reinforces the actual users' attitude concerning the wisdom of their choice.

Of course, usage or consumption of the brand is the primary objective of the marketer – there being a well-established relationship between profitability and market share. Doyle cites the well-known PIMS (Profit Implications of Market Strategy) findings (Buzzell and Gale, 1987)[9] which showed that brands with a market share of 40% generated three times the profit or return on investment of those with a market share of 10%, which increased to four times when the ratio was increased to 60:10, as shown in Figure 9.4.

These findings have been supported by research in many other countries (Q.V. Doyle, 1980) and explain the sellers' concern to build successful brands with large market shares. A note of caution is appropriate. During the late 1980s research into the actual performance of companies seeking to build or improve market

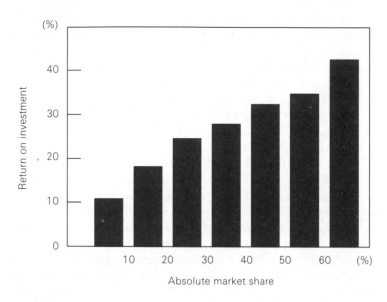

Figure 9.4   The relationship between market share and profitability

Source: R.D. Buzzell and B.T. Gale, *The PIMS Principles: Linking Strategy to Performance* (London: Collier Macmillan, 1987).

share showed that many of them became less profitable (or even unprofitable) than they had been with their original market share. This observation suggests that when you enjoy a large market share you are likely to be the most profitable player in that market, but if you are seeking to win market share from established brands the costs of doing so will very probably eliminate the profits anticipated from the increased volume. Clearly, this finding reinforces Ries and Trout's advice to be the firstest with the mostest, or the more general observation that much marketing expenditure should be regarded as an investment rather than an expense on the basis that the benefits are likely to be distant and long-term rather than immediate and short-term. Indeed it has been estimated that as a working rule of thumb it costs six times as much money to win a new customer as to retain an existing customer's loyalty (Peters, 1988)[10]. With odds like these, winning the brand share war against a strongly entrenched and preferred competitor is bound to prove very expensive and to be undertaken only if one has considerable confidence that the market is likely to survive well into the future. Most evidence suggests that such markets are most often found in the realm of consumer goods where the brand leaders have sustained a dominant position for decades. (Research in 1975 showed that 19 out of 25 leading brands in the USA were the same as in 1925, fifty years earlier!)

Long-term brand leadership of this kind is most usual where *product differentiation opportunities are less available*, i.e. where it is difficult to reposition a product through technological innovation without actually changing the nature of the product/market. This is not to say that product improvement will not occur but the markets for carbonated beverages like Coca Cola, for breakfast cereals like corn flakes, or for soap products have been characterised by evolutionary rather than revolutionary change, mainly led by the companies with the dominant market shares. In markets where revolutionary change is possible through technological innovation the incidence of long-lived 'brand leaders' is much less. One reason for this is undoubtedly the 'marketing myopia' diagnosed by Ted Levitt,[11] which arises from too close involvement with a past or present way of doing things and an unwillingness to accept the displacement of such established ways with new ways. The irony of this is that all experience points to the fact that the perceived credibility and standing of a market leader offers the greatest likelihood of success in launching a new product, i.e. the 'halo' effect of a house brand like IBM or Marks & Spencer will help reduce much of the risk which a potential user would perceive if invited to try the same new product launched by an unknown company without such an established reputation. How then should one set about building a brand reputation?

■ Building a Brand Reputation

Implicit in our model of choice behaviour is the belief that a rational person or organisation will always prefer *objective* and *tangible evidence* to subjective and intangible evidence in selecting between competing offerings. This belief is not equivalent to the proposal of a mechanistic process in which a third party could automatically determine another's preferred choice (as suggested in economic theory) for, as we have seen, the selection and interpretation of both objective and subjective data is mediated by the attitudes, opinions, beliefs and experience (habit) of the chooser. Nonetheless, the model does allow us to identify some *necessary* conditions, albeit that they may not be *sufficient* to predict brand choice. Further, we can see that choice is the outcome of a sequential process which may be aborted at any stage between awareness of a need and the adoption/rejection of a specific solution. These ideas are encapsulated in a modified version of Levitt's concept of the brand[12], and illustrated in Figure 9.5.

At the heart of the product are the essential characteristics which enable users to identify it as a possible solution to their consumption need. This essential or 'core' product/service is largely defined by its performance characteristics, i.e. what it will do for the owner. For the industrial or organisational buyer seeking to purchase a complex offering it will be defined in detail in the formal specification, whether it be for the building of an off-shore rig or the supply of a catering service in a new residential management centre. Associated with the core product will be a cluster of other attributes such as its design, appearance, packaging and identification (the brand) which enable potential users to differentiate between the offerings of competing suppliers. Without such

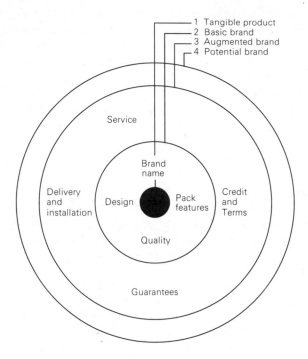

1 Tangible product
2 Basic brand
3 Augmented brand
4 Potential brand

Service

Brand
name

Delivery
and
installation

Design

Pack
features

Credit
and
Terms

Quality

Guarantees

Figure 9.5   What is a brand?

Source: Adapted by the author from T. Levitt, *The Marketing Imagination* (London: Collier
Macmillan, 1983).

attributes the product would become a commodity like wool, wheat, iron ore,
etc. where the only rational basis for purchase is cost–benefit: i.e. how much in
time and space will I secure for any given expenditure? While attributes such as
design, packaging and quality will all assist the potential buyer to discriminate
between products at the point of purchase, increasing competition and a concern
for the user's needs has led to the development of what Levitt terms the
'augmented' product.

Augmented products reflect the seller's concern for the actual performance of
the product and offer additional benefits to the intending buyer. Many of these
benefits, such as guarantees and the provision of after-sales service, help to reduce
the perceived risk which the buyer experiences in selecting a durable product or
service whose benefits will be enjoyed over a period of time, like a piece of
machinery, or else are intended to mature if a particular event such as damage,
loss or theft occurs (insurance). Similarly, delivery, assistance with installation
and the provision of credit are all additional incentives which add value and
enable buyers to discriminate between objectively similar products.

Finally, the 'outer shell' of the product is the 'potential brand' which Doyle defines[13] as 'anything that conceivably could be done to build customer preference and loyalty'. Despite Ries and Trout's assertion quoted earlier that advertising is a weak force and incapable of achieving major change in buying behaviour, there can be no doubt that advertising and promotion have a great deal to do with creating the Just Noticeable Difference (JND) factor which mediates the decision-maker's final behavioural response (BR in our model of buyer behaviour). Advertising and promotion are important at the beginning of the purchase decision because they attract our attention and help move us from a state of subconscious readiness to one of conscious awareness, i.e. they make us aware of a *possible need*. Having secured our attention, advertising and promotion can then provide information which can prompt us to further action – information search for high-involvement products and even purchase for low-involvement goods.

Advertising also helps reinforce our existing patterns of behaviour and provides reassurance that such behaviour is to our greatest benefit. All these attributes add value to the brand. In many instances, they create and sustain subjective associations which are the very essence of actual preference. In our model of buyer behaviour these are often the factors which enable buyers to tip the balance between augmented brands where competing suppliers have matched each other exactly in terms of all the performance factors and service attributes. Naturally, these marginal distinctions, which are usually highly specific to the individual decision-makers, will come into play only where alternatives appear identical in every other respect. Because the subjective associations created by advertising have this ability to influence the final choice critics claim that advertising is manipulative. Such claims are clearly specious and do a grave disservice to the buyer who has performed a careful comparative assessment of the merits of available alternatives and, being unable to distinguish between them, instead of tossing the statistician's coin selects the offering in which he or she has the greatest confidence.

In suggesting that a brand has a core and up to three 'skins', we are reflecting the view that decision-making is a sequential process in which one uses increasingly selective criteria in order to make a final choice. It is clear that if the core product is sufficiently distinctive then would-be buyers will not need to have recourse to second, third or even fourth order factors to position their offerings in the mind of prospective consumers. But, given the increase in global competition referred to in Chapter 2 and the turbulent and rapidly changing environment discussed in Chapter 6, it is obvious that more and more suppliers in all types of business must give careful attention to all aspects of the brand.

That said, some dimensions are more important than others and Doyle (1969) proposes that these are:

1   Quality.
2   Superior service.
3   Get there first.
4   Look for differentiation.

In the case of quality Doyle cites Buzzell and Gale's (1987) analysis of the PIMS data which showed a similar relationship between perceived quality and return on sales and investment as that noted earlier for market share (see Figure 9.6).

Because products can be copied so readily Doyle argues that 'service is perhaps the most sustainable differential advantage'. Service is, of course, an intrinsic element of the exchange process and thus much more difficult to replicate than physical features or attributes like delivery, credit terms, etc. As we noted in Chapter 2, when discussing the contribution of marketing to competitive success, in the final analysis 'It ain't what you do, it's the way that you do it'. In Chapter 18 we discuss the role of service in the particular and in Chapter 19 we examine how successful organisations develop cultures which create added values for themselves and their customers. 'Get there first' was Ries and Trout's primary recommendation and Doyle quotes Clifford & Cavanagh's (1985)[14] study which provides formal evidence to support this advice (see Figure 9.7). Doyle also suggests that there are at least five ways of getting there first:

(a)   Exploiting new technology (e.g. Xerox, IBM).
(b)   New positioning concepts (e.g. Body Shop, Fosters Lager).
(c)   New distribution channels (e.g. Argos).
(d)   New market segments (e.g. Amstrad).
(e)   Exploiting gaps created by sudden environmental changes (e.g. egg substitutes – a reference to a scare about infected eggs in the UK in 1990).

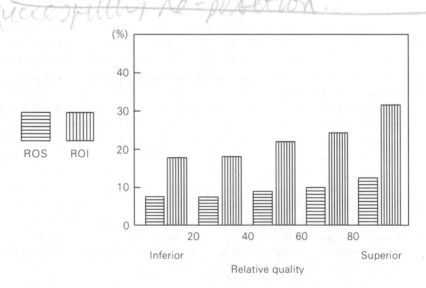

Figure 9.6   Quality and Profitability

Source: R. D. Buzzell and B.T. Gale, *The PIMS Principles: Linking Strategy to Performance* (London: Collier Macmillan, 1987).

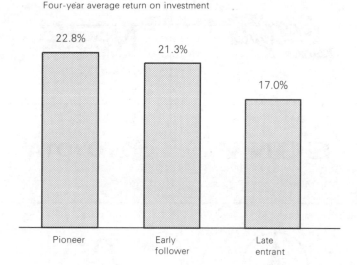

Figure 9.7   Timing of market entry and business

Source: D. K. Clifford and R. E. Caveanagh, *The Winning Performance: How America's high growth midsize companies succeed* (London: Sidgwick and Jackson, 1985).

Doyle's fourth element – differentiation – is, of course, what branding is all about. As John Murphy observed[15] a brand is the product or service of a particular supplier which is differentiated by its name and presentation. Thus any manufacturer can produce a cola drink but only the Coca-Cola Company can produce Coke. Indeed, the only feature which a determined and well resourced competitor would be unable convincingly to replicate is the brand itself. A brand is therefore more than the actual product, it is the unique product of a specific owner which has been developed over time to embrace a set of values, both tangible and intangible, meaningfully and appropriately to differentiate products which may otherwise be very similar.

In a survey undertaken by Landor Associates of the strength of major corporate, service and consumer brand names across international markets and industry categories the world's 'Top Ten' brands were as shown in Figure 9.8. For the UK, the Top Ten brands are shown in Figure 9.9.

As implied by Murphy's comments, branding has been considered primarily at the level of the individual product or service. More recently, however, the distinguished marketing practitioner Stephen King[16] has argued cogently that in the 1990s it will be more important to consider the actual company as a brand. In *Marketing* (5th edn, 1991) I included a summary of the article which Stephen wrote for the *Journal of Marketing Management* which I edit. In view of its relevance and importance the essence of this summary is reproduced below.

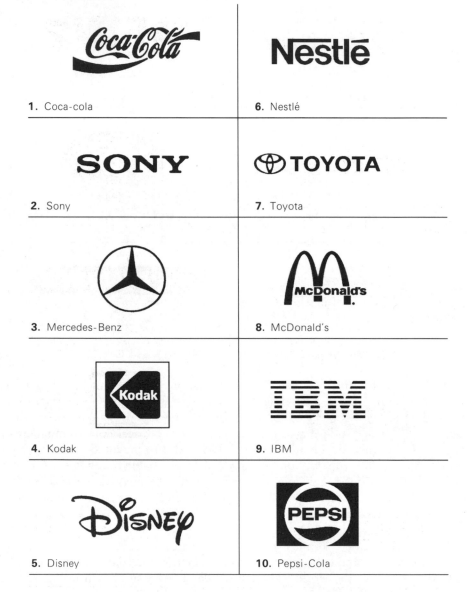

1. Coca-cola

6. Nestlé

2. Sony

7. Toyota

3. Mercedes-Benz

8. McDonald's

4. Kodak

9. IBM

5. Disney

10. Pepsi-Cola

Figure 9.8   The global top 10

Source: The Landor ImagePower Survey 1990, Landor Associates.

1. Marks & Spencers

6. Heinz

2. Kellogg's

7. Boots

3. Cadbury

8. McVitie's

4. BBC

9. Yellow Pages

5. Nescafé

10. W.H.Smith

Figure 9.9   The top 10 brands in the UK

Source: The Landor ImagePower Survey 1990, Landor Associates.

■ The Company as a Brand

In 'Brand Building in the 1990s' (*Journal of Marketing Management*, 7(1), 1991) Stephen King identifies six areas of change which are exerting pressure on companies and which are likely to intensify over the next few years:

- More confident consumers.
- New concepts of quality.
- Shortage of skills.
- Tightening of the competitive screw.
- The side effects of New Technology.
- Restructuring.

In respect of consumers King points out they have become more confident, readier to experiment and trust their own judgement, have more disposable income and are more worldly wise. They have a greater understanding of 'marketing' in all its activities and this understanding will help ensure customers in business-to-business marketing become more demanding too.

Consumers have strong views on what gives them satisfaction and are less tolerant of goods and services that don't live up to their expectations. Finally, and probably as a consequence of the preceding changes, they have become more independent and closer to the highest level of Maslow's need hierarchy – self-actualisation. The world may be a global market, but its tribes and their members still have a need to distinguish themselves from one another to express their growing individualism. Nowhere is this more the case than in consumers' increasing demand for quality and a quality founded on real values which go together to make up 'the good life', such as green products rather than products which consume non-replaceable resources, pollute the atmosphere or cause pain or suffering to other species.

Satisfying the needs of these 'new' consumers will call for radical changes on the supply side but here skills shortages, due to declining birth rates, and insufficient education and training pose a threat to our ability to make these changes. However, international competition looks certain to intensify and will become even more acute as the leading players seek to secure the necessary labour inputs.

While it has become a cliché to talk of accelerating technological change the trend persists. As King observes 'Constant innovation will be a necessary part of normal commercial life, but few companies will be able to rely on having any *demonstrable* product or service advantage for more than a few months'. In the absence of objective criteria to guide the choice decisions, then, the *relationship* between seller and buyer will assume even greater importance. In consumer markets King believes this will reinforce the retailer's position as the consumer's friend at the expense of the manufacturer.

Faced with changes of the kind discussed above, producers will continue to restructure in an effect to secure economies of scale in manufacturing and marketing. In many cases this will involve margers and takeovers, in others the striking of strategic alliances. Inevitably it will result in still greater concentration of market power in the hands of a small number of global players in the majority of industries. In order to survive, King, amongst others, is of the opinion that success will depend critically on *brand-building* which he defines as 'using all the company's particular assets to create unique entities that certain consumers really want; entities which have a lasting personality, based on a special combination of physical, functional and psychological values; and which have competitive advantage in at least one area of marketing (raw materials/sourcing, product/ design/patents, production systems, supply/sales/service networks, depth of understanding of consumers, style/fashion, and so on)'. Only through brand building will it be possible to:

- build stable, long-term demand;
- add value looked for by customers;
- develop a sound base for future growth and expansion;
- recruit the growing power of intermediaries;
- become recognised as a company with a reputation and going places that people will want to work with and for.

However, King believes that brand-building in the 1990s will be quite different from that of the past which led to the emergence and dominance of classic single-line brands like Coke, Pepsi, Marlboro, Persil, Oxo, Kit-Kat, and Andrex. As King points out, in 1969 19 of the 25 top spending brands in the UK were repeat purchase packaged goods; in 1989 it was just 1. Now the trend is to the *company brand*, in which it is the subjective, difficult-to-define aspects of service and reputation associated with a company which will position it in the consumer's mind and the market place. 'In essence, brand-building in the 1990s will involve designing and controlling all aspects of a company, leading people and activities well beyond the traditional skill of the marketing department and the agencies that it employs. It will be a lot closer to the marketing of services (such as airlines, hotels, retailers, building societies) than to the brand-building of the classic brands'.

But such brand-building will have to be very different from most managers' current perception of 'brands' as fmcg or possibly the company's logo and corporate identity programme. In future the company 'brand' will have to encapsulate and communicate what an organisation *is* and what it *stands for* – its mission, culture and aspirations. In doing so it will be as important for the internal marketing of the firm as it is for its efforts to win a distinguished and distinctive place in the perception of its actual and prospective customers. To achieve this will require organisations to be market-orientated and customer-driven in a manner which embraces all members and functions of the organisation.

Clearly, many companies are already seeking to implement this advice and have developed *positioning statements* which seek to encapsulate the values which the company subscribes to and offers its customers. Examples include:

- 'Access your flexible friend'.
- 'It's you we answer to' (British Telecom).
- 'We won't make a drama out of a crisis' (Commercial Union).
- 'Everything we do is driven by you' (Ford).
- 'Helping you control your world' (Honeywell).

■ Summary

In Chapter 9 we have looked at the need for firms to position themselves in the market place. Positioning is the development of a distinctive and unique selling proposition (USP) which enables a seller to differentiate himself from all other sellers who are seeking to serve the same market segment.

The need for positioning has arisen due to increased international (and domestic) competition and the erosion of the ability to develop objectively different products based upon technological innovation. Given the proliferation of available solutions to the firm's/individual's consumption needs, and the intensity of the competitive effort clamouring for attention, it is unsurprising that buyers have developed decision rules to simplify the complexity of the situation. In such an environment the brand – product, service, and especially the company – has become a convenient shorthand to summarise a multiplicity of both objective and subjective attributes that have to be considered when making choice decisions. The nature and importance of these diverse attributes has been reviewed, as have techniques such as perceptual mapping which enable sellers to capture and analyse this complexity as the basis for developing differentiated marketing strategies.

Situation Analysis: The Marketing Audit

Learning Goals

The issues to be addressed in Chapter 10 include:

1 The *nature* and *purpose* of the marketing audit.
2 *Competitor analysis.*
3 *Sales forecasting.*

After reading Chapter 10 you will be able to:

1 *Define* a marketing audit.
2 Spell out the *scope* and *major elements* of a marketing audit.
3 Explain the *importance* of competitor analysis.
4 Define the *nature* and *purpose* of sales forecasting.
5 Set out the steps in *preparing* a sales forecast.
6 Review the main sales forecasting *methods* and summarise their *advantages* and *disadvantages*.

■ Introduction

Up to this point in the book we have been concerned primarily with developing a conceptual understanding of the nature of *marketing strategy* and the forces external to the firm which influence and shape the *strategic options* available to it. In Chapter 10 we mark the transition from strategy to management by exploring how the firm can assess its own *competitive standing* in relation to its external environment and the current state of competition in the markets in which it intends to compete.

The discussion this far has focused upon developing the theme that strategic marketing planning (SMP) is a prerequisite for success. We have examined a number of analytical frameworks, theories and techniques which provide a foundation for developing an SMP system. It is clear, however, that while diagnosis and prognosis are essential to the formulation of strategic plans it is the quality of the *implementation* which determines the degree of success enjoyed by the firm. As we pointed out in Chapter 6, when considering the relative importance of environmental analysis *vis à vis* an analysis of industry structure, all firms face a *common external environment* and it is their interaction with each other which determines their actual degree of success.

Implementation is the responsibility of the firm's management and there is clear evidence that in our present turbulent environment a careful analysis of the firm's strengths and weaknesses in relation to the external opportunities and threats is a necessary, albeit not sufficient, condition for long-run competitive success. Some of the underlying forces which influence the external environment were explored in Chapter 6. In this chapter we concentrate primarily upon the assessment and measurement of the firm's *internal strengths and weaknesses* which comprise the other 'half' of a technique usually referred to as the marketing audit. While we shall present the marketing audit as a mechanism for enabling the organisation to conduct a situation or SWOT analysis in which it seeks to relate its strengths to market opportunities, avoid threats and remedy weakness we shall also suggest that it provides an ideal basis for assessing these organisation's competitors. Accordingly, the second section of the chapter deals with competitor analysis.

The third section of the chapter also reflects its transitional nature and deals with the topic of sales forecasting. Sales forecasting is an important technique for bringing the broadly-based environmental analysis into the sharper focus which is essential for detailed planning purposes. As such, it is a vital and necessary input to the preparation of annual or short-term marketing plans, which is a subject that we return to later in Chapter 20.

■ Marketing Audits

'A marketing audit is a systematic and thorough examination of a company's marketing position.'[1]

A marketing audit is a 'systematic, critical, and impartial review and appraisal of the total marketing operation: of the basic objectives and policies and the assumptions which underlie them as well as the methods, procedures, personnel, and organisation employed to implement the policies and achieve the objectives'.[2]

Kotler[3] offers a similar but more extensive definition:

> A marketing audit is an independent examination of the entire marketing effort of a company, or some specific marketing activity, covering objectives, programme, implementation, and organisation, for the triple purpose of determining what is being done, appraising what is being done, and recommending what should be done in the future.

Marketing audits are necessary to monitor changes in the environment in which the organisation conducts its business, and should take into account both the external and internal situation. In addition to evaluating both past performance and present practices the marketing audit should also help identify *future* threats and opportunities and so provide a basis for policy formulation and planning. Thus the marketing audit should be regarded as an input to the overall corporate planning function and the foundation of the detailed marketing plan. An excellent tabulation of the scope and components of the marketing audit is provided by Kotler, Gregor and Rogers,[4] and is reproduced as Table 10.1.

Table 10.1 The marketing audit

MARKETING ENVIRONMENT AUDIT

I. Macro-environment

Economic-Demographic
1.   What does the company expect in the way of inflation, material shortages, unemployment, and credit availability in the short run, intermediate run, and long run?
2.   What effect will forecasted trends in the size, age distribution, and regional distribution of population have on the business?

Technology
1.   What major changes are occurring in product technology? In process technology?
2.   What are the major generic substitutes that might replace this product?

Political-Legal
1.   What laws are being proposed that may affect marketing strategy and tactics?
2.   What federal, state, and local agency actions should be watched? What is happening in the areas of pollution control, equal employment opportunity, product safety, advertising, price control, etc. that is relevant to marketing planning?

Social-Cultural
1.   What attitude is the public taking toward business and toward products such as those produced by the company?
2.   What changes are occurring in consumer life styles and values that have a bearing on the company's target markets and marketing methods?

II. Task environment

Markets
1.   What is happening to market size, growth, geographical distribution, and profits?
2.   What are the major market segments? What are their expected rates of growth? Which are high opportunity and low opportunity segments?

Customers
1.   How do current customers and prospects rate the company and its competitors, particularly with respect to reputation, product quality, service, sales force, and price?
2.   How do different classes of customers make their buying decisions?
3.   What are the evolving needs and satisfactions being sought by the buyers in this market?

Competitors
1.   Who are the major competitors? What are the objectives and strategy of each major competitor? What are their strengths and weaknesses? What are the sizes and trends in market shares?
2.   What trends can be foreseen in future competition and substitutes for this product?

Distribution and Dealers
1.   What are the main trade channels bringing products to customers?
2.   What are the efficiency levels and growth potentials of the different trade channels?

Suppliers
1.   What is the outlook for the availability of different key resources used in production?
2.   What trends are occurring among suppliers in their pattern of selling?

Facilitators
1.   What is the outlook for the cost and availability of transportation services?
2.   What is the outlook for the cost and availability of warehousing facilities?
3.   What is the outlook for the cost and availability of financial resources?
4.   How effectively is the advertising agency performing? What trends are occurring in advertising agency services?

MARKETING STRATEGY AUDIT

Marketing Objectives
1.   Are the corporate objectives clearly stated and do they lead logically to the marketing objectives?
2.   Are the marketing objectives stated in a clear form to guide marketing planning and subsequent performance measurement?
3.   Are the marketing objectives appropriate, given the company's competitive position, resources, and opportunities? Is the appropriate strategic objective to build, hold, harvest, or terminate this business?

Strategy
1.   What is the core marketing strategy for achieving the objectives? Is it a sound marketing strategy?
2.   Are enough resources (or too much resources) budgeted to accomplish the marketing objectives?
3.   Are the marketing resources allocated optimally to prime market segments, territories, and products of the organisation?
4.   Are the marketing resources allocated optimally to the major elements of the marketing mix, i.e. product quality, service, sales force, advertising, promotion, and distribution?

MARKETING ORGANISATION AUDIT

Formal Structure
1.   Is there a high-level marketing officer with adequate authority and responsibility over those company activities that affect the customer's satisfaction?
2.   Are the marketing responsibilities optimally structured along functional product, end user, and territorial lines?

Functional Efficiency
1.   Are there good communication and working relations between marketing and sales?
2.   Is the product management system working effectively? Are the product managers able to plan profits or only sales volume?
3.   Are there any groups in marketing that need more training, motivation, supervision, or evaluation?

Interface Efficiency
1.   Are there any problems between marketing and manufacturing that need attention?
2.   What about marketing and R & D?
3.   What about marketing and financial management?
4.   What about marketing and purchasing?

MARKETING SYSTEMS AUDIT

Marketing Information System
1. Is the marketing intelligence system producing accurate, sufficient, and timely information about developments in the marketplace?
2. Is marketing research being adequately used by company decision makers?

Marketing Planning System
1. Is the marketing planning system well-conceived and effective?
2. Is sales forecasting and market potential measurement soundly carried out?
3. Are sales quotas set on a proper basis?

Marketing Control System
1. Are the control procedures (monthly, quarterly, etc.) adequate to ensure that the annual plan objectives are being achieved?
2. Is provision made to analyse periodically the profitability of different products, markets, territories, and channels of distribution?
3. Is provision made to examine and validate periodically various marketing costs?

New Product Development System
1. Is the company well-organised to gather, generate, and screen new product ideas?
2. Does the company do adequate concept research and business analysis before investing heavily in a new idea?
3. Does the company carry out adequate product and market testing before launching a new product?

MARKETING PRODUCTIVITY AUDIT

Profitability Analysis
1. What is the profitability of the company's different products, served markets, territories, and channels of distribution?
2. Should the company enter, expand, contract, or withdraw from any business segments and what would be the short- and long-run profit consequences?

Cost-Effectiveness Analysis
1. Do any marketing activities seem to have excessive costs? Are these costs valid? Can cost-reducing steps be taken?

MARKETING FUNCTION AUDIT

Products
1. What are the product line objectives? Are these objectives sound? Is the current product line meeting these objectives?
2. Are there particular products that should be phased out?
3. Are there new products that are worth adding?
4. Are any products able to benefit from quality, feature, or style improvements?

Price
1. What are the pricing objectives, policies, strategies, and procedures? To what extent are prices set on sound cost, demand, and competitive criteria?
3. Does the company use price promotions effectively?

Distribution
1. What are the distribution objectives and strategies?
2. Is there adequate market coverage and service?
3. Should the company consider changing its degree of reliance on distributors, sales reps, and direct selling?

Sales Force
1. What are the organisation's sales force objectives?
2. Is the sales force large enough to accomplish the company's objectives?
3. Is the sales force organised along the proper principle(s) of specialisation (territory, market, product)?
4. Does the sales force show high morale, ability, and effort? Are they sufficiently trained and incentivised?
5. Are the procedures adequate for setting quotas and evaluating performances?
6. How is the company's sales force perceived in relation to competitors' sales forces?

Advertising, Promotion, and Publicity
1. What are the organisation's advertising objectives? Are they sound?
2. Is the right amount being spent on advertising? How is the budget determined?
3. Are the ad themes and copy effective? What do customers and the public think about the advertising?
4. Are the advertising media well-chosen?
5. Is sales promotion used effectively?
6. Is there a well-conceived publicity program?

Source: P. Kotler, W. Gregor and W. Rogers, 'The MA Comes of Age', *Sloan Management Review*, 18(1) (Winter 1977).

Despite its comprehensiveness the checklist contained in Table 10.1 is illustrative only. While it covers the broad scope of a marketing audit it is lacking in the detail which would be necessary in gathering the appropriate level of detail for the preparation of a marketing plan. However there are numerous books which provide such checklists and offer the level of detail required. For example Makens[5] and Stapleton[6] provide extensive examples of documentation to be used in undertaking a marketing audit. Table 10.2, from Stapleton's book, deals with the specific issue of a consumption audit and is but one of a large number of tables designed to ensure a comprehensive analysis.

It should also be noted that Table 10.1 dates back to the 1970s and so does not include a specific reference to service under the final marketing function audit, which it certainly would do if it were being prepared today.

The frequency with which marketing audits are undertaken is a function of several variables, including the firm's planning frame (monthly, annual, biennial, etc.), the nature of its business and the rate of change in the environment. The optimum approach is probably to undertake a standardised audit at regular intervals and supplement these with special *ad hoc* surveys as conditions dictate. Similarly, the scope of the audit may be varied with certain key areas being assessed with a high frequency with more detailed, in-depth analysis being undertaken less often. Such detailed inquiry into specific topics, e.g. pricing policy, may well be amenable to some form of *rota*, so that all areas will be covered within the duration of a planning cycle. For example, if the firm normally operates on an annual cycle then it may be convenient to monitor key indicators such as sales, prices, market share, etc., on a monthly basis and the 'mix' elements on a bi-monthly rota, e.g.:

Table 10.2   Consumption audit

1	Is the total market in decline?
2	Is the brand share in decline?
3	In what position does the brand rank?
4	Will brand share increase if promoted?
5	Can retail selling price bear an increase?
6	Can production economies be achieved?
7	Can range be reduced?
8	What other markets are possible?
9	What is the profit contribution?
10	What is the break-even point?
11	Can the brand be revitalised?
12	Can the brand be sold off?
A	Who are the potential buyers?
B	What is the size and scope of the potential market?
C	What is the distribution of the potential market?
D	What are the needs, habits, and buying motives of the potential market?
E	What related products will/do people buy?
F	What is the expected buying frequency?
G	What is the likely buying quantity?
H	Who is the purchasing agent in the target audience family?
I	Who influences brand choice decisions?
J	What price differentials are possible among market segments?
K	Is the buying derived from some other purchase?
L	Is the buying on impulse or predetermined?
M	Is the demand likely to be elastic?
N	Is the brand likely to be price sensitive?
O	Is the demand going to be dependent on merchandising?
P	What factors are likely to limit demand?
Q	What is the effect of fashion/technological changes?
R	What seasonal factors are apparent?
S	What is likely to be the average rate of consumption?
T	What factors are likely to affect the consumption rate?
U	What emotive/psychological factors need to be taken into account?
V	What current legislation exists: safety, packaging, labelling, weights?
W	How are problems related to pre-sales and after-sales?
X	What additional credit/financing is likely to be required?
Y	What guarantees/warranties are appropriate?
Z	What are marked preferences for choice of outlet?

Source: John Stapleton, *How to Prepare a Marketing Plan* (Aldershot: Gower, 1989) 4th edn.

- Month 2   Pricing.
- Month 4   Packaging.
- Month 6   Promotion.
- Month 8   Distribution.
- Month 10   Sales.
- Month 12   Market research.

Crisp [7] suggests six alternative sources of audit:

1 *Self-audit.*
2 *Audit-from-across* – persons in related activities on the same functional level audit each other.
3 *Audit-from-above.*
4 *Company auditing office.*
5 *Company task-force audit* – a team is appointed on an *ad hoc* basis from within the company's staff.
6 *Outside audit.*

While Crisp prefers the last option on the grounds of greater objectivity and freedom from internal operating pressures, there would seem to be merit in a composite approach involving more than one option, for example, the appointment of an external auditor to validate and integrate self-audit by managers with functional and/or departmental responsibility. Such a composite approach could well permit the benefits of external objectivity with the greater detail and frequency of data collection possible with internal systems.

Grashof[8] suggests that a marketing audit falls into three phases – information assembly, information analysis and the formulation of recommendations – and that these central phases will be preceded by a planning stage (pre-audit activities) and followed by an implementation phase (post-audit activities). Phase I (Information Assembly) consists of the identification and acquisition of information bearing upon the major areas which affect a firm's marketing programme, including:

1 The industry.
2 The firm.
3 The market.
4 The product.
5 Distribution.
6 Promotion.
7 Pricing.

A similar approach is proposed by Cannon,[9] and recognises five steps:

		Key elements *Develop:*
Step One:	Define the market	1 Statement of purpose in terms of benefits. 2 Product scope. 3 Size, growth rate, maturity state, need for primary vs selective strategies. 4 Requirements for success. 5 Divergent definitions of the above by competitors. 6 Definition to be used by the company.
Step Two:	Determine performance differentials	1 Evaluate industry performance and company differences. 2 Determine differences in products, applications, geography, and distribution channels. 3 Determine differences by customer set.
Step Three:	Determine differences in competitive programmes	Identify and evaluate individual companies for their: 1 Market development strategies. 2 Product development strategies. 3 Financing and administrative strategies and support.
Step Four:	Profile the strategies of competitors	1 Profile each significant competitor and/or distinct type of competitive strategy. 2 Compare own and competitive strategies.
Step Five:	Determine strategic planning structure	When size and complexity are adequate: 1 Establish planning units or cells and designate prime and subordinate strategies. 2 Make organisational assignments to product managers, industry managers, and others.

In the view of Douglas Brownlie of the Glasgow Business School there is a danger that the growing emphasis being given to external environmental factors may distract management from undertaking an equally rigorous review of their internal environment. This danger may well be exaggerated by the assumption that of course everyone knows what is going on inside the firm and so takes less care to document this thoroughly. In his article in the *Journal of Marketing Management*[10] Brownlie offers a wide-ranging review of the execution of an internal appraisal and its role in the overall strategic management of the firm. The paper also introduces a conceptual framework which integrates tasks of defining, identifying and evaluating the firm's strengths and weaknesses. In doing so it also looks at functional areas of the firm and gives examples of the strengths and weaknesses to be found in each. The paper contains extensive references, and so is an ideal starting point for readers wishing to explore this topic in greater detail.

■ Competitor Analysis

From the discussion of competition in Chapter 2 and the subsequent discussion of competitive strategy in Chapter 3 it has become clear that the firm's ultimate success or failure depends upon its ability to position itself effectively, *vis-à-vis* other firms seeking to serve the same end-use markets. It follows that a vital element in terms of the situation analysis prior to the formulation of a marketing plan is an assessment of the competition and their strengths and weaknesses. In an ideal world one would seek to document competitive firms in the same detail as suggested by the internal marketing audit described in the previous section, and in oligopolistic markets characterised by a small number of similar sized competitors this may be partially possible. However, the cost of acquiring and maintaining a database on competitive firms may far exceed the worth of the actual data and the cost of acquiring it. For example, in August 1991 the *Sunday Times* reported that ICI had spent over £10 million in documenting the activities of Hanson Trust as a basis for a defence against a possible takeover. In the view of some city analysts such expenditures were regarded as at best misguided and at worse a misappropriation of shareholders' funds.

If, therefore, one is to undertake a reasonable assessment on one's competitors one must first establish what are the most appropriate *performance indicators*, and then select those that can be documented most cost effectively.

In John Stapleton's book (1987), it is suggested that the most appropriate means for assessing competition is in truly financial terms as this enables comparisons to be made and a standard to be developed against which the firm's own performance can be measured. To structure such an analysis Stapleton proposes nine different indicators. The first of these, which he calls 'Financial Performance', is a simple chart intended to highlight the profitability in growth of significant suppliers and compare their performance against each other. At a minimum, this requires recording of data for sales, net income, total assets, and number of ordinary shares together with net profit expressed as a percentage return on sales, total assets and ordinary shares. Superficially it would appear very simple to obtain such data either from the company's own published accounts or else from companies such as Dun & Bradstreet which specialise in the compilation of such information. Of course, the problem is that the more readily available such data is the more likely it becomes that the firm has multiple products on sale in multiple markets. But, as our discussion of strategy has indicated, the important criterion is the definition of *market segments* within which the firm has chosen to compete. Accordingly unless the financial data relates to a single-product firm operating in only one market it will offer only the most generalised form of comparative data.

Much the same criticism applies to the second of Stapleton's analyses, which he calls 'Standard Comparison'. This comprises recording the entries one would find in a detailed profit and loss account for each main competitor.

Stapleton's third checklist/chart is reproduced as Table 10.3, and may be used at either the firm or at the specific product market level. As the headings suggest what is called for here is that the appraiser seeks to rate his own company's performance on a number of critical success factors and then performs the same analysis on the major competitive firms. Table 10.3 is included for illustrative purposes as the nature and number of critical success factors to be rated will depend very much upon the firm and industry to which it belongs. The remaining documentation provided by Stapleton deals with Price and Market Share Relationships, Geographical Sales Distribution, Penetration of Sales Outlets, Competitive Pricing, etc. While it may not be possible to get precise data on each of these factors, this is the kind of grass roots market data which one might reasonably expect the salesforce to collect as part of its day-to-day activity.

Information of the kind discused in the preceding paragraphs comprises an essential element of the firm's *Marketing Information System* (MkIS). The MkIS is itself a sub-set of the larger Management Information System (MIS) which will contain the firm's financial information system, production information system, etc. Most MkISs will contain a number of separate modules dealing with sales, forecasting, product planning, market research, distribution, pricing, promotion and new product development. The objective of the MkIS is to synthesise and make readily available all the information which the firm possesses which is relevant to its marketing activities. To achieve this it is usual for a person (or persons) to be made responsible for collecting and collating the data and entering it into the database which is the heart of the system. Implicit in the previous paragraph is recognition that inputs to the MkIS may come from a number of different sources.

As we shall see in Chapter 12, marketing data is usually classified as being either primary or secondary in origin. Secondary data is that which is available from published sources while primary data is usually collected for a specific purpose, for example by using the salesforce or commissioning professional marketing research. Some of these issues are discussed in Chapter 12 but readers requiring a more extensive coverage of the objectives and methods of collection should consult *Research for Marketing* (1991)[11].

As Makens (1989) observes[12] 'The task of gathering and analysing competitive information is generally less difficult than knowing what to do with the acquired data. Managers within many industries find themselves flooded with competitive information, but seem to be baffled concerning what to do'. Makens accordingly

Table 10.3 Weighted services and performance

Date _____ Prepared by _____

Company	Price	Technical specification	Delivery service	Packaging	Supporting services	Company reputation	Product reputation	Reciprocal trade agreements	Captive markets	Personal relationships	Outside influences	Product performance	Finish design	Length of service	Advertising and public relations	Merchandising	Sales strength	Sales ability	Channels of distribution	Total assessment
Own company	Sales				£$															
	Sales				£$				% total sales							Market share				
	Sales				£$				% total sales							Market share				
	Sales				£$				% total sales							Market share				
	Sales				£$				% total sales							Market share				
	Sales				£$				% total sales							Market share				
Comments																				

Source: John Stapleton, *How to Prepare a Marketing Plan* (Aldershot: Gower, 1989) 4th edn.

suggests a number of key indicators to help distinguish the important from the unimportant.

First, Makens emphasises the importance of monitoring *trends* rather than responding to particular occurrences as and when they occur. Thus a lowering of price may be a temporary promotional device to move stock and help improve cash flows. However, a trend of consistently lowered prices may indicate that a firm is following an experience curve, production–pricing strategy, in an effort to gain market share and achieve new economies of scale. Of course an alternative interpretation of a firm consistently lowering its prices is that it is in deep competitive trouble in terms of its product performance and so can maintain sales only by giving away margins. In monitoring trends, therefore, one is seeking to establish consistency over time and also to be able to identify – and, hopefully, explain – variances from secular trends.

Other indicators which Makens recommends one should monitor are shake-ups in management, as these frequently anticipate major changes in policy and strategy. Similarly stock market changes such as a change in share prices, in gearing or price–earnings ratios often reflect advanced knowledge of forthcoming changes in a firm's fortunes.

In sum, while it is important to monitor competitor activity one has to be careful to avoid the trap of 'paralysis by analysis'. This phenomenon occurs when those responsible for creating and maintaining databases lose sight of the marginal value of information. When this occurs information overload is inevitable and the analyst becomes paralysed by his inability to distinguish the important from the unimportant. While it may be tempting to squirrel away every little bit of information on one's market and competitors a much more selective approach emphasising the number of key performance indicators which are regularly used, and are of proven relevance, is to be preferred.

■ Sales Forecasting

A continuing problem faced by all types of organisation is that of projecting *future demand* for their goods and services, for it is upon such projections that policy and strategy must be based.

Although the actual time horizon will vary according to the nature of the firm's business it is convenient to think of forecasting for the short, medium, and long term for which appropriate time spans might be 1 to 2 years, 2 to 5 years, more than 5 years. Clearly the further into the future one looks the less certain one can be of the accuracy of one's projections. However, long-range forecasting is an essential input to top management's thinking, for it provides a basis for deciding upon the direction in which an organisation is to go and so influences long-term capital investment decisions. It is also important to recognise that in this sense forecasting has a material effect upon future events – for example, if it takes 5 years to build an integrated steel plant with a life-expectancy of 15 years then a decision taken today about the construction of such a plant will directly affect the availability of steel for a period 5 to 20 years from now. Similarly, our ability to sell products and services today is the consequence of past decisions to provide and sell such products and services.

It follows from the foregoing observation that an organisation's ability to change direction will be very limited in the short term, in that its alternatives will be constrained by its *existing structure and product–service mix*, while in the very long run its ability to change is almost infinite. For the purpose of this section we are concerned with the short to medium term in which an organisation is concerned with specific market opportunities open to it by virtue of its structure and skills, its product–service mix, its geographical scope, etc. and will ignore the problems of long-range forecasting and policy formulation.[13]

■ Some Definitions . . .

- '*Forecasting* is the systematic analysis of market data, the purpose of which is to make firm quantitative estimates of the size of consumer demand for a product at specified dates in the future' (John Treasure, personal correspondence).
- *Sales forecast* – 'the basic planning document of the typical firm' (Koonz and O'Donnell, 1980).[14]
- *Company sales forecast* – 'is the expected level of company sales based on a chosen marketing plan and assumed environmental conditions' (Kotler, 1967).[15]
- *Forecasting* – 'is a basic and inescapable responsibility of business management. The systematic marshalling of facts and judgement for gauging future company prospects is essential for sound decision-making, planning, and control. Most important of all in this process, for most firms, is the determination of future sales volume' (NICB, *Forecasting Sales*).
- *Sales quota* – 'the sales goal set for a product line, company division or company agent. It is primarily a managerial device for defining and stimulating sales effort' (Kotler, 1967).
- *Sales budget* – 'is a conservative estimate of the expected volume of sales and is used primarily for making current purchasing, production, and cash flow decisions' (Kotler, 1967).

. . . and an Explanation

These definitions of forecasting emphasise that the objective is the systematic preparation of a *quantified* statement of expected demand for a specified future time period. Second, they emphasise that the forecast is the basis for planning and thereby for *control* through the comparison of actual performance against projected performance. Third, forecasting requires the combination of *facts* and *judgement*.

In order to develop a forecast for a specific product or service it is usually necessary first to make a broad forecast of the general business or economic climate, for the performance of any industry sector is closely tied to the performance of the economy as a whole. Similarly, an industry forecast is a necessary prerequisite for a company sales forecast as the individual supplier can assess his own potential performance only in light of the total demand for products or services of the type he can supply and the competition from other suppliers for a share of this demand.

Once a company forecast has been prepared then management can assess what action will be necessary to permit its achievement and embody these in a plan for a specified future period. Within this plan the sales quota represents the target performance while the sales budget spells out the financial implications of operating at this designated level.

■ Preparing a Sales Forecast

The NICB survey referred to among our definitions suggests the following eleven steps in the preparation of a sales forecast:

1 Determine purposes for which forecasts are to be used.
2 Divide company products into homogeneous groups.
3 Determine factors affecting sales of each product group and their relative importance.
4 Choose forecasting method or methods best suited to job.
5 Gather all available data.
6 Analyse data.
7 Check and cross-check deductions resulting from analysis.
8 Make assumptions regarding effect of factors that cannot be measured or forecast.
9 Convert deductions and assumptions into specific product and territorial forecasts and quotas.
10 Apply these to company operation.
11 Review performance and revise forecast periodically.

From this list it is apparent that steps 3 and 4 are of central importance. Among the many variables which must be taken into account (step 3) Buyers and Holmes suggest the following.[16]

(a) The firm's own sales and those of its competitors area by area.
(b) Whether its share of business is increasing or decreasing.
(c) Seasonal fluctuations.
(d) The effect of past or potential population movements.
(e) Changing consumer tastes.
(f) The effect of introducing new products by the concern itself or by competitors.
(g) Increases or decreases to be made in the advertising budget.
(h) The effect of sales promotion schemes planned by the firm itself or by its competitors (so far as is known).

(i)   The effects of any planned improvement in existing products or of their discontinuation.
(j)   The possibility of selling in new territories or of discontinuing sales in existing ones.

It should be stressed that this check list is suggestive not definitive and items may be added or deleted by the forecaster, depending upon the particular requirements of his industry.

In turn, this decision will be heavily influenced by the method chosen for developing a forecast.

■ Sales Forecasting Methods

Among the more common forecasting techniques are the following:

1   Jury of executive opinion (expert opinion).
2   Sales force composite.
3   Buyers' intentions (users' expectations).
4   Time series analysis.
5   Other mathematical techniques.

□ Jury of Executive Opinion

The NICB survey, *Forecasting Sales*, cites the following pros and cons of this method:

> The process of combining and averaging or otherwise evaluating the opinion of top executives is one of the oldest methods of forecasting. It reflects a tendency to broaden the base of predicting. Any firm operating under such a system usually brings together executives from the sales, manufacturing, finance, purchasing, and administrative fields to secure a wide coverage of experience and opinion.

The advantages and disadvantages of this method are summarised by the NICB as follows:

● *Advantages*:

1   Can provide forecasts easily and quickly.
2   May not require the preparation of elaborate statistics.
3   Brings a variety of specialised viewpoints together for a pooling of experience and judgement.
4   May be the only feasible means of forecasting especially in the absence of adequate data.

- *Disadvantages*:

1 Is inferior to a more factual basis of forecasting, since it is based too heavily on opinion.
2 Requires costly executive time.
3 Is not necessarily more accurate because opinion is averaged.
4 Disperses responsibility for accurate forecasting.
5 Presents difficulties in making breakdowns by products, time intervals, or markets for operating purposes.

☐ Sales Force Composite

As the name suggests, this approach consists of pooling information from members of the sales force and modifying it in light of the judgement of successive levels of sales management (e.g. area, district, national) to arrive at an overall assessment. A reversal of this procedure is then followed in setting quotas. The NICB assesses this method as follows:

- *Advantages*:

1 Uses specialised knowledge of people closest to the market.
2 Places responsibility for the forecast in the hands of those who must produce the results.
3 Gives sales force greater confidence in quotas developed from forecasts.
4 Tends to give results greater stability because of the magnitude of the sample.
5 Lends itself to the easy development of product, territory, customer, or salesmen breakdowns.

- *Disadvantages*:

1 Salesmen are poor estimators, often being either more optimistic or more pessimistic than conditions warrant.
2 If estimates are used as a basis for setting quotas, salesmen are inclined to understate the demand in order to make the goal easier to achieve.
3 Salesmen are often unaware of the broad economic patterns shaping future sales and are thus incapable of forecasting trends for extended periods.
4 Since sales forecasting is a subsidiary function of the sales force, sufficient time may not be made available for it.
5 Requires an extensive expenditure of time by executives and sales force.
6 Elaborate schemes are sometimes necessary to keep estimates realistic and free from bias.

☐ Buyers' Intentions

Simplistically this approach consists of asking customers, or a representative cross-section of them, what their buying intentions are for a future period.

The strengths and weaknesses of this technique include:

- *Advantages*

1 Bases forecast on information obtained direct from product users, whose buying actions will actually determine sales.
2 Gives forecaster a subjective feel of the market and of the thinking behind users' buying intentions.
3 Bypasses published or other indirect sources, enabling the inquiring company to obtain its information in the form and detail required.
4 Offers a possible way of making a forecast where other methods may be inadequate or impossible to use – e.g. forecasting demand for a new industrial product for which no previous sales record is available.

- *Disadvantages*:

1 Is difficult to employ in markets where users are numerous or not easily located.
2 Depends on the judgement and co-operation of product users, some of whom may be ill-informed or uncooperative.
3 Bases forecast on expectations, which are subject to subsequent change.
4 Requires considerable expenditure of time and manpower.

☐ Time Series Analysis

The logic underlying time series analysis is that past results reflect a causal relationship between actions, e.g. buying, and trends in the environment which are likely to continue into the future. If, therefore, we can forecast changes in the underlying trends then we should be able to forecast the future behaviour of the action we are trying to predict.

Four factors are generally recognised as likely to affect sales on a month-by-month basis:

(a) Secular trends – i.e. the long-term tendency of sales to increase or decrease as a result of changes in disposable income, population, etc.
(b) Seasonal variations.
(c) Cyclical trends associated with the overall level of activity in the business cycle.
(d) Random, accidental or residual fluctuations – such as a strike of Spanish aircraft controllers!

A battery of statistical techniques has been devised for adjusting data to allow for changes in these factors and a number of texts describe their use. Fundamentally, however, the final results are as good only as the data used in the calculations, so that the quality of the information used remains of critical importance.

■ Summary

As noted in the Introduction, Chapter 10 marks the transition from the strategic aspects of marketing planning to their application in practice. To begin with, we looked at the marketing audit as a systematic procedure for documenting both the strengths and weaknesses of an organisation and assessing the opportunities and threats in its competitive environment – hence the SWOT analysis referred to earlier in Chapter 5.

Once an organisation has committed itself to a given industry and market then it is the 'jockeying for position' with the immediate competitors in that market which will largely determine its success, or otherwise. It follows that one should monitor carefully the characteristics and behaviour of these competitors and it was suggested that the same factors should be considered as in the firm's own internal audit.

Finally, we examined some of the issues associated with forecasting demand in the short to medium term. In earlier chapters the emphasis has been upon the need to devise strategies based upon the firm's vision of the business it is in and where it wants to be in the long term. The more distant the future the greater the uncertainty and the more speculative the forecasts and scenarios which planners can devise. But, having determined the firm's goal and its broad strategy for achieving it, the role of management is to devise a series of short-term operational plans to move the firm towards that goal while compensating for changing circumstances as they become better understood. It is here that sales forecasting comes into play and we reviewed the better known techniques and their various advantages and disadvantages.

CHAPTER 11
The Marketing Mix

Learning Goals

The issues to be addressed in Chapter 11 include:

1 The *concept* of the marketing mix.
2 Identification of the mix *ingredients*.
3 *Selection* of a marketing mix.
4 *Management* of the marketing mix.

After reading Chapter 11 you will be able to:

1 Explain the *concept* of the marketing mix.
2 Describe the *elements or ingredients* which make up the marketing mix and critique some of the different *classificatory schemes*.
3 Discuss the factors which influence the *relative importance* of mix elements and their selection and use.
4 Suggest some possible *mix patterns* according to industry type and stage of the product life-cycle.

■ Introduction

In common with many other professions the practice of marketing is often made complex and difficult due to the sheer diversity of the problems with which it is confronted. To a large degree this diversity is due to the fact that the principal actors in exchange processes are people, or organisations comprised of people, and so exhibit the dynamic and interactive behaviour associated with human beings. If human beings rarely became unwell and then only from a small range of causes, we would have need for many fewer doctors than at present. Similarly, if disagreements between parties leading to litigation were limited in their origins then we would have a need for many fewer lawyers. However, like marketing, these two professions have to deal with an enormous variety of factors which might give rise to a need for medical care or litigation. Accordingly, professions all have a need for *diagnostic frameworks* which help them to isolate the most likely causes of the problem to be solved, so that these may become the focus of detailed examination.

260

In marketing, one such conceptual framework which is particularly useful in helping practitioners structure their thinking about marketing problems, is that of the so-called 'marketing mix'. To devise a product or service which will be seen as different in the eyes of prospective customers, to the point where they will prefer it to all competing substitutes, is obviously the ultimate objective of the marketer. In devising this unique selling proposition or bundle of benefits the marketer has four basic ingredients which he can combine in an almost infinite number of ways to achieve different end results. These four basic ingredients are frequently referred to as the 4 'Ps' of marketing following the classification first proposed by McCarthy.[1] These 4 'Ps' – Product, Price, Place (or distribution) and Promotion are the subject of separate treatment in later chapters. At this juncture our primary aim is to review how they may be combined to create a distinctive marketing mix.

According to John O'Shaughnessey (1984)[2] 'Product, price, promotion and distribution are factors that, within limits, are capable of being influenced or controlled. Marketing strategy can be viewed as reflecting a *marketing mix* of these four elements. Every market has its own logic whereby excellence on one element of the mix, whether product, price, promotion or distribution, is often a necessary condition for success . . . Knowing the key factor in the marketing mix is crucial in drawing up a marketing strategy since it means knowing what to emphasise' (p. 54).

■ The Evolution of the Marketing Mix Concept

Although marketers have always experimented with different combinations of product, price, place and promotion, it is only comparatively recently that serious attempts have been made to see if any particular combinations give better or worse results than others. Clearly, if this is the case, then such combinations are to be preferred or avoided as the case may be. One of the earliest studies of this kind was undertaken by the Harvard Business School Bureau of Business Research in 1929 which sought to determine if there were any common relationships to be found in the expenses on various marketing functions of a sample of food manufacturing companies. Almost two decades later James Culliton[3] set out to discover whether a bigger sample and more careful classification of companies would yield a different result from that found in the earlier study (in the 1929 study, no common figures had been found which could be used for predictive purposes). Despite Culliton's more rigorous and larger-scale investigation the results were the same, and it was this which led Culliton to describe the business executive as a 'decider', 'an artist' – a 'mixer of ingredients who sometimes follows a recipe to the ingredients immediately available, and sometimes experiments with or invents ingredients no-one else has tried'. This description of a marketing executive as a mixer of ingredients appealed greatly to his fellow Harvard Professor, Neil Borden[4], who began to use the term 'marketing mix' to describe the results. Borden wrote that 'Culliton's description . . . appealed to me as an apt and easily understandable phrase, far better than my previous references to the marketing man as an empiricist seeking in any situation, to devise a profitable "pattern" or "formula" of marketing operations from among the many procedures and policies that were open to him. If he was a "mixer of ingredients", what he designed was a "marketing mix"!' Given this idea of a marketing mix it follows that the next step is to identify and classify the various ingredients available to the marketer and the uses to which they may be put.

▌ Identifying the Ingredients of the Marketing Mix

A search of the available literature concerned with the marketing mix components reveals that there is a wide diversity among marketers on what elements compose the marketing mix.

Many checklists and guides featuring different elements of the marketing mix have been proposed since the concept first came into being. These checklists, as Borden indicates, can be long or short, depending on how far one wishes to go on in the classification and sub-classification of the marketing procedures and policies with which marketing managements deal when devising marketing programmes.

However, a brief review of the literature suggests that there are many classifications of the marketing mix elements ranging from the narrow classification (e.g. two-way classification) to the broadest one (the twelve-way classification).

Albert Frey[5], uses two dimensions: the *offering* (product, package and so forth) and the *tools* (e.g. advertising and personal selling and so forth).

Lazer and Kelley[6] and Lazer, Culley and Staudt[7] use a threefold classification:

1 The *product and service mix*, which includes many factors such as the number of product lines carried, as well as the product planning, product development, size, colour, price, packaging, warranties and guarantees, branding, labelling and the service of each individual's product.
2 The *distribution mix*, which comprises two components, the channels of distribution, and the activities of physical distribution.
3 The *communication mix*, which pertains to the strategic combination of advertising, personal selling, sales promotion and other promotional tools used in communicating with the marketplace.

McCarthy,[8] Stanton,[9] and Lipson and Darling,[10] among others, have used a four-way classification, namely, product, price, place and promotion.

Lipson and Darling, for example, divide the marketing mix elements into four components, namely, product component mix, terms of sale component mix, communication component mix, and distribution component mix. Figure 11.1 indicates these sub-mixes. Each of the major components may consist of four dimensions or major variables, which is directed at a particular market segment.

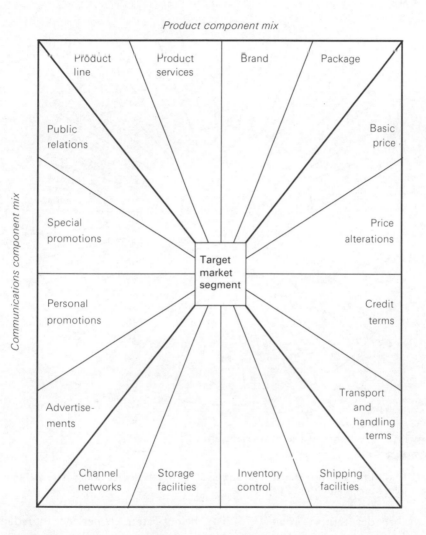

Figure 11.1   **Model of the customer market offering dimensions of the marketing mix**

Source: H. A. Lipson and J. R. Darling, *Introduction to Marketing: an administrative approach* (New York: John Wiley & Sons, 1971).

By contrast John Martin[11] argues that the purpose of the marketing mix is to communicate with targeted buyers or buying groups when he places at the centre of his conceptualisation of the marketing mix, as shown in Figure 11.2.

Figure 11.2   Elements of the marketing mix

Source: J. Martin, 'The Best Practice of Business', in *Marketing Planning*, vol. 5 (London: John Martin Publishing, 1978).

In the broadest terms Borden (1975) lists the important elements or ingredients that make up marketing programmes. He distinguishes twelve sub-divisions:

1   *Merchandising – Product Planning*:

    (a)   Determination of product (or service to be sold – qualities, design, etc.). To whom, when, where, and in what quantities?

    (b)   Determination of new product programme – research and development, merger.

(c) Determination of marketing research programme.

2 *Pricing*:

(a) Determination of level of prices.
(b) Determination of psychological aspects of price, e.g. odd or even.
(c) Determination of pricing policy, e.g. one price or varying price, use of price maintenance, etc.
(d) Determination of margins: freedom in setting?

3 *Branding*:

(a) Determination of brand policy, e.g. individual brand or family brand.

4 *Channels of Distribution*:

(a) Determination of channels to use – direct sale to user, direct sale to retailers or user, sources of purchase, e.g. supply houses.
(b) Determination of degree of selectivity among dealers.
(c) Devising of programmes to secure channel cooperation.

5 *Personal Selling*:

(a) Determination of burden to be placed on personal selling and methods to be employed.
   (1) For manufacturer's organisation.
   (2) For wholesalers.
   (3) For retailers.
(b) Organisation, selection, training and guidance of sales force at various levels of distribution.

6 *Advertising*:

(a) Determination of appropriation burden to be placed on advertising.
(b) Determination of copy policy.
(c) Determination of mix of advertising:
   (1) To trade.
   (2) To consumers.
(d) Determination of media.

7 *Promotions*:

(a) Determination of burden to place on special selling plans or devices and formulation of promotions:
   (1) To trade.
   (2) To consumers.

8 *Packaging*:

(a) Determination of importance of packaging and formulation of packages.

9 *Display*:

   (a) Determination of importance and devising of procedures.

10 *Servicing*:

   (a) Determination of importance of service and devising of procedures to meet consumer needs and desires.

11 *Physical Handling*: Warehousing – Transportation – Stock policy.

12 *Fact-finding and Analysis*: Marketing research.

With regard to the marketing forces bearing upon the marketing mix, Borden divides them into four categories, namely, consumer attitudes and habits, trade attitudes and methods, competition and government control, all of which govern the blending of the marketing elements.

From the above review of the different approaches to the marketing mix components, it can be argued that there is no widely accepted list that can be used by marketers. Some of them talk of the marketing mix in terms of the four 'Ps', i.e. product, price, place and promotion. Some others add a fifth element, i.e. after-sales service, while some marketers talk about seven 'Ps' and one A –, price, promotion, packaging, personal selling, publicity, physical distribution and advertising.

■ Selecting the Right Mix

These ingredients of the mix are valid in most situations. None the less, there are environments in which the mix ingredients must be adapted to the specific needs of the market-place. For a cosmetic manufacturer, packaging and advertising may be so important that they deserve classification as separate marketing activities, while storage may be so unimportant as not to deserve separate classification. Each marketer should set up his own classification of marketing activities, emphasising those important to the operation's success, de-emphasising others.

Simon Majaro[12] identifies three of the factors which help the marketer to make a decision as to whether a specific ingredient deserves a separate existence in the mix.

1 *The level of expenditure spent on a given ingredient*
   Every ingredient involving a significant expenditure would normally earn its separate identity. Basically, it is a question of resources allocated to each ingredient which matter. Thus, a firm that spends an insignificant amount of money on packaging would not bother to give this ingredient a separate existence, but will attach it to the product or the 'promotional' mix, whichever appears more appropriate in the circumstances.

2 *The perceived level of elasticity and consumer responsiveness*
Where the marketer knows that a change in the level of expenditure (up or down) of a given ingredient will affect results, it must be treated as a separate tool in the mix. For example, if the marketer is able to alter the supply–demand relationship through price changes, this element deserves a separate place in the mix. On the other hand, for a firm enjoying a monopoly or where the price is fixed by government edict, the price will be less important or may be removed from the mix.

3 *Allocation of the responsibilities*
A well-defined and well-structured marketing mix reflects a clear-cut allocation of responsibilities. Thus, where the firm requires the services of a specialist to help to develop or design new packaging, as in the case of cosmetics firms, it is perfectly proper to say that 'packaging' is an important and integral part of the mix and deserves a separate existence therein.

So while the ingredients of the mix described above are valid in most situations, the mix elements and their relative importance may differ from industry to industry, from company to company and quite often during the life of the product itself. Furthermore, the marketing mix must take full cognisance of the major *environmental dimensions* that prevail in the market-place. This latter point adds a dynamic flavour to the marketing mix in so far as it has to be changed from time to time in response to new factors in the marketing scene.

Generally, in striving to maintain or improve his profit position, the marketer is an empiricist trying changes in the several procedures and policies which make up what we call a 'marketing programme'. His success depends to a large extent on his understanding of the forces of the market which bear upon any product or product line and his skill in devising a 'mix' of marketing methods that conforms and adjusts to these forces in ways that produce a satisfactory net profit figure.

A study of the marketing programmes or mixes that have been evolved under this empirical approach shows a tremendous variation in their patterns. This variation is reflected in the operating statements of manufacturers, e.g. Profit and Loss Account and Balance Sheets. As Culliton found among such statements there is little uniformity, even among manufacturers in the same industry. There are no common figures of expense that have much meaning as standards, as holds true for many retail and wholesale trades, where the methods of operation tend to greater uniformity. Instead, the ratios of sales devoted to the various functions of marketing are widely diverse. This diversity in methods and in expenditures by categories even within an industry is accounted for largely by the fact that products, the volume of sales, the market covered, and the other facts that govern operations of each company tend to be unique and not conducive to uniformity with the operational methods of other companies, although there are tendencies towards uniformity among companies whose product lines are subject to the same market forces. As noted, in any category of expenses the percentage of sales spent may cover wide ranges. For instance, the advertising expense figure, which reflects the burden placed upon advertising in the marketing programme, will be found to vary among manufacturers from almost 0% to over 50%. Similarly, the percentages of sales devoted to personal selling will cover a wide range among different businesses.

To illustrate, proprietary medicine manufacturers often have no salesforce at all. Advertising is used to sell the product to consumers and advertising literally 'pulls' the product through the channels of distribution. At the retail level little or no effort is made to secure selling support. In contrast, manufacturers of other types of products, e.g. heavy machinery, often put relatively little of the burden of selling upon advertising and rely primarily on the 'push' of personal selling by either salesforce or the salesforce of distributors.

The part played in the marketing programme by the distributive trades varies markedly. Sometimes the trade plays a considerable part in the sales programme and the close support and co-operation of the trade is sought, as has generally been true with heavy appliances. In other instances the part played by the trade is not highly important and little effort is devoted to securing trade support, as is true among the proprietary medicine companies cited above. Likewise, the employment of sales promotional devices and of point of purchase effort in marketing programmes varies widely.

In the matter of pricing and pricing policy, wide variation is likely to be found. In some instances competition is carried out largely on price and margins are narrow. In other instances prices are set with wide margins and competition is carried out on non-price bases, such as product quality or services or advertising. In some instances resale prices are maintained; in others they are not.

It is possible to go on citing wide differences in the practices of branding, packaging and servicing that have been evolved.

In short, the elements of marketing programmes can be combined in many ways. Or, stated another way, the 'marketing mixes' for different types of products vary widely, and even for the same class of product competing companies may employ different mixes. In the course of time a company may change its marketing mix for a product, for in a dynamic world the marketer must adjust to the changing forces of the market. The search of business in any instance is to find a mix that will prove profitable. To attain this end, the various elements have to be combined in a logically integrated programme to conform to market forces bearing on the individual product. Guptara (1990)[13] provides a useful summary of variation in the marketing mix as illustrated in Figure 11.3.

To summarise, the concept of the marketing mix is a schematic plan to guide analysis of marketing problems through utilisation of:

(a) A list of the important forces emanating from the market which bear upon the marketing operations of an enterprise.
(b) A list of the elements (procedures and policies) of marketing programmes.

The marketing mix thus refers to the apportionment of effort, the combination, the designing, and the integration of the elements of marketing into a

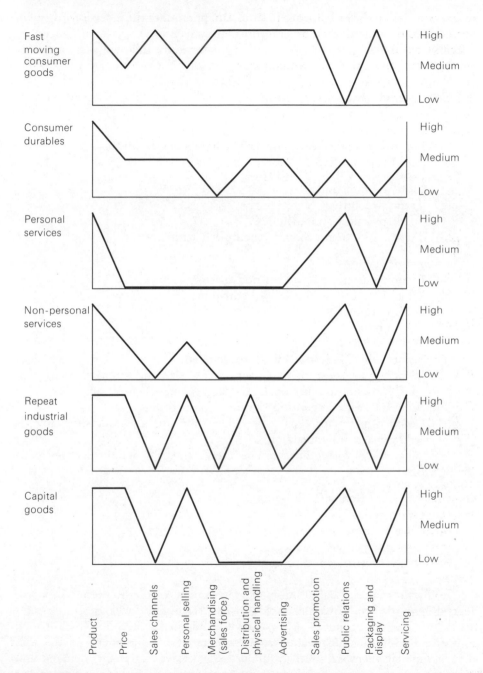

Figure 11.3 Typical marketing mix patterns by industry type

Source: P. Guptara, *The Basic Arts of Marketing* (London: Hutchinson, 1990).

programme or 'mix' which, on the basis of an appraisal of the market forces, will best achieve the objectives of an enterprise at a given time.

In his original conceptualisation, Borden suggested the following list of market forces bearing upon the marketing mix.

1   *Consumer Attitudes and Habits*:
    (a)   Motivation of users.
    (b)   Buying habits and attitudes.
    (c)   Important trends bearing on living habits and attitudes.

2   *Trade Attitudes and Methods*:
    (a)   Motivation of trade.
    (b)   Trade structure.
    (c)   Trade practices and attitudes.
    (d)   Trends in trade procedures, methods, attitudes.

3   *Competition*:
    (a)   Is competition on a price or non-price basis?
    (b)   What are the choices afforded consumers:
          (1) In product?
          (2) In price?
          (3) In service?
    (c)   What is the relation of supply to demand?
    (d)   What is your position in the market – size and strength relative to competitors? – number of firms – degree of concentration.
    (e)   What indirect competition vs direct competition?
    (f)   Competitors' plans – what new developments in products, pricing, or selling plans are impending?
    (g)   What moves will competition be likely to make to actions taken by your firm?

4   *Governmental Controls*:
    (a)   Over product.
    (b)   Over pricing.
    (c)   Over competitive practices.
    (d)   Over advertising and promotion.

It follows that the actual design and management of the marketing mix will depend upon the firm's own perception of its strengths and weaknesses *vis-à-vis* the threats and opportunities in the markets and environment in which it is to compete. In forming judgements as to the tactical deployment of the mix elements management will need to undertake a closer analysis of demand and supply than that provided by the environmental review discussed in Chapter 6 or the broad discussion of buyer behaviour in Chapter 7. Two key inputs to detailed marketing planning within the framework of SMP are sales forecasting and the execution of a marketing audit, as discussed in Chapter 10.

■ Managing the Mix

In Chapter 14 of *The Marketing Book* (1991)[14] Professor Peter Doyle provides a clear exposition of the key issues involved in managing the marketing mix. As he points out 'There are two key decisions which are central to marketing management: the selection of target markets which determine where the firm will compete and the design of the marketing mix (product, price, promotion, and distribution method) which will determine its success in these markets'.

To this point, the emphasis has been upon defining the *context* within which exchange or marketing occurs; of the forces – economic, behavioural, technological, political and legal – which *shape* and *influence* the exchange process; and of procedures for *analysing* and *interpreting* all these factors as a basis for developing a coherent and viable strategy. But, as we have seen, strategy identifies future objectives to which the firm aspires and which are likely to be modified due to changing circumstances. Thus strategy charts a direction to be followed to achieve a destination that will probably be changed as we approach it. However, to ensure that we remain on course we will set a series of sub-objectives which represent points along the way from where we are to where we want to be. Given the convention of reporting financial performance on an annual basis it has also become conventional to set performance targets on an annual basis and develop short-term plans for their achievement. In turn, short-term (1-year plans) are usually a sub-set of a medium-term (3 to 5 year) plan equivalent to the Kitchin or inventory cycle described in Chapter 6.

Short-term plans and, to a less extent, medium-term plans, are clearly the domain of operational management. It is this operational management which is responsible for translating the strategy into plans and for devising marketing mixes for their realisation. Where a firm is practising *undifferentiated* or *concentrated* marketing it will have only a single marketing mix but, where it is practising *differentiated* marketing it will have several. Irrespective of whether it has one or several mixes the objective is the same – to develop and maintain a *sustainable differential advantage* (SDA). In order to do this it is necessary to undertake the kinds of analysis described in earlier chapters.

Simply analysing problems is not enough – as we have observed on several occasions it is a necessary, but not sufficient, condition for success. Marshalling evidence is a precondition for analysis but it does not follow that all decision-makers will draw the same conclusion from a given data set (selective perception strikes again!). What matters is the quality of the plan devised by the manager based upon his analysis and the quality of the implementation. Central to all this is the understanding and deployment of the mix elements. Doyle (1991) provides a useful diagram to illustrate the nature of the matching process which ensures that the marketing mix is consistent with the needs of customers in the target market (see Figure 11.4).

Similarly, Chester Wasson (1974)[15] provided an excellent summary of the use of the various mix elements in accordance with the phases of the PLC as illustrated in Table 11.1.

Table 11.1   Wasson's Hypotheses about Appropriate Strategies over the Product Life-Cycle

DYNAMIC COMPETITIVE STRATEGY AND THE MARKET LIFE CYCLE

	MARKET DEVELOPMENT (Introductory period for high learning products only)	RAPID GROWTH (Normal introductory pattern for a very low learning product)	COMPETITIVE TURBULENCE	SATURATION (Maturity)	DECLINE
Strategy Objective	Minimize learning requirements locate and remedy offering defects quickly, develop widespread awareness of benefits, and gain trial by early adopters	To establish a strong brand market and distribution niche as quickly as possible	To maintain and strengthen the market niche achieved through dealer and consumer loyalty	To defend brand position against competing brands and product category against other potential products, through constant attention to product improvement opportunities and fresh promotional and distribution approaches.	To milk the offering dry of all possible profit
Outlook for Competition	None is likely to be attracted in the early, unprofitable stages	Early entrance of numerous aggressive emulators	Price and distribution squeezes on the industry, shaking out the weaker entrants	Competition stabilized, with few or no new entrants and market shares not subject to substantial change in the absence of a substantial perceived improvement in some brand	Similar competition declining and dropping out because of decrease in consumer interest
Product design objectives	Limited number of models with physical product and offering designs both focused on	Modular design to facilitate flexible addition of variants to appeal to every new	Intensified attention to product improvement, tighten up of line	A constant alert for market pyramiding opportunities through either bold cost- and price-penetration of new	Constant pruning of line to eliminate any items not

	minimizing learning requirements Designs cost- and use-engineered to appeal to most receptive segment / Utmost attention to quality control and quick elimination of market-reveled defects in design	segment and new use- system as fast as discovered	to eliminate unnecessary specialities with little market appeal	markets or major product changes. Introduction of flanker products. Constant attention to possibilities for product improvement and cost cutting / Reexamination of necessity of design compromises	returning a direct profit
Pricing objective	To impose the minimum of value perception learning and to match the value reference perception of the most receptive segments High trade discounts and sampling advisable	A price line for every taste, from low-end to premium models Customary trade discounts Aggressive promotional pricing, with prices cut as fast as costs decline due to accumulated production experience	Increased attention to market-broadening and promotional pricing opportunities	Defensive pricing to preserve product category franchise Search for incremental pricing opportunities, including private label contracts, to boost volume and gain in experience	Maintenance of profit level pricing with complete disregard of any effect on market share
Promotional guidelines Communications objectives	(a) Create widespread awareness and understanding of offering benefits (b) Gain trial by early adopters	Create and strengthen brand preference among trade and final users Stimulate general trial	Maintain consumer franchise and strengthen dealer ties	Maintain consumer and trade loyalty, with strong emphasis on dealers and distributors Promotion of greater use frequence	Phase out, keeping just enough to maintain profitable distribution
Most valuble media mix	In order of value: Publicity Personal sales Mass communications	Mass media Personal sales Sales promotions, including sampling Publicity	Mass media Dealer promotions Personal selling to dealers Sales promotion Publicity	Mass media Dealer-orientated promotions	Cut down all media to the bone—use no sales promotions of any kind
Distribution policy	Exclusive or selective, with distributor margins high enough to justify heavy promotional spending	Intensive and extensive with, dealer margins just high enough to keep them interested Close attention to rapid resupply of distributor stocks	Intensive and extensive, and a strong emphasis on keeping dealer well supplied, but with minimum inventory cost to him	Intensive and extensive, with strong emphasis on keeping dealer well supplied, but at minimum inventory cost to him	Phase out outlets as they become marginal

| **Intelligence** focus | To identify actual development use-systems and to uncover any product weakness | and heavy inventories at all levels

Detailed attention to brand position, to gaps in model and market coverage, and to opportunities for market segmentation | Close attention to product improvement needs, to market-broadening chances, and to possible fresh promotion themes | Intensified attention to possible product improvements. Sharp alert for potential new inter- product competition and for signs of beginning production decline | Information helping to identify the point at which the product should be phased out |

Note: Strictly speaking, this is the cycle of the category market, and only a high learning introduction passes through all phases indicated above. The term, *product life cycle* is sometimes applied indiscriminately to both brand cycles and category cycles. Most new brands are only emulative of other products already on the market, have a much shorter life than the product category, and must follow a strategy similar to any low learning product.

Roger A. Kerin, *Perspectives on Strategic Marketing Management* (Cambridge Mass.: Allyn & Bacon, 1980) 2nd edn.

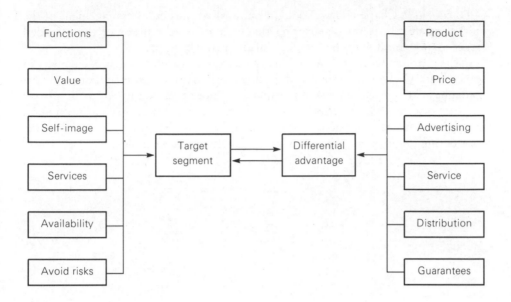

Figure 11.4 The marketing mix and differential advantage: matching customer service wants

Source: P. Doyle, in M.J. Baker (ed.), *The Marketing Book* (London: Butterworth-Heinemann, 1991).

■ Summary

Chapter 11 marked the transition from the strategic aspects of marketing planning to their application in practice. In Chapter 11 we have been concerned with a conceptual framework which has proved to be particularly helpful in assisting practitioners to do this – the idea of the *marketing mix*. This idea is essentially simple and practical and proposes that in seeking to develop a differentiated and competitive product the marketing manager will have recourse to a variety of 'ingredients' which he can 'mix' together to create a unique 'recipe' or marketing plan.

Having traced the origins of the concept we looked at a variety of different approaches to classifying the ingredients of the marketing mix. Our review identified very simple models containing only two factors – the *offering* and the *tools* – through McCarthy's well known 4 Ps to Borden's original conceptualisation of 12 factors. Clearly, there is no single or definitive statement of the mix elements and the practitioner must select the elements which are most important to the product-market situation with which he is concerned. Advice on how to do this was considered, together with a discussion of the factors which impact on this decision.

To conclude Chapter 11 we took a brief look at the actual management of the marketing mix in terms of ensuring that it matches the needs of the intended target markets and over the life-cycle of the product itself.

In the chapters which follow in Part II we examine each of the mix elements in some detail. We would remind readers, however, that it is assumed that they have read a basic text book or have practical experience of marketing. Accordingly we have not discussed the descriptive aspects of the subject but have concentrated on the policy and management issues which need to be borne in mind when considering *deployment* and *use* of the individual mix variables.

Part II

MANAGING THE MARKETING FUNCTION

CHAPTER 12

Marketing Research

Learning Goals

The issues to be addressed in Chapter 12 include:

1 The *role* and *nature* of marketing research.
2 The distinction between *qualitative* and *quantitative* research.
3 *Sources of data* and *methods of data collection*.
4 The *analysis* and *reporting* of data.
5 *Bayesian analysis* as an aid to decision-making under conditions of uncertainty.

After reading Chapter 12 you will be able to:

1 Explain the *importance* of marketing research and its contribution to competitive success.
2 Describe the differences between *quantitative* and *qualitative* research, when to use them and how they complement each other.
3 Identify the role of *secondary data* sources as an input to market analysis.
4 Define the nature of *primary data* and describe the methods by which it can be collected – observation, experimentation, simulation and sample survey.
5 Suggest a checklist for assessing a *market's worth*.
6 Explain the process for *analysing* sample data and drawing *inferences* from it.
7 Discuss *probabilistic approaches* to decision-making under conditions of uncertainty, following the principles of Bayesian analysis.
8 Show how to *structure* problems, identify alternatives, develop decision trees, select a decision criterion and *solve* problems by combining facts and judgement.

■ Introduction

Although 'Fact-finding and Analysis' was the twelfth and final item on Borden's listing of the marketing mix elements we considered in Chapter 11 above, and

Marketing Research does not even appear on most authors' typologies, it must be the foundation for all SMP. Indeed all of the preceding chapters have assumed, implicitly or explicitly, that decision-makers are defining options and alternative courses of actions based upon consideration of relevant information. So where does this information come from if it is not captured and synthesised in some formal way?

As we shall see in Chapter 12, not all firms do take formal steps to gather, analyse and store market data. We shall also provide evidence that those that do so perform better than those that don't. A vital ingredient in this process is marketing research and the establishment of a Marketing Information System (MkIS) as an integral part of the firm's larger Management Information System (MIS).

In a broadly-based book of this kind one can provide only a limited introduction to what is a major sub-field of the marketing discipline. An extended and detailed description/analysis of the role and uses of marketing research is to be found in *Research for Marketing*,[1] which was written specifically for users of research to illuminate and help solve marketing problems (as opposed to a book for practitioners emphasising technique and procedure). In this chapter we will seek to establish why marketing research is so important, together with providing evidence of the reasons why it is believed to make such an important contribution to overall competitive success. We will also examine some of the criticisms of formal marketing research and distinguish the differences between quantitative and qualitative approaches.

Having established the nature and scope of marketing research we examine the distinction between secondary and primary data and review briefly the main methods of primary data collection. Next we provide a checklist for assessing market potential – the heart of marketing research – before discussing data reduction and analysis as a necessary discipline to reduce potential information overload to manageable proportions. Finally, we present an extended review of the Bayesian methodology which enables decision-makers to combine facts and judgement and so make decisions under conditions of uncertainty – the primary activity of managers and the one which distinguishes their role from all others.

■ The Need for Marketing Research

In their book *Marketing Decisions: a Bayesian approach* Enis and Broome[2] identify three sets of factors which create particular difficulties in applying formal analytical procedures to marketing decisions:

> First, many marketing problems are more or less unique. A new product, for example, is offered to the market only once. There are no historical data from which long-run relative frequencies can be calculated for traditional statistical analysis. Consequently, past experience often provides only general guidelines for decision making. Secondly, marketing's interface with buyers results in problems not found in

other areas of business. The buyer can think for himself. He may, therefore, change his mind, reorder his priorities, or otherwise alter his behaviour patterns. By contrast, the production manager may feel reasonably confident that his raw materials will not refuse to become part of the product he is manufacturing.

A third barrier to formal analysis of marketing problems is the complexity of such problems.

It is because of these difficulties that many managers dismiss the relevance of the more formal decision-making procedures which depend upon basic statistical laws such as the Law of Statistical Regularity and the Law of Inertia of Large Numbers. Similarly, such managers have little patience for the techniques developed by Operational Researchers even though many of these are eminently suitable to many classes of marketing problems as shown by Arthur Meidan[3] and summarised in his Taxonomy of OR Methods which is reproduced as Figure 12.1.

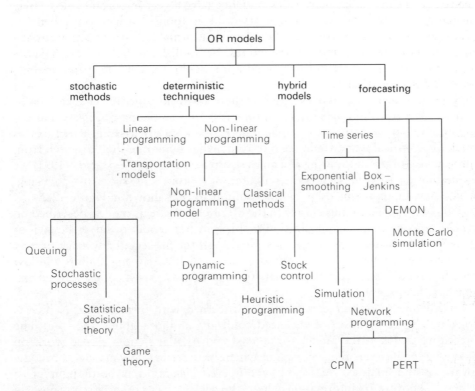

Figure 12.1   Operational research (OR) methods – a taxonomy

Source: A. Meidan, *Marketing Application of Operational Research Techniques* (1981).

In part rejection of these models and approaches is felt to arise from the intrinsic fear which a significant proportion of managers exhibit when faced with anything which calls for a quantitative analysis. (The prevalence of this fear is well established, but it is difficult to understand particularly when one considers the nature of the Graduate Test for Studies in Business which seeks to measure performance in terms of both numeracy and verbal skills. Candidates are awarded a composite score which reflects their performance in terms of both these dimensions which many persons regard as mutually exclusive. Assuming the dimensions are equally weighted it is clear that to come in the top 10% of all performers if you gain full marks on one dimension then you must still score not less than 80% in the other – in other words high performers tend to be good on both verbal and quantitative tests.) Because of this fear there is a proclivity to stress judgemental approaches and emphasise the importance of 'experience' as a basis for informed decision-taking where there are genuine doubts about expected outcomes

Because of the novelty, complexity and dynamic nature of marketing problems referred to earlier, judgement and experience have a very important role to play in managerial decision-making, but it would be foolish to ignore the benefits which accrue if such skills are combined with a formal and structured approach to problem-solving. Similarly, it would be foolish to ignore the benefits associated with a formal and structured approach to the collection and analysis of marketing information.

Naturally all managers seek to keep themselves informed of changes in the market place and their own organisation – it is an essential part of the manager's job and a vital input to strategic planning of the kind discussed in Part I of this book. The critical issue would seem to be at what point one should switch from informal to formal monitoring and analysis. In *Research for Marketing* (1991) we argue that decision-making is the outcome of a process of 'successive focusing' which may be represented by a funnel similar to that shown in Figure 12.2.

This funnel corresponds closely to the hierarchy of effects models described on p. 174 and the sequence of decision-making in our model of buyer behaviour (p. 179). Of course, one may decide to break off the process at any stage or may short-circuit it when, say, undirected viewing such as passing a shop window reminds us of a need which we can satisfy by a purchase based upon a learned and routinised response.

Strictly speaking, market research is concerned with formal search which is triggered by recognition of the need to find out more about an issue. The preceding stages in the model are taken from Aguilar's[4] now classic work on *Scanning the Business Environment* in which he describes how managers become aware of and analyse issues. Thus *undirected viewing* may be thought of as general exposure to information where the viewer has no specific purpose in mind save the recognition that one needs to monitor the environment in case there is something of possible interest going on. In other words undirected viewing is a stage of general *awareness*. As a result of such undirected viewing some cue or stimulus may attract the conscious *attention* of the scanner and lead

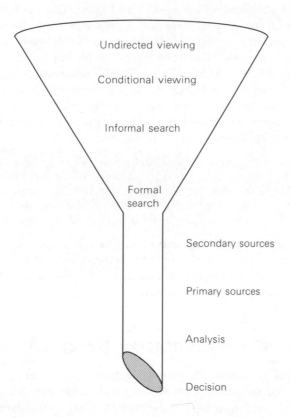

Figure 12.2   Successive focusing

Source: M. J. Baker *Research for Marketing* (London: Macmillan, 1991).

them to a state of *conditional viewing*, i.e. they will examine the information that has attracted their attention to see if it is really of any *interest*. If the information is of interest then the viewer will move on to an *informal search*, which may be defined as a relatively limited and unstructured effort to obtain specific information or information for a specific purpose. This stage we may character-ise as *keeping an eye on things*. If this further stimulates the viewer's interest, then it is likely he or she will institute a formal search. In marketing, this is where marketing research will come into play. The danger, as we have hinted earlier, is that if managers believe they are rewarded for exercising judgement they may short-circuit the process without going to the effort (and cost) of a formal search.

As long ago as 1964 the National Industrial Conference Board (NICB)[5] in the United States published the results of a survey into the causes of product failure which clearly showed that the major reason for such failure was an incomplete and/or inadequate understanding of market and competitive conditions, precisely the kind of information which marketing research could have provided. Numerous studies since have confirmed the view that expenditure on marketing research can easily be justified on the grounds of improved competitive performance. Thus, in 1984, Hooley and West[6] undertook a wide-ranging survey of the use of marketing research in the UK from which they concluded there was 'a clear association between conducting marketing research and improved company performance both in terms of profit margin achieved and self-assessed performance'. They went on to say:

> While the research cannot prove that the higher levels of usage have caused better performance the high level of association found does indicate that strong inferences can be drawn. The relationship between usage of marketing research and performance suggests that those companies with zero or low usage could significantly improve their performance by making better use of marketing research.

The findings of the survey by Baker and Hart[7] led to precisely this conclusion. Indeed out of over 60,000 possible relationships between marketing practices and improved performance greater use of marketing research was one of the very few where a significant correlation was detected.

■ Quantitative or Qualitative Research?

Earlier we caricatured the reluctance of managers to use marketing research as arising from a fear of the mathematical/statistical techniques which seem to dominate the subject, reinforced by a preference for their own judgement based upon experience. This division between quantitative and qualitative approaches is also apparent within the practice of marketing research itself.

In *Research for Marketing* (pp. 32ff) we present a table which appears to suggest that quantitative and qualitative research may be regarded as polar and mutually exclusive alternatives, as can be seen from Table 12.1.

But, as our discussion then points out, more recently a more balanced approach has emerged in which both kinds of researcher admit the contribution of the other. In parallel with this trend (or perhaps because of it) there has developed a growing recognition amongst the users of research that qualitative research is essential to address questions of what, how (process) and why, while quantitative research is appropriate to answer questions of who, where, when and how (quantity).

In very broad terms one should use qualitative research:

1   To define the parameters of the market.
2   To understand the nature of the decision-making process.
3   To elicit attitudinal and motivational factors which influence behaviour.
4   To help understand why people behave the way they do.

Table 12.1   Qualitative versus quantitative research

Qualitative	Quantitative
Soft	Hard
Dry	Wet
Flexible	Fixed
Grounded	Abstract
Descriptive/exploratory	Explanatory
Pre-scientific	Scientific
Subjective	Objective
Inductive	Deductive
Speculative/illustrative	Hypothesis testing
Political	Value free
Non-rigorous	Rigorous
Idiographic	Nomothetic
Holistic	Atomistic
Interpretivist	Positivist
Exposes actors' meanings	Imposes sociological theory
Phenomenological	Empiricist/behaviourist
Relativistic case study	Universalistic survey
Good	Bad
Bad	Good

Source: P. Halfpenny, 'The Analysis of Qualitative Data', *Sociological Review*, 27 (4) (1979).

Overall qualitative research is best suited to areas calling for a flexible approach while quantitative research is necessary to define more precisely the issues identified through qualitative methods. According to Peter Sampson[8] the areas calling for a flexible approach may be summarised as:

1 Concept identification and exploration.
2 Identification of relevant behavioural attitudes.
3 Establishing priority among and between categories of behaviour, attitudes, etc.
4 Defining problem areas more fully and formulating hypotheses for further investigation.

More recently, Wendy Gordon and Roy Langmaid (1988)[9] have suggested that the most important areas for qualitative research are:

- Basic exploratory studies.
- New product development.
- Creative development.
- Diagnostic studies.
- Tactical research projects.

Exploratory studies are usually called for when seeking to identify market opportunities for new product development, to monitor changes in consumption patterns and behaviour, to help define the parameters and characteristics of newly emerging markets or when seeking to enter established markets of which one has no prior experience. Gordon and Langmaid[10] indicate five specific types of information which may be obtained from studies of this kind, namely:

1   *To define consumer perceptions of the market or product field* in order to help understand the competitive relationships between different types of product and/or brand in any product category – from the consumer's point of view rather than the manufacturer's.
2   *To define consumer segmentations in relation to a product category or brand*, e.g. psychographics and life-style segmentations.
3   *To understand the dimensions which differentiate between brands*, specifically on the basis of rational criteria and emotional beliefs. Where objective differences can be developed between products, rationality will predispose consumers to select these which conform most closely with their own preferences or criteria. Unsurprisingly, objective differences are comparatively easy to emulate with the result that emotional beliefs have come to play an increasingly important part in purchase decisions – industrial as well as consumer.
4   *To understand the purchase decision-making process and/or usage patterns.*
5   *Hypothesis generation.*

As a broad generalisation, then, qualitative research is an essential prerequisite to most quantitative research in that it will help clarify the issues to be addressed, the parameters to be defined and measured and the likely relationships between them.

The distinction between quantitative and qualitative research, and their mutual dependence, was illustrated by an article by Johansson and Nonaka entitled 'Market Research the Japanese Way'.[11] In this article, the authors report Japanese disdain for the volume of formal market research conducted in the USA. They point out that when Sony researched the market for a lightweight portable cassette player the results indicated that consumers would only buy one with a recording facility. Akio Morita ignored this finding and the Walkman is history. Citing examples such as Matsushita and Canon the authors report how Japanese companies depend upon a combination of 'soft data' gathered by managers actually visiting customers and distributors and 'hard data' about shipments, inventory levels and retail sales. However, the authors also cite evidence of Japanese failures in American markets which they attribute to a lack of understanding of the attitudes and opinions of American consumers which could have been established by use of some of the survey techniques which they have eschewed. The conclusion is that both kinds of research are called for. Clearly with highly innovative and novel products it is unlikely that consumers could conceptualise the possibilities for a portable, personal entertainment system such as the Walkman. But, once the technological possibilities have become apparent and markets begin to grow and mature then the need to segment markets and position products will call for the kind of quantitative data which is unavailable when developing wholly new product concepts.

■ Data Collection

Given that one is persuaded of the desirability of conducting marketing research and setting up a MkIS the obvious question is: how does one set about collecting the necessary data? A cursory examination of any basic textbook quickly reveals there is a wide range of techniques and procedures available. Discussion of these is well beyond the scope of a book of this kind but, in Table 12.2, we have summarised the major approaches one is likely to encounter. A brief summary of the more important areas is also given but for a detailed explanation one should consult *Research for Marketing*.

■ Secondary Sources of Data

Secondary sources consist of existing data and it is common sense to identify and consult these first. The starting point for research into these sources will evidently depend upon how novel the product and/or market are in relation to the firm's existing product range. Clearly, if one is considering modification to existing products or marketing practices then the firm's existing records will be a logical and fruitful place to start. On the other hand if one is diversifying into a completely new market with a radically different product one will need to look for other published sources of information when the initial difficulty is more likely to be the apparent wealth of information rather than the absence of it. We say 'apparent' advisedly for closer inspection often reveals that relatively little information bears directly upon one's problems. However, there is some truth in the cliché that there is nothing new under the sun for, in a basic sense, even major innovations are a substitute for a previous product for which data is available. Thus xerography is but the latest in a long line of copying devices, the market for which was well documented at the time the Xerox process was introduced. Obviously, what was not known was the penetration that the new product would achieve, i.e. share of existing market, nor the effect it would have on the growth of the market. In the event, xerography revolutionised the copying business and both attracted demand from alternative methods of reproduction, e.g. stencils and duplicators, while expanding total usage due to its simplicity and cleanliness of operation and the quality of the finished product. Of course, few products are as successful or so well protected by patents (which effectively limit direct competition), as Xerox was, but it is worth bearing in mind that radically new or improved products may lead to an increase in total demand by suggesting new uses and by converting latent demand into effective demand.

Broadly speaking sources of published data fall into five categories:

288

Table 12.2   Methods of data collection

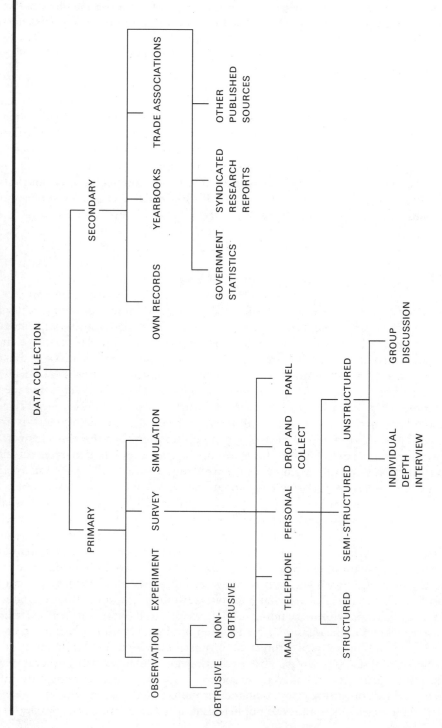

1   Government publications – both domestic and foreign. Salient among the former are the various *Censuses* of *Population, Production* and *Distribution*, the *Monthly Digest of Statistics*, the *Annual Abstract of Statistics, Trade and Industry* and *Business Monitor*. Major foreign sources are the various publications of the EEC and the ECSC, the International Monetary Fund, the OECD, the UN, and, of course, the foreign governments and their agencies.
2   Trade Associations and Chambers of Commerce. Trade Associations tend to publish highly specific data about their own industry, Chambers of Commerce more generalised information about business opportunities.
3   Universities and non-profit research organisations, e.g. *Oxford Bulletin of Statistics*, Stanford Research Institute. This category also includes the various academic journals.
4   Commercial Research Organisations, e.g. Economist Intelligence Unit, Attwood Statistics, Arthur D. Little, Booz, Allen & Hamilton, Gallup, etc.
5   The Press, both general, e.g. the *Financial Times*, and specific, e.g. *Fortune, Business Week*, etc.

From sources such as these the researcher should be able to build up a fair picture of the market for the product he is considering developing, at least in quantitative terms, e.g. total size, growth trends, seasonality, location, number of buyers, usage and replacement rates, etc. However, such parameters only serve to define past and current demand for other, albeit related products. While this may be sufficient to justify development of some products, e.g. where the risk is small or can be made so, as for example in a joint development with a prospective buyer, a very significant cost/ price or quality/price advantage, etc., in many cases the developer will want to know much more about the operation of the market than is apparent in bare statistics. In order to obtain this information, and/or to fill the gaps in the published data, it is usually necessary to engage in field research to collect this original or primary data.

■ The Collection of Primary Data

Primary or original data may be collected by one, or a combination of four methods – observation, experimentation, sample survey and simulation.

While observation of buying and usage behaviour may yield useful clues to consumer needs which may be incorporated in the product design, packaging, promotion policies, etc., it is not a particularly useful source of information on market size or potential. Much the same is true of both experimentation and simulation as techniques. Thus, by a process of elimination, the major source of primary data is the sample survey. In theory, of course, the ideal method of acquiring information about a 'population' (e.g. all potential purchasers of a new product) is to conduct a census of that population. In practice this is rarely feasible due to the size of the population and the time and cost of establishing contact with it. In fact experience of censuses suggests that 100% response is impossible of achievement and that a figure nearer 90% is more realistic. Accordingly, because of the time and expense involved in attempting a census, the knowledge that 100% response is unattainable, and the delay and cost involved in processing the mass of information yielded by the census,[12] most researchers prefer to conduct a sample survey. The only exceptions are the few cases where the population is small, easily identified and accessible, e.g. buyers of steel-making plant in Europe.

Sample surveys, or, as they are popularly known, 'opinion polls', are a familiar part of our daily life and generally accepted as a fairly accurate reflection of opinion at large, despite occasional lapses in predicting the outcomes of elections. However, as the pollsters point out, in many elections a swing of 2–3% will give an opposite result from that predicted while in most commercial situations, a level of accuracy of 97–98% would be more than adequate for decision-making purposes. In fact, if greater precision is required this can usually be achieved by increasing the sample size, always bearing in mind that costs tend to increase geometrically and accuracy only arithmetically, making the expected value of the additional information a very real issue.

Fundamentally, sampling theory rests upon two statistical 'laws' – the 'Law of Statistical Regularity' and the 'Law of Inertia of Large Numbers'. The first law states that any set of objects taken from a large group of such objects will tend to have the same characteristics as that larger group, while the second law holds that large groups are more stable than small groups because deviations about the mean tend to cancel each other out. Simplistically, therefore, if we can identify the members of a population in which we are interested (electors, buyers, etc.), then a given portion or sample of them should be representative of the whole, and the bigger the sample the more representative it will become. Sampling theory is now highly developed and the subject of many books in specialised fields such as operations research, production management, marketing research, etc. Reference should be made to these specialist treatments by those wishing to explore the subject further; for our purposes we must confine our comments to a brief description of the types of survey used in marketing research to establish market potential.

■ Probability Samples

Broadly speaking, sample designs fall into two categories – those based on probability theory and those which are not. Samples based on probability theory tend to be better known and are essential if one wishes to use the results for predictive purposes. In a probability based sample the chance that any given unit will be selected may be assigned a definite, non-zero probability. Given this knowledge it is possible to state within determinate limits, or 'degree of confidence' how likely it is that the sample results are an accurate reflection of the population from which the sample has been drawn. Among the better-known types of probability sample four are used fairly often by market researchers, namely:

(a) *Random samples* in which, theoretically, every member of the universe has an equal chance of being selected. In fact it may not be possible to pre-identify every member of a population as is possible when sampling, say, units of output in a factory, but it is usually possible to draw a sample that can be treated as unbiased for all practical purposes.

(b) *Systematic sample*. Unlike the true random sample, where every unit is identified, allocated a number and selected by a random process (cf. Ernie and Premium Bonds), the systematic sample is drawn by selecting units at a predetermined interval from a chosen starting point, e.g. every eighth house, every third member on a list.

(c) *Stratified samples*. The population is segmented into strata and random samples drawn from each stratum by either method (a) or (b).

(d) *Area sampling*. An area, usually a country, is broken down into sub-areas. A sample of sub-areas is then drawn and these are then sampled using one of the three preceding methods. This approach is followed for most national surveys.

We have already noted one difficulty in using probability sampling in a marketing situation – that of pre-identifying all members of the population. A second difficulty arises from the non homogeneous nature of the units which comprise populations of interest to marketers. This lack of homogeneity is particularly marked in the case of usage or consumption patterns and is illustrated by what has been termed the 'heavy half' syndrome.

This phenomenon is apparent both in industrial and consumer markets where it can usually be shown that a relatively small proportion of all users account for a disproportionately large share of total consumption. Thus one may find that the two or three largest firms in an industry of several hundreds, or even thousands, account for half of the usage of a given product, while in consumer markets it is often contended that 20% of the users account for 80% of the consumption while the remaining 80% of consumers account for the balance of 20%. Clearly, from a marketing point of view we are primarily interested in the heavy users, while, from a sampling point of view, we are concerned that our sample should be representative. If, however, every unit has an equal chance of being included it also has an equal chance of being excluded such that, if we are faced with a population in which the parameter we wish to measure is not distributed normally, there is a strong likelihood that our sample will be unrepresentative. For example, it would be like Lucas, with thousands of customers, trying to forecast demand for a new electrical component having drawn a sample which excluded the major car manufacturers. It is because of this possibility that marketing researchers make extensive use of non-probabilistic sampling methods.

■ Non-probability Samples

Three types of non-probability sample are in common use. The most basic and the crudest method is the *convenience sample* in which one solicits information from any convenient group which may have views pertinent to the subject of inquiry, e.g. one could ask Saturday afternoon shoppers for their views on pedestrian-only precincts, off-street parking facilities, adequacy of public transportation services, etc. This method is usually only used in the design stage of a survey to obtain a cross-section of opinion. A slight refinement of the convenience sample is the *judgement sample* in which the interviewer deliberately sets out to pick out a representative cross-section of opinion. For example, one would anticipate somewhat different attitudes to banning cars from city centres from non-car owners, car owners who use them for pleasure purposes and car owners who use them for business. Accordingly one would seek opinions from each of these categories.

Although both the foregoing methods provide a useful insight into opinions, attitudes and behaviour, one would be hesitant to extrapolate from such a survey. Under certain circumstances, however, one would be prepared to make market projections from the third type of non-probability sample – the *quota sample*. Quota sampling recognises that certain characteristics in which the researcher is interested are distributed through the population in a particular way and so draws a sample in which quotas are set that reflect this distribution. For example, in the case of our electrical component for a motor-car we might set our quotas so as to reflect past purchase patterns for a similar item and poll all the car manufacturers, most major retailers such as Halfords, a fair number of the major garage chains and car distributorships, and a very small proportion of all the independent garages that install and sell spare parts. Due to problems of bias arising from non-response in probability based samples it is quite possible that a well-designed and executed quota sample will yield equivalent if not better results.

It is clear that selection of a sample is a matter requiring both skill and judgement. The same attributes are equally necessary in selecting the method for establishing contact with respondents.

■ Field Survey Methods

Once a firm has identified the nature of the information required (usually the points unanswered by desk research), and the identity of members of the population which can supply this information, it must be decided *who* it will approach (sample design) and *how* it will approach them.

Basically, there are three main methods of administering a questionnaire, by post, by telephone and by personal interview. Each method has its advantages and disadvantages, and these we consider briefly below.

The major advantage of the mail questionnaire is its ability to reach named individuals, household or business establishments anywhere in the country at very low cost. (Cost depends on the length of the questionnaire, number of follow-ups, etc., but normally is in the range of £2–£5 per completed interview.) Other advantages are that mail questionnaires can convey complex information for evaluation using pictures, diagrams, etc.; this gives the respondents time to reflect before answering, i.e. the respondent is not 'under pressure' when a 'don't know' might be given to difficult questions, and they are not subject to interviewer bias, i.e. the respondent is not influenced or led by the interviewer. However, set against these are a number of corresponding disadvantages. In the final analysis the relevant cost criterion is, 'How much per usable response?'. Obviously if each questionnaire costs £2.00 to administer and the response rate is 10% then the true cost is £20. Unfortunately, low response rates are typical of mail surveys and 20%–30% would be considered good. Naturally, there are ways of increasing response rates, but these usually cost money and require simplification of the questionnaire itself to the point where its information yield is very small. If, therefore, only a limited proportion respond we must be immediately sensitive to the fact that perhaps people who answer mail questionnaires are different from those that do not – in other words the possibility of bias is very high and steps must be taken to check on reasons for non-response. In the absence of an interviewer to prompt, explain and generally maintain interest, questionnaires must be short and unambiguous – their value is correspondingly reduced.

An alternative to the mail questionnaire which has been shown to achieve very high response rates at a reasonable cost is the 'Drop and Collect' survey. Using this method an 'interviewer' physically delivers a structured questionnaire to intended respondents and asks them to complete it by a given date when the interviewer will call back.

Some of these difficulties may be overcome by using the telephone when the interviewer can interact with the respondent while, at the same time, executing interviews quickly and at low cost. Telephone interviewing is especially useful in the industrial market and increasingly so in consumer surveys where possession of a telephone is now estimated at 87% of all households. Like postal questionnaires, telephone interviews are best kept short and explicit. Perhaps their greatest ability is a back-up to postal or personal interviews when the telephone may be used to locate respondents, to check-up on non-respondents and validate completed interviews.

It is largely because of the deficiencies of postal and telephone surveys that researchers depend heavily upon personal, face-to-face interviews. In general such interviews may be structured, semi-structured or open-ended. Open-ended interviews (also known as unstructured and/or non-directive interviews) fall into two broad categories. Superficially both appear to be loose discussions about a theme, which is generally true in the exploratory stage of a research problem when one is seeking to define the scope and parameters of the problem. In these circumstances both interviewer and respondent are unsure what the discussions will generate, which is rather different from the open-ended interview where the interviewer is very familiar with the ground which he wishes to cover with the respondent, but is sufficiently skilful to do this in an apparently spontaneous manner, using one set of responses as a lead into the next series of questions. Open-ended discussions, particularly with a group of people, are very helpful as both a source of ideas and for concept testing. As an interviewing technique it is very dependent upon the skill of the interviewer but, when executed properly, is usually the most fruitful due to the freedom given the interviewer to interact with the respondent.

At the other extreme from the open-ended interview is the totally structured questionnaire in which all the questions are set in advance. Not only is the content of the questions predetermined, so also is the precise wording and sequence of the questions. The interviewer is allowed no discretion in executing such an interview. As a result of this standardisation, structured questionnaires should elicit directly comparable data and be largely free of the bias which interviewers may create in less formal interviewing situations. These features make the structured questionnaire a virtual must in consumer research where very large samples are necessary and less skilled interviewers have to be used because of the number of interviews involved.

However, because of its standardisation the structured questionnaire lacks the flexibility to cope with many of the problems which arise in opinion research, e.g. defining what is meant where the form of words used is ambiguous or not understood, probing the reasons for a given response, etc. Accordingly, where the subject is complex, the numbers to be interviewed are not excessive, and trained interviewers are available, many researchers prefer the semi-structured questionnaire. These, too, vary in terms of the degree of standardisation followed from a set sequence of open-ended questions where the respondent's answers are noted verbatim and probed when necessary, to a mere *aide-mémoire* or check list of points to be covered with no restrictions as to wording or sequence.

Clearly, selection of a sample design and execution of a survey are matters demanding considerable skill. With the exception of the very largest organisations, few companies possess these skills 'in house' and, even where they do, they are likely to use the services of a specialised marketing research agency to supplement their own resources. The benefits of using an agency are considerable and include access to:

(a)   Specialist knowledge of methodology and techniques.
(b)   Specialist skills, e.g. interviewers, psychologists.
(c)   Specialist facilities, e.g. laboratories for product testing.
(d)   An objective and fresh approach to one's problems.
(e)   Experience in related, or even the same product area.

A further benefit of using an agency is that many of them produce regular reports on a syndicated or subscription basis. Much of this data is collected from *panels* of respondents (e.g. housewives, doctors, retail stores) who keep diaries of their purchase/sales activities and so allow the researcher to track buying and selling behaviour on a continuous basis.

However, if a firm is to derive the maximum benefit from the skills and resources available in a marketing research organisation then it is essential that it be able to specify its needs clearly and that it will be willing to take the agency into its full confidence. Thus, even in the firm without marketing research personnel of any kind it is important that an executive be nominated to liaise with the agency. It will be helpful, therefore, if we summarise the basic types of information which the company may need in order to decide whether a market is worth exploiting and as a basis for developing a research strategy.

■ Market Assessment, Research Checklist

1   What are the possible uses for the proposed product?
    The intent is to identify *who* might use the product, *how*, in *what circumstances* and under *what conditions* as a basis for specifying different end-use markets or market segments.
2   What are the salient characteristics of each of the markets/segments?

(a) *Size*

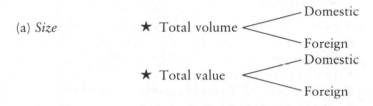

★ Volume and value of sub-divisions within the market

- by type of user
- by size of user
- by location
- by preferred product characteristics (size, price, quality, grade)

★ Size of markets for close substitutes.
★ Trends in each of the above last year, last five years.

(b) *Structure*

★ Number of suppliers
★ Number of consumers/users
★ Concentration ratios[13]
★ Changes in user and/or supplier industries likely to affect competitive structure.

(c) *Demand*

★ Elastic or inelastic in terms of
- Price
- Quality
- Near substitutes

★ Seasonality
★ Cyclical characteristics
★ By category of user
★ Durability, i.e. what is life-cycle of typical product?
★ Trends in the above.

(d) *Competition*   ★ The nature of competition is implicit in many of the above factors, none the less an explicit statement should be made in terms of the basic policies followed by the major competitors in each market covering

● Price
● Packaging
● Promotion
● Distribution
● Selling
● Financing
● Service
● Reciprocity

(e) *Buying practices*   ★ Individual or group responsibility
★ Frequency of purchase
★ Size of purchase
★ Inventory practices
★ Criteria used (cf. Demand conditioning factors)
★ Conditions imposed – e.g. Delivery, quality, etc.

The above points serve only as an indication of the broad areas to be documented and analysed. For a more explicit and much lengthier check list the reader is referred to Appendix A in Aubrey Wilson's book.[14] However, in the final analysis, and as indicated in the introduction to this chapter, the firm's decision ultimately depends upon its interpretation of the information at its disposal which is the subject of the next section.

■ Data Reduction and Analysis

With the advent of the computer the old complaint of 'insufficient information' has become less common and in some instances has been replaced by criticisms of 'too much information' – usually from overburdened executives whose desks are groaning under huge piles of computer printout. As with so many things it is not the quantity of information which is so important as the quality, and in this section we review some of the techniques and methods which enable one both to reduce data into a useful and meaningful input to a decision as well as to determine the value or importance to be attached to the data themselves.

In preceding sections we have discussed the collection of data from both secondary, or published sources, and direct from respondents by means of some type of survey (primary research). In the case of secondary data it was noted that such information may not have been collected for precisely the purpose which the inquirer is concerned with or that there may be uncertainty about the actual methods used which cast doubts on its accuracy, validity, etc. Further, it is unlikely that the data will be published in a format which corresponds with the researcher's needs. While these problems should be much less in the case of primary data, on the grounds that they have been collected for a specific purpose, there still exist problems in arranging the raw data in a style suited to the needs of the decision-taker. Problems such as these are a subject in their own right and numerous books are available which deal with them. For readers wishing to explore the topic in more detail there is a short bibliography at the end of the chapter, but for our immediate purposes we can do no better than quote from Green and Tull's[15] standard work on marketing research.

The overall process of analysing sample data and drawing inferences from it can be considered as involving a number of separate and sequential steps:

1 *Ordering the data into appropriate categories* – organising the data into forms which give it meaning within the context of the problem at hand and the initial hypotheses to be examined.
2 *Summarising the categorised data* – using summarising measures to provide economy of description and so to facilitate understanding and manipulation of the data.
3 *Formulating additional working hypotheses* – arriving at tentative explanations of behaviour or relationships among variables that were not originally considered in the problem statement.
4 *Inferring whether meaningful differences exist among categories* – drawing inferences concerning whether observed differences among categories are the results of chance variation due to sampling process or reflect actual differences in the population being studied.
5 *Inferring relationships among variables* – arriving at conclusions concerning the nature and existence of underlying relationships among the variables involved.

Ideally, one establishes categories prior to data collection but this is not always possible particularly when one is undertaking exploratory research using depth interviews, open-ended questions, projective techniques, etc. However, whether one establishes categories *ante* or *post hoc* it is generally agreed that they must satisfy four conditions:

1 Data *within* categories must be sufficiently similar as to be considered homogeneous.
2 Data *between* categories must be sufficiently different to merit a distinction being drawn between the categories.

3   Each category should be based upon only *one relevant criterion*.
4   The categories defined should be *mutually exclusive* and *collectively exhaustive*.

For example, when using Age as a basis for classification one might well use the following categories:

* 0–4
* 5–15
* 16–24
* 25–45
* 46–64
* 65 and over.

These divisions are purely arbitrary but reflect the following descriptive labels (again largely arbitrary).

* Pre school
* School age
* Young adult
* Family life
* Empty nest
* Senior citizen.

Categories such as these may be predetermined and there is a large number of such divisions which have become accepted through custom and practice thus ensuring that data collected at different times can be easily compared without having to reorganise the basic classificatory system, e.g. social class groupings. On the other hand when conducting primary research one may prefer not to anticipate patterns in the data and so only establish categories when these appear of their own accord. Indeed the advent of the computer and the ability to manipulate very large and complex data bases have led to a rather promiscuous approach to research in which everything is collected without prior justification and order is imposed through processes such as factor analysis. This is not to decry the power of techniques such as factor analysis, but to advocate the perhaps old-fashioned scientific method which presumes that one is pursuing research with a particular purpose in mind and so has some working hypotheses against which to test one's observations.

The statement of categories permits one to organise the data in tabular form and relate different factors to each other through the process of cross-tabulation, e.g. using our age categories we could examine, say, the consumption of milk to determine if there is any pattern or apparent association between age and milk consumption. It also becomes possible to develop so-called *summary statistics* which provide a concise statement of the distribution of data within and between the different categories. Summary or *descriptive* statistics fall into two main groups – *measures of central tendency* and *measures of dispersion*. Measures of central tendency comprise the arithmetic *mean*, the *median* and the *mode* while the measures of dispersion include the *range, standard deviation, variance* and *coefficient of variation*, definitions and descriptions of which are to be found in any statistics textbook.

The third step is formal analysis in the development of additional hypotheses – 'additional' because, as we argued earlier, research is intended to provide answers to questions (i.e. hypotheses) suggested by previously observed data. Clearly, if we had a sufficiently high prior probability concerning a particular hypothesis then the expected value of further information would probably be so low that it would preclude further research. Thus, most marketing research is 'designed to reduce areas of uncertainty surrounding business decisions' and it would be surprising if new information did not suggest new questions and solutions.

The final step in analysis is to establish whether any observed differences are real or are the result of chance, and, if real, draw conclusions concerning the relationship between the variables involved. Hypothesis testing traditionally involves four elements.[16]

1 A probability distribution of the sample statistic to be tested.
2 A null and alternate hypothesis which contain predictions of the population value against which the sample statistic is to be tested.
3 A test statistic.
4 A rejection region in the probability distribution.

Under this practice there is a tendency to prefer inaction to action by only rejecting the null hypothesis (i.e. no difference exists) given very high levels of certainty or significance (often as high as 0.95). But, in the managerial sciences in general and marketing in the particular, it is rare to find such high levels of certainty, and one must be prepared to reduce one's criterion. (Technically, one should consider Type II errors more important than Type I errors which is the opposite of the approach favoured by basic researchers.)[17]

Analysis of data is a subject in its own right, and dealt with at length in many texts on Quantitative Methods. A review of methods used in analysing marketing data is to be found in *Research for Marketing*, Chapter 9, Green and Tull[18] and Tull and Albaum (chapter 9 particularly)[19] and readers should refer to these for further information.

■ Bayesian Analysis

■ Introduction

It will often happen that even if it is possible to collect the complete facts on a situation the cost of so doing would be so prohibitive that absolute certainty is not worth while and the decision-maker will accept the risk involved in acting on only some of the facts. However, there are many situations in which even if the decision maker so wished he would be unable to collect perfect information and so would be left with an irreducible element of uncertainty concerning the decision to be taken. Thus the decision-maker can be in one of three states.

(a) *Certainty* – he has perfect information and *knows* the outcome of a given combination of events with the result that he can predict these precisely – e.g. an eclipse of the sun, high water at Tower Bridge in a month's time, the behaviour of falling objects, etc.

(b) *Risk* – the decision-maker has extensive past experience (personal or vicarious) of similar events to the extent that he can predict the general outcome but not the specific result of any given event. For example, O-level passes were based on the expectation that students in the top 40% of the ability range would be able to gain them. It follows that if I predict any given child will fail I have a 60% chance of being right.

(c) *Uncertainty* – as with risk there are several possible outcomes, but in this case one has little or no prior experience and so cannot assign an *objective* probability to the possible outcomes.

Of course an inability to assign an objective probability does not prevent us from developing subjective expectations as to the likelihood of a given event and from acting upon our judgement. In the real world of decision-making this is normal everyday practice but ordinary mortals should not be deluded into thinking it is as simple as it looks. If ever there were a case of natural selection then judgemental decision-making is it – those who are able to do it (intuitively or otherwise) succeed and those that can't fail and are not usually allowed to repeat the mistake – hence Napoleon's quest for 'lucky' generals. Fortunately, we can learn from those who appear to have an innate ability and by following a similar approach learn to combine facts and judgement to arrive at a decision which is consistent with our overall attitude to risk. In essence the key to successful decision-making would seem to lie in an ability to specify the alternatives, the likelihood of their occurrence and the consequences associated with each. In the case of important decisions it is likely that we will seek to obtain evidence to test the validity of our expectations – in other words we will undertake marketing research – and then seek to synthesise the two pieces of information into a single composite 'decision'. To assist managers to improve their decision-making ability a new school of decision theorists has developed in the last twenty years or so who, following the lead of Raiffa and Schlaifer at the Harvard Business School in emphasising the role of probability in decision-making, have developed the concept of decision 'trees' and have resurrected Bayes' Theorem as a means of combining prior estimates with new information to generate a set of revised or posterior probabilities. It is the particular power of this latter technique which has led to the generic term 'Bayesian' being applied to probabilistic approaches to problem-solving.

■ Problem Specification

It is often claimed that problem definition constitutes 90% of the difficulty in problem-solving. Experience shows this often to be the case in the sense that once a decision-maker has clearly articulated his objectives it becomes possible to assess the factors which will hinder or encourage their achievement and so determine the possible courses of action open to him. Depending upon the decision-maker's confidence in his ability to predict the likely outcome of each of the alternatives he will either make his decision or defer it pending the acquisition of further information up to the point where the marginal cost of further information is equal to its perceived value. This sequence of events is illustrated in Figure 12.3 from Enis and Broome.

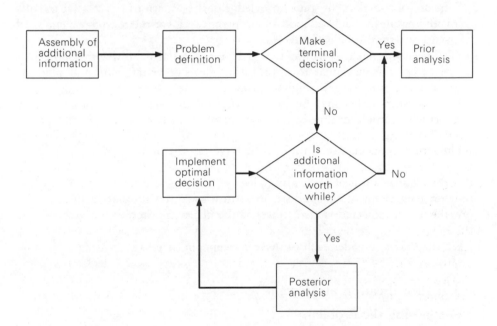

Figure 12.3   A Bayesian view of the decision process

Source: B. M. Enis and C. L. Broome, *Marketing Decisions: a Bayesian approac*h (Aylesbury: Intertext, 1973).

From Figure 12.3 it is clear that if the decision-maker is satisfied with his *prior* analysis then he will automatically select the alternative which appears optimal to him and implement his decision. But, if there is an element of doubt about the outcome, he may well reflect upon the advisability of spending resources (time and money) in improving the information available to him – in Bayesian terminology this is called *pre-posterior* analysis. If the likely cost exceeds the expected value then the decision will be taken but if it is thought the expected value exceeds the cost then more information will be collected and analysed through a *posterior* analysis. The procedure will then recycle and a decision be made or deferred pending more data acquisition. Enis and Broome summarise[20] this Bayesian approach as consisting of five elements, namely:

1   The decision-maker is involved in a situation in which there are at least two alternative ways of reaching a specific objective(s), and he has the power to decide among the alternatives.
2   The decision-maker is uncertain as to which decision alternative to select, because he does not know the set of environmental conditions (state of nature) which will actually prevail at the time the decision is implemented.
3   The decision-maker has some knowledge of the situation, e.g. relative payoffs of alternatives, and likelihood of occurrence of various events or states of nature which affect these payoffs.
4   The decision-maker is willing to use expected value as his decision criterion, i.e. accept the view that to optimise his decision making he will take the course of action with the highest expected value (utility).
5   The decision-maker may be able to obtain additional information (at some cost) which might change his assessment of the situation.

Thus three concepts are central to the Bayesian methodology:

(a)   the identification of alternatives;
(b)   the assignment of probabilistic expectations to the alternatives;
(c)   the use of expected value (utility) as the decision criterion.

We shall now consider each of these concepts in turn.

■ The Identification of Alternatives
□ Diagnosing the Problem

Unless and until one has specified the possible courses of action open to the decision-maker it is impossible to express a judgement on the likelihood of occurrence of any one of them for the simple reason that the combined likelihood of an exhaustive set of alternatives must always add up to 1.00 where occurrence is mutually exclusive. Thus, even if one cannot specify fully all the possible alternatives one should still be able to assign an expectation to the residual and unspecified alternatives which will express one's expectations about them *vis-à-vis* those of which one is aware.

In order to develop alternatives one must first define and diagnose the nature of the problem itself. According to George F. Huber[21] there are three tendencies which frequently interfere with adequate problem exploration:

1   The tendency to define the problem in terms of a proposed solution.
2   The tendency to focus on narrow, lower order goals.
3   The tendency to diagnose the problem in terms of its symptoms.

The first tendency is a widespread and pervasive phenomenon which has sometimes been characterised as 'a solution searching for a problem'. The more 'expert' a person is the greater the likelihood that they will fall victim of this fallacy and tend to recast or interpret the facts in terms of their own selective perception. Thus all problems become seen as a manifestation of the problem-solver's own expertise and it is no accident that as top managers emerge from given disciplines and functions they tend to view all the problems they encounter from that perspective and classify them as 'finance', 'marketing' or 'production' problems. (This tendency becomes even more dangerous when the decision-maker seeks to avoid 'guilt by association' and shifts the onus to another functional area solely to divert attention from his own possible culpability.) The greatest danger of this approach is that it provides a focus and so excludes consideration of other possibilities.

The second tendency is also commonplace among managers who seek to reduce problems to a comfortable order of magnitude which falls well within their existing experience and competence. Such managers will be happy with fine tuning the marketing mix, but will shy away from a radical programme of innovation and new product development which will lead them into new and unfamiliar markets.

The third tendency of diagnosing problems in terms of their symptoms is also familiar but much less dangerous than the two previous diversions from the search for alternatives. Indeed in many circumstances good diagnosis must be a sequential process in which you relate the symptoms to the most likely cause and prescribe accordingly. Most headaches are temporary and acute phenomena which may rise from any of a large number of causes which are equally temporary and acute. The need is to alleviate the symptoms and monitor their progression. If after 24 hours all is well and the symptoms do not return we will discount the cause as unimportant. But, if the symptoms persist we will probe more deeply and try other remedies until, by a process of trial and error, we discover the true cause. Such a procedure exemplifies well the concept of the expected value of information for, in the absence of highly distinctive and unmistakable symptoms one does not admit to hospital for a brain scan every person who complains of a headache.

Huber argues that these tendencies are part of a defensive mechanism designed to reduce tension among problem-solvers by enabling them to move on to steps which help to alleviate the discomfort which problem recognition creates. Conversely, generating alternatives may only exacerbate the problem and suggesting that a man with a headache may have a brain tumour is unlikely to be seen as a helpful suggestion. Clearly, a narrow path has to be trodden and experience suggests that the development of decision trees has much to commend it in that the creation of alternatives occurs sequentially in an ordered manner which is psychologically less stressful than less structured, open-ended listing and ordering techniques such as brainstorming.

■ Developing a Decision Tree

One of the clearest and earliest explanations of the use of decision trees in problem-solving is to be found in John F. Magee's article.[22] This article has seldom been equalled and never bettered and provides the basis of this section.

Magee starts with a simple example to illustrate the salient characteristics of the decision-tree approach by posing the problem of what to do on an overcast Saturday afternoon when 75 people are coming round for cocktails. This he describes as follows:

> You and your wife feel it is time you returned some hospitality by holding a party.
> You have a pleasant garden and your house is not too large; so if the weather permits,
> you would like to set up the refreshments in the garden and have the party there. It
> would be more pleasant, and your guests would be more comfortable. On the other
> hand, if you set up the party for the garden and after all the guests are assembled it
> begins to rain, the refreshments will be ruined, your guests will be damp and you will
> heartily wish you had decided to have the party in the house . . . What should you
> do? This particular decision can be represented in the form of a 'pay-off' table:

	Events and results	
Choices	*Rain*	*No rain*
Outdoors	Disaster	Real comfort
Indoors	Mild discomfort, but happy	Mild discomfort, but regrets

> In turn the information in the pay-off table can be represented pictorially by means of
> a decision tree [see Figure 12.4]:

As Magee comments:

> The tree is made up of a series of nodes and branches. At the first node on the left, the
> host has the choice of having the party inside or outside. Each branch represents an
> alternative course of action or decision. At the end of each branch or alternative
> course is another mode representing a chance event – whether or not it will rain. Each
> subsequent alternative course to the right represents an alternative outcome of this
> chance event. Associated with each complete alternative course through the tree is a
> pay-off, shown at the end of the rightmost or terminal branch of the course.

From this description it is clear that a decision tree will always combine action choices with different possible events or outcomes which are subject to some degree or other to chance (distinguished by different symbols for emphasis).

In the case of the relatively simple decision discussed so far one probably needs neither a pay-off table nor a decision tree to help one come to a decision. But, given more complex decisions where several alternatives are available it is easy to

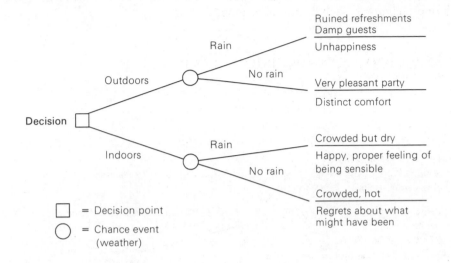

Figure 12.4 **An exercise in decision-making, showing the possible results of a**
■■■■■■■■ **chance event**

Source: J. F. Magee, 'Decision Trees for Decision Making', *Harvard Business Review* (July–
August 1964).

understand how the content of a pay-off table could confuse rather than
illuminate while a decision tree would help disaggregate the problem in a clear
and meaningful way. Magee presents such a tree when he analyses the familiar
marketing problem of whether or not to invest in product development. Although
he does not pursue the analysis of this tree further in his article its relevance to
marketing is such that it is used as the basis for the discussion which follows.

The inevitability of change and the pressures which it creates for a continuing
process of new product development have already been touched on in looking at
the nature of competition and are central to the theme of the next chapter which
is concerned with product policy. Faced with the decision of whether or not to
commit funds to the improvement or replacement of an existing product in order
to maintain or improve market share the marketing manager may well come up
with a decision tree such as that in Figure 12.5. Clearly, this tree does not cover all
possible eventualities. For example, if the development fails you may decide that
you cannot wait and see what your competitor does and so will immediately
recycle to the initial decision point and commit additional funds to further
development. However, it is sufficient to illustrate the application of the
technique.

As it stands our decision tree has already served a useful purpose in making
clear the alternatives open – it now remains to show how one can use the
decision-maker's knowledge and expectations to reach a decision.

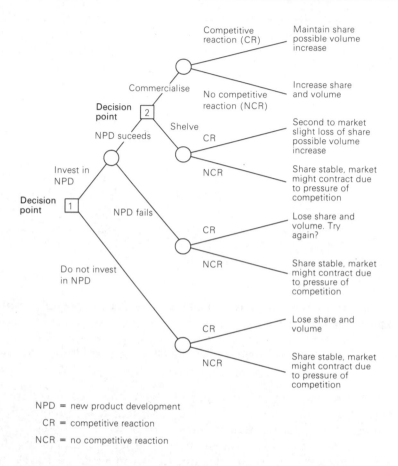

NPD = new product development

CR = competitive reaction

NCR = no competitive reaction

Figure 12.5   The new product development decision

■ Probability

Earlier in the chapter we referred explicitly to the distinction between 'certainty', 'risk' and 'uncertainty' and since then have used terms such as 'expectations', 'likelihood' and 'outcomes' in a rather loose way. In order to make our decision tree operational and understand the application of Bayes' Theorem it is necessary now to review briefly the concept of probability.

In simple terms probability reflects the likelihood of an event expressed on a scale which runs from certain to impossible to which, by convention, have been assigned the values 1.0 and 0.0 respectively. Intermediate points are assigned values which reflect the frequency with which they are expected to occur and the critical issue is the basis upon which the expectation is founded. In his book

Howard Thomas[23] identifies three methods of assessing probability with which the manager should be familiar – *a priori, relative frequency* and *subjective.*

An *a priori* probability expresses the frequency with which an event may occur in terms of the total number of possible outcomes so that the *a priori* probability of a head in coin tossing is ½ or 0.5, of a six on a single throw of a dice 1/6 or 0.166, of the ace of spades on a single draw from a pack of cards 1/52 or 0.019 and so on. However, as Thomas observes, 'This concept of probability, based on equally likely outcomes, has little application as a means of measuring probability other than in games of chance.'

The *relative frequency* method of assigning probabilities is much more useful and is the technique used when defining risk in the sense in which we defined it earlier. As the term suggests, probabilities of this kind are based upon knowledge concerning the frequency with which an event has occurred in the past, thus enabling one to express a view as to the likelihood of its reoccurrence in the future. This concept is central to the whole theory of sampling, which is a procedure used extensively in marketing research and reviewed briefly in an earlier section.

However, the use of relative frequencies depends upon the availability of objective information concerning previous occurrences of events identical to the one which we are trying to predict. But, as we saw when defining uncertainty, the dynamic and interactive nature of most marketing activities tends to militate against identical occurrences and it is this which makes prediction of marketing events so difficult. For this reason we have to depend upon the skill and experience of the decision-maker himself and use his *subjective* expectation of the occurrence of an event as the basis for an actual decision.

From Figure 12.3, illustrating the Bayesian view of the decision process and our new product development decision tree, it is clear that most decisions are not just simple 'either or' choices, but involve multiple, mutually exclusive but inter-dependent alternatives. It follows that we need some rules to explain how probabilities will interact given a compound decision of the kind most likely to be encountered in marketing. Statements of the rules of probability are to be found in most statistics textbooks and also in books on managerial decision-making (see, for example, Thomas[24]) and are beyond the scope of this chapter. However, analysis of our decision tree will throw some light on the rules and demonstrate that in very simple terms probabilities may be added or multiplied, but their sum must always be unity. But, before we can solve our decision problem we must first agree upon the criterion to be used and show how one's expectations can be converted into probabilistic statements.

■ The Decision Criterion

Although a number of possible decision criteria are available theorists are unanimous in recommending that one should seek to '*maximise the expected utility*' *(MEU)* flowing from a decision. Utility is usually thought of as an objective, economic concept, but, in reality, it is subjective and relative. In cases where decision-makers are acting solely on their own behalf the distinction between objective and subjective is irrelevant, but when one is acting on behalf of an organisation or in conjunction with a number of other decision-makers it is important that all of them handle risk in a similar way.

One of the best and earliest discussions of the application of utility theory in decision-making was that contained in the *Harvard Business Review* by Ralph O. Swalm.[25] In this article Swalm focuses clearly on the issue of the decision criterion in his opening paragraphs:

> Suppose that you were lucky enough to be offered the following alternatives:
>
> (1)   Accept the payment of a tax free gift of $1 million.
> (2)   Toss a fair coin. If heads come up, you get nothing; if tails come up you get a tax free gift of $3 million.
>
> Which would you choose? Would it be the certain $1 million, or the 50–50 chance of $3 million or nothing.

When confronted with this choice, most people say they would choose the certain $1 million, even though the gamble has what is called an 'expected value' of $1.5 million. (The term 'expected value', often used in quantitative analysis, is the product of the hoped for gain and the probability of winning it $3\,000\,000 \times 0.5$ in this case.)

Swalm continues to speculate that most people would probably continue to take the certain $1 million even if the odds were increased to $5 million if tails came up. Clearly, this is not the sort of objective behaviour you would expect of businessmen — or is it? According to two of the founding fathers of decision analysis, John von Neumann and Oskar Morgenstern, it is, and is defined by them as *cardinal utility theory*. Swalm comments: 'oversimplifying a bit, this concept proposes that each individual attempts to optimise the expected value of something which is defined as utility, and that for each individual a relationship between utility and dollars can be found.'

The remainder of Swalm's paper is concerned with a further explanation of cardinal utility theory and the doubt which it casts on 'the classical notion of the American businessman as a risk taker and on the validity of many control systems set up to monitor manager behaviour'. Following a description of a methodology for developing an individual's utility function, Swalm reports the results of an experiment which illustrates vividly the wide variation in attitudes to risk which may be found among executives in the same corporation. Because of these discrepancies Swalm (and numerous others since him) advocates the use of cardinal utility theory as a means of making explicit different decision-makers' attitude to risk thereby providing a basis for reconciling such differences and encouraging a more objective and realistic attitude to risk.

Despite these exhortations it is clear that much still remains to be done. Writing in 1980, Bob Hayes and Bill Abernathy[26] attributed the lacklustre performance of the US economy since the Second World War to the short-term risk-avoiding tactics of most American managers. In that the same condition is to be found in most of the advanced industrial countries it is small wonder that Hayes and Abernathy's diagnosis has received widespread support. To a large degree 'milking the investment' is encouraged by an emphasis upon short-term planning horizons and the accounting mentality which has come to afflict so much of professional management. If marketers are to avoid falling into the same trap they must take a long-term view of success and be prepared to adjust their own risk behaviour to bring it in line with the more objective approach which takes into account the expected value of alternative courses of action. To this end we recommend the use of expected value as its decision criterion. (Because expected value is usually expressed in terms of money it is usual to use the term EMV or *'expected monetary value'*).

■ Analysing the Decision Tree

We are now in a position to add some rational data to our new product development decision tree and describe the process known as 'rollback' to indicate what decision should be taken. In Figure 12.6 we have added the costs of new product development and our best expectations about likely events and the ultimate financial consequences to us of each end-position as described earlier and shown in Figure 12.4 Because we are a successful firm and good at NPD we assess the likelihood of success as 0.8. However, past experience suggests that markets often change during the course of NPD, so we consider that having invested £500 000 in development there is a 0.2 chance we will put our innovation 'on the shelf', leaving a 0.8 probability that we will commercialise it.

Given that we do launch our new product we believe strongly (0.8) that our competitors will try to launch a 'me-too' product so that the net benefit would be approximately 1 million. On the other hand, if they do not, the rewards will be very considerable indeed (5 million). Assuming that we have shelved a product because we think the time for a launch is unpropitious we have a fairly high expectation (0.7) that no one else will do so and it seems reasonable that because the signs are unpropitious and there is no aggressive marketing action the overall market will contract and our sales with it. Conversely, if we are mistaken and a competitor livens up the market with a new product launch we will have ours ready in the wings and will be able to gain some benefit from the revitalisation of consumer interest.

Should we fail in developing our new product then it could be that a competitor could take advantage of the opportunity which would have led us to launch a new product if we had one. We estimate this as a 50–50 chance and the same applies if we had not attempted to develop a new product ourself in the first place although in the latter case we would have saved the £500 000 on NPD. So what should we do? Figure 12.7 makes it quite clear that we must go ahead with new product development. If we do not, the expected outcome is a loss to us of £2 750 000 whereas if we go ahead the exercise will yield an expected value of £70 000 net of

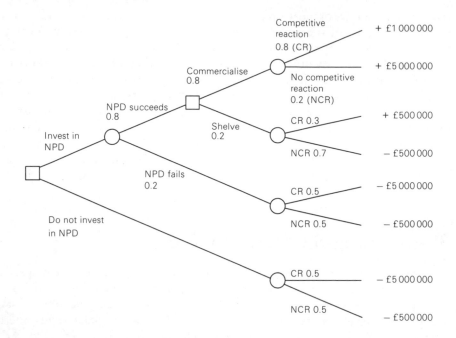

Figure 12.6 Expected outcomes for NPD

£500 000 development costs. These figures are arrived at by the simple process of computing the likelihood of any given outcome by multiplying the probabilities associated with it and relating them to the expected value of that outcome. We then 'roll back' the tree from the end-points to the decision-point, enabling us to assign a value to the basic choice of developing or not developing a new product in the first place.

This analysis also highlights the application of the concept of the expected value of information, for at the point where we have succeeded in developing a new product we can decide whether to alter our original 80-20, produce or shelve decision, and whether or not it would be worth spending money on market research to firm up our expectations.

■ Summary

The Bayesian approach to decision-making has widespread application to the type of problems which predominate in marketing, which Philip Kotler has described as having to be made 'in the context of insufficient information about processes that are dynamic, non-linear, lagged, stochastic, interactive, and downright difficult'. The treatment in Chapter 12 can do no more than sketch

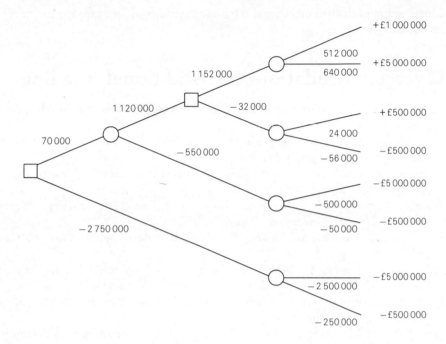

Figure 12.7 Decision for roll-back

in some of the salient features of the technique and the procedures associated with it, but the reader is strongly recommended to consult at least some of the sources cited.

In addition we have also attempted to provide an overview of the sources of data available to the manager (primary and secondary) and summarised the major methods of data collection – observation, experimentation and sample survey. The discussion of sample survey methodology suggested that in most cases only the largest and most sophisticated companies are likely to have a marketing research function of their own, so that most work of this kind will be sub-contracted to a specialist agency. (This is also true of large companies in the case of large-scale field surveys.) However, to ensure the maximum benefit from such contracted-out research it is important that the organisation should have a clear view of its research needs and appoint someone to liaise directly with the market research agency.

Some consideration was also given to the problems of too much information and the means of classifying and categorising this in order to reduce it to meaningful and usable proportions. From this review it became clear that, despite the apparent information overload, decision-makers are often faced with situations where objective data are not available and they need to combine the 'facts' with their own judgement to arrive at a decision. In doing so the construction of decision trees and Bayesian methods of analysis appear to offer a useful framework.

■ Recommendations for Additional Reading

Bryan Carsberg, *Economics of Business Decisions* (Harmondsworth: *Penguin* Books, 1975).

Paul Goodwin and George Wright, *Decision Analysis for Management Judgement* (Chichester: John Wiley, 1991).

Mark R. Greene, 'How to rationalise your marketing risks', *Harvard Business Review (May–June* 1969).

John S. Hammond III, 'Better decisions with preference theory', *Harvard Business Review* (November–December 1967).

K.F. Jackson, *The Art of Solving Problems* (London: Teach Yourself Books, 1977).

P.G. Moore and H. Thomas, *The Anatomy of Decisions* (Harmondsworth: *Penguin* Books, 1976).

Philip A. Schedule Jr, 'ROI for new product planning'. *Harvard Business Review* (November–December 1964).

D.S. Tull and G.S. Albaum, *Survey Research: A Decisional Approach* (Intertext Books, 1975).

CHAPTER 13
Product¹ Policy

Learning Goals

The issues to be addressed in Chapter 13 include:

1 The role of the *product* in marketing.
2 The relationship between *user needs* and *product characteristics*.
3 The *classification* of products.
4 The *nature* of *product policy*.
5 The *importance* of *product development*
6 The *normative theory* of *new product development*
7 The management of the *product life-cycle* (PLC)
8 The monitoring of *product performance*.

After reading Chapter 13 you will able to:

1 Explain the *central role played by products* in the development of marketing strategy.
2 Define the major terms associated with *product management*.
3 Identify the *four basic growth strategies* proposed by Ansoff, and their implications for product policy and management.
4 Describe and illustrate the *normative theory of new product development*.
5 Specify the actions most appropriate to the management of products at *different stages of their life-cycles*.
6 Suggest procedures for *monitoring product performance*.

Introduction

According to the marketing concept – and in an ideal world – the primary focus of economic activity should be the market, for it is the market which mirrors demand and it is demand which reflects human needs. Thus textbook writers – and even some entrepreneurs – can start with the proposition that identification and selection of market opportunities should be the starting-point for business activity. But, in the real world, things are very different. Most resources, or factors of production, are already committed to the creation of specific goods and services and a comparatively small surplus exists at any point in time which is available for new investment. Of course, in deciding the best use to which this surplus may be put the normative theory of market planning will be of inestimable value in identifying market opportunities and selecting between them. Even so, choices will be severely proscribed, for existing organisations will usually seek to retain contact with one or other major dimension of their current operation (products or customers) and retain a common thread. Similarly, entrepreneurs rarely undertake a formal analysis of market opportunities and respond to a demand pull – usually they are implementing a strong drive to make and/or sell something for which they *believe* there is a need.

As a consequence of all these forces the primary concern of most organisations is product policy and management rather than market policy and management. Once a firm has committed itself to a given market all else flows from it and the decision is difficult if not impossible to reverse. As Corey[2] has pointed out, choice of market 'builds a set of relationships with customers that are at once a major source of strength and a major commitment. The commitment carries with it the responsibility to serve customers well, to stay in the technical and product development race, and to grow in pace with growing market demand.'

Given the central role played by the product as the focus of the exchange process it is clear that a single chapter in a book can only introduce some of the more important ideas and suggest where the reader may find more detailed information and explanation. To this end the chapter will open with a discussion of the role of the product in marketing and build upon earlier analyses of buyer behaviour and product portfolio planning. An attempt will also be made to define some of the terms used in the literature of product management.

Although we have argued that existing firms may be preoccupied with, or even locked into, certain products, the inexorable pressures of change will require them to determine how they can best position themselves to meet future needs. In turn, this will invariably require them to modify, update and even replace existing products with new ones and so will focus attention upon product development as a key strategic function. Our own analysis of product development will first look at it in the abstract as a process and will then seek to show how product policy and management will vary according to the different stages of the life-cycle – introduction, growth, maturity and decline. Finally in this chapter we will look at methods for monitoring product performance.

■ The Role of the Product in Marketing

For many years previous to the birth of the electronic watch a classic case study in the armoury of any business school teacher offering a course in Business Policy, General Management or Marketing Strategy was 'Hamilton Watch'. Almost without exception the first question posed on this case study was 'What is a watch?' and the answer would encompass a wide range from 'a scientific instrument for measuring time' through 'a gift' to 'a status symbol', thus allowing the instructor to make *the* basic point about any product, namely, that it is a bundle of attributes and that it is the need and perception of the consumer or user which will determine which of these definitions is most apposite in any given set of circumstances. Such an insight is fundamental to the marketing concept, underlies the reason why product differentiation became the basic competitive strategy in the 1920s and explains why market segmentation has assumed such importance in the mature and saturated markets of the advanced industrialised economies.

As we attempted to show in Chapter 7, when addressing the question of how buyers select between alternatives, choice behaviour is conditioned by both objective and subjective factors. In recent years recognition that the objective factors which are intrinsic to the product (performance and price) are relatively easy to copy has led to much greater emphasis upon the qualitative and subjective dimensions which will become determinant when objective parity is perceived to exist. We say 'perceived' advisedly for our analysis has shown that people have difficulty in distinguishing very small differences to the extent that in business a useful working rule-of-thumb is that a difference must be at least 10% between the objects which are being compared if it is to become 'noticeable', i.e. 10% bigger, smaller, faster, more efficient, etc. Two consequences flow from this:

1 Producers wrongly assume that small differentiating features will be perceived when they won't, with the result that:
2 Greater emphasis is given to creating subjective differences between competitive products through service and promotional efforts.

The net outcome of these trends is that the recent literature on marketing has tended to give little specific attention to product characteristics and product differentiation and has concentrated more upon user characteristics and market segmentation. Such a change in emphasis is believed to have gone too far, for the simple reason that objective differences are easier to develop, control and sustain than subjective differences and, if they exist, will largely eliminate the need to try and create such subjective differences.

As H. V. Thompson observed in his book *Product Strategy*:[3] 'You can change products: it is a comparatively simple matter of decision and cost. You can't change people – but you can influence them – but seldom if ever cheaply. It is far easier – and thus far more economical – to find out what people want and to supply it than it is to influence them to want what you make.' A sentiment echoing those of Ries and Trout in Chapter 9 on Positioning.

Support for the view that too much attention has been given to market 'need' as opposed to product content is to be found in a forceful article by Bennett and Cooper.[4] Citing the automobile industry as a microcosm of the American economy Bennett and Cooper claim that lower cost and better fuel economy are simplistic explanations of the 30% market share secured by Japanese and European imports. In their view 'The Europeans and Japanese car makers have simply been better competitors; they anticipated market needs; they built a better product – one that is more reliable, has better workmanship, and is better engineered; and they did it effectively. In short, these manufacturers delivered better value to the American consumer.'

Several similar instances (tv tubes, motorcycles, etc.) are cited and lead to the conclusion that:

> The failure to deliver product value to the customer is the prime reason for this lack of competitiveness. Twenty years of adherence to the marketing concept may have taken its toll of an American enterprise. The marketing concept has diverted our attention from the product and its manufacture; instead we have focused our strategy on responses to market wants and have become preoccupied with advertising, selling, and promotion. And in the process, product value has suffered.

Similarly it is a truism to state that consumers will always prefer a better product at the same price or the same product at a lower price, but both observations underline the importance of trying to create objective product differences before resorting to the intangible and subjective elements. Satisfaction is the end, but the product or service is the means by which it is achieved. As Lawrence Abbott[5] has pointed out, 'what people really desire are not the products but satisfying experiences', but 'experiences are attained through activities. In order that activities may be carried out physical objects or the services of human beings are usually needed. Here lies the connecting-link between man's inner world and the outer world of economic activity. People want products because they want the experience-bringing services which they hope the products will render.'

■ User Needs and Product Characteristics

Ultimately it seems to me to be irrelevant whether one first identifies user needs and develops product characteristics to match them or, alternatively, creates a product and then seeks out customers whose needs match these characteristics. In the final analysis the process is circular and subject to continuous adjustment. That said, there will be clear benefits if one can spell out some of the basic dimensions of user needs as this will make it that much easier to develop the appropriate product characteristics. A very helpful approach to this process is to be found in a monograph published by the Design Council by Rothwell, Gardiner and Schott[6] which provides a framework for this section.

Rothwell *et al.* argue that user needs can be thought of as having four dimensions which they define as follows;

- *Need elements*: An indication of the overall price and specific performance characteristics required by customers.
- *Need intensity*: A measure of the degree of importance given to each need element by potential users.

- *Need stability*: A measure of the degree to which the need remains unchanged over time.
- *Need diffusion*: A measure of how widely felt the need is. This defines the size of the potential market.

Thus 'need elements' define the properties which a product must contain and/or deliver while 'need intensity' specifies the relative importance which consumers will attach to any given element. As we have seen when analysing how buyers choose, many properties are assumed to exist as they are intrinsic to the product and it would not qualify for consideration at all if it didn't possess them. Further, buyers will often use a single performance or benefit criterion as a surrogate for a large number of individual product characteristics when assessing suitability or fitness for purpose, e.g. few buyers of machine tools will evaluate the metallurgical analysis of the materials used nor the precise tolerances used in constructing the tool – they will assess its suitability in terms of its output potential. By the same token the purchaser of a TV set rarely inquires into the nature of the electronic gadgetry contained in the 'box'; he is concerned with the quality of the sound and picture which these components deliver. Of course there will always be exceptions to these generalisations and it is for this reason that it is felt more attention should be given to spelling out the product's characteristics, for only by cataloguing them fully will we be able to establish whether our product possesses features others don't and, if so, whether these features will have appeal to a sufficient number of potential customers to constitute a viable market segment.

In Table 13.1 an attempt has been made to provide a consolidated listing of product characteristics or attributes to act as a check list for assessing existing or proposed new products. Several sources have been used in an attempt to make the listing suitable for all categories of products.

In Figure 13.1 we reproduce a simple bar chart which illustrates well how need elements and need intensity can be combined to give a quick visualisation of the product configuration desired by a particular market segment. Such pictograms should be constructed for each market segment and, when combined with an evaluation of the need stability and need diffusion, will enable the planner to decide which offer the best opportunities in terms of his own aspirations and supply capabilities.

While physical attributes are a necessary condition for purchase they are not usually sufficient, particularly where there is little to distinguish one physical product from another.[7] In these circumstances our model of buyer behaviour predicates that subjective/behavioural influences will become determinant in enabling the individual to discriminate between competitive offerings. As we noted earlier, the creation of subjective perceived differences is likely to prove more difficult and more costly than the creation of objective differences, but the likelihood of being able to achieve this will be greatly enhanced if one adopts a marketing approach and defines one's products in terms of the benefit/satisfaction it provides rather than the function it performs. Levitt first propounded this

Table 13.1   Product characteristics

Technical	Economic Non-price	Price
Size	Servicing costs	List price
Shape		
Weight	Availability of	Sale price
Consistency	parts and service	
Materials used in	Running costs	Net price after
construction		trade-in allowance
Complexity		
Power source	Breakdown costs	Financing or leasing
Power output		arrangements
Speed/Production rate	Depreciation	
Reliability		Discounts
Flexibility/Adaptability	User training facilities	
Ease of use		Sale or return
Ease of maintenance	Instructions	
Safety		Special offers
Appearance/Design features	Delivery	
Smell		
Taste		

Source: R. Rothwell, P. Gardiner and K. Schott, *Design and the Economy* (London: The Design Council, 1983). J.R. Evans and B. Berman, *Marketing* (New York: Macmillan, 1982).

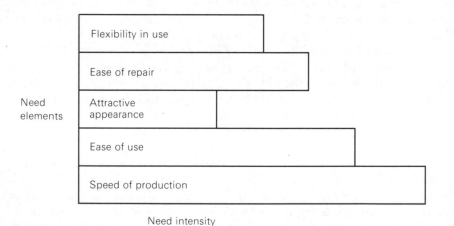

Figure 13.1   **Bar chart showing need elements and need intensity**

Source: R. Rothwell, P. Gardiner and K. Schott, *Design and the Economy* (London: The Design Council, 1983).

philosophy in his famous 'Marketing Myopia', but elaborated on it in a subsequent contribution entitled 'The Augmented Product Concept'[8] in which he wrote:

> One million quarter-inch drills were sold not because people wanted quarter-inch drills, but because they wanted quarter-inch holes.

Levitt also quoted the President of Melville Shoes as saying:

> People no longer buy shoes to keep their feet warm and dry. They buy them because of the way the shoes make them feel – masculine, feminine, rugged, different, sophisticated, young, glamorous, in. Buying shoes has become an emotional experience. *Our business now is selling excitement rather than shoes* (emphasis mine).

This, of course, is an extreme statement and not to be taken too seriously. Clearly, people still do buy shoes to keep their feet warm and dry and have quite clear expectations as to the functions shoes must perform. But, the point is well made that different images and associations may well encourage people to buy more shoes, to suit different moods and situations, than are required for the sole purpose of protecting one's feet.

▮ Product Classification and Marketing Strategy

Experience suggests that it is possible to classify types of products in terms of the relative emphasis which should be or is accorded to their objective and subjective characteristics and the manner in which they are bought. If this is so then such classification will provide a useful basis for specifying the appropriate strategy to be used in the markets into which the different classes of goods are sold.

Perhaps the simplest and most obvious approach to product classification are the dichotomies industrial goods v. consumer goods, and durable v. non-durable goods. However, as Avlonitis[9] has pointed out, these are at best approximations and a more sophisticated classificatory system is necessary to enable rational marketing strategy decisions to be made. He then reviews the three best-known schemata in the following terms:

> Historically, one of the most widely accepted classifications of products has been proposed by Copeland.[10] He proposed a trichotomy: convenience goods, shopping goods and speciality goods based on consumer buying habits. Although his concern was with consumer goods his scheme may be easily generalised to include industrial goods as well.
>
> Although this classification yields some anomalies and is not altogether satisfactory, it tends to be quite useful in guiding the development of marketing strategy. For instance convenience goods tend to require relatively heavy advertising and competitive pricing to achieve product differentiation and large distributive and selling organisation to deal with the need for widespread points of sale. Shopping goods that are of a higher unit value than convenience goods, and are purchased less

frequently after deliberate comparison of alternatives, suggest more personal selling, selective distribution and quality conscious pricing. Speciality goods, because they are 'unique' in some regard so that special effort is required for their acquisition, suggest restricted promotion, exclusive distribution, perhaps to the point of exclusive franchises and conformable pricing.

An alternative product classification scheme was introduced by Aspinwall.[11] He proposed a trichotomy: Pure red goods (roughly parallel to convenience goods), Pure yellow goods (roughly parallel to shopping goods) and Orange goods (lying between the red and yellow goods) based on such characteristics as the Replacement rate, Gross margin, Adjustment (services applied to goods in order to meet the exact needs of the consumer), Time of consumption (durability) and Searching time (time and distance from source of supply).

Aspinwall's scheme is useful for relating products to promotion and distribution strategy. For instance, the Red goods, because of the high replacement rate and low searching time required for their acquisition, suggest an intensive distribution system with long channels and mass advertising to pull products through the extensive channel network. The Yellow goods because of the adjustments required and the low replacement rates suggest more selective outlets. Also because customers desire to search out and compare alternative Yellow goods, personal selling becomes a better communication vehicle for this type of goods.

Aspinwall's work was revised and extended by Miracle, who delineates five product groups instead of three by specifying nine product characteristics instead of five.[12] The nine product partitioning characteristics are:

(a)   Unit value.
(b)   Significance of each individual purchase to the customer.
(c)   Time and effort spent purchasing by customers.
(d)   Rate of technological change including fashion change.
(e)   Technical complexity.
(f)   Customer need for service before, during and after the sale.
(g)   Frequency of purchase.
(h)   Rapidity of consumption.
(i)   Extent of usage or variety of ways in which the product provides utility.

When products are rated from very high to very low for each of these characteristics, certain combinations of rating occur together regularly for specific groups of products. On this basis, Miracle suggests that five product groups can be established. Having established product groups and their characteristics he then proceeds to recommend a marketing strategy for each group including the product variable (Degree of Product Variety) the price variable (Degree of control and variation in price) the distribution variable (Degree of distribution intensiveness) and promotion variable (Degree of emphasis between advertising and personal selling).

For Group I (cigarettes, candy bars, razor blades and soft drinks) little effort on product development, considerable effort on advertising with little or no personal selling, intensive distribution and little effort to control and adjust prices is required. At the other extreme, for Group V, the mix would consist of a custom-designed product sold directly from manufacturer to user, promoted through personal selling and transacted on the basis of an individually negotiated price. This Group includes electronic office equipment, steam turbines and specialised machine tools.

Marketing mix strategies for products in Groups II (groceries and small hardware items), III (radio and television sets) and IV (automobiles, high-quality household furniture) would reflect modifications of the mixes in Groups I and V.

Avlonitis proceeds to review some marginal refinements to Miracle's work, but these add little to the basic approach and can be ignored for our purposes.

While classifying products in this way will provide a useful first cut at selecting a marketing strategy it is clear that other important considerations must also be borne in mind. Foremost among these is the stage of the product life-cycle and much of the remainder of this chapter will be concerned with identifying the influence and effect this will have on product policy and management. However, before turning to this subject it will be helpful to define some of the terms in common currency in the product management literature and then review the broad policy alternatives which are available.

■ Some Definitions of the 'Product'

From the foregoing review of product characteristics it is clear that there can be no simple or single definition of such a complex phenomenon as 'a product'. Indeed a central concern of our discussion to date has been an avoidance of such simple unidimensional definitions on the grounds that by adopting a particular slant we may exclude equally important alternatives. That said, the word 'product' is used quite specifically in a number of contexts in the marketing literature and it will be helpful to summarise and define these according to the common usage of the terms.

- *A Product* is a combination of objective (tangible) and subjective (intangible) properties designed or intended to provide need satisfying experiences to consumers.
- *A Product Line* consists of a group of products with similar physical characteristics and/or similar end-use applications, e.g. lubricating oils, lathes, detergents, cosmetics.
- *The Product Mix* comprises all the product lines of an organisation. With the emergence of the SBU as the basic planning unit, definition of the product mix is usually confined to the SBU. The product mix is usually assessed in terms of three dimensions – width, depth and consistency.
- *Width* is defined in terms of the number of different product lines; *Depth* measures the number of distinct products within a product line; and
- *Consistency* reflects the degree to which the various product lines enjoy similar end-uses and marketing mixes.

For the sake of convenience products may be distinguished as industrial or consumer. Industrial products are usually classified as falling into one of four basic categories:

- *Raw materials*: Those industrial materials which in part or in whole become a portion of the physical product but which have undergone no more processing than is required for convenience, protection, economy in storing, transportation or handling. Threshed grain, natural rubber and crushed ore fall into this category.
- *Equipment*: Those industrial goods which do not become part of the physical product and which are exhausted only after repeated use, such as major installations or installations equipment, and auxiliary accessories or auxiliary equipment. Installations equipment includes such items as boilers, presses, power lathes, bank vaults, etc., while auxiliary equipment includes trucks, office furniture, hand tools and the like.
- *Fabricated materials*: Those industrial goods which become a part of the finished product and which have undergone processing beyond that required for raw materials, but not so much as finished parts. Steel, plastic moulding powders, cement and flour fit this description.
- *Supplies*: Those industrial goods which do not become a part of the physical product or which are continually exhausted in facilitating the operation of an enterprise. Examples of supplies include fuel, stationery and cleaning materials.

Consumer goods, as we saw earlier, may be classified in several ways. The most common distinction is between consumption goods which are consumed at the time or soon after purchase, and durable goods which may be used repeatedly like industrial equipment, e.g. cars, TVs, washing machines.

■ Product Policy

In the preceding sections we have attempted to strike a balance between emphasising the physical characteristics of products and the needs which they satisfy to show that in reality they are two faces of the same coin. It follows that undue emphasis upon one to the neglect of the other may well be counter-productive. However, in seeking to achieve balance, one must be careful that one does not end up 'sitting on the fence' and taking no positive action to shape the direction of the organisation through a clear statement of policy.

In Chapter 3 we adopted the assumption that growth is a prime objective of most companies on the basis that the opposite condition – contraction – is essentially inimical to the most fundamental corporate objective of all – *survival*. (Given the rate of change in the environment stability is considered too risky an objective.) Based upon this assumption we then introduced Igor Ansoff's now famous growth vector matrix which is based upon joint consideration of the implications of change in the product (technology) and/or the market, as perhaps the simplest and most basic statement of the strategic alternatives open to the firm. It will be recalled that the matrix appeared as in Figure 13.2, and that the four basic strategies were defined as:

1 Market Penetration: the company seeks increased sales for its present products in its present markets through more aggressive promotion and distribution.
2 Market Development: the company seeks increased sales by taking its present products into new markets (a market segmentation approach)
3 Product Development: the company seeks increased sales by developing improved products for its present markets (a product differentiation approach)
4 Diversification: the company seeks increased sales by developing new products for new markets (a composite strategy).

The first three of these strategies hold constant one or both of the core strategic variables – product and market – and so sustains the common thread of the business. But, by definition, the fourth alternative of diversification breaks the thread and projects the firm into a totally new situation where it has experience of neither technology nor user needs.

		Product	
		Present	*New*
Mission	*Present*	Market penetration	Product development
	New	Market development	Diversification

Figure 13.2 Ansoff's growth vector matrix

Source: I. Ansoff, *Corporate Strategy* (New York: McGraw-Hill, 1965); 'Strategies for Diversification', *Harvard Business Review* (September–October 1957).

Ansoff's definition of a 'common thread' is based upon three factors:[13]

1 *the product-market scope* which specifies the particular industries to which the company confines its product-market position;
2 the growth vector which indicates the direction in which the company is moving with respect to its current product-market position;

3   *the competitive advantage* which seeks to identify particular properties of
    individual product markets that will give the company a strong competitive
    position.

Once again there is a tendency to project maintenance of a common thread as a
straight 'either/or' proposition when in reality what is needed is a judicious blend
of both. A recurring theme of this book is that the firm must develop a portfolio
of products, that these products should ideally be at different stages of their
individual PLCs to provide a balance between new and declining products with
their varying cash needs and profit potential and that the firm should pursue
distinctly different strategies for new, mature and declining products (what we
term '3-in-1 marketing'). Frequent reference has also been made to the radical
changes which took place in the environment in the 1970s and early 1980s one
consequence of which has been a significant shift in managerial attitudes to
corporate risk. Perhaps the most influential statement concerning this shift in
attitudes is that published by Hayes and Abernathy.[14] The essential thesis of this
article is that, as more and more firms come under the control of professional
managers as opposed to entrepreneurs, there is a marked tendency to avoid
uncertainty by concentrating on short-term projects with low-risk and known
pay-offs. As a consequence less and less effort is devoted to basic and applied
research and more and more is concentrated on the development of existing
products. Much of the latter investment is seen as trivial and gives rise to minor
competitive advantages which are quickly eroded.

Almost simultaneously with Hayes and Abernathy's article Peter Riesz
published a very similar view[15] but was much more specific in his diagnosis of
the causes of these changes, which he attributed to a marketing orientation.
Specifically, Riesz's argument is that by moving from a 'science push' (production
orientation) to a 'market pull' (marketing orientation) American firms have
sacrificed much creativity, technological parity, thoughtful product strategy and
commanding market positions particularly to countries like Japan which have
been stepping up their R & D effort. In support of his argument Riesz states:

> During the past decade, more than half of the 30% of research and development
> budgets previously spent on major innovation has shifted toward more conservative,
> shorter-term, less uncertain projects. Of an estimated $38.2 billion in research and
> development expenditures in 1976, 61% was for development, 27% was for applied
> research, while the remaining 12% was allocated to basic research.
>
> Much of today's research and development is focused on the existing product,
> market, or process base rather than on the development of new ventures or
> technologies. Firms are increasingly reluctant to make new commitments that
> require complex technologies, heavy start-up costs, or previously untried marketing
> concepts. Rather research and development activity seems much more committed to
> building on what is called the 'common thread' of business.

Like Hayes and Abernathy, Reisz attributes much of this trend to the 'MBA
syndrome' which 'is alleged to have produced super cautious managers who are

unwilling to gamble on anything but a sure thing'. Other deterrents to innovation include low incentives to entrepreneurs, consumerism, government interference and regulation and the greater uncertainty which is associated with current environmental turbulence. Even more serious is the widespread tendency to regard R & D expenditure solely as a cost centre with the result that, like investment in advertising where benefits are often long-term, future, stream of earnings, such expenditures are among the first to be cut when short-term profit margins are squeezed.

In our view the indictment of all MBAs and professional managers as a basic cause of this short-sighted approach to business is mistaken. During the 1960s and 1970s there was a marked emphasis upon the finance function and many of the best paid and most attractive appointments were to be found in this area. At the same time many MBAs chose to major in Production, OR, Marketing, etc., but were less influential in determining corporate strategy than those with a short-term profit-maximising objective. There are now clear signs that this trend is being reversed. Many MBAs are now anxious to work in small business and set up on their own account. In addition there is a much clearer appreciation that most accounting conventions are just that and arbitrary as well. Hopefully this realisation will help reverse the decision of the USA Financial Accounting Standards Board which ruled that R & D expenditures could no longer be treated in the balance-sheet but must be accounted for as direct profit or loss items in the year spent.

However the main thrust of Riesz's argument is that whereas a marketing orientation appears to be desirable and logical in that it focuses upon satisfying felt needs, such a 'shift from "science push" to "market pull" can have negative effects both on the firm and on public policy'. According to Riesz the deficiencies in a market-pull orientation arise from at least four sources.

First, there are the well-known weaknesses in research methodology centring on issues such as sampling, survey design and response bias. However, in our view the fact that these weaknesses are known means that they can be anticipated and allowed for.

Second, the average customer is usually unable to articulate significant improvements in ways of satisfying their felt needs and is even less likely to be able to specify vaguely felt latent needs. This is more true of consumers than it is of organisational buyers.

The third weakness in the marketing orientation is the potential risk that failure to undertake basic R & D will result in the firm losing contact with and access to the scientific and technological community. In turn this increases the probability that the firm will be unaware of likely changes in the market due to technological innovation and so be by-passed by innovator firms.

Collectively Riesz believes that these weaknesses will lead to a diminution in marketing's contribution to corporate strategy because: 'Among strategic variables which enable the firm to adjust to an ever-changing external environment, product policy is almost always identified as being crucial to the long-term survival and development of the firm.'[16]

Riesz's views find strong support in the analysis of Bennett and Cooper referred to earlier. In developing their claim that adoption of a marketing orientation has led many firms to neglect product value Bennett and Cooper[17] tend to polarise the issues into an 'either/or' situation. This is particularly the case in their discussion of *market pull* and *technological push* as opposing models of technological innovation ('The market pull model is the antithesis of the technology push approach'). Bennett and Cooper provide an excellent cameo of the market-pull model (reproduced as Table 13.2) which is contrasted with technology push where 'scientific discovery or the availability of new technology leads to the development of a product'. Ideas come from scientists and engineers, not from consumers.

Table 13.2   The market-pull model

The market pull model has been perfected by the packaged goods industry. They search the market for clues and examine people's needs exhaustively. The result is usually a carefully focused product that is moderately successful. As an example, consider the market-pull model for the development of a new breakfast food by a hypothetical company:

Step 1. Do extensive market research to identify an unsatisfied need, segment, or niche in the marketplace. Using sophisticated market research tools if necessary (multidimensional scaling, tradeoff analysis, and so on), determine the ideal product's attributes. Let the market 'design' the product, e.g., a semi-sweet, easily prepared, baked breakfast product, with attributes somewhere between toast and a sweet roll.

Step 2. Ask the R & D group to develop a product that meets these market specifications exactly. No technological breakthroughs or inventions are necessary – just give the market what it says it wants. In our example, the result might be a waffle-like product, frozen, suitable for a toaster, with a sweet filling.

Step 3. Refine the product design (including consumer preference taste tests) and verify the financial attractiveness of the project (test marketing, for example).

Step 4. Launch the product. Position it in people's minds as a great-tasting, 'fun' breakfast food that is easy to prepare (hot from your toaster). Give it a name to reflect its position: 'Pop-Toasties.' Package it attractively and saturation advertise on television.

Source: R.C. Bennett and R.G. Cooper, 'The Misuse of Marketing: an American tragedy', *McKinsey Quarterly* (Autumn 1982) p. 55.

But as we have argued earlier, firms with a portfolio of products at different stages of their life-cycles will require a combination of both market pull to ensure that developing products remain competitive and to rejuvenate mature lines, while more basic research and technology push will be pursued in the hope of achieving a significant breakthrough which will allow the firm to by-pass its rivals. It is also important to recognise that even apparently superficial changes in a product form of the kind implied in Bennett and Cooper's 'market-pull model' depend upon significant advances in food technology, in packaging and in distribution – freeze dried products like coffee may seem little different from instant coffee but the technology is radically different.

Thus while it is quite true to assert that 'A market-oriented R&D strategy necessarily leads to low-risk product modifications, extensions and style changes', it is also true that 'understanding user needs' and the 'customer-active' model of new product developments (NPD) have been conclusively shown to be associated with successful innovation whereas a much higher proportion of technology push products fail. Successful management of a product portfolio demands that we balance the risks and, as the Boston Box clearly shows 'Question marks' and, to a lesser extent, 'Stars' depend on the cash-generating 'Cows' to sustain them. Clearly the longer we can prolong the useful life of the 'cash cows' the greater the opportunity to underwrite more radical R&D.

Thus, the essence of our argument is that market penetration, market development, product development and diversification are not mutually exclusive options from which the firm must select one. Rather they are interdependent and mutually reinforcing alternatives and the management task lies in achieving the optimum balance between them. To this end the approach proposed by Samuel C. Johnson and Conrad Jones probably offers more to the practising manager as it recognises an intermediate state between old and new – namely the 'improved' product and the strengthened' market.[18] Johnson and Jones's model is reproduced as Figure 13.3 and is considered to be self-explanatory. (In passing it is interesting to note that this schemata antedates Ansoff by four months in the same publication.) The model also makes it clear that some form of product development is intrinsic to most positive strategies.

	New market	New use	Market extension	Diversification
	Extended market	Re-merchandise	Improved product	Product line extension
Increase market newness	No change	Present position	Re-formulation	Replacement
		No change	Improved technology	New technology

Increasing technological newness

Figure 13.3   The technology market matrix

Source: Samuel C. Johnson and Conrad Jones, 'How to Organize for New Products', *Harvard Business Review*, (May–Jane 1957).

■ Product Development

While much product development is an on-going process which involves modifications and adjustments to existing products most textbooks concentrate on describing the full cycle of events in bringing a new product to the market-place. Such an approach has much to recommend it, for it establishes both a chronology and a procedure for developing new products from scratch as well as distinguishing discrete stages which may also be involved in product modification and improvement. Accordingly this section will trace the normative theory of new product development or NPD as a statement of how it *should* be done.

If, as we have claimed, product differentiation has become a basic competitive strategy then two direct and immediate consequences become apparent:

1 It increases the relevance and importance of the product development function; and
2 It is likely to lead to more rapid product obsolescence and a shortening of product life-cycles.

In my book *Market Development* I presented a table which illustrates both these consequences and this is reproduced as Table 13.3. Additional evidence is also to be found in the 1981 report from the consulting firm of Booz, Allen & Hamilton, which has long specialised in documenting the contribution of NPD to corporate success.

Based upon 150 in-depth interviews and 700 replies to a mail survey Booz, Allen & Hamilton documented 13,311 items which had been introduced between 1976 and 1981. Of these, 35% were unsuccessful, marginally up on the rate for 1963–8, but the remainder accounted for 28% of sales growth and 22% of profits for the period. Approximately half the 'new' products were either additions to or modifications of existing products and only 10% were 'new to the world'. Significantly, 27% of the most successful products came from the 'new to the world' category. Looking ahead the respondents forecast that new products would play an even more important role over the next five years with 37% of sales growth and 31% of profits expected to come from them.

While data and projections such as these provide impressive evidence of the contribution which NPD makes to the growth and success of firms it is important to bear in mind that the net contribution is much greater for, in the absence of continuous product development, the forces of competition and the inevitability of the PLC would result in a contraction in the firm's market share and a corresponding decline in its profitability. Guiltinan and Paul[19] suggest that, taking into account corporate strategy, portfolio analysis and product life-cycle analysis, managers can have at least five other objectives in addition to market-share growth, namely:

● Market-share maintenance.
● Cash-flow maximisation.

- Sustaining profitability.
- Harvesting.
- Establishing an initial market position.

The suitability and relevance of these objectives will become clear when we review the management of the product over its life-cycle later in the chapter. However, before doing so it will be useful to describe the classic NPD cycle.

Table 13.3   Inter-industry variations in dependence on new products
(Source: M. J. Baker and S. T. Parkinson, 'An Analysis of the Significance of Innovation', appendix to SSRC *Report 1974*.) **Where does the largest proportion of your own sales come from?**

Industry	Products launched within the last five years		Products launched more than five years ago		Totals	
	%	n	%	n	%	n
Building and construction	45	13	55	16	100	29
Chemicals/allied products	29	12	71	30	100	42
Clothing	67	19	33	9	100	28
Electrical machinery	38	13	62	21	100	34
Engineering/general machinery	41	71	59	102	100	173
Fabricated metal	21	8	79	30	100	38
Food, drink, tobacco	11	68	94	9	100	55
Furniture and fixtures	57	8	43	36	100	14
Iron and steel	21	6	79	22	100	28
Leather	54	7	46	6	100	13
Paper	24	5	76	16	100	21
Plastics	50	9	50	9	100	18
Printing and publishing	38	8	62	13	100	21
Textiles	50	33	50	33	100	66
Miscellaneous	64	9	36	5	100	14
Stone, glass, clay	24	5	76	16	100	21
Total	38%	232	62%	383	100%	N = 615

Source: M. J. Baker, *Market Development*, (Harmondsworth: Penguin Books, 1983) p. 14.

■ The New Product Development (NPD) cycle

In my book *Market Development* the NPD cycle is described in the following terms (pp. 20–30):

The development of a new product is seen as a sequential process normally containing six distinct phases. While some models contain additional sub-phases and may employ slightly different terminology, the most widely accepted sequence proposed by Booz, Allen & Hamilton, based on their experience with several hundred companies, is:

Exploration → Screening → Business Analysis →
Development → Testing → Commercialization

Like the PLC concept the NPD model is of greatest value when regarded as a framework or structure to guide one's own approach. Clearly no single, simple process model can allow for all the complications and problems likely to be encountered by the firm which sets out to manage NPD, nor is such a model appropriate to many radical innovations or to situations where technology 'push' is dominant. That said, however, all phases are recommended and are usually found to be present in case histories of NPD. Hence a brief review of each will be helpful.

The exploration phase, sometimes termed 'idea generation', may be structured, unstructured or serendipitous. A structured procedure for new product ideas may rest upon continuous market research into consumer reactions, both to one's own product and to those of one's competitors in order to give early warning of failing interest or dissatisfaction or, more positively, to suggest areas for improvement which will enhance the product's standing with its target audience.

Monitoring competitive activity has assumed increasing importance in recent years with the growing popularity of what is termed 'the strategy of the fast second' whereby firms depend more on their ability to copy or improve upon a new product and cash in on the market as it moves into the growth phase than on being the first to market with a new product. The Japanese are past masters of this strategy, and are imitative innovators of the first order across almost all classes of goods, depending upon an enhanced product, competitive prices and excellent distribution and after-sales service to ensure a dominant position in almost all the world's growth markets. Significantly, the Japanese have been responsible for no major technological innovations themselves.

A specific example of the strategy of the fast second is to be found in the competition between Seagram and Showering in the UK market for sparkling wines. Seagram pursued a classic NPD strategy in that they realised the need to broaden their product line as a means of achieving wider distribution for their range of spirits, and commissioned research to try and find a gap in the market which they might fill. The research suggested that females in the age range 18-25 would appreciate a drink which was less alcoholic than spirits, more glamorous than beer and more exciting than wine. Showering already marketed a product which met this specification – a champagne perry called Babycham – but the research indicated that the target group regarded this as an old-fashioned product more appropriate for their mothers than themselves.

Seagram went through the exploration phase armed with a clear picture of the sort of product characteristics desired by the market segment they wished to reach and, after screening a number of possibilities, settled upon a sparkling white wine. Research had also underlined the importance of packaging and branding to products of this nature to convey the necessary associations of glamour and excitement, and after extensive testing the company settled upon a green, single-portion size bottle with a foil cap and named the product Crocodilo.

Equipped with their new, tested product, Seagram moved into the recommended test market phase in which the product is marketed on a regional basis with the sort of support it would receive if launched nationally. The test market in East Anglia proved very successful and encouraged Seagram to 'go national' in late 1980.

Within two weeks of the announcement, Showering introduced a directly competitive product 'Green Dragon', and put it into widespread distribution through the holding company's (Allied Breweries) tied outlets and elsewhere as Babycham's 'little sister'. Showering's strategy is not hard to appreciate. If they (unilaterally) had launched a new sparkling wine drink, they would only have competed with themselves and could well have cannibalised sales of the existing product. But faced with a competitive threat on a regional basis the obvious thing to do is monitor the success or otherwise of the newcomer and plan accordingly. This Showering did very effectively, for they came up with a sparkling wine that was clearly preferred in blind taste tests, which gave them a better product, in addition to the other advantages they already enjoyed as an established supplier of drinks of this type with effective national distribution. One can only speculate at this time that all Seagram's promotional efforts will serve to build primary demand for a new product on which the 'fast second' will capitalise.

Unstructured idea generation tends to be more typical of firms with a single product or small range of products experiencing a decline in their current profitability – that is, the firm does not have a formal NPD function, but operates on an *ad hoc* basis. Brainstorming is a frequently used technique in these circumstances in which the second phase of screening or sifting the ideas assumes particular importance. An unstructured approach is also often associated with serendipity when an idea for a new product occurs by chance – as a by-product of research into something else, for example, or as the result of an approach by a prospective user asking if you could make something to meet a specific need.

Once the firm has generated a portfolio of ideas for new products it is essential that these be 'screened' to ensure that only the most promising are subjected to thorough analysis, if for no other reason than that the further one proceeds with any given idea the greater the expense involved, as shown in Figure 13.4. Screening is an essentially subjective procedure in which managers use their knowledge and experience to weed out the obvious non-starters. Beyond doubt, managers are most confident when applying their knowledge of internal constraints and will eliminate many ideas as being inconsistent with the firm's product policies and objectives, with the existing skills and resources and so on. In the same way, ideas which are incompatible with the firm's existing markets and its knowledge of its current users and customers are likely to be screened out at this phase as the firm seeks to build upon its existing strengths.

Given a short-list of 'possible' ideas, the next step is to subject these to a more formal analysis – a task which will be greatly improved if an explicit check list is developed, setting out the criteria and their relative importance one to another. In general this evaluation should assess each of the ideas in terms of its technology and its 'fit' with the production system, its marketability and its competitiveness, and finally in terms of the financial implications of proceeding with it further.

Assuming that evaluation indicates that development of the product appears feasible, that forecasted sales and budgeted costs promise a satisfactory return on investment, and that the company is satisfied it can gain access to the target market, then the next phase in the process is technical development. At this juncture the objective is to establish if it is physically possible to produce an object with the desired performance characteristics within the cost constraints indicated by the

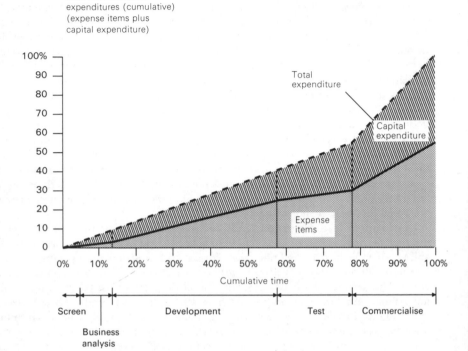

% of total evolution
expenditures (cumulative)
(expense items plus
capital expenditure)

Figure 13.4   New Product Development costs

Source: Management Research Department, Booz, Allen & Hamilton Inc.

forecast demand schedule. Usually this phase is the longest in the whole process, and it is vitally important that, throughout development, the innovator should continue critically to observe events and changes in the proposed target market. In the case of one of the classic new product failures – the Edsel – its downfall arose, not from an incorrect assessment of a market opportunity, but because the market need changed during the course of the development of the car.[20]

In addition to updating the product concept to reflect changes in the market, the development phase should also provide for testing the product under real-world usage conditions to ensure that it will deliver the promised satisfactions. The more complex the product, and the more radical the behavioural change required of the end user, the more important this phase becomes. Indeed, with many capital, material and consumer durable innovations, the development phase frequently continues well into the market launch stage on the grounds that deficiencies and defects in the final product will only become apparent once it is exposed to a broad spectrum of usage situations. For example, in the case of the JCB 110 the relocation of the engine behind the operator resulted in numerous engine failures caused by severe overheating. The cause of this overheating was the fact that, in confined working conditions, many drivers reversed until stopped by piles of spoil excavated from the foundations and so forth, on which the machine was working. By reversing into this spoil the ventilator grilles became blocked, leading to overheating and engine seizure. Once the problem was known, a fairly simple redesign was all that was required to rectify it, but, as is so often the case, extensive usage was necessary to sensitise the makers to the intrinsic design fault.

With complex products, the development phase may well proceed in parallel with physical and market testing, but in other cases, such as that of Crocodilo considered earlier, the test phase may be a discrete activity in its own right. Obviously testing is a risk-reduction strategy as the firm's commitment is limited and a final go/no-go decision can be deferred pending the test results. With a major and complex new product, marketing on a small scale to iron out the bugs has much to commend it, but, with less sophisticated products such as Crocodilo, test marketing can give the game away to one's competitors and allow them to counter your full-scale launch with a strong competitive reaction. Indeed, with many consumer goods test marketing can be a complete waste of effort as competitors create abnormal trading conditions in the test area so that little or no reliance can be placed on the results.

The final phase of the NPD process is commercialisation when the product is launched in the market, thus initiating its life-cycle, and it is this phase which is the main focus of *Market Development*. As can be seen from Figure 13.4 above, commercialisation increases the firm's financial commitment by several orders of magnitude. Capacity must be installed to cater for the anticipated demand; inventory must be built up to ensure that supplies can be made available to the distribution channel; intensive selling-in must take place to ensure widespread availability at the point of sale or to canvass orders from prospective buyers; maintenance and servicing facilities may be necessary and a large promotional investment will be needed to create awareness of the new product's existence. Given the importance of this phase, one might reasonably expect discussions of it to dominate texts dealing with the subject, but it only requires a cursory examination to reveal that this stage rarely receives equal treatment with the preceding phases and attracts comparatively little attention.

The problems involved in introducing new products into the market-place is the theme of *Market Development*, which also seeks to provide empirical support for the composite model of buying behaviour introduced in Chapter 7, and persons interested in these topics are recommended to consult this source.

■ Organisation for New Product Development

If the firm is to practise 3-in-1 marketing then it will require a different organisational style to cope with the three distinct time horizons. Evidence from research by Axel Johne[21] shows that successful firms appear to be able to operate in different modes and that managers can 'change gear' from an organic to a mechanistic style and back again. Other evidence and experience would seem to suggest that such transitions will be facilitated by certain organisational devices and in this section we shall look briefly at four of them:

- New product committees
- Venture teams
- New product departments
- Product managers

A new product committee probably represents the lowest level of recognition that conventional organisational structures of a functional kind are not best suited to the task of NPD. Such committees are usually, but not always, *ad hoc* and are established to evaluate specific product development proposals. Members with relevant expertise will be drawn from the various functional areas and their brief will usually be to reach conclusions on proposed courses of action and then ensure that action is co-ordinated and integrated between the departments involved. Such an arrangement may well be adequate for firms with small product portfolios operating in markets where change is slow and life-cycles are prolonged. Where the rate of change is faster and/or the product line is bigger then such a committee may be established on a standing basis. This arrangement may also suit a multidivisional firm where the top management requires advice on the comparative merits of proposals from divisions operating in radically different markets.

Venture teams are similar to new product committees in the sense that they are usually composed of experts drawn from different areas of the organisation and that they are formed for a specific purpose. However, while the new product committee's role is solely advisory, the new venture team assumes responsibility for the execution of the proposal too. Thus members will have to be seconded from their normal duties for the life of the project and the approach may best be thought of as establishing a new business in its own right.

New product departments are usually found only in large organisations with big product lines subject to frequent change. The advantages of setting up a department with sole responsibilities for developing new products right up to the commercialisation phase when they can be handed over to the operating divisions are obvious. However, the efficiencies which may be expected to accompany task specialisation may well be diluted or completely negated unless communication between the partners is first class. Where it is not, an 'us and them' mentality may well arise and there is considerable evidence to suggest that new products succeed best where they are the responsibility of a single-product champion who will see them through all the way from conceptualisation to commercialisation and beyond.

In recognition of this evidence many multi-product firms have chosen to give full responsibility for the management of discrete products and product lines to a single product or brand manager. Such a manager will be responsible both for introducing new products and for managing them throughout their life-cycle. There is a very large literature which deals with the advantages and disadvantages of the product manager system, particularly as compared with the alternative of organising around markets as the common factor.[22] From this literature it is clear that there are many different kinds of product management and that there is considerable difference of opinion as to the merits and demerits of the system. Many of the problems are a direct consequence of the difficulty in assigning product managers sufficient authority commensurate with their responsibility. A great deal certainly depends upon the calibre of the persons appointed to this position and many firms regard the product manager's job as a proving ground for aspirant general managers, which is hardly surprising given the seven roles which Luck and Ferrell[23] suggest he must play:

1 A *coordinator* of the various functions and department operations, so that they synchronise relative to the particular product(s) and programs.
2 An *entrepreneur* or profit centre within the corporation who develops and is responsible for an area of the business, the assigned product(s).
3 An *expediter* who sees that tasks get done, products are distributed, crises are met, etc., relative to the product(s).
4 An *expert* information center who is most knowledgeable about his or her products and their markets, serving as advisor and source of information about them.
5 A *forecaster* who studies the markets, competition, etc., and projects the likely effects of plans, expenditure, and demand changes on the product(s).
6 An *innovator* who finds or creates new ideas regarding the product(s), their marketing, etc.
7 An *integrator* who brings together the ideas, plans and viewpoints of others into a systematic product plan.

Ultimately the decision as to the most appropriate organisational form must represent a judicious balance between the frequency and importance of NPD, the homogeneity/diversity of the products and markets involved and the personal preferences of those with overall responsibility. In this section we can only indicate the broad alternatives available, and point to sources where more detailed analysis can be found.

■ Managing the Product Life-cycle

Just as it was helpful to consider NPD as a process so it will assist understanding of the most appropriate strategy for product management if we trace the product through its life-cycle. Some reference has already been made to the application of major mix elements as the product moves from introduction through growth and maturity to senility (see pp. 100ff), but in this and succeeding 'mix' chapters we shall analyse the appropriate tactics in rather greater depth. By doing so we run the risk of giving the impression that one can manipulate a particular mix element while holding the others constant which is rarely the case. On the other hand by concentrating upon one element at a time we hope to isolate the major options so that we can then determine how combination with the other elements may affect the relevance in any given set of circumstances.

■ Market Introduction

Over the years a great deal of my own interest and research has been concentrated upon the problems of introducing new products into the marketplace. As we saw in earlier chapters, this interest is founded upon the proposition that product life-cycles represent an underlying process whereby innovations diffuse or spread through a population of adopters, from which it follows that there is a functional relationship between the time to first acceptance and full diffusion. Hence the more quickly one can achieve initial penetration the more rapidly sales will build up, the greater the opportunity to establish a commanding position before imitators can climb on the bandwagon, and the more quickly one can recoup one's initial investment and move into profitability. In order to achieve this more rapid penetration it was argued that one should pay particular attention to the manner in which selective perception might result in a mismatch between the seller's view of the benefits offered by his new product and the prospective purchaser's interpretation of them so that one can concentrate the launch effort on those potential users most likely to see 'eye to eye' with the seller.

An explicit assumption throughout this work is that the marketer has a problem in penetrating the market and it would be as well at this juncture to make it equally plain that this is by no means always the case. As Chester Wasson[24] has shown so clearly, many products proceed almost instantaneously from introduction to rapid growth and so present the seller with quite different problems from those associated with slow penetration. Wasson differentiates between products with a protracted introduction phase and those with almost no introduction phase in terms of the amount of consumer learning which is necessary to comprehend the benefits offered by the new product – high learning and low learning introductions respectively. It follows that the first step in devising a new product launch strategy is to decide whether the product requires high or low learning by the consumer.

In seeking to make such a distinction one has to be careful to avoid circular reasoning, and it is not much help to suggest that something which it is easy to understand will require less learning than something which is hard to understand! Notwithstanding this difficulty one of the most distinguished writers on innovation, Everett Rogers,[25] offers us five product characteristics which have been found to determine whether or not a new product will require much consumer learning:

- Relative advantage
- Compatibility
- Complexity
- Divisibility
- Communicability

With the possible exception of divisibility all of these factors are comparative rather than absolute in value, in that they depend upon the potential user's existing status. From this it can be deduced that the more closely a new product approximates that existing status the less learning will be required and the faster the prospect's reaction to the new product.

Based upon our earlier discussion of the 'just noticeable difference' it should also be apparent that new products which are very similar to old ones may not be seen as different at all and certainly not as sufficiently different to merit the switching costs and possible dissonance which a change of purchasing behaviour may occasion. Slow sales build-up for low learning products obviously has quite different implications than it has for radically new innovations with high learning requirements.

Depending upon one's assessment of the learning requirements for the new product, one can evaluate the relative merits of an undifferentiated, differentiated or concentrated marketing strategy with the logical relationship being that depicted in Figure 13.5.

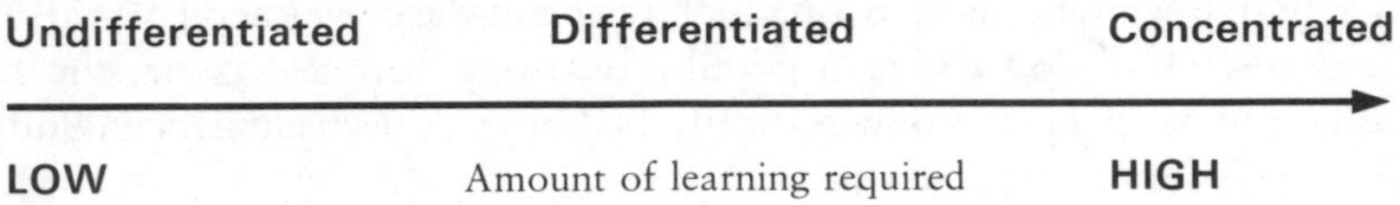

Undifferentiated   **Differentiated**   **Concentrated**

LOW   Amount of learning required   **HIGH**

Figure 13.5 Marketing strategy: relationships

Of course other factors will also have to be taken into account, not least of which is the firm's existing competitive strength for this will strongly influence the investment in launch inventory, the physical distribution that can be achieved and the promotional effort possible. Another consideration is the novelty of the technology, for if this is difficult to replicate and/or enjoys patent protection then the innovator may wish to control the speed of the product launch to optimise his investment and cash flows. (A radically new technology does not necessarily imply that consumers will need a lot of learning to appreciate it – given availability and a low price products such as TVs, VCRs, and pocket calculators could have diffused almost instantaneously!)

To sum up, the greater the product differentiation and the stronger the marketer's proprietorial rights in the differentiating factor the greater the control he can exercise over his introductory marketing strategy. From this observation it follows that only very large and well-established firms can hope to survive on a policy of trivial incremental product innovation by depending upon economies of scale in volume (cost/price), in distribution and in promotion. Conversely, the only hope for the small firm to break such an established market leadership is to 'by-pass' the competition through radical product innovation.

■ Growth

Assuming that a product survives the introductory phase, the PLC concept predicts that it will enter upon a period of accelerating growth which will be signalled by a distinct upward inflexion on the sales curve. In determining when a product has 'taken off' it is important to differentiate between low and high learning products for in the case of the former the introductory phase may be very short or non-existent. For example, in *Market Development* the case histories show that the benefits of needled woven polypropylene, coaxial tomography (the body scanner) and Ambush (an insecticide) were so obvious that almost the only constraint on take-up was physical availability. Conversely, superplastic aluminium, the JCB 110, and vinyl floor products required more learning and sales only built up slowly.

It is also important to consider the replacement rate for, where this is short as in the case of most consumer goods, one is liable to find extensive sampling of new products on a trial basis. (Short replacement cycles are almost always associated with low unit costs and/or a high rating in the consumer's overall scale of preferences.) It follows that it would be premature to assess the sales performance of such new products until the repeat purchasing behaviour of the early buyers becomes apparent.

A third important consideration when determining the appropriate product strategy during the growth phase is to bear in mind that the actual rate of growth is the outcome of both demand and supply factors – of both a contagion and a bandwagon effect. Contagion results from the increased physical visibility of the product in the hands of consumers (the 'new car at the kerbside' effect) and from the word-of-mouth activities of early buyers who seek to reduce possible post-purchase dissonance by telling their contacts of the benefits they are experiencing from ownership of the new thing. Bandwagon effects are the consequence of new suppliers entering the market and increasing the physical availability of the new product for purchase. Often this increased availability is accompanied by price cutting/discounting/sales promotion as the different suppliers seek to build up their individual market shares.

Of course the ability of new suppliers to enter the market will depend very much upon the existence or otherwise of barriers to entry (see pp. 24–6 for a summary of these) and the precise nature of these barriers. As a simple rule-of-thumb ease of entry is inversely related to the degree of product differentiation, from which it follows that the product strategy alternatives are:

1　Differentiate the product and create a monopoly for it, or,
2　Accept that differentiation is difficult and concentrate on manufacturing and distribution efficiencies in order to keep costs down so that one can use price and dealer margins to build up market share and secure the benefits of the scale and experience effects (see p. 118).

Where a firm does have a monopoly of a new product or process it is likely that it will have adopted a concentrated or skimming strategy on introduction and used price to restrict demand and enhance profit margins. To deter competition and/or to avoid investigation by regulatory agencies the firm will not want to be seen to exploit its monopoly for too long by earning excessive profit margins and so will seek to increase total profits by taking a smaller margin on an increased volume – usually by cutting price and 'sliding down the demand curve'. In order to make such price reductions acceptable to the early buyers who paid the full price the seller would be well advised to modify the product and offer an economy model or perhaps introduce a new deluxe model so that the original can be seen as marginally out of date and so deserving of a lower price. Obviously this latter approach has the double advantage that it may encourage the original buyers to trade-up and so maintain their feelings of exclusivity and innovativeness.

Overall, however, the product variable may be expected to be fairly low key during the growth phase as the rapidly expanding demand suggests buyers are seeking to satisfy primary needs. Thus they may well find the claims of competing models on points of detail are more a source of confusion than clarification and emphasise availability, price and promotion rather than minor product features when making a choice.

■ Maturity

Once sales level off and stabilise the product is considered to have reached the mature stage of its life-cycle. However, before coming to this conclusion it is important to determine whether there are any other geographic areas which are as yet unexploited and/or whether there may be alternative uses to which the product may be put. Thus by simply increasing the geographical availability of a product one may stimulate renewed sales growth and defer the onset of maturity. Alternatively, as we saw earlier when discussing the PLC for nylon (p. 107), it may be possible to find complete new uses for a product and so expand the total demand for it.

In most texts extending coverage and/or finding new uses are discussed as strategies for the mature phase of the life-cycle. In our opinion this is wrong for if such possibilities exist they should have been pre-identified and constitute approaches for extending the growth phase. Only when these alternatives have been fully exploited and sales have levelled off should we consider the product to have reached full maturity. Of course, this is a counsel for perfection and in the real world most individuals and organisations appear to expect growth to continue unchecked indefinitely. So, it is only when growth stops that much effort is given to finding out why and what may be done about it. As a result of such inquiry new markets and new uses may be found that result in a renewal of growth but, by definition, they don't require a product change. For example, the frequently quoted case of Johnson's Baby Powder shows how sales were increased substantially by promoting its use to adults, but with no change in the product, its price, distribution or packaging.

Another similar case with an interesting twist is Church & Dwight's Arm & Hammer brand of baking soda which has been on sale in the USA for well over 100 years. The makers knew that baking soda will absorb food odours in refrigerators, but their initial attempts to establish whether there would be interest in this use indicated there was no interest. Essentially the problem was that housewives were asked if they had an odour problem in their refrigerator and, not surprisingly, they said 'No'. Accordingly the use was not promoted until the company decided to ignore the early research and put out an ad suggesting the use. The response was immediate and very large – as an insurance policy or a cure it was a very inexpensive and simple solution.

Once a product has truly reached the mature stage then clearly the prime objectives are to sustain this for as long as possible and to secure as large a share as possible of the available market. Both ends will be served through a policy of continuous product improvement which may involve an actual change in the product itself or in the services associated with its delivery and/or consumption.

Examples of improvements in mature products are not difficult to come by as can be seen by scanning almost any newspaper or magazine. Taking the *South China Morning Post* for 13 October 1984 as a case in point, three advertisements illustrated the point clearly. (The author was in Hong Kong when he wrote this!).

First, there was the Zebra Twinball Pen as an example of a fast-moving convenience good which most people take for granted and consider to be fully developed. Yet the advertisement offered two significant improvements – it is leak-proof and will write upside down. Second, there was a consumer durable, the Braun micron 2000 electric shaver, which offered three new product features – it can be used as a mains shaver or as a rechargeable free from the cord; it automatically adapts to every AC voltage and cycle frequency the world over and it is the first model with 'stainless steel housing and soft knobs for better grip'. Third, there was the Boeing 747 SP, advertised by Pan-Am, which is designed to 'fly quieter, faster, further and higher than any other commercial airplane' and allows Pan-Am to offer the only non-stop service from Hong Kong to San Francisco.

All of these products offer the kind of improvement which is unlikely to result in any marked change in overall demand, but could well secure an increased market share for the innovator and may well prolong the product life-cycle. Improved ballpoints will help resist the inroads of fibre-tip pens; a 'use anywhere' electric razor might persuade the users of razor blades to switch, whereas disposable razors had stimulated a trend in the opposite direction; and a 'stretched' Jumbo will both delay the demand for the SST and pave the way for it.

Similarly, design and style changes may encourage people to replace products more quickly and maintain interest in them while discouraging competitors from seeking to develop radically different means of satisfying the consumer's basic need. However, despite their best efforts to sustain mature products, sooner or later new and improved products will appear, initiating a decline in sales.

■ Decline

Given that most new products are substitutes for existing products – hence the popularity of the 'what business are we in' approach to long-term strategic planning – one should not be surprised if cumulative sales curves are reasonably symmetrical. In other words all the factors which may delay or accelerate a new product's acceptance are just as likely to work for or against it when a substitute for it is subsequently introduced to the market. However, whether or not one anticipates that the decline phase of the life cycle will be gradual or sudden one must have a clear policy for dealing with the ailing product.

Until recently comparatively little interest has been shown in the decline phase and in 1984 there were only about five[26] articles which dealt with the subject in any depth and most of these were rather dated and failed to address adequately the practical problems of implementation. However in the early 1980s my former colleague George Avlonitis published a number of articles on the topic dealing with both the theoretical considerations and the practicalities using extensive research into the UK engineering industry as an empirical foundation and launched a renewed interest in the topic.

While most writers on product elimination see it as a straight choice between phasing it out slowly – variously referred to as milking, harvesting, run-out and product petrification – and immediate withdrawal Avlonitis identifies two further alternatives:

1   Drop from the standard range and reintroduce as a 'special'.
2   Sell out to another manufacturer ('Divert').

Avlonitis believes that the ability to reintroduce a product as a special is probably unique to the industrial market, but otherwise the strategies would seem to be equally appropriate to both consumer and industrial products. That said, such evidence as there is points to a tendency for industrial goods to be phased out gradually while consumer goods are more prone to immediate withdrawal.

Of course much will depend on whether the seller's production equipment is specific or non-specific and the extent to which it has been depreciated. Where the production equipment can be put to other uses or is near the end of its useful life an immediate drop decision is much more likely than a slow phase-out and vice versa. Further, in the case of durable goods the seller will have to give careful attention to service and maintenance obligations and the provision of spare parts and components. For such products Avlonitis provides a very helpful flow diagram of the product-elimination decision and this is reproduced as Figure 13.6.

Once it has been decided to phase a product out then the guiding principle must be to extract the maximum benefit at the minimum cost and Luck provides an excellent set of strategic steps for accomplishing this:

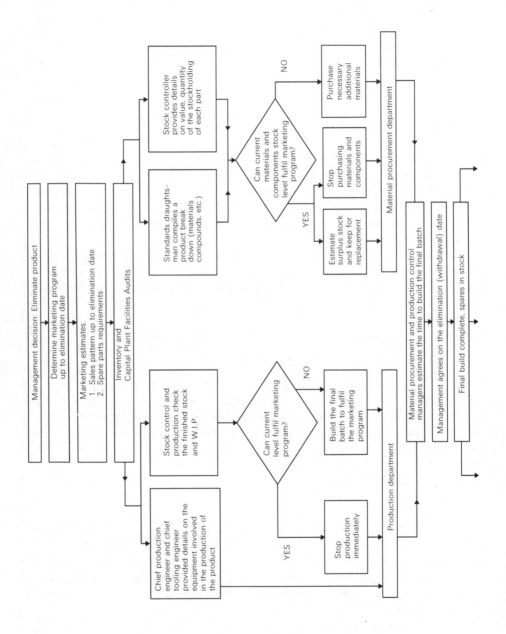

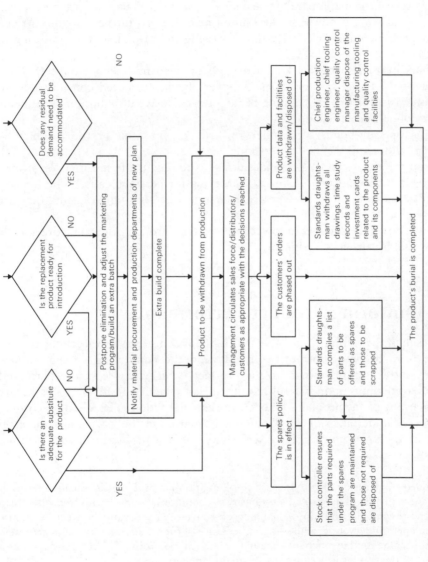

Figure 13.6 A sequential flow diagram for the implementation of the product-elimination decision

Source: George J. Avlonitis, 'The Product-Elimination Decision and Strategies', *Industrial Marketing Management*, 12 (1983) pp. 31–43.

1   Simplify the product line to the best selling items and, if workable, those that yield the higher gross profit margins.
2   Dress up the product with relatively inexpensive styling and feature changes that create a fresh impression.
3   Bring all marketing efforts into a narrower focus by determining which portions of the market are the heavier and more loyal users or are best served by the existing product. Make limited resources go further in concentrated markets, including selectivity in advertising media and sharper tailoring of appeals.
4   Concentrate also on market areas and on distributors that have the best potentials. If the specific types of buyers being promoted consider the old brand as speciality in shopping behaviour, exclusive distribution agreements may obtain dealer support.
5   Offer special bonuses or other rewards for pushing of the product by distributors and their sales personnel.
6   Limit the always costly personal sales calls to only the best outlets or buyers. Substitute more telephone or mail ordering for personal calls.
7   Utilise more economical wholesale channels by shifting to agents that are shared with other products.
8   Trade down the product to lower price buyers through price reductions made possible by austerity actions.[27]

■ Monitoring Product Performance

As a result of the emphasis upon NPD as a major competitive strategy the risks of failure have become substantial. In addition the continuing stream of new offerings poses serious threats to the products which they seek to replace and so puts a premium upon careful monitoring of product performance to secure early warning of any problems and permit remedial action to be taken. According to a survey undertaken by the Conference Board[28] in the USA many managements have shown much greater sensitivity to such problems in recent years. They observe:

> Added emphasis on identifying and resolving product problems is often the result of management's reaction to adverse business conditions, coupled with the widespread trend towards integration of planning objectives and programs between corporate and operating levels. Product-line surveillance of the vitality of each significant item has become routine practice in many firms. Such monitoring is often conducted as a part of the regular procedures for formal planning.

This survey also showed that the concept of portfolio management was gaining support and that it was proving particularly useful in highlighting both potential problem areas and opportunities.

The Conference Board survey found that the wider use for formal planning combined with concepts of product portfolios has focused specific attention on the product on at least four dimensions:[29]

- The progression of time (usually through annual plans, either freestanding year after year, or as a first year instalment rolled over into a longer range plan).
- The product's intrinsic characteristics (e.g. its unique strengths and weaknesses from the standpoint of customer acceptance, distribution, pricing, technology and the like).
- The product's external environment (e.g. market potential, possible threats from competitors, changes in the economy, and so on).
- The compatibility of the strategy for each individual product with the needs, resources, and longer term objectives of the entire operating unit or corporation.

While Hopkins[30] accepts that the product has always occupied a central place in corporate planning, at least in theory, he argues that the survey shows much greater commitment in practice at senior levels than was apparent in earlier years. Similarly, the survey also provides empirical support for the kind of procedures advocated earlier in this book – especially environmental and marketing audits – as the basis for a 'product surveillance' system.

In determining the product's state of health profitability, sales volume and market share are the usual criteria. Of course, profitability may be measured in a number of ways and the survey found considerable variety in practice including the following:

- An operating margin on sales.
- A return on investment (ROI) for each product line.
- A contribution to advertising and promotion above all fixed and variable costs above a minimum level.
- A ratio of direct costs to sales price above a minimum level.
- A return on assets (ROA).

Sales volume provides both an absolute and a relative measure of performance, and most firms would wish to consider both before making specific marketing decisions, e.g. to boost promotion, extend distribution, cut price, etc. Thus one needs to monitor the industry sales/market demand for the product to provide a yardstick with which to measure one's own comparative performance. However, in some product areas with very high fixed investments management may fix a minimum sales volume below which it is unattractive to stay in that market. This does not mean that firms will drop immediately any product which falls below such a minimum sales volume as much will depend upon whether the resources can be transferred to other uses and how quickly. In the short-term even sick products make a contribution to fixed and operating costs and one needs to be certain of an equivalent or larger contribution from other uses of one's resources before making any change.

The importance of market share as an indicator of both performance and profitability has been discussed earlier (Chapter 4, p. 85) and appears to be used by an increasing number of companies for monitoring individual products. While the conventional wisdom is that one should seek to dominate a market so that one can exercise leadership over it, it requires only a moment's reflection to realise that if all firms believed this then all industries would be monopolistic. Of course a great deal depends upon how one defines a market and it is quite clear that small firms may concentrate all their energies upon a small but discrete market segment and dominate it while only achieving a fraction of industry sales for the product as a whole.

In addition to the three usual criteria of profits, volume and share, the Conference Board Survey also identified several other factors which management use in assessing product potential, which may be summarised as:

- Synergy
- Cash-needs
- Technology
- Availability of bought-in supplies
- Legislation/regulation

Obviously the ideal product will be complementary to one's other products and markets, will have low cash needs, be technologically advanced, use freely available materials and components and be unlikely to attract any adverse public or governmental attention.

In our previous discussion of the management of products at different stages in their life-cycle there was an implicit assumption of a smooth progression through the four stages. In reality this is unlikely to occur for individual offerings and the purpose of monitoring is to permit remedial action to be taken at any stage of a product's life. Thus it may be that the competitive reaction to a new product may be so strong that one may decide to opt out of the race while the market is still growing rapidly. Two examples of this in *Market Development* are the vinyl floor products and body scanner cases. In the former, Delaware Floor Products realised that it had not the resources to compete with either of the major linoleum manufacturers once they had decided to enter the market and so sold its interests to one of them. Similarly, EMI neglected further technological development of its invention and was overtaken by other companies who also had a much better understanding of the market for X-Ray equipment. EMI, too, sold out long before the market for body scanners reached maturity. If EMI had been less complacent and monitored product developments better, it may well have retained its leadership – a salutary lesson that monitoring performance is an essential activity to be performed continuously.

■ Summary

In Chapter 13 we have only scratched the surface of the issues involved in formulating and implementing a product policy. Hopefully, however, we have succeeded in communicating the belief that the product is at the very heart of the marketing process and deserves greater attention than it appears to have enjoyed in recent years. That said, we have also tried to demonstrate that the product has to match market needs, that the functions of supply and demand are mutually interdependent and that neither is of much consequence unless it stimulates a reaction from the other. (There are just as many if not more demands which suppliers do not consider it worth their while to satisfy as there are products which consumers are unwilling to buy.)

Because of competitive pressures, and in recognition of our maxim that 'the act of consumption changes the consumer', more and more firms are turning to product differentiation as a means of sustaining or improving their position. This has resulted in growing interest in the process of NPD and the normative approach to this has been described and discussed, as have organisational structures to promote the process.

Following our adoption of the product life-cycle as the basic analytical and planning framework we looked next at the implications of this for the product variable. Our review suggests that product considerations will be important throughout, but are most critical in the introduction and decline phases. Notwithstanding this generalisation we consider it important to monitor the product's performance on a continuous basis and the chapter has concluded with a brief overview of approaches to this.

CHAPTER 14

▌Packaging

┌─ Learning Goals ───────────────────────────────────────┐

The issues to be addressed in Chapter 14 include:

1 The role of packaging as a *strategic element* in the marketing mix.
2 The factors to be considered in *developing* a package.

After reading Chapter 14 you will be able to:

1 Explain the *four roles played by packaging* in marketing.
2 Describe the five criteria to be considered in *developing* a package –
   appearance, protection, function, cost and disposability.
3 Spell out the steps to be followed in *designing a pack* and achieving a
   balance between the five functional criteria.

└──┘

▌Introduction

In Chapter 7, when discussing 'How do buyers choose?', it was argued that both individuals and organisations are often faced with situations in which two or more competing offerings appear equivalent in terms of their performance characteristics and the cost benefits associated with their acquisition and use. Under such circumstances, even relatively small perceived differences may result in the prospective buyer preferring one product to another. One element of the marketing mix which offers considerable scope for creating a 'just discernible difference' or 'determinant factor' is packaging, and in this chapter we shall look first at the functions of packaging, then at the factors involved in developing a pack, and finally at the use of packaging in the marketing mix. Although packaging has an important role to play in the marketing of all types of product, it is clear that its overall influence is greatest in the field of fast-moving consumer goods and such products will tend to dominate the discussion in this chapter. That said, it should not be overlooked that design features which comprise the 'packaging' of many industrial goods, e.g. use of colour on machinery, operator comfort features, etc., play an increasingly important part in many industrial buying decisions.

■ Definitions

While there are many books concerned with technical aspects of packaging, comparatively few of these deal with the managerial aspects of the function which are of prime importance to the marketer. One of the few that does, by J. H. Briston and T. J. Neill,[1] offers three definitions of packaging as follows:

1 'Packaging is the art, science and technology of preparing goods for transport and sale.'
2 'Packaging may be defined as the means of ensuring the safe delivery of a product to the ultimate consumer in sound condition, at the minimum overall cost.'
3 'Packaging must protect what it sells, and sell what it protects.'

In the standard reference work edited by Frey (*Marketing Handbook*)[2] packaging is defined in terms of the role it plays in marketing and divided into four categories as follows:

1 *Primary packaging* is the 'essential container enveloping the product[which] remains with the product from the time of its manufacture or preparation at least through distribution to retailers, and very often continues through the entire life of the product'.
2 *Secondary packaging* refers to the additional containers and wrappings that are added for protective or marketing requirements
3 *Display packaging* is packaging intended for displaying the product at the point of sale.
4 *Shipping packaging* is intended primarily for protecting goods in transit and storage.

All four categories of packaging are of major importance in marketing, bearing in mind that the manufacturer is concerned not only with protecting his goods until they are safely delivered to the final user, but also with his relationships with intermediaries in the channels of distribution. Well-designed packaging performs a number of distinct purposes, each of which will vary in importance for these different persons in the distributive chain from producer to user, and a review of these will indicate a number of ways in which packaging may be used as both a tactical and strategic variable in the marketing mix.

■ Packaging Criteria

Briston and Neill (1972) distinguish five criteria which have to be considered in developing a package:

● Appearance
● Protection
● Function

- Cost
- Disposability

The *appearance* of a product is of vital importance to the vast range of fast-moving consumer goods (f.m.c.g.) which are sold through self-service outlets. Given that most retailers will carry three or four different brands of a given product, the package provides a critical visual cue at the point of sale, acting both as a reminder (most purchases of convenience goods are unplanned in the sense that the shopper does not enter the outlet with a prior intention to buy specific products, but relies on the display to act as a signal or prompt to suggest or recall specific needs) and a distinguishing feature between the product and closely competitive offerings. In addition to providing a distinctive and appealing means of identification, the pack must also provide the user with information concerning its contents. Some of this information may be required by law, while the remainder must communicate not only the identity but also facts concerning method of use, etc.

Protection[3] of the contents is probably the single most important criterion involved in pack design and construction. Damage may arise from physical and/or chemical causes of which the most important are:

- *Chemical*

    (i)   Interaction between the container and its contents;
    (ii) Ingress of vapours or liquids;
    (iii) Ingress of micro-organisms;
    (iv) Loss of liquid or vapour.

- *Physical*

    (i)   Compression/impact/vibration/puncturing;
    (ii) Effect of temperature;
    (iii) Effect of light;
    (iv) Attack by insects/rodents etc.;
    (v)   Pilferage/tampering.

During 1982 the importance of packaging as a means of protecting a product was strongly emphasised when several people died in the USA as a result of illegal tampering with a number of well-known packaged products. In the first instance cases were confined to a brand of painkiller to which a lethal ingredient was added, but the publicity given to the incident sparked off a spate of copy-cat incidents which culminated in the UK with claims that poultry on sale in a number of chain stores had been infected with a poison so that all the merchandise had to be withdrawn and stringently tested. In 1984 Mars was threatened by a group of animal rights activists who stated their intention of poisoning the company's lines of confectionery. Although a hoax, sales plummeted. A similar claim about Lucozade in November 1991 forced the company to withdraw millions of bottles for fear that they had been contaminated.

Cases such as these have led to renewed interest in ensuring that packaging was tamper-resistant and to a reversal of the trend towards simplicity, easy opening and cost/ material reduction. Thus, at the major packaging show – Pack Expo – held in Chicago during October 1982 a special supplementary catalogue was issued listing companies claiming to offer packaging which would provide visible evidence if it had been tampered with. As Allen observed 'Most packaging suppliers were careful to specify that their products achieved tamper-evidence or tamper-resistance, *not* tamper-proofing'. No pack can be tamper-proof, but precautions can be taken with many types of packaging to ensure that it is obvious if an attempt has been made to violate its integrity. These range from heat-seal banding of bottlenecks, through print which is removed from its substrata when the label is pulled off, to a tear-off strip attached to plastic screw caps.

A major area of concern which exemplifies well the dilemma between security of contents and simplicity in use is provided by the packaging of products which may be harmful if used incorrectly, particularly by children. Thus, the British Pharmaceutical Society recommends that all prescription drugs should be sold in child-resistant containers (CRCs) which are difficult for small children to open but are easily opened by adults. Examples of such packs are the 'press-and-turn' closure found on many pill bottles, and lids which can only be opened after lining up matching marks on the lid and body of the container.

According to Briston and Neill,[4] packaging performs two basic *functions*:

(a)   those concerned with its end use, and
(b)   those concerned with its behaviour on the packaging/filling line.

Of the end-use factors, the most important are seen as display, ease of opening, convenience and dispensing. By *display* is meant making the contents visible to the prospective user rather than appearance of the pack itself which has already been touched upon. While it is not always possible to use packaging which displays the contents, e.g. where a light-resistant pack is used to protect the contents, such as unexposed photographic film, from damage, the majority of users like to be able to examine an object prior to purchase. This instinct is firmly grounded in the injunction not to buy 'a pig in a poke' and frequently creates a conflict between the seller, who is anxious to protect his stock from damage, and the buyer, who is loath to buy something which he has been unable to inspect closely, such as books sealed in shrinkwrap. In circumstances such as these it may be necessary to have a display or demonstration model available, with the remainder of the stock being sold in sealed containers.

The question of *ease of opening* has already been reviewed when describing the need to protect products from being tampered with or misused. The problem of ease of opening is a very real one and has become acute in the case of many products which use new packaging materials such as plastic and foil pouches and foil-sealed plastic containers such as those used for yoghurt or portions of butter, jam, etc. Similar problems of opening may be experienced with tear-off sealing strips on liquid containers and can be a source of considerable frustration to users.

Many of these new approaches to packaging have been developed in an attempt to achieve the third function of *convenience*, often to the extent that product and package have become completely integrated, as is clearly the case with packaging in aerosol containers and TV dinners on a foil or plastic tray. Similarly, *dispensing* the product is closely related to ease of opening and convenience and provides numerous opportunities for manufacturers to differentiate their product through close attention to these features.

The second basic group of factors which the manufacturers must take into account when making a decision on packaging is concerned with its behaviour on the packaging or filling line. It follows that the greater the standardisation and the more basic the pack the greater are the production economies open to the producer. Most packaging equipment and machinery is extremely sophisticated and therefore costly. Conversely, such standardisation may be in direct conflict with the desire to cater for user needs and has led to considerable emphasis upon contract packaging.

In *Market Development*[5] I include a case study which describes the launch of the widemouth bottle in the UK. As is so often the case, the innovators concentrated their initial selling-in efforts on the largest potential users of the new pack, and only after a singular lack of success did they turn their attention to the small breweries. The latter were quick to see that the new pack offered them an opportunity to distinguish their product at the point of sale from that of their main competitors, whose products were sold mainly in cans with the balance in conventional bottles, and adopted the innovation enthusiastically. Looking back on this experience, and with the benefit of hindsight, the marketing director explained the initial lack of success to the fact that the big breweries had very large investments in their existing packaging plants and could not afford to make this obsolete prematurely by taking up a new type of pack.

This dilemma faces many manufacturers, especially of fast-moving convenience goods. On the one hand, packaging offers an opportunity to differentiate their product at the point of sale, but, on the other, it can represent a significant on-cost and so encourages the producer to standardise his packaging to achieve the maximum economies of scale. One solution to such an impasse is to subcontract part of one's output to an outside agency.

Writing in *Marketing* in 1982 Richard Lawson[6] estimates that 15–20% of all fast-moving consumer goods are packed by outside contractors, rising to 20–25% for food, 50% for aerosols and 80% for portion packs. Lawson observes:

> The business is likely to continue to grow as manufacturers pay closer attention to segmented markets and as the resulting production runs become shorter. This is because it is uneconomical for manufacturers to put in their own expensive packing machinery if it is not used more or less continuously. For relatively short runs, the

only way they can get the benefits of economies of scale is to go to a specialist packing contractor whose equipment is used to service a number of manufacturers.

Lawson goes on to describe a number of specific situations where using the services of a contract packer may be particularly advantageous. These may be summarised as:

1 *New Product Development* (NPD). As noted earlier, the capital cost of a specialised packing plant can represent a significant element in the total cost of production. By using a contract packer, one can experiment with a variety of sizes and designs before taking a final decision.
2 *Production of sample packs*, e.g. for sales promotion purposes.
3 *Cross-branding promotions*, i.e. where one pack contains a brand from another manufacturer, e.g. a sachet of Bick hamburger relish in a pack of Bird's Eye hamburgers.
4 *Multipackaging*. Where products are offered in non-standard packs for promotional purposes or as 'banded' i.e. joint, offers.
5 *Portion packing*, i.e. miniature containers of jam, butter, etc.
6 *Demand seasonality*. Where demand fluctuates according to the season of the year the manufacturer may install only base-line capacity and contract-out peak demands.
7 *Exporting*. Export packaging is often different from that used in domestic markets. Depending on the scale of foreign sales it may be more economical to subcontract the packaging rather than change one's own facilities. Frequently such packaging may be undertaken in the export country itself.

It seems clear that faced with shorter runs due to increased competition and an accelerated rate of NPD, not to mention the changes in packaging technology and materials, manufacturers will depend increasingly upon packing contractors for some or all of their requirements.

The importance of careful assessment of *cost–benefit* is obviously a major factor underlying all packaging decisions. Briston and Neill[7] identify (p. 20) four areas where packaging is of significant importance to the marketing of the product and packaging costs must be closely controlled:

1 Where the cost of the packaging is high relative to the product costs, e.g. cosmetics, toiletries and specialty goods.
2 Annual expenditure on packaging materials is high: household cleaning products, tobacco and cigarettes, and food products.
3 The unit product cost is high: electrical appliances, watches, specialty chemicals and wines/spirits.
4 A large number of items are handled: automobile spare parts, private label products, etc.

Cost-control procedures for packaging are very similar to those used for the manufacturing process as a whole and demand a fine balance between perceived value added, losses due to inadequate packaging and the actual costs incurred. However, readers wishing to explore this topic further will find full coverage in Chapter 8 of Briston and Neill's text.

The final criterion which it was suggested should be borne in mind when developing packaging was the *disposability* of the pack. This factor has become of particular importance in recent years due to increased public awareness of the need to protect the environment from litter and pollution caused by discarded packaging, accompanied by concern as to the wastage implicit in disposing of much packaging material. While comparatively few consumers would actually reject a product because its packaging was not actually biodegradable or capable of being recycled (but probably still sufficient to warrant serious consideration as a distinct market segment!), the potentially bad effects caused by litter bearing distinctive brand names warrants careful consideration of ways of avoiding such criticism and will accelerate the search for new materials which will reduce or eliminate the problem. Meantime, bottle banks, waste paper collection and incentives to recycle tinplate and aluminium containers provide a partial solution.

Although Frey's discussion of criteria to be taken into account in developing a package differs in detail from those proposed by Briston and Neill, there is a high measure of agreement, as can be seen from Frey's statement of the 'Characteristics of a good package',[8] which should be:

1 Economical
   a. to manufacture (on standard equipment by regular suppliers);
   b. to fill (on standard equipment within the plant);
   c. to move (on conventional carriers at normal cost).
2 Functional
   a. in transit (for protection);
   b. in stores (for merchandising);
   c. at home (for convenience).
3 Communicative
   a. of brand (to distinguish from competitors);
   b. of product (to identify contents);
   c. of usage (to point out special uses).
4 Attractive
   a. in colour (appropriate to nature of product);
   b. in design (readily distinguishable from competitors);
   c. in graphic impact (to gain attention and hold interest).

■ Developing the Pack

Whereas a great deal of packaging development is concerned with modifying, improving and up-dating existing packaging, it will be useful to assume that one is starting from scratch with an entirely new product. By adopting this assumption (as we did when discussing NPD) we will take into account all of the steps and procedures/techniques involved in the complete process and so provide a framework for deciding which parts are relevant when considering whether to modify an existing pack.

In broad terms the sequence to be followed is similar to that for all other problem-solving situations:

1 Problem recognition.
2 Statement of objectives.
3 Collection of relevant information.
4 Assessment of alternatives.
5 Selection of a course of action.
6 Implementation.
7 Evaluation and feedback.

In the case of a completely new product the need to design a pack which will complement the product and enable it to satisfy the five criteria reviewed in the preceding section is clear-cut, and the major problem is deciding on the relative emphasis to give the pack *vis-à-vis* the other mix elements. To a large extent the questions to be considered are the same as those which will be asked in developing the new product itself, i.e. Who will buy the product? When and where will they buy it? How will the product be consumed and what role will the pack play in dispensing, protecting and storing the product in use? What information needs to be conveyed on the pack – by law – for purposes of brand identification, to ensure correct use, etc.? What packaging are competitors using? What needs does the channel of distribution have? Are we going to package ourselves – what constraints does this impose – or do we intend to sub-contract?

With an existing product, determining the cause of lack lustre performance is not always easy, and while giving the packaging a 'face lift' may bolster declining sales, it will be insufficient to make good serious deficiencies in other elements of the marketing mix. In turn, setting objectives will usually require one to specify some order of priority for the five criteria (appearance, protection, function, cost and disposability) – e.g. if economy or cost reduction is the prime objective, then basic packs, as used by Gateway for their own label brands, will be preferred; if protection, then perhaps cost factors will be subordinated, e.g. packing malt whisky bottles in stiff cardboard cylinders.

With regard to collecting relevant information, the *Marketing Handbook* cites nine factors which have to be taken into account, each of which may encompass a number of sub-factors:

1 Size

★ Contents
★ Trade Customs
★ Price
★ Consumer Convenience • portability
                                                                • use
                                                                 • storage

		★ Dealer Convenience
		★ Available Packaging Machinery
2	Shape	★ Tradition
		★ Cost
		★ Space Requirements
		★ Utility
		★ Eye Appeal
3	Material	★ Protective Quality
		★ Cost Factors
		★ Sales Appeal
		★ Tradition and Fads
		★ Impression of Quality
		★ Transparency
4	Construction	★ Costs
		★ Protection of Contents
		★ Utility
		★ Sales Appeal
5	Closure	★ Durability
		★ Ease of Opening
		★ Ease of Closing
		★ Aid to Use of Contents
		★ Attractiveness
		★ Capacity for Carrying Copy
		★ Cost Factors

6 Surface Design

7 Legal Requirements

8 Packing

9 Distribution

Most of these topic headings are self-evident and need little elaboration, but it may be helpful to say a little more about design and the economics of packaging (cost factors) as these dimensions are common to all the others.

Reference has already been made to the fact that often the pack constitutes the just discernible difference which attracts attention at the point of sale and prompts purchase. Bearing in mind that the average supermarket is likely to have more than 20 000 products on display at any one time, it is clear that outstanding design is essential if it is to capture the customer's attention. Two articles in the 5 August 1982 issue of *Marketing* serve to underline this fact and emphasise the amount of detail which is necessary in designing a pack.

Consider, for example, a product as ordinary as the cracker biscuit. As can be seen from Table 14.1, taken from 'Shedding Light on Design' by Richard Head,[9] there are at least 24 brands available and there are at least four different ways in which the product could be displayed at the point of sale. As Head comments:

Table 14.1   Example of facings analysis: cracker market

Brand	Facings				
	Front	Side	End/Top	Back	Total
Ryvita	126	127	121	11	385
Jacob's Cream Crackers	100	84	101	23	308
Ry-King	71	51	63	2	187
Krackawheat	44	72	66	1	183
Cornish Wafers	26	61	73	41	64
Jacob's Water Biscuits	72	14	40	11	27
Energen	30	91	75	1	197
Scanda Crisp	13	16	23	1	53
Vita Wheat	27	31	37	1	96
Carr's Table Water Biscuits	25	20	42	0	87
Crawford's Cream Crackers	28	8	29	3	68
Macvita	13	19	30	0	62
Butter Puffs	6	1	3	0	10
Daily Break	13	7	45	2	67
Rakusen's	34	3	15	3	55
Primula Rye Bread	11	13	16	1	41
Sainsbury's Rye Crispbread	9	16	16	0	41
Burton's Hippodrome C.C.	15	9	13	0	37
Sainsbury's Cream Crackers	18	2	5	0	25
Mac Cream Crackers	12	3	7	0	22
Lyons' Rye Crackers	4	2	6	0	12
International C.C.	4	2	0	0	6
Tesco Cream Crackers	3	0	2	1	6
Tesco Snack Crackers	1	0	0	0	1
Total	705	652	828	552	2,240

Source: R. Head, 'Shedding Light on Design', Marketing, (5 August 1982) p. 31.

[The table] shows that the next thing to be determined is which faces of the pack are actually being seen by the shopper. It is absolutely futile to choose as the major face of the package design the one that is the largest, if it is not going to be seen by the customer. The research must establish the number of faces (front, sides, ends and back) on view, so that it is possible to predict which faces the retailer is going to choose to display to the customer.

These faces should be counted whether or not they contain branding, because they are still branding opportunities. And if they are not being used, then they should be used. The analysis of facings in the cracker market shown . . . indicates that there is really very little to choose between the different faces. Ends and tops are seen more than any other facing, but they are closely followed by fronts, which in film are closely followed by sides. What this makes clear is that wherever the design is placed an adequate job must be done on ends and sides as well as front panels.

This point is even more important in the cake market, where the main panels are hardly seen at all, leaving the branding job almost entirely to the sides and end panels. In this case Mr Kipling has excelled himself.

In the second article, by Colin Wiltshire,[10] the illustration makes the central point: 'Here is a clear idea very simply expressed – it attracts the shopper's attention and stands out in a competitive situation' far better than any amount of copy (see Figure 14.1 for an example).

Figure 14.1   Packaging that stands out from the competition: simple designs and vivid colours attract the shopper's attention

The influence which packaging has upon consumer perceptions of the product itself was highlighted in the leader in the 17 February 1982 issue of *Marketing*[11] which quoted a recent A.C. Nielsen survey in the US in which 46% of a representative sample of consumers said they had discarded or returned a product because of defective packaging in the previous twelve months. Of these dissatisfied consumers, 19% said they would never buy the same brand again, and 24% said they would 'shop more cautiously' or 'buy a different type of package'.

In another American survey, consumers were asked to list the package characteristics of most importance to them. The answers were: storage life of the unused portion; ability to recognise the contents by looking at the package graphics; resealability and ease of storage.

An article by Sara Macdougall in the same issue of *Marketing*[12] reported the results of a UK consumer attitudes survey commissioned by INCPEN (the Industry Committee on Packaging and the Environment). The research carried out by Market Behaviour showed that consumers found bulky packs irritating, especially when rigid cartons were found to be only three-quarters full, as were cereal and soap boxes. Again it was believed that superfluous packaging ... cost unnecessary money. Examples given included tubes in boxes, board sleeves on beer cans and margarine tubs, and triple layers of packaging for multipack Kitkats.

While [the consumers'] concerns were found to be primarily functional, the economic and aesthetic aspects of packaging were also important. These criteria were often found to conflict with each other. Consumers' awareness of the benefits of packaging did not prevent a significant number of them from expressing dissatisfaction with some aspects.

■ Summary

In Chapter 14 we have been concerned with two broad issues:

1   The role of packaging as a *strategic element* in the marketing mix
2   The factors to be considered in *developing* a package.

With respect to the first issue we considered first the basic roles played by packaging – *primary, secondary, display* and *shipping* – and their importance in protecting the product in distribution and use as well as acting as a source of information and brand identification for prospective buyers.

Next we reviewed the five criteria to be considered in developing a package – *appearance, protection, function, cost* and *disposability*. It was noted that current concerns with environmentalism have focused increased attention on packaging and especially the disposability and protection criteria.

Finally, we returned to the role played by packaging as a strategic element in the marketing mix where it may become the 'just noticeable difference' or JND factor which enables intending consumers to differentiate between products or services with very similar performance characteristics (cf Chapter 7, Buyer Behaviour and Chapter 9, Positioning).

Pricing Policy and Management

— Learning Goals —

The issues to be discussed in Chapter 15 include:

1 The *theoretical foundations* of pricing behaviour and their contribution and limitations in practice.
2 The nature of *pricing objectives* and their relationship to profit and sales (market share) objectives.
3 Major pricing objectives *in practice*.
4 Approaches to *price determination* – cost-plus, flexible mark-up and marginal-cost.
5 The role of pricing in the *marketing mix*.
6 Alternative *pricing strategies*.

After reading Chapter 15 you will be able to:

1 Explain the *economic theory of price* and its role in achieving a balance between supply and demand.
2 Describe the concept of *elasticity*.
3 Suggest the limitations of price theory as an explanation of real world behaviour, but its contribution to understanding *policy* and *procedure*.
4 Spell out the *objectives of price-policy* and distinguish particularly between profit and sales oriented objectives.
5 Define and describe *three basic approaches* to pricing – cost-plus, flexible mark-up and marginal-cost pricing.
6 Discuss the role of price as an *element in the marketing mix*.
7 Review the *pricing strategies* available to the firm.

■ Introduction

In economic theory the concept of price is of central importance as the mechanism through which supply and demand are adjusted in order to ensure that resources are allocated to those uses which will maximise overall satisfaction. Prices and price policy are also of major importance to the business man for, as Kuhlmeijer[1] has pointed out, price is the only marketing strategy variable that generates income. All the other variables in the mix – advertising, product development, sales promotion, distribution and packaging – generate costs. Hopefully these activities will generate or sustain demand, but price, while also affecting demand, is a direct determinant of the pool of revenue out of which marketing and other costs will have to be recovered. But, while price is a very flexible marketing tool, it is also very visible to both customers and competitors alike to the extent that the distinguished economist Fellner has described it as 'the blunt instrument of competition'.[2]

Under conditions of perfect competition the seller cannot be a price-maker, but is a price-taker. At any price above that prevailing in the market-place he will sell none of his output, while to sell below the going market price would be irrational, as it would result in a lesser level of profit than that obtainable by accepting the market price. However, as we have seen in earlier chapters, few if any markets correspond precisely to those in which competition is deemed to be perfect by the theoretical economist. Instead, we are more likely to find a state of oligopoly or competition between the few with a very large proportion of total output being accounted for by a relatively small number of firms, with the balance of supply being accounted for by a large number of small firms. Under these conditions price competition is usually unattractive and has led to the anonymous observation that price competition is like cutting your competitor's throat and bleeding to death yourself. Indeed, it is often claimed that the unpopularity of price competition led to the emergence of non-price factors as a basis for competition and it was this which led to an emphasis upon a marketing orientation.

In Chapter 15 we shall examine some of the theoretical foundations to the theory of pricing as a basis for examining broad pricing objectives open to the firm. Next we shall examine the way in which prices are determined and discuss the three broad brush approaches which have been observed in practice – marginalism, cost-based approaches and trial and error. Finally, we shall turn to an assessment of the role of price in the marketing mix.

■ Theoretical Foundations

One of the earlier and still popular definitions of marketing is 'identifying needs of consumers and satisfying them at a profit'. If this is so, and many practitioners have argued strongly in favour of such a basic definition in preference to the more diffuse and broadly based ones which emphasise mutually satisfying exchange relationships, then clearly the nature of demand is the primary concern of the marketer. In theory, demand concerns the relation between quantity and price and considers the demand for a product as a function of its price, the prices of substitutes and complements, consumers' tastes and incomes. Assuming that these latter determinants of demand (income, consumer tastes and the price of substitutes) are held constant then the law of demand indicates an inverse relationship between price and quantity with the result that demand curves have a negative slope, implying that the higher the price the smaller will be the quantity demanded.

In developing their theory of demand economists have evolved a number of very useful concepts which help the practitioner understand better how demand and therefore price may influence his freedom for action. A basic and very important distinction made by economists is that between short-run and long-run demand. Short-run demand refers to existing demand, with its immediate reaction to price changes, income fluctuations, etc., whereas long-run demand is that which will ultimately exist as a result of changes in pricing, promotion or product improvement, after enough time is allowed to let the market adjust itself to the new situation. The importance of this distinction is that it proscribes the competitive options available. In the short run the basic question is whether competitors will react to the fall in demand by changing their prices in an attempt to maintain their market share, with the almost inevitable result that everybody else will follow suit and so maintain their market share, but at a lower margin of profit. In the long run, of course, structural change becomes possible and companies may either enter or leave the market depending upon whether demand is expanding or contracting, while both consumers and suppliers may explore the possibility of substitute products as an alternative to the product for which demand has changed. Joel Dean[3] proposes two groups of factors which may give rise to the distinction between long- and short-run changes in demand: (i) Cultural lags in information and experience. A price change today starts a chain of adjustment in customers' attitudes and competitors' prices that may not be completed for years, even if nothing further occurs. This is partly a matter of market information. There may be delay in learning about changes in relative prices among substitutes, but there is also delay in acting on these new prices because use patterns are sticky; (ii) Capital investment required of buyers to shift consumption patterns. For example, the mass consumption of frozen food required an investment by producers and consumers in new refrigerators designed with double- or triple-sized freezer compartments. Products that require a large initial investment in consumption equipment quite commonly meet sticky and price-intensive buying habits in established markets. In such cases, industry's promotional effort in expanding sales may aim at selling the equipment rather than the product.

A second and very important distinction in demand theory is that between industry and company demand. By definition an industry demand schedule reflects the relationship of price to the quantity that will be bought from all firms. Of course, the usefulness of the industry demand schedule as a bench-mark for evaluating the demand available to any individual seller depends very much upon the degree to which prospective buyers perceive the output of the different firms as close substitutes for each other. To the extent that suppliers can differentiate their product in the minds of potential users, they can create a demand schedule which is particular to themselves. As we saw earlier in Chapter 2 when discussing competition, a major difficulty associated with product portfolio planning and market-share analysis is determining which firms and products are in direct competition with one another. Similarly, one of the main reasons underlying the emphasis upon non-price competition and particularly the practice of product differentiation, is that the supplier is attempting to create a unique position for himself in the minds of potential buyers and thereby establish a monopoly over their demand.

Another concept from the economic theory of demand which is of particular usefulness to practitioners is the concept of elasticity. As originally conceived the concept of elasticity refers only to price/sales ratios (price elasticity of demand), but it has now become generalised to apply to each demand determinant such as consumer income, advertising expenditures, etc. Thus, in the abstract, elasticity is the ratio of the relative change in the dependent variable (demand) to the relative change in an independent variable (price, consumer income). Thus, demand is said to be elastic when the relative change in the independent factor is greater than the relative change in the quantity demanded, and inelastic when it is less than the relative change in the quantity demanded. Graphically these differences are reflected in the slope of the demand curve, with totally inelastic demand being represented by a vertical line and infinitely elastic demand by a horizontal line. These differences are indicated in Figures 15.1 and 15.2 respectively, while 15.3 represents the type of demand curve typically found in which elasticity will vary according to price. As can be seen from Figure 15.3 a minority of users have a very strong demand for the product and therefore price is inelastic for them. However, as price falls more and more users will become willing to buy units of the product and demand becomes very elastic relative to price. This tendency continues until the market approaches saturation, at which point even drastic reductions in price are unlikely to result in very much more demand so that the price elasticity once again is inelastic.

Another very important dimension of demand is known as 'cross-elasticity'. Cross-elasticity of demand measures one of the most important demand relationships – namely the closeness of substitutes or the degree of complementarity of demand. A high cross-elasticity means that the commodities are close substitutes for each other (Ford and Toyota), while a zero cross-elasticity means that they are independent of each other in the market (TVs and washing machines). Finally, a negative cross-elasticity means that the goods are complementary in the market in that one stimulates the sales of the other (cars and petrol).

A final demand theory concept of great usefulness to the practitioner is the distinction between direct and derived demand. By derived demand is meant that the demand for one product is the result of the more fundamental or direct demand for another product. Thus, the demand for all manufacturing equipment is ultimately determined by the demand for the products which that equipment is designed to produce. Similarly, the utilisation of such manufacturing equipment in turn determines the level of demand for basic raw materials such as steel.

The second major area of economic theory related to demand, from which practitioners can derive some useful concepts, is that related to cost. As with

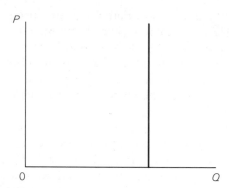

Figure 15.1   Perfect inelasticity (elasticity = zero)

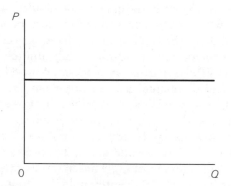

Figure 15.2   Perfect elasticity (elasticity = infinity

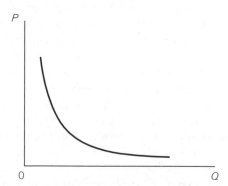

Figure 15.3   Unit elasticity

demand, the first and perhaps most important distinction is that drawn between the short-run and long-run costs. In the short run some of the variables in a problem may change, but not all of them. But, in the long run virtually all the economic variables in the problem may change with the exception of those which are related to the overall growth of an industry or group of industries. Thus, short-run costs are those associated with changes in the utilisation of fixed plant or other facilities whereas long-run cost behaviour encompasses changes in the size and kind of plant. The distinction between the short and long run leads naturally to the distinction between variable and fixed costs. Thus, variable costs are all those which do vary as output varies, whereas fixed costs are usually defined as all those costs which do not vary with output.

From these definitions it follows that the total cost of any given output in the short run is equivalent to the sum of all the fixed and variable costs of the firm, from which it follows that the average cost is the total cost divided by the output. A third type of cost of particular importance to marketers is the marginal cost, which measures the exact rate of change of total cost as output changes. Finally, there is the opportunity cost, by which is understood the sacrifice of alternatives as the result of making any given decision. Thus, in money terms it takes the profits from alternative ventures which are forgone by using resources in a particular way. (For a fuller discussion of these costs and their use in budgeting the reader should refer to Chapter 21.)

Two additional concepts which are central to economic price theory and of importance to marketers are those concerned with profit maximisation and market structures. We have already reviewed in some detail theories of competition and market structure in Chapter 2 and so will not review concepts of perfect and imperfect competition in this chapter. However, these ideas are absolutely fundamental to an understanding of the pricing alternatives open to the marketers, and the reader should review Chapter 2 in conjunction with the present chapter.

The assumption of profit maximisation is an essential axiom on which the economist's theory of price rests. Basically this assumption states that entrepreneurs strive always to earn larger profits and are therefore motivated by the desire to maximise profit. To do so the entrepreneur will behave as a marginalist and seek to achieve that price–output combination at which marginal cost equals marginal revenue. This assumption of profit maximisation has been subject to much criticism, as it presumes an ability to forecast accurately both demand and cost in a manner which is usually extremely difficult, if not impossible, in the real world. Further, as we shall see when discussing pricing objectives, it is clear that many entrepreneurs are motivated by other goals related to sales, security, etc.

■ Limitations and Contributions of Price Theory

As an explanation of pricing in the real world, price theory suffers from a number of limitations which may be summarised as follows:

1   The theory usually rests on the assumptions of profit maximisation which, as Stephen Enke[4] has pointed out, does not provide the entrepreneur with a single and unequivocal criterion for selecting one policy from another in the face of future uncertainty. Similarly, as Kotler has pointed out, the problem of pricing over the product life-cycle requires a more sophisticated model than one which has only a single criterion.

2   The theory does not distinguish clearly between long and short-run effects of price changes. Haynes[5] states that traditional theory does not deal adequately with the dynamics of pricing: the theory has little to say about the effect of today's prices on future profits and the usual graphs for short-run pricing show today's demand and cost curves and suggest that managers price to equate marginal cost and marginal revenue. However, when an entrepreneur is seeking to penetrate a market and build up an image of low price, he may well prefer to sacrifice current profit for future profit and the theory does not deal with this problem.

3   The theory does not face the problem of uncertainty and assumes that entrepreneurs know their demand and cost functions. There are grave statistical problems which handicap the determination of actual demand and cost functions for new and established products.

4   The theory fails to view the firm as an organisation in which pricing decisions are influenced by a variety of persons with varied objectives and motives.

5   The theory assumes that the only significant group to consider in the pricing of a product is the firm's customers. But, in reality, several parties have to be considered simultaneously, including rivals, suppliers, distributors, government and other business executives.

6   The theory assumes that price is the businessman's chief policy instrument, even when it is admitted that he may sometimes have others to rely upon such as product quality, sales promotion and distribution activities.

7   The theory regards price solely as a device for obtaining financial objectives, as viewed by economists, namely pricing decisions should reflect cost and demand functions and balance them to the firm's greatest advantage. What is overlooked by price theory is that price can be used as a communication device to communicate facts to the market participants about the firm, its products and its capabilities in the manner that might increase sales, raise prices or reduce costs. These communication benefits achievable by price are often central to the profitability of business.

Despite all these criticisms, and the perceived limitations which they place upon the use of price theory, it still would seem that the theory has some contribution to make to price-setters and is basic to an understanding of price policy and procedures.

In the analysis of how an individual firm sets its prices, price theory is helpful to the extent that it sets forth the general forces which affect pricing. In addition, it assumes the isolation of separate influences on prices where there are many influences operating simultaneously, and it brings to light a number of questions that the price-maker should take into account.

Price theory provides a useful standardised terminology for the discussion of cost and demand concepts. Oxenfeldt[6] states that the theory has produced a highly penetrating and useful analysis of the manner in which costs are affected by the volume of output, and developing the cost concept and the manner of each kind of cost are of great value to pricing executives in enabling them to set prices at the right level. Joel Dean[7] asserts that the main contribution to practical pricing of theoretical analysis is the kind of demand and cost relations and showing how these functional relations should be used to indicate the most profitable price.

In addition, the discussion of market structures provides useful guidelines for the pricing executive. In the first place it should focus his attention upon the importance in any price decision of the similarity of products offered by his rivals and of the number of sellers offering similar products. Second, it places a heavy emphasis on the selection of pricing strategies and on the recognition that most of the time he is matching wits with others who are intent on outsmarting him: that is, his competitors presumably are operating on the basis of carefully considered strategies designed, at least in part, to eliminate him as a competitor.

■ Pricing Objectives

A recurring theme of this book is the need for the firm to articulate clearly what its precise objectives are. In that pricing is but a means to the overall aim of an organisation, it is clear that pricing objectives are but a means to an end and therefore should be consistent with the overall objectives of the firm.

Like all other elements of the marketing mix, price should serve and help attain the firm's objectives. In the short run price has a direct and immediate influence on the firm's short-run profitability through its effect on sales volume, which in turn affects sales revenue and possibly unit cost of production and marketing as well. Further, in the medium to long run there is an indirect connection between prices and the firm's profit objectives as prices affect the firm's cash flow, its inventories, its customers' inventories, its brand image, its quality image, the competitiveness of its markets, the likelihood of government regulation and customer awareness of, and concern with, price.

In discussing the multiple implications which price has for a firm's goal achievement, Alfred Oxenfeldt[8] sets out a number of hierarchies which should help executives construct a list of goals that their firms can pursue through the intelligent use of price.

The first hierarchy which is reproduced as Figure 15.4 indicates the ultimate objectives of most firms which he defines as 'value judgements on the part of a firm's top management and large owners. They are the outcomes that those persons want "simply because they want them". That is, they are not desired because they lead to some other results. They are ends in themselves'.

Figure 15.4   Hierarchy of business objectives

Source: A. Oxenfeldt, *Pricing Strategies* (New York: AMACOM, 1975) p. 43.

Oxenfeldt then proceeds to develop each of the four generalised ultimate business objectives showing how pricing strategy impinges upon them. However, before looking at pricing strategies ourselves it would be helpful first if we were to examine the general objectives themselves in somewhat greater detail.

Again, it is important to distinguish between the short and long run, particularly as we have already argued that short-run objectives may sometimes contradict long-run objectives. For example, maximising long-run profits may be achieved by restraining profits in the short run with a lower price, a higher product quality, or a more extensive promotional campaign than the one that would maximise short-run profits. Because of the inevitable uncertainty which surrounds the future there is a tendency for most pricing methods to concentrate on the short rather than the long run. Thus, Lawrence Fisher[9] offers the following list of short-run pricing objectives:

1   To penetrate and preempt the market for a product by charging a low price.
2   To cream the market and obtain early profits and liquidity by charging a high price.
3   To assist in phasing out an obsolescent product by making it unattractively expensive.
4   To discourage competition from entering the market.
5   To avoid customer and political criticism.
6   To support a company image.
7   To encourage market expansion by a low price/high volume policy.
8   To avoid unduly provocative action which could lead to prices falling to a level inconsistent with long-term profitability.

Clearly, while these are proposed as short-run objectives, only one of them, 3, is intrinsically incompatible with a long-run pricing objective, and even this may be seen as such in an indirect way in that disposing of an obsolescent product enables one to divert resources to new and potentially more profitable ends.

Irrespective of the time perspective, however, it is generally agreed that a business firm is an organisation designed to make profits and profits are the primary measure of its success. As Joel Dean points out, social criteria of business performance usually relate to the quality of products, rate of progress and behaviour of prices. But these are tests of the desirability of the whole profit system within which profits are the acid test of the individual firm's performance. This being so, it will be helpful now to examine in more detail some profit objectives.

■ Profit Objectives

The whole of the early theory of the firm, and even the bulk of the modern development of it, identifies the profit motive as aiming for the maximum attainable amount over any given time period. The principal of total profit maximisation demands that price should be set at the level at which a small change in total cost would just equal the change in total revenue. As Kotler[10] has pointed out, advocates of the thesis that firms always seek to maximise their profits above any other goal depend on one or more of three arguments:

1 Profit maximisation is the formal purpose for which companies are established.
2 The competitive pursuit of maximum profits creates the greatest economic welfare.
3 Profit maximisation provides management with a relatively unambiguous criterion for business decision making.

Kotler then cites Henry Ford II,[11] who expresses succinctly what has now become known as the Friedmanite economic doctrine. 'There is no such thing as planning for a minimal return less than the best you can imagine, not if you want to survive in a competitive market. It is like asking a professional football team to win by only one point, a sure formula for losing. There is only one way to compete successfully all out. If believing this makes you a greedy capitalist lusting after bloated profits, then I plead guilty. The worst sin I can commit as a business man is to fail to seek maximum long-term profitability by all decent and lawful means. To do so is to subvert economic reason.'

However, as Gabor and others[12] have argued, there are at least four ways of interpreting what is meant by maximising profits. First, there is the absolute interpretation which means that capital would be poured into a firm until the increase in total profit due to the last increment was equal to the interest charge on that capital, irrespective of any other more favourable investment opportunity. The second interpretation is that one maximises the mark-up rate; the third that one maximises the rate of return on that part of capital only which belongs to the owners of the firm; and, fourth, that one maximises the rate of return on the total assets of the firm irrespective of the origin of the funds. Gabor concludes that this latter is the most appropriate objective and also makes a telling point when he observes that maximising profits has usually been interpreted by business men as the desire to achieve larger profits. Thus he observes 'a larger profit will always be preferable to a smaller one'. This is what we meant by profit maximisation. It follows that it is not the same thing as striving for excessive profits at the expense of all other considerations.

There is a large amount of empirical evidence to support Gabor's contention and this has led to the emergence of an alternative thesis of profit-seeking behaviour which has been termed 'satisficing' as opposed to 'maximising'. The view that entrepreneurs seek to make satisfactory profits rather than pursue a goal of profit maximisation owes much to the seminal work of Simon.[13] In one of his earlier contributions Simon[14] observes that the notion of satiation plays no role in classical economic theory, while it enters rather prominently in the treatment of motivation in psychology. In most psychological theories the motive to act stems from drive, and action terminates when the drive is satisfied. Moreover, the conditions for satisfying the drive are not necessarily fixed, but may be specified by an aspiration level that self-adjusts upward or downward on the basis of experience. Simon[15] argues that to explain business behaviour in terms of this theory we must expect the firm's goals to be not maximising profit, but attaining a certain level or rate of profit, holding a certain share of the market or a certain level of sales. Firms do try to satisfice rather than to maximise.

Baumol[16] argues that the business man, knowing his own limitations and the limited accuracy of the data and calculation procedures available to him, adopts a more modest goal. He wishes to obtain conditions that are thoroughly viable, but which offer no assurance of producing for him the best of all possible worlds. Thus, the failure to scan all of the relevant possibilities before reaching a decision, far from constituting an imperfection in the business man's procedures, is a logical consequence of the nature of his aspirations.

Cyert and March[17] state that when firms satisfice they do not try to find that course of action which brings them as close as possible to a particular objective. Instead they set a minimum level of performance in each of a number of different fields say, a return of 10% on capital employed, a market share of 25% and a production running at 90% of existing capacity. These minimum levels of performance are often described as 'aspiration levels'.

Two things usually seem to happen. First, the firm takes no non-routine decisions at all as long as the aspiration levels set for a product, department or, indeed, for the whole firm are being achieved. (Management by exception.) Only if the firm fails to earn the required rate of return on capital employed, or to reach the required market share, will special action be taken. So long as all aspiration levels are being met it will seem unnecessary. The firm may or may not be exceeding the minimum level of achievement which it has set for itself, but, so long as it is not achieving less, managers will be content to leave things as they are. Second, if any aspiration level does cease to be met, the firm will then take some remedial action. In taking this action it will not seek to optimise anything: it will make no attempt to find the best solution.

From the foregoing discussion it is clear that many, if not all, firms will pursue a policy at variance with that predicated by classical economic theory. This is not to say that firms do not set themselves profit objectives, nor that they do not strive to increase the overall level of profit earned. Rather, it is to argue that they are likely to state their overall objective in more general terms. Frequently these terms or objectives are related to sales goals, and it is these which we shall now review.

■ Sales-Oriented Objectives

W. J. Baumol[18] is generally recognised as having first suggested that firms often seek to maximise the money value of their sales, i.e. their sales revenue subject to a constraint that their profits do not fall short of some minimum level which is just on the border-line of acceptability. In other words, so long as profits are at a satisfactory level management will devote the bulk of its energy and efforts to the expansion of sales. Such a goal may be explained perhaps by the business man's desire to maintain his competitive position which is partly dependent on the sheer size of his enterprise, or it may be a matter of the interested management, since management's salaries may be related more closely to the size of the firm's operations than to its profits, or it may simply be a matter of prestige. It is also Baumol's view that short-run revenue maximisation may be consistent with long-run profit maximisation, and revenue maximisation can be regarded as a long-run goal in many oligopolistic firms. Baumol also reasons that high sales attract customers to the popular product, cause banks to be receptive to the firm's financial needs, encourage distributors and make it easier to retain and attract good employees.

However, the sales revenue maximisation theory has been criticised by Ragoff and Lynn,[19] who state that it is probably inefficient and leads to fat in operations. When sales are growing there is less motivation for cost control and there might be a tendency to let things slide, to approve questionable expenditure, to postpone decisions to terminate unproductive personnel, etc. However, in an earlier paper Lynn[20] had suggested that unit volume is an especially important pricing goal where profit requirements are not high and where cost and demand combine to permit relatively ample gross margins. The attainment of high unit volume appeals to firms in a number of different situations:

1 The product has a high level of visibility to consumers.
2 A threshold of sales is needed to make a firm a significant element in an industry.
3 High unit sales may facilitate the recruiting and the retention of desirable dealers.
4 Records of unit sales volume are publicised so management cannot afford to ignore unit volume.
5 Brand loyalty or store loyalty once obtained is strong.

6   Repeat sales are important.
7   Organisational growth is sought.

Either sales revenue or unit volume is usually the criterion used for making comparative assessments between one firm and another competing in the same industry in the form of a statement concerning their respective market shares. As we have seen earlier, when discussing portfolio planning models, the assessment of market share is difficult. None the less, as Oxenfeldt[21] claims, market share is a convenient goal because it differentiates the changes in sales due to a firm's action from those due to external forces. Further, it is a fair and reasonable measure, as it is related to total industry sales and not to the performance of the best competitors only, and is more relevant as an index for measuring market effectiveness, because it eliminates most of the influence of forces on which marketing people have little or no control compared to both sales and profit measures.

Although market-share goals now enjoy considerably popularity with top management, they possess a number of disadvantages, as Chevalier and Carty[22] have pointed out:

1   Market share used as a performance index does not itself reveal the cost at which it has been gained, 'buying market share' through huge discounts and promotion, or the profit at which it has been lost.
2   Market share disregards potential knowledge about companies' idiosyncrasies, because it assumes that they are comparable in many qualitative characteristics such as management ability, cash flow availability or advertising effectiveness. It assumes too that outside forces affect them in the same way, whereas it is well known that the impact of a recession or a regulation on company's share is not uniform, and depends on their previous marketing actions which more or less prepared them to face the new constraints.
3   Market share figures may be biased performance indices if the market or company sales definition do not correspond to the responsibility of the manager.
4   Market share is not a universal way to state objectives in the sense that its feasibility is linked to the stage of the life cycle of the product. Market share may not be used for a new brand in a new market; in this case, the innovator company is the only seller and primary and secondary demand are equal. Sales, profits, or even distribution objectives may seem more appropriate under such conditions. Despite this, market share is often used for a new brand in an existing market in order to stress the need to capture business from competitors and reach a minimum sales level to break even or to take advantage of possible economies of scale.

As we have seen in Chapter 2, it is the pursuit of the economies of scale and the so-called 'experience effect' which prompt many firms to set market-share objectives. The pursuit of such a strategy requires one to be prepared to accept negative results in the short run in the expectation of long-run profit maximisation.

In addition to the foregoing major goals which are most often found as the basis for a firm's pricing strategy, one may also discern a small number of other objectives. For example, some firms may pursue an image goal in the belief that high prices will be associated with high quality or prestige and thereby ensure acceptance in a market. In other industries where demand can fluctuate frequently and sometimes violently a price leader may emerge which perceives its role as one of keeping prices stable. In such industries price stability may be seen as a corollary for earning a target return on investment. Third, in small firms it is often found that mark-up is a major goal as it provides a convenient guide for decision-making and can be justified by reference to other objectives such as profits or ethics. It is also prevalent among wholesalers and retailers who have difficulty in making an accurate allocation of many operating expenses to specific products. These problems combine to encourage the use of workable rules-of-thumb, and attainment of conventional mark-up is one of these rules. Finally, some pricing decisions are affected by ethical considerations in which the business man's personal views mediate decisions based on commercial expediency.

■ Pricing Objectives in Practice

Despite the enormous literature on price theory, comparatively little of this is based upon empirical research and even less upon the implications of pricing in a marketing context. Thus, Laric[23] comments: 'There is a relative dearth of articles dealing with strategic pricing aspects and with demand aspects.' It is hardly surprising therefore that older references such as Joel Dean's article[24] on new product pricing policies and the Brookings study of pricing objectives are still standard citations in any work on pricing. Although the study of pricing objectives by the Brookings Institution[25] was first reported in 1958, it still remains the most important study of pricing objectives. The study indicates that in almost no instance did a firm state that its goal was to maximise profits by charging all the traffic would bear over the long run. In the twenty large companies which comprised the sample for the study many firms were found to have both principal and collateral goals, among which the major pricing objectives identified were:

1 Pricing to achieve a target return on investment
2 Stabilisation of price and margin
3 Pricing to realise a target market share
4 Pricing to meet or prevent competition

that is, the same as Oxenfeldt's 'ultimate objectives', cited earlier.

   Pricing to achieve a target rate of return was the most common pricing goal, with two conditions generally being present when this goal was selected. First, these firms were leaders in their respective industries and, second, this objective was typical in companies with new products and low unit price, standardised and high volume items. Among the reasons offered by executives in the respondent companies selecting this goal were the following:

1   That it is a fair or reasonable objective, both in the public eye and because the firm's pricing structure is of great interest to the Justice Department.
2   Industry tradition.
3   It was representative of what the company thought it could get in the long run.

Another principal pricing goal often mentioned by firms was that of keeping or improving their share of the market. This objective is preferred in some companies because it relates the company's operation to the size of the market. That is, the firm may have a healthy return on investment or sales, while it is suffering from a continual shrinking of its market share. Some companies, however, may choose to limit their market share in order to avoid any confrontation with the government and the anti-trust authorities.

Stabilising prices as a goal was generally chosen by those firms that prefer to avoid price wars, even during the period of decline in demand. Furthermore, those industries characterised by having a 'price leader' generally selected this pricing objective.

Meeting or preventing competition is selected by a large number of companies as a pricing system. It can be said that these firms have no pricing objective *per se*, because they cannot control the goal and the tools used to achieve it.

These findings are largely supported by subsequent research undertaken by Pass, Hague, Haynes, Barback, and Hall and Hitch,[26] and leads to the almost universal conclusion that firms do not maximise their profit by charging what the market will bear, but pursue several objectives simultaneously related to objectives of profitability, sales and stability.

■ Price Determination

Given that business men pursue other objectives than profit maximisation, it is clear that they do not follow the rule of marginalism as propounded by economists when deciding their price and output decisions. Accordingly, we shall not examine the economists' approach to marginal pricing any further, although a variant of it will be reviewed when discussing the cost approach to price determination which appears to be the method pursued by the great majority of business organisations. Basically three different approaches may be distinguished: cost-plus pricing, flexible mark-up pricing and marginal-cost pricing. We shall deal with each of these in turn. (Note that an extended discussion of costs, break-even and contribution analysis is contained in Chapter 21 on Control.)

■ Cost-plus Pricing

Cost-plus pricing embraces all methods of setting prices with exclusive reference to cost and is the practice of adding to an estimated product cost an amount of money to arrive at a selling price.

As we have seen earlier when discussing the nature of costs, considerable judgement is frequently exercised in their determination and assignment. As a consequence, at least two variants of cost-plus pricing may be distinguished and it is important that one determines which approach is being followed in any given situation. These two approaches are (a) absorption-cost pricing and (b) rate-of-return pricing.

With absorption costing all the costs associated with the business are related to the output of manufacture and are said to be absorbed at the time the product is manufactured or sold, and the unit cost is normally arrived at by dividing the total of the production, administrative and selling expenses by the estimated volume of output. Once such a unit cost has been determined then a percentage is added to provide the business with a profit. By contrast, when using a rate-of-return approach one first seeks to estimate the total cost of a year's normal production allowing for ups and downs of the business cycle. This sum is called 'capital turnover' and by multiplying it by the goal rate of return one arrives at the mark-up percentage to be added to standard cost. This mark-up is an average, both among products and through time.

Cost-plus pricing has been criticised extensively on the following grounds:

1   It ignores demand.
2   It fails to reflect competition adequately.
3   It overplays the precision of allocated costs.
4   It is based upon a concept of cost that is frequently not relevant for the pricing decision.
5   The concept of profit as an addition to unit costs is a false one.
6   It assumes that all products should absorb the fixed expenses of the business at the same rate.
7   Instead of pricing being fixed in relation to the competitive requirements of the particular market, and the overhead structure of the business being attuned to those requirements, the reverse procedure is adopted, prices are adjusted to the existing overhead structure by including in each unit cost a share of fixed expenses.
8   It is inappropriate during a period of cost inflation.
9   The system often becomes too mechanical and decisions are made at too low a management level and often lead to friction between sales and manufacturing division.
10 The method takes no account of the capital backing the different lines.

To overcome some of these deficiencies many sellers have developed a system of flexible mark-up pricing by which they arrive at their price by adding one of several margins to their base cost. The margin added depends upon the seller's view of demand conditions with the result that sellers add larger margins when business conditions are buoyant and lower margins during periods of recession and depression. Thus, flexible mark-ups can reflect demand, profit and competition in an indirect manner. Clearly, if one is to pursue an effective flexible mark-up pricing strategy it must be based upon extensive research of demand, competition and market activity, and a realistic appraisal of one's own strength and weaknesses *vis-à-vis* these forces. Pursuit of a flexible mark-up pricing strategy is usually referred to as 'charging what the market will bear'.

■ The Contribution Approach

Although the economist's approach to marginal costing has been largely discounted as a basis for business pricing decisions, management accountants have developed a very useful variant of it. While this is often referred to as 'marginal cost pricing', it is more correct to refer to it as the 'contribution approach'. As Bates and Parkinson[27] have pointed out, the philosophy underlying this approach to costing is that fixed costs are unavoidable and that what matters is to cover variable cost and make some contribution to fixed costs. Whether or not to accept an order depends on what contribution will be made to fixed costs after variable costs are covered. Thus, the approach is an attempt to take account of the fact that it is difficult to allocate fixed overhead costs to production on a basis varying with the level of output and the recognition that the resources available for meeting the fixed expenses of a business depend directly on the contribution, which is the difference between sales revenue and variable costs. It follows that the firm should seek to fix its prices so as to maximise its total contribution.

A useful product of the marginal-cost approach to pricing is break-even analysis. A business may be said to break even when its total revenue equals its total cost and this point can be calculated via marginal-cost analysis through calculations of the contribution per unit of sales made to fixed costs and thereby determining how many units of output are necessary for a firm to cover its fixed costs and hence break even.

Readers requiring a fuller treatment of marginal-cost pricing should refer to the articles by Sizer[28] and Johnston[29] given in the recommendations for additional reading at the end of the chapter. Between them these authors offer the following reasons for claiming that marginal-cost pricing is superior to full-cost pricing:

1 Marginal-cost pricing is more effective in the short run than full costing due to the multi-product, multi-process and multi-market characteristics of most business firms and the rapid rate of change in the environment which makes long run situations highly unpredictable.
2 It lends a marketing rather than a costing orientation to pricing policy.

3   Marginal cost is more relevant to pricing decisions than absorption cost because it reflects future as distinct from present cost levels and cost relationships. When making a pricing decision one is interested in the changes in costs which will result from that decision and marginal cost represents these changes.
4   Marginal cost pricing permits a manufacturer to develop a policy to make prices more differentiated and more flexible through time, which leads to higher sales and possibly reduced marginal costs through increased marginal physical productivity and lower input factor prices.
5   It is a practical prelude to price determination or modification and provides the courage to refuse business, to 'back-off', to withdraw from territories, and to drop products.

The two major criticisms of marginal pricing are that it may encourage price instability and that the practice is prevented by the lack of accurate demand information. Sizer[30] discounts the argument about price instability on the grounds that there are other more powerful forces which prevent firms from making frequent and minor changes in prices.

With regard to the second criticism, whilst one accepts the difficulty of forecasting demand, one should perhaps take the view that if the contribution approach offers the benefits claimed for it then this is an even stronger argument for attempting an accurate demand forecast.

It now remains to consider the relative role of pricing as a component of the marketing mix, together with a brief description of the pricing strategies which appear to be open to the company.

■ The Role of Pricing in the Marketing Mix

As we have seen at a number of points in this chapter, the majority of studies concerned with the relative importance of price as a competitive weapon are at variance with the doctrine of economic theory in which price is the sole competitive weapon. Thus price is only one element of the marketing mix and, as numerous studies in the past thirty years have shown, its importance is likely to vary considerably according to a wide range of situational and environmental factors.

In Udell's (1964)[31] study to explore the relative importance of the different elements of the marketing mix considered by American business men as most important to their success, pricing was only ranked sixth in order of importance. This finding was confirmed in the UK by Pass's[32] study which was reported in 1970, but was contradicted by the findings of a further study undertaken by Robicheaux[33] in 1975. More recently (1981) Dr Hanaa Said[34] undertook a large-scale investigation of pricing policies and practices in UK industry and came up with findings very similar to those of Robicheaux. This can be seen from Table 15.1 in which the findings of the four studies are reproduced together.

Table 15.1   A comparison of the Said, Robicheaux, Pass and Udell studies

	Said study 1981	Robicheaux study 1975	Pass study 1970	Udell study 1964
Pricing	1	1	6	6
Customer services	2	2	4	5
Product research and development	3	4	1	1
Product services	4	–	3	–
Sales management	5	3	7	3
Physical distribution	6	6	8	11
Advertising and sales promotion	7	9	5	4
Marketing research	8	7	2	2
Marketing cost, budgeting and control	9	5	11	9
Distribution channels control	10	10	9	8
Extending customer credit	11	11	12	10
Public relations	12	12	13	12
Organisational structure	–	8	10	7

Source: Hanaa Said, 'The Relevance of Price Theory to Pricing Practice: an investigation of pricing policies and practices in UK industry', Ph.D. dissertation, University of Strathclyde (1981).

While many factors account for the differences in these findings, it seems reasonable to assume that the inflationary and recessionary trends which became so marked in the middle 1970s would have had a significant effect upon the perceived importance of pricing in the marketing mix.

In a major literary review of articles published in the years 1964 to 1980 dealing with pricing, Michael Laric[35] summarised the situation by suggesting that prices will tend to increase in importance when:

1   The item is offered for the first time (a new task buying situation).
2   The company needs to raise prices (a return to modified re-buy situation).
3   Competition reduces prices and makes direct offers to one's buyers.
4   The products involved are directly input into the end product of the buyer and their cost is therefore fixed per end product.
5   The buyer sells to a government agency which is primarily concerned with price.

Conversely, price will tend to be less important when:

1   The item is bought on a regular basis (routinised re-buy pricing).
2   The seller has a high/unique reputation and the product's failure to perform may cause severe handicaps to the buyer.
3   The purchase represents an overhead on direct cost to the buyer.
4   The cost of the item can be easily concealed in an overall budget, as in the case of a small machine within a large budget.
5   In government markets when the budget was not yet appropriated.

An important dimension of many of these generalisations is that they reflect the perception of the prospective purchaser, i.e. the price elasticity of demand, and thus reinforce the desirability of undertaking research to determine how buyers perceive price, rather than by attempting to set prices through the addition of predetermined mark-ups to one's own costs.

Recent evidence on the use of pricing in the marketing mix is contained in an article by Barbara J. Coe entitled 'Strategy in Retreat: Pricing Drops Out'.[36] In this article the author reports the findings of an eight-year study into six SIC industries covering Accessory Equipment (3573), Installations (3721), Fabricating Materials and Parts (2819), Corrugated and Solid Fibre Boxes (2653), Paints (2851) and Ready Mix Concrete (3273) in which the issues addressed included:

1   What is the strategic role of pricing in the marketing mix of industrial firms, and has it changed in the 1980–8 period?
2   What are the general and specific pricing objectives, and have these changed in the 1980–8 period?
3   What pricing approaches are used, and have these changed in the 1980–8 period?
4   How do external and internal factors impact the pricing decision within the industrial firm, and has the importance of each changed during the 1980–8 period?
5   What other marketing strategies play an important role in the marketing mix of industrial firms, and have these strategies changed in the 1980–8 period?

Professor Coe's findings make dismal reading and are a confirmation of Hayes and Abernathy's[37] indictment of American management 'managing its way to economic decline'. According to Coe, having retreated from aggressive product development strategies to hold and build market share in the face of foreign competition, American business resorted to aggressive pricing strategies. But her research reveals these too have been dropped in exchange for 'a self-defeating focus on internal demands for short-term profits. Driven by a quick-fix mentality, fuelled, in part, by internal politics, many in American management have ignored competitive realities in the marketplace and heeded only demands for quick profits. Management appears to be in a three-dimensional "Catch-22" situation. First, they perceive that venture capitalists and short-term traders, both important in today's financial markets, demand quick, short-term profits. In addition, management's own compensation schemes are based on their ability to generate quick, short-term profits. Finally, management's fears concerning potential takeovers also spur demand for quick, short-term profits. Yet the sacrifice of short-term profits is seen as necessary to build a long-term strategy for survival and profitability.' As a result, pricing has ceased to be a strategy in the marketing mix of many firms.

Professor Coe's findings are summarised in Figure 15.5, from which it can be seen that in 1982 57 of the 60 respondent firms regarded pricing as a core or major support strategy (5%). By 1988, 78% of the respondents did not regard pricing as

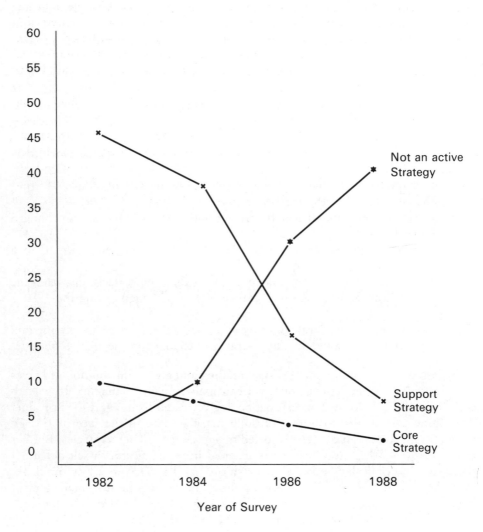

Figure 15.5   Role of pricing in marketing mix – 1980–8

Source: Barbara J. Coe, 'Strategy in Retreat: Pricing Drops Out', *The Journal of Business and International Marketing*, vol. 5, no. 1, (Winter–Spring, 1990).

an active element in their marketing mix strategy. Over the same period profit displaced competition and market share as the primary objective and the preferred pricing approach shifted from a preference for market penetration and competitive pricing (56%) to a strong preference for cost-based pricing. Concurrent with this shift was a change in emphasis from external (competitive) considerations to a preoccupation with internal factors mainly associated with short-term profitability.

Comparing these findings with those summarised in Table 15.1 it is clear that the relative importance of the mix elements varies markedly over time. That said, we should recall the point made in Chapter 7 when discussing 'Buyer Behaviour' and Chapter 9, 'Positioning', that consumers' self-interest will always predispose them to look for the 'mostest for the leastest'. As such, price is an important criterion in shaping the prospective buyer's perception of *value*. It follows that successful firms must have an active and flexible approach to the role of price in the marketing mix if they are to maintain their competitive edge.

In his influential analysis *Price Management* (1989)[38] Henry Simon cites six important reasons why price is of major importance to marketers:

1   For a large number of products empirical research shows that price elasticity is about twenty time greater than advertising elasticity (Lambin, 1976).[39] That is, a 1% price change has a sales effect twenty time as big as a 1% change in the advertising budget.

2   The sales effect of a price change shows up relatively quickly (Ehrenberg and England, 1987),[40] while variations of other variables may take longer to affect sales, e.g. there are significant time lags of advertising effects, while this is rarely the case for price.

3   In contrast to almost all other marketing measures, pricing actions can be taken without much preparatory work. A price change can be implemented immediately. Changes in product and advertising strategy take much more time. This time aspect applies also to competitive price reactions.

4   Empirical reaction elasticities of competitors are almost twice as high for a price change as for an advertising change (Lambin *et al.*, 1975; Lambin, 1976).[41] This result is consistent with points 2 and 3 above. At the same time, it allows for the reverse conclusion that competitors expect especially strong effects from a price change.

5   Price is the only marketing instrument whose use does not require an initially negative cash flow. An optimal value can usually be realised even in a tight financial situation (e.g. start-up companies, new products). Often this is not possible in the case of advertising or sales-force activities, which initially incur only expenses.

6   Price is the only marketing device – besides the product program – that plays a major role in strategic planning concepts, especially in connection with the experience curve (Abell and Hammond, 1979;[42] Henderson, 1974, 1979[43]).

Simon also lists a number of factors which reinforce the importance of price as an element in the marketing mix, including:

- Recession and inflation
- Increased competition
- Market saturation and over capacity
- New competitors
- Consumerism
- Elimination of resale price maintenance

Taken together, these factors reinforce the view that price is a critical element in the marketing mix. However, they also suggest why firms should seek to avoid the rigours of price competition and so have tended to emphasise non-price factors in developing marketing strategies.

■ Pricing strategies

Andre Gabor[44] defined a pricing strategy as 'the application of a pricing principal to a particular situation over a certain time period'. Until recently only two broad strategic approaches to prices have been recognised, namely skimming and penetration. As the names suggest, skimming recognises that in almost all markets there is a 'hard core' of demand for whom the product in question has a particular importance. Because of the strength of their perceived need such users tend to be relatively insensitive to price and this insensitivity can be exploited through a policy of setting a very high price and thus skimming the cream off the market. By contrast, a penetration strategy is based on the assumption that if you can produce a similar product to your competitor and under-price him, then you will take away some or all of his market share. As a result of economies of scale and the experience effect the strategist, using a penetration policy, hopes to reduce his initial cost structure to a point at which he can support the penetration price profitably.

The skimming policy may be appropriate in a number of situations and Philip Kotler[45] identifies the following:

1 There are enough buyers whose demand is relatively inelastic.
2 The unit production and distribution costs of producing a smaller volume are not so high that they cancel out the advantage of charging what some of the traffic will bear.
3 There is little danger that high price will stimulate the emergence of rival firms.
4 High price creates an impression of a superior product.

With regard to a penetration strategy, Joel Dean[46] sees the following three conditions as being necessary.

1 The market appears to be highly price-sensitive and therefore a low price will stimulate more rapid market growth.

2 The unit costs of production and distribution fall with accumulated production experience.
3 A low price will discourage actual and potential competition.

More recently, a number of authors have begun to suggest an alternative value-based strategy. As we have noted elsewhere, value is both a subjective and relative concept and in the case of pricing, implies that the appropriate concept is the perceived value held by the customer. This approach to value pricing was promoted by Shapiro and Jackson[47] in an article in which they wrote: 'the marketer must determine the highest price that the customer would be willing to pay for the product'. One could view that as

Benefits – Cost other than price = Highest price the customer will pay

To determine that price the marketer needs to understand the customer's perception of benefits as well as his or her perception of the costs other than price.

The marketer also needs to remember that his or her cost is unimportant in determining the customer's perceptions. The customer cares about the marketer's price not cost. In fact, to make the statement even more accurate, the customer cares about his or her own costs much more than about the marketer's price.

More recently Forbis and Mehta[48] have extended this proposal and defined economic value to the customer as 'The relative value a given product offers to a specific customer in a particular application, that is, the maximum amount a customer should be willing to pay, assuming that he is fully informed about the product and the offerings of competitors'. In the view of these authors significant differences in EVC (economic value to customer) arise from the ways in which customers use and derive value from their respective reference products and may be used as a basis for segmenting a market and developing a unique advantage over their competitors. 3M and Hewlett Packard are cited as examples of companies which have established a dominant position through the use of a value-based strategy.

Such an approach would seem to have much in common with charging 'what the market will bear', which Said[49] found to be the most widely used pricing strategy in her survey of pricing practices in UK manufacturing industry.

■ Summary

In Chapter 15 we have looked at pricing in both theory and practice. Pricing plays a central role in economic theory and a number of concepts developed by economists have proved to be valuable in analysing and explaining real-world behaviour. For example, the distinction between the long and short term and the effect this has on the competitive options available to the firm in manipulating its marketing mix is very valuable, as is the concept of elasticity of demand.

However, the theory possesses some severe limitations with its assumption of profit maximisation, its failure to deal with the problem of uncertainty, its assumption that price is the businessman's chief policy instrument, and so on.

Having established some of the limitations and contributions of price theory we looked next at the objectives of pricing strategy. According to classical economic theory profit maximisation is the primary objective of business, so firms should price to realise this goal. In reality, they do not, for a variety of reasons which we reviewed briefly before suggesting that firms often seek to maximise the money value of their sales through the pursuit of market share. While empirical research into pricing practice is limited such as is available supports the findings of the study by the Brookings Institution in 1958[50] which identified four major pricing objectives:

1 Pricing to achieve a target return on investment.
2 Stabilisation of price and margin.
3 Pricing to realise a target market share.
4 Pricing to meet or prevent competition.

Empirical research also suggests that firms pursue several objectives simultaneously. In doing so, they use three main approaches to price determination – cost-plus, flexible mark-up and marginal-cost. Each of these was reviewed in some detail before examining the recent evidence on how price is used in the marketing mix.

Finally, we looked briefly at the alternative pricing strategies of skimming and penetration before concluding that ultimately price is determined by the buyer's perception of value.

■ Recommendations for Additional Reading

André Gabor, *Pricing, Concepts and Methods for Effective Marketing* (Aldershot: Gower, 1988).

Gordon Johnston, 'The Pricing of Consumer Goods', in B. Taylor and G. Wills, *Pricing Strategies*, (London: Staples Press, 1969).

H. Simon, *Price Management* (Amsterdam: Elsevier Science Publishers B.V., 1989).

J. Sizer, 'The Accountant's Contribution to Pricing Decisions', in B. Taylor and G. Wills, *Pricing Strategies* (London: Staples Press, 1969).

Distribution and Sales Policy

Learning Goals

The issues to be addressed in Chapter 16 include:

1 The *nature* of marketing channels and the *functions* they perform.
2 Factors which influence *channel structure*.
3 The *selection* of distribution channels.
4 The formulation of *distribution policy*.
5 The role of *personal selling*.
6 Distribution strategy and the *PLC*.

After reading Chapter 16 you will be able to:

1 Explain why distribution channels *develop* and the *role* they play in linking producers and consumers.
2 Describe the *functions* performed by the distribution channel.
3 Review the forces which *influence channel structure*.
4 Relate *distribution strategy options* to the basic marketing strategies – undifferentiated, differentiated and concentrated.
5 Explain the *trade-off between cost and control* in channel selection.
6 Distinguish between *'push' and 'pull' as distribution alternatives*.
7 Account for the *decline of the role of personal selling* as a marketing function.
8 Suggest how distribution policy may vary in accordance with the *stages of the PLC*.

■ Introduction

In an article[1] published some years ago I suggested that an important marketing maxim is that 'Consumption is a function of availability' and went so far as to suggest that brand shares are a self-fulfilling prophecy. This latter suggestion was based on the following anecdotal analysis.

The basic assumption is that with 20,000 or more items to stock in a supermarket the store manager allocates the display space available in accordance with the expected yield (profit) of each product category such that the marginal return on each will be the same. Having assigned space to the product category the store manager will then divide this up between the brands he has decided to stock. Basically the brandstocking decision will be arrived at by taking into account the national brand share, any known local or regional variations and the retailer's policy on own or generic brands. Such an analysis could result in the following much simplified scenario for baked beans.

Baked beans are to receive ten facings with the following shares:

- Brand A   5 facings
- Brand B   3 facings
- Own Brand   2 facings

The first two customers for baked beans prefer the own brand and select it, leaving only Brands A and B available. Customers 3,4,5 would also prefer the own brand but, as it is not available, little Johnny wants his tea and there isn't much difference between them, they select their second choice, Brand B. Customers 6-10 inclusive would all prefer the own brand, failing which they would choose Brand B. However as neither is available they take the acceptable substitute, Brand A. At the end of the day the store manager notes with satisfaction that he has sold ten cans of beans in the proportions 5:3:2 and restocks accordingly.

Clearly this interpretation maligns both the sophistication of store management and the discriminatory powers of consumers, but hopefully it makes the point that for products which are near substitutes for one another availability will determine consumption patterns and decision-makers are quite likely to extrapolate these when making future decisions.

However, while availability is a necessary condition for consumption, it is by no means a sufficient one and we are not seeking to reestablish the now largely discredited Say's Law, which holds that supply creates demand. Indeed, we would go so far as to claim that the current practice of marketing resulted directly from the realisation that the creation of a supply did not guarantee consumption and acceptance of the fact that suppliers have to compete for the customer's patronage.

But, despite its obvious importance, distribution remains a largely neglected topic in marketing. In a famous article in the 1960s Peter Drucker[2] characterised distribution as 'The Economy's Dark Continent' and pointed out that while the distribution function accounted for between 30–50% of the total cost of manufactured goods it received comparatively little attention compared with the other major business functions. Thirty years later very little has changed – distribution activities account for substantial costs and provide extensive employment but with the exception of a few prophets like Martin Christopher, Maureen Guirdham and Christina Fulop, few marketing academics, or practitioners, give the subject much attention. This neglect is even more surprising when one considers that much of the early marketing literature has a distribution focus.

Perhaps distribution remains unexplored because it lacks the interest and excitement associated with the other marketing functions – especially product development and promotion. Yet while lacking in glamour, effective distribution is a *sine qua non* of marketing success, as the following example shows:

> In the early part of 1970, after several months and substantial expenditure, Walls withdrew from the yoghurt market and sold their fleet of chill-refrigerated vehicles to Eden Vale, their main competitors in the market. This decision meant, in effect, that Walls were abandoning the rapidly expanding chilled prepared-food market, which includes prepared salads and ready-to-serve puddings. They had been unable to obtain enough sales to warrant the high cost of distribution of these products. Underlying the poor sales performance was Walls' inability to get their chilled product distributed through enough of the high-volume outlets – the supermarkets.[3]

By the same token the tremendous success of ICI's Ambush insecticide in securing almost 50% of total sales to US cotton growers in its launch year was largely attributable to ICI signing up the most influential distributors throughout the cotton belt.[4]

Distribution is a key policy area in the formulation of marketing strategy, and in this chapter we will attempt to cover some of the more important issues. First we shall examine the reasons underlying the development of marketing channels and the functions they perform. This will lead naturally into a consideration of the various channels and the factors which will influence the choice of any particular option.

As we have noted earlier, the producer has only two basic options with regard to a distribution policy – he can either seek to work closely with intermediaries or else assume their functions and 'push' his product through the channel, or he can seek to establish a franchise with ultimate consumers and so 'pull' his product through the channel. Push strategies tend to lay greater emphasis upon personal selling; pull strategies emphasise advertising and promotion. Accordingly we will look at some of the major aspects of the selling function in this chapter while leaving advertising to Chapter 17.

Finally, in keeping with our adoption of the product life-cycle as an organising concept, we shall look at the role which sales and distribution have to play at the various stages of product development.

■ Why do Channels Develop?

The basic and most primitive form of economic organisation is the self-sufficient community in which the overall standard of living or quality of life depends directly upon the abilities, skills and resources available to the community.

Improvements in the efficiency of such communities occur when the members recognise the benefits of task specialisation in increasing both productivity and the quality of output and adopt a basis for exchanging surpluses in excess of the producer's own needs. In time still greater improvements are achieved through the application of technology to the production function and through the division of labour such that individuals perform only one or few of the many tasks involved in translating raw materials into consumable products. However, a direct consequence of the very large increments in output which result from task specialisation and the division of labour is that the production unit can supply more than can be consumed by persons with direct access to that production unit. Thus it becomes necessary to gain access to consumers who are physically distant from the production unit and this will depend upon the creation of physical means of distribution together with the development of institutions and institutional devices to serve and manage these distribution 'channels'.

Of course improved transportation not only permits the distribution of finished goods to users, it also facilitates the movement of people and raw materials so that whole industries begin to concentrate in those areas which offer the highest comparative advantage, with classical examples being the Yorkshire woollen industry, the Lancashire cotton industry and the Potteries. Such industrial concentration results in an even greater physical separation between producer and consumer and creates a concomitant increase in the dependence upon the distribution channel. As a general rule-of-thumb, the greater the number of consumers the more widely they are dispersed and the greater their frequency of purchase the more attenuated and complex will be the channel linking producer and consumer.

Unfortunately, while the value added by production has long been recognised and accepted the functions of 'merchants' who organise and manage the distribution channel has been poorly understood and subject to considerable criticism. Indeed the less the physical movement and handling involved and the more indirect the channel the more strident the criticism. Faced with such unfavourable attitudes it is perhaps unsurprising that distribution has been regarded as the least accepted and least glamorous aspect of marketing. During the 1980s there were signs, however, that this status was changing as the balance of power between manufacturer and retailer moved in favour of the latter.

It is especially ironic that the pursuit of economies of scale in production – which is seen as laudable and to be encouraged – tends to lead to diseconomies in distribution, particularly as distribution costs are variable and only occur when manufacture is complete. In addition, and much more difficult to quantify, is the reduction in the satisfaction received by the consumer due to his separation from the producer. Because of this separation producers tend to lose contact with the specific needs of consumers and lack the feedback which contact provides. The rediscovery of marketing and the growth of consumerism are the obvious consequences of this deterioration in contact.

From the producers' point of view the loss of contact can become even more serious when their identity becomes submerged or lost in the identity of intermediaries in the distribution channel. While this tends to happen most often with consumer goods – e.g. Marks & Spencer, Sainsbury, Mothercare – it is also apparent in the case of many industrial raw materials and supplies where the distributor becomes the dominant force. While such a loss of identity may protect the producer from direct criticism, it also isolates him from the feedback which this provides with the result that it may be impossible to retrieve a situation where his product has become unsatisfactory.

To restore this loss of franchise with ultimate consumers many producers have resorted to one or some combination of the following alternative courses of action:

1 Integrate forward into distribution – breweries, oil producers, shoe manu-facturers.
2 Shorten the channel by seeking to deal direct with consumers through a greater emphasis upon personal selling.
3 Speak directly with the end consumer through their promotional effort.

However, the extent to which producers will be willing to or able to manage their own distribution activities will depend ultimately upon their perception of the costs and benefits involved. Accordingly, it seems likely that given channels and forms of distribution will only survive if they are more effective in marketing the product, and to establish this one must first identify the functions which the channel performs.

■ Functions of a Channel

The foregoing discussion has shown that the primary function of a channel of distribution is to provide a link between production and consumption by filling any gap or discontinuity which exists between them. Discontinuities between producers and consumers may arise from a number of causes including the following:

(a) *Geographical separation.* As noted, the application of the theory of comparative advantage has led to considerable concentration of production on both a national and international scale. At the same time population and economic growth have resulted in many more widely dispersed consumers wanting access to these products. Distribution creates utilities in place availability.
(b) *Time.* Production and consumption rarely occur simultaneously (with the exception of personal services) and channels of distribution help even out fluctuations in supply and demand by holding stocks and through the provision of credit. These activities create time utilities.
(c) *Information.* The information needs of consumers vary widely and channel intermediaries can provide a valuable service in advising producers of the

needs of consumers and advising consumers of the specific characteristics of the offerings of different producers.

(d) *Ownership*. In addition to making goods physically available (possession) channels also provide the mechanism whereby transfer of the legal title to ownership may be accomplished.

(e) *Sorting*. 'Sorting' is the term used by Wroe Alderson[5] to describe a number of channel functions which are implicit in creating the time, place and possession utilities described above. According to Alderson, sorting comprises four distinct activities:

1 'Sorting out' which means 'breaking down a heterogeneous supply into separate stocks which are relatively homogeneous', e.g. agricultural products.
2 'Accumulation'.
3 'Allocation' which 'consists of breaking a homogeneous supply down into smaller and smaller lots'.
4 'Assorting' which means 'building up assortments of items for use in association with each other'.

In addition to plugging potential gaps which may arise between producer and consumer due to the above factors, Alderson (1954) also shows how channels can increase consumer satisfaction through improving efficiency and thereby reducing cost, and also by reducing uncertainty through routinisation of transactions.

As Alderson observes:

> *Economic analysis of the factors in price equilibrium generally rests on the assumption that exchange transactions are costless. Marketing analysis directed toward an understanding of trade channels must begin with a recognition of the costs involved in the creation of time, place, and possession utilities* (emphasis in original).

Alderson proceeds to demonstrate:

> The number of transactions necessary to carry out decentralised exchange is $n(n-1)/2$ where n is the number of producers and each makes only one article. Since the number of transactions required is only n if the central market is operated by a dealer, the ratio of advantage is $(n-1)/2$. Thus if the number of producers is raised from 5 to 25, the ratio of advantage in favour of an intermediary increases from 2 to 12. With 125 producers the ratio of advantage is 62.

Given our earlier claim that the average supermarket stocks over 20,000 different items, even allowing for the fact that these will come from significantly fewer producers, the cost advantage of dealing through such an intermediary is immediately apparent.

With regard to routinisation Alderson argues that this will reduce transaction costs to the minimum as it will eliminate the costs involved in searching for and approaching sources of supply on an *ad hoc* basis. Further, by reducing much purchase behaviour to a routine exchange one will eliminate the uncertainty which the potential buyer experiences in new buy or modified rebuy situations. Thus many buyers regard the industrial distributor or the retail outlet as the guarantee of satisfactory performance and leaves it to the intermediary to undertake the search, evaluation and trial aspects of a purchase on their behalf.

Thus we can see that the functions of a channel of distribution not only improve the flow of physical goods, but also create flows in finance, information and ownership.

■ Channel Composition

Channels of distribution vary considerably in their complexity with the simplest involving a direct exchange between producer and consumer, while the most complex may involve several different kinds of intermediaries. The possible combinations and permutations are considerable for, of course, a supplier may make use of multiple channels simultaneously and not just depend upon a single approach to the market. Most of the major alternatives are illustrated in Figure 16.1.

From Figure 16.1 it is clear that the producer can have access to a variety of different intermediaries, each of whom will provide different kinds of services. Most basic textbooks devote considerable coverage to describing the similarities and differences which exist between different categories of intermediary together with an evaluation of their merits and disadvantages. We do not propose to pursue these further here as the choice of a particular kind of intermediary is more of a tactical decision than a strategic one and will be highly situation specific. Accordingly our own focus will be upon the basic choice between direct and indirect distribution and, if indirect, the length and complexity of the channel and its functions rather than the precise designation of the intermediaries.

■ Factors Influencing Channel Structure

With rare exceptions most producers will find themselves faced with a number of different channels through which they might seek to reach their target market. Some understanding of the broad influences which give rise to these different channel structures will provide a useful insight when deciding which of the alternatives to use.

In reviewing various explanations of channel structure Lambert (see Figure 16.1) notes that there is no consensus of opinion, with some theories stressing the product life-cycle, others the characteristics of goods and still others the size of firm. Among these theories perhaps the most detailed and best-known is that put forward by Bucklin[6] which rests upon the economic relationships between channel members and the concepts of substitutability, postponement and speculation.

392

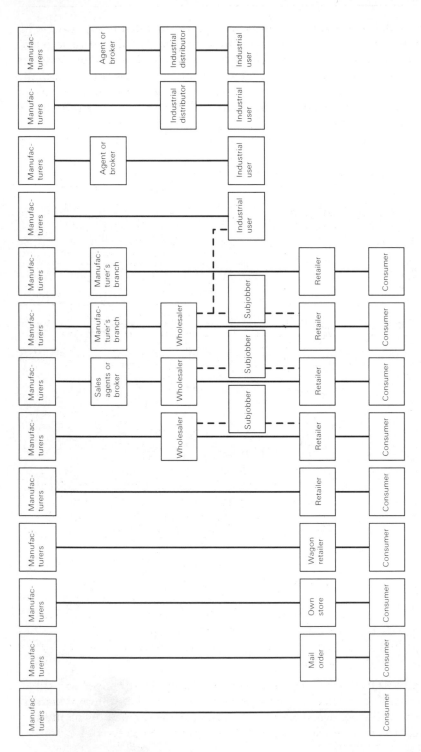

Figure 16.1 Alternative channels of distribution

Source: D. M. Lambert, *The Distribution Channels Decision* (New YokK: The Society of Management Accountants and National Society of Accountants, 1978).

According to Bucklin[7] marketing functions are substitutable for one another in much the same way as the basic factors of production and 'This substitutability permits the work load of one function to be shrunk and shifted to another without affecting the output of the channel'. He continues later: 'In essence, the concept of substitutability states that under competitive conditions institutions of the channel will interchange the work load among functions, not to minimise the cost of some individual function, but the total costs of the channel.'

Postponement and speculation are the converse of each other in that the principle of postponement 'states that changes in form and inventory location are to be delayed to the latest possible moment' while 'the principle of speculation holds that changes in form, and the movement of goods to forward inventories, should be made at the earliest possible time in the marketing flow in order to reduce the costs of the marketing system', e.g. through economies of scale.

Based upon these three principles, Bucklin argues that consumer demand will determine what services are required and what value is placed upon them, and this will result in the evolution of the most efficient and cost-effective channel structure. Thus for convenience goods ready and widespread availability is a *sine qua non* and we are likely to find the producer using multiple channels involving both direct and indirect sales to achieve the maximum market coverage. Conversely, for many industrial goods and consumer shopping goods the variation in consumer demand will lead to greater postponement so that precise needs can be articulated and will frequently result in shorter channels and a greater dependence upon personal interaction between buyer and seller.

However, as producers and distributors jockey for position to satisfy the ultimate customer one must anticipate an ebb and flow in the competitive standing of the channel members. Lambert provides a useful synopsis of Bruce Mallen's[8] analysis of the competitive forces which are likely to result in structural change in the channel, as follows:

1   A producer will spin-off a marketing function to a marketing intermediary(s) if the latter can perform the function more efficiently than the former.
2   If there are continual economies to be obtained within a wide range of volume changes, the middleman portion of the industry (and perhaps individual middlemen) will become bigger and bigger.
3   A producer will keep a marketing function if the producer can perform the functions at least as efficiently as the intermediary.
4   If a producer is more efficient in one market, the producer will perform the marketing function; if in another market the middleman is more efficient, then the middleman will perform the function.
5   If there are not economies of scale in a growing market, more firms may be expected to join the channel.

Of course, changes in the competitive standing of producers and distributive intermediaries will be subject to the complex interplay of the environmental forces reviewed in Chapter 6 and underlines the importance of monitoring these if one is to select the most efficient channel – a subject to which we turn next.

■ Selecting the Distribution Channel

Thus far the analysis of the factors governing the functions and structure of distribution channels has laid most emphasis upon cost efficiency, particularly as distribution represents such a significant proportion of the final cost to the consumer. However, we have also referred to 'effectiveness' and to consumer satisfaction, both of which tend to be of a subjective and qualitative nature. To some extent cost efficiency and maximising consumer satisfaction are conflicting objectives and lead to the classic dilemma in choosing channels of distribution – the trade-off between cost versus control.

Louis Stern[9] defines channel control and its implications succinctly when he writes:

> Channel control[signifies] the ability of one member of a marketing channel for a given product (or brand) to stipulate marketing policies to other members. For example, in a simple channel where a buyer interacts directly with a seller, the party gaining control in the bargaining process either through the use of sheer economic power, political or legal means, superior knowledge, more subtle promotional aids, or other methods, obtains a major advantage in all aspects of their relationship. When marketing policies may be stipulated by any one party, this may have a marked influence on the efficiencies of both. Their goals may not be totally compatible; therefore, by complying with the dictates of buyers, for example, sellers may frequently be forced to alter their methods of operation in a manner that is not often profitable for them.

Obviously there are many situations where the seller will have to accept an inevitable discrepancy in bargaining power between himself and his customer, but equally there are many other situations where a creative marketing approach may minimise or eliminate control over one's affairs. This is particularly true of the distribution function where it may be possible to retain a larger measure of control by performing channel functions oneself rather than using the more cost-effective services of an intermediary, e.g. in the level of servicing and/or maintenance provided, of the inventory held, etc. In turn, by providing greater user satisfaction one may be able to secure a higher price and so offset the additional costs.

As noted earlier, when selecting a channel of distribution one must pay particular attention to the environmental situation, to the product and market characteristics and the company's own strengths and weaknesses. While these factors have been the subject of extensive discussion in earlier chapters, it will be helpful to summarise the major points to be considered and provide some elaboration of them here in general terms.

Environmental
Market structure   ★ number and location of both suppliers
                                             and users

Market conduct	★ degree of concentration and nature of competition
Market performance	
Legislation/regulation	
Institutional infrastructure	★ what channels are available and what are their distinguishing characteristics
Product characteristics	
	★ Class of product
	★ Bulk/volume
	★ Price/value
	★ Durability/perishability
	★ Seasonality
	★ Service requirements
Market characteristics	
	★ Benefits looked for
	★ Geographic location
	★ Discernible segments
Company strengths and weaknesses	
	★ Size
	★ Competitive standing
	★ Goodwill – how much with whom
	★ Service and technical abilities

Consideration of these factors will inevitably lead one to consider the relative merits of our three basic strategies: undifferentiated, differentiated and concentrated marketing with their associated distribution strategies: intensive, selective and exclusive distribution.

As we have seen, an undifferentiated strategy rests on the assumption of user homogeneity and/or an implicit acceptance that one has no prior ability to segment a market and so must appeal to all of it. Either way, maximum distributive coverage is called for that almost invariably will require one to use the services of intermediaries to secure it.

By contrast differentiated marketing implies an ability to segment a market and to cater for the varying needs of the different segments. In these circumstances some segments are likely to be much more important to a given producer than others, and so justify a direct approach, while intermediaries may be used to reach more dispersed segments or those with particular needs best served by another channel member, e.g. a manufacturer of industrial equipment might sell direct to major users and through distributors or agents to increase geographical coverage.

Finally, concentrated marketing calls for highly selective distribution. It also implies a smaller supplier, hence the concentration on only one segment, and so will require the use of intermediaries in all but the most geographically concentrated markets. The implications of these three strategies for distribution are summarised succinctly in J.R. Evans and B. Berman's[10] overview of distribution planning reproduced below as Table 16.1.

Table 16.1   Intensity of channel coverage

Characteristics	Exclusive distribution	Selective distribution	Intensive distribution
Objectives	Strong image, channel control and loyalty, price stability	Moderate market coverage, solid image, some channel control and loyalty	Widespread market coverage, channel acceptance, volume sales
Channel members	Few in number, well-established, reputable stores	Moderate in number, well-established, better stores	Many in number, all types of outlets
Customers	Few in number, trend setters, willing to travel to store, brand loyal	Moderate in number, brand conscious, somewhat willing to travel to store	Many in number, convenience-oriented
Marketing emphasis	Personal selling, pleasant shopping conditions, good service	Promotional mix, pleasant shopping conditions, good service	Mass advertising, nearby location, items in stock
Examples	Automobiles, designer clothes, caviar	Furniture, clothing, watches	Groceries, household products, magazines

Source: J.R. Evans and B. Berman, *Marketing Management* (New York: Macmillan, 1982).

In their text book R.M. Gaedeke and D. Tootelian[11] provide a very useful summary table of the factors which are likely to influence the length of the channel and, therefore, the number of intermediate functions to be performed between production and consumption. These data are reproduced in Table 16.2.

However, notwithstanding the implications of these generalisations there are numerous instances where channels will differ from the normative prescription. Such variation may reflect a conscious decision to adopt a different approach to distribution in order to position the firm in a distinctive way, i.e. using distribution as the key variable in a competitive strategy, or it may simply reflect inertia or neglect. Like so many other areas of activity, while the underlying trend may be towards homeostasis or equilibrium, the state may never be reached and conditions will approach then swing away from the central state rather in the manner of a pendulum.

In the sphere of retailing these fluctuations have been characterised as a 'wheel' in which different approaches will dominate from time to time only to be displaced by alternative forms until the wheel comes full circle. The concept of a

Table 16.2   Summary of factors influencing channel length

Channel consideration	Favouring long channels	Favouring short channels
Market or customer characteristics		
1. Size of purchasing unit	Small	Large
2. Number of customers	Many	Few
3. Location of customers	Geographically dispersed	Geographically concentrated
4. Customer knowledge	Considerable and widely dispersed	Limited and concentrated
5. Installation and servicing assistance	None required	Help required
Producer characteristics		
1. Size of firm	Small	Large
2. Length of time in business	New to market	Old and established in the market
3. Financial resources	Limited	Abundant
4. Location to the market	Not centrally located	Centrally located
5. Control over marketing program	Unimportant	Important
6. Overall resource position	Weak	Strong
7. Market coverage desired	Intensive	Exclusive
8. Managerial capabilities	Weak	Strong
9. Market information availability	Limited	Abundant and expensive
10. Power	Weak	Strong
11. Policy toward pushing product	Passive	Aggressive
Environmental characteristics		
1. Number of competitors	Many	Few
2. Number of resources controlled	Few	Many
3. Economic conditions	Recessionary	Booming
4. Entry and exit of producers	Easy	Limited
5. Economic customs and traditions	Stable	Dynamic
6. Location of competitors	Geographically dispersed	Geographically concentrated
7. Laws and regulations	Tight	Loose
8. Competition among customers	Weak	Strong
9. Market to be served	New	Old
Product characteristics		
1. Perishability	Low	High
2. Fashionability	Low	High
3. Size of product	Small	Large
4. Value of product	Low	High
5. Weight of product	Light	Heavy
6. Complexity of product	Technically simple	Technically complex
a Special knowledge for sale	None	Considerable
b Installation	Not necessary	Required
c Maintenance	Not required	Frequent or regular
d Service	Not required	Frequent or regular

Channel consideration	Favouring long channels	Favouring short channels
7. Risk of obsolescence	Low	High
8. Age of product	Old	New
9. Production process	Standard	Custom-built
10. Order size (quantities purchased)	Small	Large
11. Appearance of product	Undifferentiated (homogeneous)	Differentiated (heterogeneous)
12. Type of product (buying characteristics)	Convenience good	Speciality good
13. Type of product (market)	Consumer good	Industry good
14. Time of purchase	Seasonal	Nonseasonal
15. Timing of purchase	Frequently	Infrequently
16. Regularity of purchase	Regular	Irregular
17. Profit margin	Low	High
18. Width of product line	Narrow	Broad
19. Availability requirements	Delayed	Immediately
20. Number of products per line	Few	Many
21. Product lines	Unrelated	Related
22. Number of alternative uses	Many	Limited

Source: Adapted from D.L. Brady, *An Analysis of Factors Affecting the Methods of Exporting Used by Small Manufacturing Firms* (University of Alabama, 1978), pp. 39–41.

'wheel of retailing' was first proposed by Professor Malcolm McNair of the Harvard Business School and hypothesises that 'new types of retailers usually enter the market as low-status, low-margin, low-price operators. Gradually, they acquire more elaborate establishments and facilities, with both increased investments and higher operating costs. Finally they mature as high-cost, high-price merchants, vulnerable to new types who, in turn, go through the same pattern.'[12]

Hollander's[13] article provides an excellent summary of the evidence for and against the theory and concludes that, while it is not valid for all retailing, it does 'describe a fairly common pattern in industrialised, expanding economies'. Certainly, firms like Marks & Spencer, Tesco and Comet would seem to conform to the hypothesis and the critical question must be: 'If the management of these organisations can recognise the applicability of the theory to their development to date – will they be able to avoid the seemingly inevitable outcome?'

Reference to retailers such as Marks & Spencer, Tesco, Comet and the like provides a useful link with the point made early in the chapter that, as a result of the attenuation of distribution channels, many retailers (and industrial distributors) have become the dominant channel member. In that this book is written from the perspective of producer organisations this immediately raises the question as to what implication this has for producers and what actions can they take.

■ Formulating a Distribution Policy

From the preceding discussion it has become clear that a very large number of factors may influence the structure of distribution channels between manufacturers and consumers. It has also become clear that the weighting given to any particular factor will vary over time due to changes in the environment and/or in accordance with the perception of the individuals or organisations who comprise the channel. Thus, while it may be possible to define and describe theoretically 'optimum' channels in terms of objective cost factors, the perception of producers, intermediaries and consumers may all conclude that such an 'optimum' arrangement will not optimise their own objectives and yield the desired satisfactions. For example, selling through Marks & Spencer by a textile manufacturer might ensure that the customer gets excellent value for money, but may be seen as inimical to that manufacturer's wish to retain some direct control over the marketing of his output. The question is, then, how does the manufacturer resolve this dilemma by assigning his own subjective weights to the key criteria? How does one establish a distribution policy?

Before attempting to answer this question it is important to stress a point made earlier that theoretical solutions are very often only intended to clarify the factors and their relationships which need to be taken into account. In doing so it will be necessary to make certain assumptions which will clean up the data and reduce the noise in the system and the greater the number of assumptions and the simplification of the data the more likely it becomes that the theoretical solution will depart from the empirical reality. Thus most textbooks describe issues of policy formulation for the mix element as if one were starting with a clean sheet of paper and had complete freedom of choice. But throughout this book we have tried to bear in mind that most businesses are already in being, are part of existing industry/market structures and enjoy established and continuing relationships with both suppliers and customers. Only occasionally do new organisations come into being to introduce a new product into the market and rarely will such an occurrence have much impact upon the prevailing industry/market structure. Even less often will a new market be created.

It follows then that many distribution decisions will be heavily influenced and proscribed by current relationships and commitments. Salient among these will be the existing and accepted channel structures and a basic policy decision will be whether to 'push' or 'pull' the product through a channel. Luck and Ferrell[14] recognise the importance of the decision when they comment: 'A fundamental strategic decision will be whether to pull the product through the channel by concentrating on final purchasers or whether to push it through by gaining the co-operation of middlemen. A decision to push or to pull the product will determine whether to aim messages or where to send sales people.' (p. 188)

Of course push and pull are not mutually exclusive alternatives, as elements of both are required in almost every buying/selling situation. Reverting to the simple hierarchy of effects models discussed in Chapter 7 (p. 174) it is clear that awareness/ interest must precede desire and action. As a working generalisation impersonal means of communication (essentially advertising) will be most cost effective in creating initial awareness and interest while personal communication (essentially salesmanship) will be most effective in translating interest into desire and action. The reason that this should be so is that as a prospect moves through the stages his interest will prompt questions particular to his own state of knowledge and precise needs all of which cannot be anticipated or covered by impersonal sources unless they assume encyclopedic proportions. By contrast the salesman will be able to respond directly to questions and so reduce the uncertainties experienced by persons contemplating a new or unfamiliar purchase. In addition the salesman can reinforce the prospect's own reasons for considering purchase and so overcome real or imagined obstacles to purchase. Clearly, then, it is a matter of emphasis and the producer's decision will hinge upon his perception of where the leverage exists in the channel *vis-à-vis* his own resources and bargaining power.

Where the producer wishes or has to use the services of an intermediary then both the intermediary *and* the final customer may be the object of promotional activity, but the intermediary will become the primary customer and the object of the direct selling effort. Further the distinction and emphasis between push and pull will tend to turn on whether the intermediary is *willing* to work with the producer or has to be 'coerced' to do so. I use the word 'coerced' advisedly because the producer may be able to buy cooperation through incentives to distributors (a 'push' tactic), but there will be circumstances where such efforts will be matched by competitors and the producer will have no option but to see if he can exert pressure on (coerce) the intermediary by developing a franchise with the ultimate consumer. Given that use of an intermediary has excluded personal selling by the producer to the ultimate customer by definition it is obvious that development of such a franchise will depend upon impersonal 'selling' or advertising/promotion – a 'pull' approach.

Many authors imply that there are basic differences between consumer and industrial products when developing distribution/promotion strategies and deciding whether to push or pull the product through the channel. I am not of this opinion as there are as many examples of industrial goods producers having to stimulate primary demand amongst end users in order to get the intermediaries to carry their line[15] or to incorporate it in their own product as there are consumer goods examples. The decision criteria and the principles are the same.

As intermediaries occupy such an important link in the chain between production and consumption, and because they are likely to be the focus of the producer's personal selling effort when he uses them, it will help to round out this chapter if we look briefly at the sales function here while leaving the subject of promotion to the next chapter. First, however, it will be useful to define and describe the concept of *vertical marketing systems* (VMS) as a possible response to the conflict and control issues which figure so large in setting distribution policy.

■ Vertical Marketing Systems

To this point, the discussion of distribution channels has conformed with the traditional view that members of such channels are autonomous and independent organisations which are pursuing their own individual objectives. Where these objectives are not congruent there is the potential for *conflict* and, to try and avoid this, the channel members with the greatest leverage will seek to superimpose their goals over other members and assume *control* of the channel. Thus, as we have seen, conflict and control are major issues in selecting a distribution policy. Further, and implicit in the word 'superimpose', there has been the expectation that channel conflict will be resolved by competition rather than cooperation.

In many cases competition between channel members leads to inefficiencies and lost profit opportunities. To avoid this, an alternative, more co-operative form of organisation has begun to emerge in recent years and has been designated the *vertical marketing system* (VMS). According to the Macmillan *Dictionary* (1990)[16] a VMS is 'A marketing channel which has achieved some degree of vertical integration involving some central control of operational practices and programmes'. Nylen (1990)[17] elaborates on this definition by suggesting that VMSs differ from conventional channels in four important respects:

1   VMSs use centrally prepared marketing programs.
2   Whether or not the members of a VMS are independent of each other their activities are directed by this central program.
3   In a VMS marketing functions are assigned to units on the basis of efficiency and effectiveness rather than on the basis of traditional roles and precedent.
4   The members in a VMS accept closer control than is usual in a conventional channel, with the result that VMSs tend to be more stable.

Following the publication of a paper by Bert C. McCammon Jr[18] it has been customary to recognise three main types of VMS – *Administered*, *Contractual* and *Corporate*. The difference between the three kinds of system is determined primarily by the means used to exercise control over the members. In an *administered* system a channel leader (sometimes termed the *channel captain*) has sufficient power to persuade the other members of the benefit of cooperation. In order to enjoy this power the leader will normally be the organisation which enjoys the strongest customer franchise. For most food products this now means the major multiples will set the lead although major brands like P&G, Lever Bros, Heinz, etc. will be able to moderate this power and are likely to give the lead in the channels which involve the smaller retailer chains and independents. Either way the leader of an administered VMS will be expected to spell out the terms of trade within the channel (discounts, allowances, trading areas, etc.) in order to provide the incentives necessary to keep the channel intact.

The second type of VMS is the *contractual* system in which the relationships between members tend to be more formalised and spelled out in official contracts. Three main kinds of contractual VMS may be distinguished – retail co-operatives, wholesale co-operatives and franchises. Retail co-operatives occur when independent retailers take the initiative to band together and set up their own wholesaling intermediary. Conversely wholesaler co-operatives occur when smaller wholesalers band together to secure the benefits of bulk buying power through pooled purchases as well as the benefits of professional advice, joint branding and advertising, etc. commonly associated with both kinds of co-operative.

Franchises occur where the owners of products or services license others to wholesale or retail them under the franchiser's name in exchange for the payment of a fee. Car dealerships, fast food outlets and soft drinks like Coca-Cola are probably the best known example. Franchises also depend upon a contractual relationship, but differ from retail and wholesale co-operatives which are forms of backward integration by intermediaries whereas franchises are cases of forward integration by producers.

Finally, *corporate* VMSs exist where a firm integrates vertically, either backwards or forwards, and so becomes responsible for the product/service from its initial conceptualisation/production right through to its consumption and after-sales service.

Nylen (1990) summarises the advantages and disadvantages of VMSs as follows:

- *Advantages*

    1 Distribution economies.
    2 Marketing control.
    3 Stability, reduction of uncertainty.

- *Disadvantages*

    1 Loss of incentive.
    2 Investment requirements.
    3 Inflexibility.

Nylen continues to suggest that the choice between VMS and conventional systems depends largely on the answers to six questions.

1 What level of power does the firm have?
2 What is the potential for economies?
3 How much marketing cooperation is needed?
4 Are appropriate channel members available?
5 Is there potential for competitive differentiation through the channel system?
6 Is there a competitive threat from integrated systems?

Clearly, the answers to these questions (like so many in marketing) will call for both formal analysis and the exercise of judgement.

■ Personal Selling

In many situations deciding what to exclude or ignore is even more difficult than deciding what to include and recognise. So it is with the subject of personal selling. Repeated reference to the present needs of the organisation and the exhortation to practise 3-in-1 marketing can leave no doubt as to the importance of the sales function and yet it is consigned here to only a section within a chapter. In part such a decision is justified on the grounds that the basic objective of selling is to exercise personal influence over buying behaviour and the latter subject was treated more fully in Chapter 7; in part it is because the goals of personal selling are the same as for other forms of promotion which will be treated at greater length in Chapter 17. Overriding both these considerations, however, is my own belief that marketing *is* selling and thus the subject of the whole book.

This latter view is not entirely a popular one because there is a great deal of truth in the cynic's view that the term 'marketing' was coined to avoid the undesirable connotations which have built up around the term 'selling'. These latter are reflected in the stereotype which Gaedeke and Tootelian (1983) report from a survey of business students taking a first marketing course in response to the question 'What do you associate with the word "salesman"?' In rank order the ten most popular replies were: (1) pushy; (2) fast talker; (3) aggressive; (4) commission; (5) money; (6) dishonest; (7) helpful; (8) persistent; (9) cars; (10) well-dressed. In addition many exponents of marketing see it as a much extended and more sophisticated function than selling, and there can be no denying this if we consider the scope of a modern marketing book or course compared with a modern book on the sales function. On the other hand if you look at a book on selling written before or immediately after the Second World War you will likely find that it deals with many of the issues of customer identification and motivation which are seen now as the province of marketing not selling. It is also as well to remember that if you go back that far you will find little or nothing on corporate planning and strategy and it is planning and strategy which are considered central to the marketing function. In other words there is good reason to believe that if we hadn't changed the name the selling 'product' would now bear a remarkable resemblance to the 'marketing' product in its composition and performance, against which must be set the possibility that the change of name was essential to gain the penetration and acceptance which 'marketing' now enjoys. Whatever the reasons there can be little doubt that personal selling is now regarded as a sub-function of marketing and the great majority of writing and thinking about it is concerned with the tactical use and management of personal selling rather than regarding it as a major strategic weapon.

While few people would deny the effectiveness of personal selling in any of its traditional functions – identifying and locating potential customers, establishing contact, determining precise needs and presenting the product so that it will be seen to meet these, handling objections, closing the sale and providing after-sales service – the real and apparent importance of the function has declined for several reasons. First, personal selling is labour-intensive and time-consuming and so represents a significant on-cost. Accordingly, as markets have grown in size and numbers, producers have looked for economies in selling cost in exactly the same way as they have pursued economies in distribution. Indeed the major economy in distribution contained in Hollander's simple formula (p. 398) is the economy in the number of personal contact points reinforced by the specialisation of the various channel intermediaries. Second, several of the salesmen's functions can now be performed more efficiently and cost effectively by other means – particularly marketing research to establish market size and characteristics, and advertising to create awareness and customer identification as well as to provide basic information on product characteristics, price and availability. Third, there is a tendency to think of selling as being performed solely by manufacturers and to forget the channel intermediaries – distributors, agents, wholesalers, retailers, etc., also perform personal selling functions and must take into account exactly the same factors as the manufacturer's sales force:

- Definition of sales territories.
- Setting sales targets/quotas.
- Determination of sales call frequencies by customer type – new prospects, established accounts.
- Interface with promotion.
- Development of a compensation plan.
- Evaluation of selling effectiveness.

Thus a great deal more personal influence or selling is involved in moving products from producers to consumers than immediately meets the eye.

▎Sales and Distribution Effort Through the Product Life-cycle

Decisions as to the most appropriate sales and distribution strategy at different stages in a product's life-cycle will be heavily influenced by the same considerations which we discussed in looking at the product variable, particularly at the launch stage. Clearly if we have a radically new product a great deal will depend upon our expectations of the resistance it might encounter and the degree of protection we enjoy from direct competition. Where the degree of protection is high, a selective and controlled distribution effort is likely to have most appeal, as by restricting supply the producer will limit his own risk exposure, i.e. through restricting investment in production and marketing activities. In addition a selective approach will enable him to focus his attention on those prospects with the greatest interest/need for the product which will be of particular value where the product is complex and requires considerable learning in use by the buyer and/or where the product is of a kind where additional product development is expected to be necessary based upon early usage experience (see, for example, the

Textile Machinery case histories in *Market Development*, pp. 128 ff.). Finally, by restricting supply the seller will be able to secure higher prices and so maximise his margins.

On the other hand where a new product is felt to have only limited advantages over its competitors and/or its features can easily be copied then the seller will usually wish to secure the widest possible distribution to reach his target market(s) as quickly as possible. To achieve this it will be necessary to offer intermediaries direct incentives (discounts) for stocking the product as well as to persuade the intermediary that one is investing in advertising and promotion to ultimate consumers to stimulate awareness and interest and help pull the product through the channel. In the case of many branded consumer products the manufacturer will be forced or will wish to limit the geographical availability of a product (a) to limit the launch risk; (b) because of finite marketing resources; (c) because concentration of effort is likely to result in deeper penetration; (d) because a launch confined to a particular geographical market may be regarded as a trial run and enable him to iron out any bugs in the product or its marketing strategy/plan; (e) because documented success in the market will prove a powerful argument for gaining dealer and consumer acceptance in other geographical areas.

Once a product has achieved recognition and acceptance then sales will take off, but, as we noted earlier, this will be as much a function of the bandwagon (increased supply) effect as of the contagion (increased demand) effect. Indeed the ultimate constraint upon the volume of sales must be the volume of production and it is likely that manufacturing and physical distribution will be seen as key strategic functions by corporate management while selling and promotion will operate in support of them. To achieve this end many producers, who may well have marketed direct during the launch phase, will want to work through intermediaries to ensure the widest possible distribution of their product. Given that the market opportunity will now be apparent to almost everybody there should be no shortage of intermediaries willing to handle the product and the important decision is to select those who offer most synergy to the manufacturer.

With the onset of maturity the major concern must be to maintain the maximum availability of the product. However, by this stage of the PLC one will have been able to make informed judgements about both the attractiveness of different market segments as well as about the effectiveness and efficiency of different channels in reaching them and may well want to phase out some of the markets and intermediaries. Also, while distribution will remain an important function, familiarity with the product is likely to lead the manufacturer to give more emphasis to product improvement and advertising and promotion to maintain the interest of both final users and intermediaries.

Much the same approach will also apply to the decline stage where the manufacturer is seeking to make a phased withdrawal at minimum risk and cost to himself and with the least inconvenience to users and distributors. Of particular importance at this stage is the manufacturer's policy on the provision of spare parts and maintenance, both of which will be an integral part of his distribution effort.

Ohmae[19] provides a compelling example of how many Japanese companies have varied their distribution policy over the product life-cycle in order to penetrate and then dominate markets.

> In the early stages of such a strategy, (penetration) the company in question still needs to achieve price competitiveness; hence, securing the economies of scale is likely to take precedence over building brand awareness. For this reason, such a company will be prepared to play the role of OEM (original equipment manufacturer) and rely parasitically on distributor sales rather than waste its resources prematurely on international marketing and sales. This enables it to gain, as quickly as possible, the volume base needed to generate manufacturing profits and thus become a recognised global competitor although not yet a completely functional company. Once it has attained the required economies of scale, such a company will gradually terminate its OEM supplier role and distributor arrangements and shift to establishing its own brand and its own distribution network (p. 256)

Examples of companies which have followed this strategy include Honda, Seiko, Sharp, Casio, Sony, Hitachi, Nikon and Yamaha, to mention but a few.

▪ Summary

In Chapter 16 we have seen that while distribution policy and decisions may lack the glamour and visibility of some other elements of the marketing mix none the less they are of central importance to marketing strategy and management. In part this importance is due to the fact that between 30% and 50% of the total cost of manufactured goods is accounted for by the distributive function. But even more important is the fact that it is the distribution channel which acts as the link between producer and user. However, while physical distribution has successfully overcome the spatial separation of manufacturer and consumer the development of marketing may be largely attributed to the failure of distribution channels to overcome the psychological separation of the parties.

To overcome the physical separation of producer and user a variety of intermediaries may be involved and, while many critics question the value added by them it seems clear that such intermediaries will only prevail when they are more cost effective than direct links. However, the use of and dependence upon intermediaries frequently faces the producer with a need to trade-off the cost savings which may be possible with the loss of control which may accompany them. Accordingly, the choice of distribution channel will call for a careful evaluation of the environment, of product and market characteristics and the company's strengths and weaknesses leading to the selection of either an undifferentiated, differentiated or concentrated strategy. Similarly the producer will have to decide whether he is to work closely with distributors and 'push' the product to the consumer or, alternatively, seek to temper the influence of the intermediary by developing a franchise with the end-user which will 'pull' his product through the channel.

The discussion of distribution led naturally to a review of the role of personal selling. In part the inclusion of this topic in a chapter on distribution was prompted by the view that the greater part of personal selling is done by distributors rather than manufacturers. However, it was also suggested that the strategic aspects of selling are inextricably a part of marketing, and so pervade the book as a whole, while selling itself is essentially a tactical activity most closely associated with distribution policy.

To conclude, the chapter has examined the most appropriate sales and distribution strategies at different stages in the product's life-cycle. In the next chapter our attention will turn to issues of promotion policy and management.

Promotion Policy and Management

Learning Goals

The issues to be addressed in Chapter 17 include:

1 The *nature* of the *communication* process.
2 The *role of advertising* and its influence on consumers' choice behaviour.
3 Selecting *promotion objectives*.
4 The development of a *promotional strategy*.
5 Setting *advertising budgets*.
6 The measurement of *advertising effectiveness*.

After reading Chapter 17 you will be able to:

1 Describe the *nature of the communication process*.
2 Explain *how advertising appears to work* in consumer decision-making and *distinguish between high- and low-involvement buying situations*.
3 Justify the view that the *primary goal of advertising is to influence attitudes* and suggest alternative strategies for achieving this.
4 Identify possible *advertising objectives*.
5 Discuss the issues involved in *developing a promotional strategy*.
6 Describe and evaluate five basic approaches *to setting the advertising budget*.
7 Suggest *methods for measuring advertising effectiveness*.

Introduction

In Chapter 16 we noted that considerable suspicion has long existed about the value added by sales and distribution activities. In the case of promotional activities, and particularly mass-media advertising, the suspicion and criticism is even more acute. Taken together sales, distribution and promotion are frequently regarded as unnecessary and cost-creating functions which contribute little or nothing to consumer satisfaction – a viewpoint neatly encapsulated in Ralph Waldo Emerson's frequently quoted assertion that:

If a man build a better mousetrap then, even though he live in a wood, the world will beat a path to his door.

Emerson was wrong. He was wrong because he did not appreciate that 'better' is a comparative statement and can only possess meaning for the consumer in terms of his current knowledge and expectations. Only if the whole population satisfied the assumptions on which the theory of perfect competition rests would 'the world' possess a homogeneous demand and so perceive the mousetrap as better. The mere existence of a marketing function is testimony that this is not the case. But Emerson was even more wrong in his assumption that the act of creation of a better product would in and of itself result in a demand for it. Awareness of the existence of a product and knowledge of its price, performance and availability are all necessary prerequisites for the creation of demand, and awareness and knowledge require the communication of information to bring them into existence. There is also the important fact that where physical and objective differentiation between goods is small or non-existent – as we saw in Chapter 7 when discussing how buyers choose – subjective factors such as image may become determinant. A major role of advertising is to create and develop such subjective associations.

As we saw in Chapter 16, physical availability and personal selling are both effective means of communicating the existence of products, but, in that they depend upon the potential consumer being exposed to the product stimulus, e.g. by seeing it at a trade exhibition or in a shop window, or a face-to-face contact with a salesman, they tend to be limited in coverage and expensive to achieve. By contrast, impersonal channels of communication using various broadcast and print media have almost universal coverage and on a cost per contact/exposure basis are very inexpensive to use.

As the creation of awareness and the dissemination of information are essential components of effective demand it would seem sensible to use the most efficient and cost-effective means of achieving this. In Chapter 17 we shall seek to show that almost invariably this will require the use of indirect and impersonal sources of communication.

Some reference to the role of communication was made in Chapter 7 when discussing models of buyer behaviour, but before turning to examine the managerial implications it will be helpful to summarise some of the key ideas which may be derived from the very extensive body of theory related to communication which have immediate application to the practice of promotion in marketing. Specifically, it will be helpful to review:

1 The nature of the communication process.
2 Further implications of selectivity in perception, attention and retention.
3 The nature of memory span and 'forgetting'.

Based upon the insights from such a review it becomes possible to identify realistic communication objectives and the optimum promotional mix for achieving them. Clearly, selecting an optimum mix requires careful consideration of the cost and effectiveness of the promotion and we shall examine both the question of setting a promotional budget and the pre-testing and post-testing of communication to establish this. First, however, it will be useful to provide some definitions of key terms.

■ The Nature of the Communication Process

(This topic is given extensive coverage in Chapter 15 of *Marketing* (5th edn, 1991) and the reader should refer to this for a survey of the theoretical underpinning of marketing communications.)

In his book Wilbur Schramm[1] defines communication as 'the process of establishing a commonness or oneness of thought between a sender and a receiver'. Thus the simplest model of the communications process would consist of only three elements:

> Sender   →   Message   →   Receiver
> (Source   Signal   Destination)

However, until thought transference becomes possible such a model is inadequate for it ignores the necessity to translate ideas into symbols so that they can be transmitted. To allow for this we must introduce encoding and decoding elements into the model, which will then appear as:

> Sender   →   Encoder   →   Message →   Decoder   →   Receiver

As Schramm points out, the model can accommodate all types of communication so that in the case of electronic communication the encoder becomes a transmitting device – microphone, teletype, etc. – and the decoder a receiver – radio or television set, telephone, etc. In the case of direct personal (face-to-face) communication, then one person is both source and encoder while the other is decoder and destination and the signal is language. It follows that if an exchange of meaning is to take place, then both source and destination must be tuned in to each other and share the same language. Put another way, there must be an overlap in the field of experience of source and destination – which Schramm illustrates as in Figure 17.1.

We must also recognise that all communication is intended to have an effect and introduce the notion of *feedback* into our model of communication, for it is through feedback that the source learns how its signals are being interpreted. In personal communication feedback is often instantaneous through verbal acknowledgement or gesture, but in impersonal communication through the mass media it may have to be inferred from other indicators, e.g. audience size, circulation, readership, or monitored by sampling opinion.

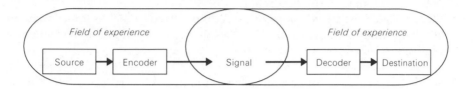

Figure 17.1 Overlap in the field of experience of source and destination

Source: W. Schramm, *The Process and Effects of Mass Communication* (Urbana: University of Illinois Press, 1955).

The final element in Schramm's model is the *channel* or, more correctly, channels, for messages are rarely transmitted through a single channel. Thus in personal communications it is not merely the words which convey the message but the intonation of our voice and the gestures which accompany them. Similarly, in the print media we lend emphasis by *italicising* keywords, by use of different typefaces, underlining, etc.

The marketer's version of Schramm's model employs slightly different terminology, but contains all of the following elements:[2]

Who...	says what...	how...	to whom...
Communicator	Message	Channel	Audience

with what effect...

Feedback

Kotler[3] defines these basic elements as follows:

Communicator: the sender or source of the message
Message: the set of meanings being sent and/or received by the audience
Channels: the ways in which the message can be carried or delivered to the audience
Audience: the receiver or destination of the message.

From his model Schramm derives four basic 'conditions of success in communication ... which must be fulfilled if the message is to arouse its intended response'. These are:

1 The message must be so designed and delivered as to gain the attention of the intended destination.
2 The message must employ signs which refer to experience common to source and destination, so as to 'get the meaning across'.

3   The message must arouse personality needs in the destination and suggest some ways to meet those needs.
4   The message must suggest a way to meet those needs which is appropriate to the group situation in which the destination finds himself at the time when he is moved to make the desired response.

Consideration of these four requirements should strike a receptive chord in the memory of the reader who is methodically working his way through the book, for they echo closely points discussed in Chapter 7 concerning hierarchy-of-effects models in consumer behaviour. In fact Schramm's four conditions are very similar to Strong's basic AIDA model – Attention, Interest, Desire and Action. It will be useful, therefore, to recapitulate on this earlier discussion, but specifically in the context of marketing communications.

■ How does Advertising Work?

The question of *how* advertising works is perhaps of less significance to the line manager than are the questions *what* can advertising do and how much will it cost to do it? That said, some understanding of what may be taking place in the 'black box' is necessary if the line executive is to judge when or when not to use advertising, and also to enable him to judge the recommendations of the advertising specialist. However, it must be admitted immediately that theoretical explanations of how advertising works are by no means complete or universally accepted. Further, in common with many other areas of research in marketing, there have been relatively few significant additions to our knowledge in the past 15–20 years although there has been considerable refinement of concepts and ideas borrowed from other behavioural sciences. Thus, in seeking to provide some answers to our question it is difficult to better the explanation provided by T. Joyce of the British Market Research Bureau[4] published as long ago as 1967 and this source will provide the framework for the discussion here (see also *Marketing*, 5th edn, Chapter 16). At the same time reference will be made to a much more recent article by Smith and Swinyard[5] which contains a comprehensive review of more recent research and proposes an 'integrated information response model' which seeks to synthesise concepts from a number of areas.

In a nutshell the nature of the problem and the basis for controversy centres upon the question of whether attitudes cause or change behaviour or whether behaviour results in the formation of attitudes. Clearly if attitude formation or change always precedes behaviour, this will be the primary focus for promotional activity. Conversely, if attitudes develop out of experience, they will be of secondary importance and the primary effort will be concentrated on encouraging and reinforcing behaviour favourable to one's product (purchase and consumption).

Hierarchical models of the kind discussed in Chapter 7 rest upon the assumption that each step is a necessary (but not sufficient) antecedent of the following step. In that liking and preference are attitudinal states such models assume that attitudes precede purchase, but much of the evidence seems to point to the opposite conclusion. Thus Smith and Swinyard cite a number of studies of the correlation between attitudes and behaviour which indicate scores between 0.00 and 0.30, which lead to the conclusion that it is more likely attitudes will not be related to actual behaviour than that they will!

As an alternative to the traditional learning model – cognition → affect → conation – Krugman[6] developed the so-called 'low-involvement model' which posits the sequence cognition → conation → affect. According to Krugman advertising for trivial products is of so little interest to consumers that they do not become actively involved in processing the information which over time and through constant repetition may well change the receiver's cognition without awareness. Accordingly when faced with a purchase situation the consumer may select a product without having formed any specific attitude towards it. Only after consumption and actual experience will attitudes be formed. Clearly, such a model (which has been empirically validated) provides powerful support for critics of advertising like Vance Packard, who would argue that advertisers are indeed hidden persuaders who condition consumers to act without conscious evaluation of their actions. In defence one might point out that the effect only applies to 'trivial' products that do not merit a high level of involvement and that in any event the purchase does not represent commitment but only a trial with limited risk to the consumer. In so far that learning from direct experience is likely to give rise to much more strongly held beliefs than will learning from indirect experience, i.e. from the claims of advertisers, one might also argue that if advertising can encourage people to try products without conscious pre-purchase evaluation and attitude formation one runs a very real risk that if the product does not live up to expectations a trial will lead to rejection and that it will be very difficult to persuade the consumer to change this belief subsequently by further advertising.

On balance, however, the low-involvement model would not seem to require us to reject the more traditional hierarchical models of the Awareness – Interest – Desire – Action (Cognition-Affect-Conation) kind. The low-involvement model provides a useful explanation of how advertising seems to work in a particular context, and it is this context – mass consumption convenience goods of low unit value – where most of the advertising expenditure and action is concentrated. That said, advertising also has an extremely important role to play in communicating information about the characteristics, performance and availability of goods which are complex, specialised and of high unit value and, presumably, may be classified as high involvement. In these cases logic and perceived risk both require the prospective customer to develop attitudes and beliefs prior to trial and possible adoption. Further, in the case of both low- and high-involvement situations much advertising is designed to *reinforce* attitudes, beliefs and behaviour rather than to change them.

In the light of these arguments the model proposed by Joyce appears to be as good a working representation of the way advertising works as it was in 1967 and

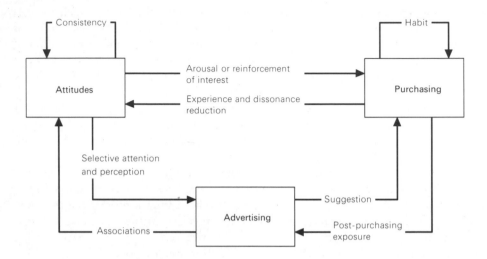

Figure 17.2 How advertising may work

Source: T. Joyce, *What Do We know about How Advertising Works?* (London: J. Walter Thompson Co., 1967).

it is reproduced here as Figure 17.2 together with Joyce's own explanation of its construction and interpretation.

> We might take as our starting-point a simple model of advertising consisting just of two arrows joining the three boxes – an arrow from 'advertising' to 'attitudes' showing that advertising changes or reinforces attitudes by investing the product with favourable associations, and an arrow from 'attitudes' to 'purchasing' showing that favourable attitudes lead to interest in the product being aroused when there is an opportunity to buy it or to a reinforcement of a purchasing habit.
>
> However, it seems that it would also be correct to put in arrows going the other way. Purchasing may influence attitudes, partly as a straightforward reflection of product experience, but partly (perhaps even before the product is consumed) by the drive to reduce dissonance, which leads to favourable attitudes in justification to oneself of the decision. Equally, the impact of advertising on the consumer is very much affected by attitudes in the sense of preconceptions: both attention and perception are selective and this selectivity is affected by attitudes.
>
> It also appears legitimate to put in arrows linking advertising and purchasing directly. We have considered the possibility that advertising may partly work by suggestion, a process in which attitudes need not necessarily function as an intermediary. Also there is evidence that the fact of having bought a particular product may in some circumstances heighten attention to advertisements for that product, again as a part of the phenomenon of the drive to reduce dissonance.
>
> Finally, it seems appropriate too to introduce two 'loops' in the system. We have

considered a certain amount of evidence that there is a drive towards consistency among attitudes even when advertising stimuli and purchasing situations are absent, and we therefore put in a loop around 'attitudes'. Also, we have recognised that much purchasing is habitual and apparently unaffected by advertising or by attitude changes, at any rate below some sort of threshold level. This is represented by a loop around purchasing.

The precise direction of the arrows and the labelling of arrows and boxes is perhaps less important than the general impression conveyed by the diagram, which is surely correct – that the advertising/purchasing system is a rather complex system of interacting variables. The model itself is tentative, but this general conclusion seems unlikely to be overthrown.

From the foregoing discussion it is clear that advertising 'works' in a number of different ways and that one must be careful to define the exact context in which advertising is to be used before one will be able to determine what may be possible. Such analysis should be an integral part of the marketing audit and will give clear indicators as to what constitutes a reasonable advertising objective which, in turn, will determine what budget or appropriation is necessary and how the effectiveness of the advertising effort may be measured.

■ Promotion Objectives

In a number of places we have given considerable support, both implicit and explicit, to the concept of hierarchies in behavioural response and particularly to Maslow's 'need hierarchy'[7] and Lavidge and Steiner's 'hierarchy of effects'.[8] Despite the fact that such hierarchies are a logical and inevitable consequence of the definitions used in formulating them, as we have seen they have not found universal favour and, as Boyd, Ray and Strong[9] point out, they have been criticised on at least two counts. First, in that sales are the ultimate objective of marketing efforts it seems reasonable that critics should be dissatisfied with promotional objectives which emphasise moving prospects up a hierarchy (awareness, recall, interest, etc.) without attempting to quantify the end-result sales. 'Second, certain behavioural scientists contended that little evidence supported the hierarchy of effects itself that is, learning does not necessarily lead to attitudinal change, nor does attitudinal change lead to behavioural change. Thus, advertising goals formed on the basis of changes in intermediate variables – such as recall or comprehension – may be of questionable value.'

With regard to the first criticism it is only natural that advertisers should want to be able to quantify and measure the sales effect of their advertising investment. It is very doubtful, however, if many advertisers (if any at all) would go to the lengths necessary to establish the possible/probable/likely effect of advertising upon sales. In 1970 Robert Buzzell and I took advantage of a natural experiment in attempting to establish that there is a positive correlation between advertising expenditure and sales. Our findings, which were reported in the *Journal of*

Advertising Research[10] were claimed by the editor to constitute the first 'proof' that advertising creates sales, but neither Buzzell nor I would be so foolhardy as to attempt to claim any particular, quantifiable advertising: sales effect.

The circumstances of our natural experiment were that the Auto workers' union had taken industrial action against Ford's in the USA immediately prior to the annual new-model launch in 1969. In the absence of new models to sell, Ford abstained from advertising and husbanded their budget for use when the strike was settled. Faced with the prospect of a delayed new-model launch by Ford, the other major auto manufacturers cut back their own advertising budgets in order to maintain a reserve for combating Ford when their campaign was mounted. Our analysis clearly showed that the reduction in sales was greater than would have been the case if advertising had no influence on the primary demand for cars (i.e. cars were available [place] with attractive features [product] and competitive prices so it was only the fourth *p* [promotion] which had been changed). However, while it was possible to distinguish a direct relationship between reduced advertising expenditures and declining sales it was clear that there was a distinct 'lag' in the effect (hence our previous argument that advertising should be considered an investment like R & D, and capitalised) and it would have been necessary to continue the 'experiment' much longer and then repeat it several times before one would have dared propose a formula to express the advertising: sales effect. Faced with such an 'academic' proposal, any sensible marketing man would tell you not to be a 'damned fool' as the lost sales revenue in establishing a relationship, which everyone implicitly accepts, could hardly be compensated for by the quantification of an effect which would be unlikely to occur again due to changes in both the environment and the other elements of the marketing mix. On these grounds alone we reject the arguments of critics who in attempting to appear pragmatic only reveal almost total insensitivity to the realities of competition and the market-place.

With regard to the second criticism the outcome has been more productive, for it has resulted in substantial evidence to support the theoretical view. Thus, it has been shown that advertising can influence attitudes and that attitudes predispose people to behave in a particular way from which it is a logical step to propose that attitudinal change may be a surrogate for purchase behaviour (sales) so that setting advertising objectives in terms of attitudinal change is both appropriate and effective.

As Boyd *et al.*[11] point out:

> Attitudes have the operationally desirable quality of being measurable, albeit with difficulty and some lack of precision. Attitudes also have long been the object of investigation by behavioural scientists, and a considerable body of knowledge has resulted from their studies and models. Today's psychologists believe that attitude includes both perceptual and preferential components; i.e. attitude is an inferred construct. When one refers to an attitude he means that a person's past experiences predispose him to respond in certain ways on the basis of certain perceptions. Attitudes, therefore, may be viewed as a variable which links psychological and behavioural components.

Since attitudes reflect perceptions, they inevitably indicate predispositions. Thus, they permit advertising strategists to design advertising inputs which will affect predispositions to respond or behave.

Perhaps even more important than hypothesising the link between attitudes and behaviour and focusing research upon it, has been the development of a whole battery of powerful techniques for measuring and stimulating both attitudinal and behavioural change. Thus while formal quantification of the precise relationship between advertising and behaviour still eludes us, it has become possible to measure attitudes and attitude change from which behavioural changes can be inferred. In keeping with our earlier assertion that objectives should be quantifiable so that we can measure our progress towards achieving them, it seems entirely reasonable to accept that the primary goal of advertising is to influence attitudinal structures. If this is the case then, as Boyd *et al.* show, the manager has five broad strategy alternatives:

He can seek to:

1   Affect those forces which influence strongly the choice criteria used for evaluating brands belonging to the product class;
2   Add characteristic(s) to those considered salient for the product class;
3   Increase/decrease the rating for a salient product class characteristic;
4   Change perception of the company's brand with regard to some particular salient product characteristic; or
5   Change perception of competitive brands with regard to some particular salient product characteristic.

Some elaboration of these rather cryptic statements seems called for.

Strategy 1 is most appropriate to those situations where the advertiser is seeking to stimulate demand for his product by increasing its saliency in the minds of potential customers *vis-à-vis* other competing product classes. In order to do this it is clear that as a minimum the advertiser must have a clear appreciation of the needs of the target market in terms of the choice criteria used to discriminate between the competing products[12] (i.e. the weighting attached to/ given to the various product characteristics and benefits discussed earlier in Chapter 13 and 8 respectively). This need profile can then be matched with that of the product and the purpose of the advertising will be to try and increase the saliency of those features in which the product enjoys some advantage over its rivals. In seeking to influence the weighting given to the various choice criteria which consumers use in developing their own scale of preferences it is important to recognise that many products are used in a specific context or as part of an 'event'. It follows that the most effective way of influencing decisions on particular products may well be to link them with the context or event and seek to modify attitudes towards the latter rather than the product which is an ingredient or part of the event.

Strategies 2 and 3 represent the basic alternatives which are available when a mismatch exists between the product and customer profile. Strategy 2 consists of adding a salient characteristic either physically, e.g. auto-focusing in cameras, solar power for calculators, numerical control to a machine tool – or, mentally by emphasising an existing feature of the product not considered salient hitherto, e.g. adults using baby powder. This strategy is particularly appropriate to the mature stage of the life-cycle by which time consumer attitudes to choice criteria will have become well-established.

Strategy 3 involves much the same approach as Strategy 1 in that it seeks to modify the consumer's perception of the saliency of specific product character-istics, i.e. rather than the saliency of the product class itself compared with other product classes. To some extent attempting to alter the saliency of a character-istic is akin to Strategy 2, but it is felt to differ significantly in the sense that Strategy 2 offered a 'new' benefit whereas Strategy 3 is seeking to reorder existing preferences. The latter is much more difficult to do and only likely to succeed where there are marked differences in terms of the characteristic between competing products within the class.

Strategies 4 and 5 are similar to Strategies 2 and 3 except that here the advertiser is not so much concerned with modifying the consumer's perception of the ideal product so that their new perception will shift towards the actual product but rather the reverse, i.e. they will seek to show how and why the actual brand corresponds (or not) to the ideal. Strategy 4 is perhaps the most traditional approach as it often comprises simply extolling the virtues of the manufacturer's brand as the ideal product. By contrast, Strategy 5 has only come into prominence in the increasingly competitive climate of the past decade when pointing out the deficiencies of the opposition (knocking copy) has become commonplace.

Boyd *et al.*'s discussion of promotion objectives focuses upon achieving changes in potential users' perceptions and attitudes and in doing so it fails to give explicit attention to the problems discussed earlier of actually achieving awareness of one's communication in a very noisy and confined environment. It also fails to recognise that many advertisers are quite happy with the consumer's existing perceptions and attitudes in so far that they favour him and so are concerned with *reminding* and *reinforcing* rather than changing these.It would seem therefore that to Boyd *et al.*'s five strategic objectives we should add three R's -

- Recognition (awareness).
- Reminder.
- Reinforcement.

To some extent the creation of awareness is implicit in Boyd's first strategy as the inference is that one has to bring a new product to the prospect's notice before he can rank order it in his overall scale of preferences. However, the emphasis is upon achieving changes in the rank order rather than the initial recognition which, by implication, might be dismissed as a low-order objective. While it is true that awareness or recognition is but the first rung on the ladder, it is also clear that the great majority of communications go completely unnoticed. With odds of the order of 99 to 1 against recognition this would seem to be a worthwhile objective in its own right. Establishing recognition also possesses the distinct advantage that it is easy both to define and measure its existence and changes in it and thereby satisfies the ever-present managerial wish to quantify both objectives and their achievement.

Once awareness has been accomplished learning theory predicates that it will be necessary to repeat the stimulus in order to achieve learning and the creation of habitual behaviour and that in doing so it will be necessary to reinforce the suitability of the response to the initial stimulus. A great deal of advertising of all types of goods and services is conceived and designed solely with the objective of reminding and reinforcing users in their existing patterns of behaviour and thereby inculcating a natural resistance to change.

Selection of an appropriate promotion objective will depend heavily on all the considerations which we have discussed in connection with the other mix elements. Rather than repeat these yet again we would prefer to emphasise the major implications of our model of buyer behaviour, namely that promotion will play a major role in –

1 Creating awareness.
2 Conditioning perceptions (of the facts).
3 Suggesting subjective associations and benefits which will prove determinant when there is an apparent objective parity between two or more competing alternatives.

To some extent all promotional activity will be directed to these ends and the specifying of an explicit objective will rest upon a careful evaluation of each and every situation on its own merits. What is important is that the choice objective be stated clearly and unequivocally, for only by doing so will it become possible to establish realistic budgets and measures for assessing effectiveness – topics to which we shall now turn.

In concluding this section we present in Table 17.1 the listing of advertising objectives which Corkindale and Kennedy derived from their extensive research into advertising in the UK in the early 1970s:

Table 17.1 Advertising objectives

Objectives related to awareness
- to inform people the product exists
- to gain or regain awareness
- to create or re-create awareness
- to buy awareness
- to create awareness in a specified section of the market

Objectives related to trial
- to gain trial
- to tempt people to try the product
- to stimulate trial
- to gain trial among a specified section of the population

Table 17.1 continued

Objectives related to education/informing (distinguished from **Messages** because of their more factual, objective bases)

- to educate people to the use of the product/an additional use of the product
- to educate people to the serving of the product
- to communicate a particular change in the product
- to show the multiple uses of the product
- to announce the variety availability
- to establish the varieties available
- to demonstrate the convenience of the product
- to give factual information about the product
- to show people how to get the best performance out of the product

Objectives related to attitudes

- to reinforce the early favourable attitudes
- to make attitudes more favourable to a particular product
- to sustain favourable attitudes
- to improve a particular attitude to the product
- to establish favourable attitudes
- to modify existing attitudes
- to improve existing negative attitudes
- to enhance certain attitudes in the target population

Objectives related to loyalty

- to retain loyal customers
- to encourage loyalty
- to keep building loyalty

Objectives related to reminding

- to remind people that the product exists

Objectives related to branding/image building

- to build an image for the product
- to improve the image of the product
- to establish the product as unique
- to establish the brand and position it in a particular way, e.g. as warm and friendly
- to retain a product quality image
- to maintain a favourable image of the product or manufacturer
- to create a brand leader in a particular market
- to create an image equal to that of the main competitor
- to establish branding
- to gain general image improvement
- to promote the corporate image and the qualities associated with the company products
- to advertise the brand
- to associate a product with the manufacturing company
- to create the right impression of the company among a particular section of the population
- to position the product for an additional section of the market
- to reassure existing users of the product
- to retain and reassure existing users of the product

Objectives of conveying a specific message

- to say that the product has a particular quality
- to establish particular associations with the product
- to convey the idea that the product is 'value for money'
- to get across the idea that the product tastes good
- to support the taste and quality claim for the product
- to convey the idea of a 'modern' product/one which is used by 'modern' people
- to state the advantages of the product compared with the competition
- to get across the idea of a unique product
- to get across the 'newness' of the product
- to say how much people like the product
- to convey a particular theme, e.g. real fruit
- to create warmth and friendliness for the product
- to emphasise the goodness of the product
- to convey the taste of the product
- to say something of the manufacturer
- to give the consumer a reason for buying the product

Source: D. Corkindale and S. Kennedy, *The Evaluation of Advertising Objectives*, Marketing Communications Research Centre, Cranfield School of Management, Report 10 (November 1974).

■ Developing a Promotional Strategy

Once the firm has established the intended objectives for its promotional activities it becomes possible to consider the strategies available for their achievement.

By virtue of the strategic analysis which precedes the formulation of a marketing plan and the selection of a marketing mix the planner/manager will have already established the market segment to be addressed, and the manner in which his brand(s) is to be positioned within that segment. As a consequence, he should have a clear picture of the intended audience, of the benefits which are important to that audience, of their present purchasing behaviour and their reaction to price inducements. In other words, whether through market research and/or prior experience the manager will have considerable information on the other major elements of the marketing mix – product, place and price.

While this might appear to make advertising something of a residual requiring much less attention than the weighty consideration given to, say, product development, this is very far from the case. In *Competitive Marketing* O'Shaughnessy[13] illustrates this forcefully in a table which is reproduced as Table 17.2.

With six major factors – Target audience, Goals (objectives), Message appeal, Message format, Media and Vehicle mix and Scheduling – and the major elements associated with each O'Shaughnessy offers 4,320 different combinations and permutations. If we were to include the 63 Advertising objectives set out in Table 17.1 in place of O'Shaughnessy's four 'goals' then the options would escalate to 68,040 and this is long before one begins to choose between different media.

Table 17.2   Advertising Strategy

Target → audience	Goals →	Message → appeal	Message → format	Media and → vehicle mix	Scheduling
Consumers/ customers	Convert Increase	Unique selling proposition	Dogmatic Emotional	TV Radio	Concentrated Continuous
Gatekeepers	Attract	(USP)	Reason-	Direct ad.	Intermittent
Opinion leaders	Maintain	Image Positioning	giving	Magazines Newspapers	
Others		*vis-à-vis* competition Buying criteria Others		Outdoor	

Source: John O'Shaughnessy, *Competitive Marketing: a Strategic Approach* (Boston: George Allen & Unwin, 1984).

Given this level of complexity it is unsurprising that the development of advertising campaigns is almost invariably delegated to the specialist advertising agencies which have developed to fill this function. In terms of O'Shaughnessy's table it is likely that the advertiser's primary input will be the articulation of the specific goals or objectives which he hopes to achieve with secondary inputs on the characteristics of the target audience and the factors which will have a bearing upon the message appeal such as their positioning *vis-à-vis* the competition, buying criteria, etc. The remaining activities are sufficiently complex to require weighty textbooks in their own right (see recommendations in the Notes & References to Chapter 7, p. 539). For a broadly based description of the advertising industry, agency selection, the characteristics of various advertising media the reader should consult Chapter 16 in *Marketing* (5th edn, 1991).

Before leaving the subject of promotional strategy it is important to reiterate the point made at the end of the preceding section, namely that promotion will play a major role in:

1 Creating awareness.
2 Conditioning perceptions (of the facts).
3 Suggesting subjective associations and benefits which will prove determinant when there is apparent objective parity between two or more competing alternatives.

It follows that promotion, and advertising particularly, are likely to be of lesser importance in industrial than in consumer markets. The survey by Hooley *et al.*

into UK marketing practices on behalf of the Institute of Marketing[14] confirmed that amongst the industrial respondents Advertising and Promotion were ranked least important of the eleven factors considered most important in gaining business in their market (see Table 17.3). However, Company/Brand Reputation was ranked fourth and clearly depends upon promotional activities, which leads Lynch and Hooley to observe that the importance of promotion may have been underestimated in the industrial marketing mix (as has marketing research!).

Table 17.3   The most important factors in gaining business in this market

	% first or second most important (N = 536)
Pricing	53.5
Product performance	47.1
Quality	43.1
Company/Brand reputation	26.1
Selling	24.8
Product design	18.6
Distribution	17.9
Service	17.4
Finance	10.1
Prior marketing research	8.5
Advertising and promotion	5.8

Source: Graham J. Hooley, Christopher J. West and James E. Lynch, *Marketing Management Today* (Cookham: Institute of Marketing, 1983).

■ Setting the Advertising Budget

Empirical observation indicates that firms use one or other of five basic approaches to setting the advertising budget. These may be characterised as:

- Percentage of sales.
- Competitive parity.
- What we can afford.
- Fixed sum per unit.
- Task and objective.

The variety of methods in use arises largely from the fact that, while ultimately advertising is intended to increase sales or, at worst, prevent one's competitors from reducing them, it is almost impossible to develop a direct measure of the advertising to sales effect. (The obvious exception is direct-mail advertising.)

In his book[15] Dr Simon Broadbent recommends that the advertiser should seek to answer four questions when setting a budget:

1   What can the product afford?
2   What is the advertising task?
3   What are competitors spending?
4   What have we learned from previous years?

As Broadbent notes, one or other of these questions will usually dominate and so give rise to one or other of the basic approaches listed above. But, that said, there is considerable merit in seeking to answer each of the questions as objectively as possible as a cross-check on their relative importance.

With regard to the question of what a product can afford Broadbent emphasises the intrinsic paradox when he says 'the advertising budget is often based on a sum which assumes that sales are fixed – yet the object after advertising is to affect this sales figure'. Another common and dangerous assumption is that advertising expenditures are a residual on-cost with the result that advertising expenditures are seen as having a much more direct influence on profit than do other costs and so become more vulnerable to cutting, as profits come under pressure which may be precisely the time when increased advertising effort is called for. Of course cash availability must represent the ultimate constraint on what the product can afford, but, as we noted previously, the assessment of cash availability is likely to be very different if one considers that advertising is a long-term investment in market share as opposed to a short-run, variable and residual marketing expense.

With regard to the question of the advertising task this should be the outcome of a careful analysis of the role promotion is to play in the overall marketing mix which will be strongly influenced by our knowledge of the way advertising works and the particular context in which it is to be used. Taken together these considerations will lead to the formulation of advertising objectives, in the manner discussed in the previous section, which Broadbent sees as leading to three specific questions:

1   What media are likely to be chosen?
2   At what cost do they reach the target?
3   What number of exposures to the target might achieve the specified effect?

Clearly, what is required here is a broad-brush review of the key characteristics of the various media available as a basis for selecting between them rather than the preparation of a detailed media plan which is the responsibility of the advertising manager and the agency within the policy guidelines contained in the marketing strategy. A much-simplified resume of the main features of the major media is contained in Table 17.4:

The third question 'of competitive parity' is often regarded as a 'cop out', but, as Broadbent[16] explains, knowledge of competitors' advertising spend is a vital input to one's own thinking. First, there is the crude but useful rule-of-thumb that: 'the sales expected for our product are the same share of the market as our advertising share'. Certainly if all the advertisers use a percentage of sales and/or

Table 17.4   Strengths and weaknesses of major media

	Strengths	*Weaknesses*
	Television	
	Broad reach	Little demographic selectivity
	Creative opportunities for demonstration	Commercial clutter
	Immediacy of messages	Short advertising life of message
	Entertainment carryover	Decreased viewing in summer
	A compelling medium	Some consumer skepticism towards claims made
	Negotiable costs	High cost
	Frequent messages	
Network	Association of prestige with programming	Long-term advertiser commitments
Local	Geographic selectivity	High reach more difficult on independent stations
	Association with programs of local origin and appeal	High cost for broad geographic coverage
	Short notice to schedule	Ad can be preempted
	Radio	
	Low cost	No visual treatment
	High frequency	Short advertising life of message
	Immediacy of message	Background sound
	Short notice to schedule	Commercial clutter
	Relatively no seasonal change in audience	
	Highly portable medium	
	Negotiable costs	
	Short-term advertiser commitments	
	Entertainment carryover	
Network	Lower absolute cost for national coverage	Difficult to accumulate reach of a large audience
		No geographic flexibility
		Limited demographic selectivity
		Limited programming variety
		Clearance problems
		Variation in audience by market
Local	Excellent demographic selectivity	High cost for broad geographic coverage
	Good geographic flexibility	
	Personality identification	
	Magazines	
	Good reproduction, especially color	Long-term advertiser commitments
	Permanence of message	Slow audience build-up

Strengths	Weaknesses

Magazines

Demographic selectivity, reaches affluent audience	Limited demonstration capacities
Regional	Less compelling than other major media like television
Local market selectivity	Lack of urgency
Special-interest possibilities	Long closing dates
Readership not seasonal	Not a frequency medium (unless used specially with multiple units in same issue)
Relatively long advertising life (one week, one month)	
Informational	
Editorially compatible environment	
Secondary readership	
Merchandising programs	

Newspapers

Geographic selectivity and flexibility	Little demographic selectivity
Short-term advertiser commitments	High absolute costs for national representation
News value and immediacy	Limited color facilities
Advertising permanence	Variable color reproduction
Readership not seasonal	Different local and national rates
High individual market coverage	Little secondary readership
Local retailer-dealer identification	
Merchandising programs	
Short closing	

Source: S. R. Fajen, 'More for Your Money from the Media', *Harvard Business Review* (September–October 1978).

fixed sum per unit approach to budgeting this will be the case. Second, an analysis of competitive expenditure will often reveal that there is an accepted ratio of advertising to sales, although this ratio is likely to vary according to the market structure and one's competitive standing, i.e. a dominant market leader will usually experience scale effects for his advertising while a small adversary will have to accept a higher advertising to sales spend in order to achieve a minimum threshold level of advertising. Of course it is always possible that the market leader will use a similar advertising: sales ratio as his smaller competitors as both a competitive weapon and a barrier to entry. Irrespective of whether you are a leader or a follower, knowledge of one's competitors' promotional strategy is a vital input to one's own planning.

Finally, there is the important question of what have we learned from previous years. By now the reader will be more than familiar with my overriding belief that a great deal of marketing can be explained in terms of a relatively small number of options or alternatives. The difficulty, challenge and excitement of managing the marketing function arises from the contextual complexity in which the variables interact and the speed with which these variables change. Thus, while it is possible to develop useful generalisations about decisions and courses of action, detailed planning and implementation must always be situation-specific and so will depend upon the experience of the manager in his particular industry/market. It follows, therefore, that decisions on future advertising strategy and expenditure should be heavily influenced by our highly specific past experience. Broadbent goes further and advocates that not only should one use previous experience as a guideline for future action, but one should actively experiment with different advertising 'treatments' to determine their effectiveness.

Ideally the provision of answers to our four questions should result in the setting of an appropriation which corresponds to the task and objective method which most authors (including myself) advocate as the most effective method. Essentially the task and objective approach consists of a series of iterations whereby the decision-maker:

1 Sets an objective
2 Specifies what is necessary to achieve this in terms of media coverage and cost
3 Compares the theoretically desirable budget with the resources actually available
4. If compatible → implement
   If *not* compatible:
   Either   – Revise the objective
   And/or – Secure new resources

As noted at the beginning of this section such a procedure may still result in the advertiser selecting, say, 'competitive parity' as his key decision factor and claiming to budget on this basis. Therefore one should be careful not to dismiss the method as lacking in objectivity until one has determined what other considerations were taken into account.

In 1985 Hooley and Lynch published findings with specific references to advertising derived from their major survey of UK marketing practice and performance. In their article, entitled 'How UK Advertisers Set Budgets',[17] the authors were concerned to establish whether a trend towards more sophisticated methods could be discerned, as it had been in the USA. The data speak for themselves and are reproduced in Tables 17.5 –17.8 below.

Clearly, the firms in this sample are making extensive use of the more sophisticated methods, and the use of such methods is highest in the larger and better performing companies. As the authors acknowledge while the 'age-old causality dilemma' exists, the results do tend to suggest that a more sophisticated approach to setting advertising budgets gives rise to improved performance.

Table 17.5   Methods used to set advertising budgets

	Use regularly (%)	Have tried it (%)	Heard of but never used (%)	Never heard of or no reply (%)
What we can afford	48.5	16.6	10.8	24.2
Objective and task	39.8	13.4	15.0	31.9
Percentage of expected sales	38.4	15.7	21.2	24.8
Experimentation	13.6	20.9	28.5	37.1
Desired share of voice	11.4	12.0	27.8	48.7
Match competition	8.3	15.5	39.8	36.4
Accept agency proposal	4.2	19.9	35.4	40.5

Figures are row percentages

Source: J. Hooley and G. Lynch, 'How UK Advertisers Set Budgets', *International Journal of Advertising*, 4 (1985).

Table 17.6   Method of setting advertising budget related to company size

Method used regularly	*Sample*	*Small*	*Medium*	*Large*
What we can afford	48.5%	45.5% (94)	47.8% (99)	52.4% (108)
Objective and task	39.8%	30.1% (76)	38.3% (96)	50.0% (126)
Percentage of expected sales	38.4%	32.6% (85)	38.8% (101)	45.1% (117)
Experimentation	13.6%	13.7% (101)	10.2% (75)	17.0% (125)
Desired share of voice	11.4%	5.7% (50)	9.5% (83)	19.2% (168)
Match competition	8.3%	5.3% (64)	5.6% (67)	13.7% (165)
Accept agency proposal	4.2%	2.5% (60)	4.1% (98)	5.5% (131)
Number of companies	1670	525	588	548
No reply	105			

Size definitions used were:

Small   – turnover less than £2.5m.
Medium – turnover £2.5–£20m.
Large   – turnover over £20m.

Percentage figures refer to column percentages.
Figures in parentheses are index figures based on the 'sample' column.

Source: J. Hooley and G. Lynch, 'How UK Advertisers Set Budgets', *International Journal of Advertising*, 4 (1985).

Table 17.7   Method of setting advertising budget related to product category

Method used regularly	Sample	Consumer durables	Fast-moving consumer goods	Repeat industrial goods	Capital industrial goods	Service
What we can afford	48.8%	48.6% (100)	51.7% (106)	55.0% (113)	52.6% (108)	41.8% (86)
Objective and task	39.6%	39.8% (101)	44.9% (113)	37.6% (95)	43.5% (110)	35.8% (90)
Percentage of expected sales	38.3%	55.1% (144)	57.7% (151)	31.3% (82)	35.9% (94)	28.7% (75)
Experimentation	13.7%	12.5% (91)	19.1% (139)	7.4% (54)	7.2% (53)	17.0% (124)
Desired share of voice	11.5%	9.3% (81)	22.5% (192)	6.3% (40)	3.8% (67)	11.3% (96)
Match competition	8.5%	6.9% (81)	16.3% (192)	3.4% (40)	5.7% (67)	8.2% (96)
Accept agency proposal	4.3%	1.4% (33)	5.6% (130)	5.4% (126)	3.3% (77)	4.1% (95)
Number of companies	1690	216	356	351	209	558
No reply	85					

Percentage figures refer to column percentages.
Figures in parentheses are index figures based on the 'Sample' column.

Source: J. Hooley and G. Lynch, 'How UK Advertisers Set Budgets', International Journal of Advertising, 4 (1985).

Table 17.8　Method of setting advertising budget related to profit margin achieved

Method used regularly	Sample	Negative	Low	Average	High
What we can afford	49.0%	59.2%	53.4%	45.4%	41.7%
		(121)	(109)	(93)	(85)
Objective and task	39.4%	33.3%	31.1%	41.1%	51.2%
		(85)	(79)	(104)	(130)
Experimentation	12.3%	10.3%	11.7%	12.5%	13.9%
		(84)	(95)	(102)	(113)
Number of companies	1386	213	412	423	338
No reply	389				

Profit margins definitions used were:

Negative – company made a loss.
Low – less than 4 per cent.
Average – 4–9.9 per cent.
High – 10 per cent or more.

Percentage figures refer to column percentages.
Figures in parentheses are index figures based on the 'Sample' column.
389 companies (22 per cent) refused to give profit or turnover figures. All percentages and index figures are based only on those companies that did supply these data.

Source:　J. Hooley and G. Lynch, 'How UK Advertisers Set Budgets', *International Journal of Advertising*, 4 (1985).

■ Measuring Advertising Effectiveness

Given the specification of clear advertising objectives and the allocation of a budget for their achievement it is only natural that one should seek to measure how effective the advertising has actually been in securing the desired results. That said, the preceding examination of how advertising works should have made it clear that this is a subject in its own right and that we can only scratch the surface here.

At the outset it is important to distinguish between pre-testing and post-testing promotion, as these have quite different roles to play. As the term suggests, pre-testing is used to try and establish the effectiveness of one or more elements of the promotional method prior to its full-scale use with the target audience, while post-testing seeks to quantify the extent to which the advertising objective has actually been achieved after implementation of the promotional programme.

The benefits and value of pre-testing were suggested in our earlier example of the nature of selective perception (Chapter 7, p. 169) in which it was shown that a campaign conceived to encourage parents not to smoke in front of children was not perceived as conveying this message by members of the target audience. Indeed it was a demonstration of the singular lack of effectiveness of this expensive and highly-thought-of (by health educationalists and other advertising professionals) campaign established by post-testing, which convinced the sponsors of the very real benefits which could accrue from pre-testing on a small scale. Thus, in advocating the task-and-objective approach pre-testing would have an important role to play in specifying precisely what message and media would provide the most cost-effective way of realising the overall objective.

With regard to post-testing the major decision will revolve around what is an appropriate measure of the agreed objective. As we have seen, the most frequently desired objectives will tend to correspond closely with our perception of the prospect's location on our hierarchy and our attempt to move them towards the ultimate goal of a satisfied repeat purchaser:

- Awareness   =   Recall product identity
- Interest   =   Recall advertising content
- Desire   =   Attitudes
    Buyer intentions
- Action   =   Purchase/Sales
    Reinforcement.

For a low-involvement product then perhaps our hierarchy would appear as:

- Awareness   =   Subconscious knowledge =
    recognition at p.o.s.
- Interest   =   Trial = sale and conscious use of advertising
- Desire   =   Beliefs about product
    Repeat purchase = reinforcement
- Action   =   Habitual behaviour
    Brand loyalty = reinforcement

With regard to specific measures of sales, attitudes, beliefs, behavioural interest, awareness and recall, Corkindale and Kennedy[18] provide the following very useful summary table (Table 17.9).

A new and sophisticated approach to measuring advertising effectiveness was reported in May 1990 when AGB announced a new development which it claimed could demonstrate not only whether a particular TV campaign had worked, but which viewers bought more products as a result of the advertising and how the budget should be deployed to bring the best sales results.[19] AGB's claim is based on the use of technique called *data fusion* which involves the integration of two existing data sources. Ideally the answer to many research questions is to use single-source data, in which a representative sample of consumers can be surveyed in terms of their purchasing behaviour related to their reading, viewing

Table 17.9   Means of assessment of advertising objectives

SALES

Own – ex factory
Sales of complementary products
Audits – home (and/or diaries)
● Outlets
Total marketing – via DTI
　　　　　　　– via pooling of all makers
Share – via own ÷ total, from published total,
　　　or pooling by all manufacturers
Share of sales through own outlets
Gains/loss special panel analysis
Penetration surveys
Special analysis of panel data (lapsed users, etc.)
Omnibus – surveys to measure 'trial'
Cost per item sold

TRADE

● Special investigation of dealer behaviour
● Trade survey (of attitudes)
● Monitor dealer response
● Salesmen's reports
● Interim comparison (of outlet's performance)

ATTITUDES

● Usage and attitude surveys
● Surveys for advertising model (St James)
● Syndicated attitude survey (API)
● Corporate image survey
● Image study

BEHAVIOUR

● U & A survey by research agency
● Survey of buyer behaviour by own field force

ADVERTISING CONTENT

● 24-hour recall
● Omnibus – on recall
● Recall survey
● Shopper survey of awareness

CONSUMER REACTION

　　　　　　　　　　　　　 formative
● Discussion groups
　　　　　　　　　　　　　 evaluative
● Depth interview
● Pre-test
● Post-test – product orientated
● Letters from consumers

AUDIENCE ACHIEVEMENT

● Media research (before)
● TV ratings achieved
● Press – forecast OTS
● Cost/1000 – forecast
　　　　　　　　– actual
● Reading and noting scores
● Comparative expenditures (MEAL)

EXPERIMENTAL AREAS

● Advertising weight tests via area tests
● Advertising content tests via area tests

COUPON RESPONSE

Coupon enquiry

Source: D. Corkindale and S. Kennedy, *The Evaluation of Advertising Objectives*, Marketing
　　　Communications Research Centre, Cranfield School of Management, Report 10
　　　(November 1974).

and listening habits. However, attempts by Central Adlab and Neilsen and
HTV's Statscan to set up sufficiently large panels to provide such data proved to
be prohibitively expensive, and had to be abandoned.

To overcome this problem BMRB launched its Target Group Ratings service in
April 1990 which is based on the fusion of TGI (which measures product usage)
and BARB (which measures viewing). The aim of Target Group Ratings is to
enable advertising agencies to plan campaigns more accurately by selecting
programmes watched by the users of their products rather than by more broadly
defined demographic groups. However, the AGB service differs in that its

primary purpose is to aid campaign evaluation by quantifying the effect of advertising on sales.

The AGB method also uses BARB data, but fuses it with information from its own TCA panel which measures product purchases in 6,500 homes. *Marketing Week*[20] reported:

> By developing a computer model of TV viewing behaviour, based on the individual viewing patterns of housewives on the BARB panel, AGB can now predict when an individual housewife on the TCA panel is likely to be watching ITV or Channel 4. From this, it can work out the number of times she is likely to have seen a particular commercial.

The model depends on certain key demographic characteristics and viewing claims, such as the fact that non-working women are much more likely to watch TV during the day than those who are out at work.

In a test on a new fmcg the fusion model showed that among heavy viewers who saw a commercial an average of 8.6 times their purchases increased by 44 per cent compared with an increase of only 29 per cent by light viewers who saw the commercial on average 2.7 times during the campaign. The analysis also showed that advertising primarily increased trial of the brand and sales to occasional buyers rather than increasing the purchase rate of regular buyers, demonstrating that the ads were much more effective with some demographic groups than others.

Clearly such results are very promising but, as *Marketing Week* cautions, they also depend heavily on the judgement and integrity of the researcher. Only when sufficient case histories are available will it be able to assess fully the potential of data fusion as a means of both campaign planning and measuring advertising effectiveness by merging existing data bases.

■ Summary

Like distribution, promotion and particularly mass-media advertising, is often regarded as a cost-creating function which adds little or nothing to the value of the product. In Chapter 17 we have sought to dispel this misconception by showing that not only is advertising the most cost-effective means of informing potential consumers about the existence of a product and generating interest in it, but it also adds value by enhancing the subjective merits of the product or service.

To this end we have reviewed the nature of the communication process and examined alternative explanations of the way in which advertising is claimed to work. While research indicated a low correlation between attitudes and behaviour (which are central to the traditional hierarchical models of advertising effect) it was suggested that this may be due to the fact that much of the reported research has been concerned with what Krugman[21] termed 'low-involvement goods'. Accordingly, our own preference was to accept the model proposed by

Joyce[22] in 1967 which recognises that while advertising may 'work' in a number of different ways, attitudes play an important role and are susceptible to influence through advertising.

Following a discussion of how individuals use selective perception, attention and retention to survive in an over-communicated society, considerable attention was given to the selection of promotion objectives as an essential precursor to setting the advertising budget. Five basic approaches to the latter problem were proposed and complemented by a summary of methods for estimating how effective such expenditure had been.

Part III

IMPLEMENTING MARKETING

Service

Learning Goals

The issues to be addressed in Chapter 18 include:

1 The *nature* and *scope* of customer service.
2 The *strategic use* of service.
3 The concept of *Total Quality Management* (TQM).
4 The *pricing* of services
5 The *measurement* of service *quality*.
6 Service as a *marketing strategy*.

After reading Chapter 18 you will be able to:

1 Define and describe the *nature* of customer service.
2 Explain how customer services can be classified as *pre-transactional*, *transactional* or *post-transactional* and the uses of this classification.
3 Suggest how service activities may be used strategically to *differentiate* and *position* products and services.
4 Define the concept of *TQM* and discuss some of the issues and problems associated with its implementation.
5 Suggest how to *price* services.
6 Discuss how to *measure* service *quality*.
7 Illustrate, through a case study example, how service may be used in formulating a *marketing strategy*.

Introduction

In the first edition (1985) we wrote:

> In our model of buyer behaviour no explicit reference was made to the role of service in motivating specific choice decisions. Similarly, little direct reference is to be found to customer service in the major marketing textbooks although it is frequently mentioned in connection with specific marketing activities – particularly physical distribution. However, in an increasingly competitive environment it seems reasonable to assume that as the potential for product differentiation is eroded one should

give added consideration to the provision of services which will enhance both the physical performance of products and their perceived value in the customer's eyes. Even more important, through the provision of support services the supplier has the opportunity to increase the strength of the bond with his existing customers and so reduce the risk of their 'switching' to alternative suppliers.[1]

In reviewing these words in the early 1990s it is clear that this was a prophetic forecast as customer service (CS) and its associated Total Quality Management (TQM) are high (if not top) of most companies' agendas. As predicted, the erosion of physical differences between competing products has required customers to depend increasingly upon a broader definition of 'fitness for purpose' which embraces the services associated with the purchase and consumption of a product or service. (It should be noted here that we are not concerned with the marketing of services *per se* which has become a fashionable sub-field of marketing in its own right – see Chapter 23 in *Marketing*, 5th edn, 1991,[2] but with service as an element of the marketing mix.) Customer concern with the *augmented product*, which includes the associated service elements, has resulted in a spate of publications dealing specifically with service as an intrinsic element of the firm's competitive offering. It follows that while the inclusion of such a chapter was commented on by reviewers of the first edition as an 'innovation' it now represents but a brief introduction to an extensive literature. Hopefully, it covers the key issues and will encourage reference to the specialist texts by those who are persuaded that Service, like Marketing Research, must be added to the simpler 4 Ps version of the marketing mix when devising successful marketing strategies.

In Chapter 18 we provide a brief review of the ways in which service activities may be used to enhance consumer/user satisfaction for both products and services. The chapter opens with some definitions of customer services and with consideration of the view that such services may be associated with three distinct phases of the buying process – pre-sale, sale and post-sale. The scope for customer service in both the industrial and consumer market will be examined, together with an evaluation of the use of service at both the strategic and tactical level, in which it will be examined as part of the broader Total Quality Management concept. The chapter concludes with a discussion of pricing services and measuring service quality.

■ The Nature of Customer Service

As noted in the Introduction, until recently comparatively little attention has been given to the role of customer service, with the result that there are no definitive statements as to the nature and scope of its functions. In one of the few British books on the subject Christopher *et al.*[3] define customer service as *'a system organised to provide a continuing link between the time that the order is placed and the goods are received with the objective of satisfying customer needs on a long-term basis'* (emphasis in original). Many would consider this too narrow a definition, as it excludes the fact that the provision of services may be highly instrumental to the actual placing of an order. This view would seem to be shared by an American Management Association Research Study[4] in which the authors comment: 'Many buyers today regard service support as a major criterion for vendor selection.'

To some extent this lack of agreement probably arises from the fact that many customer services are inextricably linked with other aspects of the marketing function and so are not seen to enjoy an existence apart from that function. For example, the provision of pre-sale information may properly be considered part of the promotion variable and seen as the responsibility of the salesman or the advertising function. Indeed the very title of Christopher *et al.*'s book links service with distribution.

However, the evidence from the AMACOM study shows clearly that product servicing is already a major and often independent function in its own right and is likely to assume even greater importance in future. On the first point Blenel and Bender state that 'More people in the United States today are engaged in technical and customer service than in industrial sales, with service organisations ranging in size from the independent repair person to corporate divisions with tens of thousands of employees' (p. 12). With regard to the second point the authors draw attention to the fact that the increased technological sophistication of many capital goods is now so great that it is beyond the competence of the user's own technicians and that he has to depend upon the manufacturer to supply the necessary service. Such dependency is clearly to the supplier's advantage and has become a deliberate policy of many manufacturers.

The broadened perspective of customer service is reflected strongly in Blenel and Bender's statement of the basic goals of service which they see as threefold:

'The first mission of service is to protect the company's customer base', a task which it accomplishes by ensuring that goods and services are delivered on time and in accordance with specification and supply and continue to supply those benefits for which they are purchased in the first place.

As noted previously, 'Service's second mission is to enhance the product's saleability, since product performance alone is no longer the only consideration of most purchasers. Many buyers today regard service support as a major criterion for vendor selection. If technology, price, delivery, and quality are comparable among vendors, *service can be the determining factor*. It can play a major role in keeping a company competitive, especially as it affects life-cycle costing and product life.' (p. 17, emphasis mine).

'The third mission of service, from the marketing perspective, is to generate income.' Blenel and Bender comment that while many services such as installation, maintenance, training, etc., were often provided at no charge, revenues from such activities can now account for up to 30% of a corporation's total revenue. Of course such services were never provided 'free', but were built into the original price to the benefit of the less-efficient and less well-organised firm and the detriment of those with better internal standards of training and maintenance. By costing these services separately the supplier is able to build up a much better understanding of his customers and concentrate on those who offer the best prospects for a mutually satisfactory long-run relationship. We return to this issue later.

It is clear that, stated in these terms, customer services are equally relevant to both consumer and industrial products, although in general the latter are emphasised more than the former. In my opinion this is due more to organisational convenience than any basic difference between the two categories of goods. As a working generalisation the more complex the product the longer its working life and the greater the financial outlay upon it the greater the need for customer service from which it follows that consumer durables like cars, washing-machines and televisions will need attention just as much as fork-lift trucks, pickling plants and computer display terminals. Similarly the major determinant of whether or not a firm will provide service directly to customers will depend upon much the same considerations that govern its choice of channel of distribution. (Indeed the close link between service and physical distribution strategies is apparent throughout Christopher *et al.*'s book.)

Accordingly, rather than preserve the traditional dichotomy between industrial and consumer goods which is supported by Blenel and Bender, we prefer to follow the distinctions based upon performance characteristics and user needs that has underlain all our analysis so far. By doing so it becomes possible to see how merchandising has been developed by manufacturers as a major service function which provides additional benefits to the retailer, who is his immediate customer, while enabling the producer to ensure that his products are displayed to the best advantage at the point of sale. Further, by following such an approach it is likely that consumer goods manufacturers will be encouraged to consider the experience of their industrial counterparts when assessing the contribution service policy may make to marketing strategy for consumer goods markets.

■ The Scope of Customer Service

Having advocated that conceptually it is not advantageous to compartmentalise marketing when considering customer service *policy* it is clear that the scope of the service function will differ considerably according to the context. This variation is illustrated well in the two organisation charts reproduced as Figures 18.1 and 18.2, which relate to durable and consumer goods respectively.

LaLonde and Zinszer[5] suggest a useful approach to classifying the elements of the service function when they assign them to the pre-transaction elements, the transaction elements and the post-transaction elements. As summarised by Christopher *et al.* these are:

> The *pre-transaction elements* of customer service relate to corporate policies or programmes, e.g. written statements of service policy, adequacy of organisational structure and system flexibility.

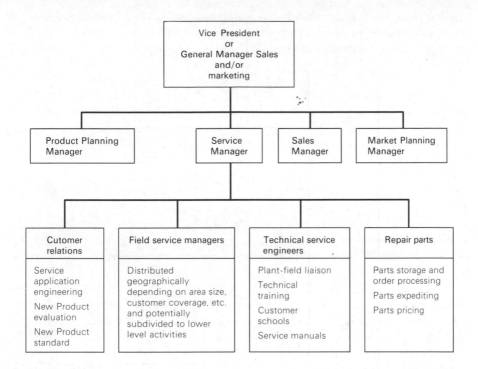

Figure 18.1 Composite service organisation for durable goods industries

Source: Reprinted from Thomas A. Gannon, ed., *Product Services Management* (New York: American Management Association, 1972) p. 76.

The *transaction elements* are those customer service variables directly involved in performing the physical distribution function. The most commonly quoted elements within this group are:

1 Product availability.
2 Order cycle time – average and consistency.
3 Order status information.
4 Order preparation.
5 Order size and order frequency.

The *post-transaction elements* of customer service are generally supportive of the product while in use. For instance, product warranty, parts and repair service, procedures for customer complaints, and product replacements.

As noted, we would wish to extend the pre-transaction elements to incorporate the provision of services which will predispose the prospective user to buy from the source providing the service. Thus many companies will supply information

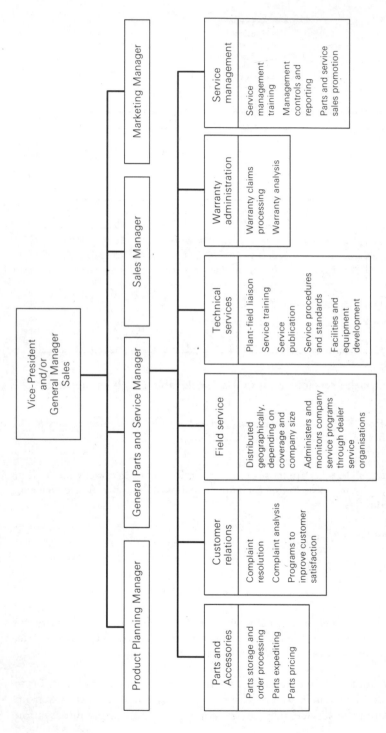

Figure 18.2 Composite service organisation for consumer goods industries

Source: Reprinted from T. A. Gannon (ed.) *Product Services Management* (New York: American Management Association, 1972) p. 76.

and advice to inquirers free of charge even though they may not have purchased the company's brand of product to which the information relates, e.g. data on the use or application of materials such as paints, lubricants, insecticides, etc. Similarly, in both the industrial and consumer markets companies will often undertake survey work to advise potential customers of the benefits which will accrue from purchase, e.g. analysis of office productivity, energy-saving and insulation surveys, need for wood treatment by firms like Rentokil.

A particular example from my own experience selling tin plate supports this point. Tin plate is essentially a homogeneous product manufactured to a precise specification. At the time in question (late 1950s early 1960s) there were only two suppliers in the UK market and the price was fixed with the result that the only factors distinguishing the two suppliers were their marketing and service. Because of the difficulty of achieving a significant long-term advantage on these two dimensions, customers exhibited considerable inertia and adopted the simple purchasing policy of buying from the two companies in proportion to their output – a ratio of 2:1. In the early 1960s demand declined due to competition from new packaging materials, just as new production facilities came on-stream resulting in excess tin-plate capacity and there developed the first real competition between the two suppliers in over twenty years. In this climate I undertook a survey of over 200 specifications used by a major tin-box manufacturer and with the help of the OR section was able to show how these could be reduced to six basic specifications which would cover all the end-use specifications. By doing this the buyer would be able to secure maximum bulk discounts and effect major savings on his raw-material purchases. The company was delighted with this proposal and as a token of its appreciation transferred 50% of its business from our competitor to ourselves.

In addition the promise of service on and after purchase may also be used very effectively to encourage active consideration of a supplier's product and secure it a place on the 'ladder' in the mind of the would-be purchaser. Whether these activities are classified as public relations, advertising, missionary selling or whatever, they clearly comprise elements of customer service and should be treated as such in the development of a service policy.

In the case of LaLonde and Zinszer's 'transaction elements' the emphasis is again on physical distribution elements which are designed to ensure the product is available as and when required. Given the frequently voiced complaints about delays in the delivery of many British manufactured goods in both domestic and foreign markets this aspect of service cannot be emphasised enough. One should also remember our maxim that consumption is a function of availability! However, the importance of physical distribution should not be allowed to distract attention from other important service elements associated with a sale. Of particular importance are:

1 Financing the sale.
2 Installation.
3 Demonstration and/or training in use.

With 'large ticket' items both industrial and consumer buyers may need to spread payments over some future time period. Because of its expertise and knowledge of its prospective customers a manufacturer or distributor may have a much better feel for their creditworthiness than do the traditional sources of credit. Thus the seller may be able to use his own credit rating and his 'bulk borrowing' capacity to offer advantageous credit terms to his customer. In addition the purchaser may find it more convenient to combine the actions of raising credit and completing a purchase into a single transaction. Credit and financing policy may well be the responsibility of the accounting/finance function, but it still comprises an important customer service which needs to be integrated into the firm's marketing strategy.

Installation may be simple – plugging-in an appliance in the home or office – or complex, fitting kitchen units or double glazing, commissioning a power station. Either way the customer benefits from the provision of such a service (which may well be an important source of revenue to the supplier), while the seller has the reassurance that the product is more likely to prove satisfactory when properly installed than would otherwise be the case. Much the same consideration attaches to demonstrating correct usage and providing training where necessary. In the absence of this the customer may well misuse the product and fail to obtain the desired output from it thus increasing the possibility of dissatisfaction and the need for more expensive post-transaction services. (See, for example, the textile machinery cases in *Marketing Development*.)

The provision of services of this kind can do much to reduce the risk perceived by a prospective purchaser and can constitute a major source of preference for one supplier over another.

In the post-transaction stage the seller has a responsibility to ensure that the customer receives the desired and promised benefits. To do so he must establish a mechanism whereby customers may receive advice and service to keep the product working – both of which will have an important effect in reducing post-purchase dissonance and in confirming the buyer in the correctness of his original decision. Such satisfaction will also ensure that the supplier will have a strong likelihood of remaining the preferred source when a replacement decision has to be made.

Suppliers must also develop a policy and mechanism for handling customer complaints. While buyers are offered extensive protection under the law, relatively few will pursue a complaint this far and prefer to adopt the simple expedient of not buying from that source again. In so far that we have defined marketing as 'selling goods that don't come back to people who do' – failure to deal efficiently and sympathetically with complaints amounts to a negation of the marketing concept. Worse still, dissatisfied customers are likely to tell others of their dissatisfaction and negative word-of-mouth can be just as harmful as positive word-of-mouth is helpful.

Evidence to support the view of the negative impact of poor service was provided by an article in *The McKinsey Quarterly*[6] by Daniel Finkelman and

Anthony Goland entitled 'How *not* to satisfy your customers'. The authors' opening paragraph endorsed the views expressed above:

> Today, a company's ability to ensure satisfaction with the entire 'customer owner-ship experience' is critical to its long-term success. As years of investment have, at least, made many firms competitive in both costs and quality, their ability to create a clear advantage based on either has been substantially reduced. Hence, the new battleground for the 1990s: providing the most satisfying ownership experience for customers – from the time shopping begins, to the buying experience itself, to the point of delivery, through the period during which the product is owned and used, and even to the customer's ultimate disposal of the product.

Finkelman and Goland cite numerous studies to support the view that customer satisfaction leads to loyalty and a high likelihood of repurchase while dissatisfied customers are likely not to complain or repurchase. However, if complaints are resolved quickly then the likelihood of repurchase increases dramatically. Figures 18.3 and 18.4 illustrate that 'A large portion of what makes up customer satisfaction for a given company or product may be entirely unrelated to product quality'. Figure 18.5 indicates that, in the case of consumer durable and industrial equipment, if product quality accounts for half of the customer's satisfaction then the remainder is attributable to a variety of service elements.

Detailed discussion of the establishment of such service policies and mechanisms is clearly beyond the scope of this book and the reader should consult the References on pp. 549–50 for information on these.

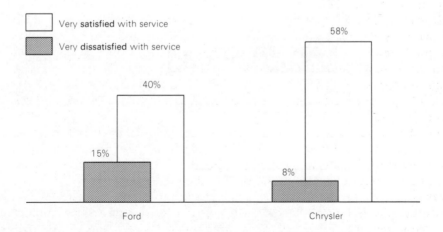

Figure 18.3 Repurchase loyalty to the retailer (new vehicle sales)

Source: McKinsey analysis.

Why industrial companies lose customers

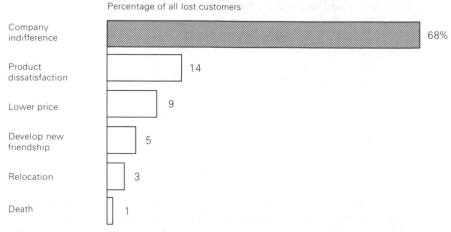

Percentage of all lost customers

Company indifference	68%
Product dissatisfaction	14
Lower price	9
Develop new friendship	5
Relocation	3
Death	1

Why customers purchase from a specific service company

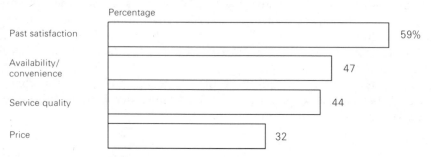

Percentage

Past satisfaction	59%
Availability/ convenience	47
Service quality	44
Price	32

Main reason for switching banks

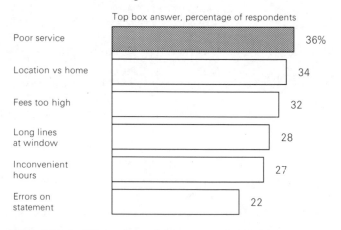

Top box answer, percentage of respondents

Poor service	36%
Location vs home	34
Fees too high	32
Long lines at window	28
Inconvenient hours	27
Errors on statement	22

Figure 18.4   The value of customer satisfaction

Source: McKinsey analysis.

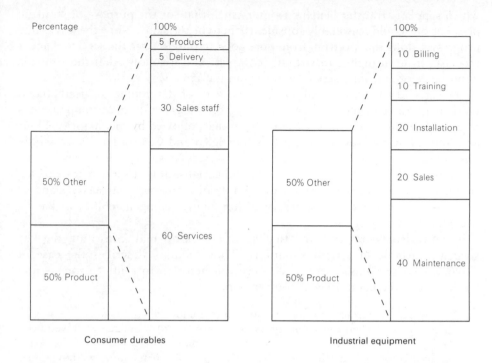

Figure 18.5 The relative importance of customer satisfaction factors

Source: McKinsey analysis.

■ The Strategic Use of Customer Service

In discussing the reasons underlying the growing importance of the service function Blenel and Bender observe that 'Besides technology, there are two other driving forces of service's growth – consumerism and legislation. Consumers today are not only more knowledgeable, they also have more alternatives.'[7]

Consumerism has been characterised, correctly in my view, as 'the shame of marketing' for clearly if suppliers were truly marketing orientated then consumers should have little cause for dissatisfaction with their efforts. By the same token the spate of legislation to protect consumers which has come into existence in recent years in most countries is an indictment of the supplier's willingness to respond voluntarily to such overt dissatisfaction.

Of course ensuring consumer satisfaction starts well before and goes far beyond the provision of customer service in a technical sense. That said, it is clear that, to a lesser or greater extent, the provision of customer service constitutes an integral component of the bundle of benefits anticipated by a purchaser. Thus in Chapter 2 we argued that products and services are part of the same spectrum by which suppliers transfer benefits to users such that for the purpose of strategic planning one could reasonably consider them to be the same. None the less as one progresses along the spectrum from pure good to pure service the service element increases from negligible to virtually complete and it follows that the strategic importance of customer service will vary in the same way.

Having said that it is apparent that one way of developing a differentiated marketing strategy which will set one apart from the general run of competition is to use a different product: service mix from that followed by the majority. Flour and lubricating oil may be pure goods but BeRo and Castrol have successfully positioned themselves by providing advisory services in support of their products. Similarly, as Ted Levitt[8] has shown, the industrialisation of service has enabled suppliers to control and guarantee the quality of many personal services and so enhance their value to consumers (e.g. automatic telling machines in banks, McDonald's hamburgers).

It must also be remembered that service back-up may constitute the key strategic variable in certain situations. Thus Ohmae[9] describes the case of Toyota, who recognised service as a critical factor to fork-lift customers and so chose it as the main basis of competition.

> This was an important strategic decision, since it entailed high fixed costs – so high that Toyota's subcritical competitors could not afford to match its investment. Today Toyota's fork-lift business has an awesome service network; the company boasts that it can despatch a service car to any part of Japan within two hours. As a result, despite its rather conventional product and pricing schemes, Toyota's share of this service hungry industry continues to climb (p. 131).

As with other aspects of marketing planning the critical questions with regard to developing a service strategy are:

1 What do customers want?
2 What do we and our competitors provide?
3 How can we improve our offering and differentiate it from our competitors?
4 What will this cost and what benefits can we anticipate from this?

With regard to the first question Kotler[10] quotes a Canadian survey in which buyers of industrial equipment ranked 13 service elements in the following rank order:

1 Delivery reliability.
2 Prompt quotation.
3 Technical advice.
4 Discounts.
5 After sales service.
6 Sales representation.
7 Ease of contact.
8 Replacement guarantee.
9 Wide range of manufacturers.

10 Pattern design.
11 Credit.
12 Test facilities.
13 Machining facilities,

It is perhaps significant that faced with a list of features in rank order the respondents emphasised general rather than specific service attributes which suggests that only if you perform satisfactorily on these will additional service factors become determinant.

Blenel and Bender[11] take a much broader and pragmatic view and state:

> *What customers want from service.* In the authors' experience, customers differ in what they most value from service. The majority consider that the most important function is to maintain the equipment so it operates well. This implies availability of spare parts, well-trained technicians, up-to-date instruction manuals, and liaison between company and customer.
>
> The next most-valued quality is a continued sales presence after the major sale. All too often service technicians must perform the after-sale function to ensure that the customer has the required re-supply items. To see that the customer gets proper and continued attention, management must make a firm decision on which unit of the company is responsible for a re-supply of expendable materials or parts, else service, unprepared though it may be, can be stuck with the task.
>
> The third most-valued quality is that service be first-rate and that it be easily accessible. The finest advertising campaign cannot convince the public that a sow's ear is a silk purse. Performance, not promise, is what is demanded. Even good equipment is often downgraded unfairly when the service organisation gives it poor support.

From these comments it is clear that one may generalise about the broad dimensions of service, but in the particular the most obvious way to determine what is required and how strong the requirement is (would you pay more for it? How much?) is to undertake research among one's customers and compare the results with the existing provision (Question 2) to see how well they match up. Only when such an analysis has been completed does it become possible to evaluate possible changes in the service strategy.

Based on their research Christopher *et al.* propose six areas in which they believe that customer service decisions differ significantly from other decision areas. While not accepting this view, as several of the 'distinctions' would seem to apply equally to other aspects of marketing, their listing is helpful in specifying factors which must be taken into account when devising a service strategy. It almost goes without saying that '*Customer service is part of the total market offering of the firm*' but the second of their propositions '*Service is perceived asymmetrically; good service is expected as a normal concomitant of business relationships; weak service becomes a highly visible negative signal*' reinforces the importance of giving as much attention to service as to the other elements of the marketing mix and of developing specific service policies.

Another important proposition, which I would qualify with the word '*Often*' is '*Customer service is directly concerned with relationships with market inter-mediary firms, rather than to final customer*'. It follows that the needs of the intermediaries in the distribution channel must be given specific attention, for they may well differ radically from the needs of the final customer and call for distinct service policies for each.

Finally, Christopher *et al.* draw an important distinction between the short- and long-run implications of customer service. In the short run service failures may result only in lost orders due to stock-outs, or to reduced margins because of the need to replace defective parts or offer compensation. In the long run repetition of such failures can put the whole organisation at risk, as customers switch to alternative sources of supply. Conversely, careful attention to service in the short run can be a powerful force in developing habitual buying behaviour and customer inertia. However, such advice begs the question as to precisely what service the supplier should provide and how he should charge for this. Before examining this issue, however, it will be useful to look at service as an integral part of the much wider concept of Total Quality Management.

■ Total Quality Management (TQM)

Total Quality Management (TQM) is well understood as a *vision* or *concept* – the challenge and the difficulty lies in translating it into *action*.

A concern for quality is enlightened self-interest. All the evidence indicates that quality reduces costs, adds value and is often the JND which differentiates between success and failure at the point of sale. Erickson[12] reports the findings of research conducted over the past decade by Opinion Research Corporation which shows that corporations ranking below average on nine key dimensions of perceived quality tend to have far lower price–earning ratios than firms with strong reputations in those areas.

However, the problems with TQM tend to emerge when its principles are extended beyond the 'hard' and objective functions such as manufacturing into the 'soft' areas which involve interpersonal relationships and the provision of services. Erickson argues that 'The way to make quality-improvement effective in such areas as customer service, marketing, and R&D is by having a clearly articulated strategy that ties all these efforts together and focuses the corporation – including top management – on strategic quality improvement. The way to ensure top management's commitment to quality is to embed quality in areas of unquestionable top management priority – the fundamental goals and priorities of the corporation'.

In order to achieve this it is argued that those responsible for the formulation of corporate strategy should change the parameters of the planning matrices which have had such a major influence on strategic business management for the past 20–30 years. Rather than emphasise the dimensions of industry maturity and competitive position (refined during the 1980s by the inclusion of concepts of

competitive advantage and intensity) it is proposed that the planning matrix for
the 1990s 'should allow organisations to articulate their objectives against the
level of customer satisfaction that they strive to achieve, as well as how their
competitors respond to similar challenges'.[13] Such a matrix is shown in Figure
18.6

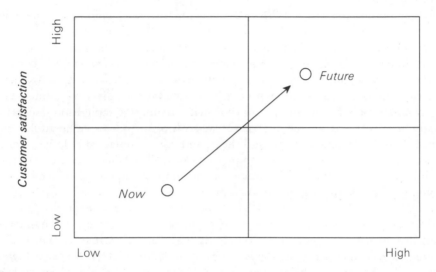

Figure 18.6 A quality-driven planning matrix: strategic response

Source: Tamara J. Erickson, 'Beyond the Quality Revolution: Linking Quality to Corporate
Strategy', *Prism* (First Quarter, 1991).

To use this matrix Erickson suggests the firm should classify and plot the
attributes of its total offering in three major categories – threshold attributes,
performance attributes, and excitement attributes. Performance attributes are
essential aspects of the product or service and, as indicated in our composite
model of choice behaviour on p. 179, will be the primary basis for discriminating
between alternatives, with 'better' performance always being preferred within
any given price bracket. By contrast, threshold attributes are those in which
additional improvements result in little added customer satisfaction and so have
little or no economic value. However, excitement attributes are defined as
'features of a service or product that consumers don't expect and in which a
modest improvement above the competitive norm can provide significantly
enhanced customer satisfaction and economic benefit'.

As the result of competition, performance and excitement attributes (which
may be thought of more as subjective values – BR in our model of choice
behaviour) may lose their distinctiveness and become threshold attributes. As and

when this occurs the firm will have to develop and introduce new attributes if it is to maintain its competitive standing. To achieve this calls for sophisticated measurement techniques and a creative understanding of customers in order to monitor and anticipate change together with tools for quality improvement. As Erickson notes 'Quality improvement tools can play a critical role in helping a firm enhance performance, lower the cost of a product, reduce lead time, and even identify new attributes and opportunities to satisfy the customer, as well as to set priorities'.

Writing in the same issue of *Prism* Diane Schmanlensee[14] emphasises the point that as quality improvement has spread from manufacturing to services so the concept of quality and its measurement have changed. Like 'satisfaction', quality is something particular to the consumer and it is their perception, not the supplier's, which matters. Perceived quality will depend heavily upon expectations such that an organisation with a modest reputation delivering good service may be rated higher than an organisation with a superior reputation delivering equally good service. In the first case expectations, and so value-added, are exceeded; in the second case they fall short, and will be reflected in lower service rating. The challenge is obvious – improved service levels increase expectations and increased expectations call for still further improvements in service levels.

In order to track and respond to customers' expectations and perceptions firms have had to develop a battery of 'soft' measures to complement the familiar 'hard' measures that quantify objective performance measures. Schmanlensee comments: 'A soft measurement is something that cannot be timed or weighed or calibrated. It is neither tangible nor physical. Rather, it is concerned with individual attitudes, beliefs, and opinion. Soft measurement allows you to hear the clear voices of your customers, employees, managers, and intermediaries. And those voices are critical not only in understanding how well you are doing, but also in determining what you should be doing next.'

Of course none of this is new to the marketer, for whom AIO (Attitude, Interest and Opinion) measurement has been a key technique in identifying market opportunities for several decades. What is new is that the Total Quality concept has provided a bridge between the traditionally hard measures of manufacturing and the soft measures of sales and marketing. In doing so, it has underlined the interdependency of the functions, and done much to break down the traditional divisions between them in a less threatening way than was seen to be the case when exhorting companies to become market-orientated.

■ Pricing Services

From the previous section it is evident that certain services may be regarded as an integral part of the product offering and their provision must be regarded as an essential cost of doing business. Clearly, such costs should be incorporated in the selling price, but what criteria should one apply to determine whether services should be priced jointly or separately? James Hauk[15] provides a useful check list:

1   Do customer needs differ significantly?
2   Do needs vary in proportion to the size of the order?
3   What is the magnitude of service cost?
4   Is it to the interest of the seller to have all buyers use the service offered?
5   What is the company's major market target?

Where customer needs are homogeneous it makes sense to incorporate the price of associated services into the price of the product – otherwise one should offer the services separately at a price, i.e. a service contract. Similarly, if the need for service varies with the size of order a joint price will ensure that clients receive what they pay for; if a fixed service is required irrespective of order size it is more equitable to charge for the service separately (or give a discount).

The third criterion seeks to relate the magnitude of the service cost to the total cost. Where this is high those customers who do not need the service would be unlikely to choose a supplier who added the service cost to the product cost and separate pricing would be appropriate. Conversely, where the service costs are small related to total cost, buyers may not perceive them and will be willing to accept a joint price.

In many cases suppliers will wish to install their products and retain responsibility for their maintenance and repair. By incorporating the service price in the selling price the supplier will limit sales to those clients willing to accept these terms and so avoid possible dissatisfaction arising from incorrect installation and maintenance. As noted earlier such a policy also enables the suppliers to develop long-term relationships with their customers and so enhance the likelihood of securing new and/or replacement sales.

Finally, the seller should consider whether the target market is price sensitive – in which case services should be priced separately – or service conscious when joint pricing is to be preferred.

In cases where services are priced separately exactly the same considerations apply as to the pricing of the product itself – namely what is the demand for the service, how price sensitive is it and what are the costs of providing any given level of service? However, one must also allow for the fact that the product and service are in *joint demand* and be prepared to modify the price for one or the other in order to optimise total revenue, e.g. you may install equipment at or below cost if it promises an attractive earnings stream from the long-term supply of services.

■ Measuring Service Quality

In the Spring 1991 edition of *Survey* Diana Brown of the Royal Mail and Roger Banks of Research International described some of the measures used by the Royal Mail to monitor the implementation of its Total Quality Management process 'Customer First'.[16] Unlike many quality assurance programmes 'Customer First' is not concerned solely with the quality of the service itself; it is seen as a way of working throughout the business based on the needs of both *internal* and *external* customers. To measure the effectiveness of this service quality two kinds of indicator are used – hard and soft.

One of the most important 'hard' measures is the End to End (E2E) programme devised by Research International which measures the time taken from pillar box to doormat. This E2E measurement system is able to provide highly localised and diagnostic feedback. However, it measures only one aspect of quality – speed of the delivery. To complement this information Royal Mail also undertakes nation-wide image studies to establish how its customers feel about the business. While this information is helpful in enabling Royal Mail to position itself against other large organisations such as BT and British Gas it is of little practical help to staff in each of Royal Mail's 64 districts around the UK.

In the words of the authors 'What was required was a comprehensive measure of performance on a range of quality issues that actually matter to business and personal customers – a measurement system that operated at the local level. And one which provided clear, unequivocal and practical guidance on how staff could consolidate in areas of strength, and improve in areas of weakness. The name of this measurement system is the Customer Perception Index (CPI)'.

Based upon qualitative group discussions with a cross-section of customers to establish key quality issues a large, nationally representative survey was undertaken to determine their relative importance. The CPI represents the third stage of the research and comprises a continuous mail survey of some 320,400 personal and business customers each year.

Reports of the survey findings are circulated every three months to each of the Districts and covers both hard and soft measures as well as comparative measures relating current to prior performance. What helps distinguish CPI from much similar market research is the effort made to action the findings by providing advice and support to District Head Postmasters so they can apply them at the local level.

■ Service as a Marketing Strategy

Writing in *Industrial Marketing Management* in 1990,[17] M.P. Singh, a business manager for the Reliance Electrical Industrial Co., provides a compelling case history of how his company has used 'offering the best service in the market as its marketing strategy to significantly increase its market share and profitability'. A synopsis of this case history provides a fitting conclusion to this chapter.

This case history reinforces many of the points made thus far. First, and perhaps most important, to succeed in business one must have a competitive edge which enables prospective customers to distinguish and prefer your offering to that of your competitors. Second, in assessing competitive offerings buyers will consider first performance factors and fitness for purpose. Having satisfied themselves that the offering will perform the functions for which it is required, buyers will compare offerings of similar functionality in terms of their cost–

■ Service as a Marketing Strategy

The case study concerns the Mechanical Group of the Reliance Electric Company, a leading supplier of power transmission equipment with world sales in excess of $1.5 billion. The Mechanical Group (MG) manufactures and markets mechanical power transmission products directly to large original equipment manufacturers (OEMs) and select users, and through distributors to other OEMs and users in USA, Canada, Mexico and Brazil. The distributors account for 'an overwhelmingly large portion of the total sales', which are mainly in the US market, and are connected with MG by computers for both information and transaction.

'The severe recession of 1982 in the US industrial economy threw the MG sales into a tailspin, and the bottom line showed big losses'. Singh describes the recession as the culmination of a series of adverse environmental and competitive trends of the kind discussed in Chapters 6 and 10 – particularly technological change and increased international competition. Singh also cites 'The traditional thinking of relating mass production to lower costs' as causing problems for marketers in that it 'resulted in 20%–30% excess capacity throughout the industrial sector of the US'. (Additional evidence that the pursuit of market share can have negative consequences, despite the fact that possession of a dominant share confers significant strategic advantage.)

Singh's analysis also lends support to our composite model of buyer choice behaviour when he distinguishes four stages in the evolution of markets which call for different emphases in marketing strategy as 'different factors assume dominant importance in customer-purchase decisions'. To begin with *technology* is most important but, as technology diffuses and becomes more widely available, so *cost* assumes dominance to be succeeded by *quality* as cost differentials disappear. Finally 'when the market leaders can offer the same (similar) costs and quality, the issue of service emerges as the dominant factor affecting the purchase. Most of today's markets are in this stage now'.

Having taken decisive action to recover from their tailspin through attention to the classic mix elements (downsizing to reduce the break-even point, increased sales and promotional efforts, accelerated plans for product improvement and NPD) MG recognised that something else was required to restore their competitive edge. 'Serving customers better' emerged as the preferred strategy.

To implement this strategy it was necessary first to define what 'Service' is. Based upon feedback from customers and internal consultation MG decided that 'Service could be measured by the ease, speed, and accuracy with which the customers can:

1 Get assistance from any employee.
2 Understand all policies and sales programs.

3   Get all the needed technical information about products and their applications.
4   Get all the needed commercial information.
5   Make the purchase.
6   Update themselves about the status of any order if there are any delays or problems expected with the shipment. (Ideally, there should not be any delays or problems.)
7   Stock and identify the products.
8   Get post-purchase service like credits and return of merchandise, etc.'.

Singh describes how MG developed the practices and procedures necessary to achieve these objectives and the outcomes, which included steady increases in market share, the best profits and ROI for its industry and reported customer perceptions that they delivered the best service in their market.

benefits, i.e. which offering represents the best *value*. If more than one offering passes this test the buyer will have to resort to other less objective criteria in order to decide between the available alternatives. Third, service provides both objective and subjective values and enhances customer satisfaction, leading to preference and loyalty.

Singh's description tends to stress the pre-transaction and transaction elements. While these are vital, we would conclude this chapter by speculating that as more and more companies use service as a strategic element in the marketing mix it will be the post-transactional elements which will become determinant.

■ Summary

As noted in the Introduction to Chapter 18 comparatively little has been written about the role of service as an element in the marketing mix. To some extent this apparent neglect may arise from the fact that many customer services are inextricably linked with other aspects of the marketing function and so are not seen to enjoy an existence separate from that function. While this is undoubtedly true the perspective of this chapter has been that the growing importance of service as a differentiating factor in the firm's strategy is such that it merits explicit treatment in its own right.

Our analysis suggests that service plays an important role in both establishing and sustaining the relationship between supplier and user. Anticipation of the user's needs and the manner in which he will 'consume' the product over time will constitute a vital input to the original design and manufacture of the product. Similarly, advice or assistance with installation and use will increase the likelihood that the product will deliver the promised performance and so provide the satisfaction which the consumer is looking for.

In turn these considerations will have a significant influence upon pricing and distribution decisions – should one set the initial price low and earn one's profits from the provision of service over the product's life-cycle or should one make one's profit on the initial sale and leave the provision of service to a third party? Clearly, there is no single or simple answer to such a question for as our analysis of the other elements of the marketing mix has shown time and again, such decisions tend to be situation-specific. That said, there is considerable evidence to suggest that in many markets, particularly for mature products, the service element will be a major factor in distinguishing between success and failure.

Developing a Marketing Culture

Learning Goals

The issues to be addressed in Chapter 19 include:

1 The relationship between *organisational structure* and *strategy formulation*.
2 The influence of *business functions* on *business orientations*.
3 The concepts of *organisational climate*, *corporate personality* and *culture* as factors affecting business organisation and practice.
4 The development of a *marketing-orientated organisation*.
5 The notions of *corporate vision, mission* and *strategic intent*.
6 *Implementing* marketing.

After reading Chapter 19 you will be able to:

1 Explain why *strategy* should determine organisational structure.
2 Describe the characteristics of the five basic *business orientations* – technology, production, sales, financial and marketing – and how these condition the conduct of the firm's business.
3 Define the concepts of *organisational climate*, *corporate personality* and *corporate culture*, and show how these shape and mediate the firm's strategy and behaviour.
4 Spell out what is involved in the development of a *marketing-orientated organisation*.
5 Explain the need for *vision*, a clear *mission* and *objectives* to clarify and communicate the firm's strategy.
6 Review some of the *obstacles* to the translation of theory into practice through effective implementation.

■ Introduction

In the Prologue (Chapter 1) we expressed the view that while some may still hold to the view that marketing is an art or craft which can be only mastered by experiential learning, the reality is that with increased professionalism there is a distinct need for formal education in the subject. We also argued that with growing recognition of the role of marketing it makes sense to train young people for careers in the function. To do so, it seems sensible to capture the extensive body of knowledge which mirrors the distilled experience of skilled and successful practitioners and record this in texts of this kind which can be used in such education and training. In the preceding chapters this is what we have attempted to do – always recognising that the treatment must be partial and eclectic and can provide only a broad overview of the subject. However, the point has now been reached in which we must address the critical question of how to put this knowledge into practice.

To begin with, it is important to consider the relationship between a firm's *structure* and its *strategy*. As we shall see, ideally, the strategy should dictate the most appropriate organisational form to ensure its effective implementation. However, with the exception of the green-field 'start-up' (which is a basic assumption of the textbook writer) organisations already possess an organisational structure, and the challenge is how to protect, modify or grow them to achieve the organisational purpose. At the outset most organisations' structures are dominated by one or other of the five basic business functions. Accordingly we are accustomed to think of firms as having a predominantly production, finance, sales or whatever orientation. From the outset this book has taken the view that while all the business functions contribute to the firm's performance this will be enhanced if it is marketing-orientated and customer-driven. Peter Doyle (1992)[1] lends considerable support to this view, as well as providing a useful diagram to help distinguish between the financial and marketing orientations. In addressing the question 'What are the excellent companies?' Doyle comments: 'The market-led approach which seeks market leadership through superiority in meeting customer needs is often associated with Japanese companies, the profit-led one with British and US ones', and cites an earlier study in which he found that in answer to the question 'How well does "Good short-term profits are the objective" describe your company?' 87% of British companies and 80% of US companies responded Yes against only 27% of the Japanese companies. The essence of the distinction between a marketing and financial orientation is aptly summarised in Figure 19.1.

The question we address is: how do we diagnose the existence of a particular bias in the firm's orientation? Existence of a dominant bias is reflected in the concepts of corporate climate and personality which, during the 1980s, became increasingly seen as a single phenomenon termed 'corporate culture'. We look at all three concepts as the basis for suggesting how one might develop a marketing-orientated organisation. Central to this objective is the articulation of a broad vision to which the members of the organisation can subscribe, and its translation into a clear mission and specific objectives which will guide and motivate them.

Finally, we explore some of the issues to be faced in implementing marketing.

460

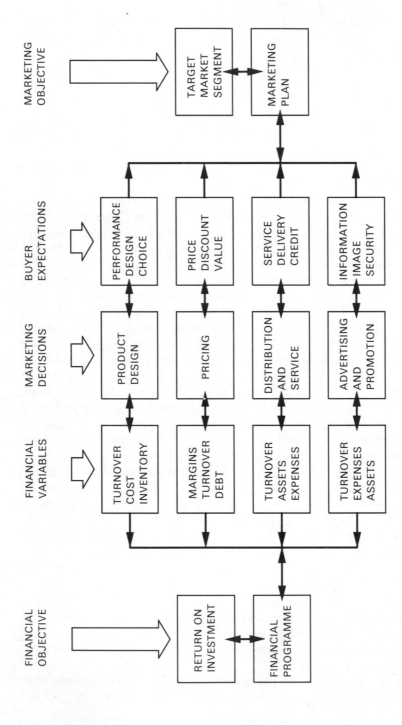

Figure 19.1 Financial vs marketing orientations

Source: P. Doyle, 'What are the excellent companies?', *Journal of Marketing Management*, 8 (2) (April 1992).

■ Organising for Marketing

The question of whether an organisation's strategy should dictate its structure or whether its structure should dictate its strategy has been the subject of much discussion between academics and practitioners alike. As with most debates, polarisation of the issues is a useful if not necessary step to tease out and make clear the arguments for and against the respective positions. In the strategy v. structure argument one of the leading exponents, if not the initiator of the debate, is Alfred Chandler Jr, whose seminal contribution – *Strategy and Structure: chapters in the history of the American industrial enterprise*[2] – has provided the stimulus for extensive inquiry into the issue. As Baligh and Burton[3] note in their very useful review of the impact of the marketing concept on the organisation's structure, 'Chandler presented the original ideas'.

In our definitions of SMP in Chapter 4 we have already cited Chandler's definition of strategy, viz: 'Strategy can be defined as the determination of the basic long-term goals and objectives of an enterprise; and the adoption of courses of action and allocation of resources necessary for carrying out these goals.' As Baligh and Burton note, this definition (along with most others) reflects 'an outside orientation for choosing what to do, i.e. which products or services to provide and how to market them'. In other words a marketing orientation. Baligh and Burton continue to cite Chandler's definition of structure: 'Structure can be defined as the design of the organisation through which the enterprise is administered' and his hypothesis: 'The thesis deduced – is then that strategy follows structure', which leads them to conclude that 'The thesis says that the internal organisation logically follows from the outside environment chosen from those available to the organisation. Neither can be optimised alone, they must be set relative to one another. This has been the statement of the proposition for some time.'

Of course, and as the existence of a debate recognises, such a clear-cut claim is overly simplistic except perhaps as a long-term objective or principle one would like to move towards. In the real world, and in the short to medium term, firms have to put up with the structures they have and the attitudes and experience of the individuals who comprise the organisation, fill its roles and perform its functions. It follows that strategy formulation will be coloured by the perception and interpretation of the people comprising the organisational structure and they can vary quite dramatically depending upon their basic business orientation.

■ Basic Business Orientations

In the conduct of business at least five distinct functions are involved, namely Research and Development, Production, Sales, Finance and Marketing. In the nature of things one or other of these functions is likely to be dominant and thus lead to the whole business being orientated towards that function. In his book

McKay[4] provides a useful summary of the key features of each of these orientations as follows:

■ Technology Orientation

An emphasis upon research and development or technology is to be found in many companies and comprises the following key features:

1   Emphasis is on research and engineering *per se*, with little recognition of economic considerations.
2   Market criteria to guide research and development are inadequate or non-existent.
3   The product is considered the responsibility of the technical organisation with little product planning influence from marketing.
4   There is a tendency to over-engineer products to satisfy internal inclinations or even whims, beyond what the customer needs or is willing to pay for.
5   Basic development, product, and facility decisions are often made between engineering and manufacturing management, without marketing participation.

■ Production Orientation

This is the classic orientation in economies where demand exceeds supply. McKay identifies seven principal characteristics:

1.   The factory floor is considered to be the business.
2   The focus and emphasis are on making products.
3   Little attention is given to marketing research and product planning.
4   There is a tendency to base price on cost and cost alone, with value and competitive considerations largely ignored.
5   Cost reduction efforts may sacrifice product quality, product performance, and customer service.
6   The role of the sales organisation is to sell whatever the factory chooses to make.
7   If customers aren't happy, the salesmen are told to go out and get some new ones.

■ Sales Orientation

McKay comments that this is often confused with a marketing orientation because it places heavy emphasis on customer considerations; however, it has fundamental differences. Its major features include:

1   The focus is on volume, not on profit.
2   The prevailing point of view is that the customer should be given whatever he wants, regardless of the cost to the business.
3   There tends to be weak linkage between true customer needs and wants and the planning of products to be offered.
4   Pricing, credit, and service policies tend to be loose.
5   Production scheduling is over-influenced by subjective estimates from the field force.
6   Market guidance of engineering and manufacturing is commonly inadequate.

■ Financial Orientation

McKay comments 'this orientation prevails frequently without being clearly recognised. Its dominance may be indirect, through the influence of the accounting, auditing, and treasury personnel on general management decisions.' In the 1980s this orientation was much more pervasive than it used to be and has been severely criticised by authors such as Hayes and Abernathy,[5] who believe that this orientation has been responsible for much of the loss in economic vigour in many western industrialised economies in the post-war period. The key features of the orientation are:

1   The emphasis tends to be on short range profit at the expense of growth and longer range profit.
2   Budgeting and forecasting frequently pre-empt business planning.
3   Efficiency may outrank effectiveness as a management criterion.
4   Pricing, cost, credit, service, and other policies may be based on false economy influences and lack of market-place realism.
5   The business focus is not on the customer and market but on internal considerations and the numbers.

■ Marketing Orientation

The basic features of this orientation are:

1   The focus is on the market-place – customers, competitors, and distribution.
2   A commercial intelligence system monitors the market.
3   It requires recognition that change is inevitable, but manageable in the business arena.
4   The business is committed to strategic business and marketing planning, and to creative product planning.
5   The emphasis is on profit – not just volume – with growth and profit kept in balance.

Clearly each of the foregoing summaries is a stereotype. None the less they contain a sufficient element of truth to indicate that an excessive bias to any one of them will significantly affect the way in which the firm interprets and responds to its environment. It follows that if we can diagnose the prevailing orientation in an organisation then we will be in a good position to predict how it might respond to competitive pressures and also to advise how it ought to respond. In attempting such a diagnosis/prognosis considerable insight and help can be gained from the findings of the field of study generally known as organisational behaviour or human behaviour in organisations (HOBO).

A fundamental principle of survival and progress is *specialisation*. In economics task specialisation and the division of labour are seen as critical to the improvement in productivity necessary to sustain growth and enhance standards of living. In the evolutionary process it is specialisation which enables organisms to adapt to changing conditions and survive. In research it is specialisation which provides the focus and the expertise which prompts discovery and invention. Clearly, specialisation is a good thing. Unfortunately it can also be wasteful and impede progress – one man's tunnel vision is another's single-mindedness of purpose! Recognition of this is implicit in the concept of synergy – the so-called $2 + 2 = 5$ effect.

The purpose of this brief homily is to warn of the dangers of specialisation to the neglect of a more broadly-based perspective, despite the fact that specialisation is often essential at the outset of one's career. Indeed the acid test which distinguishes between successful functional managers and those responsible for the overall direction and control of an organisation is the ability to generalise and perceive the linkages between superficially disparate functions or bodies of knowledge. In Chapter 7 when we discussed buyer behaviour we observed that there were at least four major disciplinary-based explanations of choice behaviour. The trouble is that none is an adequate explanation of the real world, and so we needed to develop a composite model applicable to issues of both individual and group/organisational buying behaviour.

A similar division is apparent in the existence of a sub-field of knowledge designated Human Behaviour in Organisations. Once one has created the sub-field there is an inevitable tendency to specialise in the particularities and lose the potential insights which might occur if one considered ideas and concepts related to the individuals who comprise the groups. It was such a consideration that prompted the author to pursue the thought that if the attitudes and personality of an individual coloured his or her reaction to innovation and new products the same might also be true of organisations. In doing so we identified the concept of *organisational climate* developed by Taguiri[6] which has now received much wider recognition in the concept of corporate culture. Taguiri pointed out that a concept such as organisational climate was an operational necessity as behavioural scientists shifted their attention from the individual to the organisation which plays such an important role in all our lives in an industrial society. As he observed:

Concepts such as climate are needed especially to explain behaviour outside the laboratory, in settings where the environment cannot be experimentally controlled or where the situation cannot be held constant.

Intuitively the concept of climate is familiar and is reflected in every-day expressions such as 'the climate of opinion', 'the industrial climate' and so on. However, precise definition presents a number of problems and in *Marketing New Industrial Products*[7] we review a number of attributes (pp. 85–6) which lead Taguiri to offer the following definition:

> Organisational climate is a relatively enduring quality of the internal environment of an organisation that (a) is experienced by its members (b) influences their behaviour, and (c) can be described in terms of the values of a particular set of characteristics (or attributes) of the organisation.

Closely allied to the idea of organisational climate is that of corporate personality and, taken together, the two concepts suggest that firms will exhibit a certain consistency in their response which will enable one to predict how they will react to particular circumstances. In a now famous study of how firms in two industries (engineering and textiles) responded to their environment Burns and Stalker[8] coined the terms 'organic' and 'mechanistic' to describe the two radically different responses which they detected. In their own words (pp. 5–6):

> There seemed to be two divergent systems of management practice. Neither was fully and consistently applied in any firm, although there was a clear division between those managements which adhered generally to the one, and those which followed the other. Neither system was openly and consciously employed as an instrument of policy, although many beliefs and empirical methods associated with one or the other were expressed. One system, to which we gave the name 'mechanistic', appeared to be appropriate to an enterprise operating under relatively stable conditions. The other, 'organic', appeared to be required for conditions of change. In terms of 'ideal types' their principal characteristics are briefly these:
>
> In mechanistic systems the problems and tasks facing the concern as a whole are broken down into specialisms. Each individual pursues his task as something distinct from the real tasks of the concern as a whole, as if it were the subject of a sub-contract. 'Somebody at the top' is responsible for seeing to its relevance. The technical methods, duties, and powers attached to each functional role are precisely defined. Interaction within management tends to be vertical, i.e. between superior and subordinate. Operations and working behaviour are governed by instructions and decisions issued by superiors. This command hierarchy is maintained by the implicit assumption that all knowledge about the situation of the firm and its tasks is, or should be, available only to the head of the firm. Management, often visualised as the complex hierarchy familiar in organisation charts, operates a simple control system, with information flowing up through a succession of filters, and decisions and instructions flowing downwards through a succession of amplifiers.
>
> Organic systems are adapted to unstable conditions, when problems and requirements for action arise which cannot be broken down and distributed among

specialist roles within a clearly defined hierarchy. Individuals have to perform their special tasks in the light of their knowledge of the tasks of the firm as a whole. Jobs lose much of their formal definition in terms of methods, duties, and powers which have to be redefined continually by interaction with others participating in a task. Interaction runs laterally as much as vertically. Communication between people of different ranks tends to resemble lateral consultation rather than vertical command. Omniscience can no longer be imputed to the head of the concern. (Burns and Stalker, op. cit. pp. 5–6).

While one can characterise an organisation as being organic or mechanistic overall it should be clear from our earlier statement of basic business orientations associated with the various functions that these will tend towards one or other of these polar opposites. Thus we could represent the various functional subsystems of an organisation as lying on a continuum similar to that depicted in Figure 19.2.

Organic				Mechanistic
R & D	Marketing	Sales	Finance	Production

Figure 19.2   Organisational sub-systems continuum

Such a diagram prompts at least two observations:

(a)   The competing claims of the various functions will lead to most firms occupying an intermediate position between the two extremes.
(b)   Overall effectiveness will depend heavily upon the extent to which the separate functions can be integrated together.

Many organisational theorists are of the opinion that both the effectiveness and efficiency of the various functions will be optimised if they assume the structural characteristics appropriate to their location on the spectrum. Thus Lawrence and Lorsch[9] have suggested 4 levels of formalised structure. See Figure 19.3.

If this is so then special devices will be necessary to achieve the overall coordination and integration desired, and much emphasis has been given to matrix structures, project teams, new venture management and the like. More recently Johne[10] has discovered that a particularly important aspect in his sample of successful firms was the ability of individual managers to 'change gear' and switch from organic to mechanistic roles and back again as the task demanded. From personal experience and observation this latter interpretation seems best to explain why some managers perform much more successfully than others who appear to be stuck in a single mode especially in the marketing and general management functions. Such an ability would seem to be particularly important if one is to practise 3-in-1 marketing as recommended earlier.

Structural characteristics	Formalised structure*			
	1	2	3	4
Average span of control	11–10 persons	9–8 persons	7–6 persons	5–3 persons
Number of levels to a shared superior	7 levels	8–9 levels	10–11 levels	12 levels
Time span of review of sub-system performance†	Less than 1 each month	Monthly	Weekly	Daily
Specificity of review of sub-system performance	General oral review	General written review	One or more general statistics	Detailed statistics
Importance of formal rules	No rules	Rules on minor routine procedures	Comprehensive rules on routine procedures and/or limited rules on operations	Comprehensive rules on all routine procedures and operations
Specificity of criteria for evaluation of role occupants	No formal evaluation	Formal evaluation – no fixed criteria	Formal evaluation – less than 5 criteria	Formal evaluation – detailed criteria – more than 5

* Scores from low to high formalised structures
† Based on shortest review period.,

Figure 19.3   Scales of structural characteristics

Source: Lawrence and Lorsch

During the 1970s international competition intensified with Japan, West Germany, and a number of NICs like Korea, Hong Kong and Singapore scoring significant gains against traditional trading nations like the UK and USA as well as penetrating their domestic markets in a major way. The lacklustre performance of American firms led to the criticisms of commentators like Hayes and Abernathy (1980)[11] and the search for increased competitiveness epitomised by the success of Peters and Waterman's *In Search of Excellence*.[12] The major consequence of this evaluation and analysis was recognition of the importance of a marketing organisation and the creation of customer-driven organisations. For many this required a change to an alternative orientation to sales, finance, production, etc. and so focused attention on the nature of corporate climate/personality within the enlarged concept of corporate *culture*.

According to the American Sociological Association[13] 'The Concept of "culture" is defined in terms of the shared beliefs, norms and traditions within the organisation'. Schwartz and Davis[14] endorse this, and explain that 'Culture . . . is a pattern of beliefs and expectations shared by the organisation's members.

These beliefs and expectations produce norms that powerfully shape the behaviour of individuals and groups in the organisation'. In other words, corporate culture defines 'how we do things around here'. As such, it is clearly a powerful force in determining what are accepted principles and practices and so will tend to reject or exclude persons who do not subscribe to these values.

This is not an appropriate place at which to discuss the issues of organisational change. That said, it is clear that if our diagnosis indicates that the organisation is not marketing-orientated (which is not the same as observing that it lacks a formal marketing function and the trappings associated with it) then the key issue is: how do we change the orientation? This question, too, is largely beyond the scope of this book, although we return to it in the final section of this chapter on implementation. We look next at some of the steps involved in developing a market-orientated organisation.

■ Developing a Market-Orientated Organisation

Our earlier review of the strategy vs structure argument indicated that ideally organisations should be structured in the manner which enables them best to implement their chosen strategy. In turn our discussion of strategy has provided strong support for the Arthur D. Little principle that *strategy should be condition-driven* and so represent a match between the firm's resources and competencies and the external environmental opportunities available to it. It follows then that the firm's structure should be orientated towards its external environment or markets – that it should be market orientated – and it is because of this emphasis that we have chosen to make little if anything of the distinction between corporate and marketing planning in this book.

However, it must be recognised that an emphasis upon marketing and marketing planning can have undesirable effects if it is seen to threaten or diminish other functional specialisations. Accordingly it is important to distinguish carefully and clearly between a market orientation and the marketing function. In so far as a market orientation requires one to look outward to the needs of one's customers *all* members of the organisation should be required to adopt such a perspective. However, in encouraging them to do so one should remember that one employs functional specialists because of their expertise and so not dismiss lightly alternative interpretations which a Finance or Production man may place upon data from the market-place. To assume that the marketing function has a monopoly of insight or wisdom when it comes to interpreting the market would be as mistaken as regarding any other function as infallible.

What we need to achieve then is a state of mind in which the marketing function is seen as providing essential intelligence and information on which to base decisions *after* taking into account the views of other functional specialists. It is no accident that much of the success of the Japanese in world markets can be traced to their efficient implementation of corporate plans for which all have accepted collective responsibility. While collective responsibility may imply consensus this is not necessarily the case and the important factor is that once a course of action has been decided on then *all* will support it fully. Achieving such commitment will clearly be easier if people have been consulted and involved even though their personal opinion may not have prevailed. It would also seem reasonable to assume that the likelihood of agreement will be improved if all employees can be persuaded to put the customers' needs first in their thoughts – which is not the same as asking them to become marketers. Indeed it may be true that the success of a marketing department/function is inversely related to its visibility in that the more marketing can be integrated with the other functions the less it will be seen to enjoy a separate and possibly 'threatening' existence of its own.

Offering such opinions is easy – putting the ideas into practice is difficult. Much advice and assistance is to be found in the extensive organisational behaviour literature mentioned earlier (see also recommended readings), but is beyond the scope of a book of this kind. The important thing is to be sensitive to the problem and to accept that inculcating a market(ing) orientation in an organisation is a different task from organising the marketing function.

McKay[15] provides an extensive analysis of the factors which influence the design of a marketing organisation (pp. 33–76) and is well worth detailed study. As a first step McKay argues that one must clearly define the scope of marketing in terms of its purpose and responsibility to the business as a whole, e.g.:

1 To formulate and recommend to the general manager long- and short-range marketing plans for the business in terms of products, customers, sales channels, and prices.
2 To formulate, execute and measure marketing programs to achieve these plans, and to integrate performance of these activities with other functions of the business.

To fulfil such terms of reference one will have to take into account all of the elements in the marketing mix set out in Chapter 11 as well as make decisions about the actual structure of the marketing function itself and its relationship with other functional areas. To accomplish this McKay proposes a five-step process as follows:

1 Determine the work to be done;
2 Establish the structural form (e.g. product or market centred);
3 Design individual positions;
4 Wrap up and document the organisation proposed;
5 Communicate and implement the organisation plan.

With the growth of interest in corporate culture there has developed a parallel interest in the view that a culture develops out of a *vision* which, in turn, will

enable an organisation to define a clear *mission* and *objectives*. The best
definition of (corporate) vision known to the author is that given by Warren
Bennis:[16]

> What is a vision? A vision should state what the future of the organisation will be
> like. It should engage our hearts and our spirits; it is an assertion about what we and
> our colleagues want to create. It is something worth going for; it provides meaning to
> the people in the organisation, in the work that they are doing. By its definition, a
> vision is a little cloudy and grand; if it were clear, it wouldn't be a vision. It is a living
> document that can always be added to; it is a starting place to get more and more
> levels of specificity.
>
> Now beyond that, when the vision statement is close to completion, the questions
> that also have to be asked in any organisation are: What is unique about us? What
> values are true priorities for the next era? What would make me personally commit
> my mind and heart to this vision over the next ten years? What does the world really
> need that our organisation can and should provide? and What do I really want my
> organisation to accomplish so that I will be committed, aligned and proud of my
> association with the institution?

From Bennis's definition it is clear that he sees it as providing an aspiration,
sense of purpose and broad direction in which to travel. Others attach somewhat
different meanings, and/or confuse the concept with mission or strategic intent.
Some attempt at definition will be helpful.

■ Mission, Vision and Strategic Intent

In the course of their 2-year research project into the nature and importance of
the concept of corporate mission, Andrew Campbell and Sally Yeung of the
Ashridge Strategic Management Centre were frequently asked to define and
distinguish between the concepts of mission, vision, and strategic intent. In an
article in the August 1991 issue of *Long Range Planning*[17] the authors offer their
preferred definitions as well as their views of the position of mission in the
strategic planning process.

Two broad definitions of mission prevail. For some organisations, mission is
conceived of primarily as an intellectual discipline and a strategic tool which is
fundamental to strategic management and addresses the key questions: 'What is
our business, and what should it be?' For others, mission is regarded 'as the
cultural "glue" which enables them to function as a collective unity'. Campbell
and Yeung take the view that mission is about *both* culture and strategy, and state
'a mission exists when strategy and culture are mutually supportive. An
organisation has a mission when its culture fits with its strategy'. They continue:

> Mission is an organisation's character, identity and reason for existence. It can be
> divided into four inter-relating parts: purpose, strategy, behaviour standards and

values. Purpose addresses why an organisation is in being: for whose benefit is all this effort being put in? Strategy considers the nature of the business, the desired positioning vs other companies and the source of competitive advantage. Behaviour standards are the norms and rules of 'the way we do things around here'. Values are the beliefs and moral principles that lie behind the behaviour standards, beliefs that have normally been formulated within the organisation by a founding dynasty or a dominant management team.

The Ashridge Mission model is depicted in Figure 19.4.

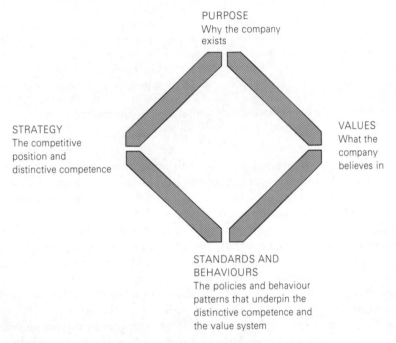

PURPOSE
Why the company
exists

STRATEGY
The competitive
position and
distinctive competence

VALUES
What the
company
believes in

STANDARDS AND
BEHAVIOURS
The policies and behaviour
patterns that underpin the
distinctive competence and
the value system

Figure 19.4   The Ashridge Mission model

Source: Andrew Campbell, Marion Devine and David Yeung, *A Sense of Mission* (London: Hutchinson Business Books Ltd, 1990).

In defining vision, Campbell and Yeung draw on the seminal work of Warren Bennis and Burt Nanus and their theory of leadership. In this theory, vision is seen as a necessary attribute of the leader who can articulate an attractive future for an organisation which will motivate its members to seek its achievement. Such visions may be vague or precise but they give the organisation a sense of purpose and direction. Campbell and Yeung believe a vision and a mission '*can* be one and the same', but suggest that the two concepts do not completely overlap one another in that visions refer to the future and may be achieved. When this occurs, a new vision will need to be articulated. By contrast, a mission is concerned with the *present* – what we are about – while remaining 'a timeless explanation of the organisation's identity and ambition'. In sum 'A vision is, therefore, more associated with a goal whereas a mission is more associated with a way of behaving'.

The third concept which overlaps with those of mission and vision is *strategic intent* – a term popularised by Gary Hamel and C. K. Prahalad's article of that title in the *Harvard Business Review*[18] Hamel and Prahalad stated that:

> On the one hand strategic intent envisions a desired leadership position and establishes the criterion the organisation will use to chart its progress. Komatsu set out to 'encircle Caterpillar'. Canon sought to 'beat Xerox', Honda strove to become a second Ford, an automotive pioneer. All are expressions of strategic intent. At the same time strategic intent is more than just unfettered ambition. (Many companies possess an ambitious strategic intent yet fall short of their goals). The concept also encompasses an active management process that includes: focussing the organisation's attention on the essence of winning; motivating people by communicating the value of the target; leaving room for individual and team contributions; sustaining enthusiasm by providing new operational definitions as circumstances change; and using intent consistently to guide resource allocations.

Given this definition, Campbell and Yeung see it as a concept containing elements of both mission and vision – goals as an integral element of vision and strategy of mission. Overall, however, intent is seen as suffering from the same deficiency as vision in that its achievement will call for restatement whereas mission or purpose have the 'advantage of being everlasting'.

Campbell and Yeung's view on mission *planning* appears to be somewhat at odds with their repeated statements that 'mission is everlasting'. If mission is 'everlasting' and 'timeless' then it should not need tinkering with on a regular basis by linking it with formalised strategic planning. Clearly the difference between mission and strategy resides in the enduring quality of the mission and the *cultural norms* and *values* it reflects and promotes. Strategy is the means whereby specific action plans (both short- and long-term) are measured against this benchmark to determine whether they conform to its requirements. Only in dire circumstances should one reformulate the mission – for, by doing so, it challenges the whole ethos of the corporate culture and 'the way we do things around here'. To achieve such a change requires great determination and courage on the part of top management and will involve considerable investment in human resource development to accomplish.

In common with our earlier discussion in Chapter 3 concerning the definition of terms like policy and strategy, the claimed similarities and differences implicit in attempts to classify concepts like mission, vision and intent inevitably degenerates into a matter of semantics. What is important is that one recognises the difference between the fundamental essence of an organisation which attracts people to it and secures and sustains their loyalty over time (its spirit) as distinct from its *modus operandi*, or strategy, which represents its best attempt to achieve its purpose according to changing times and circumstances. In the next section we look specifically at the nature of the mission statement.

■ The Mission Statement

During 1989 Mary Klemm, Stuart Sanderson and George Luffman of the University of Bradford Management Centre undertook a survey among UK companies of the types of mission statement issued by companies, their content, usage, and value to managers. Their findings were reported in the June 1991 issue of *Long Range Planning*, 'Selling Corporate Values to Employees'.[19]

Klemm *et al.* indicate that there are two simple views of the purpose of mission statements. The first is that mission statements are primarily for external public relations; the second is that they are meant to motivate employees. Obviously, the purposes are not mutually exclusive, but the question is: 'Which is the primary purpose?'

One of the earliest writers to refer to the mission statement was Philip Selznick who, writing on leadership in 1957, saw its purpose as defining the organisation's distinctive competence.[20] However, the authors suggest that 'Current thinking on mission statements could be said to originate in the 1970s when Peter Drucker[21] focused on the need for a business to define its purpose'. (Students of marketing would suggest that it was Ted Levitt who first prompted this concern in 1960 with the publication of 'Marketing Myopia'[22]). Over time, this concern with purpose has been expanded to embrace the firm's philosophy as reflected in its culture and value systems (see the Ashridge Model in Figure 19.4, p. 471).

In practice, Klemm *et al.* found that there is no single definition of a mission statement, and that companies use a variety of terms to embrace the concept:

- Mission statement
- Corporate statement
- Aims and values
- Purpose
- Principles
- Objectives
- Goals
- Responsibilities and obligations

The research also confirmed work in the USA by David[23] into the content of mission statements which indicated nine elements: products or services, customers, philosophy, self-concept, public image, location, technology, employees and concern for survival. However, the UK research suggested that these elements were frequently ordered into a hierarchy, which Klemm *el al.* defined as follows:

Statement 1   The Mission
A statement of the long term purpose of the organisation reflecting deeply held corporate views.

Statement 2   Strategic Objectives
A statement of long-term strategic objectives outlining desired direction and performance in broad terms.

Statement 3   Quantified Planning Targets
Objectives in the form of quantified planning targets over a specific period.

Statement 4   The Business Definition
A statement outlining the scope and activities of the company in terms of industry and geographical spread.

While Klemm *et al*'s survey comprised only 59 companies from the Times 1000 it showed that two-thirds of the respondents had both a mission and strategic objectives statement. 80% had a published business definition. Another significant finding was that 70% of the respondents with mission statements had drawn them up since 1985 and a number were in the process of composing them at the time of the survey.

Based upon their analysis the authors conclude that 'mission statements are seen by managers as more important *internally* than externally. They are more likely to be published to staff than outside the firm, more likely to be revised as a result of a change in senior management than a change in the external environment and seen as most valuable in giving leadership and motivating staff'.

In Figure 19.5 we reproduce the Mission Statement of Marks & Spencer plc – a leading British retailer renowned for its long-run success based on a marketing orientation – together with those for British Airways and Cable & Wireless as published in their 1991 *Annual Report and accounts*.

MISSION STATEMENT OF MARKS AND SPENCER plc

Our three great assets are:

1. The goodwill and confidence of the public.
2. The loyalty and devotion of management and staff throughout the system.
3. The confidence and co-operation of our suppliers.

The principles upon which the business is built are:

1. To offer our customers a selective range of high-quality well-designed and attractive merchandise at reasonable prices.
2. To encourage our suppliers to use the most modern and efficient techniques of production and quality control dictated by the latest discoveries in science and technology.
3. With the co-operation of our suppliers, to enforce the highest standard of quality control.
4. To plan the expansion of our stores for the better display of a widening range of goods and for the convenience of our customers.
5. To foster *good human relations* with customers, suppliers and staff.

Figure 19.5   Marks & Spencer plc: mission statement

Source: Marks & Spencer, *Report and Accounts* (1991).

OUR MISSION

To be the best and most successful company in the airline industry.

OUR GOALS

Safe and Secure:

To be a safe and secure airline.

Financially Strong:

To deliver a strong and consistent financial performance.

Global Leader:

To secure a leading share of air travel business worldwide with a significant presence in all major geographical markets.

Service and Value:

To provide overall superior service and good value for money in every market segment in which we compete.

Customer Driven:

To excel in anticipating and quickly responding to customer needs and competitor activity.

Good Employer:

To sustain a working environment that attracts, retains and develops committed employees who share in the success of the company.

Good Neighbour:

To be a good neighbour, concerned for the community and the environment.

Figure 19.6   British Airways plc: mission statement

Source: British Airways plc, *Report and Accounts* (1991).

■ Implementing Marketing

A recurrent theme throughout this book has been that the processes and techniques associated with marketing strategy and management are a necessary but not sufficient condition for competitive success. Any manager or organisation which is not familiar with the concepts and ideas discussed this far is bound to be at an immediate competitive disadvantage compared with someone who is. However, unless you have opened this book at this page purely by chance, the likelihood is that you are but one of several thousands who have read it from the beginning, one of hundreds of thousands who have read a book or books on

Cable & Wireless is a world leader in the field of telecommunications. For over 120 years, we have provided telecommunications services, networks and equipment to business and residential customers around the world.

We are committed to meeting the growing and changing needs of our customers. We are flexible and responsive to their needs and we offer them a first-class service.

Our policy is to recruit and retain high quality people, offering them every opportunity to develop their skills and their careers. We are also dedicated to the welfare of the communities we serve and the environment we share with them.

We aim to be a leader in every part of the market that we address. We invest to create further value for shareholders over the long-term and to benefit customers, employees and the societies where we operate.

Figure 19.7   Cable & Wireless: corporate statement

Source: Cable & Wireless, *Report and Accounts*.

marketing strategy, or one of millions who have read the works of Peter Drucker, Igor Ansoff, Peters and Waterman or Michael Porter. In other words the knowledge, and the wisdom and experience it represents, is widely available to all. This being so it is clear that knowledge alone is insufficient for success and the critical factor which discriminates between levels of performance is the quality of *implementation*.

While this fact has been explicitly recognised in numerous studies of competitive success published in the 1980s few of these studies offer much by the way of advice of how to put theory, or even currently useful generalisations (CUGs) to work in practice. True, there are books on leadership and numerous autobiographies detailing how successful businessmen like Buck Rogers (IBM), Lee Iacocca (Chrysler) or John Harvey-Jones (ICI) 'made it happen' in their organisations. While interesting, and often inspirational to read, most of these books are short on specific advice on *how* to do it and, especially, in the particular.

It was recognition of this gap in the literature which prompted my friend Nigel Piercy to write *Market-Led Strategic Change (Making Marketing Happen in Your Organisation)*.[24] As he states in the Preface 'The primary goal of this book is to provide managers with a number of new practical tools for evaluating the marketing performance of their organisations and, as a result of that evaluation, for identifying how best to improve marketing performance'. In this section, we seek to capture Piercy's essential advice on making marketing happen.

First, you have to know what marketing is, and what you want it to do for you. As Piercy acknowledges, you don't have to read books or attend courses on marketing in order to be successful in business, in much the same way as you don't need to be able to define prose to use it in communication. That said, one has only to consider that enormously successful marketer Henry Ford I to appreciate that while he intuitively knew what the market wanted in 1908, by 1918 he was losing touch with it and by 1925 had been upstaged by General Motors who discovered the importance of differentiated as opposed to undifferentiated marketing. Perhaps some knowledge of consumer behaviour and product life cycles might have helped Ford with his problem! For most people, therefore, some formal introduction to the nature, scope, processes and techniques of marketing would seem to be a worthwhile foundation for successful practice.

That said, 'what we cannot do is to provide an easy managerial "quick-fix". The sad truth is that there are no easy answers. We can provide new tools, and we can identify the issues and areas where they can be used, but actually using them, and achieving the objective of making our marketing work, is likely to be uncomfortable, painful, messy, imperfect, unpopular, and just plain difficult. There is really no escaping this conclusion' (pp. 17–18).

So what is one to do? Piercy suggests that in very simple terms there are two kinds of manager – transactional and transformational. Transactional managers operate on the basis that if you do something for them they will do something for you (pay you). By contrast transformational leaders (like the three cited earlier) have the ability to motivate people to achieve their vision of the organisation's potential and future. This they do by managing the *context* so that people have a sense of direction, a wish to make things happen and are allowed – and encouraged – to make things happen. Of course, such charismatic and transformational leaders are in short supply. Accordingly Piercy's aim is to help managers evaluate, manage and design better the *context* that is needed to make marketing happen in organisations. He summarises the central issues to be confronted by managers in managing the *context* of marketing as being:

- A focus on *customer satisfaction* (by painstaking example and substantial action, not the easier option of advocacy, 'quick-fix' programmes, and lip-service by us to others).
- Getting *marketing strategies and programs* together (explicitly, in integrated form, and linked to actions in the market-place – no implicit, grandiose, managerial ego-massaging which sounds impressive in meetings and reports, but leads nowhere in the reality of the marketplace as far as the customer is concerned).
- *Organising* to show we believe in marketing to customers, that we want and intend for it to happen, and to remove at least some of the most blatant organisational barriers to serving customers, which seem to exist everywhere.
- Collecting and communicating *information* and intelligence about customers, competitors, the changing environment, and our performance, to help shape – and if necessary change – the way executives perceive, and hence cope with, their market environment.
- Designing critical decision-making *processes* (namely in our case strategic marketing planning and marketing budgeting) to achieve the effects we want both in the company and in the market.

- Facing up to the realities in *implementing* marketing strategies early enough, honestly enough, and explicitly enough that it is possible to do something about barriers, and adapt our strategies to match the realities of what we can actually do as an organisation.

Each of these issues is dealt with in detail by Piercy (as, hopefully, they are in this book) with the difference that he emphasises the *context* whereas most conventional books emphasise the *content*. Of course, Piercy does detail the content, but in addition, he provides numerous diagnostic questionnaires developed from research at the Cardiff Business School into how managers implement marketing in practice, supplemented by feedback from using these questionnaires with practising managers.

As Piercy notes in his penultimate chapter 'the real marketing problems for virtually all organizations are incredibly obvious and straightforward. The real problems are not about the lack of sophisticated marketing skills and techniques. They are about the following obvious and basic issues:

- The *attitude* of our company, its culture, our managers, and our employees to the paying *customer*, and the results in how we treat that paying customer. Not what we say – what we do.
- The incredible competitive power which comes from something as simple as listening to the customer and getting better at doing the things that matter most to the *customer*.
- Getting the *marketing act together*, so the fine words and strategies are turned into the practical delivery of service and product to the customer.
- Organizing ourselves to make it easier to make marketing happen, not creating barriers and obstacles to effective marketing.
- Intelligence that challenges our underlying strategic assumptions and how we look at the world (i.e. the customer), so we stay in touch and get better at coping with the changes, threats, and challenges in the outside world.
- Managing *processes* like marketing planning and resource allocation to get 'ownership', commitment, and action – because our people want and are determined to make marketing happen.
- Taking the issue of marketing *implementation*, and the strategic organizational *change* it creates, seriously enough that we plan it, resource it, and make it part of our strategic thinking in the first place.'

In Nigel Piercy's book you will find much useful and practical advice on implementing marketing. That said, one must remember the earlier caution that there are no 'quick-fixes'. One of the reasons that the Harvard Business School perseveres with its case method approach is the recognition that case studies provide both content and context. The case method enables managers (actual or potential) to apply their knowledge and experience to the solution of specific problems, subject to the scrutiny and criticisms of their peers. By simulating the decision-making process in a wide variety of contexts participants learn diagnostic, analytic and communication skills, all of which are crucial to effective implementation. But even Harvard Business School recognises that 'wisdom can't be told', it is something one acquires by combining knowledge with experience. Accordingly, even highly practical books like Nigel Piercy's cannot implement anything for you – they can only suggest options and possibilities which may help in practice.

■ Summary

In Chapter 19 we have explored some of the organisational implications of becoming marketing-orientated and customer-driven.

First we considered the view that strategy should determine an organisation's structure. In most cases, however, this reasoning is circular for the simple reason that it is largely existing organisations that are concerned with strategy and planning so it would be surprising if their strategic decisions were not heavily influenced by what they already are. As we have seen, planning is the process for determining how we should get from where we are to where we want to be based upon a careful evaluation of both the internal factors (including our current orientation and organisational structure) and changes in the external environment in which we have to operate. Clearly, if the change in the external environment threatens our current organisation and objectives we will have to reconsider them or else accept the threat to our continued survival.

Much evidence suggests that with increased competition firms which are orientated towards the market are more likely to succeed than organisations which are more orientated to internal concerns such as R & D, Production, Finance or Sales. Some diagnostic tests were suggested to help determine the firm's current orientation and advice was offered on how to develop a marketing-orientated organisation.

Central to the task of developing a successful organisation is the definition of a vision which will motivate members to strive for its achievement. Such a vision helps define the corporate culture, and it is from this that we derive the specific mission and objectives that underpin the firm's strategy.

Ultimately, however, success is not only a matter of analysis, evaluation and planning, it is a matter of implementation. In the final section we considered some of the factors which needed to be taken into account and concluded that while 'wisdom can't be told', knowledge is an essential foundation for successful practice.

CHAPTER 20

The (Short-term) Marketing Plan

Learning Goals

The issues to be addressed in Chapter 20 include:

1 The need for *formal plans*.
2 A *framework* for marketing planning.
3 The essential *components* of a marketing plan.

After reading Chapter 20 you will be able to:

1 Explain the role of the *short-term marketing plan* within the strategic planning process.
2 Describe and justify a *normative framework* for marketing planning.
3 Set out the *conditions to be satisfied* if an organisation is to produce a marketing plan successfully.
4 Outline the key *elements* of a formal marketing plan and provide reasons to support their inclusion.

■ Introduction

To this point our main concern has been with the broad sweep of strategic thinking and analysis in order to spell out the basic parameters within which the firm must operate. In addition we have been concerned to stress the inevitability of change and the importance of continuity. Thus we do not see marketing and a marketing orientation as separate or divorced from production and a production orientation, or technology and an R & D orientation, but rather as essential elements of an organic institution attempting to cope with the varying pressures of quite different time horizons.

In the short term, survival is the name of the game and the preoccupation of management is to extract the maximum return from their existing resources and opportunities largely through tactical manipulation and manoeuvring. However, if the firm is to survive then it must have some expectation or concept of the future for which it is seeking to survive – it must have a sense of purpose and direction and it is for this reason that we have advocated so strongly the need for and the benefits flowing from SMP. Clearly, once we have defined our present status and our future aspirations then we are in a position to make plans to move us from where we are to where we want to be. This is the purpose of the marketing plan, and the primary task of marketing management.

As a key document in the implementation of marketing strategy it will be useful to set out the essential components of a marketing plan for this will serve to review and reinforce some of the key strategic elements already discussed as well as review the kind of issues with which the marketing manager has to grapple. It should also be reiterated that the development of a marketing plan is seen as a formal process and that its product should be a clear written statement available to all responsible for its implementation.

That said it is important to repeat the caveat made in Chapter 4 that plans should not be regarded as immutable or as a managerial strait-jacket. Rather they represent one's aspirations and means of achieving them in light of the knowledge one possessed at some time in the past. Accordingly as one progresses and new information comes to light, one should be prepared to revise and modify both the plan and its implementation to allow for these changes. In the absence of a plan, and a clear statement of the information and assumptions on which it is based, it is difficult to see how one can diagnose and explain change for one does not possess a bench-mark or reference-point for assessing the direction and magnitude of the change for which one has to allow. A written plan provides such a point of reference and so allows one to make judgements as to the action to be taken when reality is different from one's expectations, as well as being able to assess the actual progress made.

■ A Framework for Marketing Planning

In Chapter 4 we introduced a number of frameworks for strategic marketing planning (pp. 78ff.), including the model developed by Malcolm McDonald.[1] This was presented as Figure 4.2 and is reproduced below as Figure 20.1 for the sake of convenience and in a slightly modified form. The modifications, which were introduced in a joint article by Leppard and McDonald (1991)[2] are contained in the box relating specifically to the marketing plan. Commenting on the model of the marketing planning process the authors have the following to say:

> Although the marketing planning process can be represented diagrammatically, as in Figure [20.1], it is not necessarily the straightforward, linear sequential operation that the diagram suggests. In reality, all the stages are highly interactive and the planning process requires the flexibility to move backwards and forwards from the general to the specific. Sometimes it is even possible for some stages in the planning process to be dealt with concurrently.

Marketing plans can also vary in their time scale and degree of complexity, both of which will be dependent upon the nature of the host company and its business.

Another variable is the degree of formality of the plan. Should it be formalised as Camillus (1975)[3] advocates, thereby making executives 'communicate, think ahead and so on'? Or should companies heed the warning of Ames (1970)[4] who found that 'an overemphasis on format and procedure leads to a lack of substance and innovative thinking'?

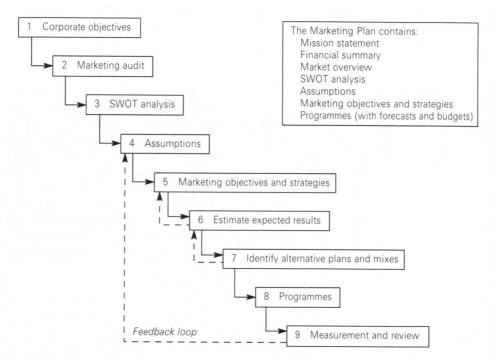

Figure 20.1   The marketing planning process

Source: J. W. Leppard and M. H. B. McDonald, 'Marketing Planning and Corporate Culture: a conceptual framework which examines management attitudes in the context of marketing planning', *Journal of Marketing Management*, 7 (3) (July 1991).

Clearly marketing planning has to be tailored to suit the style and situation of the company, while steering a course between the Scylla of good intentions and the Charybdis of bureaucracy.

Nevertheless, it is possible to describe a marketing planning process which is more or less universally accepted.

1   There is an *information gathering stage* which addresses itself to the company's internal operations and its external environment (the marketing audit).

2   The major strengths, weaknesses, opportunities and threats are identified from the *marketing audit* (the SWOT analysis).
3   Basic *assumptions* are made about the company and its situation.
4   *Marketing objectives* are set for the business, taking into account steps 1–3.
5   *Strategies* are devised about how best to attain the marketing objectives.
6   *Programmes* are formulated which identify timing, responsibilities and costs.
7   The marketing plan is *monitored* and *reviewed* at regular intervals.

Leppard and McDonald's article is based upon empirical research into the actual use and application of marketing planning in a sample of British companies. Probably their major finding is that marketing planning is more than a simple set of procedural steps and that its successful application depends upon a set of underlying values and assumptions. Only in more developed and mature organisations is one likely to find a culture capable of sustaining these values. From their analysis the authors conclude that:

A company will only be able to produce a complete marketing plan if

1.   It has the required body of knowledge, the bulk of which is concerned with understanding planning, marketing and various conceptual analytical marketing 'tools'.
2.   It can translate this knowledge into practical working skills and procedures.
3.   Adequate resources are allocated to the planning process in terms of people, time and back-up support.
4.   There is an adequate data bank and data retrieval system.
5.   The plan or planning process is perceived as necessary and not wasteful of time and effort, i.e. there is a belief in planning.
6.   There is a corporate plan to provide a context for the marketing plan.
7.   Personnel are willing to own up to problems or disclose where existing situations could be improved.
8.   Roles are made clear regarding who does what.
9.   Facts outweigh opinions.
10. Senior executives value and pay due cognizance to the information that emerges from the planning process, to the extent that they will act upon it.

Overall it would seem that such a company sees marketing to be an important function and addresses the implications of being marketing orientated in a mature and rational manner.

On the basis of these conclusions it is clear that successful marketing planning calls for a major commitment on the part of an organisation if it is not to degenerate into the 'trappings' described so vividly by Ames (1970)[5] in his explanation of the apparent failure of marketing in industrial companies.

Before leaving Leppard and McDonald's framework for marketing planning it is worth highlighting the modifications proposed for the actual marketing plan contained in Figure 20.1. Compared with the earlier model (Figure 4.2, p. 82) the following additions have been made:

- Mission statement.
- Financial summary.
- Market overview.
- Forecasts.

The importance of an explicit mission statement was discussed in Chapter 19, and its inclusion in the formal marketing plan is now regarded as providing both the context and direction for all that follows.

In Chapter 21 we shall examine some of the financial indicators which help monitor and control the firm's performance. The inclusion of a summary of these financial targets and appropriate performance indicators is vital to enable line management to determine how effectively they are implementing the plan. Similarly, a market overview or situation analysis is important to provide both context and perspective to the detailed action plans derived from management's analysis of the situation and the tasks which face them over the period of the plan.

Finally, the inclusion of forecasts in association with the budgetary process is necessary to enable management to monitor implementation and determine if variances are due to changes from the forecasts (assumptions), or to competitive activity.

What, then, should the short-term marketing plan contain?

Essential Components of the Short-term Marketing Plan

While there is considerable variation in the recommendations of various authors as to the detailed content of the marketing plan there is little or no disagreement that its essential components are:

- Executive summary.
- Situation analysis (or market overview):

    ★ External environmental audit
    ★ Industry audit
    ★ Internal evaluation (market audit).
- Conclusions and key assumptions.
- Objectives.
- Core strategy.
- Key policies:

    ★ Product
    ★ Price
    ★ Place
    ★ Promotion.

- Administration and control.
- Communication.
- Timing.

In general the information to be contained in each section should be along the following lines:

■ Executive Summary

With the recent developments in information technology the potential for information overload has grown alarmingly and most managers are having to become increasingly selective in terms of what they read. For this reason alone it is essential that any complex document should be prefaced with a clear and concise summary of the key issues contained in the main body of the document. While executive summaries are generally prepared for managers who are not directly concerned with the subject of a report, either as a specialist or as some one responsible for the detailed implementation of its findings, one should not overlook their value to such persons in providing an overview which will help guide more detailed analysis.

Writing executive summaries demands the exercise of considerable judgement. On the one hand they must not be too long or else they will fail on the conciseness criterion, while if they are too short they may be discarded as superficial and lacking in conviction. To some extent these conflicting requirements can be reconciled through judicious cross-referencing so that persons requiring substantiation of a point or argument can turn to the appropriate section in the main body of the report, e.g. 'It is unlikely that any new sources of raw materials can be brought on stream within the next 5 years so that costs may be anticipated to increase by 5% per annum over the period, net of inflation. (para. 53.1.1–3.4.2)'.

■ Situation Analysis

As discussed in this and preceding chapters a situation analysis should proceed from the general to the particular and from the external to internal. Given that one cannot possibly evaluate every single factor which may affect the firm, it is particularly important that one not only justifies those which are included in the analysis, but also that one outlines the reasoning which led one to exclude others. For example, one might list all those eventualities which are thought to have an individual likelihood of occurrence of 0.05 or less. In doing so one reminds oneself of influences which need to be taken into account, specifies a criterion for not doing so and informs third parties that one has not overlooked certain possibilities, but merely discarded them on the grounds of irrelevance or unimportance.

Having painted a general scenario summarising one's expectations about the overall environment one should undertake an analysis of potential changes in one's industry and markets whether arising from external pressures or the interplay of competitive forces. In doing so particular attention must be given to the market segments in which the firm competes or expects to compete.

Finally, the situation analysis should be completed by an audit of the firm itself summarising its major strengths and weaknesses in relation to the threats and opportunities identified in the two preceding stages.

An excellent example of what such a situation or SWOT analysis might look like is provided by Ken Gofton's article,[6] describing how the Federation Brewery in Newcastle on Tyne responded to competition in its traditional market:

■ Why it paid to SWOT

New senior management at the Federation Brewery moved quickly last year [1983] to analyse its market situation according to its strengths, weaknesses, opportunities and threats (SWOT). This was an internal document, but it is not difficult to guess its main outline:

Strengths: Good quality products, including two medal winning lagers. Low prices, because that's what the Fed's shareholders, the clubs, expect. A nationwide reputation among the 4,500 clubs and 4 million members of the Clubs and Institutes Union. A 30% share of the 'free' trade in the North-east. And – slightly tongue in cheek – ample capacity. 'This new brewery has a capacity of some 20,000 barrels a week, which could be doubled or trebled with very little extra outlay,' says national sales manager Geoff Doswell. We are not doing 20,000 barrels a week, but very few breweries are working flat out these days.

Weaknesses: No history of marketing, therefore no effective branding. A weak, confused image among consumers, especially the young. Too few sales reps. Glaring gaps in the product portfolio. Too much dependence on the declining on-trade, and almost no involvement in the expanding take-home business. Poor distribution outside the North-east, which accounts for 90% of sales.

Opportunities: There is scope for increasing sales: through promotion; through filling out the product range; through attacking the take-home trade via existing club outlets and also via the multiples; and through expanding the geographical distribution.

Threats: UK beer production has declined from 41.2 million barrels in 1979 to 36.5 million barrels in 1982, though it now seems to have stabilised. This means more competition for a smaller cake. Other breweries want to increase their share of the free trade, and see the clubs as easy pickings. Internally, there could be a long-term threat in the fact that many clubs do little to attract the younger generation.

■ Conclusions and Key Assumptions

While the conclusions from a SWOT analysis may seem self-evident it is vital that they be made explicit and set out in a comprehensive list. As a result of this discipline it will be easier to identify the gaps in one's knowledge and either to draw inferences which will make these good or else to state assumptions which reflect one's expectations about future and uncertain events.

In *Marketing* (1991)[7] we discuss the importance of formulating assumptions and making them explicit at some length. Part of that discussion is drawn on here.

McKonkey[8] argues that the formulation of assumptions should proceed in orderly steps and proposes the following sequence:

1 Isolate those future events that are most likely to have a significant effect on the company's business.
2 Evaluate as accurately as possible the probable effects of these events.
3 Determine whether an assumption is necessary; if so, formulate the assumption.
4 Record all assumptions.
5 Continuously track the validity of all assumptions.
6 Revise the assumptions and plans, and take corrective action when assumptions prove to be incorrect.

From this, it is clear that assumptions represent our best guess as to the future state of affairs at the time we are drawing up or revising our strategic plan. With the passage of time these future events become nearer, and the information available to us becomes more certain. It follows, therefore, that we should monitor the accuracy of our original assumptions and be prepared to adjust our plans to reflect changes in them.

When formulating assumptions it will also be helpful to try and quantify how likely or probable it is that a given assumption will materialise. Initially most people are more willing to express the likelihood of an outcome in qualitative or verbal terms such as 'Very unlikely', 'Likely', 'Unlikely', or 'Very unlikely'. When pressed, however, it is surprising how wide a discrepancy may exist between two different people's expectations of a given outcome when required to quantify this. Thus one person may consider an event 'likely' when it is better than an evens (50/50) chance whereas another would consider it 'likely' only if the odds were 3 to 2 on (0.75 or 75% probability). For planning purposes it is vital that all the decision-makers share the *same scale of values*, albeit that these values will be subjective (i.e. particular to each individual decision-maker) rather than objective, in which case there would be a known or certain outcome for a given event.

In addition to formulating probability estimates McKonkey also recommends that one should assign a confidence factor, especially when dealing with highly critical assumptions upon which major investment decisions may be made. In this context 'confidence' refers to the amount of confidence the manager has in the data on which his probability estimate was made so that even though a manager might consider that a given event was very likely (90% chance of occurrence) if he had no facts on which to base this assumption then it would have a low confidence value. Under such circumstances – a strong 'hunch' that such and such would happen – the manager would be likely to increase his efforts to secure more and better information to test his belief.

As noted earlier, only if we make our assumptions explicit will we be able to diagnose the possible causes of variances between actual and planned performance.

Objectives (Objectives were discussed at length in Chapter 4, pp. 75–8)

Objectives should be stated for both the long and short term. As we have seen, long-term objectives tend to be broadly worded statements of intent which point the direction in which the organisation is headed. Conversely, the short-term objectives should be closely defined and explicit goals set to be attained through implementation of the short-term plan. These should represent steps to move the firm from where it is to where it wants to be. On a year-to-year basis long-term objectives may vary very little, but short-term objectives require continuous reappraisal and updating.

■ Core Strategy

In Chapters 2 and 3 it became clear that while there is only a limited number of competitive strategies there is a much larger number of 'labels' attached to them. While it matters little which label one uses it matters a great deal that the core strategy should be made crystal clear in a statement such as the following:

> The firm will achieve its objective of 5% increase in the XYZ market during the coming financial year through increased market penetration using a pull strategy based on lower prices and increased promotion.

Once stated in these terms the remainder of the plan becomes a detailed statement and explanation of how this core strategy is to be implemented.

■ Key Policies

Although the core strategy will usually make it clear which of the mix variables is to be emphasised, this in no way reduces the necessity to set out policies for all the others. Only by developing the fullest possible statement will it become possible to judge whether one's plan is internally consistent. For example, our core strategy stated above could easily be seen as inconsistent unless we can show that economies of scale in production and distribution will enable us to cut costs so that we can lower prices and increase the promotional spend. Thus we need to look at the interaction of each of the mix variables to ensure that they reinforce rather than counteract one another. Much of Part II was concerned with an in-depth survey of these considerations in terms of each of the 4 Ps.

■ Administration and Control

In this section of the plan it must be set out who is to be responsible for implementing the proposals contained in it, together with a clear statement of areas of responsibility and authority. Lines of reporting and control must be spelt out as must the type and frequency of measures which will be used to monitor performance. While separate budgets for the major mix policy areas will have been included in the discussion of these, the administration and control section is the one in which they should be integrated into a complete budget for the marketing function.

■ Communication

This heading is not often found in books on market planning, probably on the grounds that formal lines of reporting should be contained under the Administration heading. Our reason for suggesting that communication merits separate treatment rests on the observation that business, like military, failures frequently arise from failures in communication. In turn, such failures may arise from a lack of communication or from mis-communication.

Lack of communication may be a simple case of someone forgetting to tell you or else wrongly assuming that you already possess the information in question. Check lists of information required, written plans and formal reporting systems should overcome this deficiency. Much more serious is the situation where the information does not exist because no one has identified the need for it and taken steps to acquire it. Clearly this is the responsibility of the marketing information system and the marketing research function, but, in the same way that Borden tacked on marketing research as the final element in his marketing mix, so most marketing planners make no explicit provision for spelling out a programme of information gathering and dissemination. In that communication is a two-way process it is essential that the firm have clear policies for both gathering and disseminating information and it is our belief that these should be set down in this section of the plan. We also believe that this is the appropriate place within the plan on the grounds that all which precedes it represents an action plan based on past information whereas the communication section is concerned with making good gaps in the past information as well as acquiring the new data needed for future plans.

It is also felt that by giving the marketing research function separate identification it will increase others' awareness of it and so reduce the potential for miscommunication.

■ Timing

While sequences and timings will have been set out for various activities in the preceding part of the plan this heading provides the opportunity to consolidate these into a single, comprehensive timetable.

■ Summary

In Chapter 20 we have been concerned with the *issues* involved in developing a short-term marketing plan. In general, we subscribe to General Eisenhower's maxim that 'Planning is everything: the plan is nothing'. But, in offering this advice, Eisenhower certainly did not intend us to infer that plans have no value. As we have seen, an over-emphasis upon formal planning in the 1970s resulted in its becoming distanced from those whose primary responsibility it should have been. The result was that line management felt no ownership for these plans, which became increasingly complex and detached from the realities of competition and the market place.

Clearly, a middle road must be found. Those responsible for implementation must be involved in planning. At the same time, their efficiency and effectiveness will be enhanced if they are familiar with the techniques and procedures described in this book. Finally, the output of the planning process needs to be captured in the preparation of a formal plan to act as both guide and reference point in moving the organisation from where it is to where it wants to be.

In this spirit we have reviewed a framework for strategic marketing planning first introduced in Chapter 4. As our discussion made clear, planning is a continuous and cyclical process and formal plans are attempts to define specific courses of action within meaningful time periods – the shorter the time period the greater the certainty about the assumptions on which the plan rests and the more precise the actions called for. Experience suggests that these actions may be set out in a formal plan and we then reviewed the essential components of such a document.

There is a wide variety of aids to formal planning from generalised check lists such as those proposed by Aubrey Wilson[9] to highly detailed work books such as those by Stapleton and Makens.[10] These should be referred to by those wishing to amplify the outline of a marketing plan provided here.

Control

Learning Goals

The issues to be addressed in Chapter 21 include:

1 The *assessment* and *measurement* of the marketing function's contribution to corporate success.
2 *Costs* and their behaviour in relation to output and profit.
3 The concepts of *cash flow* and *net present value*.
4 *Summary measures of performance.*
5 *Management ratios* and their use in diagnosing a firm's financial health.

After reading Chapter 21 you will be able to:

1 Suggest why *profitability alone* is an insufficient measure of a firm's performance and potential.
2 Explain the difference between *fixed* and *variable costs* and how these behave over time.
3 Undertake a *break-even analysis.*
4 Describe *other cost concepts* and their use in diagnosis.
5 Explain and exemplify the nature and use of *contribution analysis.*
6 Define and describe the concepts of *cash flow* and *net present value.*
7 Suggest how *management ratios* may be used to diagnose a firm's financial health.
8 Justify the importance of control in *implementing marketing strategy.*

■ Introduction

The primary objective of strategy formulation, and the development of plans for its implementation, is that one wishes to exercise control over an organisation and its activities and so give it direction and purpose. However, the degree of control which management can achieve will vary enormously. As we saw in Chapter 6 when discussing the marketing environment, the ultimate constraint upon a firm's freedom of action must be the social, economic, cultural, political and technological framework within which it must operate, for while the firm may have some influence upon these factors it is unlikely that it will be able to control them. Thus the purpose of environmental analysis is to determine what opportunities are available to the firm to be exploited and what threats are to be avoided. Once these boundary conditions have been established the decision-maker is in a position to select the strategy which he feels will best enable him to achieve the organisation's corporate objectives and from this articulate policies for integration of the marketing-mix elements in the most effective way.

In principle, management of the marketing function is under the control of the organisation and this will be reflected in the establishment of specific objectives supported, wherever possible, by quantified targets for achievement. But, in setting down such objectives and targets in one's marketing plan it is always necessary to bear in mind that achievement will depend upon performance by the individuals responsible and the absence of any significant change in the assumptions upon which the targets and objectives are based. Recognising that most of these assumptions will relate to external factors beyond the firm's direct control, it is clear that objective measures of performance will only be possible provided one can quantify any changes between the assumed and actual conditions in the market-place. Given such information one will be able to establish how well the organisation is performing, what factors may account for any under- or over-performance and what modification may be necessary to correct or take advantage of discrepancies between planned and actual achievement.

At various places in our discussion of the management of the marketing function we have considered appropriate objectives for the major mix elements and also suggested ways in which the achievement of these may be assessed. Basically all the methods reviewed possess the common aim of seeking to quantify the benefits flowing from or expected to flow from incurring costs or expenditures on different kinds of marketing activities with the ultimate objective of selecting that combination or mix which will yield the maximum return for any given outlay. In this chapter our primary concern is with those techniques and approaches which will enable one to assess the overall contribution of the marketing function to corporate success. To this end the main focus will be on costs and the way these behave in relation to output or volume and profit. Attention will also be given to the concept of cash flow and net present value, as these are of vital importance in assessing the advantages and disadvantages of different courses of action; this leads naturally to an examination of the relevance of various summary measures of performance such as ROI and payback. In that one's assessment of competitive standing will depend upon an appreciation of financial standing, some reference will also be made to methods of assessing an organisation's financial health from its published statements through the computation of a series of management ratios.

■ Profits and Performance

In the final analysis perhaps the simplest and most basic way of judging the effectiveness of a business organisation is by examining its profitability both in absolute terms and as a return on the capital employed. To assess profit (or loss) we need to look at two parameters – Revenue and Costs – and it is immediately apparent that while we may have almost complete control over our costs, revenue represents the market's assessment of the value of the goods or services which we offer to it. Clearly in deciding whether it is worth while to incur costs through creating a supply of anything, one needs to have some feeling for the nature of a demand schedule which indicates the quantity which will be consumed at any given price. Much of the content of this book has been concerned directly with this problem and, if nothing else, should have made it clear that predicting future purchase behaviour is a complex and difficult task. Given the uncertainty involved in forecasting demand it is unsurprising that many managers feel happier dealing with production and supply, for here there are assured and reliable methods of measuring output and cost and of exercising direct control over them.

Further, as we have attempted to show in several places, the greater the external turbulence and uncertainty the greater the inclination for corporate management to reduce risk by adopting a short-term outlook and giving particular attention to milking their past investment. Such milking tactics give added weight to the importance of controlling costs and lead to the development of a financial orientation of the kind described in Chapter 19. In and of itself careful cost control is a necessary and laudable objective, but without a proper appreciation of the nature of costs and the way in which they vary according to the volume of output one may easily be tempted to adopt measures which in the short run will reduce costs (and so appear to increase profits) but in the long run will prove counter-productive as they discourage future sales. A simple (and true) example will help make the point.

A major international hotel group had a policy of rotating its managers between different hotels in order to broaden their experience. Based upon their performance, good managers got promoted to bigger and more important hotels and less successful managers got demoted and possibly fired. The group was concerned that its overall performance and standing was declining in comparison with that of its major competitors.

A consumer survey revealed that many former clients had switched to competing hotels which they felt offered better value for money and when questioned on how they assessed this indicated a wide range of factors including decor, facilities, service, quality of food, etc. Clearly, these were all the responsibility of the hotel management and raised the question as to how a policy of promoting the most successful managers could result in such poor management at the top.

Analysis revealed that performance was judged by the bottom line of the accounts (i.e. the profitability) and probing soon indicated that, in the short term, the quickest way to enhance profits is to cut costs. Investigation showed that managers who were being judged as successful were enhancing their profits through cost avoidance – don't redecorate or refurbish, cut the number of personnel, provide less food in the restaurants, etc. Now hotels, in common with all businesses, depend heavily upon repeat purchase, which, as the quality of the product declined, began to fall away, resulting in a diminishing revenue. But, as long as you could cut costs faster you still appeared to be making better profits. Eventually, of course, such a policy will lead to the inevitable conclusion, but what happens if you promote the 'successful' manager before profits actually dip? Well, his successor will finish up the scapegoat and the better a manager he is, the worse his performance will seem. On taking over a rundown establishment with a dwindling customer base the good manager will realise that he will have to improve the product before he can win back any customers. To do so will require expenditure and take time and it is not difficult to see how at the end of his tour he will be judged 'unsuccessful' and demoted while handing over a concern ripe for 'milking'.

While a little poetic licence has been used to stress the point it is clear that the hotel group's control system was having almost the diametrically opposite effect to that desired because it was depending upon a single criterion – profit – and in computing this it failed to inquire into the nature of the costs involved or the purposes for which they were incurred. To avoid such problems one must have a clear understanding of the nature of costs.

■ Cost Analysis

Conventionally costs are divided into two types – *fixed* and *variable* – but it will be helpful to distinguish a third and intermediate category which may be labelled *semi-fixed, semi-variable*, or *'mixed'*.

In defining and classifying costs the major criterion is their behaviour in relation to a given output over *time*. Again by convention as accounts are usually prepared on an annual basis, then costs which do not change from year to year will be considered *fixed*, while those which do and/or fluctuate with output will be considered *variable*. Semi-fixed costs are those which can be changed during the accounting period, but usually result in a step function due to an intrinsic lack of divisibility, e.g. the acquisition of an additional member of staff. In economics the distinction between fixed and variable cost is defined more precisely by reference to the definition of the 'short-run' and the 'long-run'. In the *short run* plant capacity cannot be altered although of course output may be varied through changes in other factor inputs, such as hours worked and efficiency/productivity. By contrast, in the long run capacity may be changed as well as the rate of output. Examples of the three kinds of costs in a marketing context might be:

Fixed	Semi-fixed	Variable
Salaried staff	Additional staff	Commissions
Advertising approp.	Merchandisers	Distribution costs
Marketing research budget	*Ad hoc* surveys	Sales promotion
Premises		Service costs
Vehicles		Financing/credit

Diagrammatically these may be represented as in Figure 21.1:

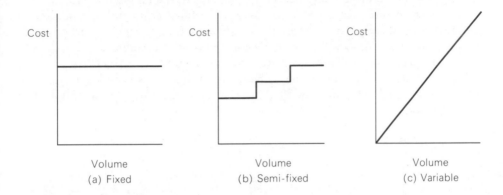

(a) Fixed (b) Semi-fixed (c) Variable

Figure 21.1 Cost curves

As John Howard,[1] *inter alia*, has pointed out, cost behaviour may be dealt with in at least three different ways. First there is the *accounting* approach which is 'much the simplest since it consists in classifying accounts into fixed, variable, and semi-variable by means of inspection and judgement. Because of its subjective nature, the method is open to serious criticism. Thus, the user of the cost data derived by the accounting method should investigate the logic used in classifying the accounts' – advice with which we agree totally. Specifically, Howard suggests that such an approach may be acceptable where three conditions exist, namely: wide fluctuation in production, detailed accounts which have been kept in the same way for a number of years and stable economic conditions. In recent years, the volatility of the economic conditions has highlighted the deficiencies of many traditional accounting practices and particularly the subjective nature of cost allocation. As a consequence a much more explicit treatment of costs has become apparent including the use of the alternative *statistical* and *engineering* approaches.

In the statistical approach much the same conditions need to apply as for the successful application of the accounting method, but a much greater degree of accuracy may be achieved by determining how costs vary with output, using techniques such as regression analysis, thereby permitting clearer definition of variable costs. In turn clearer definition of variable costs enables more precise identification of fixed costs.

Where the conditions do not satisfy the three criteria set out, the engineering approach will be appropriate. Essentially this method represents a return to basic principles as one first spells out the physical relations involved in creating output, i.e. the combination of plant and equipment, labour and materials, and the costs associated with their use.

As we have noted on numerous occasions the great majority of business is transacted by existing organisations which already comprise a collection of resources which represent its fixed costs. As a result the minimal objective must be to generate sufficient revenue to cover these fixed costs and any additional variable costs which may be necessary to generate that revenue. In other words the firm will want to 'break even'. However, in order to establish its break-even point the firm will probably need to compute a number of calculations using different assumptions about the behaviour of both costs and revenues. In undertaking such an analysis, the breakeven chart provides a simple but powerful tool to help clarify the relationships.

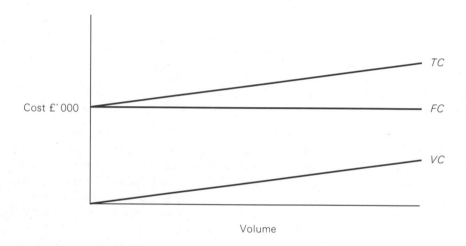

Figure 21.2   Simplified break-even chart

Most representations of break-even charts, including the one given here, adopt the simplifying but usually incorrect assumption that variable costs are constant per unit of output and so may be represented by a straight line as in Figure 21.2. In reality one expects the economies of scale and experience discussed in Chapter 6 to come into operation, which would result in a curvilinear variable cost curve as shown in Figure 21.3.

Clearly accurate representation of the variable-cost schedule and curve is of much greater importance when making strategic decisions when one will wish to explore the implications of additional increments in fixed costs in the light of one's expectations about the price elasticity of demand. Within the short term, and with a given fixed cost, declining variable cost is less likely and a straight line will be an acceptable compromise, particularly as it is likely to suggest a higher break-even than will actually be required. In order to plot the break-even point, first one will need to compute the total cost curve as shown in the following schedule and in Figure 21.4.

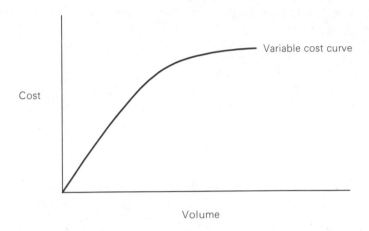

Figure 21.3   Curvilinear variable cost curve

Output	Fixed cost	Variable cost	Total cost
1	10 000	1	10 001
100	10 000	100	10 100
1 000	10 000	1 000	11 000
2 000	10 000	2 000	12 000

(This schedule assumes a single product. In a multi-product firm each product would have to be assigned its 'share' of the fixed costs in order to determine its individual break-even point. As noted previously, cost classification is often subjective in nature while allocation is arbitrary. It is for these reasons that we prefer the contribution or marginal approach, discussed later in the chapter.)

In the case of an existing product one will probably have some feel for the price elasticity of demand and will certainly know the going market price for competitive products. On the basis of this knowledge one can construct a Revenue curve by the simple expedient of calculating Volume X Price and, by plotting this curve, determine the break-even point at its intersection with the total-cost curve. Thus if it is assumed that in the case of our theoretical product the going market price is 8, our product is closely comparable to our competitors, who are numerous, we have adequate distribution and promotion and demand is buoyant it is reasonable to assume we can sell all our output at this price with the outcome plotted in Figure 21.4.

On the other hand where the product is new, knowledge of the total-cost curve will provide a useful starting-point for constructing a demand schedule and selecting a price–volume relationship which will meet the firm's profit objectives best.

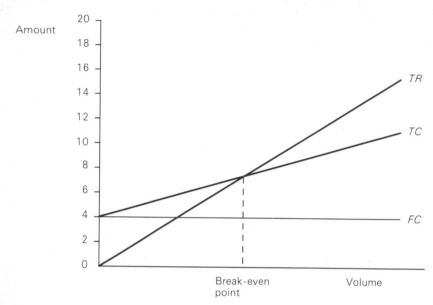

Figure 21.4   Break-even

■ Other Important Cost Concepts

While the concept of fixed and variable cost is probably the best-known and most widely used in making marketing decisions, there are a number of other cost concepts which are to be found in the economic and accountancy literature, and a brief review of them may prove useful. Perhaps one of the best accounts of the relevance of cost analysis to marketing decision is that published by John Howard as long ago as 1957[2] and our summary draws heavily on this source.

To begin with, Howard provides an excellent summary table which is reproduced in Table 21.1.

The distinction between outlay and opportunity cost is a particularly important one, but probably enjoys greater observance in theory than it does in practice. In essence an outlay cost is an actual expenditure whereas an opportunity cost represents the value which would be placed upon a factor in its most productive alternative use. While the outlay and opportunity cost may often be the same, e.g. when evaluating a future investment, they can also differ significantly, particularly when considering the redeployment of resources. A case in point which we have already touched on is the treatment of 'dogs' in the product portfolio where their status as pets may well prevent objective assessment of their true status. If one considers the actual outlay it may not seem unreasonable, particularly by comparison with other products and the

Table 21.1   Cost distinctions

Concepts		Basis of distinction
Outlay	Opportunity	Nature of the sacrifice
Future	Historical	Degree of anticipation
Short-run	Long-run	Degree of adaptation to present output
Variable	Fixed	Relation to output
Incremental	Marginal	Type of added activity
Traceable	Common	Traceability to a part of the company
Direct	Indirect	Traceability to different products

Source: J. A. Howard, *Marketing Management* (Homewood, Ill.:Irwin, 1st edn, 1957; rev. edn 1963) p. 173.

overall profitability of the firm. The trouble is that the below-average performance of the dogs will depress the overall profitability of the firm by dragging it down to its level, whereas consideration of the earnings which would flow if the same investment were made in its most productive alternative use might give a totally different picture. As Howard emphasises: '*Opportunity cost is always the appropriate concept.*'

As a consequence of the rampant inflation of the 1970s and 1980s the obvious but neglected distinction between *historical* and *future* costs has become much more apparent. In that decisions only involve future costs, it is important that historical costs only be used as indicators and even then treated with great caution. Such advice is especially pertinent to the New Product Development (NPD) process where one of the most frequently cited causes of failure is 'higher costs than anticipated', which is usually equivalent to saying that one budgeted one's projections using past cost data without adjusting them for likely changes between the commercial analysis and launch phases. Conversely, one should be careful not to discontinue new products prematurely because their costs appear too high, as these may fall quite dramatically due to the scale and experience effect as the market 'takes off'.[3]

The concepts of *traceable – common* and *direct* and *indirect* – costs are closely related. As the terms imply, traceable costs can be allocated directly to the activity engendering the cost whereas common costs are those which arise from or in support of a number of activities simultaneously and contribute indirectly to them all. For purposes of judging the comparative performance of activities, e.g. different products in the product line, the more clearly one can trace the costs involved the better the evaluation. A full description of techniques for assigning costs is given by Howard and is to be found in any basic cost-accountancy text.

We have left the concepts of *incremental* versus *marginal* cost until last because these provide a natural lead into the subject of contribution analysis which is the method preferred by most marketers. Defined precisely, the marginal cost is that which will be incurred by adding one more unit of output to the existing output. In the same way that one more straw will break the camel's back so one additional unit of output may create the need for an increase in fixed investment or some other discontinuity in the cost, but, so long as the income derived from the sale of the marginal unit exceeds its marginal cost, its production and sale should be undertaken to maximise profits (see Figure 21.5).

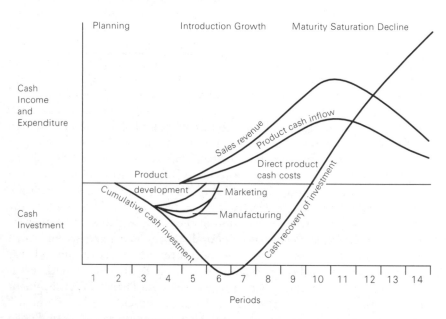

Figure 21.5   Investment life-cycle of hypothetical new product

Source: John Sizer, *An Insight into Management Accounting* (Harmondsworth: Penguin Books, 1979) p. 394.

While the concept of marginal cost strictly is confined to increases in output it tends to be used loosely to cover what properly should be termed 'incremental cost' which relates to any added activity and can encompass the addition of several units rather than one. The latter situation relates to most changes in marketing activity and so will be the appropriate concept to use.

■ Contribution Analysis

Perhaps the simplest way to highlight the difference between the conventional and contribution approaches to accounting is by means of a simple example.

The General Manager of Sporting Promotions Ltd has called a meeting with his accountant, production and sales managers to discuss problems related to stocks of goods carried forward from the previous year's trading which he considers to be worthless. The two lines in question differ quite significantly. Line A, which has sold successfully for many years, consists of a cricket score book in which enthusiasts can keep their own record of their Championship team's performance. The covers of the book are embossed with the team's name and the season, but otherwise are completely standard. Internally the first twelve pages consist of information about the County, its performance last season, and the players signed for the coming season together with the fixture list, while the remaining eighty-four pages are preprinted but completely standard for all seventeen counties. Sales are usually handled through the club itself. Once the season is over, these score books are out of date with regard to the printed information and, while some could still be sold at a reduced price as ordinary score books the company considers this might cannibalise future sales and declines to do so. While the blank pages could be reused the costs involved in remaking the books closely approximates a new print run and is not considered worth the effort.

Line B consists of an extensive range of booklets covering all the teams in the Football League. Basically the books all serve the same purpose, which is to provide information about the League fixture list and the club's past performance and future prospects. Space is also provided so that a record may be kept of the Cup and any other special games in which the team may be involved. However, the basic product is 'packaged' in a number of different formats and sizes and can be personalised for use as 'give aways' by firms to their customers as well as being sold through sporting good and CTN outlets.

At the meeting the following information is tabled, summarising the performance of the two lines.

	Line A Cricket		Line B Football	
Sales		100 000		220 000
Cost of goods sold				
Labour	30 000		100 000	
Material	30 000		60 000	
Fixed overheads	40 000		40 000	
Total cost	100 000		200 000	
Stock at cost	10 000		20 000	
	90 000	90 000	180 000	180 000
Gross margin		10 000		40 000
Selling and admin exp.		15 000		35 000
Profit (Loss)		(£5 000)		£5 000

Faced with these figures the accountant argues that both lines should be discontinued immediately, as his figures show that the cricket line is a loss-maker and the profit on the football line is hardly worth the effort. The sales manager disputes this and states that it is the cricket line which has made the loss and the football line is showing a profit, which he is confident will increase next year. The production manager admitted the gross margin on the football line was better, but argued that all the specials disrupted his production schedule and that the cricket line was more homogeneous and easier to control.

The General Manager pointed out that as the stock is worthless both lines show the same loss of 15 000 each and suggests that it would be more helpful to consider the contribution of the two lines which consist of the sales for each line less their direct variable cost:

	Line A		Line B	
Sales		100 000		220 000
Labour	30 000		100 000	
Material	30 000		60 000	
		60 000		160 000
Contribution		40 000		60 000

From this analysis it is clear that both lines make a very significant contribution to the fixed (overhead) and semi-fixed (selling and administration) costs of the company and that to drop either line immediately would only exacerbate the situation unless other new products can be brought on stream immediately using the same fixed assets. It is also apparent that the cricket lines make a bigger contribution per unit of sales than do the football lines and it is open to question whether the fixed and semi-fixed cost allocations are appropriate. For instance there are only seventeen cricket clubs to call on but there are 130 UK football league teams not to mention the other sales outlets used and the wide range of options available. Similarly, the fact that the football lines require more hand-finishing (higher unit labour cost) and so make less use of machinery does not necessarily justify an equal allocation of fixed costs between the two lines.

Clearly, in deciding how to proceed the management team needs much more information on the reasons why sales were less than forecast and what the prospects are for the coming year, e.g. if it was a very wet cricket season with well below average attendances what is the likelihood of this occurring again, etc. That said it is also clear that the contribution analysis gives a much better picture of the comparative performance of the two lines and emphasises the need for much more careful budgeting and cost control, particularly in terms of the criteria used for allocating the fixed and semi-fixed costs.

In an article entitled 'Profitability Analysis by Market Segments' Leland Beik and Stephen Buzby[4] suggest that the contribution approach will be of even greater value as a control mechanism when the analysis is extended beyond the product line to the different market segments in which it is sold. This is illustrated in Tables 21.2 and 21.3 below, the first of which provides a breakdown by product type for the company's line of adding machines while the second exhibit carries the analysis a stage further and distinguishes the segments at which the products are targeted in terms of their characteristics and product benefits:

- Full keyboard   =   Banks
- Deluxe Ten Key =   Manufacturing firms
- Basic Ten Key   =   Retailers

Table 21.2   Break-down by product type

	Company total	Full keyboard	Deluxe ten key	Basic ten key
Net sales	$10 000	$5 000	$3 000	$2 000
Variable manufacturing costs	5 100	2 500	1 375	1 225
Mfg contribution	$ 4 900	$2 500	$1 625	$ 775
Marketing costs				
Variable:				
Sales commissions	450	225	135	90
Variable contribution	$ 4 450	$2 275	$1 490	$ 685
Assignable:				
Salaries – salesmen	1 600	770	630	200
Salary – Marketing Manager	100	50	25	25
Product advertising	1 000	670	200	130
Total	$ 2 700	$1 490	$ 855	$ 355
Product contribution	$ 1 750	$ 785	$ 635	$ 330
Nonassignable:				
Institutional advertising	150			
Marketing contribution	$ 1 600			
Fixed-joint costs				
General administration	300			
Manufacturing	900			
Total	$ 1 200			
Net profits	$ 400			

Table 21.3 Product characteristics and product benefits segments

	Company total	Full keyboard Bank seg.	Full keyboard Nonseg.	Deluxe ten key Mfg. seg.	Deluxe ten key Nonseg.	Basic ten key Retail seg.
Net sales	$10 000	$3 750	$1 250	$2 550	$450	$2 000
Variable manufacturing costs	5 100	1 875	625	1 169	206	1 225
Mfg contribution	$ 4 900	$1 875	$ 625	$1 381	$ 244	$ 775
Marketing costs Variable:						
Sales commissions	450	169	56	115	20	90
Variable contribution	$ 4 450	$1 706	$ 569	$1 266	$ 224	$ 685
Assignable:						
Salaries – salesmen	1 600	630	140	420	210	200
Salary – marketing Manager	100	38	12	19	6	25
Product advertising	1 000	670	—	200	—	130
Total	$ 2 700	$1 338	$ 152	$ 639	$ 216	$ 355
Segment contribution	$ 1 750	$ 368	$ 417	$ 627	$ 8	$ 330
Nonassignable: Institutional advertising	150					
Marketing contribution	$ 1 600					
Fixed-joint costs General administration	300					
Manufacturing	900					
Total	$ 1 200					
Net profits	400					

In the case of the first two segments, customers other than the prime targets also buy the machines (labelled 'nonseg') and the analysis enables one to compare the comparative performance of the primary customer *vis-à-vis* the others. From such a breakdown it becomes clear that the bank segment is showing a poor return for the marketing effort expended on it which calls for further investigation and explanation that could well lead to changes in the marketing strategy.

Without such an analysis the disparity between the prime customers and the rest may well have gone unremarked.

■ Cash Flow and Net Present Value

When considering the concept of the product portfolio (Chapter 5) reference was made to the differing cash needs of products at different stages of their life-cycle. From this discussion it should be clear that a full understanding of the nature of cash flow is vital to the whole process of marketing planning, for otherwise the enterprise may be put at risk due to expenditures exceeding revenue in the short to medium term without adequate provision for such an imbalance.

Strictly speaking the calculation of cash flow is one of three methods used by financial accountants to assess and quantify the likely return from a possible investment (the others being the marginal or contribution approach discussed in the preceding section and the conventional calculation of profits after the deduction of overheads attributable to the project). Texts on financial and management accounting stress that cash flow is not the same as profit and will only become the same when a business is finally wound up. It follows that using cash flow to measure the worth of an investment may give quite a different picture from the calculation of profit.[5] Specifically, profits are likely to exceed cash flow in the early years of a project, but fall below it in later years due to the inclusion of depreciation.

Because the different approaches may yield different results it would seem prudent to use them all before deciding which is most appropriate to the particular circumstances of the firm and its decision-makers. However, as hinted earlier, in the case of new product development (NPD) it is considered particularly important that one should seek to specify as clearly as possible a sales forecast and expected revenues for comparison with one's budget for the launch of the product. Initially the cash flow will be negative as the manufacturer has to invest in inventory, secure distribution, promote the availability of the product, etc., while sales will take time to build up. As noted in Chapter 13 with low learning products or 'fashion' goods there may be only a short time lag between introduction and volume sales, but in the case of high learning products the introduction phase may extend over many years and require considerable underwriting which will have to be funded by the positive cash flow from established products and/or other sources.

Due to the fact that many investment projects will have lives extending over many years it is important that one discount the cash flow or future earnings stream to establish its net present value. As Taylor and Shearing[5] point out, the two major problems involved in discounting cash flows are (a) to decide on the period over which the calculations are to be made, and (b) to assess the appropriate rate of interest or discount to be used. However, once decisions on these two parameters have been made, and one can always compute a number of alternatives and subject them to a sensitivity analysis, the actual calculation is straightforward as the appropriate discount factors are readily available in published tables. For example a 5% interest rate has the following factors:

Year 1   0.9524
Year 2   0.9070
Year 3   0.8638
Year 4   0.8227

The application of discounted cash-flow analysis in selecting a product portfolio, which also incorporates a Bayesian approach to handling uncertainty concerning future outcomes, is described fully in an article by Gottlieb and Roshwalb and is recommended reading for anyone wishing to pursue this topic further.[6]

However, before leaving the topic of cash-flow analysis, it is worth mentioning that such calculations are frequently used to determine the *pay-back* period for different projects. Pay-back is a very simple concept, as it merely states how long it will take to recover one's initial investment in a project. Under conditions of inflation and uncertainty such as existed in the UK (and elsewhere!) in the late 1970s and early 1980s the temptation to invest only in projects with short-term pay-back periods became almost overwhelming, resulting in the inadequate investment in R & D and long-term strategic projects which has been commented on in several places in this book. As with most summary statistics one must be careful not to place too much reliance on a single measure without full consideration of all its implications – advice which also applies to the use of management ratios when assessing the general financial health of an organisation.

Pay-back is calculated by the simple formula:

$$\text{Pay-back} = \frac{\text{Net investment}}{\text{Average annual operating cash flow}}$$

The pay-back period is often used in determining whether an investment can be recouped within its economic life, but can be misleading unless one builds into the calculations an amount equivalent to the opportunity cost of using the funds, e.g. purchase of a machine tool with a life of six years at a cost of £50 000 and current interest rates of 15% should be calculated as follows:

Year	Opening balance	Earnings @ 15%	Cash flow	Closing balance	
1	50 000	7 500	12 500	45 000	
2	45 000	6 750	12 500	39 250	
3	39 250	5 888	12 500	32 638	
4	32 638	4 896	12 500	25 034	= pay-back
5	25 034	3 755	12 500	16 289	
6	16 289	2 443	12 500	6 232	

From this calculation it can be seen that the crude pay-back indicates pay-back in four years, but the calculation of the opportunity cost of the investment assuming interest rates will remain steady on average 15% shows that it will record a net loss of £6 232 when the machine has to be scrapped.

The position is even more complicated when the cash flow varies, which is usually the case, when pay-back can give quite erroneous indications of the merits of alternative investments.

■ Management Ratios

In so far as marketing is primarily concerned with *competitive* activity it follows that one should seek to learn as much as possible about those with whom one is competing. In that all registered organisations are required to lodge annual statements of their accounts with the Registrar of Companies and public companies publish them widely, evaluation of such statements should comprise an essential ingredient in one's strategic planning. It goes without saying that one should also apply the same evaluation to one's own accounts in order to assess the health and progress of the organisation. In doing so one should be sensitive to the six reasons set out in Table 21.4 why such comparisons may be of limited

Cont. p. 510

Table 21.4   Reasons why comparisons of individual annual statements of accounts may be of limited value

1. At the present time the accounts are prepared on a historical cost basis.

2. There are a number of permitted accounting rules for dealing with particular items of revenue, expenditure, assets, and liabilities. As no two companies employ exactly the same set of accounting rules, the rates of return of any two companies may not be intrinsically comparable.

3. If a company is a subsidiary of a large group, it is often difficult to separate the financing of the subsidiary from its trading activities.

4. If the company is a member of a vertically integrated group of companies, where the end products of one company become the raw materials of another company, the *transfer prices* from one company to another may not be market prices and the profits of individual companies in the group may not be meaningful.

5. In a vertically integrated group of companies, one company in the group may accept an export order at a loss, but for the group as a whole the order may be profitable. A comparison with the company accepting the export order at a loss would be of limited value.

6. In a group of companies a single product line might be produced by several subsidiary companies, each of which also produces several other products, while the parent company absorbs all research and development costs.

Source: J. Sizer, 'Investment Life Cycle of a Hypothetical New Product', in *An Insight into Management Accounting* (Harmondsworth: Penguin Books, 1979) p. 185.

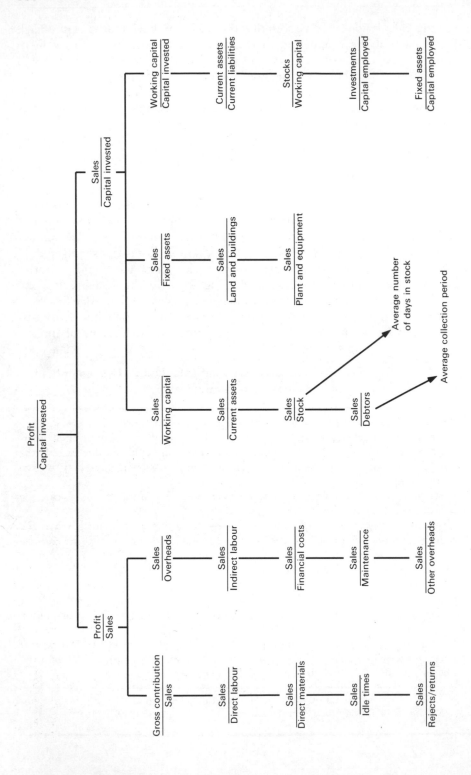

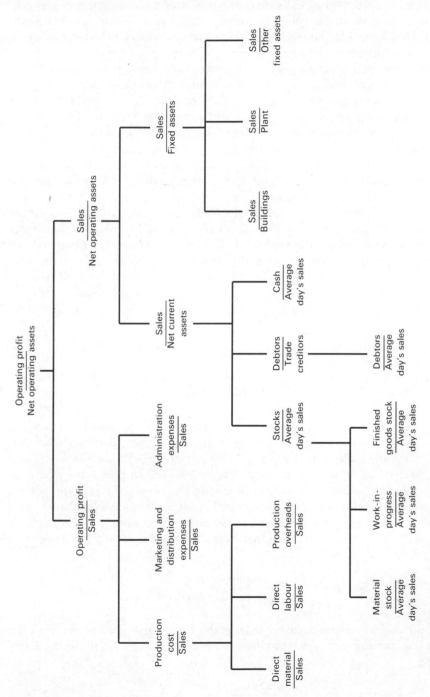

Figure 21.6 Control and operating ratios

Source: J. Sizer, *An Insight into Management Accounting* (Harmondsworth: Penguin Books, 1979) p. 394.

value when conducted on an individual basis. However, as Sizer also points out, there are a number of consolidated returns such as Interfirm Comparisons, *Business Monitors, The Times 1000*, etc., which provide a useful yardstick of competitive achievement.

A major tool for such evaluation is the use of ratio analysis.

As noted above, management ratios are summary statistics and must be treated with caution. Their main value lies in the fact that ratios express relative rather than absolute values and so make it possible to compare results over time. Most books on financial management and control suggest a pyramid of ratios similar to that reproduced in Figure 21.6. The apex of the pyramid is the most basic measure of performance – Return on Investment – and each lower level measures the component parts which go to make up or influence the summary measures on the level above. Thus if ROI is unsatisfactory this may be because Profit on Sales is inadequate or it may be that while Profit Margins on Sales are satisfactory the actual volume of sales is too low in relation to the capital employed. Whichever appears to be the cause, one can then work downwards through the pyramid until the root cause or causes is found. A full discussion of how to use ratios in this way is to be found in R.M.S. Wilson's *Management Controls and Marketing Planning*[7] or John Sizer's *An Insight into Management Accounting*.[8]

For those unable to consult these or similar sources the main ratios and their uses are:

1 *Measures of liquidity*, i.e. of the funds available for use in the business.

(a) *The current ratio* $= \dfrac{\text{current assets}}{\text{current liabilities}}$

This ratio measures the extent to which the firm is able to meet claims upon it from its creditors. A ratio of *2:1* is generally regarded as 'about right' in that the firm could experience a severe (50%) reduction in its current assets and still meet its liabilities and continue trading. While a higher ratio would no doubt please creditors, it could well indicate poor control as it might consist of excessive inventories which might be difficult to dispose of in an emergency and/or too generous a credit policy. In the latter case a need to call in payment may well reflect a general downturn in trading conditions and an inability of the debtors to pay up.

(b) *The 'acid-test' ratio* $= \dfrac{\text{liquid assets}}{\text{current liabilities}}$

'Liquid assets' comprise cash + marketable securities + receivables and the acid test measures the firm's ability to cover its current liabilities in a real crisis.

(c) *Stockturn* $= \dfrac{\text{annual sales}}{\text{average stock}}$

$$\text{or} \qquad = \frac{\text{average stock}}{\text{annual sales}} \times 12$$

(d) *Receivables* $\qquad = \dfrac{\text{debtors/receivables}}{\text{sales}} \times 12$

A measure of the length of credit extended to customers.

(e) *Payables* $\qquad = \dfrac{\text{creditors/payables}}{\text{sales}} \times 12$

A measure of the credit extended by suppliers.

2 *Measures of profitability.* While the pursuit of profit has been much qualified as a corporate objective in recent years there can be no doubt that it still remains the primary aim of the business organisation. John Sizer cites Peter Drucker's *The Practice of Management*, which points out that profit serves three purposes:[9]

1. It measures the net effectiveness and soundness of a business's effort.
2. It is the premium that covers the cost of staying in business – replacement, obsolescence, market and technical risk and uncertainty. Seen from this point of view it may be argued that there is no such thing as profit; there are only the costs of being and staying in business. These are the costs of survival. The management of a business has to provide adequately for these costs by generating sufficient profit.
3. It ensures the supply of future capital for innovation and expansion, either directly, by providing the means of self-financing out of retained profits, or indirectly, through providing sufficient inducement for new outside capital in the form which will optimise the company's capital structure and optimise its cost of capital.

While most if not all managers would agree to these three propositions, because of the qualification of the profit objective alluded to there is no single method of computing a firm's profit or its profitability and the statistic is subject to considerable ambiguity. Perhaps the most obvious comment is that profit *per se* is meaningless unless it is related to the magnitude of the resources used in generating that profit which suggests that one should first compute:

(a) *The Return on Investment* or *ROI*. Depending upon the authority consulted several methods are suggested for calculating this ratio. The most basic expression of it (and the top ratio in the pyramid) is:

$$\frac{\text{Net profit}}{\text{Capital employed}}$$

But while Sizer would define this precisely as Profit after Taxation and Interest and after Deduction of

$$\frac{\text{Profit attributable to minority and preference shareholders}}{\text{Equity shareholders' investment}}$$

many other sources are much less explicit and suggest the ratios:

$$\frac{\text{Net profit (after tax)}}{\text{Total net assets}}$$

$$\frac{\text{Net profit (after tax)}}{\text{Fixed assets}}$$

(b) *Gross profit* (or gross margin)

$$\frac{\text{Gross profit}}{\text{Sales}}$$

This ratio emphasises the contribution of sales to the selling, general and administrative expense and thus subjects them to close scrutiny, particularly when compared with:

(c) *Net profit*

$$\frac{\text{Net profit}}{\text{Sales}}$$

(d) *Earnings per Share* (EPS)

$$\frac{\text{Profit attributable to equity shareholders}}{\text{Number of equity shares}}$$

This ratio is much favoured by investors and financial analysts as a performance measure, and is usually reported in conjunction with share prices as a:

(e) *Price–Earnings (P–E) ratio:*

$$\frac{\text{Price per share}}{\text{EPS}}$$

From the above selection of ratios it should be obvious that one can compute an almost infinite number of ratios. As noted earlier, the usefulness of such ratios will vary considerably and their main value lies in highlighting changes in direction which can then be subjected to closer and more careful scrutiny.

Summary: The Importance of Control in Marketing

The foregoing discussion of financial controls and measures may seem somewhat misplaced in a book on marketing strategy and management, particularly as it is so selective and essentially superficial. However, the intention is not to provide a primer in managerial accounting, but to emphasise the basic point that finance and control are integral parts of the marketing function and that the marketing manager must have a sound understanding of both if he is to discharge his duties effectively. The truth of this claim is clearly indicated in Figure 21.7 overleaf, which is a diagrammatic representation of the business system.

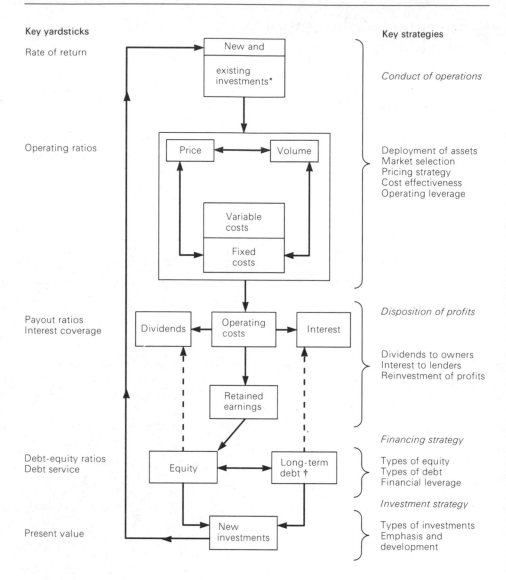

Key yardsticks

Rate of return

Operating ratios

Payout ratios
Interest coverage

Debt-equity ratios
Debt service

Present value

Key strategies

Conduct of operations

Deployment of assets
Market selection
Pricing strategy
Cost effectiveness
Operating leverage

Disposition of profits

Dividends to owners
Interest to lenders
Reinvestment of profits

Financing strategy
Types of equity
Types of debt
Financial leverage

Investment strategy
Types of investments
Emphasis and
development

Figure 21.7   The business system: an overview

* Assumes an amount equal to depreciation invested here
† Assumes continuous rollover, with no reduction through repayments

Source: E. A. Helfert, *Techniques of Financial Analysis*, 5th ed. (Homewood. Ill.: Irwin, 1982).

CHAPTER 22

Recapitulation

■ Introduction

This book has been concerned with a description and analysis of the application of strategic planning to the marketing function and the translation of the resultant marketing strategies into operational plans. Thus we have looked at the nature of strategy in general and marketing strategy in particular, and have recognised that marketing is constrained by the environment within which its activities must be performed. Within this overriding constraint we have acknowledged that the particular performance of the individual organisation will depend upon its ability to identify and satisfy the highly specific needs of individual consumers and that the degree of success which it will enjoy will depend in turn upon its ability to differentiate itself in the minds of prospective customers from the offerings of its competitors. Success in achieving this will be determined by its degree of understanding of the way in which buyers choose and the extent to which it can put this knowledge to good effect by identifying and developing profitable market segments.

Once the firm has decided upon its basic objectives in terms of the products and markets which it intends to deal in it must develop an internally consistent set of policies for the management of its marketing mix. Part II of the book has been concerned specifically with a review of the managerial dimensions of the marketing research function and the four Ps – Product, Price, Place and Promotion – building upon the assumption that the reader is already familiar with the descriptive aspects of these topics. Finally we have just looked at the problems associated with implementing marketing and the need for monitoring and controlling the marketing function in order to provide the feedback which closes the circle of marketing strategy and management. In this concluding chapter we shall seek to tease out those ideas which we consider provide the framework for the development of marketing strategy and the management of the marketing function. In doing so we are conscious that, while oversimplification can be dangerous, our earlier discussion of selective perception and retention and the concept of memory span provides a forceful argument for restricting our own listing of currently useful generalisations to the smallest reasonable number. To this end we examine first the four elements which comprise the 'virtuous circle of best marketing practice'. Next we review the contribution of marketing to competitive success. This is expanded into a set of maxims for marketing and we conclude by proposing a 'Baker's dozen' of key concepts.

The 'Virtuous Circle' of Best Marketing Practice

During 1983 the Institute of Marketing, the University of Bradford Management Centre and Industrial Market Research Ltd joined forces to undertake a major investigation into the role and practice of marketing management in the UK. Based upon the response of over 1800 senior marketing executives the authors[1] concluded that: 'The best companies and the most successful managers combine an unwavering commitment to classic marketing principles with a significantly heightened sensitivity and responsiveness to environment signals.' These factors are depicted diagrammatically in what Hooley *et al.* call the 'virtuous circle of best marketing practice' as shown in Figure 22.1.

This study presents a starkly realistic overview of the difficulties facing British managers as they attempt to cope with an unprecedentedly difficult environment. It must be said at the outset that the study provides no easy answers. None the less, it is possible to isolate certain key features which characterise the more successful organisations. These features, which are illustrated in Figure 22.1, provide clear guidelines for improved marketing effectiveness.

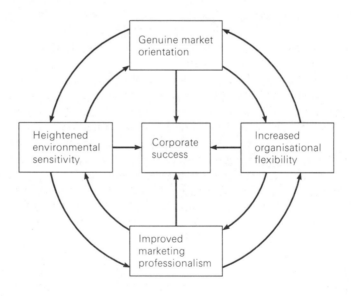

Figure 22.1   Virtuous circles of marketing practice

The key elements in this virtuous circle may be summarised as follows:

1   Marketing orientation

Despite radical changes in the environment a marketing orientation still offers the best likelihood of commercial success.

> The key to marketing success is the development of clear-cut and competitively defensible market position. This is based upon the isolation of a market segment or segments where an organisation's distinctive capabilities and competences find a match with unsatisfied consumer needs. The best performing companies demonstrate an unwavering focus upon the market place and relate all their major operating decisions to the dictates of customer needs.[2]

Market research is seen as an essential prerequisite of the identification and selection of suitable market opportunities, but it is believed that far too few firms make use of this essential marketing tool.

2   Organisational flexibility and adaptability

Flexibility and adaptability in a firm's systems, attitudes and structures are also seen as vital to survival in a turbulent environment. Thus, 'successful companies recognise the need for a flexible planning system which can encompass a wide range of possible scenarios'.

Flexibility also arises from the development of product portfolios which allows the firm to spread its risks across different markets.

3   Heightened environmental sensitivity

The UK survey confirms and supports the findings of Ansoff,[3] Argenti[4] and others that survival depends upon the development of suitable environmental scanning systems to enable the firm to monitor and respond to the 'speed, complexity and discontinuity of change'.

4   Increased marketing professionalism

'The best organisations show a commitment to the training of their personnel and a willingness to experiment with new ideas and concepts.' In other words a 'seat of the pants' approach to marketing is no longer sufficient to cope with current conditions.

While Hooley *et al.* were concerned primarily with the role and practice of *marketing management* one would expect that if marketing plays such an important role in the corporation's overall strategy (as is claimed in this book), any survey of corporate success would also show support for these factors. In one of the most influential management books in recent years Peters and Waterman provide such confirmation.[5] Although the eight attributes which they define as characteristic of the excellent and innovative company cover the whole range of general management, getting 'close to the customer', 'productivity through people' adaptability and flexibility are all seen as central to success.

■ Marketing and Competitive Success

Throughout the 1980s competitiveness was a major preoccupation of managers and academics alike. Extensive research has been undertaken on the topic and numerous books and articles on the subject produced. Of necessity, the treatment of the topic in the summary of a book of this kind can only be eclectic and the reader should be aware that this is the case.

In Chapter 2 we summarised the main thesis of Michael Porter's *The Competitive Advantage of Nations* (1990).[6] A major conclusion of this study of the performance of national economies was that, while a generous endowment of physical resources is an undoubted advantage, history appears to show that it is the *human factor* which is critical to sustained competitive success. Indeed, the emergence of the industrial revolution in Britain and the Japanese economic miracle following the second World War appear to owe much to a determination to overcome a scarcity of physical resources. This is especially the case through involvement in international trade as a means of exporting human skills as 'value-added' in exchange for imports of raw materials and commodities.

In Chapter 2 we also reported some of the findings of the study undertaken by Dr Susan Hart and myself and published as *Marketing and Competitive Success* (1989).[7] This study attempted to address the criticisms levelled against many earlier analyses – particularly that such studies tended to be partial and/or anecdotal. In our study we deliberately set out to analyse a sample of industries, covering those in the growth and mature/decline stages of development – the so-called 'sunrise' and 'sunset' industries. Further, we collected data from both successful and unsuccessful firms judged against the performance criteria appropriate to their own industry.

Based on data collected in the mid-to-late 1980s, it was clear that all our sample possessed an important and distinctive characteristic – they had all survived the recession of the late 1970s and early 1980s. It also became clear that the great majority were aware of the claimed benefits of strategic planning and of the techniques and procedures of the kind discussed in this book. Inevitably we are drawn to the conclusion that it is the *quality of implementation* which differentiates between more and less successful firms. *Knowledge of the kind contained in this book is a necessary but NOT sufficient condition for success.* To recognise this, the discussion of strategy and structure was expanded in this edition and formed the subject of a separate Chapter 19 *Developing a Marketing Culture*.

During the late 1980s James Lynch and his colleagues Graham Hooley and Jenny Shepherd of the University of Bradford Management Centre undertook a follow-up study to that reported in the previous section. Funded by the Economic and Social Science Research Council (ESRC) the objective of the study was to explore *The Effectiveness of British Marketing* and, in particular, the activities and attitudes of the more successful organisations.[8]

Following a series of preliminary depth interviews with senior marketing executives a questionnaire was mailed to 5,416 firms from a list provided by Dun

& Bradstreet and marked 'for the attention of the Chief Marketing Executive'. The effective mailout was 5,121 which, after a follow-up, yielded 1,380 replies (27%) 'broadly representative both in size and SIC of British Industry, including both manufacturing and service sectors'.

The major conclusions were that:

1 There is no magic formula which will guarantee marketing effectiveness ... 'The key to success, it would appear, may be not so much in *what* is done but in *how* it is done'. This finding clearly confirms those of MACS.
2 'In broad terms, the survey suggests both a rise in the perceived importance of marketing's role in organisational success in the last five years and a growing appreciation of the major marketing concepts'. However, the improvement is not universal and leaves much scope for further progress.

In their analysis, Lynch *et al.* isolated the 'Better Performers', who comprised approximately 12% of the sample and reported better performance than their competitors across a range of financial and market-based measures, and then compared these with the remainder:

> Detailed analysis of the research results suggests that the key differentiators between the top performers and the rest are probably not so much issues of strategy or tactics as questions of commitment, cultural consistency and leadership where marketing is concerned. In specific terms, the top performers show a greater marketing grasp and a stronger and more clearly worked-out commitment to marketing principle.

To assess their general orientation to business respondents were asked to select one of three statements 'which best describes the marketing approach of your company?'. As Table 22.1 shows, almost two-thirds selected the third option which reflects a *marketing* orientation, while 18% chose a *selling* orientation emphasising advertising and selling, with the remaining 16% favouring a *production* orientation.

This pattern is confirmed in the response to the statement that 'Marketing is seen as a guiding philosophy for the whole organisation', as shown in Table 22.2.

Additional attitudinal statements indicated that:-

- there is a stronger level of marketing commitment on the part of the Chief Executives of the top performing organisations;
- the top performers reported significantly more aggressive objectives over the last five years than their less successful counterparts, with much greater emphasis on growth and expansion;
- top performers are more likely to have adopted a longer-term marketing objective rather than short-term financial goals;
- top performers attach much greater importance to marketing training.

In terms of organisational structure the key findings are summarised in Figure 22.2.

Table 22.1   'Which of the following best describes the marketing approach of your company?'

	Total Sample (1346) (%)	Better Performers (162) (%)	Others (1184) (%)	Better Performer variation from Others (%)
Make what we can and sell to whoever will buy	16.3	9.9	17.1	− 42
Place major emphasis on advertising and selling	18.2	16.0	18.5	− 14
Place major emphasis on prior analysis of market needs adapting our products and services to meet them if necessary	65.5	74.1	65.4	+ 15

Notes:
1. Percentage figures are column percentages.
2. 'Better performer variation from others' shows the extent to which the two groups differed. The variation is calculated by dividing the Better performers' percentage by that of the others. Where the Better performers adopt a particular answer more often a positive variation is noted, where they adopt one less often a negative variation results. The 'flags' show visually the extent of the variation.

Source: J. Lynch, G. Hooley and J. Shepherd, *Effectiveness of British Marketing*, University of Bradford Management Centre.

Table 22.2   'How well does the following statement describe the role of marketing in your company?'

'*Marketing is seen as a guiding philosophy for the whole organisation*'

	Total Sample (1125) (%)	Better Performers (148) (%)	Others (997) (%)	Better Performer variation from Others (%)
Exactly	29.4	41.2	27.6	+ 49
To some extent	48.9	43.9	49.6	− 11
Not at all	21.7	14.9	22.7	− 34

Source: J. Lynch, G. Hooley and J. Shepherd, *Effectiveness of British Marketing*, University of Bradford Management Centre.

- More likely to have a marketing department
- More likely to have marketing represented directly at board level
- More likely to adopt a market-based organisational structure
- Work more closely with the other functional areas:
  Finance
  Production
  Sales
  Research & Development

Figure 22.2   Top performer organisation

In terms of operational practice – what the firms actually do in the market place – several important differences emerged, which are summarised in Figure 22.3.

- A greater input from marketing to overall strategic planning
- Greater tendency to formal long-term marketing planning
- More aggressive marketing objectives
- Prepared to attack the whole market and take on any competition
- More prepared to take a calculated risk
- Superior quality, high-price positioning strategies
- Build competitive advantages through reputation and quality
- More active in new product development to lead their markets

Figure 22.3   Top performer marketing activities

Based upon their analysis, Lynch *et al.* conclude 'that it is possible to isolate four basic orientations towards marketing on the part of respondent to the survey'. Taking the *Function* and *Philosophy* as the two key dimensions of their classification the four categories are respresented diagrammatically as in Figure 22.4, and are defined as follows.

1 *The Sales Supporters* (9%) – demonstrated a very narrow view of marketing's role and sphere of influence within the organisation. For this group marketing, where it exists at all, is perceived as essentially a support function to the central task of making the sale.
2 *The Unsures* (24%) – appeared to be in a state of flux and some uncertainty concerning marketing's role in their organisation. The Unsures see marketing to some extent as a sales supporting function but it is also believed to have some involvement in identifying and meeting customer needs.
3 *The Departmental Marketers* (26%) – are characterised above all else by the belief that marketing is a departmental activity confined to the activities of the marketing people in the organisation.

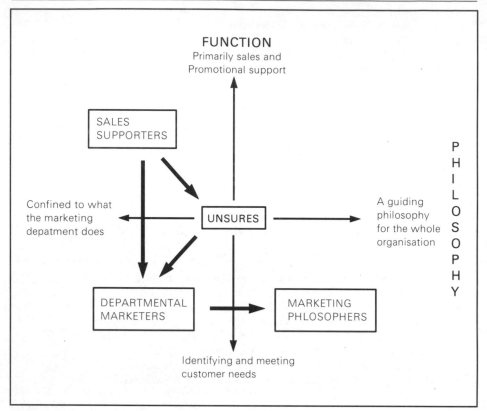

Figure 22.4   Marketing approaches and evolutionary patterns

4   *The Marketing Philosophers* (41%) – clearly distinguish between philosophy and function and, very significantly, 91% of the CEOs of these firms see marketing as the guiding approach for the whole organisation (vs 53% amongst the Departmental Marketers, 45% among the Unsures and 25% among the Sales Supporters).

The researchers conclude that these categories reflect

> an evolutionary pattern of organisational marketing effectiveness. We judge that organisations initially see marketing as a simple adjunct to selling (the Sales Supporters). This narrow view over time often changes to a wider but more uncertain sense of marketing's broader potential (the Unsures). In those organisations where additional evolution occurs, the next stage gives greater prominence to marketing but confines it strictly to the activities of the marketing people in the business (the Departmental Marketers). The final stage involves the recognition that marketing is more than just a function. It is an attitude and a philosophy which should guide all the organisation's activities and is centred upon customer focus, competitive advantage, environmental sensitivity and a healthy commitment to the financial bottom line (the Marketing Philosophers).

Lynch *et al.*'s findings support those of Peters and Waterman, Baker and Hart and many others in their emphasis upon a number of basic principles and excellence in their implementation. From an analysis of marketing practice certain themes occur and re-occur with a frequency which seems to suggest that there is a nucleus of concepts and ideas that have near-universal validity. Indeed, the robust and durable nature of these CUGs is such that they may be articulated as a series of maxims for marketers.

■ Maxims for Marketers[9]

In reviewing what I consider to be among the most important of these 'marketing maxims', it appears that the early development of marketing thought and practice has been characterised by a predilection for over-statement. Whereas such overstatement may have been necessary in the 1950s and 1960s to distinguish the new marketing orientation from the sales and production orientations which preceded it, during the 1970s and 1980s such hyperbole became misleading to the point of being counterproductive and underlines the need for a clear statement of just what marketing is really all about.

Maxim 1 Marketing is both a philosophy of business and a business function.

It seems to me that many of the difficulties which hinder understanding and acceptance of the marketing concept derive from a failure to distinguish clearly between marketing as a state of mind concerning the optimum approach to business, and the activities whereby such ideas are translated into practice.

It is probably true to say that successful entrepreneurs have always been marketing orientated, in the sense that they have recognised that success depends upon having the right goods at the right price at the right place at the right time. More important still, they have recognised that what is 'right' depends upon the consumer, for it is he who casts his money votes in the market-place and thereby exercises his sovereignty. For a variety of reasons which I discuss below in the context of other maxims, the emphasis in recent years has moved away from the 'what' and 'where', and the 'when', to the 'who', and 'why', and the 'how', and it is this change of emphasis which has led to the stress on the marketing function and marketing practice and, particularly, upon personal selling and promotion. To a large degree the latter activities appear to be the antithesis of product design and development, and the efficient management of production and distribution, which dominated earlier phases of post-industrial revolution market development, all of which appear objective and quantifiable. By contrast, selling and advertising appear to be subjective and non-quantifiable, and it is hardly surprising that this strong difference should alienate managers brought up in the scientific school of management. In turn, this alienation against marketing practice has tended to prejudice acceptance of the marketing concept, despite the intuitive attraction of this approach – thus, as the need for marketing has grown greater so also has antipathy to the means whereby concept should be translated into practice.

The main reason why there has been a need for a change in marketing practice is to be found in:

Maxim 2   The act of consumption changes the consumer.

On reflection the validity of this maxim is so obvious that it hardly seems worth stating it. Unfortunately many successful entrepreneurs have ignored the implications of this principle, and often with dire consequences. Probably the most eloquent and well-known analysis of this phenomenon is Ted Levitt's *Marketing Myopia*,[10] in which he makes the trenchant observation 'that every declining industry was once a growth industry' – you have to rise before you can fall. To rise you have to be able to recognise a market opportunity – to know what the customer wants – in other words, to be marketing orientated. However, the seeds of self-destruction and failure are built into every successful product, for it introduces the user to standards and aspirations hitherto dormant and unsatisfied. Railways made it possible to move people and freight across continents with a speed, economy and comfort unknown in the days of horse-drawn traffic and beyond the capabilities of canals and rivers. But, while the railway moguls became complacent, their customers began to perceive certain disadvantages in this new mode of transport, not least of which was the need to travel when it suited the railways, and to start your journey from their premises, not your own. The internal combustion engine, cars and lorries, provided the flexibility and convenience which the consumer was looking for, and Henry Ford knew exactly what he was doing when he set out to mass produce a basic car at a price nearly anyone could afford.

Indeed, Henry Ford was so successful that not only did he stimulate an enormous expansion in the market, but in twenty years he moved from an insignificant share of the market to a dominant position with over 60 per cent. Unfortunately Henry Ford forgot the insight which gave rise to this success, and he failed to observe that once everyone had a Model T, many wanted something better. The product planning committee of General Motors understood this, and they were also sensitive to:

Maxim 3   Downward-sloping demand curves reflect differences in preferences and purchasing power.
    To this one might add the corollary that 'The vast majority of demand curves for products and services slope downward'.

Now the mistake of the tyro economist (and of Henry Ford) is to assume that those with the strongest demand and/or most purchasing power would behave in exactly the same way if the price were reduced, i.e. they would continue to consume the same volume of the product as before, now that it had become available to more users at a lower price. For some goods this may be so, but, for most, those with the strongest preferences (inelastic demand) will look for a differentiated product. The explanation for this is to be found in Maxim 2. When new products are introduced, both supply and demand tend to be relatively small and prices high, due to the absence of economies of scale in production, distribution and marketing, coupled with the innovator's desire to capitalise his investment in R & D early on in the life of the innovation. Because of its relatively high price, only those with a very strong preference and/or high levels of disposable income are able to afford supplies. As awareness of the product grows and demand expands, producers are able to 'slide down the demand curve', offering lower prices as they achieve scale economies. By this time the early buyers have become familiar with the product, and look for improvements in it. In other words, willingness to pay different prices implies a desire for different product configurations. General Motors understood this, and evolved the concept of market segmentation, providing different types and qualities of motor-car at different prices.

Two further maxims derive directly from the rapid growth of supply and demand associated with any successful NPD:

Maxim 4   The greater the separation between producer and consumer, the greater the propensity for distortion in communication between them.

Maxim 5   The more sophisticated the demand, the less self-evident it becomes.

As markets grow there is a tendency for concentration to develop on the supply side, as the more efficient firms eliminate their less efficient competitors. Once achieved, such concentration is usually self-sustaining, as it provides scale economies in production and marketing. However, as noted earlier, a dominant position can result in complacency and loss of touch with the consumer, and it is this which can lead to a failure by the supplier to be aware of and respond to the changing needs of his customers.

By the same token, broad basic needs – food, drink, shelter, clothing, transportation etc. – are easy to detect and even to quantify in general terms. But, in the particular, this is far from the case, and in a free market suppliers expend considerable energy and ingenuity in attempting to create differentiated supplies which will appeal to a non-homogeneous collection of potential buyers.

Separation and sophistication both predicate the need to monitor carefully and continuously the nature of demand, and underline the need for marketing research.

As a consequence of Maxim 2 the act of consumption changes the consumer – of competition and concentration, we may identify –

Maxim 6 Change is inevitable – to which, parenthetically, we might add 'and difficult to predict'.

The validity of this maxim is particularly well-exemplified by one of the few genuine marketing concepts – the idea of the product life-cycle. Although the concept of a product life-cycle has been subject to much criticism, I believe this arises from attempts to use it, often unsuccessfully, to develop specific sales forecasts, rather than regarding it for what it is – a generalised predictive device of the way in which the sales of *successful* products will grow, stabilise and stagnate. The emphasis upon 'successful' is important, for one obviously cannot anticipate a period of rapid growth for a deficient product which is doomed to failure from its inception. Similarly, just as the length of any given phase of a biological life-cycle will vary according to the species, so will it vary according to the type of product under consideration.

It is also important to remember that, while change is ultimately inevitable, it is possible to influence the shape of the 'normal' product life-cycle through deliberate action. Thus, much of my own research has been concerned with ways and means of speeding up market penetration by better pre-identification of the best prospects for new products. In the same way, many others have proposed methods of extending the mature phase through policies of incremental product improvement and market extension, and there is even a modest literature on avoiding the debilitating effects of old age through programmes of planned euthanasia.

The reason why every manager should have a framed diagram of the product life-cycle on his desk or office wall is to remind him that sooner or later, for better or worse, the status quo will change. It is the manager's responsibility to be sensitive and to plan for this eventuality. Better still, he should consciously seek to influence and control the future – an assertion which leads to:

Maxim 7   Marketing is accountable for the present and responsible for the future.

One of the worst effects of the excessive enthusiasm for 'marketing' in the 1960s and 1970s was the emphasis it placed upon marketing's role in anticipating and planning for the future. A direct consequence of this was to play down or even undermine the sales function, which, hitherto, had been the mainstay of most marketing effort. This tendency still prevails, and it is not without significance that selling and sales management is not to be found enjoying the same status as other marketing functions such as advertising, marketing research, public relations, etc., in the curricula of business schools and professionally orientated courses. This attitude is irresponsible, for today is yesterday's future, and if we want to claim the privilege of planning the future we must be prepared to accept accountability for it when it arrives. Clearly, in the short term it is necessary to sell what you can make – widely derided as the antithesis of the marketing concept – in order to realise the capital invested in production facilities, so that this may be reinvested in new facilities to produce new products. It follows that the marketer must achieve a balance between the time and effort expended upon monitoring change in the market-place and translating this into plans for future action, and maximising the return from the present product-market mix.

In order to maximise sales it is necessary to give full attention to the facts discussed in the introduction to Chapter 16, namely:

Maxim 8   Consumption is a function of availability.

This maxim is essentially a restatement of the now largely discredited Say's Law that 'supply creates demand'. Despite the inevitable logic of the proposition that one can only consume products and services that are available, many commentators assert that seeing markets as supply-led is to ignore consumer sovereignty, with the result that they neglect production and distribution while stressing advertising and sales promotion. Of course, the mere creation of supply is not in itself a sufficient condition to ensure consumption, and it is for this reason that the marketing concept has so much to offer in reminding us that consumer preferences change, and that we need to keep a careful check of these changes, and modify our output accordingly. That said, however, it is clear that many potential sales are lost through non-availability, and that the less distinctive the product the greater the probability that such non-availability will result in consumers changing their preferred supplier. This is not only true of convenience goods like detergents, baked beans and the like, where brand shares are frequently a self-fulfilling prophecy (i.e. retailers stock brands in the proportions of their reported brand shares, so that, assuming total stocks for a given period roughly equate sales, it is not surprising that actual brand shares mirror predicted brand shares) it is also true of standardised industrial materials – basic chemicals, steel, etc. – components and supplies, especially when made to a well-recognised specification. Indeed, a number of surveys of industrial buyers have shown that quality and reliability are much more important determinants of buyer preference than the economists' preferred discriminator – price. This leads us to:

Maxim 9   In a true-choice situation it is the subjective marketing factors which are determinant.

Most analyses of buyer behaviour, whether it be industrial buyers or ultimate consumers, are agreed that purchasing is an essentially rational process in which the potential buyer seeks to discriminate between possible solutions to his felt need through the application of objective criteria. Of these objective criteria, performance characteristics and the cost-benefit of any given purchase are considered first. However, given the potential to create excess supplies in the advanced industrialised economies, there is frequently intense competition between suppliers of near-identical products, such that price and performance factors do not point to any clearly preferred alternative. Under such circumstances, the potential buyer is still faced with the need to make a choice, and his wish to appear rational requires that he find a criterion to justify his eventual selection. Given that objective and measurable factors have been exhausted in arriving at the short list from which a choice is to be made, it is the subjective elements which condition the final selection, and it is the subjective elements which are most sensitive to marketing activities. This is especially true of promotional activity, whether it is by impersonal communication through the media, or personal communication by salesmen, or word-of-mouth recommendation by opinion leaders.

Unfortunately this determinant role of marketing only comes into operation when all else is equal, a fact which is increasingly overlooked by those who seem to regard marketing as a panacea for all other deficiencies – in product design, in product quality, in price and in availability.

Marketing is only one factor, albeit a critical one, in ensuring commercial success. In proposing nine marketing maxims I have tried to isolate what I consider to be key considerations in the philosophy and practice of marketing, and to emphasise that true success can only occur where those responsible for the direction of the enterprise are marketing orientated, and ensure that the marketing function is fully integrated with the other key business functions – research and development, production, finance and control.

■ A Baker's Dozen of Key Concepts

In the preceding section we have looked at a nucleus of ideas which occur over and over again in any discussion or analysis of the real essence of marketing. These 'maxims' (as we have designated them) summarise some of the more important philosophical underpinnings of the marketing concept and their acceptance is essential to the development of a marketing orientation. However, as this book has attempted to show, above all else marketing is something which you *do* and in this final section we identify thirteen key concepts which are seen as intrinsic to the effective practice of marketing, namely:

1 Generic product definition.
2 The product life-cycle.
3 Limited strategic alternatives.
4 Business portfolio analysis.
5 The marketing audit.
6 Selective perception.
7 Customer diversity.
8 Market segmentation and positioning.
9 Differential advantage.
10 The marketing mix.
11 Integrated marketing planning.
12 Control and feedback.
13 3-in-1 marketing.

To some extent these key concepts are an extension of the marketing maxims, the essential difference being that they represent a sequence of operational guidelines for marketing managers.

Generic product definition is a term coined by Kotler and Levy[11] to encapsulate the most basic marketing principle of all – that one should define market opportunities in terms of the underlying need to be served rather than in terms of the product currently available to serve that need. To paraphrase Levitt (see Maxim 1), who first counselled firms to think of themselves as being in the transportation business rather than in railroads, in entertainment rather than movies, and energy rather than oil, 'people buy ¼" drills, but they *need* ¼" holes'. Clearly, with the development of laser technology conventional twist drills may soon become a thing of the past – has the hole-making industry reflected on the implications of this? Or, to take another example, consider those doyens of consumer goods marketing, the detergent manufacturers. Have Unilever and Procter & Gamble reflected on the fact that consumers don't particularly want detergent and water; their real objective is clean clothes so that an ultrasonic 'washing-machine' which requires neither would serve their needs just as well as would disposable or non-soil clothing.

It follows that the starting-point for all strategic marketing planning must be a clear and explicit statement of the benefit or satisfaction which the customer is seeking and this is so whether the customer is a firm or an individual and irrespective of whether the means of delivery is a product or a service.

As was seen in Maxims 2 and 6, a clear corollary of identifying the long-term and enduring needs of the customer is the *Product life-cycle* concept which underlines forcefully the inevitability of change and the fact that while basic needs continue almost indefinitely the means of satisfying them change continuously. Not only do products come and go, but there is a clearly discernible pattern to the life of every successful product as it passes from introduction, to growth, maturity, decline and withdrawal. So consistent is this pattern that it provides a clear set of guidelines for managing the product as it progresses from birth to decay. Thus while it cannot predict the duration or strength of any individual phase, it should sensitise the planner to the need for carefully monitoring the sales performance of his product so that he can identify changes at an early stage and take the appropriate managerial action.

Limited strategic alternatives is a simple idea which postulates that there is only a small number of basic strategies open to a firm.

- Do nothing
- Direct competition
- Indirect competition

- Innovation
- Withdrawal

★ Peaceful co-existence
★ Price
★ Product differentiation
★ Promotional differentiation
★ Distribution differentiation
★ Changing the rules of the game

The concept indicates that only rarely will it be possible to pursue a do-nothing strategy successfully due to the continuous change taking place in the market (see Maxim 6). Similarly direct or price competition is only feasible when the firm possesses a significant cost advantage and is willing to use this to secure a dominant market share and further economies of scale. Tactically, however, smaller firms may use price as a competitive weapon in the knowledge that the major suppliers are unlikely to offer a similar discount on their much larger sales volume.

In an attempt to avoid direct competition most firms have chosen to compete indirectly through differentiation of the other elements of the marketing mix – product, promotion and distribution. Through indirect competition the firm hopes to secure a monopoly over a segment of the market and so be able to exercise a degree of control over that segment particularly in terms of price policy.

However, monopolies arising from indirect competition are often uncertain, fragile and short-lived, and this encourages many firms to pursue a strategy of innovation in the hope of establishing a genuine monopoly with a radically different product or service.

The fourth key concept – *Business portfolio analysis* – is a natural extension of the preceding concept in that it recognises that while there is only a limited set of strategic alternatives these are not mutually exclusive. While it is true that there are many firms which survive and even prosper on the basis of a single product they are either very large – electricity generation, telecommunications – or very small with a particular niche in the market that no one else would wish to compete for. For the majority of firms survival and prosperity depend upon their having a range of products at different stages in their life-cycle so that as old products are withdrawn new ones are introduced to replace them. As a consequence the multi-product, multi-market firm with a portfolio of products at different stages in their life-cycle may well be pursuing *all* of the strategic alternatives simultaneously with a broadly based portfolio model such as the Boston Box or Shell's Directional Policy Matrix providing the framework for its strategic planning.

An essential ingredient to such strategic planning is the *Marketing audit* or SWOT analysis through which the firm seeks to identify threats and opportunities in the external environment as a basis for maximising its own corporate strengths and minimising its weaknesses. In undertaking such an audit, and indeed in every aspect of marketing, one must be continuously aware of the nature and effects of *Selective perception*.

The importance of this phenomenon was underlined in the discussion of how buyers (and sellers) make decisions, from which it became clear that we all tend to interpret 'facts' in terms of our own background, experience and value systems with the result that different individuals are likely to place quite different interpretations on a given piece of objective information. Accordingly one must be ever sensitive to the dangers of the self-reference criterion and of assuming that the rest of the world sees, believes and acts in the same way as ourselves. We must recognise that because of *Customer diversity* there is rarely, if ever, a homogeneous demand for the product.

However, the fact that individuals do differ from one another does not mean that there are no similarities between them, and a key activity for the marketing planner is the identification of groupings of consumers which are sufficiently alike and of sufficient size to constitute a worth-while market in their own right. As was seen in Chapter 8, there are many diverse approaches to *Market segmentation*, but behavioural differences resulting from selective perception stand out as a major source of customer diversity.

Given that markets can be segmented or subdivided on the basis of a variety of different criteria the objective of the marketing planner must be to position himself so that his offering will be seen as matching most closely the distinctive needs of the segment for which he has chosen to compete. To do so effectively the seller's product or service must be seen as offering some *Differential advantage* over those of his competitors. In our model of buyer behaviour it was seen that objective, physical and measurable differences are to be preferred, but it also recognised that such differences are also the easiest to match or copy. Thus in many markets, and particularly industrial and institutional markets, products and services are objectively the same and differentiation between them must depend upon intangible and subjective factors such as design, quality, reputation, and, increasingly, service.

In order to cater for the distinctive needs of different market segments and maximise such differential advantage as one possesses the marketer will need to develop a unique combination of the basic marketing ingredients – product, price, place and promotion. In other words, one must create a *Marketing mix* which is perceived as both different and better by a sufficient number of prospective users to comprise a worth-while market in its own right. To achieve such a marketing mix it is vital that the firm practise *Integrated marketing planning*, for it is only by doing so that synergy can be created and a competitive edge be achieved and maintained. While systems and procedures are important our discussion of managerial orientations and organisational structures indicate that successful implementation is most likely to occur when all members of the organisation subscribe to a philosophy of customer satisfaction – a marketing orientation – and that this is reflected in the values, mission and objectives (corporate culture) of the organisation.

But the road to hell is paved with good intentions. Sophisticated marketing planning procedures are irrelevant and useless unless stringent efforts are made to monitor performance through *Control and feedback* mechanisms. It is through such mechanisms that the planner is able to detect what is working and what is not, and so make the continuous adjustments necessary to maintain the integrity of the operation and ensure its successful continuation.

And, finally, we return to *3-in-1 marketing*, which is a plea to marketers to remember that while long-range strategic marketing planning is challenging, creative, demanding and exciting it will be of no avail if we lose sight of the need to manage the short- and medium-term future efficiently and effectively. Thus we must pay much more attention to the cinderellas of marketing – selling and distribution – for these are the means whereby we will recoup our past investments and earn the profits on which the future will depend.

Notes and References

■ Preface to the Second Edition

1. P. Kotler, *Marketing Management* (Englewood Cliffs, N.J.: Prentice-Hall, 1972) 2nd edn.
2. Martin L. Bell, *Marketing: Concepts and Strategy* (Boston: Houghton-Mifflin, 1972) 2nd edn.
3. E. Jerome McCarthy and William D. Perault, Jr, *Basic Marketing* (Homewood, Ill.: Irwin, 1984) 8th edn.
4. William M. Pride and O. C. Ferrell, *Marketing* (Boston: Houghton-Mifflin, 1987) 5th edn.

■ 1   Prologue

1. 'Marketing Strategy: new directions of theory and research'.
2. These are discussed at some length in Chapter 19.

■ 2   Marketing and Competition

1. Michael E. Porter, *Competitive Strategy: Techniques for Analyzing Industries and Competitors* (New York: Free Press, 1980).
   Michael E. Porter, *Competitive Advantage: creating and sustaining superior performance* (New York: Free Press, 1985).
   Michael E. Porter, *The Competitive Advantage of Nations* (London: Macmillan, 1990).
2. F. M. Scherer and D. Ross, *Industrial Market Structure and Economic Performance* (Boston: Houghton-Mifflin, 1990) 3rd edn.
3. Adam Smith, *An Enquiry into the Nature and Causes of the Wealth of Nations* (1776).
4. T. Levitt, 'Marketing Myopia', *Harvard Business Review* (July–August 1960) p. 45.
5. Porter (1980, 1985, 1990) see n. 1 above.
6. We cannot claim consumer democracy unless it is possible with disproportionate representation, for different consumers have widely different claims or titles to economic wealth. But sovereignty does exist, albeit in the negative sense that consumers within controlled supply economies choose not to consume, rather than accept someone else's interpretation of what constitutes a satisfying product.
7. Lawrence Abbott, *Quality and Competition* (New York: Columbia University Press, 1955).
8. Michael J. Baker, *Marketing: An Introductory Text* (London: Macmillan, 1974) 2nd edn.
9. Scherer and Ross (1990) see n. 2 above.

10. See n. 1 above.
11. 5th edn (1991).
12. Michael E. Porter, 'How Competitive Forces Shape Strategy', *Harvard Business Review* (March–April 1979).
13. A. Maslow, 'A Theory of Human Motivation', *Psychological Review*, 50 (1943).
14. See n. 4 above.
15. Everett M. Rogers, *Diffusion of Innovations* (New York: Free Press, 1962).
16. Michael E. Porter, 'The Competitive Advantage of Nations', *Harvard Business Review* (March–April 1990).
17. *Best of Business International.*
18. Thomas Peters and Robert Waterman, *In Search of Excellence* (New York: Harper & Row, 1982).
19. Michael J. Baker and Susan Hart, *Marketing and Competitive Success* (London: Philip Allen, 1989).
20. See n. 18 above.
21. McKinsey and Co., 'The Winning Performance of the Midsized Growth Companies', American Business Conference (May) (London: McKinsey and Co.).
22. Veronica Wong, John Saunders and Peter Doyle, 'The Effectiveness of Marketing Implementation: functional managers' views of practices in their firm', in M. J. Baker, *Perspectives on Marketing Management*, vol. II (Chichester: John Wiley, 1992).
23. David Ricardo, *The Principles of Political Economy and Taxation* (1817).

■ 3   Marketing and Corporate Strategy

1. An extended discussion of the salient characteristics of the major business orientations is to be found in Chapter 19.
2. Igor Ansoff, *Corporate Strategy* (Harmondsworth: Penguin Books, 1968).
3. Howard Raiffa, *Decision Analysis* (Reading, Mass.: Addison-Wesley, 1968).
4. Robert O. Schlaifer, *The Analysis of Decisions under Uncertainty* (New York: McGraw Hill, 1967).
5. Martin Bell, *Marketing Concepts and Strategy* (London: Macmillan, 1966). It is acknowledged that many authors still prefer to maintain a distinction between policy and strategy. Thus, Martin Bell writes: 'Strategy is not the same as policy, and is always subordinate to it. Military strategy in the United States in planned within the framework of national defence policy. This policy is established by the President of the United States in line with the basic foreign relations objectives of his administration.' Clearly, Bell regards policy as superior to strategy, while Ansoff regards it as inferior, and most authors use the terms as if they were interchangeable. Our own view, as with the definition of marketing, is that semantics are less important than appreciation of the distinction between objectives and courses of action to achieve them.
6. Kenneth R. Andrews, *The Concept of Corporate Strategy* (Homewood, Ill.: Dow Jones–Irwin, 1971).
7. Barton A. Weitz and Robin Wensley, *Strategic Marketing* (Boston, Mass.: New-Publishing, 1984).
8. George Steiner and John Miner, Management Policy and Strategy: Text, Readings and Case (New York: Macmillan, 1977).

9. Donald Melville 'Top Management's Role in Strategic Planning', in Roger A. Kerin and Robert A. Peterson (eds), *Perspectives on Strategic Marketing Management* (Boston: Allyn & Bacon, 1983).

10. See, for example, H. V. Hodson, *The Diseconomics of Growth* (London: Pan/ Ballantyne, 1972).

11. *Corporate Strategy*, p. 95 (see n. 2 above).

12. Michael J. Baker, *Marketing New Industrial Products* (London: Macmillan, 1975) especially Chapter 2.

13. E. Raymond Corey, *The Development of Markets for New Materials* (Boston: Harvard University Press, 1956).

14. For example, linoleum manufacturers did not see vinyl flooring as the logical development in the smooth floor-covering market; they regarded it as a suicidal means of highlighting the disadvantages of linoleum, thereby making their investment obsolete. The manufacturers of van trailers could see no benefit in substituting aluminium for timber and steel, with which they were familiar, as the potential increase in load capacity accrued to the operators. Only when the latter demanded the lighter van was the change made.

15. Michael J. Baker, *Marketing New Industrial Products* and *Market Development* (Harmondsworth: Penguin, 1983).

16. Michael J. Porter *The Competitive Advantage of Nations* (London: Macmillan, 1990).

17. Philip Kotler, *Marketing Management* (Englewood Cliffs, N.J.: Prentice-Hall, 1972) 2nd edn.

■ 4   Principles of Strategic Marketing Planning

1. This summary, and many of the key concepts and ideas discussed in this chapter, draw heavily upon the work of the Arthur D. Little consulting organisation, which has long been in the forefront of developments in this field of corporate planning and management.

2. Robert H. Hayes and William J. Abernathy, 'Managing our way to economic decline', *Harvard Business Review* (July–August 1980).

3. Michael E. Porter, *Competitive Strategy* (New York: Free Press, 1980).

4. Lewis Gunn, teaching notes (University of Strathclyde 1991).

5. Douglas Brownlie, 'Analytical Frameworks for Strategic Marketing Planning', Chapter 11 in *Marketing: Theory and Practice* (London: Macmillan, 1983) 2nd edn. Michael J. Baker *et al*. See also D. F. Abell and J. S. Hammond, *Strategic Marketing Planning* (Englewood Cliffs, N.J.: Prentice-Hall, 1979).

6. M. H. B. McDonald, 'The Theory and Practice of Marketing Planning for Industrial Goods in International Markets', Ph.D. dissertation, Cranfield Institute of Technology (1982). this section borrows extensively on this source. The thesis was published as *Marketing Plans* (London: Heinemann, 1984).

7. Igor Ansoff, *Corporate Strategy* (Harmondsworth: Penguin, 1968).

8. Edward S. McKay, *The Marketing Mystique* (New York: American Management Association, 1972).

9. Peter Drucker, *The Practice of Management* (London: Heinemann, 1968).

10. *Harvard Business Review* (July–August 1960).

11. P. Drucker, 'The Big Power of Little Ideas', *Harvard Business Review* (May–June 1964).
12. Bernard Taylor, 'Managing the Process of Corporate Development', *Long Range Planning* (June 1976).
13. January–February 1986.
14. 'The State of Strategic Thinking' (23 May 1987).
15. See n. 6 above.
16. B. Charles Ames, 'Trappings versus Substance in Industrial Marketing', *Harvard Business Review*, (July–August 1970).
17. Thomas G. Marx, 'Removing the Obstacles to Effective Strategic Planning', *Long Range Planning*, 24 (August 1991).
18. F. Gluck, S. Kaufman and A. S. Walleck, 'The Four Phases of Strategic Management', *The Journal of Business Strategy* (Winter 1982).
19. 31 December 1990.

■ 5 Analytical Frameworks for Strategic Marketing Planning

1. B. Charles Ames, 'Trappings versus Substance in Industrial Marketing', *Harvard Business Review* (July–August 1970).
2. N. K. Dhalla and S. Yuspeh, 'Forget the Product Life Cycle Concept!', *Harvard Business Review* (January–February 1976).
3. See, for example, the discussion in Michael J. Baker, *Marketing New Industrial Products* (London: Macmillan, 1975), together with the graphical representations of the recorded life-cycles of numerous products (pp. 24–47), and also Chapter 3 in Michael J. Baker, *Market Development* (Harmondsworth: Penguin, 1983).
4. R. D. Buzzell, 'Competitive behaviour and the product life cycle', in J. S. Wright and J. L. Goldstrucker (eds), *New Ideas for Successful Marketing*, Proceedings of the 1966 World Congress (American Marketing Association, 1966).
5. William D. Wells and George Gubar, 'Life Cycle Concepts in Marketing Research', *Journal of Marketing Research* (November 1966) pp. 355–63.
6. P. Kotler, *Marketing Management* (Englewood Cliffs, N.J.: Prentice-Hall, 1980) 4th edn.
7. C. Firth, 'New Approaches to Strategic Marketing Planning', unpublished MBA dissertation (University of Bradford, 1980); Everett M. Rogers, *Diffusion of Innovations* (New York: Free Press, 1962).
8. Heinz Wolff, reported in 'Is the Future so Frightening?', *International Management* (October 1979).
9. Everett M. Rogers, *Diffusion of Innovations* (New York: Free Press, 1962).
10. T. Levitt, 'Marketing Myopia', *Harvard Business Review* (July–August 1960).
11. (1975).
12. H. Earl Pemberton, 'The Curve of Culture Diffusion Rate', *American Sociological Review*, 1 (August 1936) pp. 547–56.
13. Derek J. de Solla Price, *Little Science, Big Science* (New York: Columbia University Press, 1963).
14. Stuart C. Dodd, 'Diffusion is Predictable: Testing Predictability Models for Laws of Interaction', *American Sociological Review*, 10(1955) pp. 392–401.
15. Zvi Griliches, 'Hybrid Corn: An Exploration in the Economics of Technological Change', *Econometrica*, 25 (October 1957) pp. 501–22.

16. Pitrim A. Sorokin, *Social and Cultural Dynamics*, 4 vols (Englewood Cliffs, N.J.: Bedminster Press, 1962).
17. Rogers, p. 152, see n. 9 above.
18. Gabriel Tarde, *The Laws of Imitation*, trans by Elsie Clews Parsons (New York: Henry Holt & Co., 1903).
19. Bryce Ryan and Neal C. Gross, 'The Diffusion of Hybrid Seed Corn in Two Iowa Communities', *Rural Sociology*, 8 (1943) pp. 15–24.
20. Harold L. Wattel (ed.), *The Dissemination of New Business Techniques*, vol. 2 (Hempstead, N.Y.: Hofstra University, 1964).
21. Edwin Mansfield, *Industrial Research and Technological Innovation* (New York: W. W. Norton, 1968).
22. G. F. Ray, 'The Diffusion of New Technology. A Study of Ten Processes in Nine Industries', *National Institute Economic Review* (March 1969) pp. 40–83.
23. C. Freeman, 'The Plastics Industry: A Comparative Study of Research and Development', *National Institute Economic Review* (November 1963) pp. 22–62.
24. Raymond Vernon, 'International Investments and International Trade in the Product Cycle', *Quarterly Journal of Economics*, 53(2) (May 1966) pp. 190–207.
25. Louis T. Wells, Jr, 'A Product Life Cycle for International Trade?', *Journal of Marketing*, 32(3) (July 1968) pp. 1–6.
26. OECD, *Gaps in Technology, Comparisons between Member Countries in Education, Research and Development, Technological Innovation, International Economic Exchanges* (Paris: 1970).
27. Frank Lynn, 'An Investigation of the Rate of Development and Diffusion of Technology in Our Modern Industrial Society', in *The Employment Impact of Technological Change*, Appendix Volume II, *Technology Automation, and Economic Progress* (Washington, D.C.: US Government Printing Office, 1966).
28. Zvi Griliches, 'Hybrid Corn: An Explanation in the Economics of Technological Change', *Econometrica*, 25 (October 1957) pp. 501–22.
29. See n. 10 above.
30. Axel Johne, 'Innovation Organisation and the Marketing of High Technology Products', unpublished Ph.D. dissertation (Strathclyde University, 1982).
31. D. F. Abell and J. S. Hammond, *Strategic Marketing Planning* (Englewood Cliffs, N.J.: Prentice-Hall, 1979).
32. See, for example, R. Wensley, 'Strategic Marketing: beta's, boxes or basics', *Journal of Marketing* (1981); G. Day, 'Diagnosing the Product Portfolio', *Journal of Marketing* (April 1977).
33. Chapter 11 in Michael J. Baker *et al.*, *Marketing: Theory and Practice* (London: Macmillan, 1983) 2nd edn.
34. 'Gaining insights through strategy analysis', *The Journal of Business Strategy* 4(1) (Summer 1983).
35. A. Ries and J. Trout, *Positioning: the battle for your mind* (New York: McGraw-Hill, 1981).
36. D. E. Hussey, 'Portfolio Analysis: Practical Experience with the Directional Policy Matrix', *Long Range Planning* (August 1978) p. 3.
37. See n. 7 for Chapter 4 above.
38. Igor Ansoff, *Implanting Strategic Management* (Englewood Cliffs, N.J.: Prentice-Hall, 1984; 2nd edn 1990).
39. W. R. Huss and E. J. Honton, 'Scenario Planning – What Style Should you Use?', *Long Range Planning* 20(4) (1987) pp. 21–9.

■ 6   The Marketing Environment

1. Chapter 2 in Michael J. Baker, *Marketing* (5th edn, 1991) provides a broad overview of this topic.
2. John Diffenbach, 'Corporate Environmental Analysis in Large U.S. Corporations', *Long Range Planning*, 16(3) (1983) pp. 107–16.
3. K. Albrecht, *Stress and the Manager* (Englewood Cliffs, N.J.: Prentice-Hall, 1979).
4. Peter F. Drucker, *The Practice of Management* (London: Heinemann, 1968).
5. J.K. Galbraith, *The Affluent Society* (Harmondsworth: Penguin, 1958).
6. Marshall MaCluhan, *Understanding Media* (London: Kegan Paul, 1964).
7. Alvin Toffler, *Future Shock* (London: The Bodley Head, 1970).
8. See Chapter 8.
9. T. Levitt, 'Marketing Myopia', *Harvard Business Review* (July–August 1960).
10. Gene Bylinsky, 'Technology in the Year 2000', *Fortune* (18 July 1988).
11. *The Long Wave in Economic Life* (London: George Allen & Unwin, 1983).
12. W. W. Rostow, *The Process of Economic Growth* (New York: W. W. Norton, 1962) 2nd edn.
13. The discussion in this section draws heavily on the work of my former student Dr Hanaa Said.
14. J. M. Clark, *Competition as a Dynamic Process* (Washington, D.C.: Brookings Institution, 1961).
15. Philip Kotler, *Marketing Management* (Englewood Cliffs, N.J.: Prentice-Hall, 1972) 2nd edn.
16. J. Udell, *Successful Marketing Strategies in American Industries* (Madison, Wisc.: Mirrer Publishers, 1972).
17. Joan Robinson, *The Economics of Imperfect Competition* (London: Macmillan, 1933).
18. E. J. Chamberlin, *The Theory of Monopolistic Competition* (Cambridge, Mass.: Harvard University Press, 1933).
19. F. Knight, *Ethics of Competition* (London: George Allen & Unwin, 1936) 2nd edn.
20. G. Stigler, *Five Lectures on Economic Problems* (London: Longman, 1948).
21. F. Machlup, *The Economics of Sellers' Competition* (Baltimore: Johns Hopkins University Press, 1953).
22. N. Borden, 'The Concept of the Marketing Mix', in G. Schwartz (ed.), *Science in Marketing* (New York: Wiley, 1965).
23. J. Udell, 'How Important is Price in Competitive Strategy', *Journal of Marketing* (January 1964).
24. This topic is the subject of a full chapter in my introductory text *Marketing: An Introductory Text* (London: Macmillan, 1985) 4th edn and so will be given only cursory treatment here.
25. K. K. Cox, 'Marketing in the 1980s: back to basics', *Business*, 30 (1980) pp. 19–23.
26. Francis J. Aguilar, *Scanning the Business Environment* (New York: Macmillan, 1967).
27. 'The Theory and Practice of Marketing Planning for Industrial Goods in International Markets', Ph.D. dissertation Cranfield (1982). Published as *Marketing Plans* (London: Heinemann, 1984).

■ 7   Buyer Behaviour

1. Philip Kotler, *Marketing Management* (Englewood Cliffs, N.J.: Prentice-Hall, 1972) 2nd edn.
2. Kotler (1972).
3. E. Dichter, *The Strategy of Desire* (New York: Doubleday, 1960).
4. J. K. Galbraith, *The Affluent Society* (Harmondsworth: Penguin, 1958).
5. Harmondsworth: Penguin Books (1957).
6. New York: Macmillan, 1899.
7. Perry Bliss, *Marketing Management and the Behavioural Environment* (Englewood Cliffs, N.J.: Prentice-Hall, 1970).
8. In Bliss (1970), see n. 7 above.
9. A. M. Hastorf and H. Cantril, 'They Saw a Game: a case history', *Journal of Abnormal and Social Psychology*, 49 (1954).
10. M. J. Baker and S. Parkinson, 'TI Superform's Academic Launch', *Marketing* (October 1978).
11. M. J. Baker, *Market Development* (Harmondsworth: Penguin, 1983).
12. New York: Row & Peterson (1957).
13. P. Robinson, C. Faris and Y. Wind, *Industrial Buying and Creative Marketing* (Boston: Allyn & Bacon, 1967).
14. Leo Aspinwall, 'The Characteristics of Goods Theory', in W. Lazer and E. Kelley (eds), *Managerial Marketing* (rev. edn) (Homewood, Ill.: Richard D. Irwin, 1962).
15. Robinson, Faris and Wind (1967).

■ 8   Market Segmentation

1. Wendell Smith, 'Product differentiation and market segmentation as alternative marketing strategies', *Journal of Marketing*, 21 (July 1956) pp. 3–8.
2. B. M. Enis, *Marketing Principles* (Santa Monica, Calif.: Goodyear Publishing Co., 1977) 3rd edn.
3. Yoram Wind, 'Issues and advances in segmentation research', *Journal of Marketing Research*, vol 15 (August 1978) pp. 317–37.
4. Martin Bliss, 'Market segmentation and environmental analysis', unpublished M.Sc. thesis, University of Strathclyde (July 1980).
5. A. J. Resnik, P. B. B. Turney and J. B. Mason, 'Marketers turn to counter segmentation', *Harvard Business Review* (September–October 1979) pp. 100–6.
6. Wind, 'Issues and Advances in Segmentation Research', see n. 3 above.
7. Wind, 'Issues and Advances in Segmentation Research', see n. 3 above.
8. Wind, 'Issues and Advances in Segmentation Research', see n. 3 above.
9. Definitions of these segments are as follows:

   Segment 1: The Buffs. Persons who are enthusiastic and very knowledgeable about the products. They are primarily concerned with quality and technical features.
   Segment 2: The Singles. Persons who live alone. Although they are less technically competent than the Buffs, they demand good performance from a product they may use more than the average consumer.
   Segment 3: The Professions. Persons who have a higher level of education and high incomes. They tend to be more independent of their occupation and to engage in

many social activities. Their purchase of the product is partially motivated by social status needs.
Segment 4: The High Earners. Persons who have high incomes but do not possess the higher level of education or occupational independence of the individuals in Segment 3.
Segment 5: Others. Persons who do not belong to the above groups. This segment represents the largest proportion of the population.

10. Paul E. Green, J. Douglas Carroll and Frank J. Carmone, 'Design Considerations in Attitude Measurement', in Y. Wind and M. Greenberg (eds), *Moving Ahead with Attitude Research* (Chicago: American Management Association, 1977) pp. 9–18.
11. G. J. Hooley, 'The Multivariate Jungle: The Academic's Playground but the Manager's Minefield', *European Journal of Marketing*, 14(7) (1980) pp. 379–86.
12. The discussion in this section draws heavily on Brian Everitt's book *Cluster Analysis* (London: Heinemann, 1974).
13. G. H. Ball, *Classification Analysis* (Stanford, Calif.: Stanford Research Institute, 1971).
14. Everitt, *Cluster Analysis*, see n. 12 above.
15. Everitt, *Cluster Analysis*, see n. 12 above.
16. Everitt, *Cluster Analysis*, see n. 12 above.
17. Everitt, *Cluster Analysis*, p. 97, see n. 12 above.
18. R. R. Frank, R. Massy and Y. Wind, *Market Segmentation* (Englewood Cliffs, N.J.: Prentice-Hall, 1972).
19. D. L. Louden and A. J. P. Bitta, *Consumer Behaviour* (New York: McGraw-Hill, 1979).
20. Philip Kotler, *Marketing Management* (Englewood Cliffs, N.J.: Prentice-Hall, 1980) 4th edn.
21. Michael Thomas, 'Market Segmentation', *Quarterly Review of Marketing*, 6(1) (Autumn 1980) pp. 25–8.
22. See 'Acorn finds new friends' by Eric Clark. *Marketing* (16 December 1982). This is an important source for many of the facts cited here.
23. Michael Rines, 'How CLS Will Work', *Marketing* (17 March 1983).
24. Francis Quinlan, 'The Use of Social Grading in Marketing', *Quarterly Review of Marketing* (Autumn 1981) pp. 16–29.
25. D. Riesman, N. Glazer and R. Dinny, *The Lonely Crowd* (New Haven, Conn.: Yale University Press, 1950).
26. K. F. McCrohan, 'An Application of the Social Character Construct in Market Segmentation', *Journal of the Market Research Society*, 22 (4) (October 1980) pp. 263–7.
27. 'Psychographics: a critical review', *Journal of Marketing Research*, 12 (1975).
28. 'How Important to Marketing Strategy is the "Heavy User?"', *Journal of Marketing* (January 1964).
29. *Journal of Marketing*, 32 (July 1968) pp. 30–5.
30. J. Choffray and G. L. Lilien, 'A New Approach to Industrial Market Segmentation', *Sloan Management Review* 19(3) (Spring 1978) pp. 17–29.
31. R. N. Cardozo, 'Situational Segmentation of Industrial Markets', *European Journal of Marketing*, 14(5/6) pp. 264–76.
32. P. Robinson, C. Faris and Y. Wind, *Industrial Buying and Creative Marketing* (Boston: Allyn & Bacon, 1967).

33. H. G. Johnson and A. Flodhammer, 'Industrial Customer Segmentation', *Industrial Marketing Management* (July 1980) pp. 201–5.
34. Frank, Massy and Wind, *Market Segmentation*, see n. 18 above.
35. R. M. Worcester and J. Downham (eds), *Consumer Market Research Handbook* (New York: Reinhold, 1978) 2nd edn.
36. Shirley Young, Leland Ott and Barbara Feigin, 'Some Practical Considerations in Market Segmentation', *Journal of Marketing Research*, 15 (August 1978) pp. 405–12.
37. Wind, 'Issues and Advances in Segmentation Research', see n. 3 above.
38. Wind, 'Issues and Advances in Segmentation Research', see n. 3 above.

■ 9 Positioning

1. Al Ries and Jack Trout, *Positioning: the Battle for your Mind* (London: McGraw-Hill International Editions, 1986) 1st edn rev.
2. Glen L. Urban and Steven H. Star, *Advanced Marketing Strategy: Phenomena, Analysis and Decisions* (Englewood Cliffs, N.J.: Prentice-Hall, 1991).
3. Michael J. Baker and Susan Hart, *Marketing and Competitive Success* (London: Philip Allen, 1989).
4. London: Paul Chapman Publishing (1989).
5. 'Meaning of Image', *Journal of Retailing*, 50 (1974).
6. See n. 1 above.
7. Philip Kotler, *Marketing Management: Analysis, Planning and Control* (Englewood Cliffs, N.J.: Prentice-Hall, 1991) 8th edn.
8. In Michael J. Baker (ed.), *The Marketing Book* (London: Butterworth Heinemann, 1991).
9. R. D. Buzzell and B. T. Gale, *The PIMS Principles: linking strategy to performance* (London: Collier Macmillan, 1987).
10. T. Peters, *Thriving on Chaos* (London: Macmillan, 1988).
11. T. Levitt, 'Marketing Myopia', *Harvard Business Review* (July–August 1960) p. 45.
12. T. Levitt, *The Marketing Imagination* (London: Collier Macmillan, 1983).
13. See n. 8 above.
14. D. K. Clifford and R. E. Cavanagh, *The Winning Performance: How America's high growth mid-size companies succeed* (London: Sidgwick & Jackson, 1985).
15. *Marketing Business* (July–August 1991).
16. Stephen King, 'Brand-building in the 1990s', *Journal of Marketing Management*, 7(1) (January 1991).

■ 10 Situation Analysis: The Marketing Audit

1. Martin L. Bell, *Marketing: Concepts and Strategies* (Boston: Houghton-Mifflin, 1972) p. 428, 2nd edn.
2. Abe Shuchman, 'The Marketing Audit: its nature, purposes and problems', *Analysing and Improving Market Performance*, Report 32 (New York: American Management Association, 1959) p. 13.

3. Philip Kotler, *Marketing Management* (Englewood Cliffs, N.J.: Prentice-Hall, 1972) 2nd edn.

4. Philip Kotler, W. Gregor and W. Rogers, 'The MA comes of age', *Sloan Management Review*, 18(1) (Winter 1977).

5. James C. Makens, *The 12-Day Marketing Plan* (New York: Thorsons Publishers, 1989).

6. John Stapleton, *How to Prepare a Marketing Plan* (London: Gower, 1987) 4th edn.

7. Richard D. Crisp, 'Auditing the Functional Elements of a Marketing Operation', American Management Association Report, 32, see n. 2 above.

8. John F. Grashof, 'Conducting and Using a Marketing Audit', in E. J. McCarthy, John F. Grashof and Andrew A. Brogowicz (eds), *Readings in Basic Marketing* (Homewood, Ill.: Irwin, 1975).

9. J. Thomas Cannon, *Business Strategy and Policy* (New York: Harcourt, Brace & World, 1968).

10. Douglas T. Brownlie, 'Scanning the Environment: impossible precept or neglected art?', *Journal of Marketing Management*, 4(3) (Spring 1989).

11. Michael J. Baker, *Research for Marketing* (London: Macmillan, 1991).

12. See n. 5 above.

13. These were discussed in Chapter 6 above.

14. H. Koontz and C. O'Donnell, *Essentials of Management* (New York: McGraw-Hill, 1980).

15. P. Kotler, *Marketing Management* (Englewood Cliffs, N.J.: Prentice-Hall, 1967) 1st edn.

16. C. I. Buyers and G. A. Holmes, *Principles of Cost Accountancy* (London: Cassell, 1959).

■ 11   The Marketing Mix

1. E. J. McCarthy, *Basic Marketing: a managerial approach* (Homewood, Ill.: Irwin, 1978) pp. 7–8, 6th edn.

2. John O'Shaughnessey, *Competitive Marketing: A strategic approach* (Winchester, Mass.: Allen & Unwin, 1984).

3. See n. 4 nelow.

4. Neil H. Borden, 'The Concept of the Marketing Mix', in E. J. McCarthy *et al.*, *Readings in Basic Marketing* (Homewood, Ill.: Irwin, 1975) pp. 72–82.

5. Albert W. Frey, *Advertising* (New York: Ronald Press, 1961) p. 30, 3rd edn.

6. William Lazer and Eugene J. Kelley, *Managerial Marketing Perspectives and Viewpoints* (Homewood, Ill.: Irwin, 1975) pp. 72–82.

7. William Lazer, James D. Culley and Thomas Staudt, 'The Concept of the Marketing Mix' in Stuart H. Britt (ed.) *Marketing Manager's Handbook* (Chicago: Dartnell Corporation, 1973) pp. 77–89.

8. See n. 1 above.

9. William Stanton, *Fundamentals of Marketing* (New York: McGraw-Hill, 1967) 2nd edn.

10. Harry A. Lipson and John R. Darling, *Introduction to Marketing: an administrative approach* (New York: John Wiley, 1971).

11. John Martin, 'The Best Practice of Business', in *Marketing Planning*, vol. v (London: John Martin Publishing, 1978).

12. Simon Majaro, *Marketing in Perspective* (London: George Allen & Unwin, 1982) pp. 20–1.
13. Prabhu Guptara, *The Basic Arts of Marketing* (London: Hutchinson, 1990).
14. In Michael J. Baker (ed.) *The Marketing Book* (London: Butterworth Heinemann, 1991), 2nd edn.
15. Chester R. Wasson, *Dynamic Competitive Strategy & Product Life Cycles* (St Charles, Ill.: Challenge Books, 1974).

■ 12 Marketing Research

1. Michael J. Baker, *Research for Marketing* (London: Macmillan, 1991).
2. Ben M. Enis and Charles L. Broome (Aylesbury: Intertext, 1973; first pub. New York, 1971).
3. *Marketing Application of Operational Research Techniques* (Bradford: MCB Publications, 1981).
4. Francis J. Aguilar, *Scanning the Business Environment* (New York: Macmillan, 1987).
5. National Industrial Conference Board, 'Why Products Fail', Conference Board Record (October 1984),
6. G. J. Hooley, J. E. Lynch and C. J. West, *Marketing in the UK: A Survey of Current Practices and Performance*, The Institute of Marketing (1984).
7. Michael J. Baker and Susan Hart, *Marketing and Competitive Success* (London: Philip Allen, 1989).
8. 'Commonsense in Qualitative Research', *Commentary*, 9(1) (January 1967).
9. Wendy Gordon and Roy Langmaid, *Qualitative Market Research: A Practitioner's and Buyer's Guide* (Aldershot: Gower, 1988).
10. See n. 9 above.
11. Johnny K. Johansson and Ikujiro Nonaka, 'Market Research the Japanese Way', *Harvard Business Review* (May–June 1987).
12. Preliminary results from the Government Census of Population, Distribution, etc. normally take 1 or 2 years to prepare, the full report 3 or more years.
13. The concentration ratio is an economic concept used for comparative analysis and to indicate the degree of competition in a market, e.g. a concentration ratio of 100% = pure monopoly. Useful in identifying 'heavy half' phenomena, major sales prospects, etc.
14. *The Assessment of Industrial Markets* (London: Hutchinson, 1968).
15. Paul E. Green and Donald S. Tull, *Research for Marketing Decisions* (Englewood Cliffs, N.J.: Prentice-Hall, 1966).
16. See D. S. Tull and F. S. Albaum, *Survey Research* (Aylesbury: Intertext, 1973).
17. See Tull and Albaum, pp. 175–82 for a full discussion (n. 16 above).
18. Paul E. Green and Donald S. Tull, *Research for Marketing Decisions* (Englewood Cliffs, N.J.: Prentice-Hall, 1978), 4th edn.
19. Tull and Albaum (1973), see n. 16 above.
20. In *Marketing Decisions: a Bayesian approach*
21. *Managerial Decision Making* (Glenview, Ill.: Scott, Foresman, 1980).
22. 'Decision Trees for Decision Making', *Harvard Business Review*, (July–August 1964).

23. *Decision Theory and the Manager* (London: Pitman, 1972).
24. *Decision Theory and the Manager*, pp. 10–18, see n. 23 above.
25. Ralph O. Swalm, 'Utility Theory – insights into risk taking', *Harvard Business Review* (November–December 1966).
26. 'Managing Our Way to Economic Decline', *Harvard Business Review* (July–August 1980).

■ 13   Product Policy

1. Throughout this chapter the terms 'product' and 'service' will be used as implying the other unless specifically stated to the contrary.
2. E. Raymond Corey, 'Key Options in Market Selection and Product Planning', *Harvard Business Review* (September–October 1975).
3. London: Business Publications (1962) p. 33.
4. Robert C. Bennett and Robert G. Cooper, 'The Misuse of Marketing: an American tragedy', *McKinsey Quarterly* (Autumn 1982) pp. 52–69.
5. Lawrence Abbott, *Quality and Competition* (New York: Columbia University Press, 1955) p. 9.
6. Roy Rothwell, Paul Gardiner and Kerry Schott, *Design and the Economy* (London: The Design Council, 1983).
7. As Levitt has shown in his article 'The Industrialisation of Service', *Harvard Business Review* (September–October 1976), virtually all services are associated with physical/objective factors which are necessary to the delivery of the service. Thus the opulence of the bank, the cleanliness of the operating theatre and the comfort of the beauty parlour will all have an important influence on the perception of the service rendered. It is for this reason that we choose not to distinguish products from services.
8. Theodore Levitt in Robert R. Rothberg (ed.), *Corporate Strategy and Product Innovation* (New York: Free Press, 1976).
9. George Avlonitis, 'An Exploratory Investigation of the Product Elimination Decision-Making Process in the UK Engineering Industry', unpublished Ph.D. thesis, University of Strathclyde (1980).
10. Melvin T. Copeland, 'Relation of Consumers' Buying Habits to Marketing Methods', *Harvard Business Review* (April 1923).
11. This was first introduced in Chapter 7 when discussing the general influence of product characteristics on choice behaviour.
12. G. E. Miracle, 'Product Characteristics and Market Strategy', *Journal of Marketing* (January 1969).
13. H. I. Ansoff, *Corporate Strategy* (Harmondsworth: Penguin, 1968).
14. 'Managing Our Way to Economic Decline', *Harvard Business Review* (July–August 1980).
15. 'Revenge of the Marketing Concept', *Business Horizons* (June 1980).
16. 'Managing Our Way to Economic Decline', see n. 14 above.
17. 'The Misuse of Marketing: an American tragedy', see n. 4 above.
18. Samuel C. Johnson and Conrad Jones, 'How to Organise for New Products', *Harvard Business Review* (May–June 1957).

19. Joseph P. Guiltinan and Gordon W. Paul, *Marketing Management: Strategies and Programs* (New York: McGraw-Hill, 1982) pp. 40–2.
20. See Michael J. Baker, *Market Development* (Harmondsworth: Penguin, 1983) for a full description.
21. Axel Johne, 'Innovation, Organisation and Marketing of High Technology Products', unpublished Ph.D. dissertation (Strathclyde University, 1982).
22. See, for example, Michael J. Baker and Ronald McTavish, *Product Policy and Management* (London: Macmillan, 1976) Chapter 5.
23. D. J. Luck and O. C. Ferrell, *Marketing Strategy and Plans* (Englewood Cliffs, N.J.: Prentice-Hall, 1979).
24. *Dynamic Competitive Strategy & Product Life Cycles* (St Charles, Ill.: Challenge Books, 1874).
25. *Diffusion of Innovations* (New York: Free Press, 1983), 3rd edn.
26. P. Kotler, 'Phasing-out weak Products', *Harvard Business Review*, (March–April 1965) pp. 108–18.
    W. J. Talley, 'Profiting from the Declining Product', *Business Horizons*, 7 (Spring 1964) pp. 77–84.
    P. Kotler, 'Harvesting Weak Products', *Business Horizons* 21 (August 1978) pp. 15–22.
    George C. Michael, 'Product Petrification – A New Stage in the Life Cycle Theory', *California Management Review*, 9 (Fall 1971) pp. 88–91.
    J. T. Rothe, 'The Product Elimination Decision', *MSU Business topics* 18 (Autumn 1970) pp. 45–52.
27. David J. Luck, *Product Policy and Strategy* (Englewood Cliffs, N.J.: Prentice-Hall, 1972) pp. 75–6.
28. David S. Hopkins, *Business Strategies for Problem Products* Report 714 (New York: The Conference Board, 1977).
29. Hopkins, *Business Strategies*, see n. 28 above.
30. Hopkins, *Business Strategies*, see n. 28 above.

■ 14 Packaging

1. *Packaging Management* (London: Gower Press, 1972).
2. Albert Wesley Frey (ed.), *Marketing Handbook* (New York: Ronald Press, 1965) 2nd edn.
3. The material in this section draws heavily on Mike Allen, 'Designs for Top Security', *Marketing* (9 December 1982).
4. Briston and Neill, *Packaging Management*, see n. 1 above.
5. Michael J. Baker, *Market Development* (Harmondsworth: Penguin, 1983).
6. 'Opting for an Outside Job', *Marketing* (9 December 1982).
7. Briston and Neill, *Packaging Management*, see n. 1 above.
8. Frey (ed.), *Marketing Handbook*, see n. 2 above.
9. 'Shedding Light on Design', *Marketing* (5 August 1982).
10. 'Images to Catch the eye', *Marketing* (5 August 1982).
11. Leader article, 'How Consumers Judge a Product by its Package', *Marketing* (17 February 1982).
12. 'The Cost of Boxing Clever', *Marketing* (17 February 1982).

■ 15   Pricing Policy and Management

1. H. J. Kuhlmeijer, *Managerial Marketing* (Leiden: H. E. Stenfert Kroese V. B., 1975).
2. William Fellner, 'The Influence of Market Structure on Technological Progress', *Quarterly Journal of Economics*, 65 (November 1951).
3. *Managerial Economics* (Englewood Cliffs, N.J.: Prentice-Hall, 1951).
4. Stephen Enke, 'On Maximising Profits', in D. Watson, *Price Theory and its Uses* (Boston: Houghton-Mifflin, 1977) 4th edn.
5. W. Haynes, *Managerial Economics* (Austin, Texas: Business Publications, 1974) 3rd edn.
6. A. Oxenfeldt, *Pricing for Marketing Executives* (Belmont, Calif.: Wadsworth, 1961).
7. Dean, *Managerial Economics*, see n. 3 above.
8. A. Oxenfeldt, *Pricing Strategies* (New York: AMACOM, 1975) p. 42.
9. Lawrence Fisher, *Industrial Marketing* (London: Business Books, 1966).
10. P. Kotler, *Marketing Management: Analysis Planning and Control* (Englewood Cliffs, N.J.: Prentice-Hall, 1972) 2nd edn.
11. Henry Ford II. 'What America Expects of Industry', in an address before the Michigan State Chamber of Commerce (October 1962).
12. A. Gabor, *Pricing Principles and Practices* (London: Heinemann, 1977); A. Gabor and C. W. J. Granger, 'A Systematic Approach to Effective Pricing', in Leslie W. Rodger, *Marketing Concept and Strategies in the Next Decade* (New York: John Wiley, 1973).
13. H. A. Simon, 'A Behavioural Model of Rational Choice', *Quarterly Journal of Economics*, 69 (1952).
14. H. A. Simon, 'Theories of Decision Making in Economics and Behavioural Science', *American Economic Review* (June 1959).
15. Simon, 'Theories of Decision Making', see n. 14 above.
16. W. J. Baumol, 'Models of Economic Competition', in H. Townsend, *Price Theory* (London: Cox & Wyman, 1971).
17. R. M. Cyert and J. G. March, *A Behavioural Theory of the Firm* (Englewood Cliffs, N.J.: Prentice-Hall, 1963).
18. W. J. Baumol, *Business Behaviour, Value and Growth* (New York: Macmillan, 1959).
19. D. Ragoff and Robert Lynn, 'Methods v. Objectives in Pricing Policy', *Management Adviser* (March–April 1972).
20. R. Lynn, 'Unit Volume as a Goal for Pricing', *Journal of Marketing* (October 1968) pp. 35–7.
21. A. Oxenfeldt, 'How to Use Market Share Measurement', *Harvard Business Review* (January–February 1959).
22. Michel Chevalier and Bernard Carty, 'Don't Misuse Your Market Share Goal', *European Business* (Winter/Spring 1974).
23. M. V. Laric, 'Pricing Strategies in Industrial Markets', *European Journal of Marketing*, 14(5/6) (1980) pp. 303–21.
24. Dean, 'HBR Classic: Pricing Policies for New Products', *Harvard Business Review* (November–December 1969).
25. A. Kaplan, J. Dirlam and R. Lanzillotti, *Pricing in Big Business* (Washington, D.C.: Brookings Institution, 1958).
26. C. Pass, 'Pricing Policies and Market Strategy: an empirical note', *European Journal of Marketing*, 5(3) (1971).

D. C. Hague, 'Economic Theory and Business Behaviour', *Review of Economic Studies* 16 (1948–9).

W. Haynes, *Pricing Decisions in Small Business* (Lexington: University of Kentucky Press, 1962).

R. Barback, *The Pricing of Manufacturers* (London: Macmillan, 1964).

R. L. Hall and C. J. Hitch, 'Economic Theory and Business Behaviour', *Oxford Economic Papers*, 2 (May 1939).

27. J. Bates and R. Parkinson, *Business Economics* (Oxford: Blackwell, 1969).

28. J. Sizer, 'The Accountant's Contribution to Pricing Decisions', in B. Taylor and G. Wills, *Pricing Strategies* (London: Staples Press, 1969).

29. Gordon Johnston, 'The Pricing of Consumer Goods', in B. Taylor and G. Wills, *Pricing Strategies*, see n. 28 above.

30. J. Sizer, 'The Accountant's Contribution to Pricing Decisions', see n. 28 above.

31. J. Udell, 'How Important is Price in Competitive Strategy?', *Journal of Marketing* (April 1964).

32. Pass, 'Pricing Policies', see n. 26 above.

33. R. A. Robicheaux, reference found in P. Kotler, *Principles of Marketing* (Englewood Cliffs, N.J.: Prentice-Hall, 1980) 4th edn, p. 398.

34. Dr Hanaa Said, 'The Relevance of Price Theory to Pricing Practice: an investigation of pricing policies and practices in UK industry', Ph.D. dissertation, University of Strathclyde (1981).

35. 'Pricing Strategies in Industrial Markets', *European Journal of Marketing*, 4–6 (1980).

36. *The Journal of Business and Industrial Marketing*, 5(1) (Winter–Spring 1990).

37. R. H. Hayes and W. J. Abernathy, 'Managing Our Way to Economic Decline', *Harvard Business Review* (July–August 1980).

38. H. Simon, *Price Management* (Amsterdam: Elsevier Publishers B.V., 1989).

39. In Simon, see n. 38 above.

40. In Simon, see n. 38 above.

41. In Simon, see n. 38 above.

42. D. F. Abell and J. S. Hammond, *Strategic Marketing Planning* (Englewood Cliffs, N.J.: Prentice-Hall, 1979).

43. In Simon, see n. 38 above.

44. 'Determining your Pricing Structure at Home and Abroad', *Marketing Industrial Products*, Pera Conference, Melton Mowbray (April 1968).

45. P. Kotler, *Marketing Management: Analysis Planning and Control* (Englewood Cliffs, N.J.: Prentice-Hall, 1980) 4th edn, p. 387.

46. Dean, 'HBR Classic', see n. 24 above.

47. B. P. Shapiro and B. B. Jackson, 'Industrial Pricing to meet Customer Needs', *Harvard Business Review* (November–December 1978).

48. J. L. Forbis and W. T. Mehta, 'Value-based Strategies for Industrial Products', *Business Horizons* (June 1981).

49. 'The Relevance of Price Theory', see n. 34 above.

50. Kaplan, Dirlam and Lanzillotti, see n. 25 above.

■ 16 Distribution and Sales Policy

1. M. J. Baker, 'Maxims for Marketing in the Eighties', *Advertising*, 66 (Winter 1980–1).

2. Peter Drucker, 'The Economy's Dark Continent', *Fortune* (April 1962).
3. Maureen Guirdham, *Marketing: the management of distribution channels* (Oxford: Pergamon Press, 1972) p. ix.
4. Michael J. Baker, *Market Development* (Harmondsworth: Penguin, 1983).
5. Wroe Alderson, 'Factors Governing the Development of Marketing Channels', in Richard M. Clewett, *Marketing Channels for Manufactured Products* (Homewood, Ill.: Irwin, 1954).
6. Louis P. Bucklin, *A Theory of Distribution Channel Structure* (University of California: Institute of Business and Economic Research, 1966).
7. 'Postponement Speculation and the Structure of Distribution Channels', *Journal of Marketing Research* 2(1) (February 1965).
8. 'Functional Spin-Off: a key to anticipating change in distribution structure', *Journal of Marketing*, 37(3) (July 1973).
9. Louis W. Stern, 'Channel Control and Interorganisation Management', in Peter D. Bennett (ed.), *Economic Development*, American Marketing Association *Proceedings* (1965).
10. *Marketing Management* (New York: Macmillan, 1982).
11. *Marketing: principles and applications* (St Paul, Minnesota: West Publishing, 1983).
12. Malcolm P. McNair, 'Significant Trends and Developments in the Postwar Period', in A. B. Smith (ed.), *Competitive Distribution in a Free, High-level Economy and its Implications for the University* (Pittsburgh: University of Pittsburgh Press, 1958).
13. Stanley C. Hollander, 'The Wheel of Retailing', *Journal of Marketing* 25 (July 1960) pp. 37–42.
14. P. J. Luck and O. C. Ferrell, *Marketing Strategy and Plans* (Englewood Cliffs, N.J.: Prentice-Hall, 1979).
15. See, for example, E. Raymond Corey, *The Development of Markets for New Materials* (Boston: Harvard University Press, 1956).
16. Michael J. Baker, *The Dictionary of Marketing and Advertising* (London: Macmillan, 1990).
17. David W. Nylen, *Marketing Decision-Making Handbook* (Englewood Cliffs, N.J.: Prentice-Hall, 1990).
18. 'Perspectives for Distribution Programming', in Louis P. Bucklin (ed.), *Vertical Marketing Systems* (Glenview, Ill.: Scott, Foresman, 1970).
19. Kenichi Ohmae, *The Mind of the Strategist* (Harmondsworth: Penguin, 1983).

■ 17   Promotion Policy and Management

1. *The Process and Effects of Mass Communications* (Urbana: University of Illinois Press, 1955).
2. See C. Shannon and W. Weaver, *The Mathematical Theory of Communication* (Urbana: University of Illinois Press, 1962).
3. Philip Kotler, *Marketing Management* (Englewood Cliffs, N.J.: Prentice-Hall, 1972) 2nd edn.
4. *What Do We Know about How Advertising Works?*, J. Walter Thompson Company Ltd, booklet 25, reprinted in C. Weinberg, P. Doyle, P. Law and K. Simmons (eds), *Advertising Management* (London: Harper & Row, 1974).

5. Robert E. Smith and William R. Swinyard, 'Information Response Models: an integrated approach', *Journal of Marketing* 46 (Winter 1982) pp. 81–93.
6. Herbert E. Krugman, 'The Impact of Televison Advertising: learning without involvement', *Public Opinion Quarterly* 20(3) pp. 349–56.
7. Abraham H. Maslow, 'A Theory of Human Motivation', *Psychological Review* 50 (1943).
8. Robert J. Lavidge and Gary A. Steiner, 'A Model for Predictive Measurements of Advertising Effectiveness', *Journal of Marketing*, 25 (October 1961).
9. Harper W. Boyd Jr, Michael L. Ray and Edward C. Strong, 'An Attitudinal Framework for Advertising Strategy', *Journal of Marketing*, 36 (April 1972) pp. 27–33.
10. R. D. Buzzell and M. J. Baker, 'Sales Effectiveness of Automobile Advertising', *Journal of Advertising Research*, 12 (3) (1970) pp. 3–8.
11. In *Journal of Marketing*, (1972), see n. 9 above.
12. The implicit assumption is that we are concerned with product classes which are reasonably close substitutes for one another, e.g. alternative forms of entertainment, of transportation or forming metals or constructing buildings, etc.
13. John O'Shaughnessy *Competitive Marketing: A Strategic Approach* (Winchester, Mass.: Allen & Unwin, 1984).
14. Graham J. Hooley, Christopher J. West and James E. Lynch, *Marketing Management Today* (Cookham: Institute of Marketing, 1983).
15. *Spending Advertising Money* (London: Business Books, 1970).
16. See n. 15 above.
17. *International Journal of Advertising*, 4 (1985).
18. D. Corkindale and S. Kennedy, *The Evaluation of Advertising Objectives*, Marketing Communications Research Centre, Cranfield School of Management, Report 10 (November 1974).
19. *Marketing Week* (1 June 1990).
20. See n. 19 above.
21. See n. 6 above.
22. See n. 4 above.

■ 18 Service

1. It will be recalled from Chapter 6 that switching costs play an important role in competition.
2. Michael J. Baker, *Marketing: An Introductory Text* (London: Macmillan, 1991) 5th edn.
3. Martin Christopher, Philip Schory and Tage Skjott-Larsen, *Customer Service and Distribution Strategy* (London: Associated Business Press, 1979).
4. William H. Blenel and Henry E. Bender, *Product Service Planning* (New York: AMACOM, 1980).
5. B. J. LaLonde and Paul H. Zinszer, *Customer Service: meaning and measurement* (Chicago: National Council of Physical Distribution Management, 1976).
6. Winter 1990.
7. *Product Service Planning*, see n. 4 above.
8. 'Production-line Approach to Service', *Harvard Business Review* (September–October 1972).

9. K. Ohmae, *The Mind of the Strategist*, (Harmondsworth: Penguin, 1983).
10. P. Kotler, *Marketing Management* (Englewood Cliffs, N.J.: Prentice-Hall, 1980) 4th edn, p. 375.
11. *Product Service Planning*, see n. 4 above.
12. Tamara J. Erickson, 'Beyond the Quality Revolution: Linking Quality to Corporate Strategy', *Prism* (First Quarter, 1991) pp. 5–21.
13. Eriksen, 'Beyond the Quality Revolution', p. 11.
14. Diane H. Schmalensee, 'Soft Measurement: A Vital Ingredient in Quality Improvement', *Prism*, (First Quarter, 1991) pp. 49–57.
15. 'The Role of Service in Effective Marketing', in Victor P. Buell and Carl C. Meyel (eds), *Handbook of Modern Marketing* (New York: McGraw-Hill, 1970).
16. Diana Brown and Roger Banks, 'Customer First', *Survey* (Spring 1991).
17. M. P. Singh, 'Service as a Marketing Strategy: A Case Study at Reliance Electric', *Industrial Marketing Management*, 19 (1990).

■ 19   Developing a Market Culture

1. P. Doyle, 'What are the Excellent Companies?', *Journal of Marketing Management*, 8(2) (April 1992).
2. Cambridge, Mass.: MIT Press (1962).
3. Helmy H. Baligh and Richard M. Burton, 'Marketing in Modernisation – The Marketing Concept and the Organisation's Structure', *Long Range Planning*, 12 (April 1979) pp. 92–6.
4. Edward S. McKay, *The Marketing Mystique* (New York: American Management Association, 1972).
5. Robert H. Hayes and William J. Abernathy, 'Managing our Way to Economic Decline', *Harvard Business Review* (July–August 1980).
6. Renato Tagiuri and George H. Litwin (eds) *Organisational Climate* (Cambridge, Mass.: Harvard Business School, 1968).
7. Michael J. Baker, *Marketing New Industrial Products* (London: Macmillan, 1975).
8. T. L. Burns and G. M. Stalker, *The Management of Innovation* (London: Tavistock Publications, 1961).
9. Paul R. Lawrence and Jay W. Lorsch, 'Differentiation and Integration in Complex Organisations', *Administrative Science Quarterly* 12(1) (June 1967) pp. 1–47.
10. F. A. Johne, 'Innovation, Organisation and the Marketing of High Technology Products', Ph.D. dissertation, University of Strathclyde, Department of Marketing (1982).
11. R. H. Hayes and W. J. Abernathy, 'Managing Our Way to Economic Decline', *Harvard Business Review* (July–August 1980).
12. T. Peters and R. Waterman, *In Search of Excellence* (New York: Harper & Row, 1982).
13. American Sociological Association.
14. Howard Schwartz and M. Stanley Davis, 'Matching a Corporate Culture and Business Strategy', *Organizational Dynamics* (Summer 1981).
15. Edward S. McKay, *The Marketing Mystique* (New York: American Management Association, 1972).
16. Warren Bennis and Burt Nanus, *Leaders: The Strategies for Taking Charge* (New York: Harper & Row, 1985).

17. 'Brief Case: Mission, Vision and Strategic Intent'.
18. (May–June 1989).
19. 'Mission Statements: Selling Corporate Values to Employees', *Long Range Planning*, 24(3) (June 1991).
20. Philip Selznick, 'Conclusion', in *Leadership in Administration* (New York: Harper & Row).
21. P. F. Drucker, *Management Tasks, Responsibilities and Pra(ctices* New York: Harper & Row, 1974).
22. T. Levitt, 'Marketing Myopia', *Harvard Business Review* (July–August 1960) p. 45.
23. F. R. David, 'How companies define their mission', *Long Range Planning*, 22 (February 1989).
24. New York: Thorsens (1991).

■ 20   The (Short-term) Marketing Plan

1. M. H. B. McDonald, 'The Theory and Practice of Marketing Planning', Ph.D. dissertation, Cranfield Institute of Technology (1982). This section borrows heavily from this source. Published as *Marketing Plans* (London: Heinemann, 1984).
2. John W. Leppard and Malcolm H. B. McDonald, 'Marketing Planning and corporate culture: a conceptual framework which examines management attitudes in the context of marketing planning', *Journal of Marketing Management*, 7(3) (July 1991).
3. J. C. Camillus, 'Evaluating the Benefits of Long-range Planning Systems', *Long Range Planning* (June 1975).
4. B. Charles Ames, see n. 4 above.
5. B. Charles Ames, 'Trappings versus Substance in Industrial Marketing', *Harvard Business Review* (July–August 1970) pp. 93–102.
6. 'The Fed loses its Reserve', *Marketing* (2 August 1984).
7. Michael J. Baker, *Marketing* (London: Macmillan, 1991) 5th edn.
8. Dale D. McKonkey, 'Planning in a changing environment', *Business Horizons* (September–October 1988).
9. Aubrey Wilson, 'Aubrey Wilson's Marketing Audit Checklists' (New York, McGraw-Hill, 1982).
10. John Stapleton, 'How to Prepare a Marketing Plan' (London: Gower 1987) 4th edn. James S. Makens, *The 12-day Marketing Plan* (New York: Thorsons Publishers, 1989).

■ 21   Control

1. John A. Howard, *Marketing Management* (Homewood, Ill.: Irwin, 1st edn 1957; rev. edn 1963) p. 207.
2. See n. 1 above.
3. See John Sizer, 'Investment Life Cycle of a Hypothetical New Product', in *An Insight into Management Accounting* (Harmondsworth: Penguin, 1979).
4. *Journal of Marketing*, 37 (July 1973) pp. 48–53.
5. A clearly worked example which highlights the difference between the two measures is to be found in A. H. Taylor and H. Shearing, *Financial and Cost Accounting for Management* (London: Macdonald & Evans, 1974) 6th edn.

6. Morris J. Gottlieb and Irving Roshwalb, 'The "Present Value" Concept in Evaluating New Products', *New Ideas for Successful Marketing*, Proceedings of the American Marketing Association, World Congress, Chicago (1966) pp. 387–400; reprinted in D. Maynard Phelps (ed.), *Product Management: selected readings* (Homewood, Ill.: Irwin, 1970).
7. London: Heinemann (1979).
8. Harmondsworth: Penguin Books, 1979.
9. P. Drucker, *The Practice of Management* (New York: Harper & Row, 1954).

■ 22   Recapitulation

1. Graham J. Hooley, Christopher J. West and James E. Lynch, *Marketing Management Today* (Cookham: Institute of Marketing, 1983).
2. Hooley, West and Lynch (1983) see n. 1 above.
3. Ansoff, *Corporate Strategy* (Harmondsworth: Penguin, 1968).
4. John Argenti, *Systematic Corporate Planning* (Sunbury on Thames: Thomas Nelson, 1974).
5. Thomas Peters and Robert Waterman, *In Search of Excellence* (New York: Harper & Row, 1982).
6. Michael E. Porter, *The Competitive Advantage of Nations* (London: Macmillan, 1990).
7. Michael J. Baker and Susan Hart, *Marketing and Competitive Success* (London: Philip Allen, 1989).
8. James Lynch, Graham Hooley and Jenny West, *The Effectiveness of British Marketing*, A Report to the ESRC, University of Bradford Management Centre (1988).
9. This section draws heavily on an article entitled 'Marketing Maxims', *Advertising* 66 (Winter 1980–1).
10. T. Levitt, 'Marketing Myopia', *Harvard Business Review* (July–August 1960).
11. Philip Kotler and Sidney J. Levy, 'Broadening the Concept of Marketing', *Journal of Marketing*, 33 (January 1969). This article was also the first to suggest a set of key concepts which apply to all types and kinds of marketing.

Index

Abbott, Lawrence 19, 46, 155–6, 316
Abell, D. F. 118–19
Abell, D. F. and Hammond, J. S. 75, 79–80, 121, 126–7
Acorn 201–3
adopter categories 113–14
adoption of innovations 183–5
advertising 233
  budget setting 423–30
  effect of 412–15
  effectiveness 430
  effectiveness measurement 430–3
  objectives 419–21
  strategies 421
age groupings 87–90
Aguilar, F. 161, 282–3
Albrecht, Karl 145–6, 149, 150
Aldersen, Wroe 390–1
alternatives, identification of 302–4
Ames, B. Charles 90–1, 99
Andrews, K. R. 49, 52
Ansoff, Igor 48, 49, 55, 56, 75, 131–2, 160–1, 322–4
area samples 291
Aspinwall, Leo 177–8, 320
assumptions 7–8, 487–8
attitudes 164ff
augmented product 232–3
automatic interaction detector (AID) 196
Avlonitis, G. 109, 319–21, 341–3

Baker, Michael J. 110, 328–9
  with Hart, S. 37, 38ff, 220, 221, 284, 518ff
Baker composite model 179–87
Baligh, H. H. and Burton, R. M. 461
bandwagon effect 338
bargaining power
  suppliers 26
  customers 26–7
barriers to entry 24–6
Baumol, W. J. 370, 371

Bayesian analysis 48, 299–310
behaviouristic segmentation 203
Beik, L. and Buzby, S. 502–5
benefit segmentation 207–9
Bennett, R. C. and Cooper, R. G. 315–16, 326
Bennis, W. 470
Bentham, Jeremy 165
Best of Business 31, 34, 37
Bliss 167, 191
Booz, Allen and Hamilton 328–9, 330, 332
Borden, Neil 10, 158, 261–2, 264–6, 270
Boston Consulting Group (BCG) 108, 116, 119
Boston Box see growth share matrix
Boulding, Kenneth 16
Boyd, H. W., Ray, M. L. and Strong, E. C. 415–17
branding 228ff
breakeven analysis 496–8
Briston, J. H. and Neill, T. J. 349–50, 351, 353
Broadbent, S. 423–4
Brookings Institution 373
Brown, D. and Banks, R. 453–4
Brownlie, D. 74, 120, 121–3, 249–50
Bucklin, L. 391, 393
building cycle 152
Burns, T. and Stalker, G. M. 465–6
business cycles 152–5
business orientations 461–8
business policy 48–9
business portfolio analysis 121, 530
buy classes 176
buy phases 176–7, 209
buyer behaviour 9–10, 163–87
buyer behaviour models 164–8, 173–4, 176–7, 179–82
Buyers, C. I. and Holmes, G. A. 255–6
buyers' intentions 257–8
Buzzell, R. 101, 415–16

Buzzell, R. and Gale, B.   229–30, 234

Campbell, A. and Young, S.   470–2
Canadian Office of Tourism   211–15
Cannon, J. T.   249
cardinal utility theory   308
Cardozo, R. N.   209–10
cash flow   505–7
Chamberlin, E.   157–8
Chandler, A.   461
channels   *see* distribution
characteristics of goods   177–8
Chevalier, M. and Carty, B.   372
Choffray, J. and Lilien, G.   209
Christopher, M. *et al.*   438–9, 449–50
Clark, J. M.   155–6
Clifford, D. K. and Cavanagh,
     R. E.   234–5
cluster analysis   195–9
'clusters', development of   34
Coe, Barbara J.   379–81
commercialisation stage of NPD   333
communication   489–90
communication process   410–12
competition   17–19, 157–9
   international   28–9
   role of chance   33
   role of government   33
   and marketing strategy   23–7
   non-price   157–9
   perfect   104, 156–7
competitive advantage   35–7, 64–5
competitive forces   24ff
competitive position   85
competitive scope   64–5
competitive success and
     marketing   518–23
competitor analysis   250–3
concentrated marketing   129, 337, 395
Conference Board   344–6
conglomerate companies   71
conjoint analysis   196
Consumer Location System (CLS)   202
consumer sovereignty   19, 20
consumerist movement   71
contract packers   352–3
contribution analysis   500–5
contribution approach   *see* pricing
control   13, 489, 491–514

control and feedback   531
convenience sample   292
Copeland, M. T.   319
core strategy   488
Corey, R.   63, 314
Corkindale, D. and Kennedy, S.   419–21,
     431–2
corporate strategy   47–52, 60–5
   formulation of   87–9
cost analysis   494–8
cost analysis contribution
     approach   500–5
cost leadership   64–5
costs
   average   365
   concepts   365, 498–500
   engineering approach   495
   fixed   365, 494
   long-run   365, 494
   marginal   365, 499–500
   opportunity   365, 498–9
   semi-fixed   494
   short-run   365, 494
   statistical approach   495
   variable   365, 494
Cox, K.   160
Crisp, R. D.   248
critical success factors (CSFs)   220, 221
cross impact analysis   135
cues   165
CUGs (currently useful
     generalisations)   18, 43, 95–6, 99,
     476, 523–8
Culliton, J.   261–2, 267
cultural factors   167–8
culture, corporate   93, 464, 468
customer orientation   54
customer service   437–57
   nature of   438–40
   pricing   452–3
   quality   453–4
   scope of   440–7
   strategic use of   447–50, 454–6
Cyert, R. M and March, J. G.   370

data collection   287–9
data fusion   431–3
data reduction and analysis   296–9
data sources   287ff

Davidson, Hugh 166
Davies, Gary and Brooks, J. 220, 222–4
Day, George 123–4
Dean, Joel 362, 366, 369, 382–3
decision criterion 307–9
decision trees 304–10
Delphi technique 141
demand 361–5
  cross-elasticity 363
  derived 363
  elasticity 363
  industry and company 362
  law of 361–2
  long-run 362
  short-run 362
  stimulation 21
demographic factors 141–5
demographic segmentation 203
descriptive statistics 298–9
development stage of NPD 331–2
Dhalla, N. K. and Yuspeh, S. 100,
  116–17
'Diamond of National Advantage' 29–32
Dichter, Ernest 166
Diffenbach, John 141
differentiated advantage 228–9, 531
differentiated marketing 129, 156, 216,
  271, 337, 395
diffusion curves 112–14
  process 109–12
  theory 109–14
directional policy matrix (DPM) 125–30
distribution 12
  and sales policy 385–407
  channel composition 391
  channel control 394
  channel development 387–9
  channel selection 394–8
  channel structure 391–3
  functions of channels 389–91
  policy formulation 399–400
diversification 56–7, 71, 74–5, 80
Doyle, Peter 22–9, 233–5, 271, 275,
  459–60
drives 166
drop and collect survey 293
Drucker, Peter 77, 80, 386, 459, 473, 511

economic cycles 152–5

economic factors 148–9
Emerson, Ralph Waldo 408–9
Enis, B. 190
Enis, B. and Broome, C. 280–1, 301–2
environmental analysis 139–62
environmental change 140–1
equipment 322
equilibrium (market) 156
Erickson, T. 450–2
Evans, J. R. and Berman, B. 396
Everitt, B. 197ff
executive summary 485
expected value 308–9
experience effects 118
exploration stage of NPD 329

fabricated materials 322
factor analysis 195
factor endowment 28–34
family life cycle 141–5
fashion 104
fast-second, strategy of 230–1
feedback 410–11
Festinger, L. 175
field survey methods 292–5
financial orientation 463
Finkelman, D. and Goland, A. 444–7
firm's business, concept of 52, 54–7
Firth, C. 102, 103, 116, 119, 128
Fisher, Lawrence 368
flexible mark-up pricing 375–6
Ford, Henry 45, 62, 524
Ford, Henry II 369
Frank, R., Massy, R. and Wind,
  Y. 210–11
Freud, Sigmund 166
Frey, A. 349, 354

Gabor, A. 369–70, 382
Gaedeke, D. M. and Tootelian,
  D. 396–8, 403
Galbraith, John 167
gap analysis 130–2
General Electric Company's business
  screen 125–30
general management 65–6
generic product definition 529
generic strategies 64–5
geographic segmentation 200–2

Glasgow Herald   143–4
Gordon, Wendy and Langmaid, R.   285–6
governmental factors   146–8
Grashof, J. F.   248
Gray, Daniel H.   89–90
green issues   146
Green, P. and Tull, D.   297–9
growth share matrix   116, 119–21
Guiltinan, J. P. and Paul, G. W.   328–9
Gunn, Lewis   71, 72, 73
Guptara, P.   268–9

Haley, Russell I.   207ff
Harnel, G. and Prahalad, C. K.   472
Harvard Business School   48, 261
Hastorf, A. and Cantril, H.   169
Hauk, J.   452–3
Hayes, R. and Abernathy, W.   71, 308–9,
    324, 467
heavy half   204, 291
Henkoff, Ronald   93–5
'hierarchy of effects'   174–5, 412
'hierarchy of needs'   173–4
Hofer, C. W. and Schendel, D. E.   50–1,
    81
Hollander, S. C.   398
Hooley, G.   121, 122, 195–6
Hooley, G. and Lynch, J.   427–30
Hooley, G., West, C. and Lynch, J.   284,
    423, 516–18
Howard, J.   495, 498–9
Huber, George P.   302–3
Hussey, D. F.   130–1

idea generation   330
implementing marketing   475–9
industrial market segmentation   209–10
industry concentration ratio   128
industry, defined   24
industry structure   152
inertia   105
innovation   28–9, 36, 94, 100, 109ff,
    183–6
intuitive logics   133–5
inventory cycle   152–5
investment cycle   152–5

Johansson, J. K. and Nonaka, I.   286
Johne, Axel   115–16, 333, 466

Johnson, S. C. and Jones, C.   327
Joyce, T.   412–14
judgement sample   292
jugular cycle   153–5
jury of executive opinion   256–7
just noticeable difference (JND
    factor)   233, 337, 348

key policies   488–9
King, Stephen   235, 238–9
Kitchin cycle   152–5
Klemm, M. *et al.*   473–4
Kondratieff cycle   152–5
Kotler, Philip   65, 101, 102, 157, 164–8,
    226–7, 242, 310, 369, 382, 411, 448
Kotler, P., Gregor, W. and Rogers,
    W.   243–6
Kotler, Philip and Levy, S.   529
Krugman, H. E.   413
Kuznets cycle   152–5

'ladders in the mind'   225–6
Lalonde, B. J. and Zinszer, P. H.   440–1
Lambert, D.   391–3
Landor Associates   235–7
Laric, M.   378
law of inertia of large numbers   281, 290
law of statistical regularity   281, 290
Lawrence, P. and Lorsch, J.   466–7
Lawson, R   352–3
learning – low and high   336–7
Levitt, Theodore   17, 29, 35, 52ff, 60, 80,
    106, 114, 231–2, 317, 319, 448, 473,
    524, 529
life-styles   145–6, 159, 167
limited strategic alternatives   57–60,
    529–30
Lindquist, J. D.   220–1
Lipson, H. A. and Darling, J. R.   262–3
Little, Arthur D. Inc. (ADL)   74, 82, 83–9
low involvement   413
Luck, D.   344
Luck, D. and Ferrell, O.   335
Lynch, J. *et al.*   518–23

McCammon, B. C.   401ff
McCarthy, E. J.   261
McDonald, M.   75, 76, 81, 82, 90, 161
    and Leppard, J. W.   481–4

McKay, E.   76, 77–8, 79, 84, 462–3, 469–70
McKinsey   42
McNair, Malcolm   398
Magee, J. F.   304–5
mail questionnaires   293
Majaro, S.   266–7
Makens, J. C.   251, 253
management ratios   507–13
management systems, development of   68–73
market assessment, checklist   295–6
market conduct   21–3
market development   56–7
Market Development   101–2, 182ff
market penetration   56–7
market performance   21–3
market pull   325–6
market segmentation   10, 188–217, 531
market segmentation bases   191–4
market segmentation methods   194–6, 199–200
market structure   21–3
marketing approach   47
marketing audits 10, 241–59, 530
marketing and competition   8
  and competitive success   38–42, 518–23
  and corporate strategy   8
marketing concept   4, 17
marketing culture   13
  developing   458–79
marketing, definitions   18–21
marketing environment   9
marketing function, development of   45–7
marketing information system (MkIS)   257
marketing management   3, 4, 65–6
marketing maxims   523–8
marketing mix   3, 10, 65, 260–76, 531
  managing   271–5
marketing myopia   29, 35, 52, 60
marketing, organising for   461
marketing-orientated organisation   468–70
marketing orientation   4, 5, 45, 46, 69ff, 463
marketing planning   *see* strategic marketing planning

marketing planning, short-term   480–90
marketing research   11, 46, 279–312
Marketing Science Institute   118
marketing strategy   4, 60–5, 337
Marshall, A.   164–5
Martin, John   264
Marx, T. G.   91–3
Maslow, A.   29, 173–4
Mason, Edward S.   21
Meidan, A.   281
Melville, Donald   52, 53
military strategy   57–60
Miller, George   225
Minzberg, H.   68
Miracle, G. E.   320–1
mission, corporate   470–2
  statement   473–5
motivational research   166–7
multidimensional scaling (MDS)   196, 220, 222–3
multiple discriminant analysis (MDA)   196
multiple regression   196
multivariate techniques   196

needs   5–6, 46–7
net present value   505–7
new product departments   334
new product development committee   334
new product development cycle   329–33
  organisation for   333–5
NICB   283–4
niche marketing   226
non-price competition   157–9
non-probability samples   292
Nylen, D. W.   401–2

objectives   6–7, 75–8, 488
  formulation   75
observation   289
Ohmae, K.   406, 448
opportunity cost   498–9
organisational climate   464
O'Shaughnessey, John   261, 421–2
Oxenfeldt, Alfred   367–8, 372

packaging   11, 348–59
  characteristics   354

packaging (*cont.*)
  criteria   349–54
  definitions   349
  development   354–9
  functions   349–50
Packard, Vance   167, 413
Pareto's Law   204ff
Pavlov, Ivan   165–6, 180
pay-back   506–7
penetration pricing   382
perceptual map   194–5
perceptual mapping   219–24
personal interviews   293–4
personal selling   403–4
Peters, T.   230
Peters, T. and Waterman, R.   32, 39
Piercy, N.   476–9
PIMS (Profit Implications of Market
  Strategy)   118, 229–30
plan, marketing   480–90
policy and strategy   48–9
political factors   146–8
Porter, Michael   8, 15, 16, 17, 23ff, 64–5,
  71, 90, 518
positioning   10, 64, 218–40
post-purchase dissonance   175, 414–15
price determination   374
price theory, limitations of   365–7
pricing
  contribution approach   376–7
  cost-plus   374–5
  objectives   367–9, 373–4
  marginal cost   376–7
  and the marketing mix   377–82
  policy   12, 360–84
  services   452–3
  strategies   382–3
primary data   251, 289–90
probability   306–7
probability samples   290–1
product characteristics   316–19
product classification   319–21
product, defined   321–2
product development   56, 328–9
product differentiation   24, 46, 157–9,
  189–91, 337, 363
product elimination   62, 109, 321,
  341
product failure, causes   283–4

product life cycle (PLC)   9, 61–3, 100–9,
  335–44, 526, 529
  decline   107–9, 340–4
  extension   339
  growth   102–5, 338–9
  introduction   101–2, 336–7
  managing   335–44
  maturity   105–8, 339–40
  use as a planning tool   114–16
  sales and distribution effort   404–6
product managers   334–5
product performance, monitoring   344–6
product policy   11, 313–47
product portfolio analysis   115–21
  criticisms of   121–4
product, role of   314–6
production orientation   45, 46, 54, 462
profit and performance   492–4
profit maximisation   365
profit objectives   369–71
Profit Implications of Market Strategy
  (PIMS)   118
promotion objectives   415–21
promotion policy and
  management   408–34
promotional strategy, developing   421–23
psychographic segmentation   203–9
push and pull strategies   387, 399–400

quantitative *v.* qualitative
  research   284–9
quota samples   292

Ragoff, D. and Lynn, R.   371–2
Raiffa, H.   48
Raiffa, H. and Schlaifer, R.   300
random samples   291
raw materials   322
Reeves, Nicola   143–4
Ricardo, David   28, 43
Ries, A. and Trout, J.   128–9, 219, 225–8,
  229, 233
Riesman, D.   203–4
Riesz, P.   324–5
rivalry   27
Robinson, P., Faris, C. and Wind,
  Y.   176
Robinson, Joan   157
Rogers, Everett   106, 336

Rostow, W. W.   154
Rothwell, R., Gardiner, P. and Schott,
   K.   316–19

Said, H.   377ff
sales force composite (forecast)   257
sales forecasting   253–8
   definitions   254
   preparing   256–7
sales forecasting methods   256–8
sales orientation   46, 462
sales-oriented objectives   371–3
Salter, M.   68–70
sample survey   289–90
Sampson, Peter   285
satisficing   370
Say's Law   104, 386
scale effects   118
scenario planning   95–6, 132–6
Scherer, F. W.   21
Scherer, F. and Ross D.   17, 21, 22, 23
Schlaifer, R.   48
Schmanlensee, D.   452
Schramm, W.   12, 410–11
Scottish Health Education Group
   (SHEG)   159, 169
screening stage of NPD   331–2
secondary data   251, 287, 289
segmentation   see market segmentation
selective perception   169–73, 179ff, 530
service   13, 437–57
services
   pricing   452–3
   quality   453–4
   as a marketing strategy   454–6
Shell's Directional Policy Matrix   125–30
SIC Codes   209
Simon, H. A.   370, 381–2
Singh, M. P.   454–6
situation analysis   241–59, 485–6
Sizer, J.   376–7, 507–12
skimming strategy   382
Smith, Adam   165
Smith, R. E. and Swinyard, W. R.   , 412
Smith, Wendell   189
social and cultural factors   145–6
sorting activities   390
specialisation   464
Stapleton, John   246–7, 250–2

statistical analysis   194–200
Steiner, G. and Miner, J.   52
Stern, Louis   394
stimulus–response theory   166
strategic business unit (SBU)   55, 74–5,
   83ff, 127
strategic centres, concept   88
strategic intent   470–2
strategic marketing planning (SMP)   8,
   67–97, 531
   criticism of/obstacles to   89–96
   definitions   73–5
   framework for   78–83, 98–138
   principles   83–6
   trends   73
   types   72
strategic overviews   125–30
strategic v. tactical decisions   52
strategic thinking   93–4
stratified sample   291
structured questionnaires   294
substitution, threat of   26
summary statistics   298–9
supplies   322
Supral   171–2
sustainable differential advantage
   (SDA)   228, 234
Swalm, Ralph O.   308
SWOT analysis   80, 136–7, 486, 530
synergy   86, 464
systematic sample   291

Taguiri, R.   464–5
Taylor, B.   80–1
technological factors   149
technology orientation   462
technology-push   326
telephone survey   293
testing stage of NPD   333
Thomas, M.   199, 200
Thompson, H. V.   315
Thomson, Howard   307
time-series analysis   258
total quality management (TQM)   450–2
trend-impact analysis   135
Twedt, Dik Warren   204–7

Udell, J.   157–9, 377ff
undifferentiated marketing   128, 337, 395

unique selling proposition (USP)   240, 261
Urban G. and Starr, S.   220, 224
usage segmentation   204–7
user needs   316–19

value-based pricing   383
values, changing   159–60
Van Duijn, J.   152–5
Veblen, Thorstein   167
venture teams   334
vertical marketing systems (VMS)   400–2
virtuous circle of best marketing
    practice   516–17
vision, corporate   470

Wasson, C.   271–4, 336
weak signal management   160–1
Webber, R.   200–1
Weitz, B. and Wensley, R.   52
Wells, William   204ff
'wheel of retailing'   398
Wilson, R. M. S.   510
Wind, Yoram   190ff
Wind, Yoram and Robertson, T. S.   3, 4,
    16
Wong, V., Saunders, J. and Doyle, P.   42
Worcester, R. M. and Downham, J.   211

Young, Shirley *et al.*   211ff